FREE Study Skills DVD

Dear Customer,

Thank you for your purchase from Mometrix! We consider it an honor and a privilege that you have purchased our product and we want to ensure your satisfaction.

As a way of showing our appreciation and to help us better serve you, we have developed a Study Skills DVD that we would like to give you for FREE. This DVD covers our *best practices* for getting ready for your exam, from how to use our study materials to how to best prepare for the day of the test.

All that we ask is that you email us with feedback that would describe your experience so far with our product. Good, bad, or indifferent, we want to know what you think!

To get your FREE Study Skills DVD, email freedvd@mometrix.com with *FREE STUDY SKILLS DVD* in the subject line and the following information in the body of the email:

- The name of the product you purchased.
- Your product rating on a scale of 1-5, with 5 being the highest rating.
- Your feedback. It can be long, short, or anything in between. We just want to know your impressions and experience so far with our product. (Good feedback might include how our study material met your needs and ways we might be able to make it even better. You could highlight features that you found helpful or features that you think we should add.)
- Your full name and shipping address where you would like us to send your free DVD.

If you have any questions or concerns, please don't hesitate to contact me directly.

Thanks again!

Sincerely,

Jay Willis
Vice President
jay.willis@mometrix.com
1-800-673-8175

OAT

Prep Book
2019 & 2020

OAT Test Prep Secrets Study Guide

Full-Length Practice Test

Step-by-Step Review Video Tutorials

Written and edited by the Mometrix Optometry School Admissions Test Team

Printed in the United States of America

This paper meets the requirements of ANSI/NISO Z39.48-1992 (Permanence of Paper).

Mometrix offers volume discount pricing to institutions. For more information or a price quote, please contact our sales department at sales@mometrix.com or 888-248-1219.

Mometrix Media LLC is not affiliated with or endorsed by any official testing organization. All organizational and test names are trademarks of their respective owners.

Paperback
ISBN 13: 978-1-5167-1144-4
ISBN 10: 1-5167-1144-0

DEAR FUTURE EXAM SUCCESS STORY

First of all, **THANK YOU** for purchasing Mometrix study materials!

Second, congratulations! You are one of the few determined test-takers who are committed to doing whatever it takes to excel on your exam. **You have come to the right place.** We developed these study materials with one goal in mind: to deliver you the information you need in a format that's concise and easy to use.

In addition to optimizing your guide for the content of the test, we've outlined our recommended steps for breaking down the preparation process into small, attainable goals so you can make sure you stay on track.

We've also analyzed the entire test-taking process, identifying the most common pitfalls and showing how you can overcome them and be ready for any curveball the test throws you.

Standardized testing is one of the biggest obstacles on your road to success, which only increases the importance of doing well in the high-pressure, high-stakes environment of test day. Your results on this test could have a significant impact on your future, and this guide provides the information and practical advice to help you achieve your full potential on test day.

Your success is our success

We would love to hear from you! If you would like to share the story of your exam success or if you have any questions or comments in regard to our products, please contact us at **800-673-8175** or **support@mometrix.com**.

Thanks again for your business and we wish you continued success!

Sincerely,
The Mometrix Test Preparation Team

Need more help? Check out our flashcards at:
http://mometrixflashcards.com/OAT

TABLE OF CONTENTS

Introduction

Thank you for purchasing this resource! You have made the choice to prepare yourself for a test that could have a huge impact on your future, and this guide is designed to help you be fully ready for test day. Obviously, it's important to have a solid understanding of the test material, but you also need to be prepared for the unique environment and stressors of the test, so that you can perform to the best of your abilities.

For this purpose, the first section that appears in this guide is the **Secret Keys**. We've devoted countless hours to meticulously researching what works and what doesn't, and we've boiled down our findings to the five most impactful steps you can take to improve your performance on the test. We start at the beginning with study planning and move through the preparation process, all the way to the testing strategies that will help you get the most out of what you know when you're finally sitting in front of the test.

We recommend that you start preparing for your test as far in advance as possible. However, if you've bought this guide as a last-minute study resource and only have a few days before your test, we recommend that you skip over the first two Secret Keys since they address a long-term study plan.

If you struggle with **test anxiety**, we strongly encourage you to check out our recommendations for how you can overcome it. Test anxiety is a formidable foe, but it can be beaten, and we want to make sure you have the tools you need to defeat it.

Secret Key #1 – Plan Big, Study Small

There's a lot riding on your performance. If you want to ace this test, you're going to need to keep your skills sharp and the material fresh in your mind. You need a plan that lets you review everything you need to know while still fitting in your schedule. We'll break this strategy down into three categories.

Information Organization

Start with the information you already have: the official test outline. From this, you can make a complete list of all the concepts you need to cover before the test. Organize these concepts into groups that can be studied together, and create a list of any related vocabulary you need to learn so you can brush up on any difficult terms. You'll want to keep this vocabulary list handy once you actually start studying since you may need to add to it along the way.

Time Management

Once you have your set of study concepts, decide how to spread them out over the time you have left before the test. Break your study plan into small, clear goals so you have a manageable task for each day and know exactly what you're doing. Then just focus on one small step at a time. When you manage your time this way, you don't need to spend hours at a time studying. Studying a small block of content for a short period each day helps you retain information better and avoid stressing over how much you have left to do. You can relax knowing that you have a plan to cover everything in time. In order for this strategy to be effective though, you have to start studying early and stick to your schedule. Avoid the exhaustion and futility that comes from last-minute cramming!

Study Environment

The environment you study in has a big impact on your learning. Studying in a coffee shop, while probably more enjoyable, is not likely to be as fruitful as studying in a quiet room. It's important to keep distractions to a minimum. You're only planning to study for a short block of time, so make the most of it. Don't pause to check your phone or get up to find a snack. It's also important to **avoid multitasking**. Research has consistently shown that multitasking will make your studying dramatically less effective. Your study area should also be comfortable and well-lit so you don't have the distraction of straining your eyes or sitting on an uncomfortable chair.

The time of day you study is also important. You want to be rested and alert. Don't wait until just before bedtime. Study when you'll be most likely to comprehend and remember. Even better, if you know what time of day your test will be, set that time aside for study. That way your brain will be used to working on that subject at that specific time and you'll have a better chance of recalling information.

Finally, it can be helpful to team up with others who are studying for the same test. Your actual studying should be done in as isolated an environment as possible, but the work of organizing the information and setting up the study plan can be divided up. In between study sessions, you can discuss with your teammates the concepts that you're all studying and quiz each other on the details. Just be sure that your teammates are as serious about the test as you are. If you find that your study time is being replaced with social time, you might need to find a new team.

2

Secret Key #2 – Make Your Studying Count

You're devoting a lot of time and effort to preparing for this test, so you want to be absolutely certain it will pay off. This means doing more than just reading the content and hoping you can remember it on test day. It's important to make every minute of study count. There are two main areas you can focus on to make your studying count:

Retention

It doesn't matter how much time you study if you can't remember the material. You need to make sure you are retaining the concepts. To check your retention of the information you're learning, try recalling it at later times with minimal prompting. Try carrying around flashcards and glance at one or two from time to time or ask a friend who's also studying for the test to quiz you.

To enhance your retention, look for ways to put the information into practice so that you can apply it rather than simply recalling it. If you're using the information in practical ways, it will be much easier to remember. Similarly, it helps to solidify a concept in your mind if you're not only reading it to yourself but also explaining it to someone else. Ask a friend to let you teach them about a concept you're a little shaky on (or speak aloud to an imaginary audience if necessary). As you try to summarize, define, give examples, and answer your friend's questions, you'll understand the concepts better and they will stay with you longer. Finally, step back for a big picture view and ask yourself how each piece of information fits with the whole subject. When you link the different concepts together and see them working together as a whole, it's easier to remember the individual components.

Finally, practice showing your work on any multi-step problems, even if you're just studying. Writing out each step you take to solve a problem will help solidify the process in your mind, and you'll be more likely to remember it during the test.

Modality

Modality simply refers to the means or method by which you study. Choosing a study modality that fits your own individual learning style is crucial. No two people learn best in exactly the same way, so it's important to know your strengths and use them to your advantage.

For example, if you learn best by visualization, focus on visualizing a concept in your mind and draw an image or a diagram. Try color-coding your notes, illustrating them, or creating symbols that will trigger your mind to recall a learned concept. If you learn best by hearing or discussing information, find a study partner who learns the same way or read aloud to yourself. Think about how to put the information in your own words. Imagine that you are giving a lecture on the topic and record yourself so you can listen to it later.

For any learning style, flashcards can be helpful. Organize the information so you can take advantage of spare moments to review. Underline key words or phrases. Use different colors for different categories. Mnemonic devices (such as creating a short list in which every item starts with the same letter) can also help with retention. Find what works best for you and use it to store the information in your mind most effectively and easily.

3

Secret Key #3 – Practice the Right Way

Your success on test day depends not only on how many hours you put into preparing, but also on whether you prepared the right way. It's good to check along the way to see if your studying is paying off. One of the most effective ways to do this is by taking practice tests to evaluate your progress. Practice tests are useful because they show exactly where you need to improve. Every time you take a practice test, pay special attention to these three groups of questions:

- The questions you got wrong
- The questions you had to guess on, even if you guessed right
- The questions you found difficult or slow to work through

This will show you exactly what your weak areas are, and where you need to devote more study time. Ask yourself why each of these questions gave you trouble. Was it because you didn't understand the material? Was it because you didn't remember the vocabulary? Do you need more repetitions on this type of question to build speed and confidence? Dig into those questions and figure out how you can strengthen your weak areas as you go back to review the material.

Additionally, many practice tests have a section explaining the answer choices. It can be tempting to read the explanation and think that you now have a good understanding of the concept. However, an explanation likely only covers part of the question's broader context. Even if the explanation makes sense, **go back and investigate** every concept related to the question until you're positive you have a thorough understanding.

As you go along, keep in mind that the practice test is just that: practice. Memorizing these questions and answers will not be very helpful on the actual test because it is unlikely to have any of the same exact questions. If you only know the right answers to the sample questions, you won't be prepared for the real thing. **Study the concepts** until you understand them fully, and then you'll be able to answer any question that shows up on the test.

It's important to wait on the practice tests until you're ready. If you take a test on your first day of study, you may be overwhelmed by the amount of material covered and how much you need to learn. Work up to it gradually.

On test day, you'll need to be prepared for answering questions, managing your time, and using the test-taking strategies you've learned. It's a lot to balance, like a mental marathon that will have a big impact on your future. Like training for a marathon, you'll need to start slowly and work your way up. When test day arrives, you'll be ready.

Start with the strategies you've read in the first two Secret Keys—plan your course and study in the way that works best for you. If you have time, consider using multiple study resources to get different approaches to the same concepts. It can be helpful to see difficult concepts from more than one angle. Then find a good source for practice tests. Many times, the test website will suggest potential study resources or provide sample tests.

Practice Test Strategy

If you're able to find at least three practice tests, we recommend this strategy:

UNTIMED AND OPEN-BOOK PRACTICE

Take the first test with no time constraints and with your notes and study guide handy. Take your time and focus on applying the strategies you've learned.

TIMED AND OPEN-BOOK PRACTICE

Take the second practice test open-book as well, but set a timer and practice pacing yourself to finish in time.

TIMED AND CLOSED-BOOK PRACTICE

Take any other practice tests as if it were test day. Set a timer and put away your study materials. Sit at a table or desk in a quiet room, imagine yourself at the testing center, and answer questions as quickly and accurately as possible.

Keep repeating timed and closed-book tests on a regular basis until you run out of practice tests or it's time for the actual test. Your mind will be ready for the schedule and stress of test day, and you'll be able to focus on recalling the material you've learned.

Secret Key #4 – Pace Yourself

Once you're fully prepared for the material on the test, your biggest challenge on test day will be managing your time. Just knowing that the clock is ticking can make you panic even if you have plenty of time left. Work on pacing yourself so you can build confidence against the time constraints of the exam. Pacing is a difficult skill to master, especially in a high-pressure environment, so **practice is vital**.

Set time expectations for your pace based on how much time is available. For example, if a section has 60 questions and the time limit is 30 minutes, you know you have to average 30 seconds or less per question in order to answer them all. Although 30 seconds is the hard limit, set 25 seconds per question as your goal, so you reserve extra time to spend on harder questions. When you budget extra time for the harder questions, you no longer have any reason to stress when those questions take longer to answer.

Don't let this time expectation distract you from working through the test at a calm, steady pace, but keep it in mind so you don't spend too much time on any one question. Recognize that taking extra time on one question you don't understand may keep you from answering two that you do understand later in the test. If your time limit for a question is up and you're still not sure of the answer, mark it and move on, and come back to it later if the time and the test format allow. If the testing format doesn't allow you to return to earlier questions, just make an educated guess; then put it out of your mind and move on.

On the easier questions, be careful not to rush. It may seem wise to hurry through them so you have more time for the challenging ones, but it's not worth missing one if you know the concept and just didn't take the time to read the question fully. Work efficiently but make sure you understand the question and have looked at all of the answer choices, since more than one may seem right at first.

Even if you're paying attention to the time, you may find yourself a little behind at some point. You should speed up to get back on track, but do so wisely. Don't panic; just take a few seconds less on each question until you're caught up. Don't guess without thinking, but do look through the answer choices and eliminate any you know are wrong. If you can get down to two choices, it is often worthwhile to guess from those. Once you've chosen an answer, move on and don't dwell on any that you skipped or had to hurry through. If a question was taking too long, chances are it was one of the harder ones, so you weren't as likely to get it right anyway.

On the other hand, if you find yourself getting ahead of schedule, it may be beneficial to slow down a little. The more quickly you work, the more likely you are to make a careless mistake that will affect your score. You've budgeted time for each question, so don't be afraid to spend that time. Practice an efficient but careful pace to get the most out of the time you have.

Secret Key #5 – Have a Plan for Guessing

When you're taking the test, you may find yourself stuck on a question. Some of the answer choices seem better than others, but you don't see the one answer choice that is obviously correct. What do you do?

The scenario described above is very common, yet most test takers have not effectively prepared for it. Developing and practicing a plan for guessing may be one of the single most effective uses of your time as you get ready for the exam.

In developing your plan for guessing, there are three questions to address:

- When should you start the guessing process?
- How should you narrow down the choices?
- Which answer should you choose?

When to Start the Guessing Process

Unless your plan for guessing is to select C every time (which, despite its merits, is not what we recommend), you need to leave yourself enough time to apply your answer elimination strategies. Since you have a limited amount of time for each question, that means that if you're going to give yourself the best shot at guessing correctly, you have to decide quickly whether or not you will guess.

Of course, the best-case scenario is that you don't have to guess at all, so first, see if you can answer the question based on your knowledge of the subject and basic reasoning skills. Focus on the key words in the question and try to jog your memory of related topics. Give yourself a chance to bring the knowledge to mind, but once you realize that you don't have (or you can't access) the knowledge you need to answer the question, it's time to start the guessing process.

It's almost always better to start the guessing process too early than too late. It only takes a few seconds to remember something and answer the question from knowledge. Carefully eliminating wrong answer choices takes longer. Plus, going through the process of eliminating answer choices can actually help jog your memory.

Summary: Start the guessing process as soon as you decide that you can't answer the question based on your knowledge.

How to Narrow Down the Choices

The next chapter in this book (**Test-Taking Strategies**) includes a wide range of strategies for how to approach questions and how to look for answer choices to eliminate. You will definitely want to read those carefully, practice them, and figure out which ones work best for you. Here though, we're going to address a mindset rather than a particular strategy.

Your chances of guessing an answer correctly depend on how many options you are choosing from.

How many choices you have	How likely you are to guess correctly
5	20%
4	25%
3	33%
2	50%
1	100%

You can see from this chart just how valuable it is to be able to eliminate incorrect answers and make an educated guess, but there are two things that many test takers do that cause them to miss out on the benefits of guessing:

- Accidentally eliminating the correct answer
- Selecting an answer based on an impression

We'll look at the first one here, and the second one in the next section.

To avoid accidentally eliminating the correct answer, we recommend a thought exercise called **the $5 challenge**. In this challenge, you only eliminate an answer choice from contention if you are willing to bet $5 on it being wrong. Why $5? Five dollars is a small but not insignificant amount of money. It's an amount you could afford to lose but wouldn't want to throw away. And while losing $5 once might not hurt too much, doing it twenty times will set you back $100. In the same way, each small decision you make—eliminating a choice here, guessing on a question there—won't by itself impact your score very much, but when you put them all together, they can make a big difference. By holding each answer choice elimination decision to a higher standard, you can reduce the risk of accidentally eliminating the correct answer.

The $5 challenge can also be applied in a positive sense: If you are willing to bet $5 that an answer choice *is* correct, go ahead and mark it as correct.

Summary: Only eliminate an answer choice if you are willing to bet $5 that it is wrong.

Which Answer to Choose

You're taking the test. You've run into a hard question and decided you'll have to guess. You've eliminated all the answer choices you're willing to bet $5 on. Now you have to pick an answer. Why do we even need to talk about this? Why can't you just pick whichever one you feel like when the time comes?

The answer to these questions is that if you don't come into the test with a plan, you'll rely on your impression to select an answer choice, and if you do that, you risk falling into a trap. The test writers know that everyone who takes their test will be guessing on some of the questions, so they intentionally write wrong answer choices to seem plausible. You still have to pick an answer though, and if the wrong answer choices are designed to look right, how can you ever be sure that you're not falling for their trap? The best solution we've found to this dilemma is to take the decision out of your hands entirely. Here is the process we recommend:

Once you've eliminated any choices that you are confident (willing to bet $5) are wrong, select the first remaining choice as your answer.

Whether you choose to select the first remaining choice, the second, or the last, the important thing is that you use some preselected standard. Using this approach guarantees that you will not be enticed into selecting an answer choice that looks right, because you are not basing your decision on how the answer choices look.

This is not meant to make you question your knowledge. Instead, it is to help you recognize the difference between your knowledge and your impressions. There's a huge difference between thinking an answer is right because of what you know, and thinking an answer is right because it looks or sounds like it should be right.

Summary: To ensure that your selection is appropriately random, make a predetermined selection from among all answer choices you have not eliminated.

Test-Taking Strategies

This section contains a list of test-taking strategies that you may find helpful as you work through the test. By taking what you know and applying logical thought, you can maximize your chances of answering any question correctly!

It is very important to realize that every question is different and every person is different: no single strategy will work on every question, and no single strategy will work for every person. That's why we've included all of them here, so you can try them out and determine which ones work best for different types of questions and which ones work best for you.

Question Strategies

READ CAREFULLY

Read the question and answer choices carefully. Don't miss the question because you misread the terms. You have plenty of time to read each question thoroughly and make sure you understand what is being asked. Yet a happy medium must be attained, so don't waste too much time. You must read carefully, but efficiently.

CONTEXTUAL CLUES

Look for contextual clues. If the question includes a word you are not familiar with, look at the immediate context for some indication of what the word might mean. Contextual clues can often give you all the information you need to decipher the meaning of an unfamiliar word. Even if you can't determine the meaning, you may be able to narrow down the possibilities enough to make a solid guess at the answer to the question.

PREFIXES

If you're having trouble with a word in the question or answer choices, try dissecting it. Take advantage of every clue that the word might include. Prefixes and suffixes can be a huge help. Usually they allow you to determine a basic meaning. Pre- means before, post- means after, pro - is positive, de- is negative. From prefixes and suffixes, you can get an idea of the general meaning of the word and try to put it into context.

HEDGE WORDS

Watch out for critical hedge words, such as *likely, may, can, sometimes, often, almost, mostly, usually, generally, rarely,* and *sometimes*. Question writers insert these hedge phrases to cover every possibility. Often an answer choice will be wrong simply because it leaves no room for exception. Be on guard for answer choices that have definitive words such as *exactly* and *always*.

SWITCHBACK WORDS

Stay alert for *switchbacks*. These are the words and phrases frequently used to alert you to shifts in thought. The most common switchback words are *but, although*, and *however*. Others include *nevertheless, on the other hand, even though, while, in spite of, despite, regardless of*. Switchback words are important to catch because they can change the direction of the question or an answer choice.

FACE VALUE

When in doubt, use common sense. Accept the situation in the problem at face value. Don't read too much into it. These problems will not require you to make wild assumptions. If you have to go beyond creativity and warp time or space in order to have an answer choice fit the question, then you should move on and consider the other answer choices. These are normal problems rooted in reality. The applicable relationship or explanation may not be readily apparent, but it is there for you to figure out. Use your common sense to interpret anything that isn't clear.

Answer Choice Strategies

ANSWER SELECTION

The most thorough way to pick an answer choice is to identify and eliminate wrong answers until only one is left, then confirm it is the correct answer. Sometimes an answer choice may immediately seem right, but be careful. The test writers will usually put more than one reasonable answer choice on each question, so take a second to read all of them and make sure that the other choices are not equally obvious. As long as you have time left, it is better to read every answer choice than to pick the first one that looks right without checking the others.

ANSWER CHOICE FAMILIES

An answer choice family consists of two (in rare cases, three) answer choices that are very similar in construction and cannot all be true at the same time. If you see two answer choices that are direct opposites or parallels, one of them is usually the correct answer. For instance, if one answer choice says that quantity x increases and another either says that quantity x decreases (opposite) or says that quantity y increases (parallel), then those answer choices would fall into the same family. An answer choice that doesn't match the construction of the answer choice family is more likely to be incorrect. Most questions will not have answer choice families, but when they do appear, you should be prepared to recognize them.

ELIMINATE ANSWERS

Eliminate answer choices as soon as you realize they are wrong, but make sure you consider all possibilities. If you are eliminating answer choices and realize that the last one you are left with is also wrong, don't panic. Start over and consider each choice again. There may be something you missed the first time that you will realize on the second pass.

AVOID FACT TRAPS

Don't be distracted by an answer choice that is factually true but doesn't answer the question. You are looking for the choice that answers the question. Stay focused on what the question is asking for so you don't accidentally pick an answer that is true but incorrect. Always go back to the question and make sure the answer choice you've selected actually answers the question and is not merely a true statement.

EXTREME STATEMENTS

In general, you should avoid answers that put forth extreme actions as standard practice or proclaim controversial ideas as established fact. An answer choice that states the "process should be used in certain situations, if…" is much more likely to be correct than one that states the "process should be discontinued completely." The first is a calm rational statement and doesn't even make a definitive, uncompromising stance, using a hedge word *if* to provide wiggle room, whereas the second choice is a radical idea and far more extreme.

BENCHMARK

As you read through the answer choices and you come across one that seems to answer the question well, mentally select that answer choice. This is not your final answer, but it's the one that will help you evaluate the other answer choices. The one that you selected is your benchmark or standard for judging each of the other answer choices. Every other answer choice must be compared to your benchmark. That choice is correct until proven otherwise by another answer choice beating it. If you find a better answer, then that one becomes your new benchmark. Once you've decided that no other choice answers the question as well as your benchmark, you have your final answer.

PREDICT THE ANSWER

Before you even start looking at the answer choices, it is often best to try to predict the answer. When you come up with the answer on your own, it is easier to avoid distractions and traps because you will know exactly what to look for. The right answer choice is unlikely to be word-for-word what you came up with, but it should be a close match. Even if you are confident that you have the right answer, you should still take the time to read each option before moving on.

General Strategies

TOUGH QUESTIONS

If you are stumped on a problem or it appears too hard or too difficult, don't waste time. Move on! Remember though, if you can quickly check for obviously incorrect answer choices, your chances of guessing correctly are greatly improved. Before you completely give up, at least try to knock out a couple of possible answers. Eliminate what you can and then guess at the remaining answer choices before moving on.

CHECK YOUR WORK

Since you will probably not know every term listed and the answer to every question, it is important that you get credit for the ones that you do know. Don't miss any questions through careless mistakes. If at all possible, try to take a second to look back over your answer selection and make sure you've selected the correct answer choice and haven't made a costly careless mistake (such as marking an answer choice that you didn't mean to mark). This quick double check should more than pay for itself in caught mistakes for the time it costs.

PACE YOURSELF

It's easy to be overwhelmed when you're looking at a page full of questions; your mind is confused and full of random thoughts, and the clock is ticking down faster than you would like. Calm down and maintain the pace that you have set for yourself. Especially as you get down to the last few minutes of the test, don't let the small numbers on the clock make you panic. As long as you are on track by monitoring your pace, you are guaranteed to have time for each question.

DON'T RUSH

It is very easy to make errors when you are in a hurry. Maintaining a fast pace in answering questions is pointless if it makes you miss questions that you would have gotten right otherwise. Test writers like to include distracting information and wrong answers that seem right. Taking a little extra time to avoid careless mistakes can make all the difference in your test score. Find a pace that allows you to be confident in the answers that you select.

KEEP MOVING

Panicking will not help you pass the test, so do your best to stay calm and keep moving. Taking deep breaths and going through the answer elimination steps you practiced can help to break through a stress barrier and keep your pace.

Final Notes

The combination of a solid foundation of content knowledge and the confidence that comes from practicing your plan for applying that knowledge is the key to maximizing your performance on test day. As your foundation of content knowledge is built up and strengthened, you'll find that the strategies included in this chapter become more and more effective in helping you quickly sift through the distractions and traps of the test to isolate the correct answer.

Now it's time to move on to the test content chapters of this book, but be sure to keep your goal in mind. As you read, think about how you will be able to apply this information on the test. If you've already seen sample questions for the test and you have an idea of the question format and style, try to come up with questions of your own that you can answer based on what you're reading. This will give you valuable practice applying your knowledge in the same ways you can expect to on test day.

Good luck and good studying!

14

Biology

Cellular and Molecular Biology

All organisms are made up of matter and display the typical physical and chemical properties of matter. Every cell of an organism is composed of molecules, atoms, and ions. Chemistry is needed to explain the structure and function of all cellular processes at the molecular level. Organic chemistry involves many large and complex molecules including the biochemical compounds carbohydrates, lipids, proteins, and nucleic acids. Chemical reactions occur in the daily function of organisms even at the cellular level. Chemical reactions that are important for life include oxidation-reduction, dehydration synthesis, hydrolysis, phosphorylation, and acid-base reactions.

THE CELL

CELL THEORY

Before the invention of the microscope, it was unknown that living organisms were composed of cells. But the observations of Robert Hooke, Anton van Leeuwenhoek, Matthias Schleiden, Theodor Schwann, and Rudolph Virchow helped to form one of the most basic principles in biology: the cell theory. In 1665, Hooke constructed a primitive compound microscope and viewed, for the first time, what he termed "cells" in a sample of cork. Leeuwenhoek was the first to observe living cells (protists in pond water). Schleiden noted that plants were made entirely of cells (and cellular products) and Schwann expanded this observation to animals. At this time (1839) it was unclear how cells were formed. Virchow believed that cells did not form spontaneously, and rather came from the division of pre-existing cells. Together, these observations formed the cell theory:

- All living organisms are made of one or more cells
- The cell is the basic unit of life
- All cells arise from pre-existing cells

This theory has been modernized to include the fact that cells contain hereditary information, and pass it on during cell division. The cell theory forms the foundation of modern biology. It has helped scientists to understand how cells function, allowing for advances in biotechnology and medicine.

CELLS

Cells are the basic structural units of all organisms. All organisms have a highly organized cellular structure. In single-celled organisms, that single cell contains all of the components necessary for life. In multicellular organisms, cells can become specialized. Different types of cells can have different functions. Life begins as a single cell whether by asexual or sexual reproduction. All cells contain DNA and RNA and can synthesize proteins. Each cell consists of nucleic acids, cytoplasm, and a cell membrane. Specialized organelles such as mitochondria and chloroplasts have specific functions within the cell.

ENERGY

All cells must obtain and use energy in order to grow, make repairs, and reproduce. Cells use energy to take in food, process that food, and eliminate wastes from this process. Cells obtain the energy they need by the breaking of bonds of molecules. Organisms differ in how they obtain food. Plants and other autotrophs produce energy through photosynthesis or chemosynthesis. Animals and other heterotrophs obtain their energy from consuming autotrophs or other heterotrophs. Cellular respiration is the process of converting nutrient molecules into energy.

15

PLANT CELLS AND ANIMAL CELLS

Plant cells and animal cells both have a nucleus, cytoplasm, cell membrane, ribosomes, mitochondria, endoplasmic reticulum, Golgi apparatus, and vacuoles. Plant cells have only one or two extremely large vacuoles. Animal cells typically have several small vacuoles. Plant cells have chloroplasts for photosynthesis because plants are autotrophs. Animal cells do not have chloroplasts because they are heterotrophs. Plant cells have a rectangular shape due to the cell wall, and animal cells have more of a circular shape. Animal cells have centrioles, but only some plant cells have centrioles.

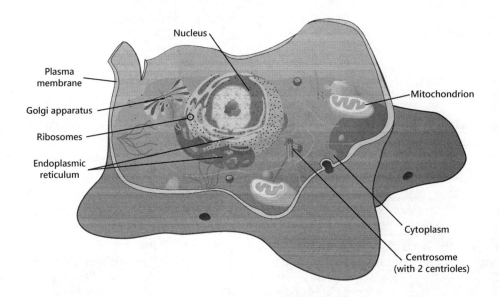

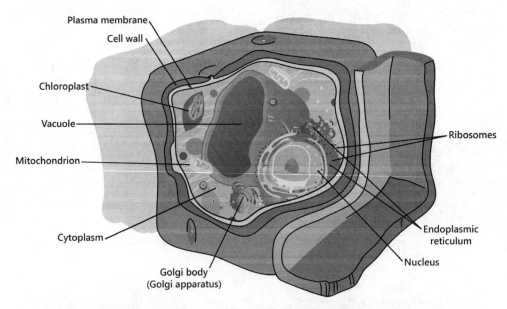

PLASMA MEMBRANE

GENERAL FUNCTION IN CELL CONTAINMENT

While the plasma membrane is involved in many functions (such as the regulation and transportation of materials, cell to cell recognition, and cell signaling), its most basic function is cell containment. The cell membrane is composed of a double layer of phospholipids that surrounds the cytoplasm of virtually all types of cells. The phospholipids form a fluid-like barrier that is reinforced by cholesterol and protein molecules. This barrier helps to contain the structures and molecules within the cell's interior, and also helps to maintain the desired concentrations of substances on either side of the membrane. Since the phospholipids orient themselves with their fatty acid chains pointed inward, the interior of the membrane is hydrophobic. This property causes the membrane to remain intact in its aqueous environment, while being somewhat impermeable to substances that are soluble in water (with the notable exception of nonpolar gases such as oxygen and carbon dioxide).

> **Review Video: Plasma Membrane**
> Visit mometrix.com/academy and enter code: 943095

LIPID COMPONENTS: PHOSPHOLIPIDS (AND PHOSPHATIDS)

A phospholipid consists of two nonpolar fatty acid chains bonded to a polar head made of glycerol, a phosphate group, and an organic R-group. (Phosphatids are the simplest phospholipids and lack the functional group on the phosphate.) Phospholipids are amphipathic, meaning that they have both hydrophilic (polar head) and hydrophobic (nonpolar tails) components. Because of this property, they arrange themselves into micelles or bilayers. A micelle is a small spherical structure made of a single layer of phospholipids with the tails pointed inward to form a hydrophobic core. They are used to transport lipid soluble materials. A bilayer is formed when the phospholipids assemble into parallel layers with the tails pointed in toward each other and the heads pointed out. Phospholipid bilayers surround liposomes and other vesicles, and also enclose the organelles in a eukaryotic cell. These bilayers also form cell membranes, which regulate the passage of materials into and out of all types of cells.

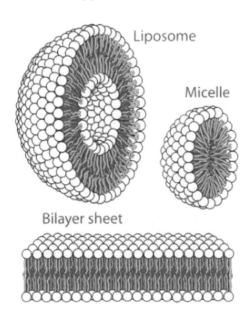

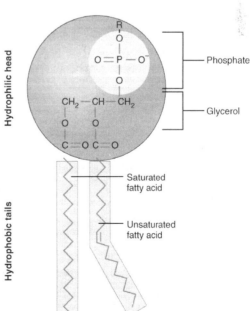

17

LIPID COMPONENTS: STEROIDS AND WAXES

Steroids are lipids that are derived from cholesterol. Cholesterol has a hydrophilic hydroxyl group and a hydrophobic region consisting of four fused hydrocarbon rings and a hydrocarbon chain. The hydrophilic region interacts with the polar heads of the phospholipids, and the hydrophobic regions interact with the nonpolar tails. Its role in the membrane is to maintain stability and proper membrane viscosity by restraining phospholipids from spreading too far apart, or packing too close together (as can occur with fluctuations in temperature).

Cholesterol:

Waxes are lipids that are offer stability to some types of cell membranes, usually in plants. They are composed of a long fatty acid chain bonded to an alcohol with a long carbon chain. Because of their highly hydrophobic property, they interact only with the tails of the phospholipids. Waxes can be used as a water repellant in many plants and some animals.

PROTEIN COMPONENTS

The proteins associated with the membrane enable most of the membrane's functions, such as the shuttling of various ions and molecules through the membrane, catalyzing reactions, joining of adjacent cells, cell signaling, cellular support and stability, and cell recognition. Some of these proteins penetrate into the hydrophobic interior of the membrane, and are called **integral** proteins. **Glycoproteins** are integral proteins with an attached sugar chain that aid in cell recognition. When integral proteins extend completely through the membrane, they are called **transmembrane** proteins, and these are often used as receptors for cell signaling. A signal molecule (like a hormone) will bind to the receptor from the extracellular side, and relay a message to the cytoplasmic side. Transmembrane proteins are also required for transport across the membrane. Some transport proteins (called **channel** proteins) have a tunnel-like conformation that allows materials to move passively, while others (**carrier** proteins) change conformation to move materials either by active or passive transport. **Peripheral proteins** are loosely bound to either side of the membrane, and often act as enzymes or receptor proteins. (Note that both of these can also be integral proteins).

FLUID MOSAIC MODEL

The currently accepted model of the plasma membrane, proposed by S.J. Singer and G.L. Nicolson in 1972, is called the **fluid mosaic model** and it describes the membrane as a fluid bilayer of phospholipids with a mosaic of proteins, cholesterol and carbohydrates associated with it. Phospholipids arrange themselves in a sandwich-like formation, with the fatty acids pointed inward and the polar heads pointed outward. They move rapidly within their layer (or "leaflet"), but only rarely flip to the opposite layer. Higher temperatures increase the fluidity and permeability of the membrane as phospholipids spread apart. (Additionally, a higher proportion of unsaturated fatty acid chains will increase fluidity; conversely saturated chains will decrease fluidity.) Proteins that extend into the hydrophobic interior of the membrane are called integral proteins, while those that are bound to either surface of the membrane are called peripheral proteins. Most proteins can drift slowly in the membrane, but some are fixed in place. Carbohydrates are only found on the exterior of the membrane, and they play a role in cell-cell recognition. They are either bound to a protein (glycoprotein) or a phospholipid (glycolipid). Cholesterol, which is found in the hydrophobic

interior of the membrane, acts as a sort of fluidity buffer, restraining phospholipids from spreading or clustering.

MEMBRANE DYNAMICS

The plasma membrane is not a rigid, static structure; nearly all of the molecules within it are in motion. Phospholipids can change locations without assistance, but certain movements are catalyzed by an enzyme. They can move very rapidly, switching places with adjacent (lateral) phospholipids without the aid of an enzyme. Uncatalyzed transbilayer diffusion (or flip-flopping from one leaflet to the other) is rarer, and occurs at a slow rate. Flippase is an enzyme that catalyzes the transfer of a phospholipid from the extracellular layer to the cytoplasmic layer, and floppase translocates it from the cytoplasmic layer to the extracellular layer. Both enzymes require the expenditure of ATP. Scramblases translocate phospholipids in either direction, and do not require ATP.

Proteins can move laterally, but not transversally, within the membrane. Integral proteins are kept within the membrane by hydrophobic interactions, but most can drift slowly within the membrane. (Some are held to the cytoskeleton and do not move.) Peripheral proteins can drift as well, as they are only loosely (and temporarily) bound to either the lipid bilayer or an integral protein.

THERMODYNAMIC CONSIDERATIONS

When solutes are transported across the membrane, they can move up or down their concentration gradients. The diffusion of solutes down the electrochemical gradient (passive transport) is a spontaneous and thermodynamically favorable process that results in a negative free energy change ($\Delta G < 0$). Diffusion will continue to occur until a state of dynamic equilibrium has been reached and the concentrations on each side of the membrane are the same. Diffusion illustrates the second law of thermodynamics, as the direction of movement is entropy-driven. Solutes move from high to low concentration, increasing entropy (ΔS). Active transport is the thermodynamically unfavorable process in which solutes are moved up their electrochemical gradients, decreasing entropy as they accumulate on one side of the membrane. Only when it is paired with an exergonic process such as the hydrolysis of ATP can active transport occur. Since energy is consumed, the free energy change is positive ($\Delta G > 0$).

PASSIVE TRANSPORT

Passive transport is the movement of substances across a cell membrane without the input of energy. Random motion of particles will lead to the net movement of substances down their concentration gradients in a spontaneous process that leads to an increase in entropy. Simple diffusion, osmosis, and facilitated diffusion are all forms of passive transport. In simple diffusion, substances cross the membrane directly, without the aid of a transport protein. Small, nonpolar molecules such as oxygen gas, carbon dioxide, and uncharged lipids are not repelled by the hydrophobic interior of the membrane.

Osmosis is the passive transport of water across the membrane. Most polar molecules cannot use simple diffusion, but water molecules are small enough to slowly squeeze between the phospholipids. Water can also use channel proteins called aquaporins to increase the rate of osmosis. When proteins are used to transport substances down their concentration gradients, this is called **facilitated diffusion**. Large, polar, and/or charged substances require shielding from the interior of the membrane, and they may use channel or carrier proteins to assist in their transport. None of these processes require ATP, and are driven by the difference in solute concentration.

Review Video: <u>Passive Transport: Diffusion and Osmosis</u>
Visit mometrix.com/academy and enter code: 642038

19

OSMOSIS

Osmosis is the diffusion of water across a semipermeable membrane. The net movement of water is down its concentration gradient, meaning it will move from an area of higher water concentration to lower, or lower solute concentration to higher. Osmosis can help to restore balance when the solute cannot cross the membrane (or if it can't cross fast enough to maintain homeostasis). When the extracellular fluid has a higher solute concentration as compared to the cytoplasm, the fluid is described as **hypertonic**. Since there are fewer free water molecules surrounding the cell, the net flow of water will be *out* of the cell. When the extracellular fluid has a lower solute concentration as compared to the cytoplasm, the fluid is described as **hypotonic**. Since there are more free water molecules on the extracellular side of the membrane, the net flow of water will be *into* the cell, causing it to swell and in some cases burst. When the extracellular fluid has the same solute concentration as the cytoplasm, the fluid is described as **isotonic**, and water will move in and out of the cell at equal rates.

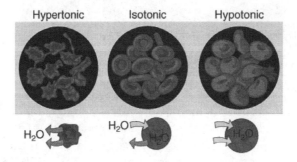

ACTIVE TRANSPORT

In **active transport**, energy is used to move solutes into or out of the cell. In most forms of active transport, substances are pumped against their concentration gradients from areas of low to high concentration. Active transport is required for processes such as the maintenance of a membrane potential, and the uptake of glucose by intestinal cells even between meals. In **primary active transport**, the pumping of solutes by a carrier protein is directly coupled to the hydrolysis of ATP. In this process, the binding of a phosphate group causes a conformational change in the protein, allowing it to transport solutes across the membrane. **Secondary active transport** relies on ATP to generate an electrochemical gradient, and it is this gradient that directly drives the active transport of a different solute. As one solute moves down its gradient, another is pumped up its gradient. When both solutes move in the same direction, it is called **symport**, and when they move in opposite directions, it is called **antiport**.

Endocytosis and **exocytosis** are types of active transport that employ vesicles to import or export substances. While these processes require ATP, they do not necessarily move solutes up their concentration gradients.

ACTIVE TRANSPORT: SODIUM/POTASSIUM PUMP

The **sodium/potassium pump** is a carrier protein that establishes a membrane potential by pumping three sodium ions (Na^+) out of the cell for every two potassium ions (K^+) that are pumped inside. The pump is an ATPase (an enzyme that hydrolyzes ATP) and the binding of a phosphate group causes a conformational change that allows the ions to be transported. Before it is phosphorylated, the pump is open to the cytoplasm and three sodium ions from the inside of the cell bind to it. Phosphorylation of the pump causes it to open to the extracellular side, and the sodium ions are released. The pump now has an affinity for potassium ions. Two potassium ions bind to the pump, stimulating the release of the phosphate group. This causes the protein to return to its original conformation, and the potassium ions are released inside the cell. The pump once

20

again has an affinity for sodium ions and the process repeats. Since three positive ions are removed for every two positive ions that enter, the intracellular space is relatively negative compared to the outside. This contributes to the negative resting membrane potential of the cell. The membrane potential can be thought of as a battery that drives cellular work. It also aids in the functioning of neurons, which rely on a membrane voltage to transmit messages.

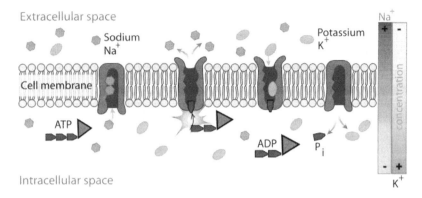

MEMBRANE CHANNELS

Membrane channels belong to a class of transport proteins that form pores to allow the passage of small, charged particles. They are specific to the solutes they transport, and act as a sort of tunnel for particles of a certain size and charge. All channels move substances down their concentration gradient by facilitated diffusion, and therefore do not require energy. Unlike carrier proteins, channels interact very weakly with the solutes they transport, allowing them to move rapidly across the membrane. Channel proteins that allow the passage of water are called aquaporins, and they are always open. Without them, osmosis would occur too slowly to accommodate the needs of the cell. Ion channels, on the other hand, are usually gated; they open and close in response to various stimuli. Voltage-gated channels respond to changes in membrane potential. These types of ion channels are vital to generating electrical impulses in nerve and cardiac cells. Ligand-gated ion channels open in response to the binding of a ligand, such as a hormone or neurotransmitter. Mechanically-gated ion channels respond to a physical stimulus, such as the stretching of the membrane, and are useful in sensory tissues.

MEMBRANE RECEPTORS

Membrane receptors are proteins (usually transmembrane) that bind extracellular molecules such as hormones and neurotransmitters. When a ligand binds, it causes a conformational change in the protein. In **ligand-gated ion channels**, the "gate" of the ion channel is opened, allowing ions to cross the membrane. **Enzyme-linked receptors** are receptor proteins that (as the name suggests) act as both receptors and enzymes. When a ligand binds, it stimulates the enzymatic activity of the receptor itself, or an associated protein. **G protein-coupled receptors** (GPCRs) are involved in a process known as signal transduction. When the GPCR changes conformation in response to the binding of a ligand, it triggers a signaling cascade in which a chemical message is passed along from molecule to molecule within the cytoplasm, until the desired response is elicited. For example, when insulin binds to its receptor, it sends a message to the cell to activate the glucose transporter, GLUT4, which aids in the uptake of sugar from the blood. Receptors are highly specific to the ligands they bind.

MEMBRANE POTENTIAL

The **membrane potential** (abbreviated V or E) is the voltage across a membrane that is determined by the relative concentrations of ions on each side of the membrane, and the permeability of the membrane to those ions. More precisely, it is the electrical potential difference between the inside and outside of a cell. Active transport mechanisms such as the sodium/potassium pump are required to maintain the membrane potential because ions use **leak channels** in an attempt to restore equilibrium. The sodium potassium pump uses ATP to pump three sodium ions out of the cell for every two potassium ions that it pumps into the cell. Most cells have a resting potential of anywhere between −30 and −90 millivolts, depending on cell type. In this state, a cell is polarized. If the inside of the cell becomes relatively positive, the membrane is said to be "depolarized", and if it becomes more negative than its resting potential, it is "hyperpolarized". Membrane potential can be calculated using the Nernst equation:

$$V = \frac{RT}{zF} \ln \frac{[K^+]_o}{[K^+]_i}$$

V (or E) = membrane potential
R = ideal gas constant (8.314 JK-1 mol-1)
T = temperature (Kelvin)
z = charge on the ion
F = Faraday's constant (96485 C mol-1)
ln = natural log
$[K^+]_o$ = ion concentration outside the cell
$[K^+]_i$ = ion concentration inside the cell

EXOCYTOSIS AND ENDOCYTOSIS

Endocytosis and exocytosis are types of vesicular transport that are used for the transport of very large particles, or bulk quantities of smaller particles. Both processes are examples of active transport because the transportation and pinching off of vesicles requires energy. (Note that particles are not necessarily moving up their concentration gradients as in other forms of active transport.) During **exocytosis**, cellular products and wastes are transported via vesicle to the cell membrane where the vesicle fuses, releasing its contents into the extracellular environment. Exocytosis is also the means by which certain membrane components (such as glycoproteins and glycolipids) become incorporated into the cell membrane. **Endocytosis** involves the ingestion of fluid, large particles, or target molecules. During this process the cell membrane folds inward, engulfing the material and pinching off into a vesicle. The ingestion of fluids is called **pinocytosis**, and it is non-specific, meaning it takes in any enzymes and nutrients that happen to be available. **Phagocytosis** is the engulfing of particles, sometimes even entire cells. Immune system cells ingest harmful bacteria by phagocytosis before destroying them. **Receptor-mediated endocytosis** is a form of endocytosis that targets certain molecules (such as LDLs, or low-density lipoproteins) that are in low concentration outside the cell. These molecules bind to receptors on the cell membrane, which then invaginates to form a vesicle.

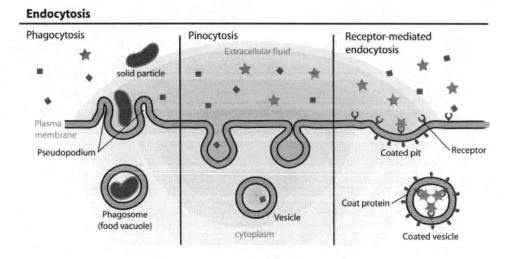

INTERCELLULAR JUNCTIONS

Intercellular junctions are structures that connect adjacent cells within a tissue. There are three main types of cell junctions found in animal tissues: gap junctions, tight junctions, and desmosomes, all of which are made of special proteins called cell adhesion molecules (CAMs).

Gap junctions are channels for water and solutes (usually ions) that allow adjacent cells to communicate. They are composed of six proteins called connexins that are arranged into a hollow cylinder called a connexon. The connexon of one cell aligns with the connexon of an adjacent cell to form a gap junction. While gap junctions are found in nearly all cell types, they are especially important in cells specialized for conductivity, such as neurons and cardiac cells. **Tight junctions** are often described as leak-proof zippers that tightly seal one cell to another via branched networks of proteins called claudins. These junctions are common in epithelial tissues; particularly those of the digestive system where they help prevent the leakage of digestive enzymes. **Desmosomes** are button-like junctions that give strength and reinforcement to tissues that stretch. They are composed of proteins called cadherins that anchor to intermediate fibers of the cytoskeleton.

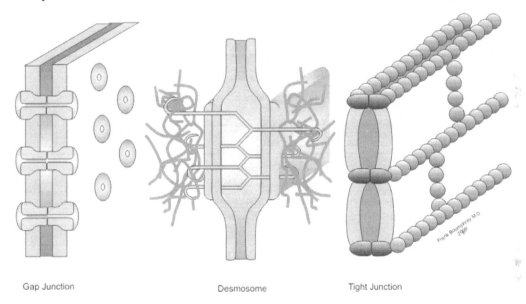

Gap Junction   Desmosome   Tight Junction

DEFINING CHARACTERISTICS OF EUKARYOTIC CELLS

Cells can be classified into two main groups based on the presence or absence of a nucleus. In fact, the terms **eukaryote** and **prokaryote** mean "true kernel" and "before the kernel," respectively. The nucleus is a membrane-bound structure that encloses nearly all the genetic material of a eukaryotic cell. Eukaryotic DNA molecules wrap around associated proteins to form linear chromosomes, and the genes within them are regulated by molecules within the nucleoplasm. For this reason, the nucleus is deemed the "control center" of the cell. Eukaryotic cells are also defined by the presence of other membrane-bound organelles, including mitochondria, endoplasmic reticulum, Golgi bodies, peroxisomes, and (in animal cells) lysosomes. Ribosomes and the cytoskeleton are not enclosed by membranes and are found in both prokaryotic and eukaryotic cells. These types of cells also differ in the way that they divide. While prokaryotes reproduce by a simple process called binary fission, eukaryotes undergo a more involved method of division called mitosis. During mitosis, duplicated chromosomes are lined up along the cell's equator and split at the centromere to form two identical daughter nuclei.

Review Video: Eukaryotic and Prokaryotic
Visit mometrix.com/academy and enter code: 231438

NUCLEUS

COMPARTMENTALIZATION, STORAGE OF GENETIC INFORMATION

The **nucleus** stores most of a cell's genetic information. (DNA is also found in mitochondria and chloroplasts.) Nuclear DNA is enclosed by the nuclear envelope: a double membrane that is perforated with pores. These pores are made of large protein complexes that regulate the passage of materials including RNA, ribosomal subunits, proteins, ions, and signaling molecules. Enclosed in the double membrane is the nucleoplasm (a semifluid), chromatin (DNA and associated histone proteins), and a non-membranous nucleolus which produces the ribosomal subunits. The inner nuclear membrane is covered by a mesh of protein filaments called the nuclear lamina which stabilizes the nucleus while regulating events such as DNA replication and cell division. The outer membrane is continuous with the endoplasmic reticulum.

The nucleus is responsible for the storage of DNA, and is also the site of DNA replication and transcription (the synthesis of RNA). Since gene expression is regulated largely at the level of transcription, the nucleus plays an important role in coordinating the activities of the cell.

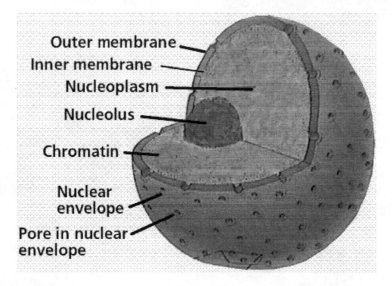

NUCLEOLUS: LOCATION AND FUNCTION

The **nucleolus** is the largest structure inside the nucleus, and it is responsible for producing ribosomal subunits. It has no membrane, and is made of three regions: two thread-like fibrillar components and one granular component. The fibrillar center (FC) is where the ribosomal RNA genes are located and transcribed. The dense fibrillar center (DFC) processes the pre-rRNA, and the immature ribosomal subunits are assembled in the granular component (GC). All rRNA is synthesized in the nucleolus except the 5S-rRNA which is made in the nucleoplasm before being incorporated into ribosomal subunits. The subunits are exported from the nucleus through the nuclear pores.

The nucleolus disappears early in mitosis (prophase) and reappears in the final stage (telophase). However, it first appears as ten small units at various chromosome sites called nucleolus organizer regions (NORs) before aggregating into one structure.

NUCLEAR ENVELOPE, NUCLEAR PORES

The **nuclear envelope** is the double membrane that encloses the nucleus, separating the nucleoplasm from the cytoplasm of the cell. There is a 20–40 nm gap between the two phospholipid bilayers called the perinuclear space, and the membranes are joined at the nuclear pores. Each pore is an octagonal aqueous channel made of hundreds of proteins called nucleoporins. These proteins interact with transporter proteins called karyopherins, which shuttle large molecules like RNA and certain proteins back and forth between the nucleus and the cytoplasm. Smaller molecules and ions are able to diffuse through the pore complex without the aid of a transporter. The pores are essential for the import of the enzymes and nucleotides that are required for DNA synthesis and transcription, and the export of mRNA, tRNA, and ribosomal subunits that are required for translation.

The outer membrane of the nuclear envelope is continuous with the endoplasmic reticulum (ER), and the lumen (inner space) of the ER is open to the perinuclear space. This allows for the easy exchange of materials between the two organelles. The nucleoplasmic side of the inner membrane is lined with a network of protein filaments called the nuclear lamina which supports the nucleus, while aiding in the organization of chromatin.

MITOCHONDRIA

Mitochondria are described as the "powerhouses" of the cell because they produce most of a cell's ATP. They have two membranes: the outer membrane, which acts a selective barrier, and the inner membrane where most of the ATP is made. The inner membrane is folded into structures called cristae, and it is within these folds that the electron transport chain of aerobic respiration is located. Between the membranes is the intermembrane space where a proton motive force is used to drive **chemiosmosis**: the synthesis of ATP. The protons that are pumped across the intermembrane space during oxidative phosphorylation re-enter the mitochondrial matrix (the interior of the mitochondrion) through the protein ATP synthase, which is located in the inner membrane. The movement of the proton's powers ATP synthase, allowing it to phosphorylate ADP. Inside the matrix are ribosomes and mitochondrial DNA. This DNA carries 37 genes (in humans) that are required for normal mitochondrion function. Mitochondria also play a role in apoptosis, or programmed cell death. Proteins associated with the inner mitochondrial membrane move into the cytoplasm in response to oxidative stress and activate other proteins that begin the degradation of the cell.

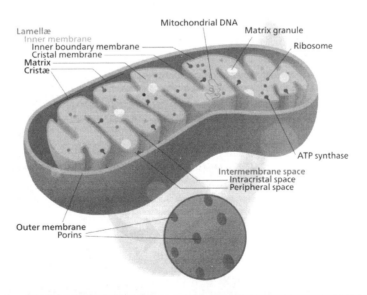

Review Video: **Mitochondria**
Visit mometrix.com/academy and enter code: 444287

<u>SELF-REPLICATION</u>

Mitochondria are described as semi-autonomous because each one has its own genome and ribosomes, and produces many of its own proteins. They also replicate in a manner similar to that of bacteria; they copy their circular DNA molecules before undergoing fission. However, mitochondria do rely on nuclear genes to produce many of the proteins required for DNA replication and other processes. These proteins are imported from the cytosol.

While the mitochondria are not fully autonomous, it is likely that they evolved from an autonomous heterotrophic prokaryote that established a symbiotic relationship with an ancestral host cell. It was probably engulfed by the host cell (hence the double membrane) and provided that cell with ATP. (This is known as the endosymbiont theory.) Its similarity to bacteria, both in structure and manner of reproduction, suggests that mitochondria were once free-living prokaryotes.

LYSOSOMES: MEMBRANE-BOUND VESICLES CONTAINING HYDROLYTIC ENZYMES

Lysosomes are organelles that function in the breakdown of various substances. They bud from the Golgi apparatus, and enclose hydrolytic enzymes that would damage the cell if not separated from the cytosol. These enzymes are active at a low pH of around 5, so hydrogen ions are pumped into the lysosome to maintain the acidic environment. Lysosomes play a vital role in cell homeostasis by dismantling various substrates and nonfunctioning intracellular components, and recycling them in a process called autophagy. Many of the substances destined for degradation are contained in a double-membrane vesicle called an autophagosome. Lysosomes can fuse with these (and with other vesicles created by endocytosis) releasing their enzymes and digesting the contents. Other substances can be transported into the lysosome directly by crossing the membrane. If enough lysosomes are damaged, the cell undergoes apoptosis, and in cases of severe damage, necrosis. Mutations of the hydrolases within the lysosomes are associated with a number of lysosomal storage diseases, including Tay Sachs.

ENDOPLASMIC RETICULUM
<u>ROUGH AND SMOOTH COMPONENTS</u>

Both the rough and smooth endoplasmic reticulum consist of a series of continuous membranes called cisternae, but each type of ER differs in both in structure and function.

The **rough ER** is continuous with the nuclear envelope, and its ribosome-studded cisternae have the appearance of flattened sacs. The ribosomes synthesize polypeptides which are then guided into the lumen of the rough ER before being modified, packaged in a vesicle, and sent to different regions within the cell, often the Golgi apparatus. The Golgi can then further modify the proteins and sort them based on their destinations. Many are shipped out of the cell via exocytosis.

The cisternae of the **smooth ER** are more tubular in shape than the rough ER, and they lack ribosomes. These membranes are continuous with the rough ER and the nucleus. Smooth ER is involved in many tasks, including the synthesis of lipids such as phospholipids and cholesterol. The smooth ER of liver cells detoxifies drugs, and the smooth ER of the muscles regulates and stores calcium ions.

<u>ROUGH ENDOPLASMIC RETICULUM SITE OF RIBOSOMES</u>

Secretory proteins (proteins destined to be exported from the cell) and proteins that are associated with the plasma membrane are synthesized on ribosomes that are bound to the cytoplasmic side of the rough endoplasmic reticulum. These ribosomes are not permanently fixed, and will bind to sites called translocons. Ribosomes that are free in the cytosol are very similar in structure to bound ribosomes, but the proteins they produce remain in the cytosol of the cell. As a polypeptide chain is

growing out of a bound ribosome during translation, the chain is fed through a tiny pore into the lumen of the rough ER, where it folds into its proper conformation. Any proteins that do not fold properly into their native shape are recycled. Enzymes in the lumen may modify proteins by covalently bonding a carbohydrate to form a glycoprotein. (The Golgi continues the posttranslational modification of proteins.) Proteins that are shipped to other parts of the cell are first packaged into transport vesicles, and the vesicle will fuse with its target.

MEMBRANE STRUCTURE

The **endoplasmic reticulum** constitutes roughly half of all the plasma membrane in a cell. The membrane system of the rough ER is connected to the outer nuclear membrane, forming flattened sacs (cisternae) that connect to each other in a manner that resembles a multi-story parking garage. These helicoidal sheets are called **Terasaki ramps**. Newly synthesized proteins are packaged in transport vesicles that are coated with protein complexes that help direct each vesicle to its destination. (COPII coating proteins, for example, coat vesicles that fuse with the cis face of the Golgi apparatus.) These vesicles bud from a region of the ER known as transitional ER, where there are few ribosomes. The smooth ER lacks ribosomes altogether, and has a branched tubular structure. Some of these tubules fuse with one another.

ROLE IN MEMBRANE BIOSYNTHESIS

Both the smooth and rough endoplasmic reticulum are involved in membrane biosynthesis. Enzymes in the smooth ER (or SER) synthesize phospholipids by joining two fatty acid chains to a molecule of glycerol. This occurs on the cytoplasmic side of the membrane. The SER is also the site of another important membrane lipid, cholesterol, which serves as a membrane fluidity buffer. The rough ER is considered the "membrane factory" of the cell because it also produces phospholipids. These lipids are then inserted into the RER's own membrane so that vesicles can bud from it and eventually fuse with the plasma membrane and other parts of the endomembrane system. Ribosomes on the RER produce the integral proteins that are incorporated into the plasma membrane of the cell, or the membranes that enclose organelles.

ROLE IN BIOSYNTHESIS OF SECRETED PROTEINS

Proteins that are to be secreted from the cell, as well as integral membrane proteins, are produced by ribosomes that are bound to the rough ER, but initially these ribosomes are free-floating in the cytosol. They are directed to the RER before translation of the protein is complete. The growing polypeptide has a "signal sequence" of amino acids on the N-terminus of the chain. This sequence is recognized by a signal-recognition particle (SRP) which carries the polypeptide and ribosome to a receptor on the rough ER. The signal sequence contains a series of hydrophobic amino acids that helps the unfolded protein to pass through the RER membrane into the lumen. Once inside the lumen, the signal sequence is cleaved off, and the protein folds into its native shape. It is then packaged into a vesicle for shipment.

GOLGI APPARATUS: GENERAL STRUCTURE AND ROLE IN PACKAGING AND SECRETION

The **Golgi apparatus** consists of a series of curved, flattened sacs called cisternae. The cis face (the stack that is nearest to the ER) receives vesicles sent by the RER that contain immature proteins. The vesicles fuse with the membrane and release the proteins into the Golgi. The proteins then move from stack to stack, budding off a new vesicle which fuses with the next cisterna layer each time. During their travels, the proteins are modified by an assortment of Golgi enzymes. Proteins that were glycosylated in the ER may have some of their sugar residues removed, or more may be added. Sulfate and phosphate groups may be added as well. These "tags" influence the structure and function of the protein, and also aid in the sorting and delivery of these proteins to their destinations. The proteins are packaged into vesicles that bud from the trans face (or exit face) of the Golgi. Some of these proteins are secreted from the cell through exocytosis, while others become part of the cell membrane. Still others serve as hydrolytic enzymes inside lysosomes.

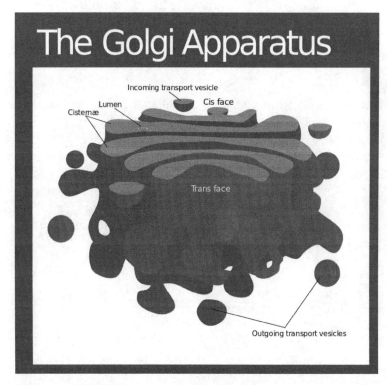

PEROXISOMES: ORGANELLES THAT COLLECT PEROXIDES

Peroxisomes are structurally similar to lysosomes; they are both membranous sacs filled with many types of enzymes. But unlike lysosomes, peroxisomes are found in all types of eukaryotic cells, and they can replicate independently using proteins that are imported from the cytosol. Their enzymes also function at a higher pH. Peroxisomes function in many metabolic processes, including biosynthesis of lipids, detoxification of alcohol, and the oxidation of amino acids and very long chain fatty acids. These oxidation reactions produce hydrogen peroxide (H_2O_2) as a byproduct, which is toxic to cells. Peroxisomes contain an enzyme called catalase that is able to break hydrogen peroxide down into water and oxygen gas. They also contain some of the enzymes involved in the pentose phosphate pathway, which produces NADPH to be used in reductive biosynthesis reactions.

CYTOSKELETON
GENERAL FUNCTION IN CELL SUPPORT AND MOVEMENT

The **cytoskeleton** is a membraneless structure found in all cell types, and it is made of various types of protein fibers. In eukaryotes, the cytoskeleton has three major components: microfilaments, intermediate fibers, and microtubules. While the cytoskeleton is known for its role in cell shape and structure, it is also involved in the movement of materials within the cell, and movement of the cell itself. The cytoskeleton is dynamic and can extend and retract, allowing cells to maintain their shape, or change shape as needed. The network of protein fibers stabilizes most of the organelles, and also provides a "railway" for motor proteins to use to direct vesicles to their destinations. Components of the cytoskeleton help anchor the cell to neighboring cells, and in some cases, form extensions such as cilia and flagella that aid in cell movement. Cell division would be

impossible without the cytoskeleton, as it is used to separate sister chromatids, and also pinches the cell into daughter cells during cytokinesis.

MICROFILAMENTS: COMPOSITION AND ROLE IN CLEAVAGE AND CONTRACTILITY

Microfilaments are the thinnest components of the cytoskeleton, averaging about 6 to 8 nm in diameter. They are composed of protein molecules called actin that join together to form two rod-like polymers which twist around each other to form flexible tension-bearing filaments. These filaments organize into either bundles or networks, and they are involved in maintaining cell shape and events like cytokinesis, muscle contraction, and movement of the cell itself.

During cytokinesis, a cleavage furrow is formed through the contraction of microfilaments. These microfilaments are organized into a ring shape which decreases in size as they contract.

The cytoplasm is constricted until the original cell pinches into two daughter cells. Microfilaments are also involved in muscle contraction. The protein myosin binds to actin filaments forming myofibrils. The two components slide past each other as the cell contracts, and the muscle shortens. Microfilaments also aid in the gross movement of a cell by elongating the plus end (actin polymerization) while shortening the minus end (actin depolymerization).

MICROTUBULES: COMPOSITION AND ROLE IN SUPPORT AND TRANSPORT

Microtubules are the thickest components of the cytoskeleton (around 25 nm in diameter). They are made of a globular protein known as tubulin, which is a dimer made of α-tubulin and β-tubulin. These dimers stack upon each other to form linear rows called protofilaments, and 13 of these protofilaments arrange themselves in a ring to form a hollow tube. Microtubules can lengthen and shorten by polymerization and depolymerization of the tubulin dimers. They extend throughout the cell, helping the cell to resist compressional forces, while also providing a framework for motor proteins to travel on. Kinesins are motor proteins that tend to "walk" toward the plus end of the microtubule and dyneins travel toward the minus end. Many of these motor proteins carry vesicles to their destinations. Microtubules are also the major components of the mitotic spindle which segregates sister chromatids during mitosis. Cilia and flagella are also formed from microtubules which group together in nine pairs that surround a central pair.

INTERMEDIATE FILAMENTS, ROLE IN SUPPORT

Intermediate fibers are components of the cytoskeleton that (at around 10 nm in diameter) are thinner than microtubules but thicker than microfilaments. They are composed of many types of proteins (over fifty), and the types of proteins are specific to certain types of cells. For example, microfilaments made of keratin are found in epithelial cells, and microfilaments made of desmin are found in muscle cells. Lamins are proteins that form the microfilaments that line the inside portion of the nuclear envelope. Unlike their cytoskeletal counterparts, they are not polar, and they are not directly responsible for cell movement. They appear to only play a role in support. They help cells adhere to one another at cell junctions known as desmosomes, and also help to anchor the nucleus and other organelles. Intermediate filaments are specialized to withstand tensile forces, and thereby help to prevent cell distortion under mechanical stress. They do not polymerize and depolymerize the way that microtubules and microfilaments do.

COMPOSITION AND FUNCTION OF CILIA AND FLAGELLA

Both cilia and flagella are structures made of microtubules that extend from some types of cells. In eukaryotic cells, these microtubules are doubled up into pairs, and nine doublets form a ring around a central pair (the "9 + 2" arrangement). Each cilium and flagellum is about 0.25 µm in diameter, but flagella are usually much longer than cilia. Cilia are almost always found in high

29

numbers, while cells rarely have more than a few flagella. Both structures are able to "wave" back and forth through the action of motor proteins called dyneins.

Some cells use cilia for locomotion while cells that are fixed within a tissue may use cilia to sweep materials along the surface. Ciliated cells of the respiratory tract move mucus out of the lungs, and cells of the female reproductive tract use cilia to mobilize the egg. Some cilia can even detect signals and transmit information to the inside of the cell. When cilia move, they do so in back-and-forth strokes, much like oars on a rowboat.

Flagella move differently; they are more whip-like with an undulating, beating pattern. Unlike cilia, they are only used for locomotion. Each human sperm uses a flagellum to move, and (like cilia) they can be found in many types of protists.

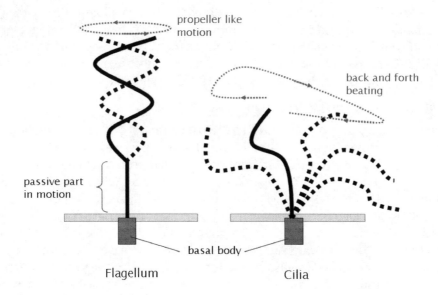

CENTRIOLES, MICROTUBULE ORGANIZING CENTERS

Centrioles are cylindrical structures that are formed from nine triplets of microtubules arranged in a circle around a hollow center. In animal cells, two perpendicular centrioles form an organelle called a **centrosome**. Other types of eukaryotic cells have simple centrosomes, but only animal cells use centrioles to organize their microtubules. Centrosomes are typically found near the nucleus, but they migrate to opposite poles of the cell during cell division. Microtubules extend from the centrioles as the plus ends grow toward the metaphase plate, forming the spindle fibers of the mitotic spindle. Polar fibers extend from one centrosome to the other, while kinetochore fibers attach to the chromosomes, pulling the sister chromatids apart during anaphase.

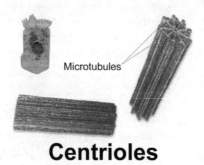

Microtubules

Centrioles

CELLULAR PROCESSES

PHOTOSYNTHESIS

Photosynthesis is a food-making process that occurs in three processes: light-capturing events, light-dependent reactions, and light-independent reactions. In light-capturing events, the thylakoids of the chloroplasts, which contain chlorophyll and accessory pigments, absorb light energy and produce excited electrons. Thylakoids also contain enzymes and electron-transport molecules. Molecules involved in this process are arranged in groups called photosystems. In light-dependent reactions, the excited electrons from the light-capturing events are moved by electron transport in a series of steps in which they are used to split water into hydrogen and oxygen ions. The oxygen is released, and the $NADP^+$ bonds with the hydrogen atoms and forms NADPH. ATP is produced from the excited electrons. The light-independent reactions use this ATP, NADPH, and carbon dioxide to produce sugars.

C3 AND C4 PHOTOSYNTHESIS

Three types of photosynthesis are C3, C4, and crassulacean acid metabolism (CAM). C3 and C4 photosynthesis are named for the type of carbon molecule (three-carbon or four-carbon) that is made during the first step of the reaction. The first step of C3 photosynthesis is the formation of two three-carbon molecules (3-phosphoglycerate) from a reaction between carbon dioxide and a five-carbon molecule (ribulose 1,5-bisphosphate). The first step of C4 photosynthesis is the formation of a four-carbon molecule (oxaloacetate) from a reaction between carbon dioxide and a three-carbon molecule (phosphoenolpyruvate). More than 95% of plants perform C3 photosynthesis. C4 photosynthesis can be used by plants in sunlight-intense regions because it helps conserve water.

CRASSULACEAN ACID METABOLISM

Crassulacean acid metabolism (CAM) is a form of photosynthesis adapted to dry environments. During nighttime, pores of the plant leaves (stomata) open to receive carbon dioxide, which combines with phosphoenolpyruvate (three-carbon molecule) to form malate (four-carbon molecule). Malate is stored in vacuoles. During the daytime, the stomata are closed and the malate is transported to chloroplasts, where malate is broken down into pyruvate (three-carbon molecule) and carbon dioxide. The carbon dioxide released from malate is used in photosynthesis during the daytime. One advantage of the CAM cycle is that it minimizes loss of water through the stomata during the daytime. A second advantage is that concentrating carbon dioxide in the chloroplasts in this manner increases the efficiency of the enzyme that converts carbon dioxide and ribulose 1,5-bisphosphate into two 3-phosphoglycerate molecules.

> **Review Video: Photosynthesis in Biology**
> Visit mometrix.com/academy and enter code: 402602

CHLOROPLASTS

Chloroplasts are large organelles that are enclosed in a double membrane. Discs called thylakoids are arranged in stacks called grana (singular, granum). The thylakoids have chlorophyll molecules on their surfaces. Stromal lamellae separate the thylakoid stacks. Sugars are formed in the stroma, which is the inner portion of the chloroplast. Chloroplasts perform photosynthesis and make food in the form of sugars for the plant. The light reaction stage of photosynthesis occurs in the grana,

31

and the dark reaction stage of photosynthesis occurs in the stroma. Chloroplasts have their own DNA and can reproduce by fission independently.

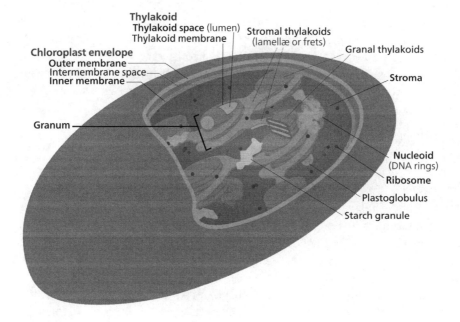

<u>PLASTIDS</u>

Plastids are major organelles found in plants and algae. Because plastids can differentiate, there are many forms of plastids. Specialized plastids can store pigments, starches, fats, or proteins. Two examples of plastids are amyloplasts and chloroplasts. Amyloplasts are the plastids that store the starch formed from long chains of glucose produced during photosynthesis. Amyloplasts synthesize and store the starch granules through the polymerization of glucose. When needed, amyloplasts also convert these starch granules back into sugar. Fruits and potato tubers have large numbers of amyloplasts. Chloroplasts can synthesize and store starch. Interestingly, amyloplasts can redifferentiate and transform into chloroplasts.

CHEMOSYNTHESIS

Chemosynthesis is the food-making process of chemoautotrophs in extreme environments such as deep-sea-vents. In general, chemosynthesis involves the oxidation of inorganic substances. Chemosynthesis is unlike photosynthesis in that chemosynthesis does not require light. Sulfur bacteria live near or in deep-sea vents. Some actually live in other organisms such as huge tube worms near the vents. Hydrogen sulfide is released from deep-sea vents. Instead of sunlight, chemosynthesis uses the energy stored in the chemical bonds of chemicals such as hydrogen sulfide. Carbon is obtained from molecules such as carbon dioxide. During chemosynthesis, the electrons that are removed from the inorganic molecules are combined with carbon possibly from the dissolved carbon dioxide in the seawater or from methane from deep-sea vents to form organic molecules in the form of carbohydrates. Some bacteria use metal ions such as iron and magnesium to obtain the needed electrons. Methanobacteria such as those found in human intestines combine carbon dioxide and hydrogen gas and release methane as a waste product. Nitrogen bacteria such as nitrogen-fixing bacteria in the nodules of legumes convert atmospheric nitrogen into nitrates.

PHOSPHORYL GROUP TRANSFERS AND ATP

ATP, or **adenosine triphosphate**, is an adenine-containing RNA nucleotide. Adenine (the nitrogenous base) is covalently bonded to the sugar ribose, which has a chain of three phosphate groups that stems from its 5' carbon. The closest phosphate group is termed "alpha," followed by "beta," and terminating with "gamma," and they are all linked by phosphoanhydride bonds. Because these groups are negatively charged, they repel each another. ATP is sometimes called "energy currency" because it drives most of the reactions in a cell, often by transferring of one of its phosphate groups to another molecule. When a molecule is phosphorylated, its function will change; it may be activated or deactivated as a result of a change in conformation.

ATP Hydrolysis $\Delta G \ll 0$

ATP is hydrolyzed to produce adenosine diphosphate (ADP) and an inorganic phosphate group in the following reaction:

$$ATP + H_2O \rightarrow ADP + P_i$$

Less commonly, two phosphate groups are removed to produce adenosine monophosphate (AMP). The free energy released by the hydrolysis of ATP is used to drive cellular work. The phosphoanhydride bonds between the phosphate groups are often described as "high energy bonds" but it is the difference in free energy between the products and the reactants that explains the output of energy, not the breaking of the bond itself.

The Gibbs free energy change (ΔG) associated with the hydrolysis of ATP (which is highly exergonic) is dependent on the surrounding conditions. Under standard conditions, it is −30.5 kJ/mol (or −7.3 kcal /mol). But under typical cellular conditions, the concentration of ATP is far below the standard 1.0 M. Also, Mg^{2+} ions in the cytosol bind to ATP and stabilize it. For this reason, ΔG can be much greater than the value at standard conditions, even double or more.

ATP Group Transfers

The hydrolysis of ATP without a coupled reaction and/or group transfer is unlikely, because it would result in simply the release of heat. Usually, the hydrolysis of ATP is coupled with a less energetically favorable reaction to help drive cellular work. ATP participates in the reaction that it is driving, usually by the covalent binding of one or more of its phosphate groups to an intermediate molecule, which is then used in the next reaction. Sometimes, part of an ATP molecule will bind to another molecule in order to change its conformation and function. The sodium potassium pump, for example, is only able to shuttle sodium ions out of the cell when a phosphate group binds to it. AMP (the molecule that remains after the removal of two phosphates from ATP, or one phosphate from ADP) can also bind to a protein to change its function.

BIOLOGICAL OXIDATION-REDUCTION

Reactions that involve the transfer of electrons are called **oxidation-reduction reactions**, or **redox reactions**. Oxidation is the process of losing electrons, and reduction is the process of gaining electrons. One reaction must be accompanied by the other; they cannot occur independently. The electron acceptor, or **oxidizing agent**, is reduced by the electron donor, or

reducing agent. Biological redox reactions are essential to all living organisms. Both photosynthesis and cellular respiration are driven by these reactions. During photosynthesis (a non-spontaneous endergonic process), electrons are transferred from water (which is oxidized) to carbon dioxide (which is reduced). During cellular respiration (a spontaneous exergonic process), glucose is oxidized, and oxygen is reduced. In both these processes, electrons are not moved directly from the starting reactants to the end products. They are transferred along intermediates via a series of enzyme-catalyzed reactions.

Reduction
$$\text{Oxidant} + e^- \longrightarrow \text{Product}$$
(Electrons **gained**; oxidation number **decreases**)

Oxidation
$$\text{Reductant} \longrightarrow \text{Product} + e^-$$
(Electrons **lost**; oxidation number **increases**)

HALF-REACTIONS

In a redox reaction, one agent is oxidized while another is reduced. A **half reaction** is only one part of a redox reaction; it is either the oxidation component (in which the agent accepts electrons) or the reduction component (in which the agent loses electrons). These are called half reactions because they are always coupled together. Separating these redox reactions into their half components allows one to determine how many electrons are being transferred. Electrons should be balanced on either side, and will cancel out to give the complete redox reaction.

Generalized format:
Complete redox reaction $X + Y \rightarrow X^+ + Y^-$
Half reaction (X is oxidized) $X \rightarrow X^+ + e^-$
Half reaction (Y is reduced) $Y + e^- \rightarrow Y^-$

Specific example:
Complete reaction Acetaldehyde $+ \text{NADH} + H^+ \rightarrow$ Ethanol $+ \text{NAD}^+$
Half reaction (acetaldehyde is reduced) Acetaldehyde $+ 2H^+ + 2e^- \rightarrow$ Ethanol
Half reaction (NADH is oxidized) $\text{NADH} \rightarrow \text{NAD}^+ + H^+ + 2e^-$

SOLUBLE ELECTRON CARRIERS

There are many molecules that function as electron carriers in the cell; some are water-soluble and some are lipid-soluble. The list below describes some of the common electron carriers that participate in metabolic pathways.

Nicotinamide adenine dinucleotide (**NAD**): accepts two electrons and a proton during glycolysis and the citric acid cycle, and donates them to establish the proton motive force that leads to the production of ATP during oxidative phosphorylation. **NADP** is a similar molecule that is used in the pathways of photosynthesis.

Flavin adenine dinucleotide (**FAD**): accepts one or two electrons and two protons. It accepts electrons during the citric acid cycle, and donates them to oxidative phosphorylation.

Ubiquinone (also called coenzyme Q): lipid soluble, accepts one or two electrons, and helps to move electrons across phospholipid bilayers.

Cytochrome c: a protein with an electron-accepting iron atom inside it called the heme group. It participates in the final stage of cellular respiration. (Cytochrome c is water soluble, but most cytochromes are lipid soluble.)

FLAVOPROTEINS

Flavoproteins are proteins that contain a prosthetic group, either flavin adenine dinucleotide (FAD) or less commonly flavin mononucleotide (FMN). FAD and FMN are derived from riboflavin, and are essential to many cellular processes, including cellular respiration, photosynthesis, fatty acid oxidation, and the activation of vitamin B. They can catalyze the transfer of either one or two electrons, and this characteristic allows them to act as cofactors for many types of enzymes. These cofactors are tightly bound, but only rarely by covalent bonds.

CARBOHYDRATES

Carbohydrates are the most abundant class of organic compounds found in nature, and the most accessible source of energy for most organisms. Each gram of carbohydrate releases around 17 kJ, or 4 kcal, of energy. Carbohydrates serve other roles as well, including cell-cell recognition, structural components in cell walls and the exoskeletons of arthropods, and intermediates in metabolic pathways.

All carbohydrates contain predictable ratios of carbon, hydrogen, and oxygen. Nearly all simple sugars have a 1:2:1 ratio of C, H, and O. Each additional sugar that is added will result in the removal of a water molecule via dehydration synthesis reaction. As such, the empirical formula for carbohydrates is $C_n(H_2O)_m$.

> **Review Video: Carbohydrates**
> Visit mometrix.com/academy and enter code: 601714

NOMENCLATURE AND CLASSIFICATION, COMMON NAMES

Carbohydrates can be classified by the number of substituent sugar units, their functional groups, and stereochemistry (L / D, R / S nomenclature).

- **Monosaccharide**: a simple sugar made of one sugar unit. These can be classified further according to the number of carbons.
    - **Triose**: Three carbons (ex: glyceraldehyde)
    - **Tetrose**: Four carbons (ex: erythrulose)
    - **Pentose**: Five carbons (ex: deoxyribose, ribose)
    - **Hexose**: Six carbons (ex: glucose, fructose, galactose)
- **Disaccharide**: a double sugar consisting of two monosaccharides (ex: sucrose, lactose, maltose)
- **Oligosaccharide**: a carbohydrate usually made of three to ten monosaccharides (ex: raffinose)
- **Polysaccharide**: a long chain (sometimes branched) of monosaccharides (ex: glycogen, starch, chitin)
- **Aldose**: contains an aldehyde functional group (ex: glucose, glyceraldehyde)
- **Ketose**: contains a ketone functional group (ex: fructose, dihydroxyacetone)

ABSOLUTE CONFIGURATION

Absolute configuration refers to the three-dimensional arrangement of the atoms that are bonded to a chiral carbon. A **chiral carbon** is an asymmetrical carbon with four different ligands. There are different ways of designating absolute configuration.

The **L / D designation** compares the configuration of the carbohydrate to glyceraldehyde, and is determined by examining the chiral carbon that is furthest from the carbonyl group. When depicted in a Fischer projection, an L enantiomer will have the OH group (hydroxide) on the left, and a D enantiomer will have the hydroxide pointing to the right. (+) enantiomers rotate plane-polarized light in the clockwise direction, and (−) enantiomers rotate it counterclockwise.

The **R / S designation** examines each ligand on a chiral carbon and assigns it a priority number, based on atomic number (1 = highest atomic number and priority, 4 = least). When the lowest priority substituent points away from the viewer, the remaining ligands will decrease either in the clockwise direction (R) or the counterclockwise direction (S).

CYCLIC STRUCTURE AND CONFORMATIONS OF HEXOSES

A monosaccharide with more than four carbons will usually arrange itself into a cyclic conformation in aqueous solution. A five-membered ring is a furanose, and a six-membered ring is a pyranose. An aldose is a monosaccharide that contains an **aldehyde**: a functional group composed of a carbon with a single bond to hydrogen and a double bond to oxygen. A ketose is a sugar that contains a **ketone group**, which has an R group in place of the hydrogen. The carbon of the aldehyde or keto group interacts with a nucleophilic hydroxyl group, and the double bond between carbon and oxygen is eliminated resulting in a more energetically favorable arrangement. Aldose sugars form hemiacetals, and ketose sugars form hemiketals. Fischer projections are commonly used to portray open-chain carbohydrates, but monosaccharides that can form rings are usually translated into Haworth projections and/or chair conformations to give a more realistic depiction of the stereochemistry and structure.

EPIMERS AND ANOMERS

Epimers are specific types of diastereomers that differ from each other at only one of the chiral carbons. D-glucose and D-mannose are epimers because they share the same chemical formula ($C_6H_{12}O_6$) but differ in the orientation of the OH group on carbon 2.

```
        CHO                        CHO
         |                          |
    H—C—OH                    HO—C—H
         |                          |
   HO—C—H                     HO—C—H
         |                          |
    H—C—OH                     H—C—OH
         |                          |
    H—C—OH                     H—C—OH
         |                          |
      CH₂OH                      CH₂OH

     D-Glucose                  D-Mannose
```

Anomers are specific types of epimers. The difference in configuration occurs at the **anomeric carbon**: the carbonyl carbon that rotates to become a chiral center and form a cyclic structure. There are two conformations that can emerge as a result of the rotation: alpha (α) and beta (β). In the α-form, the OH group is on the opposite side of the ring from CH_2OH, and in the β-form, it is on the same side. (See the example below of α-D-glucose and β-D-glucose.)

HYDROLYSIS OF THE GLYCOSIDE LINKAGE

A **glycosidic linkage** is a covalent bond formed between the anomeric hydroxyl and the hydroxyl group of another compound (often another sugar). These bonds link individual sugar units together to form disaccharides and polysaccharides, and also link a nitrogenous base to the pentose in a nucleotide. When an anomeric center participates in a glycosidic bond, it can no longer revert back and forth between the α and β form as it did when it was free. These bonds are stable, but they can be broken in an acidic aqueous environment. Water is split to give a hydrogen back to one unit and an OH back to the other. Enzymes called **hydrolases** can help to cleave these bonds. They are specific, in that a particular enzyme can only act on α-linkages *or* β linkages. For example, the hydrolase known as α-amylase can break the α(1→4) linkages between glucose subunits of starch, but not the β(1→4) linkages of cellulose. This explains why humans cannot digest cellulose. Other animals rely on microbes to hydrolyze these bonds. Another enzyme called glycosylase assists in the cleavage of the nitrogen base from the sugar in a nucleotide.

MONOSACCHARIDES

Monosaccharides are the simplest sugars. They cannot be broken down into smaller carbohydrates, but they can bond together via glycosidic linkage to form larger ones. Nearly all monosaccharides share the same general formula $(CH_2O)_n$, where n is greater than or equal to three. (The notable exception is deoxyribose $(C_5H_{10}O_4)$, which lacks an oxygen on the 2' carbon.) Monosaccharides differ in the number of carbons, and how the atoms are arranged. Below are some common monosaccharides.

- Trioses: glyceraldehyde, dihydroxyacetone
- Tetroses: erythrose, erythrulose
- Pentoses: deoxyribose, ribose, arabinose
- Hexoses: glucose, mannose, fructose, galactose
- Heptoses: glucoheptose, mannoheptulose

Monosaccharides can be oxidized to release energy (as seen in the oxidation of glucose during cellular respiration). In fact, all monosaccharides are considered "reducing sugars" because they either have aldehyde groups that are oxidized, or they can tautomerize to form aldehyde groups in solution. Non-reducing sugars lack a hydroxyl group on the anomeric carbon. Reducing sugars can be detected by various reagents. Benedict's solution oxidizes the aldehyde to produce an orange precipitate, Cu_2O. Tollens' reagent contains Ag^+ ions which are reduced by the aldehyde to produce a silver color.

<u>DISACCHARIDES</u>

Disaccharides are composed of two monosaccharides linked by a glycosidic bond. The general formula for a disaccharide is $C_n(H_2O)_m$. While monosaccharides almost always have a 1:2:1 ratio of carbon, hydrogen, and oxygen (respectively), disaccharides are formed via dehydration synthesis, and therefore a water molecule is subtracted from the formula. The formula for nearly all disaccharides is $C_{12}H_{22}O_{11}$.

The glycosidic linkage between monosaccharides can vary, even when both of the sugar subunits are the same. This is because the linkage can stem from any OH group, and be in the α or β form. For example, maltose, cellobiose, and trehalose are each made of two glucoses linked together in different ways to give rise to sugars with different properties. An α(1→4) linkage produces maltose, β(1→4) produces cellobiose, and α, α(1→1) produces trehalose.

Some disaccharides, such as maltose, lactose, and cellobiose, are reducing sugars because only one anomeric carbon participates in the glycosidic bond. This allows one of the subunits to take an open chain form and free up an aldehyde, which can then be oxidized. Other disaccharides, such as trehalose and sucrose, are nonreducing sugars because both anomeric carbons are involved in the glycosidic linkage.

<u>POLYSACCHARIDES</u>

Polysaccharides are large carbohydrates with at least ten monosaccharides, but they typically contain hundreds to thousands of monosaccharides. Like disaccharides, the sugar subunits are joined by glycosidic bonds, and the general formula for the whole unit is $C_n(H_2O)_m$. The most common polysaccharides include starch, glycogen, cellulose, and chitin, all of which are polymers of glucose. Since they are composed of only one type of monosaccharide, they are all homopolysaccharides. Heteropolysaccharides have more than one type of monosaccharide, and are less common.

Some polysaccharides (ex: starch, glycogen) function as a source of fuel, and others form structural components (ex: cellulose, chitin). Starch is a storage polysaccharide in plants, and is an important part of the human diet. It is made up of two polymers: **amylose** and the branched polymer **amylopectin**. Glycogen is a storage polysaccharide in animals and fungi. Like amylopectin, it a branched polymer of glucose, but the branches are shorter and more frequent. Most of the bonds between the subunits of these storage polysaccharides are α(1→4), with the exception of branch points which are α(1→6). Cellulose is a structural polysaccharide found in the cell walls of plants. The glucose monomers are joined by β(1→4) linkages. Chitin is a component in fungal cell walls and the exoskeleton of arthropods. It is structurally similar to cellulose, but each glucose has a nitrogen-containing appendage.

GLYCOLYSIS, GLUCONEOGENESIS, AND THE PENTOSE PHOSPHATE PATHWAY

Glycolysis is a process that metabolizes glucose to produce pyruvate and ATP. The process is inefficient, producing only two net ATP per glucose. However, the breakdown of glucose can continue with the citric acid cycle and oxidative phosphorylation if oxygen is present. In the absence of oxygen, pyruvate is reduced into lactate (or in some cells, ethanol). The overall reaction for glycolysis is:

$$\overset{\text{glucose}}{C_6H_{12}O_6} + 2NAD^+ + 2P_i + 2ADP \rightarrow 2\overset{\text{pyruvate}}{C_3H_4O_3} + 2NADH + 2ATP + 2H^+ + 2H_2O$$

Glycolysis can be divided into three main stages:

- Stage 1: Two ATP are invested to convert glucose into fructose 1,6-biphosphate.
- Stage 2: Fructose 1,6-biphosphate is split into two phosphorylated 3-carbon compounds called glyceraldehyde-3-phosphate, or G3P.
- Stage 3: G3P is oxidized, resulting in two 3-carbon compounds called pyruvate. Four ATP and two NADH are made during this stage. Since two ATP were invested in stage 1, there is a net production of two ATP.

The ten steps of glycolysis:

Step	Substrate	Catalyzed by	Product
1 (irreversible)	Glucose	Hexokinase	Glucose 6-phosphate
2	Glucose 6-phosphate	Phosphogluco-isomerase	Fructose 6-phosphate
3 (irreversible)	Fructose 6-phosphate	Phosphofructo-kinase	Fructose 1, 6-biphosphate
4	Fructose 1, 6-biphosphate	Aldolase	Dihydroxyacetone phosphate
5	Dihydroxyacetone phosphate	Triose phosphate isomerase	Glyceraldehyde 3-phosphate (isomer of dihydroxyacetone phosphate)
6	Glyceraldehyde 3-phosphate	Triose phosphate dehydrogenase	1,3-Biphosphoglycerate
7	1,3-Biphosphoglycerate	Phosphoglycero-kinase	3-Phosphoglycerate
8	3-Phosphoglycerate	Phosphoglycero-mutase	2-Phosphoglycerate
9	2-Phosphoglycerate	Enolase	Phosphoenolpyruvate
10 (irreversible)	Phosphoenolpyruvate	Pyruvate kinase	Pyruvate

FEEDER PATHWAYS: GLYCOGEN, STARCH METABOLISM

A **feeder pathway** for glycolysis describes the entrance of glucose or another reactant into glycolysis. Glucose is not the only carbohydrate that can enter glycolysis. Other hexoses such as fructose and galactose can enter the pathway as well. Fructose is phosphorylated by the enzyme hexokinase to produce fructose 1,6-bisphosphate, which is an intermediate in glycolysis and the process continues from there. In the liver, fructose is metabolized in a different pathway. It is phosphorylated by fructokinase and then cleaved to produce glyceraldehyde 3-phosphate and dihydroxyacetone phosphate, which are intermediates in glycolysis.

Not all non-glucose hexoses are converted to intermediates. A series of reactions can convert galactose into glucose 1-phosphate, which is then converted into glucose 6-phosphate for entry into glycolysis. Disaccharides can be cleaved, and their substituents fed into glycolysis in the manner described above. The polysaccharides, glycogen and starch, can be catabolized into their substituents to feed glucose into glycolysis. Phosphorylase breaks the $\alpha(1\rightarrow4)$ bond between the last glucose in a branch to produce glucose 1-phosphate, before the enzyme phosphoglucomutase converts it to glucose 6-phosphate.

FERMENTATION (ANAEROBIC GLYCOLYSIS)

Anaerobic respiration is one way in which certain organisms can metabolize sugar in the absence of oxygen. It is similar to aerobic respiration, but the final electron acceptor is not oxygen. (Often, it is sulfate or nitrate). Other organisms rely on fermentation to break down sugar when oxygen is not available. In **fermentation**, glycolysis is the only pathway that releases some of the energy stored in glucose; it is not followed by the citric acid cycle or the electron transport chain as in anaerobic respiration. Instead, the pyruvate that is made at the end of glycolysis is reduced to either lactate or ethanol, depending on the type of cell.

Both types of fermentation occur in the cytosol and produce two ATP per molecule of glucose and two NAD^+. NAD^+ is important because it is recycled back into glycolysis to act as an electron acceptor, allowing glycolysis to continually operate in the absence of oxygen. Fermentation is only about 2% efficient, releasing 14.6 kcal from the 686 kcal stored in a mole of ATP.

Lactic acid fermentation occurs in animal cells, often during exertion when the supply of oxygen is too low to keep up with the expenditure of ATP. It also occurs in some types of bacteria, and can be used to make products such as yogurt and cheese. The reversible reaction (beginning with pyruvate) is catalyzed by the enzyme lactate dehydrogenase.

$$\overbrace{C_3H_4O_3}^{\text{pyruvate}} + NADH + H^+ \leftrightarrow \overbrace{C_3H_4O_3}^{\text{lactic acid}} + NAD^+$$

Alcoholic fermentation occurs in yeast cells, and some types of bacteria. This form of fermentation is used in the production of alcoholic beverages and bread-making. There are two steps in this process: the formation of acetaldehyde by pyruvate decarboxylase (irreversible), followed by the reduction of acetaldehyde by alcohol dehydrogenase to form ethanol (reversible). The reactions are summarized below. Note that in the first reaction, CO_2 is produced as a waste product.

$$\overbrace{C_3H_4O_3}^{\text{pyruvate}} \rightarrow \overbrace{C_2H_4O}^{\text{acetaldehyde}} + NADH + H^+ + CO_2 \leftrightarrow \overbrace{C_2H_6O}^{\text{ethanol}} + NAD^+$$

GLUCONEOGENESIS

Gluconeogenesis (GNG) is the biosynthesis of glucose from non-carbohydrate substrates; i.e. not from glycogen or starch. It is essentially the reverse of glycolysis. This valuable but energetically expensive metabolic pathway occurs when glucose levels are low. In humans it occurs mostly in the liver, but also occurs in the small intestine, kidneys, and muscle. Precursors to glucose include lactate, pyruvate, glycerol, and glucogenic amino acids. In fact, all amino acids except lysine and leucine (which are purely ketogenic) can be converted to glucose, and alanine and glutamine are the most commonly used. The net reaction of gluconeogenesis is as follows:

$$2\,\overbrace{C_3H_4O_3}^{\text{pyruvate}} + 4ATP + 2GTP + 2NADH + 2H^+ + 6H_2O \rightarrow \overbrace{C_6H_{12}O_6}^{\text{glucose}} + 4ADP + 2GDP + 2NAD^+ + 6P_i.$$

Gluconeogenesis is described as the reverse of glycolysis, but three of the ten steps of glycolysis are highly energetically favorable (large negative ΔG) and therefore irreversible.

The steps of glycolysis that must be bypassed are:

- Step 1: the phosphorylation of glucose to form glucose 6-phosphate.
  - *Bypass accomplished by the use of the enzyme glucose 6-phosphatase.
- Step 3: the phosphorylation of fructose-6-phosphate to form fructose 1,6-bisphosphate
  - *Bypass accomplished by the use of the enzyme fructose 1,6-bisphosphatase.

- Step 10: the transfer of a phosphate from phosphoenolpyruvate (PEP) to ADP to form pyruvate.
  - *Bypass accomplished through a series of reactions that convert pyruvate to oxaloacetate to PEP.

PENTOSE PHOSPHATE PATHWAY

The **pentose phosphate pathway** is an alternative pathway to glycolysis that occurs in the cytosol of certain cells. It is sometimes referred to as the hexose monophosphate shunt. This pathway degrades glucose to generate NADPH and ribose 5-phosphate. NADPH is used in reductive reactions within the cell, and is necessary for the anabolism of fatty acids and steroidogenesis. It also donates electrons to antioxidants. Ribose 5-phosphate is required for the synthesis of nucleotides.

This pathway consists of two phases: the oxidative phase and the non-oxidative phase. The oxidative phase is irreversible and produces CO_2, NADPH, and ribulose 5-phosphate from glucose 6-phosphate. The nonoxidative phase is reversible and generates ribose 5-phosphate, as well as fructose 6-phosphate and glyceraldehyde 3-phosphate which can be used in glycolysis. Note that no ATP are produced or expended during either phase.

NET (MAXIMUM) MOLECULAR AND ENERGETIC RESULTS OF RESPIRATION PROCESSES

Glycolysis requires the investment of energy in order to produce a net amount of ATP. One ATP is needed to power step 1 of glycolysis, where glucose is phosphorylated to produce glucose 6-phosphate. ATP is also utilized in step 3, where phosphofructokinase catalyzes the phosphorylation of fructose 6-phosphate to produce fructose 1,6-bisphosphate. Step 6 produces two NADH molecules when two molecules of glyceraldehyde 3-phosphate are oxidized to give way to 1,3-biphosphoglycerate. ATP is produced during step 7 when a phosphate group is removed from each of two molecules of 1,3-biphosphoglycerate and transferred to ADP, producing two ATP and two 3-phosphoglycerate. Two more ATP are made during step 10, when a phosphate group from each of two molecules of 1,3-biphosphoglycerate is transferred to ADP, forming pyruvate.

To summarize, two ATP are invested, and four ATP are produced, resulting in a net output of two ATP, two NADH, and two pyruvate per glucose. This process is only about 2% efficient, assuming the standard free energy change of −7.3 kcal/mol for the hydrolysis of ATP, and −686 kcal/mol for the complete oxidation of glucose. However, under cellular conditions, the efficiency may be as high as 4%. The chemical equation for glycolysis is as follows:

$$\overbrace{C_6H_{12}O_6}^{glucose} + 2NAD^+ + 2P_i + 2ADP \rightarrow 2\overbrace{C_3H_4O_3}^{pyruvate} + 2NADH + 2ATP + 2H^+ + 2H_2O$$

PRINCIPLES OF METABOLIC REGULATION

A **metabolic pathway** is a series of connected reactions that result in the synthesis or breakdown of molecules. The product of one reaction is used as a substrate in the next reaction. These pathways must be monitored and regulated so that the immediate demands of a cell can be met. Enzymes play a critical role in this process by increasing the rate of these reactions. Furthermore, activators and inhibitor molecules can control the activity of the enzyme as a way to turn a reaction on or off.

Dynamic steady state is a condition in which a system remains constant as a result of the work being done to maintain that condition. Free energy enters and leaves biological systems, and the system has a higher energy level than its surroundings. This is in contrast to static equilibrium, in which there *is* a stable condition, but no input of energy is required to keep it that way. A cell's metabolism is a steady state condition because the concentrations of reactants and products remains constant, but new substrates are entering the pathway as products are removed.

REGULATION OF GLYCOLYSIS AND GLUCONEOGENESIS

During glycolysis, glucose is used to form pyruvate, and during gluconeogenesis, pyruvate is used to form glucose. These processes are reciprocally regulated so that when one pathway is operating, the other is inhibited. The reason for this becomes clear when examining the production and expenditure of ATP in each process. In glycolysis, 2 ATP are *produced*, while in gluconeogenesis, 4 ATP and 2 GTP are *used*. If both processes occurred at the same time, then the effects of glycolysis would be negated.

Allosteric enzymes are responsible for coordinating these processes. If the cell has high amounts of ATP (relative to AMP) there is no need for glycolysis, and phosphofructokinase is inhibited. High amounts of GTP will inhibit hexokinase. Without these enzymes, glycolysis will not proceed. The surplus of ATP is then used in gluconeogenesis to make glucose, which is then built up into glycogen for later use. Gluconeogenesis is inhibited when AMP builds up in a cell. AMP inhibits the activity of fructose 1,6-bisphosphatase, and ADP inhibits pyruvate carboxylase and phosphoenolpyruvate carboxykinase.

METABOLISM OF GLYCOGEN

Glycogenolysis is the breakdown of glycogen. It begins with the action of the enzyme **glycogen phosphorylase**, which catalyzes the hydrolysis of the terminal $\alpha(1\rightarrow4)$ glycosidic linkage, releasing glucose 1-phosphate. This process continues until a branch point within the glycogen macromolecule is reached. Glycogen phosphorylase cannot hydrolyze the $\alpha(1\rightarrow6)$ linkage at the branch point, so **glycogen debranching enzyme** (GDE) breaks the bond. The glucose 1-phosphates that are clipped from glycogen must then be converted to glucose 6-phosphates for further breakdown. This is achieved by the enzyme **phosphoglucomutase**, which transfers a phosphate to carbon 6 of glucose 1-phosphate to produce glucose 1,6-bisphosphate. The phosphate on carbon 1 is then transferred to phosphoglucomutase, and glucose 6-phosphate is formed. (Note that these processes do not require the hydrolysis of ATP.) Glucose 6-phosphate can be converted to glucose in the liver, kidneys, and small intestine, but not the skeletal muscles.

Glycogenesis, or the synthesis of glycogen, begins with the phosphorylation of glucose to form glucose 6-phosphate (G6P). ATP provides the phosphate, and the reaction is catalyzed by **hexokinase** (in the muscle) or **glucokinase** (in the liver). G6P is then converted to glucose 1-phosphate by **phosphoglucomutase**. The enzyme **UDP-glucose phosphorylase** (UGPP) attaches glucose-1-phosphate with uridine triphosphate (UTP) to form uridine diphosphate glucose (UDP glucose). The enzyme **glycogenin** then attaches carbon 1 of UDP glucose to one of its tyrosine residues via $\alpha(1\rightarrow4)$ glycosidic linkage to begin the formation of a primer. Once the primer has around eight UDP-glucose residues, the enzyme **glycogen synthase** takes over, linking carbon 1 UDP-glucose to carbon 4 of the non-reducing end of glycogen via $\alpha(1\rightarrow4)$ bonds. Branch points are handled by **glycogen branching enzyme** (GBE). This metabolic pathway occurs in the liver and muscle cells.

REGULATION OF GLYCOGEN SYNTHESIS AND BREAKDOWN

Glycogenesis and glycogenolysis must be coordinated so that both processes do not occur simultaneously and cancel each other out. This complex process is achieved through both allosteric control (which acts at the level of the cell) and hormonal control (which acts at the level of the organism). Enzymes such as glycogen synthase and glycogen phosphorylase are allosterically activated or inhibited by molecules that signal the needs of the cell. For example, both glucose-6 phosphate and ATP inhibit glycogen phosphorylase, which is the primary enzyme involved in the

42

degradation of glycogen. It can be also be controlled by the hormones glucagon, epinephrine, and insulin. Glucagon and epinephrine activate glycogen phosphorylase (and therefore glycogenolysis) while insulin deactivates it. This is accomplished through second messenger systems in which the hormone binds to receptors in the cell membrane, causing a cascade of events that affect the concentrations of cAMP. cAMP plays a role in the activation of protein kinase A (PKA) which in turn plays a role in activating the enzymes directly involved in glycogenesis and glycogenolysis by phosphorylation or dephosphorylation.

ANALYSIS OF METABOLIC CONTROL

Metabolic control analysis (MCA) quantifies the control of a specific enzyme over the flux (the rate of the pathway as a whole) and concentration of metabolites. "Control" in this context refers to the degree that an enzyme can alter a pathway. This analysis calculates the effects of the enzyme quantitatively, rather than describing it qualitatively in terms of rate limitation or rate determining steps. For example, instead of labeling a step along the pathway as simply rate-limiting, MCA is used to determine the *amount* that flux varies in response to a change in enzyme activity, and to study the relationship between the *control coefficient* of an enzyme and its *elasticity*. The **control coefficient** is a measure of the effects of flux or concentration on the system as a whole. **Elasticity** measures the effect of metabolite concentration on a local reaction. Elasticity is positive for metabolites that increase the reaction rate, and negative for metabolites that inhibit it. If the flux control coefficient is multiplied by the elasticity for every enzyme in the pathway, they will add up to zero, as stated by the connectivity theorem.

CITRIC ACID CYCLE

ACETYL-COA PRODUCTION

There are various ways in which acetyl coenzyme A (acetyl-CoA) is produced, including the β-oxidation of fatty acids, the breakdown of amino acids, and the oxidative decarboxylation of the pyruvate that was made during glycolysis. Oxidative decarboxylation occurs in the matrix of the mitochondria through the action of the pyruvate dehydrogenase complex. This complex consists of the enzymes pyruvate dehydrogenase, dihydrolipoyl transacetylase, and dihydrolipoyl dehydrogenase. The main events of oxidative decarboxylation occur as follows. First, a carboxyl group is removed from 3-carbon pyruvate in the form of carbon dioxide. The resulting two-carbon acetyl group is oxidized, as NAD^+ accepts two electrons and two hydrogens to form NADH. The acetyl group combines with a derivative of pantothenic acid called coenzyme A, resulting in acetyl-CoA (two acetyl-CoA molecules per glucose). Acetyl-CoA is then catabolized in the citric acid cycle. The overall reaction for the production of acetyl-CoA via oxidative decarboxylation is:

$$\overbrace{C_3H_4O_3}^{\text{pyruvate}} + CoA + NAD^+ \rightarrow \text{acetyl-CoA} + NADH + CO_2$$

REACTIONS OF THE CYCLE, SUBSTRATES AND PRODUCTS

The **citric acid cycle** (also called the Krebs cycle) occurs in the mitochondrial matrix and transfers the energy stored in acetyl-CoA into molecules that are used in oxidative phosphorylation. Some of the important products are 3 NADH, 1 $FADH_2$, and 1 ATP (per molecule of acetyl-CoA).

The cycle begins when the enzyme citrate synthase combines acetyl-CoA with 4-carbon oxaloacetate to form 6-carbon **citric acid**. A hydroxyl group changes location on the citric acid molecule by the enzyme aconitase to form **isocitrate**. The enzyme isocitrate dehydrogenase oxidizes isocitrate to produce 5-carbon **α-ketoglutarate**, as a carbon is released in the form of carbon dioxide. NAD^+ accepts the electrons to make NADH. A similar reaction occurs through the action of α-ketoglutarate dehydrogenase, except when carbon is removed, it is replaced by coenzyme A. NADH and 4-carbon **succinyl** *CoA* are formed. The enzyme succinyl-CoA synthetase catalyzes the next reaction in which a phosphate group replaces coenzyme A on succinyl CoA, before being transferred to GDP to make GTP, and then transferred again from GTP to ADP to form ATP. **Succinate** is produced during the reaction. The transfer of two hydrogens to FAD (forming $FADH_2$) is catalyzed by succinate dehydrogenase, yielding **fumarate**. Fumarase adds water to fumarate to form **malate**, which is then oxidized to regenerate **oxaloacetate**. NAD^+ accepts the electrons and forms NADH.

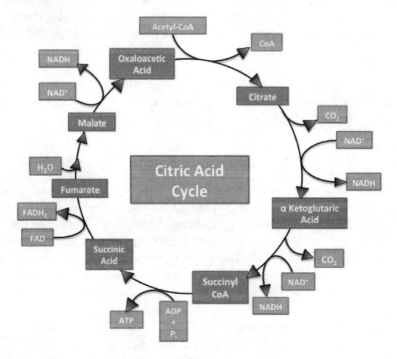

REGULATION OF THE CYCLE

The citric acid cycle is regulated at many levels. The production of acetyl-CoA can be controlled before the cycle begins, and then there are different control points within the cycle itself that can be regulated.

The production of acetyl-CoA (the initiator of the citric acid cycle) is catalyzed by the pyruvate dehydrogenase complex. Pyruvate dehydrogenase can be activated or deactivated in response to levels of NADH, ATP, and acetyl-CoA. High concentrations of these molecules promote phosphorylation of the enzyme, effectively turning it off when energy-rich molecules are in abundance. The enzyme can be activated by high levels of calcium.

Three enzymes within the citric acid cycle also serve as regulation points: citrate synthase, isocitrate dehydrogenase, and α-ketoglutarate dehydrogenase. When NADH is in high concentration, these enzymes are inhibited. They are further regulated by other factors. Both ATP and Succinyl-CoA (an intermediate of the citric acid cycle) inhibit citrate synthase and α-ketoglutarate dehydrogenase. High levels of calcium, ADP and NAD^+ promote the citric acid cycle.

NET (MAXIMUM) MOLECULAR AND ENERGETIC RESULTS OF RESPIRATION PROCESSES

The citric acid cycle alone produces 3 NADH, 1 $FADH_2$, and 1 GTP (later converted to ATP) per cycle. Since two cycles run per glucose molecule, these numbers can be doubled when considering the molecular and energetic results of the cycle. Half of the reactions of the cycle are oxidation reactions, and the energy is conserved in NADH and $FADH_2$. These molecules are used during the next stage (oxidative phosphorylation) to produce more ATP. The maximum ATP yield per NADH and $FADH_2$ is 3 and 2, respectively, but actual yields are closer to 2.5 ATP per NADH and 1.5 per $FADH_2$. Using the maximum values, one acetyl CoA will give rise to 12 ATP when NADH and $FADH_2$ are considered. 2 CO_2 molecules (per molecule of acetyl-CoA) are released as waste products during the cycle. The overall reaction for the citric acid cycle is:

$$\text{acetyl-CoA} + 3NAD^+ + FAD + GDP + P_i + 2H_2O$$
$$\rightarrow 2CO_2 + \text{CoA-SH} + 3NADH + FADH_2 + GTP + 3H^+$$

METABOLISM OF FATTY ACIDS AND PROTEINS

DESCRIPTION OF FATTY ACIDS

A **fatty acid** is a carboxylic acid with a hydrophobic hydrocarbon chain. The carboxyl group (COOH) is the component that participates in chemical reactions. Dehydration synthesis results in an ester linkage between the carboxyl group and a hydroxyl group of an alcohol, often glycerol.

The aliphatic (non-aromatic) chain can be saturated or unsaturated. Saturated fatty acids contain only single bonds, and are therefore "saturated" with hydrogens at every position. Unsaturated fatty acids have at least one double bond. In a **cis** configuration, both hydrogens on either side of the double bond point in the same direction, resulting in a kink in the chain. In a **trans** configuration, the adjacent hydrogens point in opposite directions and the chain has little to no bend.

Chains also vary in the number of carbons, and they are almost always even numbers.

- Short-chain fatty acids (SCFA): fewer than six carbons
- Medium-chain fatty acids (MCFA): 6–12 carbons
- Long-chain fatty acids (LCFA): 13–21
- Very long chain fatty acids (VLCFA) more than 22 carbons.

Fatty acids have many important roles in the body. They can be built up into triglycerides to store energy, and serve as a source of fuel when oxidized. They also make up phospholipids, the main components of plasma membranes. The nonpolar nature of the fatty acids prevents the passage of certain substances across the membrane. The outer leaflets of membranes also contain glycolipids, which aid in cell recognition and membrane stability. Intracellular proteins are often tagged with a lipid to help direct them to their destinations in the membrane. Fatty acids can also act as signaling molecules. For example, some fatty acids regulate transcription factors, and thereby play a role in gene expression.

DIGESTION, MOBILIZATION, AND TRANSPORT OF FATS

Triacylglycerols (or TAGs) are the most common source of fat in the body. They are insoluble in aqueous solution, and group together to form droplets. The liver secretes bile to break down these droplets into micelles so that enzymes have more surface area to act on. Lipases are secreted mainly by the pancreas and empty into the small intestine. These enzymes break the ester linkages within a TAG, producing a free glycerol molecule and 3 fatty acid chains. The subunits are then small enough to be absorbed by the cells of the small intestine. Once in the intestinal wall, they can recombine into TAGs again. These hydrophobic fats must then be transported by a specialized lipoprotein called a chylomicron which carries fats within its core. Since the proteins are too large to enter the blood capillaries directly, they are taken up by lymphatic capillaries before draining into thoracic ducts, which in turn drain into veins. Enzymes known as lipoprotein lipases break down the chylomicron and the TAGs within, which are then taken up by various tissues within the body. Adipose tissue stores fat in large droplets, and can release fatty acids in response to hormonal signals. Other tissues, with the exception of cells of the central nervous system and red blood cells, extract the energy by oxidation of the fatty acids. First, the fatty acids are activated by combining with coenzyme A to form fatty acyl-CoA. This activated form can be transported into the mitochondria via the carnitine carrier system for oxidation.

OXIDATION OF SATURATED FATTY ACIDS

The β-oxidation of saturated fatty acids begins with the oxidation of α and β carbons (C2 and C3) via acyl-CoA-dehydrogenase to form a trans double bond between those carbons. The accompanying reduction reaction produces $FADH_2$ from FAD, and the resulting molecule is called trans-Δ^2-enoyl CoA. In the next reaction, enoyl-CoA hydratase catalyzes the hydration of the double bond to produce L-3-hydroxyacyl CoA. The newly added hydroxyl group on the β-carbon is then oxidized by 3-hydroxyacyl CoA dehydrogenase to form 3-ketoacyl CoA, and NAD^+ is reduced to NADH. In the final reaction, the bond between the α and β carbon is cleaved when the thiol group of coenzyme A is added between the α and β carbons via β-ketothiolase, releasing acetyl-CoA which can then enter the citric acid cycle. The remaining shortened fatty acid will then be put through the same set of reactions repeatedly until all the carbons have been released as acetyl-CoA. An 18-C fatty acid, for example, would eventually give rise to nine molecules of acetyl-CoA. Nine citric acid cycles (at 12 ATP per cycle), plus 9 NADH (3 ATP max, per NADH), plus 9 $FADH_2$ (2 ATP max, per $FADH_2$), would produce a theoretical maximum of 153 ATP for a fatty acid of this length.

OXIDATION OF UNSATURATED FATTY ACIDS

The β-oxidation of unsaturated fatty acids is a similar pathway to that of saturated fatty acids, but additional enzymes are required any time a double bond is encountered. The double bonds of most unsaturated fatty acids are **cis** bonds, meaning the hydrogen atoms on either side of the double bond are on the same side. If there is an odd number of double bonds, as in a monounsaturated fat such as palmitoleate, the enzyme enoyl CoA isomerase converts the cis double bond to a trans double bond to produce **trans-Δ^2-enoyl CoA**: a normal substrate in the β-oxidation pathway that can be acted on by enoyl-CoA hydratase. In the case of an even number of bonds, an intermediate called 2,4 dienoyl-CoA is formed that requires an additional enzyme (2,4 dienoyl CoA reductase) before it can be acted on by enoyl CoA isomerase. 2,4 dienoyl-CoA is reduced (and NADPH is oxidized) to form trans-Δ3-enoyl CoA. Isomerase can now act on this molecule, allowing it to be fed into the β-oxidation pathway.

KETONE BODIES

Ketone bodies are byproducts of the breakdown of fatty acids that can be used as sources of energy when carbohydrates are scarce (as in starvation). Acetoacetate, β-hydroxybutyrate, and acetone are all ketone bodies, but only acetoacetate and β-hydroxybutyrate are catabolized for energy; acetone is simply excreted from the body. The production of ketone bodies (ketogenesis) occurs in the mitochondria of liver cells when acetyl-CoA begins to accumulate. Two acetyl-CoA molecules combine to form acetoacetyl-CoA, which combines with another acetyl-CoA molecule via HMG-CoA synthase to form HMG-CoA. The enzyme HMG-CoA lyase then breaks down HMG-CoA to produce acetoacetate, which can give rise to both β-hydroxybutyrate and acetone. Ketoacidosis will occur when high amounts of ketone bodies bring the pH of the body to dangerously low levels. The liver cannot use the ketone bodies it produces because it lacks the enzyme thiophorase (also known as succinyl CoA-acetoacetate CoA transferase) which oxidizes β-hydroxybutyrate to form acetoacetate. This active form can be metabolized in the mitochondria to yield energy.

ANABOLISM OF FATS

Fatty acids are constructed from acetyl-CoA, mainly in the cytoplasm of liver and fat cells. Acetyl-CoA cannot cross the mitochondrial membrane into the cytoplasm, but citrate can. Once citrate is in the cytoplasm, it is split apart by the enzyme **citrate lyase** into acetyl-CoA and oxaloacetate. Acetyl-CoA can now be incorporated into a fatty acid. It is activated by the enzyme **acetyl-CoA carboxylase** by adding CO_2 to produce malonyl-CoA. This process requpass-throughenditure of ATP, and the cofactor biotin. The enzyme complex **fatty acid synthase** (which requires vitamin B_5) then catalyzes a series of reactions, including the reduction of the carboxyl group, as NADPH is oxidized. Water is removed, creating a double bond which is reduced by a second NADPH. The 2-carbon compound is incorporated into the elongating fatty acid chain until it is 16 carbons in length. This compound is known as **palmitate**, and is the only fatty acid produced by humans from simple starting materials. To form a triacylglycerol, three fatty acid chains must form ester linkages to glycerol 3-phosphate. As with fatty acid synthesis, triacylglycerol formation occurs mostly in the liver and adipose tissue.

Overall reaction for fatty acid synthesis:

$$8\text{acetyl-CoA} + 7\text{ATP} + 14\text{NADPH} + 14\text{H}^+$$
$$\rightarrow \text{palmitate} + 7\text{CO}_2 + 7\text{ADP} + 7\text{P}_i + 8\text{CoA} + 14\text{NADP}^+ + 6\text{H}_2\text{O}$$

METABOLISM OF PROTEINS

When proteins are digested, the amino acids are usually incorporated into new proteins (during translation), but they can be metabolized for energy as a last resort.

Protein digestion begins in the stomach with the enzyme pepsin, which denatures the protein and begins hydrolyzing some of the peptide bonds. Polypeptides and free amino acids will stimulate the secretion of cholecystokinin (CCK), which in turn stimulates the release of pancreatic proteases trypsin, chymotrypsin, and carboxypeptidases, each with its own specificity. They are activated in the small intestine with the help of enteropeptidase and continue to hydrolyze the peptide bonds. Aminopeptidase is an enzyme found in the plasma membrane of the cells of the small intestine that finishes the degradation of the protein into units no longer than a tripeptide. The amino acids, dipeptides, and tripeptides are actively transported into the cells and then released into the blood.

Proteins are only metabolized as a source of energy in extreme circumstances when carbohydrates and lipids are not available. For this to happen, the amino group must be removed from the amino acid in a process called deamination. The amino group is converted to ammonia (which is then converted to urea and excreted), and the remaining molecule (a keto acid) can be used as a source of fuel.

OXIDATIVE PHOSPHORYLATION
ELECTRON TRANSPORT CHAIN AND OXIDATIVE PHOSPHORYLATION, SUBSTRATES AND PRODUCTS, GENERAL FEATURES OF THE PATHWAY

Oxidative phosphorylation refers to the combined processes of the electron transport chain and chemiosmosis. This pathway produces more ATP than any other stage of cellular respiration. In the electron transport chain (located in the cristae), a series of redox reactions helps to generate a proton gradient. NADH and $FADH_2$ (products of previous stages) are oxidized, and their electrons passed along a chain of four enzyme complexes: NADH dehydrogenase (I), succinate dehydrogenase (II), Q-cytochrome c oxidoreductase (III), and cytochrome c oxidase (IV). Electrons from NADH enter the chain at complex I (more specifically to a prosthetic group on the complex called flavin mononucleotide or FMN), while electrons from $FADH_2$ enter at complex II. Electrons from both NADH and $FADH_2$ are passed onto a carrier called ubiquinone (also called coenzyme Q) which transports them to complex III. Cytochrome C carries the electrons to complex IV, where oxygen (the final electron acceptor) is reduced to form water. The energy that is lost by the moving electrons is used by complexes I, III, and IV to pump protons from the mitochondrial matrix to the intermembrane space. This establishes an electrochemical gradient, and the protons re-enter the matrix through an enzyme called ATP synthase. As they flow through the enzyme, they turn a portion of it like a water wheel, allowing it to add a phosphate to ADP, forming ATP (1 ATP per 3 protons).

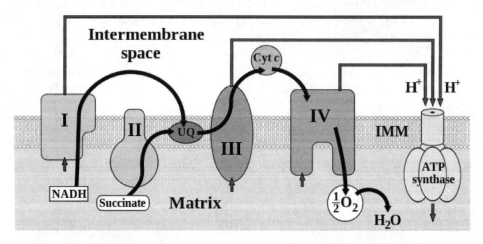

ELECTRON TRANSFER IN MITOCHONDRIA

First, NADH is oxidized to NAD^+, donating two electrons to complex I. The electrons are passed to ubiquinone (which becomes ubiquinol, or QH_2 in its reduced form). Complex 1 pumps four protons out of the matrix into the intermembrane space. $FADH_2$ donates two electrons to complex II, which also passes them onto ubiquinone. The electrons then travel from ubiquinone to complex III (which pumps out another four protons), where they are carried by cytochrome C to complex IV (which pumps out two protons). The final electron acceptor is oxygen, which splits apart and combines with hydrogen ions to form water.

Nicotinamide adenine dinucleotide (NADH) is a coenzyme that can switch back and forth between its reduced form (NADH) and its oxidized form (NAD^+). Its role in oxidative phosphorylation is vital, as it shuttles electrons to the electron transport chain, where the energy of those electrons is harvested to synthesize ATP. NADH donates two electrons to complex I of the electron transport chain within the inner mitochondrial membrane. Each subsequent complex (II, III, and then IV) is more electron-hungry than the last, so the electrons are transferred through a series of redox reactions before being accepted by O_2.

Nicotinamide adenine dinucleotide phosphate $NADP^+$ is another coenzyme that can cycle between its reduced (NADPH) and oxidized ($NADP^+$) forms. While NADH is often employed in catabolic reactions, NADPH is a reducing agent in many anabolic reactions. In photosynthesis, it is produced in the redox reactions of the electron transport chain of the thylakoid membrane, and used to reduce intermediates within the Calvin cycle (where sugars are made).

Flavoproteins are one of the many types of electron carriers found in the electron transport chain. They contain a flavin nucleotide such as flavin adenine dinucleotide (FAD) or flavin mononucleotide (FMN). These prosthetic groups transfer electrons and protons during many cellular processes, including cellular respiration. Both NADH dehydrogenase (complex I) and succinate-dehydrogenase (complex II) contain flavoproteins. NADH donates two electrons to FMN of complex 1, reducing it to $FMNH_2$. The flavoprotein within complex II contains FAD, which is reduced to $FADH_2$. There is also an electron transfer flavoprotein complex within the mitochondrial membrane that accepts electrons from primary dehydrogenases.

Cytochromes are electron carriers that contain a heme group (with a central iron atom) that allows it to transfer electrons. They are found in complexes III and IV. When electrons are transferred to complex III (Q-cytochrome c oxidoreductase), they are passed to cytochrome c, and then to complex IV (cytochrome c oxidase). Complex IV accepts one electron at a time, but transfers four electrons to oxygen at once.

ATP SYNTHASE, CHEMIOSMOTIC COUPLING

ATP synthase is an enzyme that uses a proton motive force to form ATP from ADP and an inorganic phosphate. It is often referred to as the world's smallest motor. This protein complex is integrated into the inner mitochondrial membrane. The proton motive force is established by pumping protons from the matrix into the intermembrane space using the energy from the electrons traveling along the electron transport chain. Complex 1 (the first of the enzyme complexes in the ETC) pumps four protons out of the matrix into the intermembrane space. Complex III pumps out four more protons and complex IV pumps out two, for a total of ten protons. The protons accumulate, and the energy stored in this electrochemical gradient is used to drive **chemiosmosis**: the process that couples the reactions of the electron transport chain to the production of ATP.

The protein complex ATP synthase consists of two main coupled regions, F_0 and F_1. The proton motive force causes the accumulated H^+ ions to move down the gradient into the F_0 portion of the enzyme. This flow of protons causes the F_0 portion to spin like a rotor, similar to the way that water turns a water wheel. Each proton completes one full revolution and is released on the opposite side of the membrane. The torque created by the rotation of the F_0 complex is transferred to the F_1 region by a shaft. The rotating shaft does not turn the F_1 region, but it does cause a conformational change, which in turn catalyzes the formation of ATP from ADP and a phosphate group. One ATP molecule is produced for every three H^+ ions that pass through ATP synthase.

NET (MAXIMUM) MOLECULAR AND ENERGETIC RESULTS OF RESPIRATION PROCESSES

Oxidative phosphorylation yields more ATP than any other pathway of cellular respiration, though it is dependent on the products of the previous reactions. The exact amount of ATP can vary depending on environmental conditions and cell type. Each NADH is capable of producing 3 ATP, however 2.5 is often used in calculations to account for suboptimal conditions and the active transport of NADH. Each $FADH_2$ can generate a maximum of 2 ATP, but 1.5 is more likely in normal conditions. To summarize the important products of each stage (per molecule of glucose):

Glycolysis: 2 ATP, 2 NADH, and 2 pyruvate

The **link reaction** (pyruvate decarboxylation): 2 NADH, 2 acetyl-CoA, and 2 CO_2 (waste)

The **citric acid cycle**: 2 ATP, 6 NADH, 2 $FADH_2$, and 4 CO_2 (waste)

49

Oxidative phosphorylation generates a maximum of 34 ATP, though the actual amount may be closer to 28 when using the more realistic yields per NADH and $FADH_2$. It also produces water when oxygen accepts electrons at the end of the electron transport chain.

Under the most ideal conditions, a eukaryotic cell could generate a maximum of 38 ATP per glucose. Using this number, the efficiency of aerobic respiration would be about 40%, assuming the standard free energy change of -7.3 kcal/mol for the hydrolysis of ATP, and -686 kcal/mol for the complete oxidation of glucose. However, it is probably closer to 34% when accounting for normal conditions.

REGULATION OF OXIDATIVE PHOSPHORYLATION

Oxidative phosphorylation is regulated mainly by O_2 and ADP, and is directly tied to the energy requirements of the cell. If oxygen levels are depleted, electrons will have nowhere to go at the end of the electron transport chain, and the redox reactions come to a halt. The electron carriers NADH and $FADH_2$ accumulate, inhibiting the citric acid cycle. If oxygen *is* present, then oxidative phosphorylation is further regulated by ADP. As ATP is consumed, the levels of ADP rise. ADP allosterically stimulates the activity of isocitrate dehydrogenase, the enzyme that catalyzes the third step of the citric acid cycle (the oxidative decarboxylation of isocitrate into alpha-ketoglutarate). The rate of the citric acid cycle increases, which in turn increases the rate of oxidative phosphorylation. If ATP is in abundance, it acts as an allosteric inhibitor of cytochrome *c* oxidase (complex IV of the electron transport chain). Complex IV can also be inhibited by carbon monoxide, cyanide, and azide. When the complex is deactivated, the proton motive force will not be established, and chemiosmosis will not occur.

MITOCHONDRIA, APOPTOSIS, OXIDATIVE STRESS

Mitochondria play a critical role in inducing apoptosis in response to oxidative stress. **Apoptosis** is programmed cell death. This mechanism targets cells that, for one reason or another, need to be eliminated, and does not refer to the demise of cells that are exposed to extreme conditions or infection. Cells singled out for apoptosis include those that have lost their anchorage to adjacent cells, have damaged DNA, or experience oxidative stress.

Oxidative stress is the loss of balance between the production of reactive oxygen species (ROS) and the antioxidants that defend against them. ROS are results of the incomplete reduction of O_2 during the processes of the electron transport chain. They are highly reactive and unstable, and include superoxide anions, peroxides, and hydroxyl radicals. Antioxidants and certain enzymes seek to neutralize them, but sometimes apoptosis is required.

To initiate apoptosis, the permeability of the outer mitochondrial membrane increases as a result of proapoptotic Bcl-2 proteins. This allows cytochrome c (part of the electron transport chain) to move into the cytoplasm and activate enzymes known as caspases. These enzymes begin the breakdown of specific intracellular components, while activating other enzymes to do the same.

HORMONAL REGULATION AND INTEGRATION OF METABOLISM
HIGHER LEVEL INTEGRATION OF HORMONE STRUCTURE AND FUNCTION

Hormones are responsible for the integration of energy metabolism. Metabolism is regulated on the cellular level, but it is important that it be regulated at a higher level, the level of the organism. The endocrine system produces hormones that work to maintain homeostasis by responding to changes in activity, food intake, or other events. They act as chemical messengers, traveling through body fluids and binding to receptors on or inside target cells. Hormones are involved with many essential functions including growth and development, reproduction, and metabolism (such as carbohydrate, lipid, and protein metabolism).

Hormones come in a variety of structures that can be grouped into three main classes: lipid-based, amino acid-derived, and peptides. Lipid hormones (such as cortisol) are usually derived from cholesterol to form steroids, and they are insoluble in water. Most amino-acid derived and peptide hormones (such as epinephrine and insulin, respectively) are water-soluble, and cannot diffuse across the plasma membrane. Water-soluble hormones act relatively quickly through second-messenger systems, while lipid-soluble hormones tend to regulate transcription and act more slowly (but with a more prolonged effect).

Tissue Specific Metabolism

The metabolic reactions that occur in various tissues can change depending on whether the body is in an absorptive state (well-fed, energy-storing) or post-absorptive state (fasting, energy-utilizing).

Liver: In the absorptive state, insulin facilitates the synthesis of glycogen and/or fatty acids from glucose. Fatty acids will be built into triglycerides and sent to adipose tissue. In the fasting state, glycogen is broken down into glucose and released in the blood. Amino acids are converted to keto acids, which the liver can metabolize for energy.

Adipose tissue: When the body is well fed, fat cells take up glucose and use it to make triglycerides. During the post-absorptive state, low levels of insulin stimulate the breakdown of triglycerides so that fatty acids can be released.

Skeletal muscle: In the absorptive state, glucose can be made into glycogen or oxidized if needed for energy, and amino acids are built into proteins. In the fasting state, glycogen is broken down into glucose, and proteins are broken down into amino acids which are taken up by the liver to form keto acids and glucose.

Cardiac muscle: In both the absorptive and post-absorptive states, fatty acids are oxidized for fuel.

Brain: The brain does not store energy. In the absorptive state, it oxidizes glucose. In a prolonged fasting state, it oxidizes both ketones and glucose.

Hormonal Regulation of Fuel Metabolism

The main hormones involved in the regulation of fuel metabolism include insulin, glucagon, epinephrine, glucocorticoids, and thyroid hormones.

During the absorptive state, insulin facilitates the uptake of glucose from the blood, and stimulates the synthesis of glycogen while inhibiting glycogenolysis. Insulin is opposed by many counterregulatory hormones, as described below.

Glucagon (in the fasting state) signals the cell to mobilize its glucose reserves, breaking down glycogen and increasing the levels of glucose in the blood.

Epinephrine stimulates glycogenolysis. Furthermore, an increase in epinephrine (and therefore a decrease in insulin) causes cells to release amino acids from muscle cells and fatty acids and glycerol from adipose tissue. The liver will use amino acids and glycerol to synthesize glucose during gluconeogenesis so that the body has a source of glucose during longer episodes of fasting. (Glycogenolysis releases glucose into the blood more quickly than gluconeogenesis.) Epinephrine is also known to raise the basal metabolic rate.

Glucocorticoids inhibit the uptake of glucose, and stimulate gluconeogenesis in response to stress by stimulating the release of amino acids and glycerol into the blood.

Thyroid hormones increase the basal metabolic rate.

<u>OBESITY AND REGULATION OF BODY MASS</u>

When caloric intake is equal to the energy expended, the body mass of an individual will not change. Excess calories result in the storage of fat in adipose tissue and an increase in body mass. Hormones such as leptin and ghrelin help to balance the intake and output of energy. Leptin is produced by adipose tissue, and binds to receptors in the hypothalamus to suppress appetite when full. Obesity can result if leptin is not produced, or if it cannot bind to the leptin receptors. Ghrelin is sometimes called the "hunger hormone" because it (like leptin) acts on the cells of the hypothalamus. But unlike leptin, ghrelin enhances hunger. It is secreted by the stomach when it is empty, but the secretion stops as the stomach stretches with food. It can also be secreted in response to stimuli such as the scent or sight of a good meal.

MITOSIS AND MEIOSIS

MITOTIC PROCESS: PROPHASE, METAPHASE, ANAPHASE, TELOPHASE, INTERPHASE

Mitosis is the stage of the cell cycle in which the nucleus divides. It alternates with a much longer stage called interphase in which the cell performs its normal functions and prepares for division by copying organelles and duplicating chromosomes. If the cell passes the two major regulatory checkpoints of interphase, it proceeds through the four phases of mitosis, as summarized in the table below (though there will be one last checkpoint prior to anaphase). Mitosis is usually followed by cytokinesis, division of the cytoplasm, and results in two genetically identical daughter cells with the same number of chromosomes as the parent cell.

Prophase	Chromatin condenses into chromosomes The nucleolus and nuclear membrane break down The mitotic spindle begins to form
Metaphase	The spindle aligns the chromosomes along the metaphase plate
Anaphase	Sister chromatids are split at the centromere and pulled toward opposite poles
Telophase	Chromosomes uncoil A nuclear membrane forms around each set of chromosomes A nucleolus forms in each new nucleus The mitotic spindle breaks down Cytokinesis begins (it may also begin during anaphase)

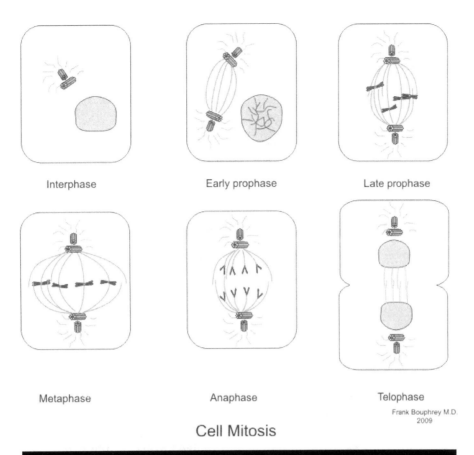

Interphase   Early prophase   Late prophase

Metaphase   Anaphase   Telophase

Frank Bouphrey M.D.
2009

Cell Mitosis

Review Video: Mitosis
Visit mometrix.com/academy and enter code: 849894

At the onset of prophase, chromatin coils tightly into discrete chromosomes that are visible under a light microscope. The chromosomes resemble the shape of an "X", with identical DNA in each sister chromatid. The sister chromatids are bound together along their entire length by protein complexes called cohesins, but by metaphase all cohesins are broken down, except those found at the centromere. As the chromatin condenses, the nuclear envelope begins to disintegrate and the nucleolus disappears. Centrosomes, the microtubule organizing centers of the cell, migrate towards opposite poles of the cell as microtubules polymerize outward. This begins the formation of the mitotic spindle, which continues until metaphase. Protein-based structures called kinetochores form at the centromere to serve as an attachment point for the kinetochore fibers (microtubules) of the spindle. As the kinetochore microtubules attach to each chromosome at the centromere, other microtubules called polar fibers overlap at the center of the cell, never interacting with the chromosomes. By the end of prophase, the nuclear envelope has completely dissolved. This tends to be the longest stage of mitosis.

During metaphase, the centrosomes are at opposite poles of the cell, and chromosomes are positioned along an imaginary line between the two centrosomes known as the metaphase plate (sometimes called the spindle equator or equatorial plate). The kinetochore fibers lengthen or shorten as needed to line up the chromosomes, and the movement is assisted by forces exerted by motor proteins. Polar fibers continue to grow until they are sufficiently overlapped in preparation for the next stage of mitosis. Anaphase will only follow metaphase if the chromosomes are properly aligned, and every kinetochore on every sister chromatid is attached to a kinetochore fiber. Metaphase is usually shorter than prophase.

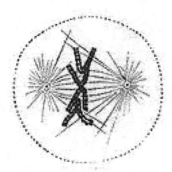

Chromosomes are at their most condensed form during anaphase. The stage begins when an enzyme known as separin cleaves the cohesins that hold sister chromatids together. The kinetochore fibers shorten as a result of depolymerization, splitting the centromeres and pulling the liberated chromosomes toward the centrosomes. As they are dragged through the cytosol, the linear chromosomes bend into a "V" shape as they trail behind the centromere. Meanwhile, the overlapping polar fibers push away from each other, causing the cell to elongate. There is now a complete set of chromosomes at each end of the cell.

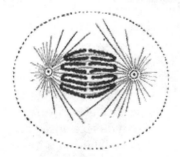

As liberated chromosomes arrive at the poles of the cell, a new nuclear membrane is formed around each group. The polar fibers continue to elongate the cell as the chromosomes uncoil and the nucleoli reform. The microtubules of the spindle are depolymerized and disappear. Cytokinesis begins during either telophase or late anaphase. A cleavage furrow forms near the site of the metaphase plate as a contractile ring of microfilaments beneath the plasma membrane begins to constrict the cell. This will continue after telophase, pinching the parent cell into two identical daughter cells.

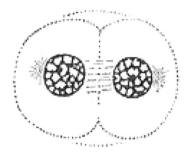

CENTRIOLES, ASTERS, SPINDLES

The mitotic spindle is responsible for segregating sister chromatids during mitosis. The assembly of the spindle begins with a structure called a **centrosome**, often described as the microtubule-organizing center of the cell. In animal cells, the microtubules are organized into structures called **centrioles**. Each centrosome is made of an amorphous matrix of proteins called pericentriolar material that encloses two centrioles that are oriented at right angles to each other. A centriole consists of nine triplets of microtubules arranged in a cylindrical shape. During the formation of the spindle, microtubules extend out from the centrioles to form spindle fibers. Some of these fibers attach to the chromosomes, and others overlap near the midline of the cell. A star-shaped array of shorter microtubules project from each centrosome to form an **aster**. Asters ensure the correct position of the mitotic spindle by anchoring the centrioles to the cell membrane at opposite poles of the cell.

Centrioles

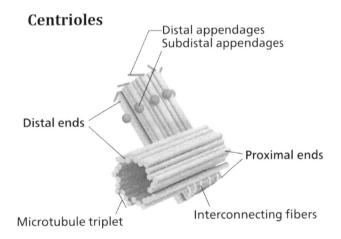

CHROMATIDS, CENTROMERES, KINETOCHORES

Chromosomes are duplicated during the S phase of the cell cycle so that a complete set of DNA can be distributed to each daughter cell during mitosis. Each "half" of a duplicated chromosome is called a **chromatid**, and they are attached to each other at the **centromere** by cohesin proteins. The centromere is characterized by repetitive sequences of DNA (centromeric DNA), and two protein complexes called **kinetochores** that form upon it. (Each chromatid has its own kinetochore.) The inner portion of a kinetochore associates with the centromeric DNA, and the outer portion provides an attachment point for the kinetochore microtubules of the mitotic spindle. When the microtubules contract, chromatids of a duplicated chromosome are separated at the centromere. They are no longer considered chromatids at this time, and are instead called chromosomes.

NUCLEAR MEMBRANE BREAKDOWN AND REORGANIZATION

In most eukaryotic cells, the nuclear membrane (also called the nuclear envelope, or NE) disappears during prophase so that the spindle fibers can access the duplicated chromosomes. It later reforms around each set of chromosomes during late anaphase or telophase. The disassembly of the NE is controlled by cyclin-dependent kinases. These enzymes phosphorylate proteins of the inner nuclear membrane, causing them to dissociate from the NE. This in turn causes the nuclear lamina (the structure that supports the nuclear envelope) to break down. Some elements from the disassembled NE diffuse into the cytosol, and others are incorporated into the endoplasmic reticulum. It is not entirely clear how the membrane reforms, but it is likely that inner membrane proteins are dephosphorylated, and parts of the endoplasmic reticulum are reorganized to form a new nuclear membrane.

MECHANISMS OF CHROMOSOME MOVEMENT

Chromosome movement is facilitated by the lengthening and shortening of microtubules, and is further aided by motor proteins. Microtubules are hollow structures made of protein dimer subunits called alpha and beta tubulin. During prophase, these dynamic structures radiate from the centrosome by adding tubulin at the plus end, while the minus end remains fixed at the centrosome. Eventually, the kinetochores of every chromosome will be "captured" by a microtubule. The chromosomes are then pushed and pulled by polymerization or depolymerization of the microtubules until they are positioned along an imaginary midline called the metaphase plate. This movement is mediated by ATP-driven motor proteins called kinesins that "walk" along the microtubules toward the plus end. When the chromosomes are aligned, the microtubules that are attached to the chromosome depolymerize by the removal of tubulin from the plus end. As the kinetochore fibers shorten, the chromosomes separate at the centromere. Meanwhile, the polar microtubules that overlap in the center of the cell lengthen and push against each other. The combined effect of the elongating polar microtubules and shortening kinetochore microtubules moves the chromosomes towards the poles of the cell.

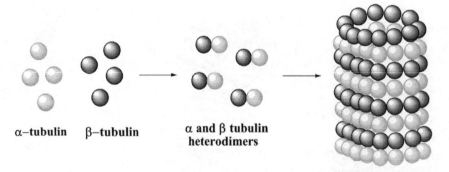

α–tubulin   β–tubulin   α and β tubulin heterodimers   Section of a Microtubule

Review Video: Chromosomes
Visit mometrix.com/academy and enter code: 132083

PHASES OF CELL CYCLE: G₀, G₁, S, G₂, M

The **cell cycle** can be described as the life of a cell, beginning with the formation of the cell, and ending with its own division. The phases of the cycle are G_1 (first gap), S (synthesis), G_2 (second gap) and M (the mitotic phase). Many cells, however, enter a non-growing G_0 state in which the cell performs its job but does not divide. This may happen for a number of reasons, and it is not always reversible. Cells that are deficient in nutrients or growth factors may be blocked from proceeding to the S phase, and only called back to the cycle when favorable conditions are restored. Mature liver cells and many adult stem cells exist in a reversible **quiescent** state, and only divide in response to stimuli such as tissue damage. Some cells leave the cell cycle permanently. A cell with damaged DNA, for example, is likely to enter an irreversible state of **senescence**. This allows the cell to avoid apoptosis (programmed cell death), but it will remain in G_0 indefinitely. Other highly differentiated cells such as nerve and cardiac muscle cells permanently leave the cell cycle because they are genetically programmed to do so.

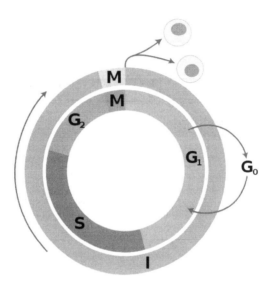

The G_1 (first gap) phase of the cell cycle is the first part of interphase, and it begins immediately after cell division. During this stage, the volume of the cell increases, and the metabolic activities that were inhibited during mitosis are accelerated. The cell begins the task of copying its organelles, synthesizing mRNA, tRNA, and rRNA, and producing the enzymes required for DNA replication, all while continuing to perform its given function. The time duration of this phase varies greatly, but it tends to be the longest phase of the cell cycle, averaging 6-12 hours. Some cells remain in this phase for years. Before the cell is allowed to proceed to the S phase, it is inspected at the G_1 checkpoint. It "passes" if it has grown enough and has sufficient nutrients and growth factors, and the DNA is not damaged. If it "fails" it enters the G_0 phase.

The S (synthesis) phase of the cell cycle falls between G_1 and G_2 of interphase. During this time (which averages 6–8 hours) each molecule of DNA is replicated, doubling the genetic content from 2n to 4n. Note that this does *not* change the ploidy of the cell; the chromosome number remains at 46. Helicases separate the two complementary strands of DNA at multiple sites along each molecule, and DNA polymerases add nucleotides at a rate of about 50 nucleotides per second. By the end of the S phase, there is an identical copy of each DNA molecule, ensuring that each daughter cell that is created during the M phase will have a complete genome. Centrosomes are duplicated during this stage as well, while transcription and protein synthesis are inhibited.

The G_2 (second gap) phase follows DNA replication, and is the final part of interphase. It is characterized by roughly 3–4 hours of cell growth, continued replication of organelles, and protein synthesis. The centrosomes that were duplicated during the S phase begin to mature, as microtubules become more organized and the centrioles elongate. As it prepares for mitosis, the cell performs its usual metabolic functions-but before the cell is allowed to divide, it must pass inspection at the G_2 checkpoint. If any errors are detected in the duplicated chromosomes, the cell cycle is arrested until the DNA can be repaired. Cells that are significantly and irreparably damaged will either enter a state of senescence, or be eliminated through programmed cell death.

Mitosis (nuclear division) and cytokinesis (cytoplasmic division) together make up the M phase of the cell cycle. There is no growth during this phase, and normal metabolic functioning is inhibited to devote the cell's resources to the division process. During mitosis, the chromosomes condense (prophase), align along the metaphase plate (metaphase), split at the centromere and segregate (anaphase), and uncoil as a new nuclear membrane is built around each full set (telophase). Cytokinesis overlaps with the final stages of mitosis.

In animal cells, cytokinesis results from the formation of a contractile ring of actin and non-muscle myosin II filaments. This ring forms around the equator of the cell, directly beneath the plasma membrane, and parallel to the metaphase plate. Myosin is a motor protein that uses ATP to move the actin filaments, causing the ring to contract like a drawstring. As this is happening, vesicles from inside the cell fuse along the cleavage furrow to form a plasma membrane. The two cells become physically separated in a process called abscission. The M phase is the shortest phase of the cell cycle, averaging 1–2 hours.

GROWTH ARREST

Cell growth can be halted in response to signals from both inside and outside the cell. For example, most cells require anchorage to neighboring cells or substrates to proliferate. Cells that exhibit anchorage dependence usually exhibit density-dependent inhibition as well. As they become crowded, the physical constraints may stop the cells from growing. Crowding may also activate signal transduction pathways that arrest cells at certain points in the cell cycle. Growth arrest may also occur in conditions of oxidative stress, infection, or depleted levels of nutrients and/or growth factors. (Growth factors are proteins that stimulate cell growth.) Finally, any cells with damaged or incompletely replicated DNA, or chromosomes that are not properly aligned along the midline of the cell during mitosis, are arrested before they divide by checkpoint proteins. If the problem can be corrected, the cell will be allowed to progress. Cells that are too damaged will either remain in an arrested state permanently, or undergo apoptosis.

CONTROL OF CELL CYCLE

There are three significant checkpoints that control the cell cycle: G_1, G_2, and M. These regulation points can be compared to traffic lights. If a cell fails inspection, then its progression to the next stage is halted. Checkpoints respond to signals from both inside the cell (such as incomplete DNA replication) and outside the cell (such as overcrowding, or a deficiency in growth factors).

Checkpoint	Assesses the cell for the following conditions:
G_1 (G_1 / S transition)	Sufficient cell growth Presence of adequate growth factors Sufficient energy reserves / nutrients DNA integrity (no damage) Side note: This checkpoint is called the "restriction point." Once the cell has passed it, the cell is committed to division.

G_2 (G$_2$ / M transition)	Completely replicated chromosomes following S phase DNA integrity (no damage)
M (metaphase of mitosis)	Chromosomes are aligned along the metaphase plate during metaphase Every kinetochore is anchored to a spindle fiber

Checkpoints are controlled by proteins, namely cyclins and cyclin-dependent kinases (CDKs) that respond to intracellular and extracellular cues. Cyclins belong to a family of proteins that activate CDKs by binding to them to form cyclin-dependent kinase complexes (CDKCs). Concentrations of cyclins fluctuate throughout the cycle to control the timing of each phase. Once a CDKC becomes enzymatically active, it can phosphorylate target proteins (such as transcription factors) within the cell cycle. Phosphorylation may increase or decrease the activity of the target, which in turn affects the progression of the cell cycle. A well-known CDKC is MPF, or maturation-promoting factor. It phosphorylates proteins in the nuclear membrane, causing it to break down at the onset of mitosis. Later, it activates APC/C. or anaphase-promoting complex, in order to initiate its own destruction and move the cell from the M phase to the G_1 phase.

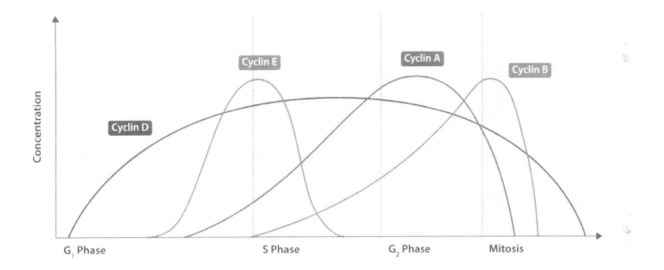

LOSS OF CELL CYCLE CONTROLS IN CANCER CELLS

Cancer cells do not respond to signals that control the cell cycle. They bypass checkpoints and proliferate in conditions that should trigger senescence or apoptosis. This can happen as a result of mutations in the genes that produce either positive or negative regulatory proteins. For example, there are tumor suppressor genes, including the RB (retinoblastoma), BRCA, and p53 genes that control the production of proteins that *inhibit* the cell cycle in unfavorable conditions. P53 is nicknamed the "guardian of the genome" because when DNA is damaged, the p53 protein (a transcription factor) triggers the synthesis of the p21 protein, which forms a complex with CDK, arresting the cell cycle before the S phase. Many incidences of cancers are associated with a p53 mutation.

Mutations can also arise in genes called proto-oncogenes that synthesize proteins that *stimulate* the cycle. For example, a mutation could transform a proto-oncogene into an oncogene that allows a CDK to function without partnering with a cyclin. In short, a mutation in any of the proteins that play a role in the cell cycle can lead to uncontrolled cell division.

SIGNIFICANCE OF MEIOSIS

Meiosis is the process by which sexually reproducing organisms create gametes, or sex cells, from a single diploid cell. The events of meiosis ensure that these gametes have half the number of chromosomes (haploid) and that each gamete has a unique combination of genes. In the first stage of meiosis (prophase I), chromatin condenses into chromosomes, and each chromosome pairs up with its homolog in a process called synapsis. One homolog then exchanges genetic material with the other. This process, known as crossing-over, results in chromosomes with new, reshuffled alleles. Sister chromatids are no longer identical, and each member of a homologous pair now has DNA from the other.

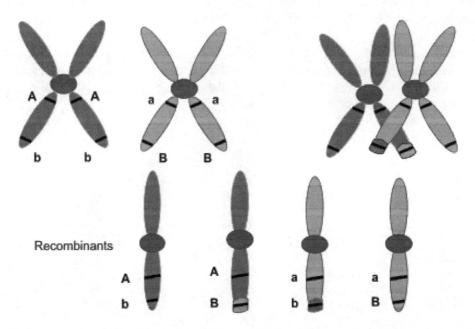

In the second stage of meiosis (metaphase I), chromosomes line up in pairs, and the orientation of the pairs is random every time. This means that gametes receive a random assortment of maternal and paternal chromosomes when homologous are split and distributed to each daughter cell in anaphase II. The events described above allow for a nearly infinite amount of genetically unique gametes.

IMPORTANT DIFFERENCES BETWEEN MEIOSIS AND MITOSIS

Mitosis is the mechanism by which a fertilized egg (zygote) grows into an adult and also the process that repairs tissues. Mitosis involves a single division of the nucleus and includes these stages: prophase, prometaphase, metaphase, anaphase, and telophase. During these stages, the chromatin condenses into chromosomes that then line up in a single line along the equator of the cell. Sister chromatids (with identical alleles) are split at the centromere and pulled toward each pole of the cell by the mitotic spindle, and a nuclear envelope forms around each group of chromosomes. Each nucleus has a complete set of DNA with the same number of chromosomes as the original cell.

Meiosis is a type of cell division that makes gametes. The process involves two divisions: meiosis I (prophase I, prometaphase I, metaphase I, anaphase I, and telophase I) and meiosis II (prophase II, etc.). During prophase I, homologous chromosomes pair up to form a tetrad and exchange genetic material before lining up in pairs along the equator of the cell during metaphase I. (Synapsis does not happen in mitosis.) These pairs are separated during anaphase I, and by the end of the first division, there are two genetically different daughter cells with half the number of chromosomes as the parent cell. These cells undergo a second division (similar to the stages of mitosis) to split the sister chromatids and produce four genetically different haploid daughter cells.

THERMODYNAMICS

Bioenergetics is the study of energy flow through biological systems. The first law of thermodynamics is a restatement of the law of conservation of energy. According to the law of conservation of energy, the total amount of energy in an isolated system remains constant. When applied to thermodynamics, the change in the internal energy of a system is equal to the amount of heat supplied to the system minus the work done by the system on the surroundings. Organisms are open systems because they are always exchanging both matter and energy with their surroundings; they are never at equilibrium. They take free energy from the surroundings either through sunlight or nutrients, and do work on the surroundings by moving, breathing, etc. Any energy that is taken in is returned to the surroundings as heat, resulting in an increase in entropy/disorder of the surroundings.

EQUILIBRIUM CONSTANT

Equilibrium describes a state of maximum stability where the rate of the forward reaction is equal to the rate of the reverse reaction. This does not mean that the concentrations of products and reactants are equal; rather there is no net change in the concentrations of the reactants or products. The equilibrium constant can predict whether the products or the reactants will be in higher concentration at equilibrium, and which direction of the reaction is favored. In other words, it relates the concentration of products to reactants.

The following equation can be used to calculate the equilibrium constant:

$$K_{eq} = \frac{[C]^c [D]^d}{[A]^a [B]^b}$$

- **C** and **D** are equilibrium product concentrations
- **A** and **B** are equilibrium reactant concentrations
- **a**, **b**, **c** and **d** are stoichiometric constants (the numbers in front of each reactant and product in the chemical equation)

When $K_{eq} = 1$, the reactants and products are equal in concentration. When $K_{eq} > 1$, the concentration of products exceeds that of the reactants, and when $K_{eq} < 1$ the concentration of products is less than that of the reactants.

FREE ENERGY: G

Free energy is a measure of the energy within a system that is available to do work. The change in Gibbs free energy (ΔG) is the usable energy that is either absorbed or released during the reaction. ΔG can be calculated using the following equation:

$$\Delta G = \Delta H - T\Delta S$$

- ΔG = change in Gibbs free energy; SI units: Joules
- ΔH = change in enthalpy
  - Enthalpy is the total heat content of a system, and the *change* in enthalpy measures the difference between the energy stored in the bonds of the reactants and the products, assuming a constant pressure. If ΔH is positive, heat is absorbed, and if ΔH is negative, heat was released.

- T = absolute temperature
  - Always positive (because it is expressed in units of Kelvins)
- ΔS = change in entropy
  - Entropy is a measure of the disorder of a system. A positive change in entropy means that the system is more disordered. If ΔS is negative, the system becomes more ordered.

RELATIONSHIP BETWEEN THE EQUILIBRIUM CONSTANT AND GIBBS FREE ENERGY

Free energy, often called Gibbs free energy (G), is the energy available to do work at a constant temperature and pressure. The notation G^0 indicates "standard" free energy, or the free energy at standard state conditions. The relationship between K_{eq} and standard Gibbs free energy is as follows:

$$\Delta G^0 = -RT \ln\left(K_{eq}\right)$$

- G^0 = standard free energy
- R = gas constant
- T = absolute temperature in Kelvins
- $\ln\left(K_{eq}\right)$ = natural log of the equilibrium constant

When $K_{eq} = 1$, then ΔG is zero and reactants and products are favored equally. When $K_{eq} > 1$, then ΔG is negative and products are favored. When $K_{eq} < 1$, then ΔG is positive and the reactants are favored at equilibrium.

SPONTANEOUS REACTIONS AND ΔG^0

When ΔG^0, or the change in free energy at standard conditions (1.0 atm, 298 Kelvin), is negative, the reaction will be exergonic and favor the formation of products. These reactions are always spontaneous. It is important to note that spontaneous reactions do not always happen quickly; it simply means that the change in free energy is negative.

When ΔG^0 is positive, the reaction will be non-spontaneous and endergonic, and favor the reactants. While all non-spontaneous reactions are endergonic, they are not always endothermic. When the entropy increases by more than ΔH, the reaction will be non-spontaneous and exothermic.

When ΔG^0 is zero, the reaction is in equilibrium; neither the reactants nor products are favored.

CONCENTRATION

Increasing the concentration of reactants will lead to more collisions per unit time between those reactants, and therefore the rate of the forward reaction increases as concentration increases. When there is a high concentration of reactants, the free energy of the reactants is greater than that of the products. As the concentration of the products increases, the rate of the reverse reaction increases. When the concentrations of the reactants and products become stable (not necessarily equal), the rate of the forward and reverse reactions are the same, and the reaction is at equilibrium.

LE CHÂTELIER'S PRINCIPLE

According to **Le Châtelier's principle**, when the equilibrium of a system is disrupted, the system will shift to restore equilibrium. For this reason, it is sometimes referred to as the equilibrium law. Factors that can disrupt equilibrium include changes in concentration, volume and pressure, and temperature. Le Châtelier's principle can be observed in biological systems, for example the metabolism of glucose. When glucose levels rise, insulin will facilitate the uptake of glucose into the cells, and stimulate glycolysis.

Variable	Change	System's response to restore equilibrium
Concentration	Reactants or products are added	The added reactants / products are consumed
	Reactants or products are removed	More reactants / products are produced to replace those that were removed
Volume	Increase (with decrease in pressure)	Shifts to the side with more moles of gas
	Decrease (with increase in pressure)	Shifts to the side with fewer moles of gas
Temperature	Increase	Endothermic reaction is favored
	Decrease	Exothermic reaction is favored

ENDOTHERMIC/EXOTHERMIC REACTIONS

An **endothermic reaction** is a reaction that absorbs heat from the surroundings, meaning the heat content of the products is greater than the reactants. An **exothermic reaction** releases heat into the surroundings; the heat content of the products is less than the reactants. These reactions cause a change in **enthalpy**, a measure of the heat content of a thermodynamic system. The change in enthalpy (ΔH) is negative for an exothermic reaction and positive for an endothermic reaction. Endothermic reactions will often cause the surroundings to decrease in temperature, as they require the addition of energy to proceed. These reactions are usually non-spontaneous. On the other hand, exothermic reactions will increase the temperature of the surroundings, and are usually spontaneous. Photosynthesis is an example of a biological endothermic process; the energy from the sun is used to build carbon dioxide into molecules of glucose. The glucose can then be oxidized during cellular respiration to produce ATP and heat. Cellular respiration is an example of an exothermic process because the bonds in glucose hold more energy than those of the products.

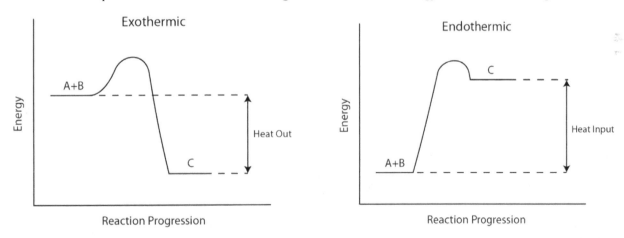

FROM CELLS TO TISSUES

EPITHELIAL CELLS

Epithelial cells come in a variety of shapes and functions, but they share the characteristic of being avascular. They are nourished by the diffusion of oxygen and nutrients from capillaries in the underlying layer of connective tissue called the basement membrane. Epithelial tissues are the lining and covering tissues of the body, and depending on their location may be involved in protection, absorption, secretion, and/or filtration. These tissues are classified according to the shape and arrangement of their cells:

Cell Shape	
flattened, scale-like	squamous
cube-shaped	Cuboidal
long, thin	Columnar
Arrangement	
single layer of cells	simple epithelia
appearance of multiple layers as a result of differences in cell shape and location	pseudostratified
multiple layers of cells	stratified epithelia

There are **many** types of epithelial tissues in the body. Stratified squamous epithelial tissues are found in locations that experience friction, such as the mouth, esophagus, and exterior skin. Simple columnar epithelia line the digestive tract, and harbor mucus-producing goblet cells. Simple squamous epithelia form membranes where filtration or diffusion occurs, such as the alveoli of the lungs. These are merely a few examples.

CONNECTIVE TISSUE CELLS

Connective tissues are the most abundant tissues in the body. Most connective tissues are highly vascular, the exceptions being ligaments, tendons, and cartilage. In general, they support and protect the body, and are characterized by the presence of a nonliving matrix. This matrix is secreted by the cells of the connective tissue and it consists of ground substance (water, proteins, and carbohydrates) and protein fibers such as collagen, elastin, or reticular fibers. The consistency of these connective tissues varies greatly from one tissue type to another. Blood is a connective tissue made of blood cells and plasma, and it transports oxygen, carbon dioxide, nutrients, and wastes. Adipose tissue is made of fat cells that cushion and insulate the body. Osseous tissue, or bone, consists of osteocytes surrounded by a hard matrix of calcium salts and collagen. Cartilage, like bone, is a connective tissue that provides support, but it is made of cells called chondrocytes, and is more flexible. Ligaments and tendons are made of dense fibrous connective tissue, which is made mostly of collagen fibers.

BIOSIGNALING

Biosignaling is a messaging system that cells use to coordinate their activities. It involves the use of receptor proteins and the signal molecules that they bind from outside the cell. Proto-oncogenes encode the information for growth factors and their receptors, and are therefore important players in the signaling pathways that regulate the cell cycle. When proto-oncogenes are over-expressed or mutated, they can accelerate the signaling pathways that promote cell division. The RAS oncogene is one of many genes commonly associated with cancer. The RAS protein is a GTPase that regulates the cell cycle by toggling back and forth between an active and inactive state. But when it is mutated, it remains in its active form, signaling the cell to divide even in the absence of growth factors. Oncogenes can also inhibit apoptosis, a natural process that eliminates damaged or unhealthy cells. When a cell is targeted to die, enzymes are released from the mitochondria which activate caspases in the cytosol, and the caspases digest the intracellular components. Oncogenes can both prevent the release of the mitochondria enzymes and directly inactivate the caspases.

EXISTENCE OF REGENERATIVE CAPACITY IN VARIOUS SPECIES

Regenerative capacity describes the ability to regrow damaged or lost tissues. There are different mechanisms by which this can happen. **Somatic cell proliferation** occurs when differentiated cells produce more of their own kind. This is used by complex organisms as a way to heal, and rarely used to grow a complex structure such as a limb. Another means of regeneration is the **differentiation** of adult stem cells. The hematopoietic stem cells that reside in the bone marrow, for example, can give rise to any type of blood cell. **Dedifferentiation** describes the ability of specialized cells to revert back to a less differentiated state. They then proceed through a similar migration pattern as seen during development to restore the injured or missing structure. Complex structures can be regenerated this way—for example, the regrowth of a salamander limb. **Transdifferentiation** is the direct differentiation of a somatic cell into a cell of a different lineage without dedifferentiation. Pancreatic cells can transdifferentiate into liver cells.

Regeneration is used by all species to varying degrees. The hydra can regenerate its entire body from just a small fragment. Many amphibians can regenerate complex structures like limbs and tails. Birds and mammals have a much narrower range of regenerative capabilities. The human liver can quickly replace lost tissue, but the heart cannot.

SENESCENCE AND AGING

Senescence is a progressive decline in function as a result of biological aging. The term can be used to describe an organism as a whole, or the irreversible state of a cell that can no longer divide but remains physiologically active. Senescence can be brought on by the activation of an oncogene or the deactivation of a tumor suppressor gene, as a way to reduce the threat of cancer. This non-proliferative state can also be induced by oxidative stress, DNA damage, and telomere shortening. **Telomeres** are repetitive non-coding sequences of DNA found at the ends of chromosomes that protect the coding sequences. Every time a cell divides, the chromosomes shorten because DNA polymerase cannot replicate the end portion. Eventually the telomeres are lost and the cell must enter a state of senescence to prevent damage to important genes. An enzyme called telomerase *can* add nucleotides to these problematic end portions, but it is only found in certain types of cells, such as embryonic stem cells, germ cells, cancerous cells, and even adult stem cells (in low amounts). The proportion of senescent cells tends to increase with age, but evidence shows that senescence is also a strategy used during embryonic development to halt the growth of certain tissues, thereby helping to shape the embryo.

GEL ELECTROPHORESIS

Gel electrophoresis is a technique used to separate macromolecules such as nucleic acids and proteins. Fragments of DNA and RNA are separated according to length. Proteins are separated according to length and charge. The technique is relatively simple. For example, to separate DNA strands, a solution containing the DNA strand is placed in a gel. When an electric current is passed through the gel, the DNA strands migrate from the negative end of the container to the positive end due to their negative charge because of their phosphate ions. Shorter DNA strands migrate faster than the longer DNA strands. This results in a series of bands. Each band contains DNA strands of a specific length. A DNA standard is placed in the gel to provide a reference to determine the strand length. Lengths are measured in base pairs (bps).

MICROSCOPY

Microscopy is used in microbiology. Bacteria, viruses, cell components, and molecules are too small to be seen by the naked eye. Several types of microscopes are available to examine these samples. There are light microscopes, which use visible light to study samples, and electron microscopes, which use beams of electrons. The light microscope (also called the compound microscope) uses

65

two types of lenses (ocular and objective) to magnify objects. These are typically used when studying samples at the cellular level. Basic compound light microscopes are typically used in high school biology classes. Other compound light microscopes such as the dark-field microscope, phase-contrast microscope, and the fluorescent microscope are available for more specific uses. For tiny samples, such as viruses, cell components, or individual molecules, electron microscopes can be used. Electron microscopes use beams of electrons instead of light. Because beams of electrons have shorter wavelengths, electron microscopes have greater resolution than light microscopes. Resolution is the ability of a lens to reveal two points as being distinct. The two types of electron microscopy are transmission electron microscopy (TEM) and scanning electron microscopy (SEM). SEM is a newer technology than TEM and produces three-dimensional images.

Genetics

CLASSICAL GENETICS

MENDEL'S CONTRIBUTIONS TO GENETICS

Johann Gregor Mendel is known as the father of genetics. Mendel was an Austrian monk who performed thousands of experiments involving the breeding of the common pea plant in the garden of his monastery. Mendel kept detailed records including seed color, pod color, seed type, flower color, and plant height for eight years and published his work in 1865. Unfortunately, his work was largely ignored until the early 1900s. Mendel's work showed that genes come in pairs and that dominant and recessive traits are inherited independently of each other. His work established the law of segregation, the law of independent assortment, and the law of dominance.

LAW OF SEGREGATION

The law of segregation states that the alleles for a trait separate when gametes are formed, which means that only one of the pair of alleles for a given trait is passed to the gamete. This can be shown in monohybrid crosses. A monohybrid cross is a genetic cross for a single trait that has two alleles. A monohybrid cross can be used to show which allele is dominant for a single trait. The first monohybrid cross typically occurs between two homozygous parents. Each parent is homozygous for a separate allele for a particular trait. For example, in pea plants, green pods (G) are dominant over yellow pods (g). In a genetic cross of two pea plants that are homozygous for pod color, the F_1 generation will be 100% heterozygous green pods.

	g	g
G	Gg	Gg
G	Gg	Gg

Review Video: Punnett Square
Visit mometrix.com/academy and enter code: 853855

MONOHYBRID CROSS FOR A CROSS BETWEEN TWO GG PARENTS

If the plants with the heterozygous green pods are crossed, the F_2 generation should be 50% heterozygous green, 25% homozygous green, and 25% homozygous yellow.

	G	g
G	GG	Gg
g	Gg	gg

LAW OF INDEPENDENT ASSORTMENT

Mendel's law of independent assortment states that alleles of one characteristic separate independently of the alleles of another characteristic. This means that traits are transmitted independently of each other. This can be shown in dihybrid crosses.

DIHYBRID CROSS FOR THE F_2 GENERATION OF A CROSS BETWEEN GGYY AND GGYY PARENTS

A dihybrid cross is a genetic cross for two traits that each have two alleles. For example, in pea plants, green pods (G) are dominant over yellow pods (g), and yellow seeds (Y) are dominant over green seeds (y). In a genetic cross of two pea plants that are homozygous for pod color and seed color, the F_1 generation will be 100% heterozygous green pods and yellow seeds (GgYy). If these F_1 plants are crossed, the resulting F_2 generation is shown below. There are nine genotypes for green-pod, yellow-seed plants: one GGYY, two GGYy, two GgYY, and four GgYy. There are three genotypes for green-pod, green-seed plants: one GGyy and two Ggyy. There are three genotypes for yellow-pod, yellow-seed plants: one ggYY and two ggYy. There is only one genotype for yellow-pod, green-seed plants: ggyy. This cross has a 9:3:3:1 ratio.

	GY	Gy	gY	gy
GY	GGYY	GGYy	GgYY	GgYy
Gy	GGYy	GGyy	GgYy	Ggyy
gY	GgYY	GgYY	ggYY	ggYy
gy	GgYy	Ggyy	ggYy	ggyy

PEDIGREE

Pedigree analysis is a type of genetic analysis in which an inherited trait is studied and traced through several generations of a family to determine how that trait is inherited. A pedigree is a chart arranged as a type of family tree using symbols for people and lines to represent the relationships between those people. Squares usually represent males, and circles represent females. Horizontal lines represent a male and female mating, and the vertical lines beneath them represent their children. Usually, family members who possess the trait are fully shaded and those that are carriers only of the trait are half-shaded. Genotypes and phenotypes are determined for each individual if possible. The pedigree below shows the family tree of a family in which the first male who was red-green color blind mated with the first female who was unaffected. They had five children. The three sons were unaffected, and the two daughters were carriers.

Inheritance of Red-Green Color Blindness:
an X-linked Recessive Trait

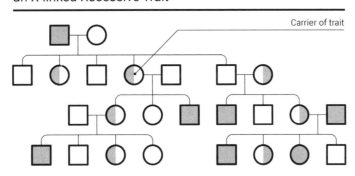

NON-MENDELIAN INHERITANCE CONCEPTS

LINKAGE

Linkage is an exception to Mendel's law of independent assortment. Linkage can occur when two genes are located on the same chromosome. Each chromosome has several genes, and those genes tend to be inherited together. Genes that are located on the same chromosome and tend to be inherited together are called linkage groups. Because the genes are on the same chromosome, they do not separate during meiosis. During meiosis, the genes in a linkage group always go into the same gamete together. Due to linkage, genes with different characteristics are inherited together more frequently than is predicted using the laws of probability. An example of a linkage group is found on chromosome number 4. This linkage group includes genes for Parkinson's disease, narcolepsy, and Huntington's disease.

SEX-LINKED INHERITANCE

Sex-linked inheritance is an exception to Mendel's law of independent assortment. In human genetics, females have two X chromosomes, and males have one X and one Y chromosome. Sex-linked traits are carried on the X chromosome. Because females have two X chromosomes, they have two copies of genes found on the X chromosome. Females may possess a recessive allele for various disorders on one X chromosome, but as long as they possess the dominant allele for normal functioning on the other X chromosome, they will not have the disorder. Females who are heterozygous for a trait such as color blindness or hemophilia are only carriers. Because males have only one X chromosome, if they possess the recessive allele for a disorder, it will be expressed. Examples of traits that are a result of sex linkage are color blindness, hemophilia, a form of muscular dystrophy, and some forms of anemia.

MULTIPLE ALLELES

Multiple alleles result in a type of non-Mendelian inheritance. In Mendelian inheritance, only two alleles for each gene exist. For example, Mendel's pea plants were either tall or short. Mendel's pea plants had either yellow or green pods. Often, there are more than two possibilities for a particular trait. For example, in human genetics, blood type has many variations. Multiple allele inheritance occurs where there are more than two different alleles of a gene for a particular trait. Even though there may be several alleles for a particular trait, each individual can still only possess two of those possible alleles. For example, the three human blood alleles are I^A (blood contains type A antigens), I^B (blood contains type B antigens), and i (blood contains neither type A nor type B antigens).

Blood types and their possible genotypes are shown below.

Blood Type (Phenotype)	Genotype
A	$I^A I^A$, $I^A I^O$
B	$I^B I^B$, $I^B I^O$
AB	$I^A I^B$
O	ii

INCOMPLETE DOMINANCE

Incomplete dominance is an exception to Mendel's law of dominance. In these situations, there is no dominant or recessive allele. Instead, both alleles of a heterozygote are expressed, and when they are, they blend or mix. For example, there are two alleles for petal color for snapdragons: red (C^R) and white (C^W). Crossing a red snapdragon with a white snapdragon yields an F_1 generation that is

100% heterozygous pink. Crossing two pink snapdragons yields an F_2 generation that is 50% heterozygous pink ($C^R C^W$), 25% homozygous white ($C^W C^W$), and 25% homozygous red ($C^R C^R$).

LAWS OF DOMINANCE AND CODOMINANCE

The law of dominance states that a dominant trait is always expressed. Codominance is an exception to the law of dominance. In codominance, a heterozygote simultaneously expresses both genes for a trait without blending. For example, in certain horses, the hair colors red (D^R) and white (D^W) are codominant. Horses with the genotype $D^R D^W$ have coats composed of red hairs and white hairs, which when mixed together causes their coats to have a golden color.

POLYGENIC INHERITANCE

Polygenic inheritance occurs when a trait is determined by the interaction of many different genes. In Mendelian genetics, traits are determined by just one pair of genes with two alleles. For example, Mendel's pea plants had either red or white flowers, and his plants were either tall or short. An example of polygenic genetic inheritance in human genetics is skin color and height. Each is controlled by at least four pairs of genes. Skin color has many variations between very light and very dark. Height has many variations between very short and very tall. Eye color and intelligence are also polygenic.

EPISTASIS

Epistasis occurs when a gene at one locus inhibits the expression of a gene at another locus. For example, in mice, black hair (B) is dominant over brown hair (b). But a different gene at a different locus determines whether or not pigment is deposited (C for deposited and c for not deposited) on the mouse hair. A black mouse with genotypes BB or Bb will only have that color deposited if the pigment genotype is CC or Cc. A black mouse with genotype BBcc will be white. A brown mouse can have genotypes bbCC or bbCc, but a mouse with genotype bbcc will also be white.

PLEIOTROPY

In Mendelian inheritance, each gene can influence only one trait. Most genes can affect many traits or have multiple phenotypes. Pleiotropy is the situation in which one gene influences several seemingly unrelated traits. A gene that affects multiple traits is pleiotropic. Pleiotropy can be due to normal or mutated genes. Genes code for proteins. Because proteins are often used in more than one tissue or more than one area of the body, a missing protein can cause many complications. For example, the hormone insulin is a protein. If the insulin receptors are faulty, then the cells cannot recognize and use the insulin. Other examples of pleiotropy include inherited diseases such as cystic fibrosis, sickle-cell anemia, phenylketonuria (PKU), and albinism.

GENETIC VARIATION

CONTRIBUTION TO GENETICS BY ALFRED HERSHEY AND MARTHA CHASE

Alfred Hershey and Martha Chase did a series of experiments in 1952 known as the Hershey-Chase experiments. These experiments showed that deoxyribonucleic acid (DNA), not protein, is the genetic material that transfers information for inheritance. The Hershey-Chase experiments used a bacteriophage, a virus that infects bacteria, to infect the bacteria *Escherichia coli*. The bacteriophage T2 is basically a small piece of DNA enclosed in a protein coating. The DNA contains phosphorus, and the protein coating contains sulfur. In the first set of experiments, the T2 was marked with radioactive phosphorus-32. In the second set of experiments, the T2 was marked with radioactive sulfur-35. For both sets of experiments, after the *E. coli* was infected by the T2, the *E. coli* was isolated using a centrifuge. In the first set of experiments, the radioactive isotope (P-32) was found in the *E. coli*, showing that the genetic information was transferred by the DNA. In the second set of

69

experiments, the radioactive isotope (S-35) was not found in the *E. coli*, showing that the genetic information was not transferred by the protein as was previously thought. Hershey and Chase conducted further experiments allowing the bacteria from the first set of experiments to reproduce, and the offspring was also found to contain the radioactive isotope (P-32) further confirming that the DNA transferred the genetic material.

MUTATIONS
MISSENSE MUTATIONS, SILENT MUTATIONS, AND NONSENSE MUTATIONS

Mutations are changes in DNA sequences. Point mutations are changes in a single nucleotide in a DNA sequence. Three types of point mutations are missense, silent, and nonsense.

- Missense mutations result in a codon for a different amino acid. An example is mutating TGT (Cysteine codon) to TGG (Tryptophan codon).
- Silent mutations result in a codon for the same amino acid as the original sequence. An example is mutating TGT (Cysteine codon) to TGC (a different Cysteine codon).
- Nonsense mutations insert a premature stop codon, typically resulting in a non-functional protein. An example is mutating TGT (Cysteine codon) to TGA (STOP codon).

FRAMESHIFT MUTATIONS AND INVERSION MUTATIONS

Deletions and insertions can result in the addition of amino acids, the removal of amino acids, or cause a frameshift mutation. A frameshift mutation changes the reading frame of the mRNA (a new group of codons will be read), resulting in the formation of a new protein product. Mutations can also occur on the chromosomal level. For example, an inversion is when a piece of the chromosome inverts or flips its orientation.

GERMLINE MUTATIONS AND SOMATIC MUTATIONS

Mutations can occur in somatic (body) cells and germ cells (egg and sperm). Somatic mutations develop after conception and occur in an organism's body cells such as bone cells, liver cells, or brain cells. Somatic mutations cannot be passed on from parent to offspring. The mutation is limited to the specific descendent of the cell in which the mutation occurred. The mutation is not in the other body cells unless they are descendants of the originally mutated cell. Somatic mutations may cause cancer or diseases. Some somatic mutations are silent. Germline mutations are present at conception and occur in an organism's germ cells, which are only egg and sperms cells. Germline mutations may be passed on from parent to offspring. Germline mutations will be present in every cell of an offspring that inherits a germline mutation. Germline mutations may cause diseases. Some germline mutations are silent.

CHROMOSOMAL ABERRATIONS

Chromosomal aberrations are changes in DNA sequences on the chromosomal level. These mutations typically involve many genes and often result in miscarriages. Chromosomal aberrations include translocations, deletions, inversions, and duplications. Translocations occur when a piece of DNA breaks off of one chromosome and is joined to another chromosome. Deletions occur when a piece of DNA breaks off on a chromosome and is lost without reattaching. Inversions occur when a piece of DNA breaks off of one chromosome and becomes reattached to that same chromosome but with an inverted or flipped orientation. Duplications occur when a piece of DNA is replicated and attached to the original piece of DNA in sequence.

CROSSING OVER

Crossing over is a major source of genetic variation. Crossing over is the exchange of equivalent segments of DNA between homologous chromosomes. Crossing over occurs during meiosis in

prophase I. During synapsis, a tetrad is formed when homologous chromosomes pair up. Also during synapsis, the chromatids are extremely close together and sometimes the chromatids swap genes. Because genes have more than one allele, this allows for an exchange of genetic information. Crossing over is that exchange of genes. Crossing over can occur several times along the length of the chromosomes. Although crossing over does not introduce new information, it does introduce new combinations of the information that is available. Without crossing over during meiosis, only two genetically different gametes can be formed. With just one instance of crossing over, four genetically different gametes can be formed. With crossing over, each gamete contains genes from both the father and the mother. Crossing over leads to variation in traits among gametes, which leads to variation in traits among offspring.

SOURCES OF GENETIC EXCHANGE

Genetic exchange, or the transfer of DNA from one organism to another, is a source of genetic variation. Three general types of genetic exchange are transduction, transformation, and conjugation. Transduction occurs when genetic material is transferred from one bacterium to another by a bacteriophage. A bacteriophage is a virus that infects a bacterium. As the new bacteriophages are replicated, some of the host bacteria DNA can be added to the virus particles. Transformation occurs when a cell obtains new genetic information from its environment or surroundings. Many bacteria take up DNA fragments such as plasmids from their surroundings to obtain new genes. Conjugation occurs when bacteria or single-celled organisms are in direct contact with each other. Genes can be transferred from one into the other while the two cells are joined.

INDEPENDENT ASSORTMENT DURING SEXUAL REPRODUCTION

Independent assortment during sexual reproduction is a source of genetic variation. Mutations originally brought about changes in DNA leading to alleles or different forms of the same gene. During sexual reproduction, these alleles are "shuffled" or "independently sorted," producing individuals with unique combinations of traits. Gametes are produced during meiosis, which consists of two cell divisions: meiosis I and meiosis II. Meiosis I is a reduction division in which the diploid parent cell divides into two haploid daughter cells. During the metaphase of meiosis I, the homologous pairs (one from the mother and one from the father) align on the equatorial plane. The orientation of the homologous pairs is random, and each placement is independent of another's placement. The number of possible arrangements increases exponentially as the number of chromosomes increases. The independent assortment of chromosomes during metaphase in meiosis I provides a variety of gametes with tremendous differences in their combinations of chromosomes.

> **Review Video: <u>Gene and Alleles</u>**
> Visit mometrix.com/academy and enter code: 363997
>
> **Review Video: <u>Gene Mutation</u>**
> Visit mometrix.com/academy and enter code: 955485

MUTAGENS

Mutagens are physical and chemical agents that cause changes or errors in DNA replication. Mutagens are external factors to an organism. Examples include ionizing radiation such as ultraviolet radiation, x-rays, and gamma radiation. Viruses and microorganisms that integrate their DNA into host chromosomes are also mutagens. Mutagens include environmental poisons such as asbestos, coal tars, tobacco, and benzene. Alcohol and diets high in fat have been shown to be mutagenic. Not all mutations are caused by mutagens. Spontaneous mutations can occur in DNA due to molecular decay.

CHROMOSOMAL CHANGES THAT LEAD TO DOWN SYNDROME

Down syndrome is a type of aneuploidy (abnormal number of chromosomes) in which an individual has three copies of chromosome 21, as shown in the karyotype below. When a gamete with an extra 21st chromosome unites with a normal gamete, the result is a group of three chromosomes instead of a diploid set. A trisomy can occur as a result of nondisjunction, which occurs when a pair of chromosomes fails to separate during meiosis in the formation of an egg or sperm cell.

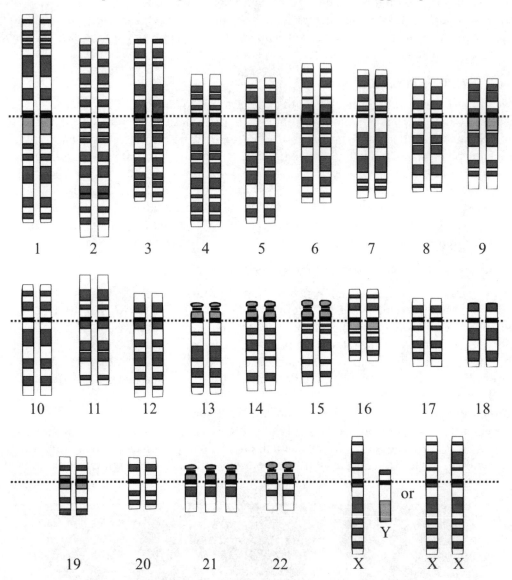

GENETICS OF SICKLE-CELL ANEMIA

Sickle cell anemia is a genetic disorder that is the result of a gene mutation. Specifically, sickle cell anemia is the result of the point mutation in which adenine is substituted for thymine. This results in a defective form of hemoglobin. Sickle-cell anemia occurs when a person is homozygous for the defective gene. Sickle-cell trait occurs when a person is heterozygous for the defective gene, and this person is a carrier but usually suffers no ill effects. Sickle cell anemia is an example of pleiotropy, in which a change in one gene affects multiple aspects of a person's health. These health problems are due to the abnormally sickle-shaped red blood cells that block the flow of blood, damaging tissues and organs. The sickle-shaped cells tend to rupture, leading to anemia.

GENETIC DRIFT

Genetic drift is a microevolutionary process that causes random changes in allele frequencies that are not the result of natural selection. Genetic drift can result in a loss of genetic diversity. Genetic drift greatly impacts small populations. Two special forms of genetic drift are the genetic bottleneck and the founder effect. A genetic bottleneck occurs when there is a drastic reduction in population due to some change such as overhunting, disease, or habitat loss. When a population is greatly reduced in size, many alleles can be lost. Even if the population size greatly increases again, the lost alleles represent lost genetic diversity. The founder effect occurs when one individual or a few individuals populate a new area such as an island. This new population is limited to the alleles of the founder(s) unless mutations occur or new individuals immigrate to the region.

GENE FLOW

Gene flow is a microevolutionary process in which alleles enter a population by immigration and leave a population by emigration. Gene flow helps counter genetic drift. When individuals from one genetically distinct population immigrate to a different genetically distinct population, alleles and their genetic information are added to the new population. The added alleles will change the gene frequencies within the population. This increases genetic diversity. If individuals with rare alleles emigrate from a population, the genetic diversity is decreased. Gene flow reduces the genetic differences between populations.

GENETICS CONCEPTS

REGULATION OF GENE EXPRESSION

ROLE OF PROMOTERS

Promoters are DNA sequences located upstream of the gene needed for transcription. Promoters signal the beginning of transcription. Special proteins called transcription factors, which bind to promoters, subsequently provide binding sites for the RNA polymerase, which is the enzyme that transcribes the RNA. Promoters in the Archaea and Eukaryota domains often contain a nucleotide sequence TATA, which is called a TATA box. The TATA box is usually 25 nucleotides upstream of the transcription start site, and it is the location at which the DNA is unwound.

ROLE OF ENHANCERS

Enhancers are DNA sequences that regulate gene expression by providing a binding site for proteins that regulate RNA polymerase in transcribing proteins. Enhancers can greatly increase the expression of genes in their range. They can be hundreds or thousands of base pairs upstream or downstream from the genes they control. Some enhancers are located within the gene they control. Enhancers are functional over large distances. Most genes are controlled by two or three enhancers, but some may be controlled by more. Enhancers provide binding sites for regulatory proteins that either promote or inhibit RNA polymerase activity. Enhancers are more common in eukaryotes than prokaryotes.

ROLE OF TRANSCRIPTION FACTORS

Transcription factors are DNA-binding proteins that help regulate gene expression in eukaryotes and prokaryotes. In eukaryotes that have promoter or enhancer regions, transcription factors bind near these regions and increase the ability of the RNA polymerase to start transcription. In eukaryotes, because genes are typically turned "off," transcription factors typically work to turn genes "on." The opposite is often true in bacteria, and transcription factors often work to turn genes off.

<u>ROLE OF OPERONS</u>

Operons are segments of DNA or groups of genes that are controlled by one promoter. Operons consist of an operator, a promoter, and structural gene(s). The operator provides a binding side for a repressor that inhibits the binding of RNA polymerase. The promoter provides the binding site for the RNA polymerase. The structural genes provide the sequence that codes for a protein. Operons are transcribed as single units and code for a single mRNA molecule, which produces proteins with related functions. Operons have been found in prokaryotes, eukaryotes, and viruses. For example, the lac (lactose) operon in certain bacteria controls the production of the enzymes needed to digest lactose. If lactose is already available in the cell, the lactose binds to the repressor protein to prevent the repressor protein from binding to the operator. The gene is transcribed, and the enzymes necessary for the digestion of the lactose are produced. If there is no lactose that needs to be digested, the repressor protein binds to the operator. The gene is not transcribed, and the enzyme is not produced. This allows the cell to only code for proteins as needed by the cell.

<u>ROLE OF EPIGENETICS</u>

Epigenetics studies factors or mechanisms that determine if genes are active (switched on) or dormant (switched off). These mechanisms can alter gene function or gene expression without altering the sequences of the DNA itself. An example is the addition of a methyl group (methylation) to the histones. Acetylation, the addition of an acetyl group, and phosphorylation, the addition of a phosphoryl group, are also modifications to the proteins associated with DNA that can switch genes on or off or affect their activity level.

DIFFERENTIAL GENE EXPRESSION

Differential gene expression is the expression of different sets of gene by cells with identical DNA molecules. The unused genes in a differentiated cell remain in the cell but are not expressed. Actually, only a few genes are expressed in each cell. For example, during mammalian embryonic development, the undifferentiated zygote undergoes cell division through mitosis. As the number of cells increases, selected cells undergo differentiation to become specialized components in the developing tissues of the embryo.

MITOCHONDRIAL INHERITANCE

Mitochondria are cellular organelles that produce energy for the cell. Mitochondria contain their own DNA consisting of 37 genes arranged in a circular structure. Mitochondrial DNA is transmitted maternally, which means that these mitochondrial genes are only inherited from the mother. The offspring's mitochondria only come from the oocyte (egg cell), not from the sperm. Sperm cells only contain mitochondria in their tails, which does not enter the egg during fertilization. Mitochondrial inheritance is not consistent with Mendelian inheritance in which the zygote derives half of the genetic material from the mother and half from the father. Most of these genes code for proteins related to muscular disorders.

STEM CELLS

Stem cells are undifferentiated cells that can divide without limit and that can differentiate to produce the specialized cells that each organism needs. Embryonic stem cells are harvested from the embryo at the blastocyst stage or from the developing gonads of the embryo. Stem cells can be pluripotent or multipotent depending on their source. Early embryonic stem cells are pluripotent. This means they have not undergone any differentiation and have the ability to become any special type of cell. After embryonic stem cells begin to differentiate, they may be limited to specializing into a specific tissue type. These stem cells are considered to be multipotent because they can only develop into a few different types of cells. Adult stem cells, also called somatic stem cells, are harvested from organs and tissues and can differentiate into those types of cells in that particular organ or tissue. Umbilical cord blood stem cells can be harvested from the umbilical cord of a newborn baby. Adult stem cells and umbilical cord blood stem cells are multipotent. Induced pluripotent cells (iPS) are somatic cells that have been manipulated to act like pluripotent cells. Experiments have shown that iPS may be useful in treating diseases.

HW EQUILIBRIUM

Hardy–Weinberg (HW) equilibrium is a theoretical concept that uses a mathematical relationship to study gene frequencies. According to HW, if specific conditions are met, the proportions of genotypes in a population can be described by the equation: $p^2 + 2pq + q^2 = 1$, in which p is the frequency of the dominant allele and q is the frequency of the recessive allele. Also, p^2 is the frequency of the homozygous dominant genotype, $2pq$ is the frequency of the heterozygous genotype, and q^2 is the frequency of the homozygous recessive genotype. In addition, the sum of p and q must be equal to one. If the frequencies on the left side of the equation have a sum of one, then the population is in equilibrium, and evolution is not taking place. If the frequencies on the left side of the equation do not have a sum of one, then evolution is taking place. Therefore, the HW equation is only true for populations that are in equilibrium. The HW equilibrium requires the following five conditions to be met: 1) The population must be very large; 2) Mating is random; 3) There are no mutations; 4) No immigration or emigration can occur; and 5) All individuals of the population have an equal chance to survive and reproduce. According to this concept, if all five conditions are met, the gene frequencies will remain constant. In reality, these five conditions are rarely met except in a laboratory situation.

CALCULATION OF ALLELE FREQUENCY

Explain how to calculate allele frequencies of a simple genetic locus at which there are two alleles (A and a) in a population of 1,000 individuals given that the population consists of 120 individuals homozygous for the dominant allele (AA), 480 heterozygous individuals (Aa), and 400 individuals homozygous for the recessive allele (aa).

To calculate the frequency of an allele, divide the total number of those alleles in the population by the total number of alleles in the population for that locus as shown in the following equation:

$$\text{allele frequency} = \frac{\text{total \# of allelles in population}}{\text{total \# of alleles in the population for that locus}}.$$

First, find the total number of each type of allele. The 120 AA individuals produce 240 A alleles. The 480 heterozygous individuals produce 480 A alleles and 480 a alleles. The 400 aa individuals produce 800 a alleles. Therefore, there is a total of 720 A alleles and 1280 a alleles. Adding the 720 and 1,280 yields a total of 2,000 alleles in the population for that locus. The allele frequency for $A = \frac{720}{2,000}$ or 0.36. The allele frequency for $a = \frac{1,280}{2,000}$ or 0.64.

PCR

The polymerase chain reaction (PCR) is a laboratory technique used to rapidly copy selected segments of DNA. PCR can be performed on the DNA from a single cell. PCR is a hot-and-cold cycled reaction that uses a special heat-tolerant polymerase. The DNA sample is combined with this special DNA polymerase, primers, and free nucleotides. Primers are synthetic strands of DNA containing just a few bases. The first step is a high-temperature denaturation step (90–95°C) that causes the DNA strands to unwind. The second step is a low-temperature annealing step (~60°C) in which the primers anneal to the single-stranded DNA. The final step is an activation step that matches the activation temperature for the heat-resistant DNA polymerase (~70°C, depending on

75

the enzyme). This final step results in the formation of newly-synthesized, double-stranded DNA. These steps will be repeated on the same sample for multiple cycles, typically ~30. The number of DNA copies generated is 2^N, where N is the number of cycles.

DNA Sequencing

DNA sequencing is a laboratory technique used to determine the order or linear sequence of nucleotides of DNA fragments. A polymerase chain reaction (PCR) is used to isolate the needed DNA segment or DNA template. During PCR, some of each of the nucleotides containing the four bases, G, C, A, and T, is chemically altered and fluorescently tagged with different colors of dye. Also, the chemically altered nucleotides have the dideoxyribose sugar, which contains one less oxygen atom than the usual deoxyribose. When synthesis begins, the polymerase randomly adds either a regular nucleotide or an altered nucleotide. If the polymerase adds an altered nucleotide, synthesis stops. This way, each DNA fragment of the same length is tagged with the same color. Then, electrophoresis is used to separate DNA fragments according to length. The DNA sequence can be read by reading the tags of the shortest fragments to the tags of the longest fragments.

Human Genome Project

In 1990, the Human Genome Project (HGP), which involved scientists from 16 laboratories located in at least 6 different countries, was launched to map the human genome. The project was completed in 2003. The human genome consists of approximately 3.12 billion paired nucleotides. The genomes of several plants, animal, fungi, protists, bacteria, viruses, and even cell organelles have also been studied and mapped. Interesting comparisons can be made between these genomes. For example, the number of genes in an organism's genome does not indicate the complexity of that organism. Humans have approximately 21,000 genes, but the simpler roundworms have approximately 26,000 genes.

Gene Therapy

Gene therapy is an experimental but promising technique that introduces new genes into an organism to correct a specific disease caused by a defective gene. In gene therapy, the defective gene is replaced by a properly functioning gene. Gene therapy is most promising for diseases that are caused by a single defective gene. For example, gene therapy was first successfully used to treat severe combined immunodeficiency (SCID). One type of SCID is caused by a single defective gene on the X chromosome. Doctors removed some bone marrow from the test subjects, injected a retrovirus that was carrying the gene, and then re-implanted the bone marrow. The bone marrow cells then have the correct DNA sequence for the production of proteins for much-needed enzymes. Unfortunately, some of the first recipients developed leukemia, and the trials were halted. Later, researchers discovered that the leukemia was related to the location of the insertion of the retroviral vectors.

Cloning

Clones are exact biological copies of genes, cells, or multicellular organisms. There are natural clones and artificial clones. Many clones are produced in nature. Animals that can reproduce asexually by fragmentation or budding produce natural clones. Some plants such as strawberries can reproduce by stolons. Typically, in biology, cloning refers to gene cloning or the cloning of organisms. Gene cloning is the process of splicing genes that are needed to code for a specific protein and introducing them into a new cell with a DNA vector. Gene cloning has been used with bacteria in the production of human insulin and a human growth hormone replacement.

Cloning can also occur with an entire organism. This type of cloning is called a somatic cell nuclear transfer. The first mammal clone was Dolly the sheep. In this procedure, a nucleus of a somatic cell

from the sheep to be cloned was transferred or injected into a denucleated egg cell of the surrogate mother sheep. The egg was stimulated to divide by electric shock, and then the embryo was implanted into the uterus of the surrogate mother. Dolly was born identical to the egg nucleus donor, not the surrogate mother. Dolly and other cloned mammals typically have serious health problems. Dolly aged prematurely possibly due to the shortened telomeres from the adult somatic cell nucleus.

Review Video: Cloning
Visit mometrix.com/academy and enter code: 289634

GENETIC ENGINEERING AND GENETICALLY ENGINEERED CELLS

Genetic engineering is the manipulation of DNA outside of normal reproduction. This modified DNA is called recombinant DNA. Genetic engineering is prevalent in gene cloning, which is used in the production of genetically modified (GM) organisms and the production of GM food. Gene cloning involves cloning a specific gene that is needed for a specific purpose. Genes can be inserted into cells of an entirely different species. Genetically engineered cells are also called transgenic cells. GM organisms such plants or crops contain recombinant DNA. Many types of organisms such as plants, animals, fungi, and bacteria have been genetically modified. GM crops such as corn and soybeans can be engineered to be herbicide resistant to ensure that herbicides kill the weeds but not the crop plants. Crops can also be modified to be pest resistant in order to kill the insects that might damage the crops. Also, several foods can be genetically modified to increase nutritional value.

Review Video: Genetic Engineering and Genetically Engineered Cells
Visit mometrix.com/academy and enter code: 548687

Diversity of Life

HISTORICAL AND CURRENT KINGDOM SYSTEMS

In 1735 Carolus Linnaeus devised a two-kingdom classification system. He placed all living things into either the *Animalia* kingdom or the *Plantae* kingdom. Fungi and algae were classified as plants. Also, Linnaeus developed the binomial nomenclature system that is still used today. In 1866, Ernst Haeckel introduced a three-kingdom classification system, adding the *Protista* kingdom to Linnaeus's animal and plant kingdoms. Bacteria were classified as protists. Cyanobacteria were still classified as plants. In 1938, Herbert Copeland introduced a four-kingdom classification system in which bacteria and cyanobacteria were moved to the *Monera* kingdom. In 1969, Robert Whittaker introduced a five-kingdom system that moved fungi from the plant kingdom to the *Fungi* kingdom. Some algae were still classified as plants. In 1977, Carl Woese introduced a six-kingdom system in which in the *Monera* kingdom was replaced with the *Eubacteria* kingdom and the *Archaebacteria* kingdom.

DOMAIN CLASSIFICATION SYSTEM

In 1990, Carl Woese introduced his domain classification system. Domains are broader groupings above the kingdom level. This system consists of three domains- *Archaea*, *Bacteria*, and *Eukarya*. All eukaryotes such as plants, animals, fungi, and protists are classified in the *Eukarya* domain. The *Bacteria* and *Archaea* domains consist of prokaryotes. Organisms previously classified in the *Monera* kingdom are now classified into either the *Bacteria* or *Archaea* domain based on their ribosomal RNA structure. Members of the *Archaea* domain often live in extremely harsh environments.

THREE DOMAINS

A three-domain system is used to classify all living organisms. These domains are Archaea, Bacteria, and Eukarya. The cell(s) of the organisms within the domain Eukarya are eukaryotic, and therefore have a nucleus and membrane-bound organelles. This domain includes the kingdoms Plantae, Animalia, Fungi, and Protista. The domains Archaea and Bacteria consist of single-celled organisms called prokaryotes. Prokaryotes share a common structure; they have a single circular chromosome that is *not* enclosed in a nucleus (it is concentrated in the nucleoid region), nor do they have membrane-bound organelles. They divide by binary fission, and do not have a mitotic spindle. They do have ribosomes (though they are smaller than eukaryotic ribosomes) and a plasma membrane, and are surrounded by a cell wall. They also have a primitive cytoskeleton. Prior to the 1970's, all prokaryotes were classified as a single kingdom (Monera) but research has shown that archaea and bacteria each have a distinct line of descent.

Phylogenetic Tree of Life

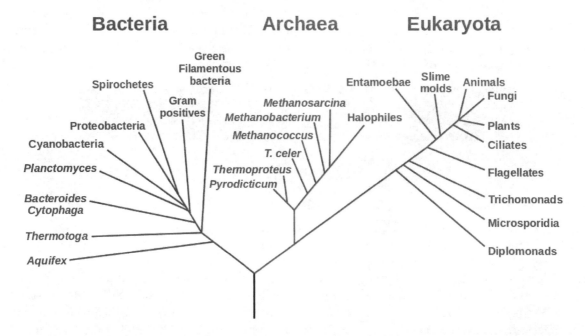

PLANTS

Plants are multicellular organisms with eukaryotic cells containing cellulose in their cell walls. Plant cells have chlorophyll and perform photosynthesis. Plants can be vascular or nonvascular. Vascular plants have true leaves, stems, and roots that contain xylem and phloem. Nonvascular plants lack true leaves, stems and roots and do not have any true vascular tissue but instead rely on diffusion and osmosis for most transport of materials. Almost all plants are autotrophic, relying on photosynthesis for food. A small number do not have chlorophyll and are parasitic, but these are extremely rare. Plants can reproduce sexually or asexually. Many plants reproduce by seeds produced in the fruits of the plants. Some plants reproduce by seeds on cones. Ferns reproduce by spores. Some plants can reproduce asexually by vegetative reproduction.

Review Video: <u>Kingdom Plantae</u>
Visit mometrix.com/academy and enter code: 710084

VASCULAR AND NONVASCULAR PLANTS

Vascular plants, also referred to as tracheophytes, have dermal tissue, meristematic tissue, ground tissues, and vascular tissues. Nonvascular plants, also referred to a bryophytes, do not have the vascular tissue xylem and phloem. Vascular plants can grow very tall, whereas nonvascular plants are short and close to the ground. Vascular plants can be found in dry regions, but nonvascular plants typically grow near or in moist areas. Vascular plants have leaves, roots, and stems, but nonvascular plants have leaflike, rootlike, and stemlike structures that do not have true vascular tissue. Vascular plants include angiosperms, gymnosperms, and ferns. Nonvascular plants include mosses and liverworts.

FLOWERING VERSUS NONFLOWERING PLANTS

Angiosperms and gymnosperms are both vascular plants. Angiosperms are flowering plants, and gymnosperms are nonflowering plants. Angiosperms reproduce by seeds that are enclosed in an ovary, usually in a fruit. Angiosperms can be further classified as either monocots or dicots. Gymnosperms reproduce by unenclosed or "naked" seeds on scales, leaves, or cones. Angiosperms include grasses, garden flowers, vegetables, and broadleaf trees such as maples, birches, elms, and oaks. Gymnosperms include conifers such as pines, spruces, cedars, and redwoods.

> **Review Video: Fruits in Flowering Plants**
> Visit mometrix.com/academy and enter code: 867090

MONOCOTS AND DICOTS

Angiosperms can be classified as either monocots or dicots. The seeds of monocots have one cotyledon, and the seeds of dicots have two cotyledons. The flowers of monocots have petals in multiples of three, and the flowers of dicots have petals in multiples of four or five. The leaves of monocots are slender with parallel veins, and the leaves of dicots are broad and flat with branching veins. The vascular bundles in monocots are distributed throughout the stem. The vascular bundles in dicots are arranged in rings. Monocots have a fibrous root system, and dicots have a taproot system.

PLANT DERMAL TISSUE

Plant dermal tissue consists of the epidermis and the dermis. The epidermis is usually a single layer of cells that covers younger plants. The epidermis protects the plant by secreting the cuticle, which is a waxy substance that helps prevent water loss and infections. The epidermis in leaves has tiny pores called stomata. Guard cells in the epidermis control the opening and closing of the stomata. The epidermis usually does not have chloroplasts. The epidermis may be replaced by periderm in older plants. The periderm is also referred to as bark. The layers of the periderm are cork cells or phellem, phelloderm, and cork cambium or phellogen. Cork is the outer layer of the periderm and consists of nonliving cells. The periderm protects the plant and provides insulation.

PLANT VASCULAR TISSUE

The two major types of plant vascular tissue are xylem and phloem. Xylem and phloem are bound together in vascular bundles. A meristem called vascular cambium is located between the xylem and phloem and produces new xylem and phloem. Xylem is made up of tracheids and vessel elements. All vascular plants contain tracheids, but only angiosperms contain vessel elements. Xylem provides support and conducts water and dissolved minerals from the root and upward throughout the plant by transpirational pull and root pressure. In woody plants, xylem is commonly referred to as wood. Phloem is made up of companion cells and sieve-tube cells. Phloem conducts nutrients including sucrose produced during photosynthesis and organic materials throughout the plant. By active transport, the companion vessels move glucose in and out of the sieve-tube cells.

PLANT GROUND TISSUE

The three major types of ground tissue are parenchyma tissue, collenchyma tissue, and sclerenchyma tissue. Most ground tissue is made up of parenchyma. Parenchyma is formed by parenchyma cells, and it provides photosynthesis, food storage, and tissue repair. The soft "filler" tissues in plants are usually parenchyma. The mesophyll in leaves is parenchyma tissue. Collenchyma is made of collenchyma cells and provides support in roots, stems, and petioles. Sclerenchyma tissue is made of sclereid cells, which are more rigid than the collenchyma cells, and provides rigid support and protection. Plant sclerenchyma tissue may contain cellulose or lignin. Fabrics such as jute, hemp, and flax are made of sclerenchyma tissue.

PLANT MERISTEMATIC TISSUE

Meristems or meristematic tissues are the regions of plant growth. The cells in meristems are undifferentiated and always remain totipotent, which means they can always develop into any type of special tissue. Meristem cells produce all the new cells in a plant and regenerate damaged parts. Cells of meristems reproduce asexually through mitosis or cell division that is regulated by hormones. The two types of meristems are lateral meristems and apical meristems. Primary growth occurs at apical meristems. Roots and shoots have meristem tissue at their tips and can grow in length. Primary meristems include the protoderm, which produces epidermis; the procambium, which produces cambium; xylem and phloem; and the ground meristem, which produces ground tissue including parenchyma. Secondary growth occurs at the lateral or secondary meristems. Secondary meristems include the vascular cambium and cork cambium. Secondary growth causes an increase in diameter.

FLOWERS

The primary function of flowers is to produce seeds for reproduction of the plant. Flowers have a pedicel or stalk with a receptacle or enlarged upper portion, which holds the developing seeds. Flowers also can have sepals and petals. Sepals are leaflike structures and protect the bud. Petals, which are collectively called the corolla, help to attract pollinators. Plants can have stamens, pistils, or both depending on the type of plant. The stamen consists of the anther and filament. The anther produces the pollen, which produces the sperm cells. The pistil consists of the stigma, style, and ovary. The ovary contains the ovules, which house the egg cells.

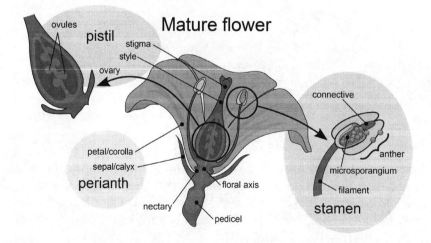

STEMS

Plants can have either woody or nonwoody (herbaceous) stems. The stem is divided into nodes and internodes. Buds are located at the nodes and may develop into leaves, roots, flowers, cones, or more stems. Stems consist of dermal tissue, ground tissue, and vascular tissue. Dicot stems have vascular bundles distributed through the stem. Monocots have rings of vascular bundles. Stems have four main functions: (1) they provide support to leaves, flowers, and fruits; (2) they transport materials in the xylem and phloem; (3) they store food; and (4) they have meristems, which provide all of the new cells for the plant.

LEAVES

The primary function of a leaf is to manufacture food through photosynthesis. The leaf consists of a flat portion called the blade and a stalk called the petiole. The edge of the leaf is called the margin and can be entire, toothed, or lobed. Veins transport food and water and make up the skeleton of the leaf. The large central vein is called the midrib. The blade has an upper and lower epidermis. The epidermis is covered by a protective cuticle. The lower epidermis contains many stomata, which are pores that allow air to enter and leave the leaf. Stomata also regulate transpiration. The middle portion of the leaf is called the mesophyll. The mesophyll consists of the palisade mesophyll and the spongy mesophyll. Most photosynthesis occurs in chloroplasts located in the palisade mesophyll.

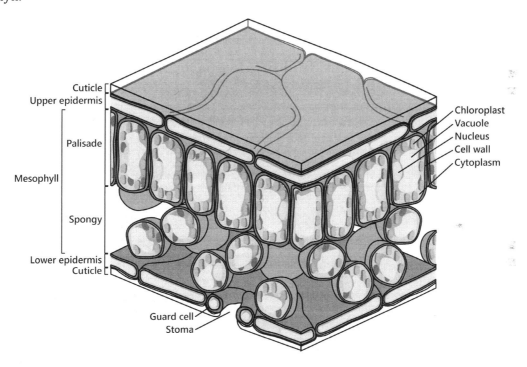

ROOTS

The primary functions of roots are to anchor the plant, absorb materials, and store food. The two basic types of root systems are taproot systems and fibrous root systems. Taproot systems have a primary root with many smaller secondary roots. Fibrous root systems, which lack a primary root, consist of a mass of many small secondary roots. The root has three main regions: the area of maturation, the area of elongation, and the area of cell division or the meristematic region. The root is covered by an epidermal cell, some of which develops into root hairs. Root hairs absorb water and minerals by osmosis, and capillary action helps move the water upward through the roots to the rest of the plant. The center of the root is the vascular cylinder, which contains the xylem and phloem. The vascular cylinder is surrounded by the cortex where the food is stored. Primary growth occurs at the root tip. Secondary growth occurs at the vascular cambium located between the xylem and phloem.

POLLINATION STRATEGIES

Pollination is the transfer of pollen from the anther of the stamen to the stigma of the pistil on the same plant or on a different plant. Pollinators can be either abiotic (not derived from a living organism) or biotic (derived from a living organism). Abiotic pollinators include wind and water. Approximately 20% of pollination occurs by abiotic pollinators. For example, grasses are typically pollinated by wind, and aquatic plants are typically pollinated by water. Biotic pollinators include insects, birds, mammals, and occasionally reptiles. Most biotic pollinators are insects. Many plants have colored petals and strong scents, which attract insects. Pollen rubs off on the insects and is transferred as they move from plant to plant.

SEED DISPERSAL METHODS

Methods of seed dispersal can be abiotic or biotic. Methods of seed dispersal include gravity, wind, water, and animals. Some plants produce seeds in fruits that get eaten by animals and then are distributed to new locations in the animals' waste. Some seeds (e.g. dandelions) have structures to aid in dispersal by wind. Some seeds have barbs that get caught in animal hair or bird feathers and are then carried to new locations by the animals. Some animals bury seeds for food storage but do not return for the seeds. The seeds of aquatic plants can be dispersed by water. The seeds of plants near rivers, streams, lakes, and beaches (e.g. coconuts) are often dispersed by water. Some plants, in a method called mechanical dispersal, can propel or shoot their seeds away from them even up to several feet. Touch-me-nots and violets can reproduce by mechanical dispersal.

ALTERNATION OF GENERATIONS

Alternation of generations, also referred to as metagenesis, contains both a sexual phase and an asexual phase in the life cycle of the plant. Mosses and ferns reproduce by alternation of generations: the sexual phase is called the gametophyte, and the asexual phase is called the sporophyte. During the sexual phase, a sperm fertilizes an egg to form a zygote. By mitosis, the zygote develops into the sporophyte. The sporangia in the sori of the sporophyte produce the spores through meiosis. The spores germinate and by mitosis produce the gametophyte.

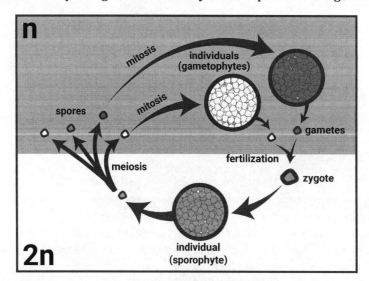

OBTAINING AND TRANSPORTING WATER AND INORGANIC NUTRIENTS

Inorganic nutrients (4) and water (5) enter plants through the root hair and travel to the xylem. Once the water, minerals, and salts have crossed the endodermis, they must be moved upward through the xylem by water uptake. Most of a plant's water is lost through the stomata (3) by transpiration. This loss is necessary to provide the tension needed to pull the water and nutrients

up through the xylem. In order to maintain the remaining water that is necessary for the functioning of the plant, guard cells (2) control the stomata. Whether an individual stoma is closed or open is controlled by two guard cells. When the guard cells lose water and become flaccid, they collapse together, closing the stoma. When the guard cells swell with water and become turgid, they move apart, opening the stoma.

USE OF ROOTS

Plant roots have numerous root hairs that absorb water and inorganic nutrients such as minerals and salts. Root hairs are thin, hairlike outgrowths of the root's epidermal cells that exponentially increase the root's surface area. Water molecules cross the cell membranes of the root hairs by osmosis and then travel on to the vascular cylinder. Inorganic nutrients are transported across the cell membranes of the root endodermis by active transport. The endodermis is a single layer of cells that the water and nutrients must pass through by osmosis or active transport. Casparian strips, which are waxy waterproof deposits, line the channels between the cells of the endodermis to prevent crossing there. Water passes through by osmosis, but mineral uptake is controlled by transport proteins.

USE OF XYLEM

The xylem contains dead, water-conducting cells called tracheids and vessels. The movement of water upward through the tracheids and vessels is explained by the cohesion-tension theory. First, water is lost through evaporation of the plant's surface through transpiration. This can occur at any surface exposed to air but is mainly through the stomata in the epidermis. This transpiration puts the water inside the xylem in a state of tension. Because water is cohesive due to the strong hydrogen bonds between molecules, the water is pulled up the xylem as long as the water is transpiring.

USE OF PHLOEM TO TRANSPORT PRODUCTS OF PHOTOSYNTHESIS

The movement of sugars and other materials from the leaves to other tissues throughout the plants is called translocation. Nutrients are translocated from sources (areas with excess sugars) such as mature leaves to sinks (areas where sugars are needed) such as flowers, fruits, developing leaves, and roots. Phloem vessels are found in the vascular bundles along with the xylem. Phloem contains conducting cells called sieve elements, which are connected end to end in sieve tubes. Sieve tubes carry sap from sugar sources to sugar sinks. Phloem sap contains mostly sucrose dissolved in water. The sap can also contain proteins, amino acids, and hormones. Some plants transport sugar alcohols. Loading the sugar into the sieve tubes causes water to enter the tubes by osmosis, creating a higher hydrostatic pressure at the source end of the tube. Sugar is removed from the sieve tube at the sink end, and water again follows by osmosis lowering the pressure. This process is referred to as the pressure-flow mechanism.

ANIMALS
STRUCTURE, ORGANIZATION, MODES OF NUTRITION, AND REPRODUCTION OF ANIMALS

Animals are multicellular organism with eukaryotic cells that do not have cell walls surrounding their plasma membranes. Animals have several possible structural body forms. Animals can be relatively simple in structure such as sponges, which do not have a nervous system. Other animals are more complex with cells organized into tissues, and tissues organized into organs, and organs even further organized into systems. Invertebrates such as arthropods, nematodes, and annelids have complex body systems. Vertebrates including fish, amphibians, reptiles, birds, and mammals are the most complex with detailed systems such as those with gills, air sacs, or lungs designed to exchange respiratory gases. All animals are heterotrophs and obtain their nutrition by consuming autotrophs or other heterotrophs. Most animals are motile, but some animals move their environment to bring food to them. All animals reproduce sexually at some point in their life cycle. Typically, this involves the union of a sperm and egg to produce a zygote.

CHARACTERISTICS OF THE MAJOR ANIMAL PHYLA

BODY PLANES

Animals can exhibit bilateral symmetry, radial symmetry, or asymmetry. With bilateral symmetry, the organism can be cut in half along only one plane to produce two identical halves. Most animals, including all vertebrates such as mammals, birds, reptiles, amphibians, and fish, exhibit bilateral symmetry. Many invertebrates including arthropods and crustaceans also exhibit bilateral symmetry. With radial symmetry, the organism can be cut in half along several planes to produce two identical halves. Starfish, sea urchins, and jellyfish exhibit radial symmetry. With asymmetry, the organism exhibits no symmetry. Very few organisms in the animal phyla exhibit asymmetry, but a few species of sponges are asymmetrical.

BODY CAVITIES

Animals can be grouped based on their types of body cavities. A coelom is a fluid-filled body cavity between the alimentary canal and the body wall. The three body plans based on the formation of the coelom are acoelomates, pseudocoelomates, and coelomates. Acoelomates do not have body cavities. Pseudocoelomates have a body cavity called a pseudocoelom. Pseudocoeloms are not considered true coeloms. Pseudocoeloms are located between mesoderm and endoderm instead of actually in the mesoderm as in a true coelom. Coelomates have a true coelom located within the mesoderm. Simple or primitive animals such as sponges, jellyfish, sea anemones, hydras, flatworms, and ribbon worms are acoelomates. Pseudocoelomates include roundworms and rotifers. Most animals including arthropods, mollusks, annelids, echinoderms, and chordates are coelomates.

MODES OF REPRODUCTION

Animals can reproduce sexually or asexually. Most animals reproduce sexually. In sexual reproduction, males and females have different reproductive organs that produce gametes. Males have testes that produce sperm, and females have ovaries that produce eggs. During fertilization, a sperm cell unites with an egg cell, forming a zygote. Fertilization can occur internally such as in most mammals and birds or externally such as aquatic animals such as fish and frogs. The zygote undergoes cell division, which develops into an embryo and eventually develops into an adult organism. Some embryos develop in eggs such as in fish, amphibians, reptiles, and birds. Some mammals are oviparous and lay eggs. Most mammals are viviparous and have a uterus in which the embryo develops. Some mammals are marsupials and give birth to an immature fetus that finishes developing in a pouch. Some animals reproduce asexually. For example, hydras reproduce by budding, and starfish and planarians can reproduce by fragmentation and regeneration. Some fish, frogs, and insects reproduce by parthenogenesis.

MODES OF TEMPERATURE REGULATION

Animals can be classified as either homeotherms or poikilotherms. Homeotherms, also called warm-blooded animals or endotherms, maintain a constant body temperature regardless of the temperature of the environment. Homeotherms such as mammals and birds have a high metabolic rate because much energy is needed to maintain the constant temperature. Poikilotherms, also called cold-blooded animals or ectotherms, do not maintain a constant body temperature. Their body temperature fluctuates with the temperature of the environment. Poikilotherms such as

84

arthropods, fish, amphibians, and reptiles have metabolic rates that fluctuate with their body temperature.

Review Video: Basic Characteristics of Organisms
Visit mometrix.com/academy and enter code: 314694

ORGANIZATIONAL HIERARCHY WITHIN MULTICELLULAR ORGANISMS

Cells are the smallest living units of organisms. Tissues are groups of cells that work together to perform a specific function. Organs are groups of tissues that work together to perform a specific function. Organ systems are groups of organs that work together to perform a specific function. An organism is an individual that contains several body systems.

TISSUES

Tissues are groups of cells that work together to perform a specific function. Tissues can be grouped into four broad categories: muscle tissue, nerve tissue, epithelial tissue, and connective tissue. Muscle tissue is involved in body movement. Muscle tissues can be composed of skeletal muscle cells, cardiac muscle cells, or smooth muscle cells. Skeletal muscles include the muscles commonly called biceps, triceps, hamstrings, and quadriceps. Cardiac muscle tissue is found only in the heart. Smooth muscle tissue provides tension in the blood vessels, controls pupil dilation, and aids in peristalsis. Nerve tissue is located in the brain, spinal cord, and nerves. Epithelial tissue makes up the layers of the skin and various membranes. Connective tissues include bone tissue, cartilage, tendons, ligaments, fat, blood, and lymph. Tissues are grouped together as organs to perform specific functions.

ORGANS AND ORGAN SYSTEMS

Organs are groups of tissues that work together to perform specific functions. Organ systems are groups of organs that work together to perform specific functions. Complex animals have several organs that are grouped together in multiple systems. In mammals, there are 11 major organ systems: integumentary system, respiratory system, cardiovascular system, endocrine system, nervous system, immune system, digestive system, excretory system, muscular system, skeletal system, and reproductive system.

Review Video: Muscular System
Visit mometrix.com/academy and enter code: 967216

CARDIOVASCULAR SYSTEM

The main functions of the cardiovascular system are gas exchange, the delivery of nutrients and hormones, and waste removal. The cardiovascular system consists primarily of the heart, blood, and blood vessels. The heart is a pump that pushes blood through the arteries. Arteries are blood vessels that carry blood away from the heart, and veins are blood vessels that carry blood back to the heart. The exchange of materials between blood and cells occur in the capillaries, which are the smallest of the blood vessels. All vertebrates and a few invertebrates including annelids, squids, and octopuses have a closed circulatory system. Mammals, birds and crocodilians have a four-chambered heart. Most amphibians and reptiles have a three-chambered heart. Fish have only a two-chambered heart. Arthropods and most mollusks have open circulatory systems. Many invertebrates do not have a cardiovascular system. For example, echinoderms have a water vascular system.

85

RESPIRATORY SYSTEM

The function of the respiratory system is to move air in and out of the body in order to facilitate the exchange of oxygen and carbon dioxide. The respiratory system consists of the nasal passages, pharynx, larynx, trachea, bronchial tubes, lungs, and diaphragm. Bronchial tubes branch into bronchioles, which end in clusters of alveoli. The alveoli are tiny sacs inside the lungs where gas exchange takes place. When the diaphragm contracts, the volume of the chest increases, which reduces the pressure in the lungs. Then, air is inhaled through the nose or mouth and passes through the pharynx, larynx, trachea, and bronchial tubes into the lungs. When the diaphragm relaxes, the volume in the chest cavity decreases, forcing the air out of the lungs.

REPRODUCTIVE SYSTEM

The main function of the reproductive system is to propagate the species. Most animals reproduce sexually at some point in their life cycle. Typically, this involves the union of a sperm and egg to produce a zygote. In complex animals, the female reproductive system includes one or more ovaries, which produce the egg cell. The male reproductive system includes one or more testes, which produce the sperm.

INTERNAL AND EXTERNAL FERTILIZATION

Eggs may be fertilized internally or externally. In internal fertilization in mammals, the sperm unites with the egg in the oviduct. In mammals, the zygote begins to divide, and the blastula implants in the uterus. In birds, after the egg is fertilized, albumen, membranes, and egg shell are added. Reptiles lay amniotic eggs covered by a leathery shell. Amphibians and most fish fertilize eggs externally. But some fish give birth to live young.

INVERTEBRATES

Most invertebrates reproduce sexually. Invertebrates may have separate sexes or be hermaphroditic, in which the organisms produces sperm and eggs either at the same time or separately at some time in their life cycle. Many invertebrates such as insects also have complex reproductive systems. Some invertebrates reproduce asexually by budding, fragmentation, or parthenogenesis.

DIGESTIVE SYSTEM

The main function of the digestive system is to process the food that is consumed by the animal. This includes mechanical and chemical processing. Depending on the animal, mechanical processes can happen in various ways. Mammals have teeth to chew their food. Saliva is secreted, which contains enzymes to begin the breakdown of starches. Many animals such as birds, earthworms, crocodilians, and crustaceans have a gizzard or gizzard-like organ that grinds the food. Many animals such as mammals, birds, reptiles, amphibians, and fish have a stomach that stores and absorbs food. Gastric juice containing enzymes and hydrochloric acid is mixed with the food. The intestine or intestines absorb nutrients and reabsorb water from the undigested material. Many animals have a liver, gallbladder, and pancreas, which aid in digestion of proteins and fats although not being part of the muscular tube through which the waste passes. Undigested wasted are eliminated from the body through an anus or cloaca.

EXCRETORY SYSTEM

All animals have some type of excretory system that has the main function of metabolizing food and eliminating metabolic wastes. In complex animals such as mammals, the excretory system consists of the kidneys, ureters, urinary bladder, and urethra. Urea and other toxic wastes must be eliminated from the body. The kidneys constantly filter the blood. The nephron is the working unit of the kidney. Each nephron functions like a tiny filter. Nephrons not only filter the blood, but they also facilitate reabsorption and secretion. Basically, the glomerulus filters the blood. Water and dissolved materials such as glucose and amino acids pass on into the Bowman's capsule. Depending on concentration gradients, water and dissolved materials can pass back into the blood primarily through the proximal convoluted tubule. Additional water can be removed at the loop of Henle. Antidiuretic hormone regulates the water that is lost or reabsorbed. Urine passes from the kidneys through the ureters to the urinary bladder where it is stored before it is expelled from the body through the urethra.

<u>KIDNEYS</u>

The kidneys are involved in blood filtration, pH balance, and the reabsorption of nutrients to maintain proper blood volume and ion balance. The nephron is the working unit of the kidney. The parts of the nephron include the glomerulus, Bowman's capsule, and loop of Henle. Filtration takes place in the nephron's glomerulus. Water and dissolved materials such as glucose and amino acids pass on into the Bowman's capsule. Depending on concentration gradients, water and dissolved materials can pass back into the blood primarily through the proximal convoluted tubule. Reabsorption and water removal occurs in the loop of Henle and the conducting duct. Urine and other nitrogenous wastes pass from the kidneys to the bladders and are expelled.

NERVOUS SYSTEM

All animals except sponges have a nervous system. The main function of the nervous system is to coordinate the activities of the body. The nervous system consists of the brain, spinal cord, peripheral nerves, and sense organs. Sense organs such as the ears, eyes, nose, taste buds, and pressure receptors receive stimuli from the environment and relay that information through nerves and the spinal cord to the brain where the information is processed. The brain sends signals through the spinal cord and peripheral nerves to the organs and muscles. The autonomic nervous system controls all routine body functions by the sympathetic and parasympathetic divisions. Reflexes, which are also part of the nervous system, may involve only a few nerve cells and bypass the brain when an immediate response is necessary.

ENDOCRINE SYSTEM

The endocrine system consists of several ductless glands, which secrete hormones directly into the bloodstream. The pituitary gland is the master gland, which controls the functions of the other glands. The pituitary gland regulates skeletal growth and the development of the reproductive organs. The pineal gland regulates sleep cycles. The thyroid gland regulates metabolism and helps regulate the calcium level in the blood. The parathyroid glands also help regulate the blood calcium level. The adrenal glands secrete the emergency hormone epinephrine, stimulate body repairs, and regulate sodium and potassium levels in the blood. The islets of Langerhans located in the pancreas secrete insulin and glucagon to regulate the blood sugar level. In females, ovaries produce estrogen, which stimulates sexual development, and progesterone, which functions during pregnancy. In males, the testes secrete testosterone, which stimulates sexual development and sperm production.

IMMUNE SYSTEM

The immune system in animals defends the body against infection and disease. The immune system can be divided into two broad categories: innate immunity and adaptive immunity. Innate immunity includes the skin and mucous membranes, which provide a physical barrier to prevent pathogens from entering the body. Special chemicals including enzymes and proteins in mucus, tears, sweat, and stomach juices destroy pathogens. Numerous white blood cells such as neutrophils and macrophages protect the body from invading pathogens. Adaptive immunity involves the body responding to a specific antigen. Typically, B-lymphocytes or B cells produce antibodies against a specific antigen, and T-lymphocytes or T-cells take special roles as helpers, regulators, or killers. Some T-cells function as memory cells.

MAINTENANCE OF HOMEOSTASIS IN ORGANISMS

ROLE OF FEEDBACK MECHANISMS

Feedback mechanisms play a major role in homeostasis in organisms. Each feedback mechanism consists of receptors, an integrator, and effectors. Receptors such as mechanoreceptors or thermoreceptors in the skin detect the stimuli. The integrator such as the brain or spinal cord receives the information concerning the stimuli and sends out signals to other parts of the body. The effectors such as muscles or glands respond to the stimulus. Basically, the receptors receive the stimuli and notify the integrator, which signals the effectors to respond. Feedback mechanisms can be negative or positive. Negative-feedback mechanisms are mechanisms that provide a decrease in response with an increase in stimulus that inhibits the stimulus, which in turn decreases the response. Positive-feedback mechanisms are mechanisms that provide an increase in response with an increase in stimulus, which actually increases the stimulus, which in turn increases the response.

ROLE OF HYPOTHALAMUS

The hypothalamus plays a major role in the homoeostasis of vertebrates. Homeostasis is regulation of internal chemistry to maintain a constant internal environment. The hypothalamus is the central portion of the brain just above the brainstem, which is linked to the endocrine system through the pituitary gland. The hypothalamus releases special hormones that influence the secretion of pituitary hormones. The hypothalamus regulates the fundamental physiological state by controlling body temperature, hunger, thirst, sleep, behaviors related to attachment, sexual development, fight-or-flight stress response, and circadian rhythms.

ROLE OF ENDOCRINE SYSTEM AND HORMONES

All vertebrates have an endocrine system that consists of numerous ductless glands that produce hormones that help coordinate many functions of the body. Hormones are signaling molecules that are received by receptors. Many hormones are secreted in response to signals from the pituitary gland and hypothalamus gland. Other hormones are secreted in response to signals from inside the body. Hormones can consist of amino acids, proteins, or lipid molecules such as steroid hormones. Hormones can affect target cells, which have the correct receptor that is able to bind to that particular hormone. Most cells have receptors for more than one type of hormone. Hormones are distributed to the target cells in the blood by the cardiovascular system. Hormones incorporate feedback mechanisms to help the body maintain homeostasis.

ROLE OF ANTIDIURETIC HORMONE

Antidiuretic hormone (ADH) helps maintain homeostasis in vertebrates. ADH is produced by the posterior pituitary gland, and it regulates the reabsorption of water in the kidneys and concentrates the urine. The stimulus in this feedback mechanism is a drop in blood volume due to water loss. This signal is picked up by the hypothalamus, which signals the pituitary gland to secrete ADH. ADH is carried by the cardiovascular system to the nephrons in the kidneys signaling them to reabsorb more water and send less out as waste. As more water is reabsorbed, the blood volume increases, which is monitored by the hypothalamus. As the blood volume reaches the set point, the hypothalamus signals for a decrease in the secretion of ADH, and the cycle continues.

ROLE OF INSULIN AND GLUCAGON

Insulin and glucagon are hormones that help maintain the glucose concentration in the blood. Insulin and glucagon are secreted by the clumps of endocrine cells called the pancreatic islets that are located in the pancreas. Insulin and glucagon work together to maintain the blood glucose level. Insulin stimulates cells to remove glucose from the blood. Glucagon stimulates the liver to convert glycogen to glucose. After eating, glucose levels increase in the blood. This stimulus signals the pancreas to stop the secretion of glucagon and to start secreting insulin. Cells respond to the insulin and remove glucose from the blood, lowering the level of glucose in the blood. Later, after eating, the level of glucose in the blood decreases further. This stimulus signals the pancreas to secrete glucagon and decrease the secretion of insulin. In response to the stimulus, the liver converts glycogen to glucose, and the level of glucose in the blood rises. When the individual eats, the cycle begins again.

THERMOREGULATION

Animals exhibit many adaptations that help them achieve homeostasis, or a stable internal environment. Some of these adaptions are behavioral. Most organisms exhibit some type of behavioral thermoregulation. Thermoregulation is the ability to keep the body temperature within certain boundaries. The type of behavioral thermoregulation depends on whether the animal is an endotherm or an ectotherm. Ectotherms are "cold-blooded," and their body temperature changes with their external environment. To regulate their temperature, ectotherms often move to an appropriate location. Fish move to warmer waters. Animals will climb to higher grounds. Diurnal ectotherms such as reptiles often bask in the sun to increase their body temperatures. Butterflies are heliotherms in that they derive nearly all of their heat from basking in the sun. Endotherms are "warm-blooded" and maintain a stable body temperature by internal means. However, many animals that live in hot environments have adapted to the nocturnal lifestyle. Desert animals are often nocturnal to escape high daytime temperatures. Other nocturnal animals sleep during the day in underground burrows or dens. Birds can spread their wings to capture heat from the sun.

GAMETE FORMATION

Gametogenesis is the formation of gametes. Gametes are reproductive cells. Gametes are produced by meiosis. Meiosis is a special type of cell division that consists of two consecutive mitotic divisions referred to as meiosis I and meiosis II. Meiosis I is a reduction division in which a diploid cell is reduced to two haploid daughter cells that contain only one of each pair of homologous chromosomes. During meiosis II, those haploid cells are further divided to form four haploid cells. Spermatogenesis in males produces four viable sperm cells from each complete cycle of meiosis. Oogenesis produces four daughter cells, but only one is a viable egg and the other three are polar bodies.

FERTILIZATION

Fertilization is the union of a sperm cell and an egg cell to produce a zygote. Many sperm may bind to an egg, but only one joins with the egg and injects its nuclei into the egg. Fertilization can be external or internal. External fertilization takes place outside of the female's body. For example, many fish, amphibians, crustaceans, mollusks, and corals reproduce externally by spawning or releasing gametes into the water simultaneously or right after each other. Reptiles and birds reproduce by internal fertilization. All mammals except monotremes (e.g. platypus) reproduce by internal fertilization.

EMBRYONIC DEVELOPMENT

Embryonic development in animals is typically divided into four stages: cleavage, patterning, differentiation, and growth. Cleavage occurs immediately after fertilization when the large single-celled zygote immediately begins to divide into smaller and smaller cells without an increase in mass. A hollow ball of cells forms a blastula. Next, during patterning, gastrulation occurs. During gastrulation, the cells are organized into three primary germ layers: ectoderm, mesoderm, and endoderm. Then, the cells in these layers differentiate into special tissues and organs. For example, the nervous system develops from the ectoderm. The muscular system develops from the mesoderm. Much of the digestive system develops from the endoderm. The final stage of embryonic development is growth and further tissue specialization. The embryo continues to grow until ready for hatching or birth.

POSTNATAL GROWTH

Postnatal growth occurs from hatching or birth until death. The length of the postnatal growth depends on the species. Elephants can live 70 years, but mice only about 4 years. Right after animals are hatched or born, they go through a period of rapid growth and development. In vertebrates, bones lengthen, muscles grow in bulk, and fat is deposited. At maturity, bones stop growing in length, but bones can grow in width and repair themselves throughout the animal's lifetime, and muscle deposition slows down. Fat cells continue to increase and decrease in size throughout the animal's life. Growth is controlled by genetics but is also influenced by nutrition and disease. Most animals are sexually mature in less than two years and can produce offspring.

PROTISTS

Protists are small, eukaryotic, single-celled organisms. Although protists are small, they are much larger than prokaryotic bacteria. Protists have three general forms, which include plantlike protists, animal-like protists, and fungus-like protists. Plantlike protists are algae that contain chlorophyll and perform photosynthesis. Animal-like protists are protozoa with no cell walls that typically lack chlorophyll and are grouped by their method of locomotion. Fungus-like protists, which do not have chitin in their cell walls, are generally grouped as either slime molds or water molds. Protists may be autotrophic or heterotrophic. Autotrophic protists include many species of algae. Heterotrophic protists include parasitic, commensalistic, and mutualistic protozoa. Slime molds are heterotrophic fungus-like protists, which consume microorganisms. Some protists reproduce sexually, but most reproduce asexually by binary fission. Some reproduce asexually by spores. Some reproduce by alternation of generations and require two hosts in their life cycle.

FUNGI

Fungi are nonmotile organisms with eukaryotic cells containing chitin in their cell walls. Most fungi are multicellular, but a few including yeast are unicellular. Fungi have multicellular filaments called hyphae that are grouped together in mycelia. Fungi do not perform photosynthesis. All fungi are heterotrophs. Fungi can be parasitic, mutualistic or free living. Free-living fungi include mushrooms and toadstools. Parasitic fungi include fungi responsible for ringworm and athlete's foot. Mycorrhizae are mutualistic fungi that live in or near plant roots increasing the roots' surface area of absorption. Almost all fungi reproduce asexually by spores, but most fungi also have a sexual phase in the production of spores. Some fungi reproduce by budding or fragmentation.

> **Review Video: Feeding Among Heterotrophs**
> Visit mometrix.com/academy and enter code: 836017
>
> **Review Video: Kingdom Fungi**
> Visit mometrix.com/academy and enter code: 315081

CLASSIFICATION AND STRUCTURE OF PROKARYOTIC CELLS

ARCHAEA VS. BACTERIA

Archaea and Bacteria both consist of unicellular prokaryotic organisms. They do not possess a nucleus or membrane-bound organelles, but they do have ribosomes, a single circular chromosome, a plasma membrane, and a cell wall. Despite these similarities, the two groups are quite different, hence the grouping into separate domains. Unlike that of bacteria, the hereditary material of archaea contains introns, and histone-like proteins are used to organize the DNA. The composition of ribosomal RNA and the cell wall is also different (only bacterial cells have peptidoglycan in their cell walls). Archaea are associated with extreme environments because many species have the ability to thrive in harsh conditions (high salt concentrations, extreme temperatures or pH, etc.). Many of them are chemosynthetic and can extract energy from inorganic sources. But archaea are not limited to extreme habitats. Some species even live in the human body, but pose no pathogenic threat. Bacteria can be beneficial to humans, but can also cause disease.

BACTERIA

Bacteria are small, prokaryotic, single-celled organisms. Bacteria have a circular loop of DNA (plasmid) that is not contained within a nuclear membrane. Bacterial ribosomes are not bound to endoplasmic reticulum, as in eukaryotes. A cell wall containing peptidoglycan surrounds the bacterial plasma membrane. Some bacteria such as pathogens are further encased in gel-like capsules. Bacteria can be autotrophs or heterotrophs. Some bacteria heterotrophs are saprophytes that function as decomposers in ecosystems, and some are pathogens. Many types of bacteria share commensal or mutualistic relationships with other organisms. Most bacteria reproduce asexually by binary fission. Two identical daughter cells are produced from one parent cell. Some bacteria can transfer genetic material to other bacteria through a process called conjugation. Some bacteria can incorporate DNA from the environment in a process called transformation.

MAJOR CLASSIFICATIONS OF BACTERIA BY SHAPE

The three major classifications of bacteria by morphology are: bacilli, spirilla, and cocci.

Bacilli are rod-shaped bacteria, and may be gram-positive or gram-negative depending on the species. They can occur as a single bacillus, pairs called diplobacilli, or chains called streptobacilli. There are also oval-shaped bacilli called coccobacilli. Common examples of bacilli include *Listeria*, *Bacillus*, *Escherichia*, and *Salmonella*.

Spirilla are gram-negative, and have a spiral shape that may or may not be flexible depending on the type. Spirochetes are flexible, and have internal flagella. *Borrelia* are spirochetes that are responsible for Lyme disease. Spirilla, such as *Helicobacter*, are more rigid, and their flagella are external.

Cocci are spherical bacteria. They can be gram-positive or negative, and have many possible arrangements: pairs (diplococci), chains (streptococci), clusters of 4 (tetrads), cubes of 8 (sarcina), and irregular clusters (staphylococci). *Staphylococcus aureus* and *streptococcus pneumoniae* are cocci that are associated with infection.

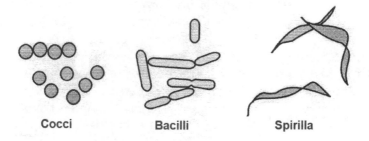

Cocci   Bacilli   Spirilla

PRESENCE OF CELL WALL IN BACTERIA

The cells of plants, fungi, archaea, and bacteria have cell walls that vary in composition. The cell wall of a bacterium is made of a polymer of polysaccharides (glycosaminoglycan) and peptide chains called peptidoglycan (or murein). The thickness of this mesh differs between gram-positive and gram-negative bacteria. Gram-positive bacteria have up to 40 layers of peptidoglycan that surround a phospholipid bilayer (together these are called the **envelope**). The cell wall of gram-positive bacteria can be up to 100 nm thick. Gram-negative bacteria have far fewer layers, with a thickness of up to 10 nm. They also have an outer membrane that surrounds the cell wall, in addition to the inner membrane. The cell walls of gram-positive bacteria stain purple when stained with a Gram stain, and gram-negative bacteria stain pink. The cell wall gives strength and support to the cell, but is flexible enough to allow for growth and fission. It also helps to regulate the passage of materials by acting as a filter.

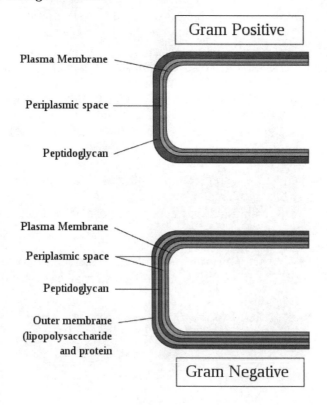

FLAGELLAR PROPULSION, MECHANISM

A **flagellum** is a whip-like structure that many types of cells use for locomotion. A bacterial flagellum is made of a single filament (composed of the protein flagellin) with a diameter of about 20 nm, and a hollow central channel. A hook connects this filament to a complex structure called the **basal body**. The basal body is embedded in the plasma membrane and acts as a motor that can rotate clockwise or counterclockwise. The torque on the filament causes it to move. This process is powered by a proton motive force; the greater the concentration gradient, the greater the flow of hydrogen ions across the bacterial plasma membrane, and the faster it rotates. Bacteria can detect various chemicals and use flagellar propulsion to propel bacteria toward or away from the source of these chemicals. This is called **chemotaxis**.

The structure and mechanism for propulsion is different for bacteria than it is for archaea and eukaryotes. The flagella of archaea and eukaryotes are powered by ATP, not a proton motive force. Eukaryotic flagella are hollow and made of microtubules, while the flagella of archaea are solid, and made of many different types of proteins.

GROWTH AND PHYSIOLOGY OF PROKARYOTIC CELLS
REPRODUCTION BY FISSION

Bacteria reproduce asexually in a process known as **binary fission**. To prepare for this process, a bacterium must grow in volume and enlarge its membrane and cell wall. It replicates its circular chromosome, beginning at the origin of replication and continuing until the entire loop is copied. Each chromosome attaches to the membrane, and the cell wall and membrane grow inward at the middle to form a transverse septum with a replicated chromosome on each side. Other components such as ribosomes are randomly distributed to each daughter cell. Unlike in mitosis, there is no formation of a spindle apparatus. Each daughter cell is identical to the parent cell. Sometimes, cytokinesis is incomplete, and the cells remain attached to each other to form arrangements such as doublets, tetrads, and chains.

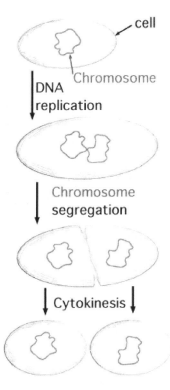

93

<u>HIGH DEGREE OF GENETIC ADAPTABILITY, ACQUISITION OF ANTIBIOTIC RESISTANCE</u>

Bacteria, despite reproducing asexually, have a high degree of genetic adaptability. Random **mutations** in their DNA can give rise to genetically unique offspring. Depending on the location of that mutation, it could impart antibiotic resistance to the mutant. Bacteria can also exchange DNA with one another in a process called **conjugation**. The donor bacterium uses a narrow tube called a pilus to attach to the recipient bacterium before transferring a plasmid: a small piece of circular DNA. The plasmid often carries favorable genes, such as antibiotic resistance. Bacteria can also acquire new genes through **transformation**. In this process, the cells uptake fragments of DNA that are present in the surroundings (often left over from dead cells). The foreign DNA can be incorporated into the bacterial chromosome and expressed. Finally, **transduction**, or the injection of viral DNA from a bacteriophage, can also alter the bacterial genome.

<u>EXPONENTIAL GROWTH</u>

The growth curve of a typical population of bacteria under favorable conditions has an exponential phase, but it usually begins with a lag phase. The **lag phase** occurs when the bacteria are introduced to a new environment. The population remains unchanged as they acclimate to the conditions, grow in size, metabolize nutrients, and perform normal functions. During the **exponential** (or log) **phase**, they divide regularly by binary fission. One cell produces two, then four, eight, sixteen, etc. This exponential growth can only continue until resources become limited and metabolic end products accumulate. This plateau in the growth curve is called the **stationary phase**. The **death phase** shows a decline in the population as the bacteria start to die off at a rate similar to the division rate in the exponential phase.

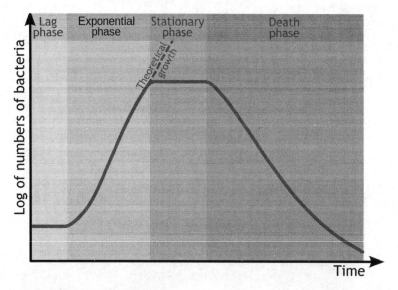

<u>EXISTENCE OF ANAEROBIC AND AEROBIC VARIANTS</u>

Bacteria can be classified into groups based on their response to oxygen. **Obligate aerobes** are bacteria that require oxygen for their metabolism. Like humans, they use glycolysis, the citric acid cycle, and oxidative phosphorylation to extract energy from organic compounds. **Obligate anaerobes**, on the other hand, cannot survive in the presence of oxygen because they lack the enzymes that protect them from oxidative damage, and must rely on either fermentation or anaerobic respiration to obtain energy. Anaerobic respiration, like aerobic respiration, involves glycolysis, the citric acid cycle, and an electron transport chain, but there is no oxidative phosphorylation. That is, oxygen is not reduced, but rather an alternative electron acceptor such as sulfate or nitrate is used. In fermentation, energy is extracted without the citric acid cycle or an electron transport chain. **Aerotolerant anaerobes** can tolerate oxygen, but do not use it in their

94

metabolic processes. **Microaerophiles** do require oxygen, but can only survive in low concentrations. **Facultative anaerobes** can use aerobic respiration in the presence of oxygen, but can switch to fermentation or anaerobic respiration when oxygen is absent.

PARASITIC AND SYMBIOTIC

Many species of bacteria can establish relationships that can benefit their host, but others can be harmful. Pathogenic bacteria grow at the expense of their host. They produce harmful toxins that result in diseases such as tetanus, tuberculosis, meningitis, and chlamydia. But far more common are mutualistic and commensal bacteria. Mutualistic bacteria benefit from their host, and the host is helped rather than harmed. For example, some bacteria in the human body keep the growth of harmful bacterial species in check. Other species in the digestive tract aid in digestion and synthesize B and K vitamins. There are also bacteria that exist in a commensalistic relationship and do not affect their host at all. *Streptococcus pyogenes* is a species that can thrive in certain body locations without causing harm, but a change in environment can lead to a variety of infections such as strep throat and impetigo.

CHEMOTAXIS

Chemotaxis is the movement of an organism (often a bacterium) in response to a chemical stimulus. The direction, but not rate, of motion is determined by the concentration gradient of the chemical. In positive chemotaxis, a bacterium moves toward a favorable stimulus such as food, while in negative chemotaxis it moves away from an unfavorable stimulus such as a toxin. The direction of motion is controlled by signal transduction processes. Receptor proteins at one or both poles of the cell relay information about the chemical to the inside of the bacterium through a series of reactions. The end result is usually a change in the direction of flagellar rotation.

GENETICS OF PROKARYOTIC CELLS

EXISTENCE OF PLASMIDS, EXTRAGENOMIC DNA

Many bacteria contain **extragenomic DNA**: DNA that is outside of their single chromosome. Plasmids, for example, are small circular strands of DNA that replicate independently and are passed onto daughter cells during cell division. (Some types of plasmids called episomes *can* get integrated into the bacterial chromosome.) While plasmids often contain genes that impart desirable traits such as antibiotic resistance or the ability to metabolize certain substances, they are rarely needed for survival under favorable conditions. A cell can contain anywhere from one to hundreds of copies of a plasmid. Sometimes, there are different types of plasmids within the same cell, assuming the plasmids are "compatible."

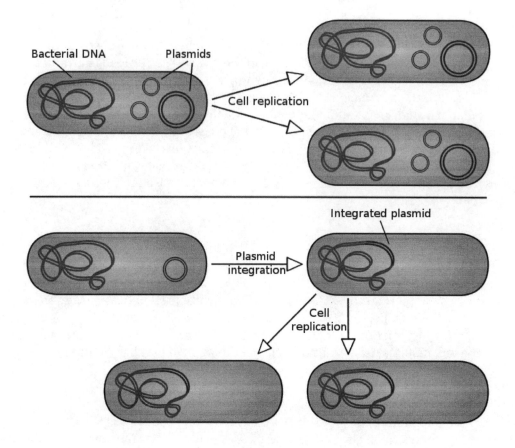

<u>TRANSFORMATION: INCORPORATION INTO BACTERIAL GENOME OF DNA FRAGMENTS FROM EXTERNAL MEDIUM</u>

When a bacterial cell dies, pieces of its DNA are released into the surrounding medium. These fragments can cross the envelope of surrounding bacteria if the cells are in a state of competence. Certain bacteria enter this state when nutrients are low, or if they are exposed to other stressful conditions. After the DNA is taken in, enzymes in the cell can either break down the fragments and use the nucleotides during DNA replication, or the fragments can be integrated into the bacterial chromosome. Any genes contained in the fragments can then be expressed by the bacterium. This is an example of horizontal gene transfer; DNA is passed between organisms, rather than from parent to offspring.

<u>CONJUGATION</u>

Conjugation is the process by which bacteria transfer DNA from one bacterium to another. Bacteria reproduce asexually, but conjugation is one mechanism for genetic recombination (the others being transformation and transduction). During conjugation, hereditary material is transferred in one direction from the donor to the recipient. For this to happen, the donor cell must have an F (fertility) plasmid which allows the donor "male" to form appendages called sex pili. The donor cell (also called the F+ cell) uses a pilus to connect to the recipient female (or F- cell). One nucleotide strand of the double stranded plasmid is given to the F- cell, while the other strand remains in the F+ cell. Once the complementary strand of each single strand is synthesized, the plasmids will be identical to each other. The recipient cell is now an F+ cell, and can donate the plasmid to another F- cell. The F plasmid can be integrated into the bacterial chromosome or remain separate.

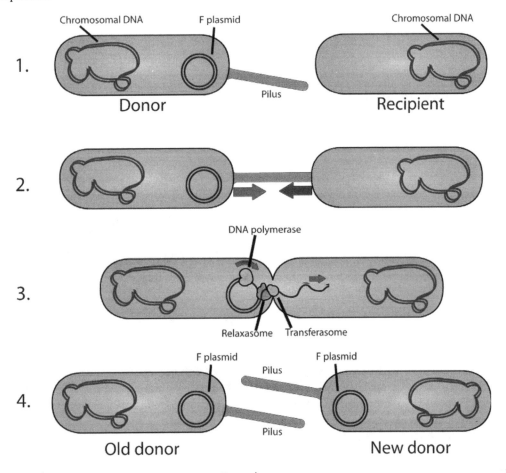

TRANSPOSONS (ALSO PRESENT IN EUKARYOTIC CELLS)

Transposons are segments of DNA that can move within the genome. They are found in both prokaryotic and eukaryotic cells. Transposons are sometimes called "jumping genes" because of their ability to translocate. They can cause mutations by interrupting gene sequences, but they can also carry their own genes. In bacteria, they often include an antibiotic resistance gene and can move back and forth between a plasmid and the chromosome.

There are two main classes of transposons: retrotransposons (class I) and DNA transposons (class II). Both encode the gene for the enzyme **transposase**, which facilitates the transfer of the genomic element from one location to another. Retrotransposons, however, are first transcribed into RNA, and then the enzyme **reverse transcriptase** synthesizes DNA from the RNA before it is inserted. DNA transposons are actually cut out of a genome before they are translocated.

VIRUS STRUCTURE

GENERAL STRUCTURAL CHARACTERISTICS (NUCLEIC ACID AND PROTEIN, ENVELOPED AND NONENVELOPED)

Viruses are particles that are classified somewhere between living and nonliving. They are made of proteins and nucleic acids, yet are acellular and entirely reliant on host cells to reproduce and to carry on metabolic processes. For this reason, viruses are described as obligate intracellular parasites. When they are outside of a host cell, they are referred to as **virions**.

Viruses share a common structure. They lack all of the organelles found in eukaryotic and prokaryotic cells, including ribosomes. They do have a protein coat called a capsid that is made of subunits called capsomeres. It encloses the viral genome, which may be DNA or RNA. The capsid comes in various shapes (such as rod and polyhedral) depending on the type of virus. Some viruses are surrounded by an envelope made of phospholipids and both bacterial and viral proteins.

LACK ORGANELLES AND NUCLEUS

Viruses contain DNA or RNA, but their genome is not enclosed in a nucleus. In fact, viruses do not have *any* organelles, and must rely on the ribosomes of the host cell to produce the proteins involved in the replication of their genome, as well as the proteins that form the capsid. It is not surprising that viruses are small, given that they are little more than a protein coat and genes. They must also be small enough to fit inside another cell so that they can replicate. They range from 20 to 400 nm in diameter, which is about 1/100 the size of a prokaryote, and 1/1000 the size of a typical eukaryotic cell.

STRUCTURAL ASPECTS OF TYPICAL BACTERIOPHAGE

A **bacteriophage** (also called a "phage") is a virus that only infects prokaryotes, and therefore bacteriophages cannot infect humans. The name is appropriate because it means "bacteria eater", and these viruses destroy the cells that they infect. Most bacteriophages have a tail sheath that they use to inject their genome, and tail fibers that allow it to recognize and attach to a specific host. Like all viruses, the genome is encapsulated by a protein coat. This protein coat is left behind on the surface of the bacterium when the genome is injected.

Bacteriophages replicate in one of two ways: the lytic or lysogenic cycle. The method used is dependent on the type of virus and/or the environmental conditions. In the lytic cycle, the virus takes over the intracellular machinery of the host cell, producing progeny and lysing the cell. A virus in the lysogenic cycle does not typically cause symptoms because the genome is integrated into the host genome, without the production of more viruses. The genome is replicated when the host cell replicates, but no progeny are created unless a change in the environment causes it to leave the host genome and enter the lytic cycle.

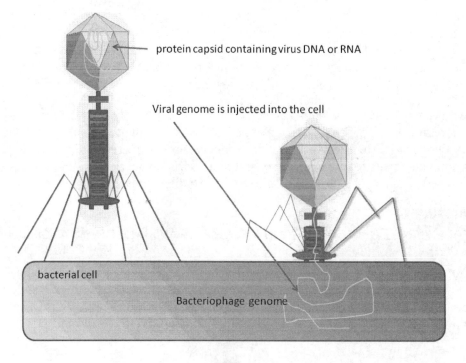

protein capsid containing virus DNA or RNA

Viral genome is injected into the cell

bacterial cell

Bacteriophage genome

GENOMIC CONTENT — RNA OR DNA

All viruses encapsulate a genome. Viral genomes vary by size, and by the type of nucleic acid they contain. The average size of a viral genome is around 40 kilobase pairs, but there is a wide range from 1–2 kbp to a few hundred kbp. Most viruses contain RNA, but some have DNA, and each type of nucleic acids may be double or single stranded. Some single stranded (ss) RNA-containing viruses are "positive-sense," meaning their genes can be translated directly into proteins using the ribosomes of the host cell. Other RNA viruses are "negative-sense," and must synthesize a complementary transcript of the ssRNA. To do this, they use the enzyme RNA polymerase which they carry inside the capsid. The synthesized complementary strand is the "messenger RNA" used in translation. Some RNA viruses (called retroviruses) synthesize DNA from their ssRNA, and the DNA is integrated into the host DNA.

VIRAL LIFE CYCLE

SELF-REPLICATING BIOLOGICAL UNITS THAT MUST REPRODUCE WITHIN SPECIFIC HOST CELL

Viruses cannot replicate outside of a host cell. To infect a cell, a virus must attach to specific receptors on the surface of a cell. If virus-specific receptors are not present, the cell cannot be penetrated. Once attached, the genome of the virus is either injected (typical of a bacteriophage), leaving the capsid behind, or the virus enters the cell intact (typical of a virus that infects eukaryotes). Once inside the host cell, the capsid (if present) is broken down, and the nucleic acid released. Many copies of the genome are produced, and the machinery of the host cell is used to make the proteins that are used in the assembly of new viruses. The genome and capsid proteins (capsomeres) spontaneously self-assemble into viral progeny. As progeny are produced, either they can bud off of the host cell (typical of enveloped viruses), or the cell may become so full of viruses that it bursts. The lysed cell dies, and virions are released to infect other cells. Cell damage and/or death, in combination with the body's immune response, account for the symptoms of a viral infection.

GENERALIZED PHAGE AND ANIMAL VIRUS LIFE CYCLES

ATTACHMENT TO HOST, PENETRATION OF CELL MEMBRANE OR CELL WALL, AND ENTRY OF VIRAL GENETIC MATERIAL

For a virus to attach to a host cell (a process called **adsorption**), it must bind to receptor proteins. The pathway for entry of the viral genome after adsorption varies according to the type of virus, and the type of host cell. Some viruses (particularly bacteriophages) use tail fibers to attach to the host cell's receptors before injecting their genome using the tail sheath. Viruses that infect eukaryotic cells tend to enter either by receptor-mediated endocytosis or by membrane fusion. In receptor-mediated endocytosis, attachment sites on the surface of the virus bind to cell surface receptors, and cell membrane invaginates around the virus, pinching off to forming a vacuole that enters the cytoplasm. Some cells mistake the virus for a desired resource, like nutrients. Enveloped viruses typically gain entry when proteins within their lipid envelope bind to receptor proteins on the cell membrane, and the envelope and membrane fuse. The virus enters, and the protein coat is degraded. If the cell does not have the specific receptor proteins used by a particular virus, then that cell cannot be infected.

USE OF HOST SYNTHETIC MECHANISM TO REPLICATE VIRAL COMPONENTS

Viruses depend on the biosynthetic machinery of the cell to replicate. They cannot copy their own genome, nor can they produce the proteins needed for the capsid. The host cell provides ATP, nucleotides, transfer RNA, amino acids, and most of the enzymes required for viral replication (though some viral genomes contain genes that are translated into enzymes). The cell's ribosomes are redirected to translate viral proteins that are used in the assembly of progeny. The cell can no longer perform its own functions, and has essentially become a virus factory.

TRANSDUCTION: TRANSFER OF GENETIC MATERIAL BY VIRUSES

Transduction is the transfer of DNA from one cell to another through the action of a virus, and is one way in which genetic recombination occurs in bacteria. When a bacteriophage infects a bacterium and replicates, the viral progeny may take parts of the bacterial genome with them when they exit the cell. The bacteriophages then inject the bacterial DNA (along with the viral genome) into new host cells. The bacterial DNA may simply be broken down by the new host cell, but if it matches up with a homologous sequence, crossover may occur, resulting in genetic recombination. There are two types of transduction. In **generalized transduction**, viruses can transfer any portion of the bacterial genome, whereas in **specialized transduction** only certain genes can be transferred.

RETROVIRUS LIFE CYCLE: INTEGRATION INTO HOST DNA, REVERSE TRANSCRIPTASE, HIV

Retroviruses are single-stranded RNA viruses that use the enzyme **reverse transcriptase** to transcribe their RNA into double-stranded DNA. The viral DNA becomes incorporated into the host cell's DNA with the help of the enzyme **integrase**. When the host cell replicates, it treats the viral DNA as its own and copies it, passing it on to each daughter cell. The viral genes within the host genome are transcribed and translated to produce the components of new viruses that bud from the cell to infect new ones. These types of viral infections are difficult to treat because once the viral DNA has been integrated into the host genome, the only way to kill it is to kill the cell itself. The human immunodeficiency virus (HIV) is an example of a retrovirus that infects white blood cells known as CD4 cells. As the number of CD4 cells declines, AIDS develops.

PRIONS AND VIROIDS: SUBVIRAL PARTICLES

Prions and viroids are tiny, non-living infectious particles that are much smaller than viruses. In fact, these pathogens are nothing more than proteins and RNA molecules, respectively.

Prions are misfolded variations of normal proteins that incubate for many years before symptoms of disease begin to show. They do not replicate, but rather prompt the misfolding of other proteins, though the mechanism is not well understood. The misfolded proteins group together, triggering the formation of even more prions. The cell cannot function normally under these conditions, and animal diseases such as mad cow disease and Creutzfeldt-Jakob disease result.

Viroids are short circular molecules (approximately 250–400 nucleobases) of ssRNA that are not translated into proteins, but replicate in host plant cells. Replication requires the enzyme RNA polymerase II, and occurs either in the nucleus or in chloroplasts. Viroids cause a number of plant diseases by silencing the normal RNA of the plant, and therefore interfering with gene expression. The human disease hepatitis D is caused by a viroid-like pathogen.

Structure and Functions of Systems

NERVOUS SYSTEM

The nervous system is responsible for coordinating and controlling all of the activities of the body. It is composed of a complex network of neurons and the neuroglial cells that support them. Neurons are responsible for carrying out the **sensory**, **integrative**, and **motor** functions of the nervous system. Sensory receptors detect changes in the internal and external environment, such as pain, pressure, light, or temperature. During integration, the information is brought to the central nervous system where it is processed and interpreted. The motor function refers to the voluntary or involuntary response that is carried out by effectors, such as the contraction of a muscle, or the secretion of products by gland cells. These rapid responses are essential for the maintenance of

homeostasis, heart rate, breathing, regulation of temperature, movement, sensations, memory, emotion, language, and more.

HIGH LEVEL CONTROL AND INTEGRATION OF BODY SYSTEMS

The nervous system is responsible for the integration of body systems. The central nervous system (CNS) consists of the brain and spinal cord. It is considered the control/integration center because it combines sensory information from various sources. It communicates with the rest of the body via the peripheral nervous system (PNS). The **afferent** division of the PNS brings information *to* the CNS, and the **efferent** division delivers messages *from* the CNS to muscles or glands.

The nervous system works particularly closely with the endocrine system. Nerve impulses send information about the condition of the body to the hypothalamus, which regulates the release of hormones from the pituitary. The pituitary, or "master gland," controls other glands of the endocrine system. All body systems ultimately require direction from the nervous system to function properly and maintain homeostasis. Heart rate, digestion, body temperature, movement, and higher functions such as cognitive ability, memory, emotion, and fine motor skills are under the control of the nervous system.

ORGANIZATION OF VERTEBRATE NERVOUS SYSTEM

The nervous system is divided into two main parts: the central nervous system (CNS), which consists of the brain and spinal cord, and the peripheral nervous system (PNS), which consists of nervous tissues (nerves, ganglia) that are outside the CNS. The CNS integrates sensory information, and the PNS sends information to and from the CNS, allowing it to communicate with the rest of the body. Afferent neurons of the PNS transmit impulses to the CNS, and efferent neurons transmit impulses to effectors.

The PNS is further divided into the autonomic system (ANS) and somatic nervous system (SNS). The SNS controls voluntary movements, such as the contraction of skeletal muscles. The ANS controls involuntary movements, such as the contraction of smooth and cardiac muscles, and glandular secretions. The ANS has two subdivisions that tend to work antagonistically (though there are exceptions). The sympathetic division activates the "fight or flight" response, preparing the body for action by increasing heart rate, dilating pupils and bronchial tubes, and suppressing functions that are not required for immediate survival. The parasympathetic division activates the "rest and digest" functions by decreasing heart rate, constricting pupils and bronchial tubes, and promoting digestion.

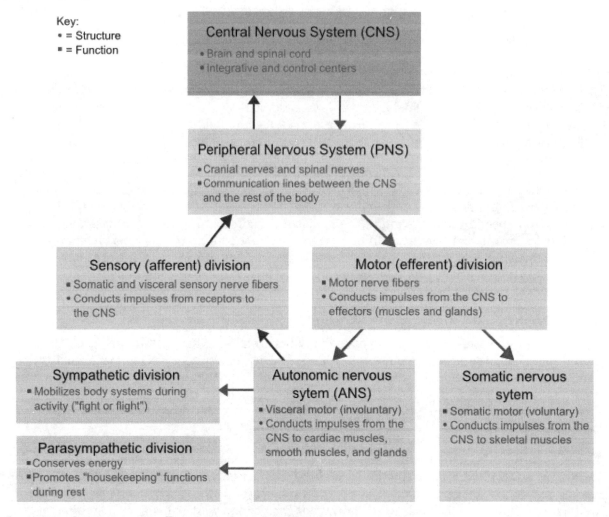

ADAPTIVE CAPABILITY TO EXTERNAL INFLUENCES

The nervous system is the first body system to respond to changes in the environment. The receptors of afferent neurons (sensory neurons) are specialized to detect certain types of stimuli, and these neurons transmit action potentials to the CNS where a motor response may be called for. Sensory receptors are found nearly everywhere in the body. They can be classified by location, morphology (free vs. encapsulated nerve endings), the nature of the stimuli they detect (pressure, chemicals, light, temperature), and rate of adaptation.

Sensory adaptation refers to the change in sensitivity that occurs when receptors are exposed to a prolonged stimulus. Adaptation rates vary greatly across the different types of receptors, but they can be classified into two main groups. **Phasic** receptors quickly adapt to a constant stimulus, meaning that action potentials decrease over time and eventually stop. This explains the loss of sensation of clothes against the skin, or how an odor seems to disappear when the source is still present. Most tactile and chemoreceptors are phasic. **Tonic** receptors adapt slowly, constantly alerting the CNS of the stimulus with action potentials. Proprioceptors (receptors that provide feedback about position and movement of the body) are tonic receptors, as are photoreceptors (light-detecting receptors) and nociceptors (pain receptors).

SENSOR AND EFFECTOR NEURONS

Sensory neurons are the afferent neurons that deliver impulses to the CNS. They are sometimes classified by the type of stimulus that they respond to. **Mechanoreceptors** respond to changes in pressure or tension. Cutaneous touch receptors such as Meissner's corpuscles, Merkel's disks, Pacinian corpuscles, and Ruffini endings are all mechanoreceptors, as are the muscle spindles that detect stretching of skeletal muscle and the receptors of the inner ear that detect vibrations. **Chemoreceptors** such as olfactory and taste receptors detect the presence of chemicals. **Photoreceptors** such as the rod and cone cells of the eye respond to light. **Thermoreceptors** sense both absolute temperature, and changes in temperature. **Nociceptors** detect pain.

Sensory neurons can also be categorized by location. **Exteroceptors** near the body surface transmit information about the external environment. **Proprioceptors** within the inner ear, skeletal muscles, and joints provide information about movement, position, and equilibrium. **Interoceptors** of visceral organs and blood vessels provide information about internal stimuli.

Once the sensory information has been processed, **effector neurons** (motor neurons) transmit the impulse away from the CNS to activate muscles and glands. All motor neurons of the somatic division run directly from the CNS to the effector without synapsing with another neuron. The autonomic division uses two-neuron pathways.

SENSORY PATHWAYS

Sensory pathways allow the brain to receive sensory information from the rest of the body. This information travels either through the spinal cord or the thalamus and is delivered to the cerebral cortex or the cerebellum. Only the conscious cortex of the brain receives this information. Examples of these pathways may include pain and temperature information or touch and pressure information.

SENSORY RECEPTORS

Sensory receptors are nerve endings that detect certain stimuli and respond to these stimuli by sending impulses to the brain. There are multiple types of sensory receptors and they are often classified by where they are located. Exteroreceptors are closer to the surface of the skin and respond to touch or other stimuli that occur outside the body. Interoreceptors are inside the body and respond to internal stimuli such as stomach pain. Proprioceptors detect unconscious stimuli such as body position and movement. Other types of receptors are classified by stimulus. Thermoreceptors respond to temperature, nociceptors respond to pain, and baroreceptors respond to pressure. Vibrations and touch are detected by mechanoreceptors, and chemical stimuli are detected by chemoreceptors, while light and visual stimuli are detected by photoreceptors.

STRUCTURES OF THE EYE

The eye is composed of many parts that work together to send visual information to the brain through the optic nerve, translating the stimuli into images. The front of the eye is clear and called the cornea. This is where light travels through and into the pupil, which is the dark center of the iris. The iris is the color of the eye, such as brown, blue, or green, and filters the light that comes in. The clear, inside structure of the eye is called the lens, and it is responsible for focusing light on the retina. The retina is a layer of nerve cells, or photoreceptors, that respond to light stimuli. The ciliary muscles help focus this light by manipulating the shape of the lens. Lastly, the middle of the eye is filled with clear fluid known as vitreous.

VISUAL PATHWAY IN THE BRAIN

In order to process vision, eyes must send the information they receive to the brain. The photoreceptors in the retina capture the visual image and send nerve impulses through the optic nerve. Each eye sends its own messages that meet up at the optic chiasm and then split up on the way to the brain. Half of the left and right optic nerve travel to the left side of the brain, while the other half of each travel to the right side.

PARALLEL PROCESSING AND FEATURE DETECTION

Parallel processing is when the brain is presented with different stimuli and must process these stimuli at the same time. An example of this would be when the brain is sent an image and it must determine the color, size, texture, and movement simultaneously. Feature detection is a theory that explains the reasons why seeing certain images or words may elicit different parts of the brain. It asserts that the nervous system is able to distinguish between significant features of the environment and irrelevant information in the background.

STRUCTURE AND FUNCTION OF THE EAR

The three main parts of the ear are classified as the external ear, the middle ear, and the inner ear. The ear canal, which is what sound travels through, and the outside of the ear drum, or tympanic membrane, are in the external ear. The bulk of the ear drum resides within the middle ear and is what sound bounces off on its way to the brain. Also, in the middle ear are the malleus, incus, and stapes or stirrup bones. These bones respond to sound waves by vibrating together, amplifying the sound and creating a wave in the fluid of the ear. This fluid is housed in the cochlea, the structure shaped like a snail containing hair cells that is located in the inner ear. The hair cells of the cochlea then send the auditory signals to the brain where they are then processed.

HAIR CELLS

Hair cells are located in the cochlea of the ear and are auditory and vestibular sensory receptors. In response to movement, the hair cells bend and prompt a discharge of neurotransmitters that send signals to the brain. In humans, hair cells are unable to regenerate, so when they are damaged, hearing loss can occur.

AUDITORY PROCESSING AND AUDITORY PATHWAYS IN THE BRAIN

Auditory processing is when sound enters through the ear and is delivered to the brain for interpretation. This sound passes through the ear canal and rebounds off the ear drum, creating vibrations in the cochlea, and is then transmitted via the auditory nerve. The message is sent to the brainstem where it can be translated into information regarding frequency, intensity, and position, and is then passed on through the temporal lobe, specifically the thalamus and auditory cortex. The auditory message is then interpreted to create a comprehensible meaning.

SOMATOSENSATION AND RECEPTOR CELLS

When the body interacts with the environment, receptor cells transmit sensory information to the brain. This process is known as somatosensation. The following three types of receptor cells are involved in this process: mechanoreceptors, thermoreceptors, and nociceptors. Respectively, these receptors involve sensations of touch, temperature, and pain.

SENSE OF TASTE

Taste receptors pick up signals from specific tastes, which are sent to the brain and translated into flavors. These different tastes include salty, sweet, bitter, sour, and "umami," also known as savory. Taste occurs through taste buds, which are spherical-shaped growths on the tongue and are linked to taste receptors. Certain chemicals in food are related to these different tastes, and if present in food, allow the brain to recognize the flavors via the taste hairs covering the taste buds. For a food to be sensed as sweet, it would contain sugar, while umami foods are meaty. Both can be detected by T1R2 and T1R3 receptors. Salt would be present and detected via sodium channels to be distinguished as salty. For bitter foods, basic chemicals such as quinine are present, and for sour foods, acidic chemicals would be present. Bitter taste is transmitted through the T2R receptors and sour taste through the transient receptor potential (TRP) channel.

SENSE OF SMELL

Within the nasal cavity, olfactory cells detect smell, called olfaction. These cells are chemoreceptors and pick up on specific chemical stimuli in order to deliver messages to the brain about smell.

OLFACTORY PATHWAYS IN THE BRAIN

When a person is exposed to something with a particular smell, this smell enters the nasal cavity. Inside the nasal cavity is the olfactory epithelium, close in proximity to the brain. Between the brain and the olfactory epithelium are the olfactory bulb and cribriform plate. The olfactory bulb has thousands of nerves and these nerves extend through the cribriform plate and into the olfactory epithelium. When a smell enters the olfactory epithelium, the cells at the end of these nerves detect the scent and send a message to the brain to interpret the particular smell.

SYMPATHETIC AND PARASYMPATHETIC NERVOUS SYSTEMS: ANTAGONISTIC CONTROL

The autonomic nervous system has two divisions, sympathetic and parasympathetic, and they tend to have antagonistic effects when they both innervate the same organ. Both divisions use a two-neuron pathway, consisting of a preganglionic neuron which runs from the CNS to a ganglion, and a postganglionic neuron which innervates the effector.

The sympathetic nervous division is responsible for triggering the "fight or flight" response. Preganglionic neurons of the sympathetic nervous system release acetylcholine (ACh), which is the stimulus for the release of norepinephrine from postganglionic neurons. Norepinephrine acts on target tissues, prompting a rapid and unified response. The heart rate increases, respiration rate increases, blood flow to the heart and skeletal muscle increases, pupils dilate, and glycogen is broken down.

The parasympathetic nervous division is responsible for the "rest and digest" response. *Both* pre- and postganglionic neurons of the parasympathetic nervous system release acetylcholine. The parasympathetic nervous system stimulates events that are slower-paced, and less essential for immediate survival. The heart rate and respiration rate decrease, blood flow is directed to digestive organs, peristalsis is promoted, pupils constrict, and glycogen is synthesized.

REFLEXES

A **reflex** is a nearly instantaneous, unconscious, and involuntary response to a stimulus. The stimulus (for example, the sensation of heat when one touches a hot stove) is detected by the receptors of afferent neurons, and sensory information is sent to interneurons in the spinal cord. (Interneurons are entirely restricted to the central nervous system, and act as bridges between sensory and motor neurons.) From here, the signal travels along motor neurons to the effectors (the muscles of the arm and hand). Before the signal for pain has reached the brain, the hand has already been withdrawn. While reflexes do not require conscious thought, some have pathways that involve the brain. The brain can sometimes override reflex actions—for example, trying not to blink during an eye exam. Sometimes, a reflex involves a direct link between the sensory and motor neuron—for example, the patellar reflex, or knee-jerk reaction. This is referred to as a monosynaptic reflex. Polysynaptic reflexes are more complex because they involve interneurons.

FEEDBACK LOOP, REFLEX ARC

A reflex arc describes a neural pathway that triggers a reflex action. It begins with a **receptor**—the site or organ that receives the stimulus. A **sensory neuron** carries the impulse along the afferent pathway to the **integration center** within the central nervous system. Interneurons process the information and pass the impulse to a **motor neuron**. The impulse travels along the efferent pathway to the **effector**—the responding muscle or gland.

Most reflexes attempt to maintain homeostasis by inhibiting a change in condition; this is called negative feedback. The maintenance of body temperature is one of many examples. As body temperature changes, thermoreceptors send information to the hypothalamus. If body temperature is too high, a command is sent to dilate blood vessels and release sweat. If the temperature is too low, the body shivers and blood vessels constrict. Positive feedback loops are less common, and sometimes harmful because they enhance the stimuli rather than inhibit them. A beneficial form of positive feedback occurs during childbirth. When the cervix is stretched by the descending fetus, impulses are sent to the pituitary, which sends a command to increase uterine contractions. The more the fetus is pushed, the more the cervix stretches. This positive feedback loop continues until birth.

ROLE OF SPINAL CORD AND SUPRASPINAL CIRCUITS

The spinal cord is a major reflex center that connects the afferent and efferent pathways. It is made of an exterior layer of white matter that surrounds an interior core of grey matter. The white matter consists of glial cells and myelinated bundles of axons that form tracts to and from the brain. There are no cell bodies or dendrites in white matter. Grey matter consists mostly of interneurons, but also contains motor neurons and glial cells. (The axons are mostly unmyelinated, giving the tissue its grey appearance.) The cell bodies of afferent neurons reside in dorsal root ganglia, just outside the spinal cord. Afferent fibers enter into the posterior/dorsal aspect of the spinal cord (a region called the posterior grey horn) through the anterior root, while efferent fibers exit on the anterior/ventral aspect (the anterior grey horn) through the posterior root. Spinal neurons usually innervate structures that are inferior to the neck.

Not all reflexes are mediated by spinal neurons. Supraspinal circuits require input from the brain or brainstem, and are involved in actions such as the blinking and gagging reflexes.

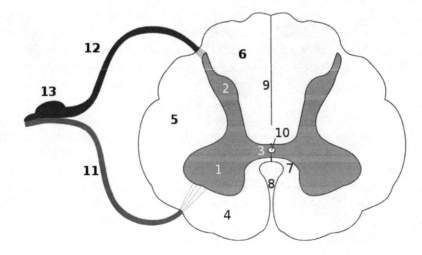

Cross section of a spinal cord		
Gray matter	White matter	Other structures
1. Anterior horn	4. Anterior funiculus	10. Central canal
2. Posterior horn	5. Lateral funiculus	11. Anterior root
3. Grey commissure	6. Posterior funiculus	12. Posterior root
	7. Anterior commissure	13. Dorsal root ganglion
	8. Anterior median fissure	
	9. Posterior median sulcus	

INTEGRATION WITH ENDOCRINE SYSTEM: FEEDBACK CONTROL

The nervous system is closely integrated with the endocrine system. Both systems control the body—the nervous system through electrical impulses, and the endocrine system though slower-acting, but longer-lasting hormones. The two systems are linked via the hypothalamus, a region in the brain that controls the autonomic nervous system as well as the pituitary gland. In fact, neurons within the hypothalamus have axons that extend through the infundibulum and terminate in the posterior pituitary. The hypothalamus produces oxytocin and antidiuretic hormone (ADH), but these hormones are stored in and secreted by the posterior pituitary. The release of other important hormones from the anterior pituitary is also regulated by the hypothalamus. Pituitary hormones go on to control other endocrine glands and body functions. Hormones travel through the bloodstream to target tissues, eliciting responses that are important for growth, development, metabolism, and the maintenance of homeostasis. An example of the interaction between the two systems can be seen in the letdown of milk during nursing. As a baby begins to nurse, the stimulus sends an impulse to the hypothalamus, causing the pituitary to release oxytocin into the blood. The hormone targets the mammary gland, inducing it to release milk.

NERVE CELL

CELL BODY: SITE OF NUCLEUS, ORGANELLES

The cell body, or soma, of a neuron contains the organelles that are responsible for the metabolic activities of the neuron. The interior of the cell body contains a nucleus with a prominent nucleolus. The DNA within the nucleus encodes the information for the many proteins that are needed for the neuron to function. The neuronal cytoplasm contains most of the organelles that are characteristic of animal cells (cytoskeleton, rough and smooth endoplasmic reticulum, Golgi bodies, lysosomes, peroxisomes, and mitochondria). There are relatively high numbers of mitochondria to support the high metabolic needs of the neuron. Granular Nissl bodies (made of rough ER and clusters of free ribosomes) synthesize proteins for use within the cell. Notably absent in mature neurons are centrioles, as differentiated neurons have lost their ability to divide. Various projections (dendrites and/or an axon) extend from the cell body, and neurons can be classified according to these structural differences.

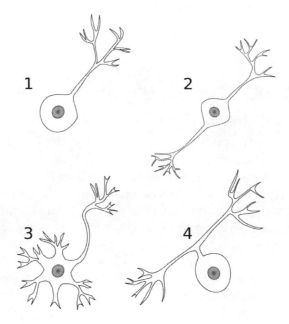

- 1: unipolar (many sensory neurons are unipolar)
- 2: bipolar (rare—associated with retina of the eyes, and inner ear)
- 3: multipolar (most common type—interneurons and motor neurons)
- 4: pseudounipolar (sensory neurons)

DENDRITES: BRANCHED EXTENSIONS OF CELL BODY

Dendrites are relatively short, branched extensions of the cell body that receive incoming chemical signals (neurotransmitters) from the other neurons. These tree-like projections taper with every branch, maximizing the surface area for synaptic inputs. Many dendrites have tiny protrusions called dendritic spines that synapse with a single axon. The cytoplasm within the dendrites contains the same organelles as the cell body, with the exception of the nucleus.

The neurotransmitters that are released from axon terminals of the presynaptic cell cross the synaptic cleft, where they bind to receptor sites on the dendrites of the postsynaptic cells. These signals may be excitatory or inhibitory, and the net effect of these signals determines whether the

neuron is inhibited or triggered to fire (in which case the chemical message will be converted to an electrical impulse that travels down the axon).

Structure of a Typical Neuron

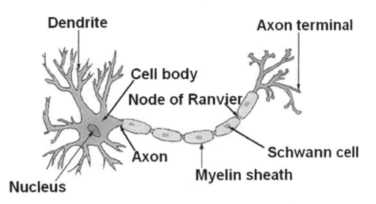

AXON: STRUCTURE AND FUNCTION

An axon is a smooth, cable-like nerve fiber that is specialized to conduct electrical impulses away from the soma. Most neurons have one long axon, but the axon's length can vary, and some neurons have no axon at all. The axon emerges from a slightly elevated structure called the **axon hillock** that connects the soma to the axon. The cytoplasm of the axon is called **axoplasm**, and it lacks the Golgi bodies, Nissl bodies, and ribosomes found in dendritic cytoplasm. Since there is little to no translation, proteins must be imported from the soma. The axon often splits into **collaterals** that allow one neuron to interact with more than one cell. At the end of each axon are highly branched structures called **axon terminals**. These club-shaped endings contain synaptic vesicles filled with neurotransmitters. When an action potential is generated at the axon hillock, it propagates along the axon. When it reaches the axon terminals, the neurotransmitters are released to a target cell.

MYELIN SHEATH, SCHWANN CELLS, INSULATION OF AXON

The axons of many neurons are sheathed in a lipid-based coating called **myelin**. Myelin insulates the axon much like the coating on electrical wire. It also increases the rate at which an impulse can travel. There are intermittent gaps in the sheath called nodes of Ranvier that allow the impulse to jump quickly from one node to the next.

Neurons of the peripheral nervous system are myelinated by **Schwann cells**. These glial cells curve around the axon, wrapping their plasma membranes around it like a bandage to form multiple lipid-rich layers. The nucleus and cytoplasm remain outside the myelin sheath, but are encased in the outer **neurilemmal** sheath of the Schwann cell. Axons of very small diameter may be supported by Schwann cells, but are not myelinated by them. These are called non-myelinating Schwann cells. **Oligodendrocytes** are responsible for sheathing the neurons of the central nervous system. Unlike Schwann cells, a single oligodendrocyte can myelinate dozens of axons by extending its membrane in multiple directions and wrapping around the axons. White matter of the CNS is made mostly of myelinated axons, while the axons associated with grey matter are unmyelinated.

Multiple sclerosis, the leukodystrophies, and many other diseases result from damaged myelin. Without the proper insulation, the neurons of affected individuals cannot effectively conduct an impulse.

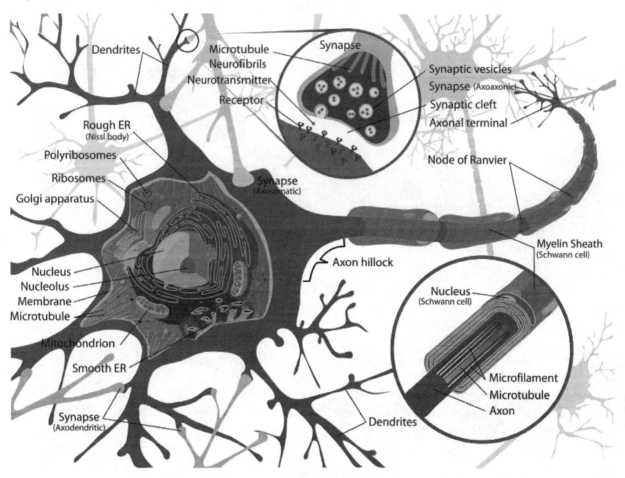

NODES OF RANVIER: PROPAGATION OF NERVE IMPULSE ALONG AXON

Nodes of Ranvier are uninsulated gaps between myelinated portions of the axon that increase the rate of conduction. These exposed portions are about 1 μm in length, and they contain a high density of voltage gated sodium and potassium channels. The channels open to allow the passage of these ions, depolarizing the membrane. Since ions are unable to diffuse through the myelin, the action potential must jump to the next node. This is called **saltatory propagation**. This type of conduction is faster and more efficient than the continuous conduction that is seen along the entire length of an unsheathed axon. Large-diameter myelinated axons conduct impulses much faster (80–120 m/s) than thin unmyelinated axons (0.5–10 m/s). While rapid conduction has its benefits, myelinated axons have less neuroplasticity than unmyelinated axons; that is, they are more limited in their ability to form new connections with other neurons.

SYNAPSE: SITE OF IMPULSE PROPAGATION BETWEEN CELLS

A **synapse** is a communicating junction between two neurons, or between a neuron and an effector (muscle or gland). The synapse consists of a presynaptic element, a tiny gap called the synaptic cleft, and a postsynaptic element. Impulses are transmitted across the synaptic cleft through the action of neurotransmitters. Synapses can be classified according to the nature of the postsynaptic element. **Axodendritic** synapses terminate on the dendrites of a postsynaptic neuron. **Axosomatic** synapses terminate on a postsynaptic soma. **Axoaxonic** synapses are rare, terminating on a postsynaptic axon.

They can also be classified by the mode in which the impulse is transmitted. Most synapses are unidirectional **chemical** junctions, using neurotransmitters to send messages to the postsynaptic cell. When the impulse reaches the axon terminals, the vesicles that store the neurotransmitters fuse with the plasma membrane, releasing the signals into the synaptic cleft before they bind to receptors on the postsynaptic target. At this point, the postsynaptic membrane will either be excited (depolarized) or inhibited (hyperpolarized). Bidirectional **electrical** synaptic junctions do not use neurotransmitters. They are linked by gap junctions that allow the flow of ions between cells. Electrical synapses are faster, always excitatory, and more rare.

Generic Neurotransmitter System

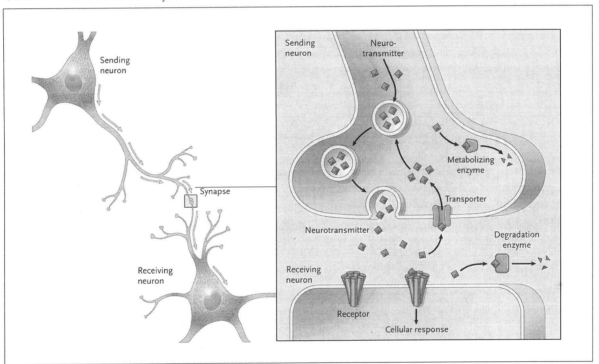

SYNAPTIC ACTIVITY: TRANSMITTER MOLECULES

When an action potential reaches the axon terminal, voltage-gated calcium channels open in response to the depolarization of the membrane. Calcium ions enter, triggering the release of neurotransmitters by exocytosis. The neurotransmitters diffuse across the synaptic cleft, binding to receptors in the target cell and eliciting either an excitatory or an inhibitory response. The neurotransmitters are then recycled back to the presynaptic cell, are degraded by enzymes, or diffuse away from the synaptic cleft to prevent overstimulation.

111

Common neurotransmitters and their actions are summarized below:

Neurotransmitter	Action
Acetylcholine (ACh)	Stimulates skeletal muscle
Norepinephrine (NE)	Influences mood and sleep patterns
Dopamine	Associated with mood, attention, reward system, and movement
Histamine	Works with the hypothalamus, promotes wakefulness
Serotonin	Many roles–mostly inhibitory. Influences sleep, mood, hunger, and arousal
GABA	The major inhibitory neurotransmitter
Glutamate	The major excitatory neurotransmitter

RESTING POTENTIAL: ELECTROCHEMICAL GRADIENT

The resting potential describes the voltage across a non-signaling neuron's membrane. It averages −70 millivolts due to an excess of negative charge in the cytoplasm as compared to the extracellular fluid. In this resting state, most of the voltage-gated sodium and potassium channels are closed. There are, however, many ungated potassium channels that allow the leakage of potassium ions (K^+) out of the cell (down the concentration gradient). There are far fewer leak channels for the sodium ions (Na^+) that are more concentrated on the outside of the cell. This differential permeability is an important factor in the establishment of the resting potential membrane. As potassium ions diffuse out of the cell, they leave behind negatively charged organic ions in the cytoplasm. Eventually their diffusion is opposed by electrical forces, and the ions are pulled back into the cell. (This combination of forces is called an electrochemical gradient.) For the difference in electric potential to be maintained, the concentration gradients of potassium and sodium must also be maintained. An ATP-powered enzyme called the sodium/potassium pump transports 3 Na^+ out of the cell for every 2 K^+ that it takes in. This counteracts the leakage of ions, maintaining a resting potential of −70 mV.

ACTION POTENTIAL

An **action potential** is the rapid change in membrane potential that occurs when an impulse is generated. At rest, the voltage-gated sodium channels of a neuron are closed, but a stimulus can cause some of them to open. The entry of Na^+ **depolarizes** the membrane; the membrane potential becomes more positive. If the stimulus meets or exceeds the threshold, more sodium channels open. The Na^+ that was concentrated outside the cell diffuses in, completely depolarizing the membrane, peaking at around +30 mV. The gates close quickly, but not before triggering nearby channels to open. A chain reaction takes the action potential down the axon.

The membrane potential is restored during **repolarization**. Voltage-gated potassium ions open as the sodium channels close, and K^+ leaves the cell, causing the inside to become negatively charged again. The membrane becomes momentarily **hyperpolarized** (around −80 mV) as more K^+ leave the cell than is necessary to establish resting potential. During the **refractory period**, the neuron either requires a greater than normal stimulus to respond (relative refractory period) or does not respond at all (absolute refractory period). The sodium-potassium pump establishes the original concentration gradients of Na$^+$ and K$^+$ by pumping sodium out and potassium in, and the neuron can fire again.

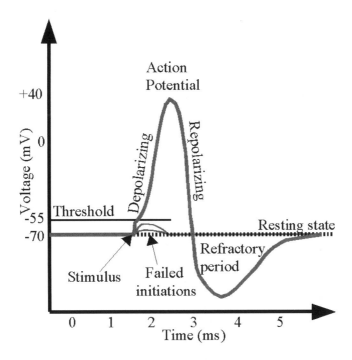

The threshold potential is the level of depolarization that is required to trigger an action potential. The average threshold value is about −55 mV. When neurotransmitters bind to the postsynaptic neuron, their effects may be excitatory or inhibitory. Whether or not the neuron fires depend on the sum of these effects. If the excitatory signals outweigh the inhibitory signals enough to reach the critical threshold, an action potential will be generated (usually at the axon hillock), sending an impulse down the neuron.

The threshold potential follows an "all-or-nothing" principle. If the stimulus is too weak to depolarize the membrane to −55 mV, then the neuron will not fire. As soon as the threshold potential is reached, the neuron will fire, and it will always fire with the same intensity - even if it overshoots the threshold. There are no "weak" or "strong" action potentials, but the neuron *can* fire more frequently as the strength of a stimulus increases.

The potential difference (or voltage) across a membrane is determined by the relative concentrations of ions on each side of the membrane. Potassium ions are more concentrated inside the cytoplasm of a neuron, and sodium ions are more concentrated on the outside. These ions diffuse down their concentration gradients through leak channels, though the membrane is far less permeable to sodium. Without some mechanism to restore the concentration gradients, the membrane would depolarize. A transmembrane protein called the sodium/potassium pump solves this problem by using active transport to pump 3 Na$^+$ out of the cell for every 2 K$^+$ that are pumped inside. Before it is phosphorylated by ATP, this electrogenic pump has an affinity for the sodium ions inside the cell. Once it is phosphorylated, it changes shape, exporting 3 Na$^+$. In this conformation, the pump now has an affinity for the potassium ions that are outside the cell. The phosphate group is released, and 2 K$^+$ enter. The imbalance of ion shuttling maintains the polarity of the membrane.

EXCITATORY AND INHIBITORY NERVE FIBERS: SUMMATION, FREQUENCY OF FIRING

A single neuron can have thousands of synapses with presynaptic neurons. Some of these synapses will have excitatory effects–increasing the probability that an action potential will be generated—, and others will have inhibitory effects—decreasing the probability that an action potential will be generated. The neurotransmitters released by an **inhibitory** nerve fiber will open potassium channels in the postsynaptic cell, allowing the *outflow* of K⁺. This leads to localized *hyperpolarization* known as an inhibitory postsynaptic potential (IPSP). The neurotransmitters released by an **excitatory** nerve fiber will open sodium channels in the postsynaptic cell, allowing the *inflow* of Na⁺. This leads to localized *depolarization* known as an excitatory postsynaptic potential (EPSP). The summation of these IPSPs and EPSPs determines whether or not the neuron will fire. **Temporal summation** is the integration of repeated signals from a single neuron over a short time, while **spatial summation** is the integration of simultaneous signals from two or more neurons. If the membrane depolarizes to threshold level, an action potential will result. The strength of the EPSP has a direct effect on the frequency of action potentials, but not on the intensity of the action potentials. For this reason, the nervous system is said to be "frequency modulated" as opposed to "amplitude modulated."

GLIAL CELLS, NEUROGLIA

Glial cells, also called neuroglia, support and protect neurons within the central and peripheral nervous system. Despite their inability to conduct impulses, there are many more glial cells than neurons within nervous tissue. Glia also have the ability to divide, and so nearly all brain tumors arise from them.

CNS Glial Cell	Structure / Characteristics	Function
Astrocytes	Star-shaped The most abundant cells found in neural tissue	Anchor neurons Facilitate the exchange of materials between capillaries and neurons Uptake excess ions and neurotransmitters
Microglia	Spider-shaped—relatively few extensions	Phagocytic—immune defense, digest dead neurons and debris
Oligodendrocytes	Structurally similar to an astrocyte, but fewer extensions Extensions wrap around axons of CNS neurons	Produce the myelin sheaths that insulate CNS neurons Speed up neurotransmission
Ependyma	Ciliated cells that form the epithelial lining of the ventricles and central canal of the spinal cord Columnar or cuboidal	Circulate cerebrospinal fluid (CSF) Facilitate the exchange of materials between the CSF and interstitial fluid of brain and spinal cord
PNS Glial Cell	Structure / Characteristics	Function
Schwann cells	Extensive lipid membranes wrap around PNS axons to form layers	Produce the myelin sheaths that insulate PNS neurons Speed up neurotransmission
Satellite cells	Flattened cells that surround the soma of neurons within PNS ganglia	Protect and cushion PNS neurons

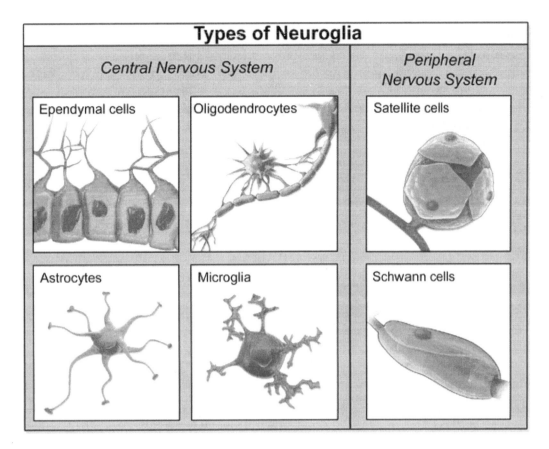

Types of Neuroglia

Central Nervous System

Ependymal cells

Oligodendrocytes

Astrocytes

Microglia

Peripheral Nervous System

Satellite cells

Schwann cells

ELECTROCHEMISTRY

CONCENTRATION CELL: DIRECTION OF ELECTRON FLOW, NERNST EQUATION

The cell membrane of a neuron can be compared to a type of a galvanic cell known as a concentration cell. The difference in concentration of ions on each side of the cell membrane sets up a voltage, much like the two half-cells of a concentration cell (each half differs only in concentration, not material). The Nernst equation relates the voltage (or Nernst potential) to the concentration gradient and charge of the ion in question (only one species of ion can be considered in the calculation.) As can be seen in the equation, if there is no difference in concentration across the membrane, then there will be no voltage, since the natural log of 1 is zero. The equation below examines potassium (K^+) but any ion can be substituted in for K.

$$V = \frac{RT}{zF} \ln \frac{\left[K^+\right]_o}{\left[K^+\right]_i}$$

- V (or E) = membrane potential
- R = ideal gas constant (8.314 JK−1 mol−1)
- T = temperature (Kelvins)
- z = charge on the ion
- F = Faraday's constant (96485 C mol−1)
- ln = natural log
- $\left[K^+\right]_o$ = potassium concentration outside the cell
- $\left[K^+\right]_i$ = potassium concentration inside the cell

115

BIOSIGNALING

GATED ION CHANNELS

Voltage-gated ion channels are transmembrane proteins that open and close in response to a change in membrane potential. Typically, these channels are highly selective, only allowing the passage of one type of ion. When an electrically excitable cell like a neuron is at its resting potential, voltage-gated channels are closed. But as a membrane depolarizes, the new electric field causes the proteins to change conformation.

Voltage-gated sodium channels have two gates: the activation gate (**gate m**) and the deactivation gate (**gate h**). These gates allow a sodium channel to shift between three conformations: closed, open, and inactivated. In the closed state (resting potential), gate m is closed, and gate h is open. Gate m opens in response to a stimulus and sodium ions diffuse into the cell, further depolarizing the membrane. At the peak of depolarization, gate h closes to block the inflow of sodium ions, and the channel is in an inactive state.

Voltage-gated potassium channels only have one gate: **gate n**. Gate n opens immediately before the sodium channels are inactivated. As potassium ions flow out of the cell, the membrane repolarizes. The potassium channel closes relatively slowly, allowing an excess of potassium ions to exit the cell.

Ligand-gated ion channels (LGICs, or ionotropic receptors) are receptor proteins that are commonly found in electrically excitable cells because they can respond very quickly to a stimulus. These transmembrane proteins undergo a rapid change in conformation in response to the binding of a particular substance, often a neurotransmitter. In a postsynaptic neuron, LGICs receive the neurotransmitters that are released from the presynaptic axon terminals. When the ligands bind, they trigger the opening of a channel within the protein that allows the flow of certain ions down their concentration gradients. These channels tend to be less specific than voltage-gated ion channels, and sometimes allow the passage of more than one type of ion. The ligand itself, however, is very specific to its receptor—fitting into it like a lock and key. As ions cross the membrane, the voltage changes, and the chemical message is translated into an electrical message. GABA, for example, is the primary inhibitory neurotransmitter in the nervous system. When it binds to its ionotropic receptor, the channel opens to allow chloride ions (Cl^-) into the cell. The cell becomes hyperpolarized and therefore less likely to fire.

RECEPTOR ENZYMES

Receptor enzymes are transmembrane proteins that act as catalysts in response to the binding of a ligand. These proteins share a common structure; they have an extracellular **ligand-binding domain**, an intracellular **enzymatic domain**, and a transmembrane domain that connects them. When a signal molecule from outside the cell binds to the ligand-binding domain, the protein undergoes a conformational change which activates the catalytic function of the enzymatic domain. This in turn triggers a signaling cascade inside the cell.

The most common class of receptor enzymes are **receptor tyrosine kinases** (RTKs). When activated by ligands (often growth factors), they phosphorylate tyrosine residues on a variety of proteins within the cytosol. These physiological changes promote differential gene expression, and help to regulate the growth and development of a cell. Neurotrophins, for example, are ligands that bind to the Trk family of RTKs. They play a critical role in the survival and proper functioning of neurons.

G PROTEIN-COUPLED RECEPTORS

G protein-coupled receptors (GPCRs) are a large class of receptor proteins that respond to a wide array of signals, including neurotransmitters, ions, light, hormones, and odor molecules. There are roughly 1,000 types of GPCRs in humans, and all share the same general structure regardless of the specific ligand that they interact with. The α-helices of the protein span the membrane seven times, with the ligand-binding site on the extracellular side. When a ligand binds, the conformation of the protein changes, activating the G protein to which it is coupled. G proteins are heterotrimeric (they consist of an alpha, beta, and gamma subunit) and are capable of binding to guanosine triphosphate (GTP) and guanosine diphosphate (GDP). When the G protein is activated, the α-subunit replaces the bound GDP with GTP. This causes the α-subunit (along with the bound GTP) to dissociate from the β- and γ-subunits, while remaining within the membrane. The G protein, depending on the type, will then go on to either stimulate or inhibit certain biosignaling pathways. G proteins are typically responsible for increasing or decreasing amounts of cyclic AMP or triggering the flow of calcium ions into the cell.

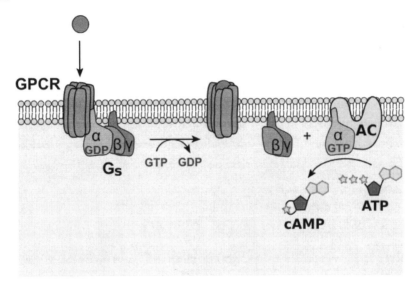

ENDOCRINE SYSTEM

LIPIDS

Lipids are a class of structurally and functionally diverse biomolecules that are characterized by their hydrophobic properties; they do not dissolve in water but do mix well with nonpolar substances. They can be classified according to structure into two main groups: saponifiable and non-saponifiable. Saponifiable lipids, such as triacylglycerols and phospholipids, contain fatty acid chains with ester linkages that can be easily hydrolyzed. Non-saponifiable lipids, such as steroids and terpenes, are non-ester lipids that lack fatty acids.

Lipids are involved in a variety of functions. Triacylglycerols can be metabolized for energy, and serve as energy storage. Phospholipids are the major structural components of cell membranes, and a type of glycolipid known as galactocerebroside forms the myelin sheaths that insulate neurons. Lipids play active roles as well, including biosignaling. Steroid hormones such as glucocorticoids, mineralocorticoids, and the sex hormones travel through the blood, diffuse into target cells, and bind to receptors that directly regulate gene expression.

> **Review Video: Lipids**
> Visit mometrix.com/academy and enter code: 269746
>
> **Review Video: Endocrine System**
> Visit mometrix.com/academy and enter code: 678939

STEROIDS

Steroids consist of four fused cycloalkane rings (three hexanes and one pentane). Cholesterol is a **sterol** (a steroid alcohol) that acts as a fluidity buffer in cell membranes. It is also the precursor to bile acids, vitamin D, and steroid hormones.

Steroid hormones include the sex hormones and corticosteroids. Sex hormones are responsible for secondary sex characteristics. They are secreted primarily by the gonads and placenta, but are also produced in small amounts by the adrenal cortex. The "female" sex hormones are the estrogens (such as estradiol), and the "male" hormones are the androgens (such as testosterone). Progesterone is produced by the corpus luteum and the placenta, and is important for the preparation and maintenance of pregnancy.

The adrenal cortex secretes glucocorticoids and mineralocorticoids. These corticosteroids help to control inflammation, electrolyte and water balance, stress responses, immune responses, and metabolism. A common glucocorticoid is the stress hormone cortisol, which acts as an anti-inflammatory. Aldosterone is a mineralocorticoid that regulates the levels of sodium and potassium in the blood, helping to maintain blood pressure.

Since these hormones are insoluble in water, they rely on plasma proteins to transport them in the bloodstream. Once released from these proteins, the hormones can diffuse through the cell membrane, bind to intracellular receptors, and directly regulate gene expression.

TERPENES AND TERPENOIDS

Terpenes are plant-made, generally odiferous lipids that can be built up into many other biological molecules, including steroids. Terpenes arise from the polymerization of **isoprene**: a hydrocarbon with the general formula C_5H_8. The formula for a terpene follows the C5 rule; it will always be a multiple of C_5H_8 or $(C_5H_8)_n$ where n = the number of linked isoprene units. Monoterpenes have two isoprene units, diterpenes have four, triterpenes have six, tetraterpenes have eight, and so on. **Squalene** ($C_{30}H_{48}$) is a triterpene that undergoes cyclization to give rise to cholesterol, which is the precursor to steroid hormones. **Terpenoids** are simply terpenes that have been modified by the addition of oxygen or the shifting or removal of methyl groups. There are over 20,000 distinct types of terpenes and terpenoids.

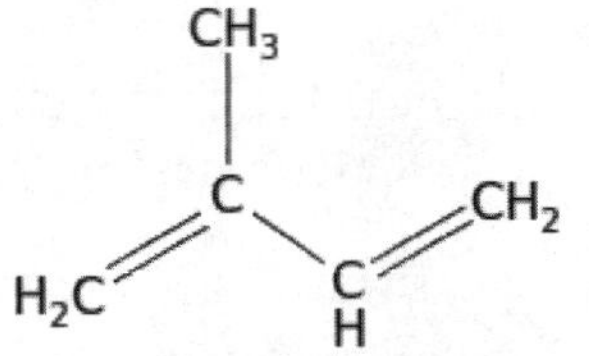

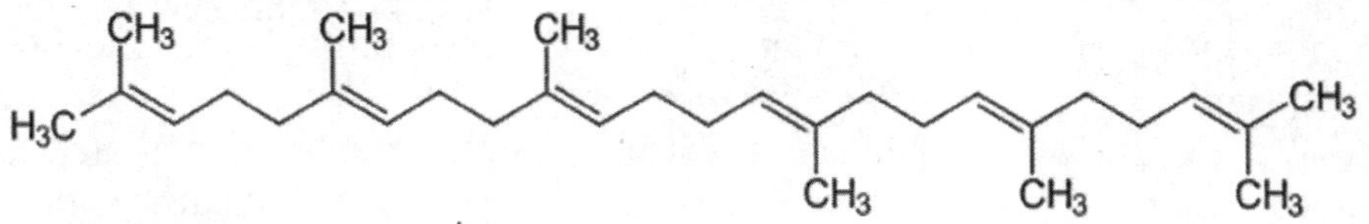

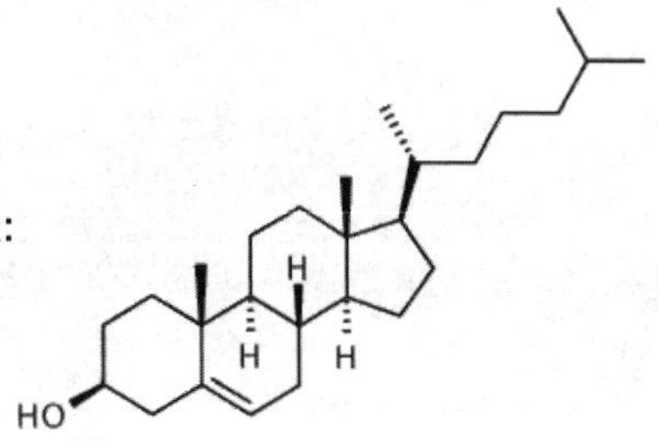

SPECIFIC CHEMICAL CONTROL AT CELL, TISSUE, AND ORGAN LEVEL

The endocrine system consists of all the glands and tissues that secrete chemical messengers called hormones. The endocrine system works closely with the faster-acting nervous system to coordinate and regulate important processes including growth, development, metabolism, immune function, reproduction, response to stress, and water and electrolyte balance. In short, the endocrine system is essential for the maintenance of homeostasis in the body. When hormones are secreted into the extracellular fluid, they diffuse into the bloodstream and are carried throughout the body. Only cells with receptors that are specific to the secreted hormones are affected. This specificity allows hormones to control targeted tissues and organs—often other endocrine glands (these are called tropic hormones). Major glands of the endocrine system include the hypothalamus, pineal gland, pituitary gland, thyroid, parathyroid glands, thymus, adrenal glands, gonads, and pancreas. Certain cells within the heart, kidneys, gastrointestinal tract, and placenta also have endocrine functions.

DEFINITIONS OF ENDOCRINE GLAND, HORMONE

An **endocrine gland** produces hormones and secretes them directly into the blood without the use of a duct. (*endo* = within, *crine* = separate or secretion.) When the hormones are first released by the gland, they enter the interstitial fluid before diffusing into nearby capillaries. The circulatory system then delivers the hormones to target organs. By contrast, **exocrine glands** release non-hormone products such as sweat, oil, tears, and bile through ducts to their target locations—usually a cavity or epithelial surface inside or outside the body. Unlike hormones, exocrine products do not bind to receptors.

Hormones are molecules that bind to receptors and deliver regulatory messages. Many of these signaling molecules are steroids derived from cholesterol. These include the sex hormones and corticosteroids. The rest are non-steroids, and include amines, peptides, and proteins.

There are also signaling molecules called eicosanoids (ex: prostaglandins) that are sometimes referred to as "local hormones," and while they do bind to receptors, they are not secreted by endocrine glands, and do not travel through the bloodstream. Paracrine signals act on target cells that are near the secreting cell, and autocrine signals target the same cell that secreted them.

HORMONES OF THE HYPOTHALAMUS AND PITUITARY

The **hypothalamus** is the link between the nervous system and the endocrine system. It is located in the brain, superior to the pituitary and inferior to the thalamus. The hypothalamus communicates with the pituitary by secreting "releasing hormones" (RH) and "inhibiting hormones" (IH). Hormones of the hypothalamus include:

Hormone	Action
GnRH - gonadotropin RH	Stimulates anterior pituitary to release LH and FSH
GHRH - growth hormone RH	Stimulates anterior pituitary to release GH
GHIH - growth hormone IH (somatostatin)	Inhibits the release of GH from the anterior pituitary
TRH - thyrotropin RH	Stimulates anterior pituitary to release thyrotropin (TSH)
PRH - prolactin RH	Stimulates anterior pituitary to release prolactin
PIH - prolactin IH (dopamine)	Inhibits the release of prolactin from the anterior pituitary
CRH - corticotropin RH	Stimulates anterior pituitary to release ACTH
Oxytocin	Targets the uterus - stimulates contractions. Targets the mammary glands - milk secretion
ADH - antidiuretic hormone (vasopressin)	Targets the kidneys and blood vessels - increases water retention

The **pituitary** is nicknamed the "master gland" because many of the hormones it secretes act on other endocrine glands. It is located within the sella turcica of the sphenoid bone, beneath the hypothalamus. This pea-sized gland hangs from a thin stalk called the infundibulum, and it consists of an anterior and posterior lobe - each with a different function.

Source	Hormone	Action
Pituitary gland (anterior)	TSH - thyroid stimulating hormone (thyrotropin)	Targets the thyroid - stimulates the secretion of thyroid hormones
	ACTH - adrenocorticotropic hormone	Targets the adrenal cortex - stimulates the release of glucocorticoids and mineralocorticoids
	GH - growth hormone	Targets muscle and bone - stimulates growth
	FSH - follicle stimulating hormone	Targets the gonads - stimulates the maturation of sperm cells and ovarian follicles
	LH - luteinizing hormone	Targets the gonads - stimulates the production of sex hormones; surge stimulates ovulation in females
	PRL - prolactin	Targets the mammary glands - stimulates production of milk
Pituitary gland (posterior)	Oxytocin (produced in hypothalamus; stored and released by posterior pituitary)	Targets the uterus - stimulates contractions Targets the mammary glands - stimulates milk secretion
	ADH - antidiuretic hormone (vasopressin) (produced in hypothalamus; stored and released by posterior pituitary)	Targets the kidneys and blood vessels - increases water retention

HORMONE SOURCES OF THE HEAD AND NECK

Source/Description	Hormone	Action
Pineal gland Situated between the two hemispheres of the brain where the two halves of the thalamus join.	Melatonin	Targets the brain - regulates daily rhythm (wake and sleep)
Thyroid gland Butterfly-shaped gland; the point of attachment between the two lobes is called the isthmus. The isthmus is on the anterior portion of the trachea, with the lobes wrapping partially around the trachea.	T_3 - triiodothyronine	Targets most cells - stimulates cellular metabolism
	T_4 - thyroxine	Targets most cells - stimulates cellular metabolism
	Calcitonin	Targets bone and kidneys - lowers blood calcium
Parathyroid gland Four small glands that are embedded in the posterior aspect of the thyroid.	PTH - Parathyroid hormone	Targets bone and kidneys - raises blood calcium

HORMONE SOURCES OF THE ABDOMEN

Source/Description	Hormone	Action
Thymus gland Located between the sternum and the heart, embedded in the mediastinum. It slowly decreases in size after puberty.	Thymosin	Targets lymphatic tissues - stimulates the production of T-cells
Pancreas The head of the pancreas is situated in the curve of the duodenum and the tail points toward the left side of the body. The pancreas is mostly posterior to the stomach.	Insulin	Targets the liver, muscle, and adipose tissue - decreases blood glucose
	Glucagon	Targets the liver - increases blood glucose
	GHIH - growth hormone IH (somatostatin)	Inhibits the secretion of insulin and glucagon
Adrenal medulla Located on top of the kidneys. The adrenal medulla is the inner part of the gland.	Epinephrine and norepinephrine	Target heart, blood vessels, liver, and lungs - increase heart rate, increase blood sugar (fight or flight response)
Adrenal cortex The adrenal cortex is the outer portion of the adrenal gland.	Mineralocorticoids (aldosterone)	Target the kidneys - increase the retention of Na^+ and excretion of K^+
	Glucocorticoids	Target most tissues - released in response to long-term stressors, increase blood glucose (but not as quickly as glucagon)
	Androgens	Target most tissues - stimulate development of secondary sex characteristics
GI tract	Gastrin	Targets the stomach - stimulates the release of HCl
	Secretin	Targets the pancreas and liver - stimulates the release of digestive enzymes and bile
	CCK - cholecystokinin	Targets the pancreas and liver - stimulates the release of digestive enzymes and bile
Kidneys	Erythropoietin	Targets the bone marrow - stimulates the production of red blood cells
	Calcitriol	Targets the intestines - increases the reabsorption of Ca^{2+}
Heart	ANP - atrial natriuretic peptide	Targets the kidneys and adrenal cortex - reduces reabsorption of Na^+, lowers blood pressure
Adipose Tissue	Leptin	Targets the brain - suppresses appetite

HORMONE SOURCES OF THE REPRODUCTIVE SYSTEM

Source/Description	Hormone	Action
Ovaries The ovaries rest in depressions in the pelvic cavity on each side of the uterus. (Note that ovaries produce testosterone in small amounts.)	Estrogen	Target the uterus, ovaries, mammary glands, brain, and other tissues - stimulate uterine lining growth, regulate menstrual cycle, facilitate the development of secondary sex characteristics
	Progesterone	Targets mainly the uterus and mammary glands - stimulates uterine lining growth, regulates menstrual cycle, required for maintenance of pregnancy
	Inhibin	Targets the anterior pituitary - inhibits the release of FSH
Placenta Attached to the wall of the uterus during pregnancy	Estrogen, progesterone, and inhibin	(See above)
	Human chorionic gonadotropin (hCG)	Targets the ovaries - stimulates the production of estrogen and progesterone
Testes Located within the scrotum, behind the penis.	Testosterone	Targets the testes and many other tissues - promotes spermatogenesis, secondary sex characteristics
	Inhibin	(See above)

MAJOR TYPES OF HORMONES

Hormones can be broadly classified into lipid-soluble hormones (steroids) and water-soluble hormones (non-steroids). Steroid hormones are derived from cholesterol, and their base structure consists of four fused carbon rings. They are released by the adrenal cortex, testes, ovaries, and the placenta. Major types of steroid hormones include the **sex hormones** (estrogens, androgens, progesterone) and the **corticosteroids** (glucocorticoids and mineralocorticoids). Since these hormones are lipid-soluble, they can diffuse through the cell membrane and bind to the nuclear receptors that regulate transcription.

Non-steroid hormones tend to elicit faster responses than steroid hormones. They cannot diffuse into the cell, and instead bind to receptors on the cell membrane, activating second-messenger systems. These hormones are classified into amines, peptides, and proteins. **Amines** are derivatives of the amino acids tyrosine or tryptophan, and include epinephrine, norepinephrine, thyroxine, and melatonin. **Peptide hormones** are short chains of amino acids. Common examples include oxytocin, somatostatin, and antidiuretic hormone. **Protein hormones** such as insulin, growth hormone, and parathyroid hormone consist of longer chains—generally over 100 amino acids. Hormones can also be **glycoproteins**. Follicle-stimulating hormone, thyroid-stimulating hormone, and luteinizing hormone all have carbohydrate attachments.

NEUROENDOCRINOLOGY — RELATION BETWEEN NEURONS AND HORMONAL SYSTEMS

Neuroendocrinology is the study of the interplay between the nervous system and endocrine system. The nervous system uses neurotransmitters to communicate, while the endocrine system uses slower-acting hormones (though the effects are longer-lasting). Hormones can trigger the firing of neurons, and neurons can stimulate the release of hormones. Both systems work together to maintain homeostasis. The physical bridge between these two systems is an almond-sized region of the brain called the hypothalamus. A slender stalk called the infundibulum extends down from the hypothalamus and connects to the pituitary gland. The hypothalamus communicates with the anterior lobe (adenohypophysis) of the pituitary through a network of capillaries, controlling the release of the six anterior pituitary hormones. The posterior lobe (neurohypophysis) is connected to the hypothalamus via neurons. It stores and releases oxytocin and ADH, which are produced by the hypothalamus. When changes in homeostasis are detected, the hypothalamus directs the pituitary to act.

CELLULAR MECHANISMS OF HORMONE ACTION

When hormones are released in response to a stimulus, they enter the bloodstream and are exposed to nearly all the cells in the body. Only cells with receptors specific to those hormones are affected. The mechanism of hormone action depends largely on the chemical nature of the hormone.

Steroid hormones are lipid-soluble, and can diffuse through the cell membrane of target cells. The hormones bind to intracellular receptors, which are usually in the nucleus but can also be in the cytoplasm. The hormone-receptor complex undergoes a conformational change, allowing it to bind to a region within the promoter sequence of DNA called the hormone-response element (HRE). This action directly controls gene activity by initiating or blocking transcription. The proteins that are translated may stimulate or inhibit certain metabolic pathways. The greater the number of hormone-receptor complexes that are formed, the greater the response from the target cell.

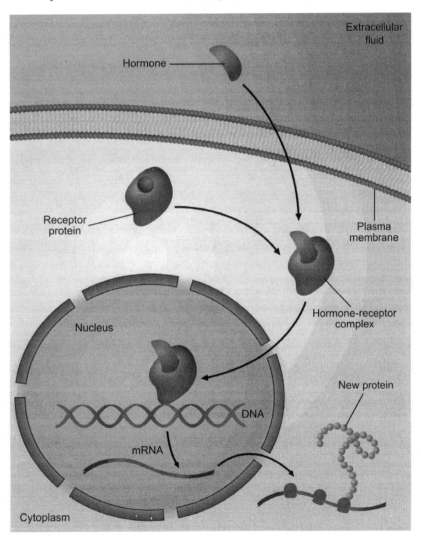

123

Non-steroid hormones are water-soluble, and (with the exception of thyroid hormones) cannot diffuse into cells. Instead, they act as first messengers by binding to receptors on the outer surface of the plasma membrane. This action activates a second messenger, which initiates a signaling cascade, ultimately changing the metabolic activities of the cell.

A common second messenger is cyclic AMP (cAMP). When the hormone binds to the receptor, it activates a G protein within the membrane. The G protein then activates the enzyme adenylate cyclase which forms cAMP from ATP. cAMP activates protein kinases, which go on to phosphorylate cytoplasmic proteins, altering their function.

Inositol triphosphate (IP_3) and diacylglycerol (DAG) are also used as second messengers. When the G protein is activated by the binding of a hormone, it activates the enzyme phospholipase C, which cleaves IP_3 off of a membrane phospholipid (PIP_2), and the remaining DAG is left within the membrane. IP_3 diffuses to the endoplasmic reticulum and triggers the release of calcium ions from the lumen. These ions activate enzymes involved in various metabolic pathways. DAG plays a role in biosignaling by activating protein kinases.

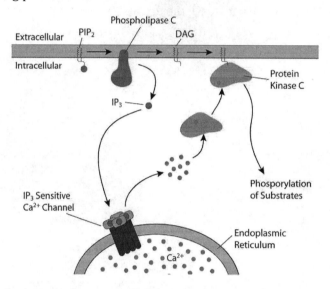

TRANSPORT OF HORMONES: BLOOD SUPPLY

Hormones are secreted from endocrine cells into in the interstitial fluid, usually through the process of exocytosis. This may occur in response to humoral stimuli (changes in the composition of extracellular fluids / blood), neural stimuli, or hormonal stimuli. The hormones diffuse into nearby capillaries and are transported to distant locations using the bloodstream. Some water-soluble hormones (most amines, peptides, and proteins) can dissolve in the blood and circulate freely, but lipid-soluble hormones (steroids and thyroid hormones) cannot. They bind loosely to carrier proteins such as albumin or globulins during transportation, and are inactive in this state. They dissociate from the carrier proteins, often in response to low hormone concentration, before binding to receptors on the target cells.

SPECIFICITY OF HORMONES: TARGET TISSUE

Hormones are able to enter systemic circulation while only affecting target tissues. Such specificity is dependent on the types of protein receptors present on or within target cells. A portion of the hormone has a shape that is nearly complementary to the binding domain of the receptor, though the receptor will flex to create a more perfect fit. Cells without the required receptors are invisible to the hormone.

The number of receptors on a target cell can change. As the number of receptors increases, the effect of the hormone increases proportionally. If the concentration of hormones in the blood is low, more receptors can be synthesized to increase the sensitivity to the hormone. This is called **up-regulation**. A prolonged increase in hormone concentration triggers a loss of receptors, desensitizing the cell to the hormone. This is called **down-regulation**.

INTEGRATION WITH NERVOUS SYSTEM: FEEDBACK CONTROL

The endocrine system is regulated primarily by negative feedback mechanisms. When the concentration of hormones in the blood is high, the release of hormones and/or production of their receptors decreases. Conversely, when concentrations are low, the hormones and/or receptors can be upregulated. Various types of stimuli can trigger the release of hormones. **Humoral** stimuli refer to changes in chemical concentrations in the blood, such as ions or glucose. **Neural** stimuli (signaling from neurons) can also cause the secretion of hormones, as seen in the fight-or-flight response. Lastly, tropic hormones can stimulate endocrine glands (**hormonal** stimuli).

When the hypothalamus detects changes in homeostasis, it signals the pituitary gland to secrete hormones into the bloodstream where they travel to their target organ. As blood concentrations increase, feedback is sent to the hypothalamus and pituitary to inhibit further signaling to the target. The nervous system has the ability to adjust the "normal" levels of a hormone for a given situation—for example, in response to stress.

RESPIRATORY SYSTEM

The respiratory system includes the nose, mouth, nasal cavity, sinuses, pharynx, larynx, trachea, bronchial tree, and lungs. These organs facilitate the delivery of oxygen to the cells of the body for use in cellular respiration. The **conductive zone** brings inhaled air to the **respiratory zone** where gas exchange occurs. As oxygen is loaded into the blood, carbon dioxide is removed. Essential to this process are the diaphragm and intercostal muscles which are used to enlarge the chest cavity during pulmonary respiration (breathing). External respiration is the exchange of gas between the lungs and the blood. Internal respiration is the exchange of gas between the blood and tissues. Secondary functions of the respiratory system include pH regulation of the blood, thermoregulation, odor detection, and the production of speech.

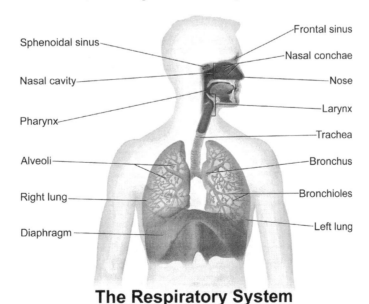

The Respiratory System

GAS EXCHANGE, THERMOREGULATION

Gas exchange is the loading of oxygen into pulmonary blood, and the removal of carbon dioxide. Inhaled air moves from through the mouth or nose to the pharynx, larynx, trachea, right / left main bronchi, and bronchioles, and then the alveoli. It is here that gases diffuse down their partial pressure gradients across a shared membrane between the capillaries and alveoli called the respiratory membrane. Oxygen diffuses into the blood where it is delivered to tissues throughout the body, and carbon dioxide diffuses out of the blood as a waste product of cellular respiration.

The respiratory system is also involved in **thermoregulation**: the regulation of body temperature. Capillaries within the respiratory tract, particularly the nasal passages and trachea, can constrict to conserve heat and dilate to release heat. The exhalation of warm, moistened air also helps to cool the body.

PROTECTION AGAINST DISEASE: PARTICULATE MATTER

A secondary role of the respiratory system is protection against disease and filtration of particulate matter. Some particles are filtered by nostril hairs and others get caught in mucus. Lysozymes within the mucus help to break down the trapped debris, and the cilia that line the respiratory tract then sweep it away. Immunoglobulin A (IgA) is also produced in the mucosal lining, and these antibodies aid in immune defenses by neutralizing pathogens. Mast cells within the respiratory tract release inflammatory chemicals that increase blood flow to the region, and alert the immune system to a threat. Large phagocytic cells called macrophages can also help to protect the lungs by engulfing small cells and particulates.

STRUCTURE OF LUNGS AND ALVEOLI

The lungs are spongy, porous organs that occupy most of the thoracic cavity. A serous membrane called the pleura lines the thoracic cavity (**parietal pleura**) as well as the surface of the lungs (**visceral pleura**). The three-lobed right lung is separated from the two-lobed left lung by the **mediastinum**. The trachea forks into primary bronchi which enter the left and right lung (along with blood and lymphatic vessels) at a region called the **hilum**. Each primary bronchus splits repeatedly into secondary bronchi, tertiary bronchi, and bronchioles to form the bronchial tree. The terminal bronchioles further divide into respiratory bronchioles, which are characterized by the presence of some alveoli. The respiratory bronchioles lead into alveolar ducts, which terminate in alveolar sacs.

126

Bronchi, Bronchial Tree, and Lungs

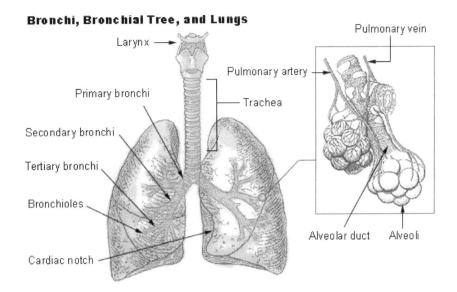

Within the alveolar sacs of the bronchi are clusters of **alveoli**: microscopic pouches where gas exchange occurs. The lungs contain hundreds of millions of these sacs, with a combined surface area that averages 70 m². The wall of each alveolus consists of a single layer of epithelial cells, most of which are type I cells. These squamous cells are involved in gas exchange. Type II cells are cuboidal cells that secrete surfactant to prevent the alveoli from collapsing. The alveolar walls are perforated by pores that connect adjacent alveoli, providing an alternate route for the passage of air in case of blocked ducts. The outer surfaces are covered with a network of capillaries. The basement membrane of a capillary fuses with the alveolar basement membrane to form the **respiratory membrane** (which also includes the capillary and alveolar epithelial cells).

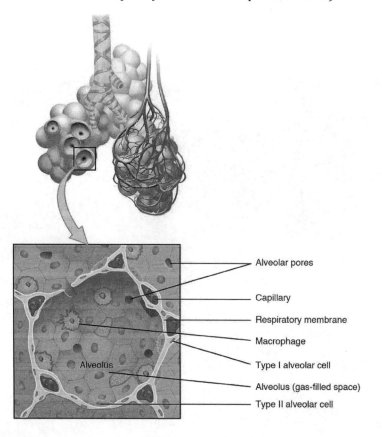

Alveolar pores
Capillary
Respiratory membrane
Macrophage
Type I alveolar cell
Alveolus (gas-filled space)
Type II alveolar cell
Alveolus

BREATHING MECHANISMS
DIAPHRAGM, RIB CAGE, DIFFERENTIAL PRESSURE

The diaphragm is a thin, dome-shaped muscle that separates the abdominal cavity from the thoracic cavity. This muscle, along with the external and internal intercostal muscles of the rib cage, are responsible for changing the volume, and therefore the pressure, of air in the lungs. This mechanism of breathing follows **Boyle's law**: the pressure and volume of a gas have an inverse relationship, assuming the temperature is constant.

When the diaphragm and external intercostals contract, the volume of the thoracic cavity increases, and the rib cage and sternum elevate and expand outward. The increase in volume results in a decrease in intrapleural pressure, and air enters the lungs in a process called **inspiration**. This is called **negative-pressure breathing** because the pressure in the lungs is lower than atmospheric pressure (and gases move down the pressure gradient). **Expiration** is usually a more passive process, and it is achieved by simply relaxing the same muscles that facilitated inhalation. As the volume of the thoracic cavity decreases, intrapleural pressure increases, and air leaves the lungs.

Air can be forcibly pushed out through the contraction of the internal intercostals and abdominal muscles.

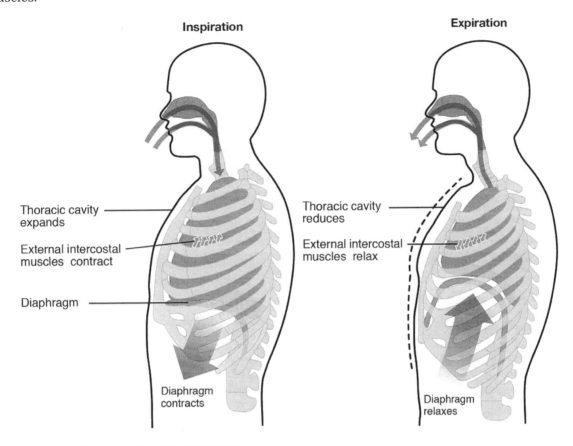

Inspiration

Thoracic cavity expands

External intercostal muscles contract

Diaphragm

Diaphragm contracts

Expiration

Thoracic cavity reduces

External intercostal muscles relax

Diaphragm relaxes

RESILIENCY AND SURFACE TENSION EFFECTS

The connective tissues of the lungs contain elastin, allowing them to bounce back after each inhalation. The greater the ability of the lung to stretch, the greater its **compliance**. Elasticity, combined with the forces of surface tension, would cause the lungs to collapse without a corrective mechanism.

The inner surface of each alveolus is coated with film of fluid. The polar water molecules at the fluid's surface are attracted to one another, and as a result of this surface tension, the volume of the alveoli is reduced. By extension, the pressure in each alveolus increases. According to the **Law of Laplace**, pressure is directly proportional to surface tension and inversely proportional to the radius ($P = \frac{2T}{r}$). Since surface tension is a constant regardless of the radius, smaller alveoli have greater pressure. Type II alveolar cells solve this problem by secreting a **surfactant**: a substance that reduces surface tension when dissolved in a liquid. The surfactant, made mostly of amphipathic lipoproteins, counteracts the cohesive forces between water molecules, making them easier to inflate. And since the surfactant has proportionally greater effects in smaller alveoli, the pressure from one alveolus to the next is somewhat uniform. Surfactant also increases the compliance of the lungs and reduces the likelihood of alveolar collapse.

THERMOREGULATION: NASAL AND TRACHEAL CAPILLARY BEDS; EVAPORATION, PANTING

A secondary role of the respiratory system is thermoregulation. In humans, body temperature is regulated mainly by vasodilation / vasoconstriction, sweating, and shivering, but breathing plays a role as well. When air is inhaled, it is exposed to the mucosa of the conducting zone, and quickly

129

equilibrates to the temperature of the blood. Most heat exchange occurs at the highly vascular nasal and tracheal epithelial lining. By the time it reaches the lungs, the air has already been warmed and moistened. During exercise, heavy breathing not only delivers more oxygen to the blood, but is also a mechanism for cooling the body. As respiratory rate increases, so does moisture evaporation along the epithelial lining. Animals that pant rely on this cooling mechanism more than non-panting species because they have little to no ability to sweat.

PARTICULATE FILTRATION: NASAL HAIRS, MUCUS/CILIA SYSTEM IN LUNGS

On average, humans inhale about 20,000 liters of air per day. This air contains particulates such as dust, pollen, mold spores, bacteria, and viruses that must be filtered and broken down. Filtration begins in the nose, where nasal hairs prevent larger particles from proceeding through the respiratory tract. The next line of defense is the mucus that lines the airways, trapping particles that were not filtered by the nose hairs. The conducting passageways of the respiratory tract are also lined with ciliated epithelial cells, and the cilia beat in a direction that pushes trapped debris and pathogens toward the throat where it is either swallowed, spat out, or expelled through the nostrils. The alveoli, however, are not coated in mucus or cilia, and they depend on white blood cells called macrophages to engulf potentially harmful particles and digest them. They also send signals to other cells of the immune system to alert them to a possible threat.

ALVEOLAR GAS EXCHANGE
DIFFUSION, DIFFERENTIAL PARTIAL PRESSURE

Exchange of gas between the air and blood occurs along the respiratory membrane of the alveoli. The blood that is brought to the alveoli via pulmonary arterioles is deoxygenated, with a concentration of carbon dioxide that is greater than that of the air. Each gas moves down its partial pressure gradient by simple diffusion. Oxygenated blood is then taken toward the heart via pulmonary venules.

Partial pressure is the pressure that one type of gas within a mixture would exert if it were to occupy the same volume as the total mixture. The partial pressure of carbon dioxide (P_{CO_2}) in the blood that enters the pulmonary capillaries is 45 mmHg, but the P_{CO_2} in the alveolar air is only 40 mmHg. Therefore, CO_2 diffuses out of the blood and into the air. The oxygen in the blood entering the capillaries has a partial pressure of 40 mmHg, but the P_{O_2} in the alveolar space is 104 mmHg. Therefore, O_2 diffuses into the blood down its partial pressure gradient. The blood that leaves the capillaries has the same partial pressures of oxygen and carbon dioxide as the air in the alveolar space.

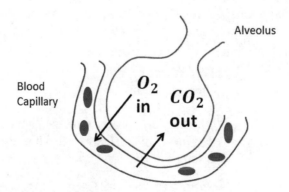

HENRY'S LAW

According to Henry's Law, the concentration of dissolved gas in a liquid is directly proportional to the solubility and partial pressure of that gas. That is, the greater the partial pressure of a gas, the greater the rate of diffusion of that gas into a liquid.

Henry's Law:

$$c = kP$$

- c = concentration of dissolved gas
- k = Henry's law constant; unique to each gas, depends on solubility
- P = partial pressure of the gas

This relationship can be used to predict the behavior of a gas (such as oxygen or carbon dioxide) when it is exposed to a liquid (such as blood). Gases move from areas of high pressure to low pressure, and the steeper the gradient, the greater the rate of diffusion. Solubility is also a factor. Carbon dioxide is more soluble in blood than oxygen, but oxygen has a steeper pressure gradient so the rates of diffusion balance out. Nitrogen has the highest partial pressure of all the atmospheric gases, but its blood concentration is very low due to its poor solubility.

PH CONTROL

The normal pH of blood ranges from 7.35 to 7.45. The lungs and kidneys each play a role in controlling these levels, as even minor disturbances can lead to serious consequences. A pH level below the normal range is called **acidemia**, and a value above the normal range is called **alkalemia**. The respiratory system uses the **bicarbonate buffer system** to balance the pH of the blood. When carbon dioxide combines with water, a weak acid (carbonic acid: H_2CO_3) is formed, before dissociating into its conjugate base (a bicarbonate ion: HCO_3^-) and a hydrogen ion (H^+) as seen in the following equation: $CO_2 + H_2O \leftrightarrow H_2CO_3 \leftrightarrow HCO_3^- + H^+$. If the pH of the blood is low (as caused by excess hydrogen ions), then the rate of respiration increases, and the reaction shifts to the left. Excess hydrogen ions are accepted by the bicarbonate ions, and the pH increases. If the pH is high, then breathing slows, the reaction shifts to the right, the concentration of hydrogen ions increases, and pH decreases. The kidneys also help to monitor blood pH, but the response is slower and longer-lasting.

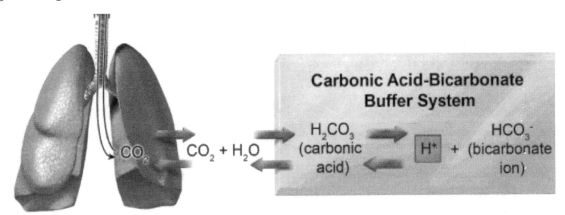

REGULATION BY NERVOUS CONTROL

The rate and depth of breathing are controlled by the nervous system, which responds to changes in the chemical composition of the blood. Carbon dioxide has the greatest effect on the rate of respiration. Chemoreceptors in the brain, specifically the medulla oblongata and pons, indirectly respond to CO_2 concentration. As levels in the blood increase, CO_2 diffuses into the cerebrospinal fluid of the brain, and reacts with water to form carbonic acid. The acid quickly ionizes to form its conjugate base and hydrogen ions. It is the hydrogen ions that stimulate the chemoreceptors of the central nervous system. The respiratory centers of the brain respond by increasing the rate of respiration, and more CO_2 is exhaled. The greater the stimulus, the greater the response.

Chemoreceptors of the peripheral nervous system, located in the aortic and carotid bodies, also regulate respiratory rate. These receptors are sensitive to CO_2, hydrogen ions, and to a lesser degree oxygen. Only when oxygen levels are critically low do receptors signal the brain to increase the rate of respiration.

CIRCULATORY SYSTEM
FUNCTIONS

The circulatory system is primarily associated with the transport of oxygen, nutrients, hormones, ions, and fluids throughout the body, as well as the removal of metabolic wastes.

Oxygen moves down its partial pressure gradient from the air into the blood of the alveolar capillaries, where most of it binds to hemoglobin molecules in the red blood cells. A small amount dissolves in the blood. Without oxygen, cells would be unable to transfer the energy in glucose to ATP during cellular respiration.

The carbon dioxide that is produced during cellular respiration is transported away from tissues and diffuses out of the alveolar capillaries. Like oxygen, carbon dioxide can dissolve in blood or bind to hemoglobin, but most travels in the form of bicarbonate ions. Other metabolic waste products such as urea are brought to the kidneys to be filtered. The kidneys also help to regulate the levels of fluids and ions in the blood.

Digested nutrients such as glucose, amino acids, and fats are circulated to target cells where they are absorbed. Hormones released by endocrine glands also reach their target cells in this way. Lipid-soluble molecules require the use of a carrier protein to be transported in blood.

ROLE IN THERMOREGULATION

The circulatory system plays an important role in thermoregulation. The human body maintains an average temperature of around 98.6 °F (37 °C), which is optimal for metabolic processes and defense against pathogens. Heat exchange occurs at the surface of the skin, where blood vessels can dilate or constrict in response to signals from the brain.

Sensory neurons called thermoreceptors detect changes in temperature and send impulses to the hypothalamus, which then sends signals to the effectors—the smooth muscles that surround cutaneous arterioles. If the body temperature is too warm, the smooth muscle relaxes, and the arterioles dilate. Vasodilation allows more blood to flow through the capillary beds near the surface of the skin, and more heat is lost to the surroundings. If the temperature is too cool, the smooth muscle contracts, and the arterioles constrict. Vasoconstriction reduces the volume of blood that flows near the body's surface, which minimizes heat loss to the surroundings. Sweating and shivering also help to control body temperature.

FOUR-CHAMBERED HEART: STRUCTURE AND FUNCTION

The wall of the heart is a composed of three layers of tissue. The outer layer is the **epicardium**, which protects the heart and secretes lubricating serous fluid. The middle layer is the muscular

myocardium, which contracts to pump blood. The innermost layer is the **endocardium**, which lines the chambers and valves.

The heart is a four-chambered organ. The superior "receiving" chambers are the atria. The **right atrium** receives blood from the vena cava, and the **left atrium** receives blood from the pulmonary veins. The muscular "discharging" chambers are the ventricles. The **right ventricle** pumps blood into the pulmonary trunk, and the **left ventricle** pumps blood into the aorta.

The **tricuspid valve** (also called the right atrioventricular valve, or right AV valve) prevents backflow into the atrium when the ventricle contracts. The **pulmonary semilunar valve** prevents the return of blood into the right ventricle. The **bicuspid valve** (also called the left AV valve, or mitral valve) prevents blood from entering the left atrium when the ventricle contracts. The **aortic semilunar valve** stops the backflow of blood into the right ventricle as it leaves through the aorta.

The path of blood through the heart is traced in the diagram below:

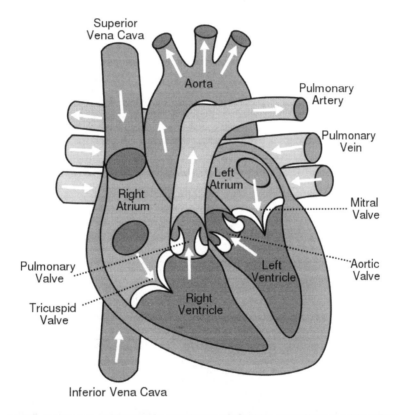

Review Video: The Heart
Visit mometrix.com/academy and enter code: 451399

ENDOTHELIAL CELLS

The thin inner lining of blood vessels (and the lymphatic vessels) is called the **endothelium**. This tissue lines the entire circulatory system, including the interior of the heart. It is composed of a single layer of squamous endothelial cells that are connected by tight junctions and adherens junctions. This allows the endothelium to act as a selectively permeable barrier between the blood and the surrounding tissue, though some vessels have pores and gaps that allow the passage of larger molecules. The smoothness of the endothelium reduces friction between the blood and the vessel wall. Endothelial cells also play a role in vasoconstriction by releasing peptides called endothelins that cause the smooth muscle within the vessel walls to contract. They also secrete chemicals that inhibit the coagulation of blood, but if the endothelium is damaged, they release different chemicals required for clot formation.

SYSTOLIC AND DIASTOLIC PRESSURE

Blood pressure is the force per unit area that is exerted by the blood on the walls of the vessels. Unless otherwise indicated, blood pressure refers specifically to the pressure within the major arteries, since arterioles, capillaries, venules, and veins have progressively less pressure. Blood pressure is often expressed as two numbers, and in units of millimeters of mercury (mmHg). The first number refers to the **systolic pressure**, or the maximum pressure that is exerted during **systole**. During this time, the ventricles contract, forcing blood into the aorta and pulmonary trunk. As the blood enters the arteries, the elastic walls stretch to accommodate the increased volume, and then return to their normal diameter during **diastole**. Diastole is the period in which the ventricles relax and blood pressure is at its lowest point. The normal average blood pressure for an adult at rest is 120/80 mmHg, where 120 is the systolic bp, and 80 is the diastolic bp. High blood pressure can damage the walls of the blood vessels and increase the risk of heart disease, heart failure, and stroke. Low blood pressure is only concerning if it occurs suddenly, or if it causes noticeable symptoms such as lightheadedness or fainting.

PULMONARY AND SYSTEMIC CIRCULATION

The **pulmonary circuit** is the part of the circulatory system that carries blood from the heart to the lungs and back to the heart. When deoxygenated blood is expelled from the right ventricle, it moves through the pulmonary trunk, which bifurcates into the right and left pulmonary arteries. Each branch extends into the lungs, eventually giving rise to arterioles and then the capillaries where gas exchange occurs by diffusion. Oxygenated blood leaves the capillaries through venules which fuse into veins, finally merging into four pulmonary veins that return blood to the left atrium. Note that in the pulmonary circuit, the arteries have *less* oxygen than the veins. Low blood oxygen in the pulmonary circuit triggers vasoconstriction, which redirects blood to better ventilated parts of the lung.

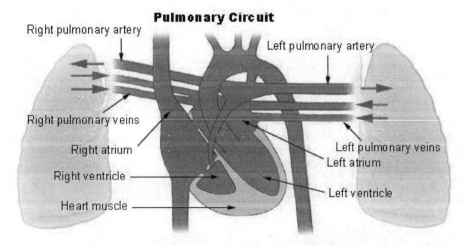

The **systemic circuit** carries blood from the muscular left ventricle of the heart to the aorta, which gives rise to the arteries that eventually branch into arterioles and then the capillary beds within the tissues of the body. Oxygen and nutrients enter the tissues, and carbon dioxide and other wastes enter the blood. Deoxygenated blood leaves the capillary beds through venules, which merge into larger veins. The blood then enters the right atrium through the superior and inferior vena cava. Because this circuit is much longer than the pulmonary circuit, blood pressure is *higher*.

Unlike the pulmonary circuit, blood in the arteries carries *more* oxygen than blood in the veins. When oxygen levels are low, vessels dilate to promote blood flow to tissues that need it.

Systemic Circuit

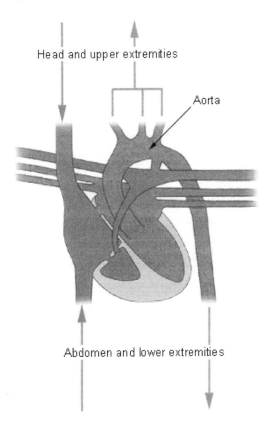

ARTERIAL AND VENOUS SYSTEMS (ARTERIES, ARTERIOLES, VENULES, VEINS)

The walls of all blood vessels (except the capillaries) consist of three layers: the innermost **tunica intima**, the **tunica media** consisting of smooth muscle cells and elastic fibers, and the outer **tunica adventitia**.

Arterial System:	Elastic arteries	Muscular arteries	Arterioles
Structure	Includes the aorta and major branches Tunica media has more elastin than any other vessels Largest vessels in the arterial system	Includes the arteries that branch off of the elastic arteries Tunica media has a higher proportion of smooth muscle cells, and fewer elastic fibers as compared to elastic arteries	Tiny vessels that lead to the capillary beds Tunica media is thin, but composed almost entirely smooth muscle cells
Function	Stretch when blood is forced out of the heart, and recoil under low pressure	Regulate blood flow by vasoconstriction / vasodilation	Primary vessels involved in vasoconstriction / vasodilation Control blood flow to capillaries

135

Venous System:	Venules	Veins
Structure	Tiny vessels that exit the capillary beds Thin, porous walls; few muscle cells and elastic fibers	Thin tunica media and tunica intima Wide lumen Valves prevent backflow of blood
Function	Empty blood into larger veins	Carry blood back to the heart

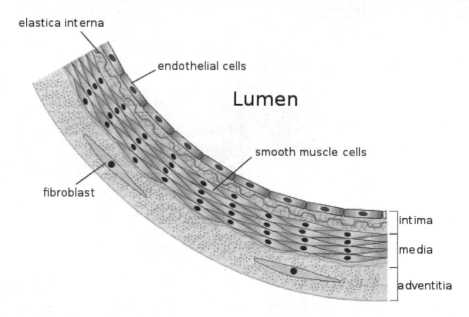

PRESSURE AND FLOW CHARACTERISTICS

Blood pressure is highest in the main arteries of the systemic circuit, particularly the aorta. The pressure decreases progressively as blood flows through the arterioles, capillaries, venules, and veins. The blood pressure is lowest in the vena cava. The steepest *drop* in blood pressure (as opposed to absolute pressure) occurs at the arterioles. The large reduction in diameter from artery to arteriole results in an increase in resistance as blood moves against the vessel wall. This slows down the flow of blood, and decreases the pressure.

Blood flow can be described as turbulent or laminar. Turbulence is an unsteady, swirling flow of blood that can occur during periods of high velocity, when the blood encounters an obstruction, or when the vessels take a sharp turn or narrow suddenly. Turbulent flow usually produces sounds, while laminar flow is silent. Laminar flow is the steady, streamlined flow of blood that occurs throughout most of the circulatory system.

CAPILLARY BEDS

MECHANISMS OF GAS AND SOLUTE EXCHANGE

Capillaries have only a single layer of endothelial cells that rest on a basement membrane. Capillary beds are groups of interconnected capillaries that facilitate the exchange of gas and solutes between the blood and interstitial fluid. Nutrients and oxygen enter the interstitial fluid, and carbon dioxide and other wastes enter the capillary blood. Gases and lipid-soluble substances can cross the endothelial cell membranes by simple diffusion, but ions and large particles often require the help of transport proteins or vesicular transport. Sometimes materials move through **intercellular clefts**: channels between adjacent endothelial cells. Capillaries with a nonporous continuous endothelium are called **continuous capillaries**. These are the most common types of capillaries in the body, and also the most impermeable. **Fenestrated capillaries** have pores that increase their permeability and are found in the kidneys and small intestine. **Sinusoidal capillaries** have a discontinuous endothelium that permits the passage of large particles and even blood cells. They are the most permeable of the capillaries.

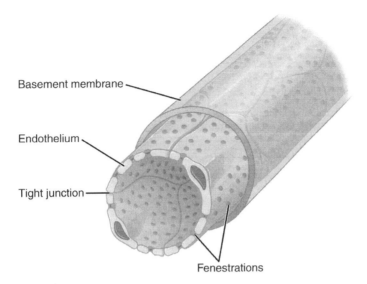

Basement membrane

Endothelium

Tight junction

Fenestrations

SOURCE OF PERIPHERAL RESISTANCE

Peripheral resistance is the resistance of the vessels to the flow of blood as a result of friction. As resistance increases, the rate of blood flow decreases. The main factors that affect peripheral resistance are diameter and length of the vessel, and volume and viscosity of the blood.

Resistance is most affected by changes in the *diameter* of the vessel. The relationship is inverse; as radius decreases, the resistance increases proportionally to the fourth power of the radius. For example, if the radius of a blood vessel is cut in half due to the buildup of plaque, resistance increases by a factor of 16. As such, vasoconstriction and vasodilation are critical to maintaining the appropriate level of resistance and flow. As *length* of the vessel increases, the resistance increases proportionally due to the increased surface area. As a person gains weight, the new blood vessels that nourish the new adipose tissue cause the total resistance of the system to increase. Blood volume and blood viscosity are usually not subject to sudden changes, but the effects of such changes are fairly intuitive. A decrease in either of these factors results in a decrease in resistance and an increase in flow rate.

COMPOSITION OF BLOOD

PLASMA, CHEMICALS, BLOOD CELLS

Blood is a mixture of plasma, chemicals, and blood cells. The clear, straw-colored liquid portion that makes up 55% of the blood is called **plasma**, and the remaining 45% consists of **formed elements**: the red and white blood cells and platelets.

Plasma is a solution of water, plasma proteins (albumin, antibodies, clotting proteins), carbohydrates, amino acids, lipids, vitamins, salts, gases, hormones, and waste products. About 92% of plasma is water.

Most of the cells in the blood are **red blood cells** (RBCs, or erythrocytes). These biconcave cells lack organelles, leaving room for hemoglobin - a protein to which oxygen and carbon dioxide can bind. The percentage of red blood cells by volume is called **hematocrit**, and averages about 42% for women and 46% for men. Less than 1% of blood consists of white blood cells and platelets. White

137

blood cells (WBCs, or leukocytes) are the only blood cells with nuclei. Unlike RBCs, they are not confined to the blood and can move in and out of vessels. There are many types of WBCs, and all are specialized to fight pathogens in different ways. **Platelets** (thrombocytes) are cell fragments that initiate clotting, and they outnumber WBCs about 40:1.

ERYTHROCYTE PRODUCTION AND DESTRUCTION; SPLEEN, BONE MARROW

Erythropoiesis (the production of red blood cells) occurs in the red bone marrow. When oxygen levels are low, the hormone **erythropoietin** (produced by the kidneys and liver) targets the marrow, stimulating **myeloid stem cells** to differentiate into **erythroblasts**. These immature RBCs divide many times, filling up with newly synthesized hemoglobin. The nuclei condense, and are ejected along with other organelles until only some endoplasmic reticulum remains. These cells are called **reticulocytes**, and they are released into the blood. After 1-2 days, the rest of the endoplasmic reticulum is lost, and mature **erythrocytes** are formed. Note that these cells are incapable of division.

After about 120 days, old and damaged RBCs are recognized and engulfed by phagocytes that are concentrated in the liver, spleen, and bone marrow. Hemoglobin is broken down into its four globin polypeptide chains and heme groups. Amino acids are released from the chains and enter the blood. The iron within the heme groups is either stored as ferritin in the liver or returned to the marrow to make more hemoglobin. The rest of the heme group is degraded to bilirubin and excreted in the bile.

REGULATION OF PLASMA VOLUME

Plasma volume is influenced by hydrostatic pressure and osmotic pressure. The pressure within the vessels and capillaries tends to be higher than the pressure of the interstitial fluid. This difference in pressure drives fluid out of the blood and into the surrounding fluid in a process called filtration. When water crosses the walls of the vessels, many solutes including plasma proteins are left behind, and the osmolarity (concentration) of the blood increases. When the osmolarity of the blood is high, water diffuses from the interstitial fluid into the blood, increasing plasma volume and decreasing osmolarity. This osmotic pressure helps to counteract the leakage of water from the capillaries.

Plasma volume is also regulated by the nervous and endocrine systems. Osmoreceptors detect changes in blood osmolarity, and baroreceptors detect changes in pressure. If solute concentration of the blood increases and/or blood volume decreases, the pituitary gland releases ADH to promote the reabsorption of water in the kidneys, rather than excreting it in urine. The adrenal cortex plays a role as well by releasing aldosterone. Aldosterone promotes the reabsorption of salt, which leads to an increase in water reabsorption, increasing the plasma volume.

COAGULATION, CLOTTING MECHANISMS

When a blood vessel is damaged, the smooth muscle constricts at the site of injury and platelets adhere to the exposed collagen of the vessel wall. The platelets develop spine-like projections, and release chemicals to attract other platelets and promote further vasoconstriction. A plug is formed as platelets aggregate, but this is rarely a sufficient fix without the coagulation of the blood.

There are two clotting mechanisms: extrinsic and intrinsic. In the extrinsic clotting mechanism, damaged tissue releases thromboplastin, which triggers a cascade of reactions that results in the production of an enzyme called prothrombin activator. Prothrombin activator is also produced by the slower-acting *intrinsic* clotting mechanism. When blood encounters a foreign substance or tissue, the Hageman factor (also called coagulation factor XII) is activated, leading to the production of prothrombin activator. From here, the clotting pathways are the same. Prothrombin activator

converts prothrombin to thrombin using calcium as a cofactor. Thrombin splits fibrinogen to form fibrin, but also stimulates its own production (a positive feedback loop). Fibrin is a fibrous protein that forms a mesh-like network that traps more platelets and red blood cells. This forms a clot that seals the injured region of the blood vessel.

OXYGEN TRANSPORT BY BLOOD

HEMOGLOBIN, HEMATOCRIT AND OXYGEN CONTENT

Almost all oxygen is transported by molecules of **hemoglobin** (Hb) that are found within erythrocytes, though 1.5% of blood oxygen is dissolved in the plasma. Hemoglobin has a protein component and a heme component. The protein component consists of four polypeptide chains known as globin (two alpha chains and two beta chains). Associated with each chain is a heme group that gives blood its red color. The heme group consists of a single iron atom surrounded by a complex organic ring called **protoporphyrin**. When blood passes through the capillaries of the lungs, it picks up oxygen. Each iron atom binds a molecule of oxygen—so one hemoglobin can bind up to four molecules of oxygen, and each erythrocyte carries around 250 million molecules of hemoglobin. The oxygenated form of hemoglobin is called **oxyhemoglobin**.

Hemoglobin can also transport up to four carbon dioxide molecules, though CO_2 binds to amino acids within the globin, not iron. Only about 23% of carbon dioxide is transported in this form, known as **carbaminohemoglobin**. Roughly 70% travels in the form of bicarbonate ions (as seen in the bicarbonate buffer system), and the rest is dissolved in the plasma.

OXYGEN AFFINITY

As the partial pressure of oxygen increases, so does the saturation level of hemoglobin. When the first oxygen molecule binds, the conformation of hemoglobin changes, making it easier for the second and third oxygen molecules to bind. The fourth and last oxygen molecule does not bind as easily, as seen in the S-shaped dissociation curve below.

Other factors can cause the curve to shift to the left (increasing affinity) or right (decreasing affinity). An increase in pH (as caused by a decrease in carbon dioxide) will also increase the affinity of hemoglobin for oxygen. Conversely, a decrease in pH (as caused by an increase in carbon dioxide) reduces affinity. This is known as the **Bohr effect**. Other factors that affect affinity include temperature, BPG, and carbon monoxide. As temperature increases, the affinity for oxygen decreases, and vice versa. BPG (2,3-bisphosphoglycerate, also called DPG) is a byproduct of glycolysis that decreases affinity for oxygen. Hemoglobin has a much higher affinity for carbon monoxide than for oxygen, and as such CO easily displaces O_2.

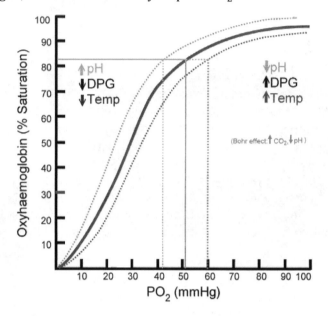

NERVOUS AND ENDOCRINE CONTROL

Heart rate and blood pressure are greatly influenced by the nervous and endocrine systems. The sympathetic division of the autonomic nervous system increases the heart rate by releasing norepinephrine (NE), which acts on the SA node of the heart. The parasympathetic division has the opposite effect. The vagus nerves that innervate the heart release acetylcholine (ACh), which slows the heart rate. Central and peripheral chemoreceptors also help to regulate heart rate by monitoring levels of pH, carbon dioxide, and oxygen.

Blood pressure is regulated by baroreceptors in the aortic arch and carotid arteries (both of which detect high blood pressure) and also the venae cavae, pulmonary veins, and atrial walls (all of which detect low blood pressure). When high blood pressure is detected, the blood vessels dilate and heart rate decreases to restore homeostasis. Blood pressure is also regulated by hormones of the endocrine system. When blood pressure drops, the kidneys secrete a hormone called renin which initiates a series of reactions that ultimately cause the release of aldosterone from the adrenal glands. Aldosterone promotes the reabsorption of water, increasing the plasma volume.

LYMPHATIC SYSTEM

STRUCTURE OF LYMPHATIC SYSTEM

The lymphatic system includes the thymus, bone marrow, tonsils, spleen, lymphatic vessels, lymph nodes, and lymph. Lymph is a clear liquid similar in composition to plasma. It is transported in one direction (toward the neck) where it is emptied into the subclavian veins. Lymph consists of white blood cells and the fluid that leaks out of the blood capillaries. Lymphatic vessels are similar in structure to veins; they have thin walls, and also have valves to prevent backflow. Their walls are more porous, however, allowing the lymph to drain into them for circulation. Lymph is moved by contractions of both smooth and skeletal muscle. Lymphatic vessels are found nearly everywhere in the body except the central nervous system and avascular tissues. The vessels are interrupted by oval-shaped masses of tissue called lymph nodes that contain lymphocytes and filter out foreign substances. The primary organs of the lymphatic system (bone marrow and thymus) produce mature lymphocytes. There are also secondary organs (such as the spleen and tonsils) that house lymphocytes. These specialized white blood cells destroy disease-causing microorganisms.

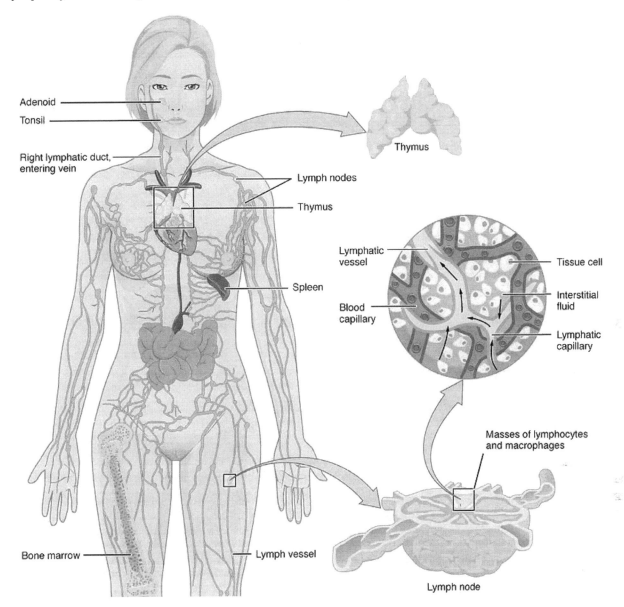

TISSUES

The functions of the major tissues and organs that play a role in the immune system:

Tissue	Function
Bone Marrow	Produces hematopoietic stem cells that give rise to all types of blood cells, including lymphocytes Site of B cell differentiation
Thymus	Site of T cell differentiation
Spleen	Splenic cords of the red pulp contain an abundance of macrophages and lymphocytes that help to filter aged blood cells, pathogens, and debris from the blood The white pulp is a lymphatic tissue that consists almost entirely of B and T cells, and provides a place for these lymphocytes to proliferate

Tissue	Function
Lymph nodes	Provide a place for lymphocytes and other WBCs to proliferate (cortex contains B cells and macrophages, medulla contains T cells) Filter the lymph of microorganisms, toxins, and wastes B cells produce antibodies that assist in the immune response
MALT	Mucosa-associated lymphoid tissue refers to the small clusters of lymphatic cells that are found in the tonsils, appendix, and Peyer's patches of the small intestine. T cells, B cells, and macrophages provide protection against pathogens

EQUALIZATION OF FLUID DISTRIBUTION AND TRANSPORT OF PROTEINS AND LARGE GLYCERIDES

One key function of the immune system is the equalization of fluid between the blood and tissues. Greater hydrostatic pressure in the blood vessels (as compared to the interstitial fluid) causes fluid to leak out of the vessels into the surrounding tissues. Porous lymphatic capillaries collect excess interstitial fluid (now called lymph) for delivery to the right and left subclavian veins. As it travels through the lymphatic system, the lymph passes through lymph nodes where it is filtered and cleansed. Eventually, it reaches either the right lymphatic duct (which drains into the right subclavian vein) or the thoracic duct (which drains into the left subclavian vein), returning fluid back into the blood. If pressure is too great in the lymphatic vessels, edema will occur as fluid leaks back into the tissues.

The lymphatic system also helps to transport certain biomolecules. The villi of the small intestine harbor specialized lymph capillaries called **lacteals** that absorb fats. These fats are transported in the form of **chylomicrons**, which give the lymph (called **chyle**) a whitish appearance. The lymphatic system is also used to return plasma proteins or cells that leaked out of the blood vessels back into the bloodstream.

PRODUCTION OF LYMPHOCYTES INVOLVED IN IMMUNE REACTIONS

The bone marrow and thymus are the "primary" lymphatic organs because they are the sites of lymphocyte production. Stem cells in the red bone marrow called **hemocytoblasts** give rise to immature lymphocytes. Lymphocytes that stay in the bone marrow differentiate into **B cells** and **natural killer (NK) cells**, and other immature lymphocytes migrate to the thymus where they differentiate into **T cells**. Lymphocytes use the bloodstream to migrate from these primary lymphatic organs to "secondary" lymphatic organs, such as the lymph nodes, spleen, and tonsils. When they make contact with antigens, the lymphocytes are activated and mature into effector cells that can participate in immune reactions.

INNATE (NON-SPECIFIC) VS. ADAPTIVE (SPECIFIC) IMMUNITY

Innate immunity refers to the nonspecific first line of defense against pathogens that is present at birth. There is no potential for this system to "learn" from previous pathogens or adapt to new threats. The first barriers to infection include mechanical barriers such as the skin and mucous membranes. Chemical barriers include the low pH of gastric juice, interferons that block viral replication, lysozyme in tears, and other antimicrobial proteins such as defensins, collectins, and complements. Pathogens can also be engulfed by phagocytes, or by the destruction of the infected cell by natural killer cells. Fever and inflammation can offer nonspecific protection as well.
Adaptive immunity develops over time. It may be slow to act initially, but the "memory" of the first encounter with an **antigen** (a toxin or a molecule on the surface of a pathogen that triggers an immune response) allows for faster responses in subsequent exposures to that same antigen. The antigen is recognized as foreign, and the appropriate type of cell is selected to combat the pathogen with which it is associated. These cells are primarily lymphocytes. Depending on the type of

lymphocyte, they respond to infection by producing antibodies, killing infected cells, or directing other immune responses.

ADAPTIVE IMMUNE SYSTEM CELLS

There are two main types of lymphocytes that are involved in adaptive immune responses: T-lymphocytes (T cells) and B-lymphocytes (B cells).

T cells mature in the thymus, and are involved in cell-mediated immunity. The initial activation of T cells occurs when they encounter their specific antigen on the surface of an antigen-presenting cell (or APC). When they bind to these APCs, they proliferate and differentiate into various types of T cells. **Cytotoxic T cells** are specialized to kill infected or abnormal cells. Some cytotoxic T cells produce **memory T cells** that respond to subsequent infections. **Helper T cells** secrete cytokines that stimulate the division of T and B cells, while alerting other types of WBCs. **Regulatory (suppressor) T cells** inhibit T and B cells to stop the immune response.

B cells mature in the bone marrow, and are involved in humoral-mediated immunity. The initial activation of B cells occurs when they encounter freely circulating antigens. (Many B cells require co-stimulation by a helper T cell.) After binding to specific antigens, B cells differentiate into plasma cells and memory B cells. **Plasma cells** secrete antibodies that bind to antigens. **Memory B cells** also produce antibodies, but only during a subsequent infection.

INNATE IMMUNE SYSTEM CELLS

There are various types of cells involved in innate immunity, many of which are phagocytes. **Neutrophils** account for most of the white blood cells in the bloodstream. These phagocytes are usually the first to arrive at the site of infection and they chase pathogens using chemotaxis. **Eosinophils** regulate inflammatory responses and release chemicals that kill foreign invaders—often parasitic worms. **Mast cells** (found in connective tissues) and **basophils** (which circulate in the blood before entering tissues) both release histamine to promote inflammation and heparin to inhibit clotting. **Macrophages** (derived from monocytes, the largest leukocytes) are large WBCs that engulf debris and pathogenic microorganisms, and function as antigen presenters to effector T cells. **Dendritic cells** function in much the same way, except they activate "naive" T cells (T cells that have not yet encountered their antigen). **Natural killer cells** are not phagocytes; they destroy cells that have been infected with a pathogen by binding to them and releasing granzymes that trigger apoptosis.

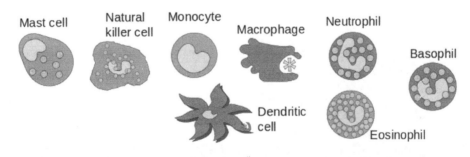

Mast cell | Natural killer cell | Monocyte | Macrophage | Neutrophil | Basophil | Dendritic cell | Eosinophil

CONCEPT OF ANTIGEN AND ANTIBODY

An **antigen** is a substance that elicits a response from the immune system. Antigens are usually large biomolecules (often proteins) that are identified as foreign or non-self. They can be found on the surfaces of antigenic substances such as viruses, bacteria, fungi, and pollen grains. **Foreign antigens** originate outside the body, and include the examples listed above. **Self-antigens** are produced by the body and rarely initiate an immune response. They often trigger a response in other people, as seen in the rejection of transplanted tissues or organs.

Antibodies (also called immunoglobulins) are products of B cells that bind to specific antigens. The binding of an antibody to an antigen can disarm the pathogen in a variety of ways. In some cases, the pathogens **agglutinate** (clump together) before being destroyed. Antibodies can also **neutralize** the antigen by blocking its ability to attach to cells, or cause it to become insoluble and **precipitate** out of solution. Sometimes, they activate **complement**—a system of proteins that enhances the effectiveness of the immune response. Other cells of the immune system can be called to action, and phagocytosis can be enhanced in a process called **opsonization**. Antibodies also promote **inflammation** to help slow the spread of infection.

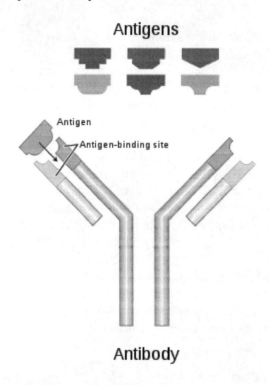

ANTIGEN PRESENTATION

T cells do not recognize free antigens, and so antigens must be presented to them by other cells. The mechanism of presentation depends on the source of the antigen.

Extracellular (exogenous) antigens are engulfed by an antigen-presenting cell, such as a macrophage or dendritic cell. Lysosomal enzymes digest the antigen into small peptides which are brought to the cell surface to be displayed. The antigen pieces are presented on glycoproteins known as **major histocompatibility complexes (MHC) class II**. Only when a helper T cell encounters an antigen presented in this manner will it activate B cells and cytotoxic T cells.

Intracellular (endogenous) antigens, such as viral proteins, are produced inside of a cell. They are digested into small peptides by proteases and then displayed on **MHC class I** molecules. These antigens are recognized by cytotoxic T cells, which go on to destroy infected or cancerous cells.

144

CLONAL SELECTION

Within the body is a large pool of lymphocytes that differ according to the antigen receptors that they possess. This varied population allows the body to be ready to defend against any antigen it may encounter. But in order to mount an effective response, the cell that is "selected" by the antigen (as determined by its capability to bind to B cell receptors [BCRs] or T cell receptors [TCRs]) must undergo clonal expansion. The selected cell divides rapidly to give rise to a large population of cells that are all equipped with the proper receptors. The clones that are produced will either be effector cells that combat the infection (such as plasma cells or cytotoxic cells), or memory cells that are prepared for a secondary response. This process occurs mainly in the lymph nodes.

STRUCTURE OF ANTIBODY MOLECULE

Antibodies are Y-shaped proteins that consists of four polypeptide chains (two identical heavy chains, and two identical light chains) linked together by disulfide bonds. At each tip of the "Y" is a variable region of amino acids that is specific to the **epitope**: the part of the antigen to which the antibody binds. The rest of the antibody is called the **constant region**. (There are five major types of antibodies [IgG, IgM, IgA, IgE, and IgD] that differ according to the constant portion of the heavy chain.)

The variable region of the antibody has a unique conformation that is complementary to the shape of a specific antigen. These specialized regions are called **antigen binding sites**. When the epitope (also called the antigenic determinant site) binds, an antigen-antibody complex is formed.

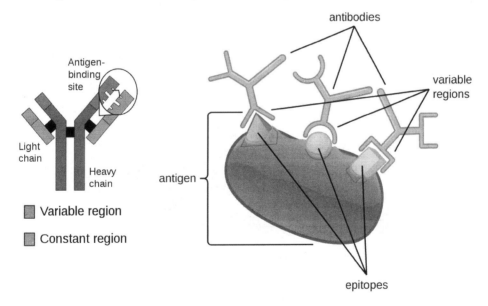

RECOGNITION OF SELF VS. NON-SELF, AUTOIMMUNE DISEASES

Self-antigens are present on all body cells, and it is important for the immune system to distinguish these antigens from foreign, or non-self, antigens. The antigen receptors on immature lymphocytes are generated randomly, and some are likely to respond to the self-antigens present in the environment. Any B cells in the bone marrow, or T cells in the thymus, that respond to self-antigens are killed in a process called negative selection. A backup mechanism is in place for any cells that escape this process, as can be seen in B cell activation. When a B cell presents an antigen on its surface, it must be activated by a helper T cell that is bound to an identical antigen. It is unlikely that the T cell will have responded to the same self-antigen, and the B cell remains inactive. Failure of this two-step verification process can result in an attack on self-cells. B cells produce antibodies and T cells act against the cells of the body. Conditions that result from such attacks are known as

145

autoimmune diseases. Common examples include rheumatoid arthritis, psoriasis, and multiple sclerosis.

MAJOR HISTOCOMPATIBILITY COMPLEX

Nearly all body cells are tagged with glycoproteins known as **major histocompatibility complexes**, or MHCs. These MHCs are different for each person (which explains the rejection of transplanted organs or tissues.) Alterations of these MHCs mark the cells as non-self.

MHC-I (MHC class I molecules) are found on nucleated cells (nearly all cells except red blood cells). Antigens produced within the cell (endogenous) are degraded, and portions of them combine with MHC-I before being displayed on the cell surface. T cells will be activated when their receptors bind to MHC-I / antigen complexes, and the antigen-presenting cell is destroyed.

MHC-II (MHC class II molecules) are found on antigen-presenting cells, such as dendritic cells, B cells, and macrophages. Antigens from extracellular pathogens (exogenous) are engulfed and broken down and the fragments combined with MHC-II before being displayed on the cell surface. This presentation alerts other immune system cells to the antigen.

DIGESTIVE SYSTEM

INGESTION

When food is ingested, it is immediately moistened by saliva. This lubricating fluid is secreted by hundreds of minor salivary glands that are scattered throughout the oral cavity, and three pairs of major salivary glands: the parotid, submandibular, and sublingual glands.

Saliva contains a variety of solutes, many of which are enzymes. **Salivary amylase** begins the chemical breakdown of polysaccharides into simpler sugars, and **lingual lipase** begins the breakdown of fats. The effects of salivary enzymes are minimal, however, compared to the digestion that occurs later in the stomach and small intestine. Saliva contains antimicrobial agents as well. **Lysozyme** is an enzyme that works together with immunoglobulin A to break down the cell walls of many bacteria. Other components of saliva include bicarbonate ions that help the saliva to maintain a pH that is optimal for salivary enzymes, as well as other ions. **Mucin** is a protein that helps to form a gel-like coating that lubricates the bolus of food.

> **Review Video: Gastrointestinal System**
> Visit mometrix.com/academy and enter code: 378740

INGESTION; ESOPHAGUS, TRANSPORT FUNCTION

The esophagus is a 25-cm tube extending from the pharynx to the stomach that functions as a passageway for food. It is not involved in digestion or absorption of nutrients, but it does secrete mucus to lubricate the esophagus and aid in the transport of food. The esophagus (and the alimentary canal that follows) has a wall that consists of four layers: the mucosa, submucosa, muscularis externa, and adventitia. Most of the digestive tract has a muscularis externa made of smooth muscle tissue, but the upper third of the esophagus is composed of skeletal muscle, and is under voluntary control. The middle portion is a mixture of both skeletal and smooth muscle, and the lower third is entirely smooth muscle. Food does not simply "fall" into the stomach; it is pushed along by **peristalsis**: an involuntary process in which the muscles in the wall of the digestive organ rhythmically contract and relax. The upper esophageal sphincter at the superior end of the esophagus and the lower esophageal sphincter at the inferior end control the passage of food by contracting and relaxing.

STOMACH

The stomach is a muscular organ located in the left superior region of the abdomen. The gastroesophageal sphincter (also called the lower esophageal or cardioesophageal sphincter) found at the junction between the esophagus and stomach helps to prevent the reflux of acidic contents. The stomach itself can be divided into four main parts: the cardiac region, the fundus, the body, and the pylorus. The **cardiac region** is the area where food is emptied into the stomach. The **fundus** is the most superior region of the stomach, and the **body** is the largest, most central region. The body curves toward the right to form a "J" shape, with a lesser curvature and a greater curvature. It then narrows into a funnel-shaped region called the **pylorus**. The wider end of the pylorus is called the pyloric antrum and the narrow portion is the pyloric canal. The pyloric sphincter is the valve that regulates the release of small amounts of chyme into the small intestine. Other features of the stomach include the gastric folds (rugae) of the mucosa that allow the stomach to stretch and expand. The stomach is also characterized by an inner oblique layer of smooth muscle that is not seen in the rest of the alimentary canal.

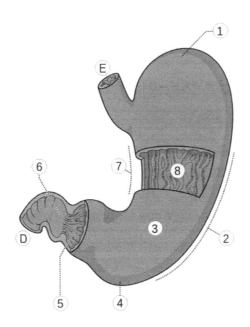

1. Fundus
2. Greater curvature
3. Body
4. Pyloric region
5. Pyloric antrum
6. Pyloric canal
7. Lesser curvature
8. Rugae
E. Esophagus
D. Duodenum of small intestine

STORAGE AND CHURNING OF FOOD

The stomach is a muscular organ that can stretch to accommodate a high volume of food. While some chemical digestion does occur, the primary role of the stomach is the storage and mechanical breakdown of food. The inner surface (mucosa) is folded into a series of ridges called rugae that allow the stomach to expand as it fills with food. The stomach holds about 1 liter after a typical meal, but can stretch to accommodate nearly four times that amount. It churns and pummels food for an average of three to four hours with the help of a third muscle layer in the muscularis externa that is unique to the stomach. As the food is mixed with gastric juices, it turns into a creamy paste called chyme. A valve called the pyloric sphincter regulates the passage of chyme into the small intestine.

PRODUCTION OF DIGESTIVE ENZYMES, SITE OF DIGESTION

The mucosa of the stomach contains gastric glands which open into numerous gastric pits. There are four types of cells in these glands: mucous cells, parietal cells, chief cells, and endocrine cells.

Endocrine cells (G cells) release hormones such as gastrin into the blood, and do not contribute to gastric juices. The rest of the glands are exocrine, and secrete their products into the stomach.

Parietal cells secrete intrinsic factor, which is required for the absorption of vitamin B_{12} in the small intestine. They also release hydrochloric acid (HCl), which lowers the pH of gastric juice to an average range of 1 to 3. This acidic environment is required for the activation of pepsinogen, which is secreted by the **chief cells**. The active form of pepsinogen is called pepsin—a digestive enzyme that breaks down proteins into smaller peptide chains. Chief cells also secrete gastric lipase, which continues the digestion of fats (though most fat and protein digestion occurs in the small intestine). The **mucus cells** secrete bicarbonate-containing mucus to protect the stomach from the acidity and digestive enzymes.

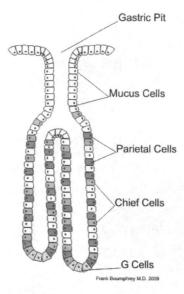

Frank Boumphrey M.D. 2009

LIVER

The liver is an essential component of the gastrointestinal system, but is not a part of the alimentary canal. This large, four-lobed organ acts as an accessory organ by performing many functions such as the production of bile, nutrient metabolism, and detoxification.

The primary digestive function of the liver is the synthesis of bile. Bile is a yellow-green solution of bile salts, pigments (mainly bilirubin from the breakdown of hemoglobin), cholesterol, and electrolytes. Only the bile salts play a role in digestion, and they do so mechanically (not enzymatically) by emulsifying fats into smaller globules called micelles that can be acted on by lipases in the small intestine. Bile also enhances the absorption of the fat-soluble vitamins A, D, E, and K. Liver cells synthesize bile salts from cholesterol.

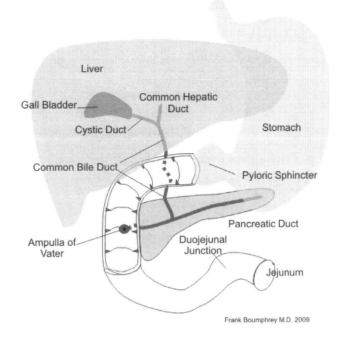

Frank Boumphrey M.D. 2009

Bile is stored and concentrated in the gallbladder. When food enters the small intestine, a hormone called cholecystokinin (CCK) signals the gallbladder to contact, and the bile is squeezed into the common bile duct. This duct joins with the pancreatic duct at the hepatopancreatic ampulla (ampulla of Vater) and bile spills into the duodenum via the duodenal papilla. Bile can also flow directly from the liver to the duodenum.

ROLE IN BLOOD GLUCOSE REGULATION, DETOXIFICATION

The liver performs many metabolic functions, including the regulation of blood glucose concentration (which averages 100 mg/dl). Blood from the digestive tract enters the liver through the hepatic portal vein. If the blood sugar is too high, the liver polymerizes glucose to form glycogen in a process called **glycogenesis**. If blood sugar is too low, liver cells break down stored glycogen and release glucose monomers in a process called **glycogenolysis**. In cases of prolonged fasting, the liver can produce glucose from non-carbohydrate sources such as proteins and fats. This is called **gluconeogenesis**.

The liver also has a vital role in detoxification. Ammonia (a toxic waste product of the metabolism of amino acids) is converted to urea in the liver and excreted by the kidneys. Hormones that are circulating in the blood are inactivated by the liver and eliminated by the kidneys as well. The liver also breaks down exogenous compounds, such as drugs and alcohol.

PANCREAS

The **pancreas** is a triangular-shaped organ with both endocrine and exocrine functions. (As an endocrine gland, it releases insulin, glucagon, and somatostatin into the blood.) It is located below the stomach, and extends from the duodenum to the spleen. Its role in digestion is the production and secretion of digestive juices. When chyme reaches the duodenum, enteroendocrine cells secrete cholecystokinin (CCK), which stimulates the acinar cells of the pancreas to release enzyme-rich juices. Secretin is secreted as well, which stimulates the duct cells to release a bicarbonate-rich solution that raises the pH. This provides the optimal environment for enzymes released by the pancreas. Pancreatic amylase digests starch, and pancreatic lipase digests fats. Proteases are released in their inactive form, but are activated in the small intestine. These activated protein-digesting enzymes include trypsin, carboxypeptidases A and B, and chymotrypsin. Nucleases digest nucleic acids. Pancreatic juice is emptied into the main pancreatic duct, which merges with the common bile duct at the hepatopancreatic ampulla. Juices enter the duodenum at the duodenal papilla. There is also an accessory pancreatic duct that empties directly into the duodenum at the minor papilla.

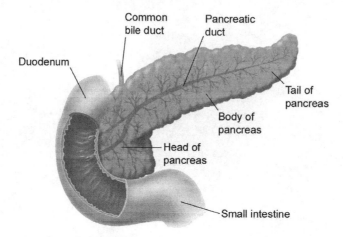

National Cancer Institute

SMALL INTESTINE

The small intestine is a long tube that extends from the pyloric sphincter to the ileocecal valve. Pancreatic enzymes and enzymes of the small intestine continue the digestion of food so the nutrients are small enough to be absorbed. These enzymes (called brush border enzymes) are embedded in the **microvilli**: tiny folds of the apical cell membrane that increase surface area. The core of each microvillus consists of actin filaments that extend out from the cytoplasm. Finger-like projections of the mucosa (villi) and deep circular folds of the mucosa and submucosa (plicae circulares) also increase the surface area available for absorption.

Absorption of water and food molecules occurs mostly in the jejunum and ileum of the small intestine. Amino acids and most sugars are taken into the intestinal cells using cotransport with sodium ions (secondary active transport). Lipid components and water are absorbed into the cells by simple diffusion. Short-chain fatty acids, sugars, amino acids, water, and electrolytes enter the bloodstream by diffusing into capillaries within the villi and traveling to the liver.

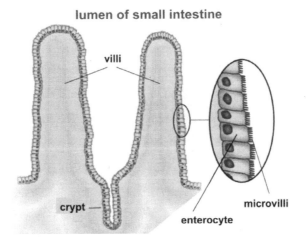

lumen of small intestine

PRODUCTION OF ENZYMES, SITE OF DIGESTION AND NEUTRALIZATION OF STOMACH ACID

Most of the chemical digestion of food occurs in the small intestine. Brush border enzymes of the microvilli (as well as pancreatic enzymes) break down carbohydrates, fats, proteins, and nucleic acids into smaller components which are then absorbed. Some mechanical digestion occurs in the small intestine as well. Peristalsis moves chyme toward the small intestine, while segmentation pushes it back and forth to help mix enzymes into the chyme. Brunner's glands in the duodenum secrete bicarbonate-containing fluid that (with the help of alkaline pancreatic juice) neutralizes the acidic chyme, providing the optimal pH for enzyme activity.

Brush border enzymes and the substrates that they break down are summarized in the table below.

Brush border enzyme	Substrate
Dextrinase	Oligosaccharides
Glucoamylase	Oligosaccharides
Maltase	Maltose (disaccharide)
Lactase	Lactose (disaccharide)
Sucrase	Sucrose (disaccharide)
Aminopeptidase	Peptides
Dipeptidase	Dipeptides
Nucleosidase	Nucleotides
Phosphatase	Nucleotides

STRUCTURE (ANATOMIC SUBDIVISIONS)

The small intestine is subdivided into three regions: the duodenum, jejunum, and ileum. At about 25 cm, the C-shaped **duodenum** is the shortest segment, but it has the widest diameter. It receives chyme from the stomach and neutralizing digestive juices from the pancreas. Most of the chemical digestion of food occurs here. It does not play a large role in absorption, with the exception of iron. The **jejunum** is the main site of absorption. It averages 2.5 meters in length, and is characterized by prominent plicae circulares, long villi, and dense microvilli. The longest segment of the small intestine is the **ileum**. It averages 3.5 meters in length, but is the narrowest in diameter. Small aggregates of lymphatic cells called Peyer's patches are common in this segment, but they can be found throughout the small intestine. The primary role of the ileum is to absorb vitamin B_{12}, bile salts, and any nutrients that were not absorbed by the jejunum. It has few circular folds, and they

151

disappear altogether in the distal region. It terminates at the ileocecal valve, which controls the movement of chyme into the large intestine.

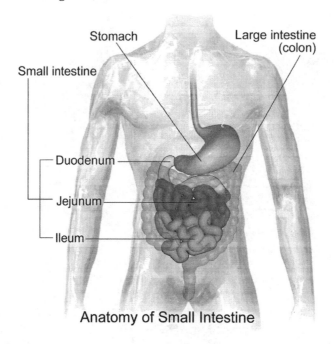

Anatomy of Small Intestine

LARGE INTESTINE

The large intestine specializes in the absorption of vitamin K, biotin, sodium ions, chloride ions, and water. By the time chyme reaches the large intestine, most of the water (approximately 80%) has already been absorbed by the small intestine. As the chyme is pushed through the colon 90% of the remaining liquid is absorbed, leaving a mass of indigestible food, water, and bacteria. If the feces are excreted before enough water is absorbed, they leave as diarrhea. Constipation results when too much water is absorbed.

BACTERIAL FLORA

The large intestine does not secrete digestive enzymes, but there are hundreds of species of resident bacteria that can digest certain materials left in chyme. These beneficial microbes are nourished by small amounts of cellulose and other carbohydrates, and they release gases such as carbon dioxide and methane as waste products of fermentation. The bacteria also release vitamin K, biotin, thiamin, riboflavin, and vitamin B_{12}. Vitamin K (required for the synthesis of clotting proteins) and biotin (a cofactor for many enzymes) are absorbed for use in the body. Resident gut flora also helps to keep populations of pathogenic bacteria in check. The appendix *may* serve as a reservoir for beneficial species of bacteria, though it is often infected with harmful microbes.

STRUCTURE (GROSS)

The large intestine is the portion of the alimentary canal that begins at the **ileocecal valve** and terminates at the anus. It is larger in diameter than the small intestine, but much shorter in length - averaging 1.5 meters. The first portion of the large intestine is a pouch called the **cecum**, and it receives chyme from the small intestine. It is also the site of a blind-ended tube called the **appendix**. The middle portion of the large intestine is the **colon**, which can be further subdivided into the ascending colon (right side of the body), transverse colon (extends across the abdominal cavity), descending colon (left side of the body), and sigmoid colon. The sigmoid colon lies in the pelvic cavity and becomes the **rectum**, which opens to the anus. There are no villi in the large intestine, but there are pouch-like sacculations called **haustra** that are separated by folds called plicae semilunares. These pouches are formed by the contraction of smooth muscle within the muscularis layer. The walls of the large intestine are lubricated by mucus, which is secreted by goblet cells.

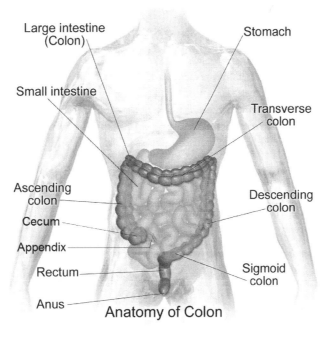

Anatomy of Colon

RECTUM: STORAGE AND ELIMINATION OF WASTE, FECES

The final 12 to 15 cm of the large intestine is called the rectum. In humans, it curves to conform to the shape of the sacrum and coccyx bone. The **anal canal** is the last portion of the rectum, and it ends with an involuntary internal sphincter and a voluntary external sphincter. A dilated region (superior to the anal canal) called the **rectal ampulla** functions as a storage area for feces before they are eliminated in the process of defecation. Feces consist of bacteria, water, undigested material, epithelial cells, and bile (which accounts for the brown coloration). As this material accumulates, the walls of the rectum expand and stretch receptors send signals that cause the rectal muscles to contract, the internal sphincter to relax, and the external sphincter to contract. At this point, the decision can be made to eliminate or delay elimination.

PERISTALSIS

Mechanical digestion begins in the mouth with the voluntary act of chewing (mastication). Skeletal muscles of the mouth and pharynx aid in swallowing (deglutition), which consists of three phases: the voluntary buccal phase and the involuntary pharyngeal and esophageal phases. The muscularis externa of the digestive tract consists of two layers of muscle tissue (three in the stomach) that contract radially and then relax to squeeze food in one direction. This involuntary propulsive process is called **peristalsis**. Peristalsis moves food from the pharynx to the esophagus to the stomach where an extra muscle layer helps to churn and mix the food. Another involuntary process called **segmentation** occurs in the intestines (in addition to peristalsis). In segmentation, non-adjacent portions of the digestive tract contract and relax to move the chyme back and forth. Haustral contractions in the large intestine are a form of segmentation that moves chyme from one haustrum to the next. Mass peristalsis describes the movements that occur two to four times a day to push large amounts of chyme toward the rectum. Movement along the digestive tract is also controlled by the gastroesophageal sphincter, pyloric sphincter, and anal sphincters.

THE ENTERIC NERVOUS SYSTEM

The network of neurons buried in the lining of the gastrointestinal tract that controls the function of the digestive system is called the **enteric nervous system** (ENS). The ENS can operate independently of the brain and spinal cord, and communicates with the CNS through the parasympathetic and sympathetic nervous systems. The parasympathetic nervous system stimulates digestive activities, while the sympathetic nervous system inhibits them.

The ENS is divided into two main parts: the submucosal and myenteric plexuses. The **submucosal plexus** is embedded in the connective tissue of the submucosa. It functions in regulating local secretions, absorption, contraction of submucosal muscle, and blood flow. The **myenteric plexus** is located between the circular and longitudinal layers of the muscularis externa. This network exerts control over the motility of the GI tract. It increases the tone, as well as the rate, intensity, and velocity of contractions.

EXCRETORY SYSTEM

ROLES IN HOMEOSTASIS

BLOOD PRESSURE

When osmoreceptors detect an increase in blood osmolality, or when baroreceptors detect a decrease in blood pressure, the pituitary gland secretes **antidiuretic hormone** (ADH). ADH stimulates the reabsorption of water in the kidney so that less water is excreted in the urine. This increases the volume and pressure of the blood.

The **renin-angiotensin-aldosterone system** (RAAS) is another mechanism by which blood pressure is regulated. When granular juxtaglomerular cells of the afferent arterioles of the kidneys detect a drop in blood pressure, they secrete an enzyme called **renin**. Renin interacts with a plasma protein called **angiotensinogen**, producing **angiotensin I**. As angiotensin I enters the capillaries of the lungs, it is acted on by another enzyme that converts it to **angiotensin II**. This hormone raises blood pressure by promoting vasoconstriction and stimulating the adrenal cortex to release **aldosterone**. Aldosterone increases the reabsorption of sodium, which increases water reabsorption, causing the blood volume and pressure to increase.

OSMOREGULATION

Osmoregulation describes the regulation of water and solute concentrations of body fluids. The primary organ involved in this process is the kidney. Dehydration or excessive salt intake will raise the osmolality of the blood. (Plasma osmolality is determined mainly by the concentrations of electrolytes, such as Na^+, Cl^-, and K^+.) When osmoreceptors in the hypothalamus detect an increase in osmolality, signals are sent to the pituitary gland to release ADH. ADH causes the collecting ducts in the kidneys to be more permeable to water, and water crosses the epithelium from the urine into the interstitium where it is returned to the blood. As a result, the blood osmolality decreases, and urine osmolality increases.

Aldosterone also plays a role in osmoregulation. When blood pressure is low, this hormone is secreted by the adrenal cortex. Aldosterone increases sodium reabsorption, which causes more water to leave the collecting tubule, thus raising blood osmolality. It also regulates the concentrations of other ions, such as potassium and chloride.

ACID–BASE BALANCE

The kidneys are key players in the maintenance of blood pH, which must be kept within a narrow range of 7.35 and 7.45. This is achieved by regulating the ratio of hydrogen ions to bicarbonate ions. (The higher the concentration of H^+ ions, the lower the pH.) Buffer systems in the body such as the phosphate, protein, and bicarbonate systems are in place to resist changes in H^+ concentration. Recall that the respiratory system helps to control pH through the bicarbonate buffer system. When carbon dioxide combines with water, carbonic acid (H_2CO_3) is formed, before dissociating into bicarbonate ions (HCO_3^-) and H^+. (Reaction: $CO_2 + H_2O \leftrightarrow H_2CO_3 \leftrightarrow HCO_3^- + H^+$) Increasing the rate of respiration decreases the concentration of H^+, which increases pH. The reverse is true when the rate of respiration decreases. The response from the *kidneys* is slower, but lasts longer. As blood pH decreases, H^+ ions are excreted by the renal tubules via urine (which is now more acidic) and bicarbonate ions are retained. The intercalated cells of the late distal tubule and collecting duct can also generate new bicarbonate ions. The kidneys lower pH by reabsorbing H^+ ions and secreting bicarbonate ions.

REMOVAL OF SOLUBLE NITROGENOUS WASTE

Nitrogen-containing wastes such as ammonia, urea, uric acid, and creatinine are excreted in urine. **Ammonia** is a toxic base that is formed during the breakdown of amino acids. Enzymes in the liver convert it to a less toxic form called **urea**. There is a high concentration of urea in the medulla because the collecting ducts are permeable to it. Much of the urea enters the interstitium, and it is then reabsorbed into the descending loop of Henle. Urea is the most abundant nitrogenous waste product in the urine, but since most of it is recycled, only a small amount is eliminated in urine. The high concentration of urea in the interstitium is helpful because it promotes the reabsorption of water. **Uric acid** is another nitrogenous waste that is excreted in the urine. It is formed as a byproduct of the catabolism of purine nucleotides, and most of it is reabsorbed in the proximal tubule by active transport. Like urea, only a small percentage is excreted. **Creatinine** is produced in the muscles as byproduct of the metabolism of creatine phosphate. It is filtered by the kidneys and excreted. Unlike urea and uric acid, creatinine is not reabsorbed by the tubules.

KIDNEY STRUCTURE

The kidneys are bean-shaped organs located in the lumbar region of the body that function in the filtering of blood and the excretion of wastes. Each kidney is surrounded by three protective layers of connective tissue: the **renal fascia**, the **adipose capsule**, and the innermost **renal capsule**. The capsule surrounds the outer region of the kidney called the **renal cortex**. The cortex contains many filtration units called **nephrons**, which have tubules that dip into the interior region called the **medulla**. The tubules in the medulla run parallel to each other and form striped cone-shaped masses of tissue called **medullary pyramids**. A cavity called the **renal sinus** contains the basin-like **renal pelvis**, which funnels the urine into the ureter. The **hilum** is the concave region of the kidney where the blood vessels and nerves enter and leave. Blood enters the kidney through the renal artery, which branches into smaller and smaller arteries until the blood reaches a tuft of capillaries called the **glomerulus**. Here, the blood is filtered before leaving the kidney through a network of veins that merge into the renal vein.

CORTEX

The renal cortex is the outer portion of the kidney, and it is the site of **ultrafiltration**: the nonspecific filtration of blood under high pressure. It is also responsible for the majority of reabsorption of water. The cortex is very vascular, and has a granular appearance due to the presence of nephrons. The renal corpuscles and the convoluted tubules of the nephrons are within the cortex (forming the **cortical labyrinth**), but the loops of Henle extend into the adjacent region known as the renal medulla. The thick, straight portions of the proximal and distal tubules, as well as the collecting ducts, form **medullary rays** that begin in the cortex and run perpendicular to the capsule. About 85% of nephrons (cortical nephrons) have short loops of Henle that extend only slightly into the medulla. The remaining 15% (juxtamedullary nephrons) have longer loops that extend deeper. Extensions of the cortex called **renal columns** dip down in between the renal pyramids of the medulla.

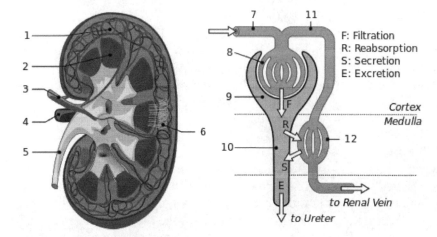

1: Renal cortex
2: Medulla
3: Renal artery
4: Renal vein
5: Ureter
6: Nephrons
7: Afferent arteriole
8: Glomerulus
9: Bowman's capsule
10: Renal tubule
11: Efferent arteriole
12: Peritubular capillaries.

MEDULLA

The adrenal medulla is the inner part of the kidney, and it continues the reabsorption of water and salts that began in the cortex. These substances enter the peritubular capillaries that are associated with the nephrons. Any filtrate that is not reclaimed by the circulatory system will leave as urine.

The medulla contains cone-shaped regions of tissue called **renal pyramids** that are separated by **renal columns**. The tips of the pyramids are oriented toward the pelvis of the kidney, and the bases face the cortex. The renal pyramids contain tubules that transport renal filtrate from the renal cortex to the apex of the pyramids. At the apex is a structure called the **renal papilla** that contains ducts that allow the processed filtrate (now called urine) to pass out of the medulla to collecting chambers called **calyces**. From here the urine passes through the renal pelvis, through the ureter, and finally into the bladder.

NEPHRON STRUCTURE

The nephron is the functional unit of the kidney. Each kidney has over a million of these microscopic structures, and each one consists of two main parts: the **renal corpuscle** (which filters the blood) and the **renal tubule** (which collects and concentrates the filtrate). The renal corpuscle consists of a cup-shaped structure called **Bowman's capsule** that wraps partially around a cluster of capillaries called the **glomerulus**. The renal tubule is a looping canal that is continuous with Bowman's capsule. It consists of different regions that differ in structure and function. The **proximal convoluted tubule** begins at Bowman's capsule and then plunges into the medulla, forming a u-shape called the **loop of Henle**. It then becomes the **distal convoluted tubule**, which is continuous with the **collecting duct**. The collecting duct is typically considered as a separate structure, and not part of the nephron.

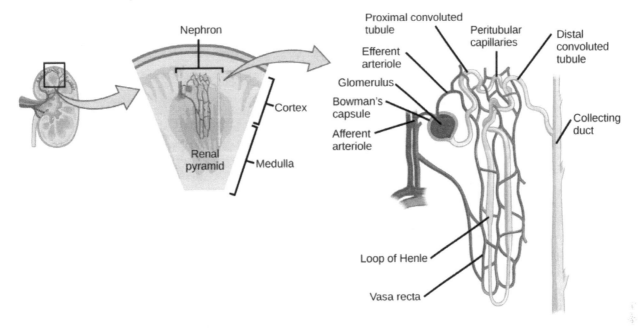

PROXIMAL TUBULE, LOOP OF HENLE, AND DISTAL TUBULE

The renal tubule is divided into three continuous regions: the proximal convoluted tubule, the loop of Henle, and the distal convoluted tubule. The **proximal convoluted tubule** extends from Bowman's capsule, and this coiled tube is characterized by cuboidal cells with dense microvilli that aid in reabsorption and secretion. There are only sparse microvilli in the rest of the tubule. The middle, hairpin-shaped portion of the renal tubule is called the **loop of Henle**, and it maintains a relatively high solute concentration in the medulla, which in turn assists in the reabsorption of water. The loop consists of a descending limb (which reabsorbs water) that plunges into the medulla, a U-turn that curves back toward the cortex, and an ascending limb (which reabsorbs ions). The ascending limb widens into a thick portion composed of larger epithelial cells. The loop is lined with simple squamous epithelial cells, with the exception of the thick ascending limb which is lined with simple cuboidal cells. This limb becomes the **distal convoluted tubule** (also lined with cuboidal cells), which is involved in absorption and secretion, but not to the extent of the proximal convoluted tubule. It is also shorter in length.

GLOMERULUS AND BOWMAN'S CAPSULE

Each renal corpuscle consists of a **glomerulus** and a **Bowman's capsule**. The glomerulus is a tangled network of blood capillaries that occupies Bowman's capsule. These fenestrated capillaries are lined with a thin layer of epithelial cells. An **afferent arteriole** takes blood to the glomerulus and an **efferent arteriole** takes it away. The smaller diameter of the efferent arteriole increases the pressure within the glomerulus, which is required for ultrafiltration. **Mesangial cells** contract to regulate blood flow, and also support the capillary network.

Bowman's capsule is a cup-like structure at the closed end of the renal tubule that encloses the glomerulus. It has an outer layer of epithelial cells that form the parietal layer, and a visceral layer of **podocytes** with processes called **pedicels** that wrap around the capillaries. Gaps between the pedicels (filtration slits) allow the passage of tiny molecules and ions. Together, the endothelial cells of the capillaries, the basement membrane, and the pedicels make up the **filtration membrane**. Fluid from the blood leaves the fenestrated capillaries and passes through the filtration membrane and collects in **Bowman's space** (the cavity between the two layers of Bowman's capsule). From here, the filtrate enters the renal tubule.

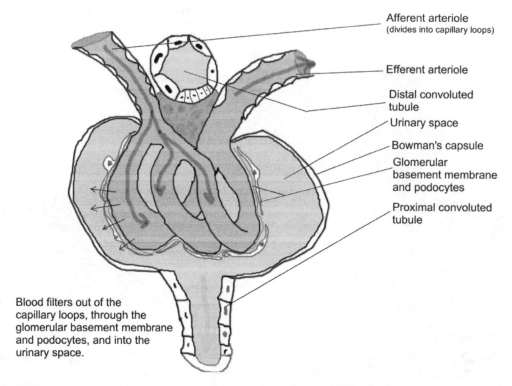

Afferent arteriole
(divides into capillary loops)

Efferent arteriole

Distal convoluted tubule

Urinary space

Bowman's capsule

Glomerular basement membrane and podocytes

Proximal convoluted tubule

Blood filters out of the capillary loops, through the glomerular basement membrane and podocytes, and into the urinary space.

COLLECTING DUCT

The collecting duct is the final site of reabsorption in the kidney, and it is shared by multiple nephrons. The distal tubule empties filtrate into the collecting tubule, which merges with other collecting tubules to form the collecting duct. Collecting tubules are lined with simple cuboidal epithelium, but these cells elongate to form columnar cells as they get closer to the duct. Some of these cells are **principal cells**, which reabsorb sodium ions and water (under ADH and aldosterone control). Other cells are **intercalated cells**, and they play an important role in acid-base balance and the reabsorption of sodium ions. Both these types of cells can also be found toward the end part of the distal tubule, but there are fewer microvilli than in the collecting duct. The filtrate that passes through the collecting duct enters the minor calyces at the apex of a medullary pyramid.

FORMATION OF URINE

The formation of urine begins with glomerular filtration. This nonspecific filtration is driven by the hydrostatic pressure of the blood. This pressure is higher than in other capillaries because the efferent arterioles that exit the glomerulus have a smaller diameter than the afferent arterioles that enter. Water and small solutes from the blood are forced through fenestrations in the capillaries, leaving behind larger particles. The fluid must pass through the 3-layered filtration membrane before entering Bowman's space as renal filtrate. The first layer is the endothelial lining of the capillaries. Fenestrations in the capillaries prevent the passage of blood cells. The second layer is the basement membrane, which excludes plasma proteins such as albumin. The third layer is the visceral lining of Bowman's capsule. Small filtration slits between the podocytes allow only the smallest of particles to pass. The concentration of a solute in the glomerular filtrate is the same as the concentration in the blood. On average, about 1/5 of the blood is filtered, but this varies depending on the pressure.

SECRETION AND REABSORPTION OF SOLUTES

Secretion removes solutes from the blood and adds them to the filtrate, while reabsorption removes solutes from the filtrate and returns them to the blood. Solutes are moved by either primary active transport, secondary active transport, or diffusion, and water is reabsorbed by osmosis. The functions of each region of the renal tubule and collecting duct are summarized in the table below:

Region	Role in Secretion
Proximal convoluted tubule	H^+, creatinine, NH_4^+, drugs, toxins—active transport
Loop of Henle—Descending limb	Urea
Distal convoluted tubule	K^+, H^+
Collecting duct	K^+, H^+
Region	Role in Reabsorption
Proximal convoluted tubule	Main site of reabsorption in the kidney; 60–70% of the volume of filtrate is reclaimed in the PCT. Glucose, amino acids, vitamins, Na^+, Cl^-, K^+, Ca^{2+}, Mg^{2+}, bicarbonate, phosphate, water, urea
Loop of Henle—Descending limb	Water
Loop of Henle—Ascending limb	Na^+, Cl^-, K^+, Mg^{2+}, Ca^{2+}
Distal convoluted tubule	Cl^-, Ca^{2+}, Na^+, Water (variable permeability—opening of Na^+ channels is dependent on aldosterone)
Collecting duct	Urea, bicarbonate, Na^+, Water (variable permeability—dependent on aldosterone and ADH)

CONCENTRATION OF URINE

The concentration of urine is influenced by the high solute concentration of the medulla, and the hormones that control the permeability of the distal convoluted tubule and collecting duct.

The **countercurrent mechanism** describes the use of active transport to move solutes out of the ascending loop of Henle (which is impermeable to water) into the medullary interstitium. The osmotic gradient that is created causes water diffuse out of the descending limb (which *is* permeable to water), concentrating the filtrate. The recycling of urea also helps to maintain a high medullary osmolarity. The descending loop of Henle and the collecting duct are both permeable to urea, but the descending limb and the distal tubule are not. Urea enters the descending loop from the interstitium, and travels through the renal tubule to the collecting duct, where it reenters the interstitium.

The concentration of urine is also regulated by hormones. The permeability of the distal convoluted tubule to sodium is dependent on aldosterone. Aldosterone promotes the reabsorption of Na^+, and since water follows the sodium, the urine becomes more concentrated. The permeability of the collecting duct is dependent on both aldosterone and ADH. ADH increases the duct's permeability by water by inserting aquaporins that allow the passage of water.

COUNTER-CURRENT MULTIPLIER MECHANISM

A countercurrent system in the loop of Henle is responsible for the generation of an osmotic gradient in the medulla that promotes the reabsorption of water. The descending limb is permeable to water, but not solutes. The ascending limb is permeable to solutes, but not water. Na^+, Cl^-, and other ions are actively transported from the ascending limb into the medullary interstitium. The concentration gradient causes water to leave the descending limb by osmosis, which increases the concentration of the filtrate in the descending limb. As the filtrate moves up the ascending limb,

159

ions are actively absorbed, raising the solute concentration in the medulla. This positive feedback loop is known as the countercurrent *multiplier* mechanism because it multiplies the concentration of the interstitial fluid as a result of the functional differences between the two limbs.

The countercurrent multiplier system is distinguished from the countercurrent *exchange* system, in which the hypertonicity of the medulla is *maintained* (not generated) by the countercurrent flow of blood in the vasa recta. As blood in the *descending* part of the vasa recta passes the *ascending* limb, it picks up ions that left the filtrate. As blood in the *ascending* vasa recta passes the *descending* limb, most of the ions diffuse back into the medulla.

STORAGE AND ELIMINATION: URETER, BLADDER, URETHRA

A **ureter** is a tubular organ that delivers urine from the kidney to the bladder for storage. The collecting ducts (the final sites of reabsorption) empty urine into the ureter, and both gravity and peristalsis move the urine into the bladder. The bladder is a bag-like organ that can store up to 600 ml of urine (though the desire to urinate begins at around 150 ml). The ureters, bladder, and superior portion of the urethra are lined with transitional epithelial tissue that allows expansion. When the organ becomes distended, the stretched epithelium appears to have fewer cell layers.

Urine is stored in the bladder until contraction of the **detrusor muscle** (the smooth muscle within the bladder wall) forces urine into the urethra. Contraction of the bladder is controlled by the parasympathetic nervous system. Stretch receptors in the bladder send impulses to the sacral region of the spinal cord. Impulses are then sent along efferent neurons to the bladder, telling it to contract. A circular smooth muscle called the internal urethral sphincter relaxes, and (if the timing is appropriate) the voluntary external urethral sphincter relaxes as well. Urine flows from the bladder, through the urethra, and out of the body in a process called micturition.

SPHINCTER MUSCLES

There are two sphincters of the urethra that delay the emptying of the bladder. The **internal urethral sphincter** (IUS) is found between the bladder and the urethra. It consists of smooth muscle and is continuous with the smooth muscle of the bladder (the detrusor muscle). The sympathetic nervous system keeps the IUS contracted until the micturition reflex is triggered. The IUS relaxes as a result of sympathetic inhibition, allowing urine to pass through. The second sphincter that controls the elimination of urine is the **external urethral sphincter** (EUS), which is made of skeletal muscle, and under the control of the somatic nervous system. A conscious decision can be made to relax the EUS under appropriate circumstances. Involuntary contraction of the detrusor forces urine out of the body, and the voluntary contraction of abdominal muscles can increase the rate of flow by compressing the bladder.

REPRODUCTIVE SYSTEM

GONADS

The gonads are the components of the reproductive system that produce gametes (sex cells) and secrete hormones. The male gonads are the **testes**. These structures are housed in the scrotum and encapsulated by a fibrous layer of connective tissue called the **tunica albuginea**. Thin layers of tissue extend from the tunica albuginea and divide the testes into 250 to 300 compartments called **lobules**. Each lobule contains –one to four **seminiferous tubules**—the sites of spermatogenesis. The epithelial lining of these tubules consists of the **spermatogenic cells** that give rise to sperm, as well the cells that nourish them (**sustentacular cells**, also called **Sertoli cells**). **Interstitial cells** (**Leydig cells**) around the seminiferous tubules produce testosterone, which stimulates the production of sperm. The seminiferous tubules join together to form a network of channels called the **rete testis** that bring maturing sperm cells to the **efferent ducts** where they exit the testes and enter the **epididymis**.

The female gonads are the **ovaries**. Ovaries are oval-shaped structures that rest in slight depressions on either side of the uterus known as the **ovarian fossae**, and they are held in position by several peritoneal ligaments. Each ovary is covered by two types of tissue: a layer of simple cuboidal epithelium known as the **germinal epithelium**, and the underlying **tunica albuginea**. The ovary is subdivided into the outer cortex and the inner medulla. The **cortex** has a granular appearance due to the presence of thousands of nourishing **follicles** in various stages of development. Each of these saclike follicles contains an oocyte. Initially, the oocyte is surrounded by a single layer of **follicular cells,** but as the follicle matures, the cells give rise to a multi-layer of estrogen-producing **granulosa cells**. After ovulation, a gland called the **corpus luteum** forms, and it secretes progesterone and small amounts of estrogen. This gland disappears unless pregnancy occurs. The interior of the ovary, or **medulla**, is made of loose areolar connective tissue, and contains many blood vessels, lymphatic vessels, and nerves that enter and leave through the **hilum**.

GENITALIA

The internal male genitalia include the epididymides, vasa deferentia, and accessory glands including the seminal vesicles, prostate gland, and Cowper's glands (the bulbourethral glands). The **epididymis** is a convoluted tube attached to the outside of a testicle that nourishes sperm as they finish maturing, and stores them until ejaculation. From here the sperm pass through the **vas deferens** (sperm duct), **ejaculatory duct**, and **urethra**, and exit through the penis. The **seminal vesicles** secrete fluid into the ejaculatory duct that makes up roughly 60% of the volume of semen. The contents of this mildly alkaline fluid include fructose, prostaglandins, and proteins. Secretions of the **prostate gland** (about 30% of semen volume) nourish the sperm and increase their motility. **Cowper's glands** secrete a lubricating fluid that makes up 2–5% of semen volume.

The external male genitalia include the penis and scrotum. The **penis** is the erectile organ responsible for delivering sperm to the female. It consists of three cylinders of spongy tissue: a pair of **corpora cavernosa** and the **corpus spongiosum** that surrounds the urethra. The **scrotum** is the sac that protects the sperm-producing testes and keeps them at the proper temperature.

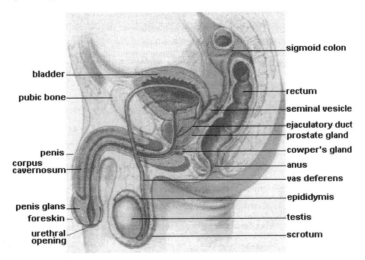

The internal female genitalia include the ovaries, the fallopian tubes, the uterus, and the vagina. The **ovaries** produce oocytes, and also secrete sex hormones. When an oocyte is released during ovulation, it is "captured" by the **fallopian tube**, also known as the uterine tube or oviduct, which is not directly connected to the ovaries. Fertilization typically occurs in the fallopian tube, and implantation of the fertilized egg usually occurs in the endometrium of the uterus. The **uterus** is a muscular, pear-shaped organ that nourishes and protects the developing embryo. The neck of the uterus that opens to the vagina is called the **cervix**. The **vagina** is a muscular canal that receives the penis during intercourse. During childbirth, the baby passes through the vagina—also called the birth canal.

The external female genitalia include the structures of the **vulva**. These include the mons pubis, the labia majora and labia minora, Bartholin's glands, and the clitoris. The **mons pubis** is a mound of fatty tissue that lies over the pubic bone. The skin folds that form the **labia** help to protect the more delicate tissues beneath. **Bartholin's glands** produce a fluid that lubricates the vagina. The **clitoris** consists of erectile tissue full of nerve endings that contribute to sexual arousal.

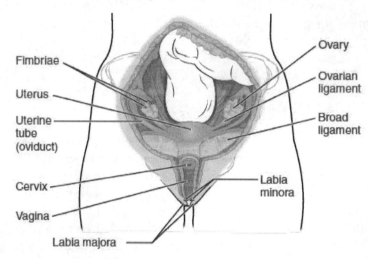

DIFFERENCES BETWEEN MALE AND FEMALE STRUCTURES

Many of the structures within the male and female reproductive are "homologous" to each other because they share a common developmental pathway. But these structures become specialized for different roles in reproduction.

The male reproductive system is designed to produce sperm and deliver it to the female for fertilization. Most of the male reproductive structures are external, which helps to keep the sperm at the optimal temperature. The testes produce much higher levels of testosterone than female gonads, and they produce millions of gametes per day after puberty. The male urethra is a common passageway for both urine and semen.

In contrast, the female reproductive system is designed to nurture a developing embryo. The reproductive structures are housed internally. The ovaries produce much higher levels of estrogen than male gonads. They contain all of the oocytes that they will ever have before birth, and only one is released per month during ovulation. The female urethra is not connected to the reproductive system.

MUSCLE SYSTEM

The muscle system is made up of skeletal, smooth, and cardiac muscles that contract to produce nearly all body movements. Skeletal muscles are used for voluntary actions. Walking, jumping, smiling, eye movements, and the maintenance of posture are all under the control of the somatic nervous system. The muscles that coordinate voluntary movements are attached to bone by tendons, and the bone is moved when the muscle shortens. Skeletal muscles also work with the tendons, ligaments, and bone to support and stabilize the joints.

Contraction of smooth muscle is involuntary, and therefore under autonomic control. Smooth muscle in the gastrointestinal tract contracts rhythmically to propel food along the gastrointestinal tract. This is called peristalsis. Blood pressure is regulated by contraction and relaxation of the smooth muscle within the vessel wall. Vasoconstriction increases blood pressure and decreases blood flow, while vasodilation decreases blood pressure and increases blood flow. Cardiac muscle of the heart contracts to pump blood throughout the body.

STRUCTURE OF THREE BASIC MUSCLE TYPES: STRIATED, SMOOTH, CARDIAC

Skeletal muscle is under somatic (voluntary) control and does not display myogenic activity. (Skeletal muscles require external stimulation to contract.) They are involved in the movement of bone, support, thermoregulation, and venous return to the heart. These muscles are **striated**; the muscle fibers have alternating regions of light and dark bands. A single skeletal myocyte is cylinder-shaped and has many nuclei.

Smooth muscle is under autonomic (involuntary) control and is capable of using myogenic mechanisms to contract (independent of nervous stimulation). Smooth muscle tissue is found in the walls of hollow organs and vessels, and aids in the movement of substances such as food and blood. The cells are spindle-shaped, non-striated, and uninucleated.

Like smooth muscle, **cardiac muscle** is under autonomic control and exhibits myogenic activity. Cardiac muscle tissue is found in the walls of the heart, and is required for the pumping of blood. The cells are branched, striated, and usually uninucleate (but may have two nuclei). They are connected to each other by intercalated discs with gap junctions that allow the cells to communicate.

THERMOREGULATION (SHIVERING REFLEX)

When thermoreceptors detect a drop in temperature, impulses are sent to the posterior hypothalamus, which then sends signals to the effectors. Smooth muscles in the walls of the cutaneous arterioles contract involuntarily to reduce the blood flow near the surface of the skin. This minimizes heat loss to the environment. Arrector pili muscles also contract, causing hairs to stand on end in an attempt to trap warm air. If the core body temperature drops, the shivering reflex is triggered by the posterior hypothalamus. Shivering is involuntary shuddering, caused by the rapid contracting and relaxing of skeletal muscles. Contraction of these muscles requires the hydrolysis of ATP, and this exothermic reaction releases energy in the form of heat. Some heat is also generated as a result of friction between the sliding filaments of the muscle.

When thermoreceptors detect a rise in temperature, the anterior hypothalamus tells the smooth muscles that surround cutaneous arterioles to relax. Vasodilation allows more blood to flow near the surface of the skin, and heat is lost to the environment.

PERIPHERAL CIRCULATORY ASSISTANCE

The return of blood to the heart is assisted by a system called the **skeletal muscle pump**. Large peripheral veins in the legs and arms have valves that prevent the backflow of blood. When the skeletal muscles around these deep veins contract, the vessel is compressed, and blood is forced through the valves in the direction of the heart. Exercising these muscle groups increases the rate of blood flow.

The **thoracic pump** also facilitates venous return. During inspiration, contraction of the diaphragm and intercostal muscles expands the thoracic cavity. The increased volume results in a decrease in pressure, which is transmitted to the right atrium. This drop in pressure helps the blood to return to the heart. Also, when the pressure in the thoracic cavity decreases, the pressure in the abdominal cavity increases, squeezing the blood in the inferior vena cava toward the heart.

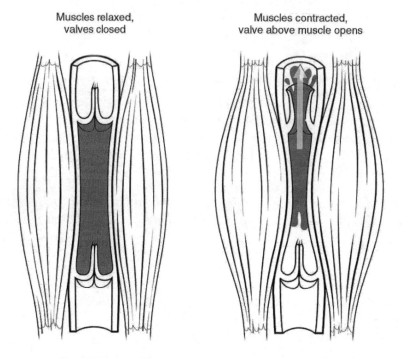

Muscles relaxed, valves closed

Muscles contracted, valve above muscle opens

MUSCLE STRUCTURE AND CONTROL OF CONTRACTION
T-TUBULE SYSTEM

Transverse tubules, or **T-tubules**, are tunnel-like invaginations of the **sarcolemma**—the plasma membrane of striated muscle cells. The membranes of this system contain a high concentration of ion channels, allowing them to play an important role in muscle contraction. When an action potential propagates along the sarcolemma, the T-tubules help to depolarize the cell by carrying the impulse to the **sarcoplasmic reticulum** (SR) that surrounds the **myofibrils** in a muscle cell. The SR is a form of smooth endoplasmic reticulum that is specialized to store and release calcium ions. The t-tubules are sandwiched between two enlarged chambers of the SR called **terminal cisternae**. This "sandwich" makes up a structure called the **triad**. When the impulse reaches the SR, the calcium channels in the SR membrane open, releasing calcium ions that ultimately cause contraction of the muscle. ATP-powered calcium pumps within the SR membrane pump Ca^{2+} back into the SR to relax the muscle.

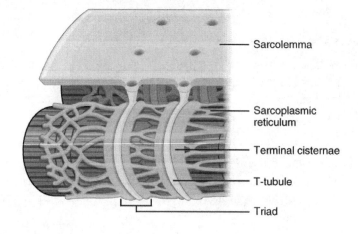

164

CONTRACTILE APPARATUS

The **contractile apparatus** describes a unit within muscle tissue that is specialized for contraction. The structure of the contractile apparatus is similar among striated muscle tissues, and consists of a repeating unit called a **sarcomere**. Tens of thousands of these sarcomeres lie end to end to form a **myofibril**. One sarcomere is separated from another by a boundary called the **Z line**, where a network of proteins serves as a point of anchorage for **actin** (thin filaments). Six thin filaments surround a single thick myosin filament. The filaments themselves do not change length during contraction; their arrangement allows them to slide over each other when myosin heads pull on the thin filaments, causing the sarcomeres to shorten, and the muscle to contract. Note that while smooth muscle cells do contain actin and myosin, the filaments are disorganized, and no sarcomeres are present.

CONTRACTILE VELOCITY OF DIFFERENT MUSCLE TYPES

There are three main types of skeletal muscle fibers: slow-twitch oxidative (SO—type I), fast-twitch oxidative-glycolytic (FOG—type IIa), and fast-twitch glycolytic (FG—type IIb). Most muscles consist of an even blend of these fibers, but the proportions vary in certain muscles, depending on function. For example, muscles associated with maintaining posture will have a high percentage of slow-twitch fibers, while muscles in the lower legs of a sprinter will have a high percentage of fast-twitch fibers.

The characteristics of each type of fiber are summarized in the following table:

	Slow Twitch, Type I	Fast Twitch, Type IIa	Fast Twitch, Type IIb
Fiber Diameter	Smaller	Intermediate	Larger
Capillary density	High	Moderate	Low
Myoglobin Concentration / Color	High / Red	Moderate / Red-Pink	Low / White
Metabolism	High aerobic capacity, low anaerobic capacity	Both aerobic and anaerobic capabilities	Low aerobic capacity, high anaerobic capacity
Concentration of Mitochondria	High	Moderate	Low
Resistance to Fatigue	High	Moderate	Low
Contractile Velocity	Slow	Rapid	Rapid
Force Production	Low	Moderate	High
General Use	Prolonged, low-intensity aerobic activities / maintenance of posture	Moderate intensity activities, such as running	Short bursts of activity, such as sprinting or heavy lifting

REGULATION OF CARDIAC MUSCLE CONTRACTION

Cardiac muscle demonstrates myogenic activity. The pacemaker cells of the sinoatrial (SA) node of the heart generate their own action potential, which then travels to the atrioventricular (AV) node (the secondary pacemaker), the bundle of His, the bundle branches, and finally the Purkinje fibers. Gap junctions between adjacent cardiac cells facilitate the transmission of the action potential from one cell to the next. As the impulse travels through the sarcolemma of a cardiac muscle cell, voltage-gated calcium ion channels open, allowing the entry of extracellular Ca^{2+}. The inflow of Ca^{2+} triggers the release of even more Ca^{2+} from the sarcoplasmic reticulum. Calcium ions cause the cardiac muscle to contract in a similar manner to skeletal muscle cells (the sliding filament mechanism). Note that skeletal muscle cells do not generate their own action potential, and the action potential is more prolonged in cardiac cells.

While the heart is autorhythmic, the muscle contraction is further regulated by the autonomic nervous system. Sympathetic stimulation increases heart rate, while parasympathetic stimulation (the vagus nerve) decreases heart rate. The endocrine system influences heart rate as well. Epinephrine secreted from the adrenal medulla and thyroxine from the thyroid gland both increase heart rate.

OXYGEN DEBT: FATIGUE

Oxygen debt is the amount of oxygen required to restore metabolic conditions to resting levels. Muscle activity is powered by the hydrolysis of ATP. In a resting state, aerobic respiration provides enough ATP for muscles to function. Stored ATP is quickly used up during intense exercise, and a molecule called **creatine phosphate** phosphorylates ADP to produce ATP. Anaerobic respiration also supplies ATP relatively quickly, but only for a short amount of time. If oxygen is available, aerobic respiration synthesizes ATP. When oxygen levels become depleted, **lactic acid** (a byproduct of anaerobic respiration) begins to accumulate. The buildup of lactic acid, along with the depletion of ATP and oxygen, causes muscle fatigue. Lactic acid that does not remain in the muscles is brought to the liver, where it is converted into glucose. The amount of oxygen required to accomplish this task, and to replenish the levels of ATP and creatine phosphate, is called oxygen debt.

NERVOUS CONTROL

The peripheral nervous system is divided into the somatic and autonomic nervous systems. Voluntary muscles are composed of skeletal muscle tissue and are under the control of the somatic nervous system. Most voluntary muscles are connected to bone. These muscles usually contract in response to a conscious thought process, but they are also involved in certain involuntary reflexes, such as the knee jerk reflex. The motor cortex of the brain is responsible for generating most of the nerve impulses that initiate voluntary movements.

Involuntary muscles are innervated by motor neurons of the autonomic nervous system. These muscles include the smooth muscles found in the walls of hollow organs such as the intestines and blood vessels, as well as the cardiac muscle of the heart. The lower part of the brainstem called the medulla oblongata sends signals to involuntary muscles that play a role in digestion, vasodilation/vasoconstriction, heart rate, respiratory rate, and other visceral functions.

MOTOR NEURONS, NEUROMUSCULAR JUNCTION, MOTOR END PLATES

The stimulus for skeletal muscle cell contraction comes from motor neurons, and the synapse between the neuron and muscle cell is called the **neuromuscular junction**. A single motor neuron can form synapses with multiple muscle cells. The neuron and the muscle cells that it innervates are collectively called a **motor unit**. This arrangement allows a large group of cells to contract together. All the motor neurons that innervate the same muscle make up a **motor pool**.

When an action potential reaches an axon terminal, voltage-gated calcium ions in the membrane are opened, and Ca^{2+} enters. These ions bind to synaptic vesicles that store acetylcholine (ACh), causing them to fuse with the membrane and release ACh into the synaptic cleft. ACh binds to nicotinic receptors on a folded portion of the sarcolemma known as the motor end plate. The permeability of the muscle cell changes, and the cell depolarizes. The action potential is taken into the muscle cell via T-tubules, causing calcium channels in the sarcoplasmic reticulum to open. The release of calcium into the sarcoplasm causes the muscle to contract.

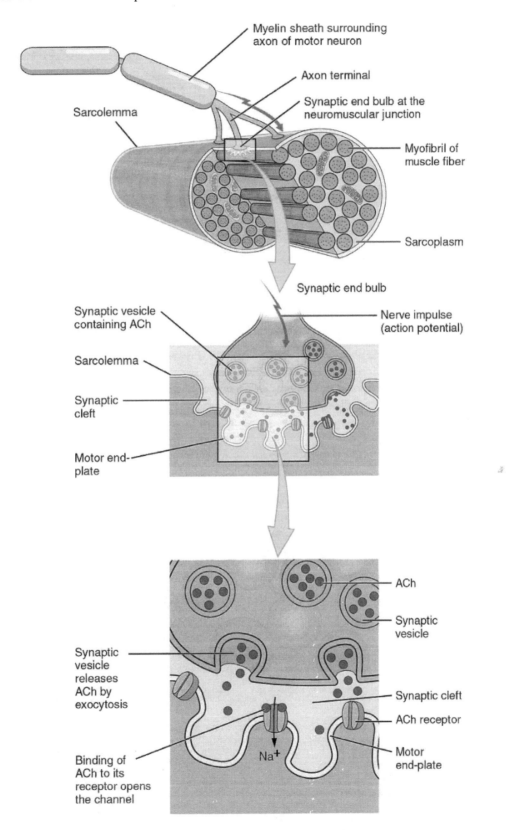

SYMPATHETIC AND PARASYMPATHETIC INNERVATION

Involuntary muscle tissues (smooth, cardiac) are innervated by motor neurons of the sympathetic and parasympathetic divisions of the autonomic nervous system. Motor pathways of the ANS consist of *two* neurons: a preganglionic and a postganglionic neuron. The cell body of a preganglionic neuron resides in the central nervous system and synapses with the cell body of one or more postganglionic neurons within an autonomic ganglion. Postganglionic nerve fibers are shorter than presynaptic fibers, and they extend to the effectors. *Pre*ganglionic neurons of both the sympathetic and parasympathetic systems release acetylcholine (ACh). *Post*ganglionic neurons of the parasympathetic division release ACh, but those of the sympathetic division release norepinephrine (NE).

In general, the sympathetic and parasympathetic systems tend to have antagonistic effects on the muscles (and glands) they innervate. The sympathetic division induces a fight or flight response, which causes the heart rate and blood pressure to increase, and blood to be diverted away from the digestive system. The parasympathetic division induces a rest and digest response, which causes the heart rate and blood pressure to decrease, and promotes digestion.

SPECIALIZED CELL - MUSCLE CELL

ORGANIZATION OF CONTRACTILE ELEMENTS: ACTIN AND MYOSIN FILAMENTS, CROSS BRIDGES, SLIDING FILAMENT MODEL

The interior of a skeletal muscle cell consists of elongated structures called **myofibrils** that run in parallel columns along the length of the cell. Myofibrils are polymers of repeating contractile units called **sarcomeres**. Within each myofibril are two types of filaments: **thin filaments** and **thick filaments**. Thin filaments are made mostly of **actin** molecules arranged in a helical configuration. Other proteins called **troponin** and **tropomyosin** can be found along the length of the filament, and they help to regulate the access of myosin to actin. **Myosin** proteins make up the thick filaments. These golf-club shaped molecules twist together, with the heads protruding out of the filament. The myosin heads form **cross bridges** when they bind to active sites on the actin filaments. The myosin changes shape, pulling the actin filament toward the middle of the sarcomere in a process called the **power stroke**. This causes the sarcomere to shorten via the **sliding filament mechanism**. ATP is required to revert the myosin heads to their original position. Cardiac muscle cells have a similar arrangement of actin and myosin, but the filaments of smooth muscle cells are less organized.

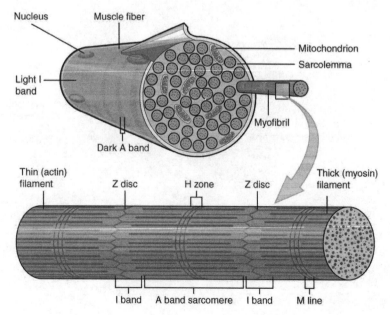

168

ABUNDANT MITOCHONDRIA IN RED MUSCLE CELLS: ATP SOURCE

Red muscle fibers are specialized for endurance activities of low intensity such as walking, light lifting, or the maintenance of posture. They are relatively slow to contract, but are resistant to fatigue and have abundant mitochondria. Mitochondria are the sites of oxidative phosphorylation. When levels of blood oxygen are insufficient, a protein called myoglobin supplies oxygen that is used in the synthesis of ATP. (Myoglobin is similar to hemoglobin, but it found in muscle tissue, has a higher affinity for oxygen, and can only carry one oxygen molecule per molecule of myoglobin.) The red coloration of these slow-twitch fibers comes from the extensive capillary network that surrounds them and the high myoglobin content. In contrast, white muscle fibers are specialized for high intensity activities, contain low amounts of mitochondria and myoglobin, and fatigue quickly.

SARCOMERES: I AND A BANDS, M AND Z LINES, H ZONE

A sarcomere is the smallest contractile unit of striated muscle that is capable of contracting. A myofibril consists of tens of thousands of sarcomeres lined up end-to-end, each one divided into various bands, lines, and zones that account for the striated appearance. The **Z-line** is made of a protein network that anchors the thin actin filaments and forms the boundary of each sarcomere. It can be seen within a light region known as the isotropic band (**I-band**) which consists only of actin filaments. An anisotropic band (**A-band**) consists of the entire length of the thick myosin filaments, including areas of overlap with the thin filaments. In the center of the A-band is the **H-zone**, made only of myosin filaments. Within the H-zone (and at the center of the sarcomere) is the **M-line**, where proteins of the cytoskeleton attach to myosin filaments. When a sarcomere is fully contracted, the ends of the actin filaments overlap, the I-bands narrow, and the H bands disappear. The lengths of the A-bands remain the same.

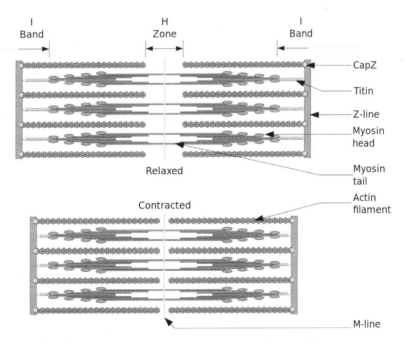

PRESENCE OF TROPONIN AND TROPOMYOSIN

Troponin and tropomyosin are regulatory proteins that initiate the contraction of striated muscles when calcium levels are high, and inhibit contraction when calcium levels drop. **Troponin** is a globular protein complex that consists of three subunits: troponin I, T, and C. **Troponin I** binds to actin filaments and inhibits the binding of myosin. **Troponin T** is bound to the protein **tropomyosin**—a fibrous, rope-like protein that winds around actin and blocks the sites where myosin heads attach to the actin filaments. **Troponin C** has a high affinity for the calcium ions that

169

regulate muscle contraction. When calcium binds to troponin C, a series of conformational changes occur that ultimately causes tropomyosin to slip out of place, allowing myosin to form cross bridges with actin and contract the sarcomere.

Note that smooth muscles lack troponin C. Instead, calcium binds to **calmodulin**, which leads to the phosphorylation of myosin and contraction of the muscle.

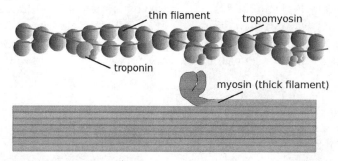

CALCIUM REGULATION OF CONTRACTION

Muscle contraction is directly tied to the concentration of calcium ions in the sarcomere. When an action potential travels from a motor neuron to a muscle cell, the sarcolemma depolarizes, and the action potential is brought into the cell by the T-tubules. Ca^{2+} is released from the sarcoplasmic reticulum (SR) at all points that come in contact with the T-tubules. Calcium ions flow into the cytoplasm of the cell (the sarcoplasm) and bind to troponin, which causes tropomyosin to reveal the myosin-binding sites on actin. When myosin binds to actin, cross bridges are formed between the myosin heads and the actin filaments. The myosin heads change shape, causing the thin actin filaments to slide past the thick myosin filaments, and the muscle fiber contracts. When the action potential is terminated, ATP-powered calcium pumps in the membrane of the sarcoplasmic reticulum pump calcium back into the SR. As the concentration of calcium ions in the sarcoplasm decreases, the sarcomeres relax.

SKELETAL SYSTEM

FUNCTIONS

The skeletal system provides a framework for the body that consists of bones, ligaments, tendons, cartilage, and other tissues. This system is essential in the support and physical protection of the body. Bones support the weight of the body, give shape to body parts, and help to keep internal organs in place. Bones also serve as attachment points for muscles, allowing for body movement. Skeletal muscles connect to bones via tendons, and bones attach to each other via ligaments. Cartilage is more flexible, and supports body parts such as the ear, the nose, the trachea, and various joints. The skeletal system also protects vital organs. The skull encloses the brain, the vertebrae surround the spinal cord, the thoracic cage protects the heart and lungs, and the pelvic girdle protects the inferior portion of the digestive system, the bladder, and the internal reproductive organs. Delicate bone marrow is also protected within the hollow spaces of certain bones.

> **Review Video: Skeletal System**
> Visit mometrix.com/academy and enter code: 256447

CALCIUM STORAGE

Bone is a reservoir for calcium. The bone cells produce a hard-acellular **matrix** composed of about 35% collagen and 65% inorganic material. Most of the inorganic matter is a type of **calcium phosphate** known as **hydroxyapatite**. Calcium is required for a number of processes, including the contraction of muscles, the conduction of a nerve impulse, and the clotting of blood. The body takes in calcium in the diet, and about 99% of absorbed calcium is stored in bones and teeth. When calcium levels are high, bone-forming cells called **osteoblasts** remove calcium from the blood and deposit it into the bone along with other components of the matrix. Eventually, these cells become surrounded by the hard, calcium-rich secretion and differentiate into mature bone cells called **osteocytes**. If blood calcium is low, cells called **osteoclasts** can break down bone and put calcium back into the blood. In a healthy individual, there is a balance between the amount of calcium deposited and the amount removed. Homeostatic imbalances result in hypercalcemia or hypocalcemia.

The calcium-regulating hormones of the endocrine system are responsible for breaking down and reabsorbing bone tissue. The kidneys produce 1,25-hydroxyvitamin D, a biologically active form of vitamin D also known as **calcitriol**. This hormone regulates levels of calcium by promoting the absorption of dietary calcium in the intestines, which increases the level of calcium in the blood. Calcitriol also stimulates osteoclasts to break down bone, which moves calcium into the blood. When blood calcium is high, the peptide hormone **calcitonin** is secreted by the parafollicular cells of the thyroid gland. Calcitonin inhibits the activity of osteoclasts, and stimulates the activity of bone-forming osteoblasts. When blood calcium is low, parathyroid glands secrete a peptide hormone known as **parathyroid hormone (PTH)**. This increases the quantity and also the activity of osteoclasts.

Calcium regulation

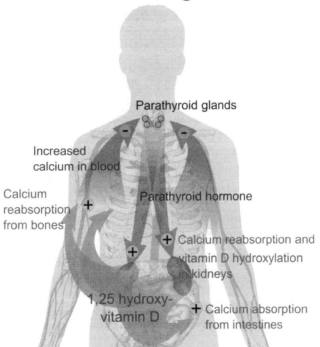

SKELETAL STRUCTURE

Bones can be classified as long, short, flat, irregular, and sesamoid. **Long bones** function primarily in movement and supporting body weight. They are rod shaped, and are longer than they are wide. The extremities of a long bone (**epiphyses**) are covered in articular cartilage, and they are wider than the shaft (**diaphysis**). Most of the bones of the upper and lower limbs are long bones, as are the collar bones. **Short bones** are roundish or cube-shaped. They have little to no role in movement, and instead function in support and stability. Examples of short bones include the carpals and tarsals of the wrist and ankle, respectively. **Flat bones** are flattened, thin bones that are usually curved. Their broad shape is suited for protection, as well as muscle attachment. The scapulae, sternum, ribs, ilia of the pelvic girdle, and certain cranial bones are all flat bones. **Irregular bones** have complex shapes that do not fit the classifications above, and their form is suited to their function. Examples of irregular bones include the vertebrae and many facial bones. **Sesamoid bones**, such as the kneecap, are found embedded in tendons where there is considerable mechanical stress.

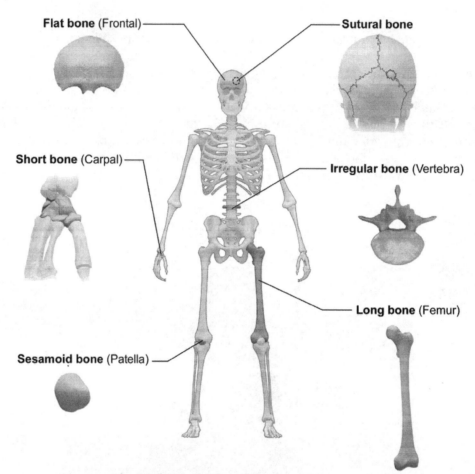

Classification of Bones by Shape

JOINT STRUCTURES

Joints are the locations where two or more elements of the skeleton connect. They can be classified according to range of motion, as well as the material that holds the joint together.

Functional classification:

Type of Joint	Description/Range of Motion	Examples
Synarthrosis	Immovable—either fibrous or cartilaginous	Skull sutures, teeth/mandible
Amphiarthrosis	Slight range of motion—either fibrous or cartilaginous	Intervertebral discs, distal tibiofibular joint
Diarthrosis	Moves freely—always synovial	Wrist, knee, shoulder

Structural classification:

Type of Joint	Material	Types	Examples
Fibrous	Held together by fibrous connective tissue	**Suture**: immovable	skull
		Gomphosis: immovable	teeth/mandible
		Syndesmosis: slightly movable	distal tibiofibular joint
Cartilaginous	Held together by cartilage	**Synchondrosis**: hyaline cartilage, nearly immovable	first rib/sternum
		Symphysis: fibrocartilage, slightly movable	intervertebral discs, pubic symphysis
Synovial	The most common type of joint; characterized by a joint cavity filled with synovial fluid	**Pivot**: allows rotation	atlantoaxial joint
		Hinge: allows movement in one plane	knee
		Saddle: allows pivoting in two planes and axial rotation	first metacarpal/ trapezium
		Gliding: allows sliding	carpals
		Condyloid: allows pivoting in two planes but no axial rotation	radiocarpal joint
		Ball-and-socket: highest range of motion	hip

BONE STRUCTURE

Compact (or cortical) bone is the hard, dense tissue that forms the outer surfaces of bones, as well as the shafts of long bones. It consists of cylindrical structures called **osteons**, also called Haversian systems. Each osteon consists of a central **Haversian canal** that contains nerve fibers and blood vessels, and these canals connect to each other via **perforating canals** (or **Volkmann's canals**). The Haversian canal is surrounded by concentric layers of calcified **lamellae** with small spaces called **lacunae**, each of which contains an **osteocyte**. Tiny channels called **canaliculi** connect the lacunae to allow oxygen and nutrients to reach the osteocytes, and wastes to be removed.

Spongy (or cancellous) bone is the porous tissue found at the ends of long bones and inside the vertebrae and flat bones. It is not as strong or abundant as compact bone, and does not contain osteons. Instead, it consists of flattened, interconnected plates called **trabeculae**. Within the spaces of the trabeculae is the **red bone marrow** that produces blood cells. There are no central canals, but osteocytes do reside in lacunae that are connected by canaliculi.

Compact Bone & Spongy (Cancellous Bone)

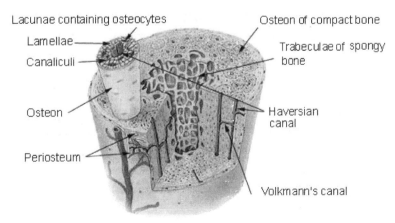

173

<u>CELLULAR COMPOSITION OF BONE</u>

Bone consists of an extracellular matrix that surrounds bone cells and functions much like reinforced concrete. The matrix consists of about 2/3 inorganic matter; mostly calcium phosphate (hydroxyapatite) with calcium carbonate and other minerals. The organic portion makes up about 1/3 of the matrix. It consists mainly of collagen, which adds strength and flexibility to the matrix, as well as ground substance proteins such as glycosaminoglycans (GAGs).

There are three types of bone cells. **Osteoblasts** (derived from osteoprogenitor cells) take calcium from the blood, and produce the matrix (including collagen fibers) that forms bone. When it is completely encased in matrix, the osteoblast differentiates into a mature bone cell called an **osteocyte**. Osteocytes are the most abundant bone cells, and they maintain the matrix by recycling calcium salts. **Osteoclasts** are large multinucleate cells that are formed by the fusion of monocytes (large white blood cells). They reside on bone surfaces and secrete acid and digestive enzymes that break down bone and return calcium to the blood.

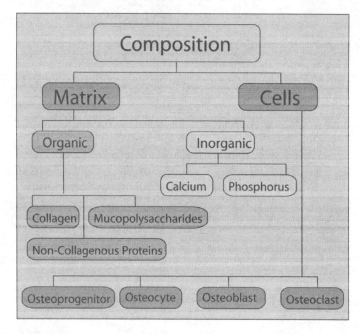

<u>ENDOSKELETON VS. EXOSKELETON</u>

An **endoskeleton** is an internal framework that supports an organism. It is derived mainly from the mesoderm, and produces bone and cartilage. Bones are made mostly of calcium and phosphorus, but they are still living tissues with various types of cells and a blood supply. An endoskeleton grows as the body grows, and is able to support a large body size.

An **exoskeleton** is a nonliving outer covering that encloses an organism. It is derived from the ectoderm, and can produce a chitinous cuticle (as seen in insects and arthropods) or calcified shells (as seen in oysters or snails), though shells are not considered "true" exoskeletons. A chitinous exoskeleton does not grow with the body, and must be shed so that a larger one can be made. These hardened coverings protect the softer living tissues that they enclose.

CARTILAGE: STRUCTURE AND FUNCTION

Cartilage is a connective tissue with a matrix that is flexible yet resistant to stretching. Cartilage is not innervated, nor does it have a blood supply, except for the **perichondrium** that forms the surfaces of nearly all cartilage. The immature cartilage cells that secrete the matrix are called **chondroblasts**. Chondroblasts give rise to mature cells called **chondrocytes** that reside in lacunae.

There are three types of cartilage: hyaline, elastic, and fibrocartilage. **Hyaline cartilage** is the most common cartilage in the body. It consists of evenly distributed collagen fibrils that explain its glassy appearance. It is found in locations that require strong support with some pliability, such as the ribs, nose, trachea, and articular surfaces. **Elastic cartilage** is similar to hyaline cartilage but is more flexible due to the presence of elastic fibers. It is found in the epiglottis and external ear. **Fibrocartilage** has collagen arranged into thick fibers, which allows it to withstand tension and compression. It is found in the jaw, in the knee, and between the vertebrae.

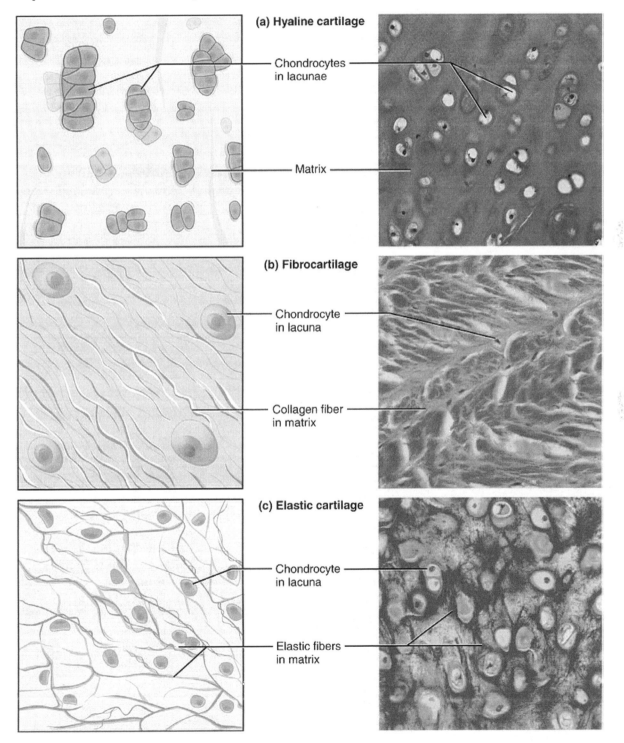

(a) Hyaline cartilage

Chondrocytes in lacunae

Matrix

(b) Fibrocartilage

Chondrocyte in lacuna

Collagen fiber in matrix

(c) Elastic cartilage

Chondrocyte in lacuna

Elastic fibers in matrix

LIGAMENTS, TENDONS

Ligaments connect bones to bones, and help to stabilize joints. **Tendons** connect muscles to bones or other structures such as the eyeballs, and facilitate movement. They are both composed of **dense regular connective tissue**, which consists of bundles of collagen fibers as well as elastic fibers. This gives them strength and resistance to stretching. The collagen fibers of tendons are more densely packed than those of ligaments. They are also arranged in parallel bundles, while the fibers of many ligaments are not. Tendons are tougher, but ligaments are more elastic. The yellowish color of certain ligaments results from the protein elastin.

INTEGUMENTARY SYSTEM

STRUCTURE

The types of cells found in the epidermis and dermis:

Cell Type	Location	Description
Keratinocytes	Epidermis	The most common type of cell in the epidermis Arise from stem cells in the stratum basale They flatten and die as they move toward the surface of the skin Produce keratin—a fibrous protein that hardens the cell and helps make the skin water resistant
Melanocytes	Epidermis	Produces melanin—a pigment that gives skin its color and protects against UV radiation
Langerhans cells	Epidermis	Antigen-presenting cells of the immune system (phagocytes) More common in the stratum spinosum than in any other layer of the epidermis
Merkel cells	Epidermis	Cutaneous receptors, detect light touch Located in the stratum basale
Fibroblasts	Dermis	Secrete collagen, elastin, glycosaminoglycans, and other components of the extracellular matrix
Adipocytes	Dermis	Fat cells
Macrophages	Dermis	Phagocytic cells that engulf potential pathogens
Mast cells	Dermis	Antigen-presenting cells that play a role in the inflammatory response (release histamine)

The **epidermis** is the outermost layer of skin. The keratinocytes of the stratum basale are the stem cells of the epidermis. The give rise to cells that differentiate as they move toward the surface.

The **stratum basale** is the deepest layer of the epidermis. It usually contains just a single layer of cuboidal or columnar cells that adhere to the basement membrane. These are the most nourished cells because they are closest to the capillaries of the dermis. The **stratum spinosum** consists of eight to ten layers of spiny cells that are connected by structures called **desmosomes**. There is limited mitotic activity in the deeper portion of this layer. The **stratum granulosum** consists of two to five layers of slightly flattened cells containing granules of keratohyalin. The cells in the superficial portion of this layer lose their nuclei. The **stratum lucidum** consists of two to five layers of dead, flattened keratinocytes, and is only present in the palms and the soles of feet. These cells contain **eleiden**—a translucent, water-resistant protein derived from keratohyalin. The **stratum**

corneum is the most superficial layer, and it consists of 15 to 30 layers of dead, keratin-containing squamous cells. This layer helps to prevent water loss from the body.

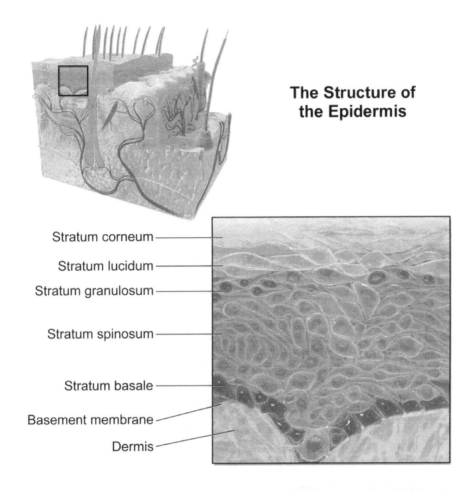

The Structure of the Epidermis

Stratum corneum
Stratum lucidum
Stratum granulosum
Stratum spinosum
Stratum basale
Basement membrane
Dermis

FUNCTIONS IN HOMEOSTASIS AND OSMOREGULATION

The skin functions in homeostasis in a variety of ways. Different types of *sensory receptors* in the skin can detect touch, pressure, temperature, and pain. This system allows the body to sense changes in the environment and to respond appropriately. As a *physical barrier*, the skin can prevent infectious microbes or harmful substances from entering the body. (Pathogens that do manage to enter are subject to a second line of defense: macrophages and other cells of the immune system.) The skin also helps to shield the body from ultraviolet radiation. When the body is exposed to the sun, melanocytes respond by increasing the production of melanin. The integumentary system has many mechanisms for *thermoregulation*, including vasoconstriction and vasodilation of superficial capillaries, and sweating and evaporation. While the skin is not the primary organ involved in *osmoregulation*, it does play an important role. The skin helps prevent water loss from the underlying tissues, as well as the excessive uptake of water from outside the body. It also excretes salts and metabolic wastes such as urea and ammonia through sweat. The ducts of eccrine sweat glands reabsorb many of the sodium ions before they are lost during perspiration.

FUNCTIONS IN THERMOREGULATION

HAIR, ERECTILE MUSCULATURE AND FAT LAYER FOR INSULATION

When the body is cold, it responds by contracting a small smooth muscle in the dermis called the **arrector pili**. This muscle pulls on the hair follicle, causing the hair to stand erect. When many hairs stand up simultaneously, it helps to trap a warm layer of air which has an insulating effect. However, this effect may be minimal in humans.

A better insulator comes in the form of adipose tissue. Beneath the dermis is a layer of subcutaneous tissue known as the **hypodermis** (which is considered separate from the skin). It helps to anchor the skin to the underlying organs, and consists mainly of loose connective tissue, specifically adipose tissue. This layer of fat cells provides insulation from heat and cold.

SWEAT GLANDS, LOCATION IN DERMIS

There are two types of sweat glands (also called sudoriferous glands) in the body: eccrine glands and apocrine glands. The secretory portion of these glands lies in the dermis. Apocrine sweat glands tend to lie deeper in the dermis than eccrine sweat glands because eccrine sweat glands secrete sweat directly onto the skin, while the ducts of apocrine glands empty into hair follicles. Apocrine sweat glands are found only in certain regions of the body, and their function is not clear; they play no role in thermoregulation. They only activate at the onset of puberty in response to sex hormones. Eccrine glands, however, are found nearly everywhere, and the secretion and evaporation of sweat helps to cool the body. The release of sweat is regulated by the hypothalamus. When body temperature rises above normal, the hypothalamus sends signals telling the eccrine sweat glands to secrete until enough heat has been removed. Hormones play a role in the degree to which the body sweats, which may explain why men sweat more than women.

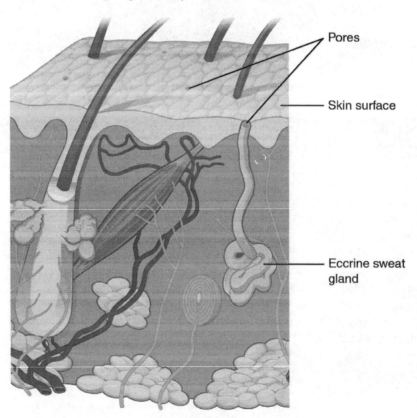

178

VASOCONSTRICTION AND VASODILATION IN SURFACE CAPILLARIES

When body temperature rises, arterioles in the dermis can promote heat loss by dilating in response to signals from the hypothalamus. This allows more blood to enter capillary beds near the surface of the skin, and heat is lost to the surroundings, primarily through radiation. Conduction and convection can also cool the body, assuming the surrounding temperature is cooler than the body. If the body temperature is too low, the adrenal medulla secretes the hormones epinephrine and norepinephrine, which act on the arterioles, causing them to constrict. This reduces the volume of warm blood that flows near the body's surface, minimizing heat loss at the skin surface.

PHYSICAL PROTECTION

NAILS, CALLUSES, HAIR

Nails are dense plates of hardened keratinocytes that protect the distal ends of fingers and toes. Each nail is composed of modified epidermal tissue that grows from the nail matrix. The nail itself does not have sensory receptors, but pressure can still be detected. Nails also aid in the grasping and manipulation of objects, while protecting delicate tissues beneath.

When a region of the skin experiences repeated mechanical abrasion, the stratum basale responds by increasing the rate of mitosis, which soon leads to an overdevelopment of the stratum corneum (hyperkeratosis). The buildup of dead cells forms a protective pad called a callus.

Hair provides a variety of protective functions as well. It shields the scalp from ultraviolet light, and offers some cushioning in case of injury. It also helps to insulate the skull. Hairs of the nostrils, ears, eyebrows, and eyelashes help to trap foreign particles. Hairs can also act as sensory receptors, allowing a quick response to possible injury.

PROTECTION AGAINST ABRASION, DISEASE ORGANISMS

The skin is continually subject to minor abrasions, but it is protected by the keratin-filled cells of the epidermis. The outer cells of the stratum corneum lose their connection to neighboring cells and slough off when exposed to mechanical stress. Keratinocytes, along with glycolipids produced by the stratum granulosum, form a seal that keeps harmful chemicals and pathogenic organisms from entering the body. The secretions of sweat and sebaceous glands mix together on the surface of the skin to form the **acid mantle**. The low pH of these secretions, along with antimicrobial agents and enzymes, helps to prevent infection. There are also beneficial microorganisms that populate the surface of the skin that outcompete harmful microbes. Within the layers of skin are dendritic cells and other white blood cells that are ready to engulf disease-causing organisms.

Developmental Biology

GAMETOGENESIS BY MEIOSIS

Gametogenesis is the process by which diploid germ cells give rise to haploid gametes (sex cells). Germ cells are produced in the early stages of embryogenesis, and migrate from the primitive streak to the gonads where they later undergo meiosis. Germ cells are distinguished from somatic cells because they can undergo both mitosis and meiosis. All other cells are restricted to mitosis, and have no potential to produce gametes. Mitosis is a single division that results in two identical cells, each with the same number of chromosomes as the parent cell. In meiosis, a germ cell undergoes two rounds of cell division (meiosis I and meiosis II). During meiosis I, homologous pairs of chromosomes exchange portions of their DNA before they are separated and distributed independently to daughter cells. These events ensure that the daughter cells are genetically unique, and the chromosome number is cut in half. The steps of meiosis II are similar to those of mitosis, and result in four haploid cells. These cells differentiate to give rise to the mature gametes that fuse during fertilization, restoring the diploid number. The production of ova and sperm is more specifically called oogenesis and spermatogenesis, respectively.

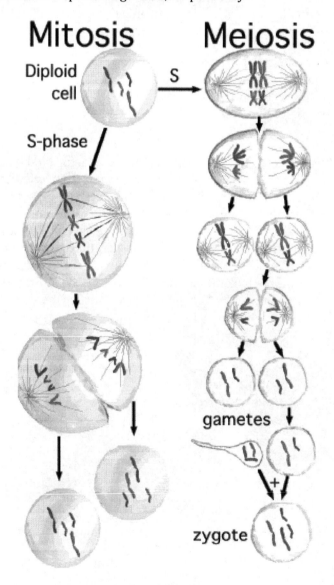

OVUM AND SPERM

Ova and sperm are reproductive cells that are produced during the processes of oogenesis and spermatogenesis, respectively. Both types of gametes are haploid (human eggs and sperm each have 23 chromosomes while somatic cells contain 46), and they originate from a diploid primordial germ cell (PGC). The development from a PGC to a mature gamete can be summarized as follows:

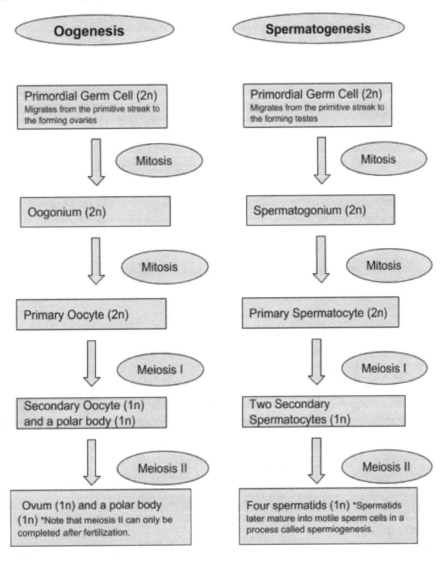

DIFFERENCES IN FORMATION

Both oogenesis and spermatogenesis begin with diploid germ cells. These diploid cells give rise to gametogonia (via mitosis), which develop into primary gametocytes (mitosis), then into secondary gametocytes (meiosis I), and then gametes (meiosis II). The differences between the processes are summarized as follows:

Oogenesis	Spermatogenesis
Nearly the entire process occurs in the ovaries; completion occurs in the oviduct	Occurs entirely in the testes
Only some oogonia develop into oocytes	All spermatogonia become spermatocytes

181

Oogenesis	Spermatogenesis
Oogonia give rise to a finite number of primary oocytes during fetal development	Spermatogonia continually give rise to primary spermatocytes at the onset of puberty (millions per day)
Nucleus does not condense; it is much larger than the nucleus of a sperm cell	Nucleus condenses to help streamline the cell
Meiosis is arrested at prophase I (resumes monthly between puberty and menopause) and arrested again at metaphase II (resumes only if sperm penetrates the secondary oocyte)	Meiosis is continuous
Cells divide unequally to produce one ovum and two or three polar bodies (polar bodies are not viable and break down)	Cells divide equally to produce four spermatids
No gametes released after menopause	Gamete production continues throughout life

DIFFERENCES IN MORPHOLOGY

An ovum is one of the largest human cells. At around 0.1 mm in diameter, it is visible to the naked eye. It is commonly confused with the follicle, a larger structure that houses an oocyte as it matures. The ovum itself is a spherical cell full of nutritional reserves for a developing embryo. The cytoplasm, nucleus, and nucleolus of the ovum are more precisely known as the **ooplasm** (or yolk), **germinal vesicle**, and **germinal spot**, respectively. **Cortical granules** near the plasma membrane help to prevent fertilization by more than one sperm. The ovum is coated in a jelly-like layer of glycoproteins called the **zona pellucida**, which plays a vital role in fertilization by triggering the reactions within a sperm cell that allow it to penetrate the ovum. This protein layer is produced by secretions from both the egg and the surrounding granulosa cells of the follicle known as the **corona radiata**. As the egg matures, the follicle enlarges until it is ejected from the ovary during ovulation.

IN THE IMAGE BELOW:

- *FC* = follicle cells of the corona radiata
- *Y* = yolk (ooplasm)
- *B* = sperm cells
- *Memb* = plasma membrane and zona pellucida
- *N* = nucleus (germinal vesicle)

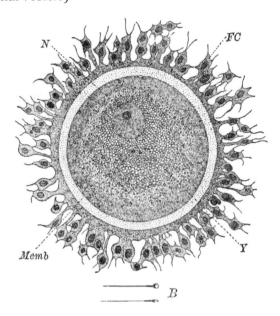

A sperm cell is the smallest of human cells, measuring about 0.05 mm in length. It has three distinct sections: the head, midpiece, and tail; its streamlined form is well suited to its function. The head contains centrioles and a compacted nucleus with tightly coiled DNA. The anterior surface of the head is capped with the **acrosome**, *a* Golgi-derived structure that is packed with enzymes that assist in the penetration of the zona pellucida, and is therefore essential for fertilization. Between 50 and 100 mitochondria spiral around the midpiece, which is the only part of the sperm that contains any mitochondria. The ATP produced by the mitochondria powers the sliding motion of the microtubules within the tail, or **flagellum**, of the sperm, which in turn causes it to undulate. The microtubule-based core of the flagellum is called the **axoneme**, and consists of nine doublets of microtubules arranged around a central pair.

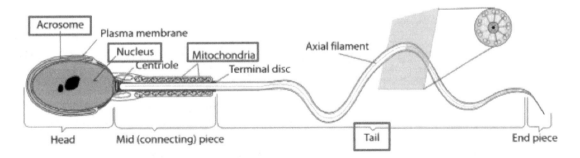

RELATIVE CONTRIBUTION TO NEXT GENERATION

When an oocyte undergoes meiosis and cytokinesis, the cytoplasm divides unequally to produce one large viable ovum. This ensures that nearly all of the resources that are required for the survival of a zygote are present. The ooplasm of the egg contains an abundance of nutrients that will sustain the zygote, and later the daughter cells (blastomeres) that are produced by mitosis. All of the molecules (enzymes, RNA) needed for protein synthesis are present as well. It also contains the organelles, with the exception of the centrioles, which are degraded during oogenesis. These structures are instead donated by the sperm cell. Sperm cells do contain mitochondria, but they are left behind when the midpiece and tail are released from the head during fertilization. Any paternal mitochondria that manage to enter the egg are quickly destroyed, leaving only maternal mitochondria. Each gamete contributes 22 autosomes (non-sex chromosomes) and one sex chromosome to the zygote. The egg always contributes an X chromosome, and the sperm contributes either an X or a Y chromosome.

REPRODUCTIVE SEQUENCE: FERTILIZATION; IMPLANTATION; DEVELOPMENT; BIRTH

Fertilization usually occurs in the fallopian tube within 24 hours of ovulation. Of the hundreds of millions of sperm that are ejaculated, an average of 200 reach the secondary oocyte. When a sperm makes contact with the oocyte, it burrows through the corona radiata and binds to receptor proteins in the zona pellucida. The acrosome releases enzymes that allow the sperm to pass through the zona pellucida to the membrane of the oocyte. Here, actin filaments extend from the sperm to form a tubular structure called the acrosomal apparatus through which its pronucleus is passed. (The midpiece and tail are left behind.) Entry of the pronucleus stimulates the cortical reaction; enzymes from cortical granules beneath the membrane of the oocyte diffuse into the zona pellucida, causing it to harden, and preventing fertilization by more than one sperm. Another block to polyspermy is the depolarization of the oocyte membrane that occurs in response to calcium ions that are released when the sperm meets the membrane. The oocyte then divides unequally by meiosis II to produce an ovum and a nonviable polar body. The pronucleus of the sperm fuses with the pronucleus of the ovum, and a zygote (fertilized egg) is formed.

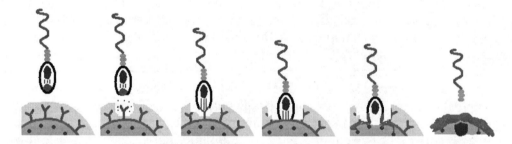

After fertilization, the zygote develops into a cluster of cells called a **morula**. The morula is pushed from the fallopian tube to the uterine cavity by peristalsis (muscle contractions) and the wave-like motions of cilia. It floats freely in the uterus for around 3 days, using uterine secretions as nourishment. The cells of the morula begin to differentiate and give rise to a blastocyst with a fluid-filled cavity and two types of cells. The inner cell mass will give rise to the embryo, and the outer trophoblasts develop into the placenta. Degeneration of the zona pellucida, followed by "zona hatching", occurs around six days after fertilization in preparation for implantation. As this transformation happens, the blastocyst secretes human chorionic gonadotropin (hCG) which stimulates the production of other hormones. These hormones help to maintain the corpus luteum (preventing menses) and prepare the endometrium for implantation. About one week after ovulation, the blastocyst (now over 200 cells) attaches to the endometrium, and outer cells of the trophoblast fuse to form large multinucleated syncytiotrophoblasts that extend like fingers (called chorionic villi) into the endometrium. Fetal blood vessels form inside these villi. About two weeks after fertilization, the blastocyst is fully implanted, and the endometrium is now called the decidua (the maternal contribution to the placenta).

During the pre-embryonic stage of development, the zygote undergoes **cleavage**, dividing mitotically to form a morula. The morula continues to divide and differentiate into a fluid-filled blastocyst. The blastocyst implants in the uterine wall, and the embryonic stage of development commences. During **gastrulation**, the cells of the embryo are reorganized to form the embryonic germ layers (ectoderm, mesoderm, and endoderm) that will produce the tissues and organs of the embryo. A neural plate derived from the ectoderm invades the mesoderm to form the neural tube in a process called **neurulation**. **Organogenesis** continues with the development of a rudimentary heart that beats at around the third week. The digestive system and other internal organs form, as well as the placenta and umbilical cord. By the end of eight weeks, the organ systems have formed and the embryo is now a fetus. During the fetal stage, development continues with the differentiation of the reproductive organs, coordinated movements of limbs, ossification of bones, and an increase of subcutaneous fat. Birth normally occurs around 40 weeks post fertilization.

The fetus must adapt quickly as it transitions from an intrauterine environment to an extrauterine environment. This transition is facilitated by hormones, notably cortisol and catecholamines. Before birth, the neonate relies on oxygen from the mother's blood, and its lungs are collapsed and fluid-filled. As labor approaches, the secretion of fluid from the fetal lungs decreases, while reabsorption increases. At birth, the lungs fill with air and the rest of the fluid leaves the lungs. This first breath triggers critical circulatory changes. Pulmonary resistance decreases, pulmonary blood flow increases, and the shunts that cause the blood to bypass the lungs and liver close or constrict. (The **foramen ovale** that bypasses the lungs closes at first breath. The **ductus arteriosus**, which also bypasses the lungs, and the **ductus venosus** that bypasses the liver, both constrict at birth and close soon after.) The neonate will no longer receive nourishment from the placenta, and will rely on mother's milk and stores of glycogen in the liver. The neonate must also expend energy to keep warm, and so increases its metabolic rate through muscle movements and the burning of brown fat.

EMBRYOGENESIS

FERTILIZATION AND CLEAVAGE

Fertilization is the fusion of a sperm and egg to create a zygote. The zygote prepares for the first mitotic division by replicating the maternal and paternal chromosomes, but does not increase in volume. Approximately thirty hours after fertilization, the zygote splits to form a two-celled embryo. These cells are called blastocysts. The cleavage process is holoblastic, meaning the division is complete (as opposed to meroblastic, or partial cleavage). These cells continue to divide rapidly. Initially, all cells divide simultaneously, but after several divisions they begin to divide independently. There is little time for growth between divisions. In fact, the G_1 and G_2 phases of the cell cycle are nearly non-existent, and the mulberry-shaped morula is the same size as the original zygote. As this period of rapid division called **cleavage** continues, the blastomeres differentiate and compact to form an inner mass surrounded by the cells of the trophoblast. By day 5, the morula has developed into a blastocyst, which implants in the uterus.

BLASTULA FORMATION

Blastulation is the development of a blastula from a morula. In mammals, a blastula is known as a **blastocyst**. Around three days after fertilization, the cells of the morula begin to compact and differentiate. These pluripotent cells are called **embryoblasts**. As they compact into an inner cell mass, a fluid-filled cavity called a **blastocoel** is formed. An outer ring of cells called the **trophoblast** creates a boundary between the blastocoel and the extracellular environment. As the blastocyst develops, the zona pellucida that once protected the egg and aided in fertilization is broken down, and the trophoblasts divide and differentiate. The inner trophoblast cells, called **cytotrophoblasts**, fuse to give rise to an outer layer of **syncytiotrophoblasts**, which form the outer portion of the **placenta**. The embryoblasts continue to differentiate as they separate from the trophoblast to form a disc of tissue that separates the blastocoel from the newly formed amniotic cavity. This **bilaminar disc** consists of two layers: the **epiblast** that is exposed to the amniotic cavity, and the **hypoblast** that is exposed to the blastocoel. The epiblasts migrate, lining the amniotic cavity to begin the formation of the amnion. The hypoblasts migrate as well, lining the blastocoel, which becomes a primitive yolk sac. The yolk sac provides nourishment to the embryo until the placenta takes over.

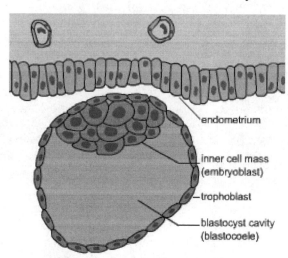

GASTRULATION: FIRST CELL MOVEMENTS

Gastrulation is the process by which the cells of an embryo are reorganized into a multi-layered gastrula. Most animals form three germ layers during gastrulation: the endoderm, mesoderm, and ectoderm. The coordinated movements of cells are under the control of signaling pathways, and the timing and pattern varies from species to species. Some common types of cell movements include:

- **Invagination** - the folding of a sheet of cells to form a pouch
- **Ingression** - the breaking away and migration of cells
- **Involution** - the rolling of a sheet of cells to form another layer
- **Epiboly** - the spreading out of cells to form a thinner layer
- **Delamination** - the splitting of one sheet of cells into two separate populations
- **Intercalation** - the rearrangement of cells from different layers to form a single layer

GASTRULATION: FORMATION OF PRIMARY GERM LAYERS (ENDODERM, MESODERM, ECTODERM)

In humans, three distinct germ layers are established in the third week of development, and it begins with the formation of the **primitive streak** on day 15. Signaling pathways trigger the coordinated movements of cells along the midline of the epiblast, defining the left and right parts of the embryo. A furrow called the **primitive groove** appears as the epiblast cells divide rapidly - more rapidly than the hypoblast cells. This causes the epiblast layer of the bilaminar disc to invaginate, and the cells begin to detach and migrate into the hypoblast. At day 16, nearly all the cells of the hypoblast layer are displaced, and there is now a layer of cells between the epiblast and hypoblast layer called the **mesoderm**. The remaining cells of the epiblast gives rise to the **ectoderm**, and the hypoblast cells give rise to the **endoderm**, forming a trilaminar embryo. The rearrangement and migration of cells also drives the formation of four extraembryonic membranes: the amnion, chorion, yolk sac, and allantois.

NEURULATION

Neurulation describes the early stages of the formation of the nervous system. It begins in the third week of development with the differentiation of cells within the mesoderm. These cells form a rod-like structure called a **notochord** that runs along the length of the embryo within the mesoderm layer. This flexible structure induces a change in the ectoderm, causing it thicken into a **neural plate**, which invaginates into the mesoderm layer. This **neural groove** deepens until the ridges on each side (**neural folds**) make contact with each other and form a cylindrical structure called the **neural tube**. This tube will later develop into the central nervous system (brain and spinal cord). **Neural crest cells** that were once at the "crest" of each neural fold break away, and will develop into the peripheral nervous system, as well as other important tissues. Neurulation (and early embryogenesis) is finished when the entire length of the neural tube is closed. Failure of the neural tube to close completely results in a disease called spina bifida.

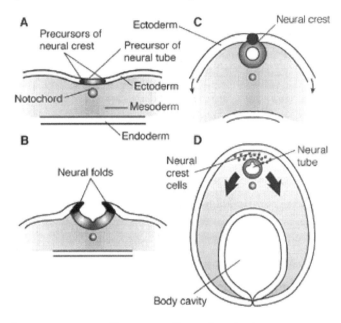

MAJOR STRUCTURES ARISING OUT OF PRIMARY GERM LAYERS

Each germ layer that forms during gastrulation contributes to specific structures and systems within the body, as described in the table below:

Primary Germ Layer	Important Derivatives
Endoderm (innermost layer)	epithelial lining of the digestive system, liver, and pancreas (excluding mouth and anus) epithelial lining of the respiratory system (excluding nasal passageways) thymus, thyroid, and parathyroid glands of the endocrine system bladder and distal urinary tract of the urinary system
Mesoderm (middle layer)	the muscular system the cardiovascular system the lymphatic system the skeletal system connective tissues of the digestive and respiratory tract dermis gonads adrenal cortex

Primary Germ Layer	Important Derivatives
Ectoderm (outermost layer)	central and peripheral nervous system epidermis and its appendages (hair, hair follicles, sweat glands, sebaceous glands) epithelial lining of the mouth, salivary glands, nasal passageways, and anus tooth enamel and dentin some skeletal elements of the jaw pituitary gland, and adrenal medulla

NEURAL CREST

Neural crest cells develop along the crests of the neural folds that arise during neurulation. When the neural tube closes, they can be found along the border of the ectoderm and neural plate (dorsal aspect). The non-neural ectoderm, neural plate, and mesoderm collectively induce the formation of these cells through a variety of signaling pathways. An important characteristic of neural crest cells is their capacity to migrate to distant locations in the body. Despite their origins in the ectoderm, these multipotent cells are sometimes called the fourth germ layer because of the many structures that they form. Neural crest cells give rise to the peripheral nervous system, including sensory ganglia, sympathetic and parasympathetic ganglia, and Schwann cells. They also contribute to other organ systems-producing the adrenal medulla, calcitonin-secreting thyroid cells, melanocytes, dentin of the tooth, smooth muscle cells, facial cartilage and bones, and a variety of other connective tissues.

ENVIRONMENT—GENE INTERACTION IN DEVELOPMENT

The development of an embryo results from complex interactions between genes and the environment. Embryogenesis is a period of accelerated gene expression that mediates the differentiation of cells, and the formation of the organ systems. Cell-cell communication, activation of transcription factors, methylation of DNA, and acetylation of histone proteins all play a role in development, and any errors in these processes can have serious consequences. Teratogens are agents that cause developmental aberrations, often by altering gene expression, which in turn may induce apoptosis or block the migration of cells. For example, high doses of vitamin A are known to interfere with the Hox genes that control the basic body plan, which disrupts the migration of neural crest cells. Other teratogenic agents include radiation, alcohol, drugs, chemicals, viruses, and bacteria.

MECHANISMS OF DEVELOPMENT

CELL SPECIALIZATION

Cell specialization is the process by which an immature cell develops into a cell with a specific form and function. The fate of a cell is determined largely by cues from surrounding tissues, and these cues drive gene expression. Cells destined to be a part of the same tissue coordinate their activities and give rise to properties not seen at the cellular level. Specialization consists of two main phases: determination and differentiation. A **determined** cell has no detectable morphological differences as compared to its derivative, but it is irreversibly committed to becoming a certain type of cell. A **differentiated** cell has specific structural characteristics (such as size and shape) and functional characteristics (such as responsiveness to signals, membrane potential, and metabolic activities). Such specialization arises not from modifications in the genome, but from selective gene expression.

DETERMINATION

Cell determination is the irreversible commitment of a cell to follow a specialized course of development. It is preceded by a less restrictive phase called specification. A **specified** cell can still be influenced by its surroundings, and its fate reversed or changed. **Determined** cells will not stray from their fates, even when placed in a foreign region of the embryo.

Determination can occur as a result of the asymmetric distribution of cytoplasmic molecules that mediate gene expression (such as transcription factors and the mRNA molecules that code for them) during cleavage. One of the daughter cells remains a stem cell, while the cell with the cytoplasmic determinants becomes committed to a specific lineage. Determination can also be caused by an external influence. Inductive signaling molecules called morphogens are secreted by nearby cells, and create a gradient as they diffuse across the tissues of the embryo. The response elicited by the cells that they act on is dependent on the concentration of the morphogen. Cells exposed to a high concentration will have a different fate than those exposed to a lower concentration. Only after a cell is determined will it begin the process of differentiation.

DIFFERENTIATION

Differentiation refers to the biochemical, structural, and functional changes that a cell undergoes as it matures into a cell with a clearly defined role. This transition from a determined cell to a specialized cell occurs as a result of differential gene expression, which in turn is driven by transcription factors. The least differentiated cells are referred to as **totipotent**, and they have the capacity to differentiate into any type of cell, including cells of the embryo and placenta. The only human totipotent cells are the zygote itself and the cells that arise in the first few divisions. Cells that give rise to the primary germ layers are **pluripotent**, because they have the capacity to form all cell types except the trophoblasts that give rise to placental structures. **Multipotent** cells are more specialized. They can still differentiate, but have limited options. Umbilical cord stem cells and the hematopoietic stem cells that give rise to blood cells are multipotent. **Oligopotent** cells are even more restricted, and finally **unipotent** cells can only produce one type of cell. It is uncertain if true unipotent cells exist.

TISSUE TYPES

Differentiation of the inner cell mass of the blastocyst produces the primary germ layers that ultimately give rise to four main tissue types: epithelial, connective, muscle, and nervous. Tissues are organized groups of cells that coordinate their activities to accomplish a specific function. The role of a tissue is mainly determined by the types of cells it contains, the arrangement and orientation of those cells, and the regulation of cell division and apoptosis.

Epithelial tissues consist of tightly packed cells that cover and line surfaces such as the skin and body cavities. These tissues are specialized for protection, secretion, absorption, and filtration. **Connective** tissues are characterized by an acellular matrix that surrounds the cells. They are the most abundant tissues in the human body, and function to support, protect, and connect body parts. Examples include bone, cartilage, adipose, and blood tissue. **Muscle** tissues, which include smooth, cardiac, and skeletal, contract to produce movement. **Nervous** tissue receives and responds to stimuli. It is composed of neurons that generate and conduct electrical impulses, and the glial cells that support them.

CELL–CELL COMMUNICATION IN DEVELOPMENT

Cell-cell communication is crucial for the proper development of an embryo. When cells are "competent" they are able to receive signals from adjacent or nearby cells, inducing them to become a certain type of cell. (Competence is not a permanent state, and may change during the course of development.) A developing cell may also secrete inducing factors of its own. Cells that secrete signal molecules are called **inducers**, and cells that differentiate in response to those signals are called **responders**. Most of these signals are growth factors that only act on cells of a specific tissue. **Autocrine** signals are self-generated; they act on the same cell that secreted them. **Paracrine** signals diffuse to cells in close proximity. **Endocrine** signals enter the blood and travel to distant tissues. **Juxtacrine** signals require direct contact between cells. When the contact is made, signals from one cell bind to the receptors of another. Sometimes, two different tissues respond to each other's signals, promoting differentiation in each other. This is called reciprocal induction.

CELL MIGRATION

Cell migration is required for normal embryonic development; it begins during gastrulation and continues throughout life. Any errors in the migration pathway can lead to malformations, diseases, or even demise of the embryo. Migration is initiated by signaling molecules that trigger the detachment of cells from their substrate. The cell polarizes to define a leading edge, while actin filaments of the cytoskeleton polymerize to push the cell forward in a crawling motion. Rearrangement of the cytoskeleton forms flat, sheet-like projections called **lamellipodia** at the leading edge. Sometimes, finger-like projections called **filopodia** extend beyond the lamellipodia in the direction of motion. Contraction of the cell occurs when actin interacts with myosin. Chemical messengers continually influence the direction and rate of motion, ensuring that cells reach the intended site in the body at the right time. Some cells migrate individually, while others (such as epithelial and mesenchymal cells) migrate collectively.

PLURIPOTENCY: STEM CELLS

Potency describes the ability of a cell to differentiate. Only totipotent cells (the zygote and cells that arise after the first few divisions) have complete potency, but pluripotent stem cells still have great differentiation potential. They can develop into any cell type, with the exception of placental cells. As the zygote and subsequent blastomeres undergo cleavage, the once totipotent cells give rise to two lineages: the cells of the trophoblast, and the embryonic stem cells that give rise to the primary germ layers (the ectoderm, mesoderm, and endoderm). All of the hundreds of types of human cells stem from these germ layers—however, pluripotent cells cannot form an entire organism because they can't produce the needed placental tissues.

Because of the malleability of pluripotent cells, they can used therapeutically in the treatment of various diseases. Researchers have identified ways to reprogram somatic cells in a way that reverses the differentiation process. These induced pluripotent stem cells, or iPS cells, provide an alternative to the harvesting of stem cells from an embryo.

GENE REGULATION IN DEVELOPMENT

Differential gene expression is the mechanism for cell specialization and ultimately the development of an organism. Many factors collectively determine which genes are expressed and *when* they are expressed. In cell-cell communication, target cells detect and respond to signals (such as growth factors) released by other cells. When a signaling molecule binds to a membrane receptor, it causes a conformational change in the receptor. The signal transduction pathway continues with the phosphorylation of cytoplasmic proteins, which leads to the activation of transcription factors. Transcription factors bind to DNA and either promote or suppress gene expression.

Other strategies exist to regulate gene expression as well. **Epigenetic regulation** involves the methylation of DNA and modification of the histone proteins that it wraps around. These heritable modifications alter the structure of the chromosome. (Regions of DNA that are more condensed are less accessible to RNA polymerase.)

Regulation continues beyond the level of transcription. For example, coding regions (exons) of messenger RNA can be spliced together in different orders to produce different proteins from the same transcript. The proteins that are produced during translation may also require activation at a later time.

PROGRAMMED CELL DEATH

Programmed cell death, or apoptosis, is an important part of embryonic development. It is induced by signals that activate proteases called caspases. Caspases cleave certain cytoplasmic proteins, setting a series of events in motion. The cell shrinks and loses its anchorage to adjacent cells. Chromatin condenses as the cell membrane bulges out into protrusions called blebs. The DNA and organelles are broken down into fragments, and the blebs break free of the cell, taking a portion of the cytoplasm with them. The blebs, now called apoptotic bodies, are engulfed and digested by phagocytic cells. No intracellular components leak out during this process (unlike necrosis, in which an injured cell releases its contents into the surroundings).

This regulated process is used to eliminate abnormal, mispositioned, or misplaced cells. It also helps to sculpt certain structures. For example, many of the precursors to neural cells are eliminated in order to create a more direct pathway for electrical impulses. Apoptosis also helps to shape the hands and feet. If the process is incomplete, toes or fingers may be fused in a condition known as syndactyly. Sometimes, apoptosis occurs as a result of teratogenic agents, leading to malformations or fetal death.

Evolution, Ecology, and Behavior

EVOLUTION

Charles Darwin's theory of evolution is the unifying concept in biology today. From 1831 to 1836, Darwin traveled as a naturalist on a five-year voyage on the *H.M.S. Beagle* around the tip of South America and to the Galápagos Islands. He studied finches, took copious amounts of meticulous notes, and collected thousands of plant and animal specimens. He collected 13 species of finches each with a unique bill for a distinct food source, which led him to believe, due to similarities between the finches, that the finches shared a common ancestor. The similarities and differences of fossils of extinct rodents and modern mammal fossils led him to believe that the mammals had changed over time. Darwin believed that these changes were the result of random genetic changes called mutations. He believed that mutations could be beneficial and eventually result in a different organism over time. In 1859, in his first book, *On the Origin of Species*, Darwin proposed that natural selection was the means by which adaptations would arise over time. He coined the term "natural selection" and said that natural selection is the mechanism of evolution. Because variety exists among individuals of a species, he stated that those individuals must compete for the same limited resources. Some would die, and others would survive. According to Darwin, evolution is a slow, gradual process. In 1871, Darwin published his second book, *Descent of Man, and Selection in Relation to Sex*, in which he discussed the evolution of man.

NATURAL SELECTION

Natural selection is the process by which individuals that are better suited to their environment survive and reproduce. It is often described as "survival of the fittest," but this description leaves out a key component: reproduction. Differential reproductive success is a driving force behind evolution, that is, a change in allele frequencies in a population over time. However, it is important to note that it is *phenotypes*, not genotypes, that are selected. For example, deer that carry the allele for albinism have the same phenotype as those that are homozygous dominant. Because both genotypes produce the same phenotype, one will not be selected over the other. But the dominant allele (which is the basis for phenotype) may increase in frequency if brown deer survive and reproduce at greater rates than white deer.

There are certain conditions that must be met for natural selection to occur: heritable variation within the population, reproduction within the population, and changing environmental conditions that lead to pressure.

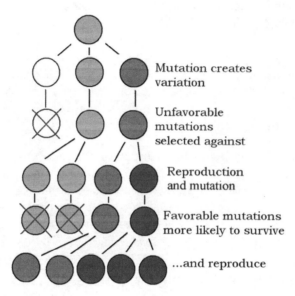

FITNESS CONCEPT

Fitness is a measure of reproductive success. The term is commonly associated with strength, agility, and speed, but *any* heritable trait that increases reproductive success will contribute to fitness. In a hot climate rabbits with oversized ears climate may be more "fit" than those with smaller ears because they can release excess heat more readily, which in turn may allow them to survive and reproduce at greater rates. Even if the long-eared rabbits have shorter life spans, they are still more fit; it is reproductive success alone that determines fitness.

There are two ways of measuring fitness. "Absolute fitness" compares the genotypic ratio before and after selection. However, "relative fitness" is more valuable when looking at natural selection because it measures the *competitive* ability of an allele. In other words, it measures the allele contribution to the next generation *relative* to others. Two forms of a gene may (in an absolute sense) both be favorable, but if one appears in greater frequency in the next generation, then it is the "fitter" of the two. At the level of the organism, an individual that produces more offspring with the favorable inherited trait is more fit than an individual that produces less.

SELECTION BY DIFFERENTIAL REPRODUCTION

Differential reproduction describes the varying degrees of reproductive success that are found in a population. Individuals with a favorable phenotype have a selective advantage; they are more likely to survive and reproduce than individuals who don't share the phenotype. This is called differential reproduction. The more "fit" individuals will produce the most offspring and (assuming the trait is heritable) transmit the alleles that contribute to the desirable phenotype. The traits that are selected by the environment will spread throughout the population, and over time that population will evolve to resemble the members with the greatest reproductive success.

CONCEPTS OF NATURAL AND GROUP SELECTION

Natural selection is normally described as acting at the level of the individual; the classic description is often as follows: "individuals with favorable traits are more likely to survive and reproduce." But it is believed by many that selection can happen at the group level as well. Whereas some argue that individuals act for self-preservation alone, others claim that altruistic behaviors may increase the reproductive success of a group, thereby favoring the fitness of the group over the individual. For example, an individual behaves altruistically when defending the group against a predator. Such action puts the individual at risk but protects the group. Other types of behaviors that may lead to group selection include maternal instincts, cooperative hunting, and predatory alert systems.

EVOLUTIONARY SUCCESS AS INCREASE IN PERCENT REPRESENTATION IN THE GENE POOL OF THE NEXT GENERATION

Evolutionary success is measured by the change in the frequency of an allele in a gene pool. If an allele's frequency in the population increases, then evolutionary success has been achieved. As alleles responsible for beneficial traits spread throughout the population, they may become fixed and lead to adaptation. Natural selection is the nonrandom mechanism by which these allele frequencies change. Members of a population that express a favorable phenotype will be more likely to survive to sexual maturity and pass their genes on to the next generation.

SPECIATION

A species is a group of genetically similar individuals that are able to breed naturally and produce viable and fertile offspring. Speciation is the formation of a new species, and this process occurs through various pathways. Anagenesis is the process by which a species changes as a single group until it is too genetically different from the original species to be considered the same. The new species completely "replaces" the original.

The more common mechanism for speciation is called cladogenesis: the process by which one species diverges into two. Cladogenesis occurs as a result of reproductive isolation. In *allopatric speciation*, the reproductive barrier is a physical separation of a population (geographic isolation). Selection and genetic drift act differently on each subpopulation, and they diverge.

If the population is not geographically isolated, but a subset of the population occupies a new niche, a new species may form in a process called *parapatric speciation*. Rarely a new species may arise from a group that occupies the same niche. This is called *sympatric speciation* and is the result of mutations that stop certain members of the population from breeding.

POLYMORPHISM

Polymorphism describes the existence of two or more alleles at the same locus within a population. Polymorphisms are distinguished from mutations because they are considered "normal" variants and are inherited (they do not arise spontaneously). Their origins, however, can be traced back to a mutation. They are not responsible for traits that have a continuous spectrum of phenotypes, such as height or hair color. Human blood groups are an example of polymorphism because the trait is controlled by a single gene with A, B, and O alleles. If the sequence of DNA at the given locus varies by only one nucleotide, then it is called a single nucleotide polymorphism (SNP). Other polymorphisms arise from deletions, insertions, duplications, and tandem repeats.

ADAPTATION AND SPECIALIZATION

Adaptation is the dynamic process by which a population changes due to natural selection. It can also refer to the result of that process, that is, the inherited feature that increases reproductive success. Adaptations are not always structural traits. Certain behaviors and abilities can be adaptations as long as they are heritable and increase fitness. They also must have arisen by natural selection for the purpose that they currently serve. Feathers, for instance, are not adaptations for flight because their original function was not flight related. Adaptations are also not the result of genetic drift (chance), even if the trait eventually proves advantageous.

Specialization is the use of an adaptation to better fill a specific niche. For example, the different species of finches that inhabit the Galapagos Islands each have a beak shape that is suited to the food sources unique to each island. But the adaptation of a nonvenomous king snake to resemble the venomous coral snake is not an example of specialization because it does not help it better fill a niche.

INBREEDING AND OUTBREEDING

Inbreeding is the mating of relatives, whereas outbreeding is the mating of nonrelatives within a species. Closely related individuals collectively have more similar genetic sequences than members who are less related. Inbreeding will produce a higher proportion of homozygous genotypes than outbreeding because there are comparatively more "like" alleles in a closely related group. Because heterozygosity is reduced, genetic diversity becomes limited. Inbred populations are more likely to express recessive disorders because relatives have a greater chance of being carriers of the same deleterious allele than a group with a robust gene pool. Outbreeding has the opposite effect of inbreeding; heterozygosity increases.

BOTTLENECKS

The bottleneck effect describes a drastic reduction in population size as a result of an environmental event such as a natural disaster, habitat destruction, or overhunting. The remaining population is unlikely to have the same proportion and variety of alleles as the original population. The population may rebound, but its gene pool will be more limited than it was. It is important to note the distinction between bottlenecking and natural selection. The survivors of a bottleneck event survived by chance, not their genetic makeup. As such, there is no improved "fitness," and the new population is unlikely to be better suited to its environment. The random change in allele frequency is known as genetic drift, and bottleneck events increase the effect of this phenomenon.

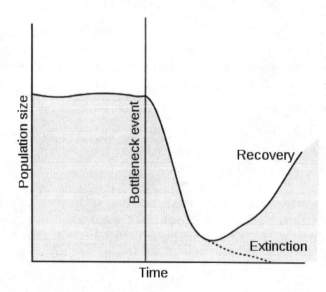

EVOLUTIONARY TIME AS MEASURED BY GRADUAL RANDOM CHANGES IN GENOME

Random mutations that are neutral (not selected by the environment) can be used as "molecular clocks" to estimate when two species diverged. DNA sequences (unless acted on by natural selection) change at a rate that is relatively constant, and therefore the number of base changes is proportional to the amount of time that has passed since a species diverged from the common ancestor.

In reality the rate of mutation is not constant. Different sections of a genome may change at different rates, or natural selection may favor one mutation over another. Nevertheless, the effects can be averaged out to approximate elapsed time. First, the molecular clock is "calibrated" by using an absolute time (as known by a historical event or fossil record) and the mutation rate of a particular gene. Once the number of mutations is graphed as a function of time, the information can be used to give estimated dates of events outside of what is directly measured.

COEVOLUTION

Coevolution describes a rare phenomenon in which two populations with a close ecological relationship undergo reciprocal adaptations simultaneously and evolve together, affecting each other's evolution. General examples of coevolution include predator and prey, or plant and pollinator, and parasites and their hosts. A specific example of coevolution is the yucca moths and the yucca plants. Yucca plants can only be pollinated by the yucca moths. The yucca moths lay their eggs in the yucca flowers, and their larvae grow inside the ovary.

ADAPTIVE RADIATION

Adaptive radiation is an evolutionary process in which a species branches out and adapts and fills numerous unoccupied ecological niches. The adaptations occur relatively quickly, driven by natural selection and resulting in new phenotypes and possibly new species eventually. An example of adaptive radiation is the finches that Darwin studied on the Galápagos Islands. Darwin recorded 13 different varieties of finches, which differed in the size and shape of their beaks. Through the process of natural selection, each type of finch adapted to the specific environment and specifically the food sources of the island to which it belonged. On newly formed islands with many unoccupied ecological niches, the adaptive radiation process occurred quickly due to the lack of competing species and predators.

Review Video: Organic Evolution
Visit mometrix.com/academy and enter code: 108959

EVIDENCE SUPPORTING EVOLUTION

MOLECULAR EVIDENCE

Because all organisms are made up of cells, all organisms are alike on a fundamental level. Cells share similar components, which are made up of molecules. Specifically, all cells contain DNA and RNA. This should indicate that all species descended from a common ancestor. Humans and chimpanzees share approximately 98% of their genes in common, and humans and bacteria share approximately 7% of their genes in common. Humans and zebra fish share approximately 85% of their genes in common. Humans and mustard greens share approximately 15% of their genes in common. Biologists have been able to use DNA sequence comparisons of modern organisms to reconstruct the "root" of the tree of life. The fact that RNA can store information, replicate itself, and code for proteins suggests that RNA could have could have evolved first, followed by DNA.

HOMOLOGY

Homology is the similarity of structures of different species based on a similar structure in a common evolutionary ancestor. The forelimbs of humans, dogs, birds, and whales all have the same basic pattern of the bones. Specifically, all of these organisms have a humerus, radius, and ulna. Tetrapods all have limbs with five digits at some stage in their development. For example, embryonic birds start with limbs with five digits, but adult bird wings have only three digits. They are all modifications of the same basic evolutionary structure from a common ancestor. Tetrapods resemble the fossils of extinct transitional animal called the *Eusthenopteron*. This would seem to indicate that evolution primarily modifies preexisting structures.

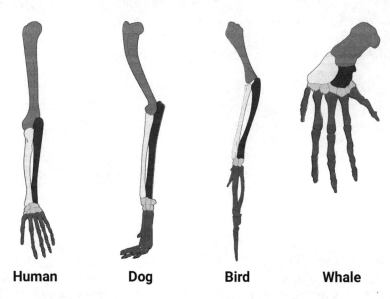

Human   **Dog**   **Bird**   **Whale**

EMBRYOLOGY

The stages of embryonic development reveal homologies between species. These homologies are evidence of a common ancestor. For example, in chicken embryos and mammalian embryos, both include a stage in which slits and arches appear in the embryo's neck region that are strikingly similar to gill slits and gill arches in fish embryos. Adult chickens and adult mammals do not have gills, but this embryonic homology indicates that birds and mammals share a common ancestor with fish. As another example, some species of toothless whales have embryos that initially develop teeth that are later absorbed, which indicates that these whales have an ancestor with teeth in the adult form. Finally, most tetrapods have five-digit limbs, but birds have three-digit limbs in their wings. However, embryonic birds initially have five-digit limbs in their wings, which develop into a three-digit wing. Tetrapods such as reptiles, mammals, and birds all share a common ancestor with five-digit limbs.

ENDOSYMBIOSIS THEORY

The endosymbiosis theory is foundational to evolution. Endosymbiosis provides the path for prokaryotes to give rise to eukaryotes. Specifically, endosymbiosis explains the development of the organelles of mitochondria in animals and chloroplasts in plants. This theory states that some eukaryotic organelles such as mitochondria and chloroplasts originated as free living cells. According to this theory, primitive, heterotrophic eukaryotes engulfed smaller, autotrophic bacteria prokaryotes, but the bacteria were not digested. Instead, the eukaryotes and the bacteria formed a symbiotic relationship. Eventually, the bacteria transformed into mitochondrion or chloroplasts.

<u>SUPPORTING EVIDENCE</u>

Several facts support the endosymbiosis theory. Mitochondria and chloroplasts contain their own DNA and can both only arise from other preexisting mitochondria and chloroplasts. The genomes of mitochondria and chloroplasts consist of single, circular DNA molecules with no histones. This is similar to bacteria genomes, not eukaryote genomes. Also, the RNA, ribosomes, and protein synthesis of mitochondria and chloroplasts are remarkably similar to those of bacteria, and both use oxygen to produce ATP. These organelles have a double phospholipid layer that is typical of engulfed bacteria. This theory also involves a secondary endosymbiosis in which the original eukaryotic cells that have engulfed the bacteria are then engulfed themselves by another free-living eukaryote.

CONVERGENT EVOLUTION

Convergent evolution is the evolutionary process in which two or more unrelated species become increasingly similar in appearance. In convergent evolution, natural selection leads to adaptation in these unrelated species belonging to the same kind of environment. For example, the mammals shown below, although found in different parts of the world, developed similar appearances due to their similar environments.

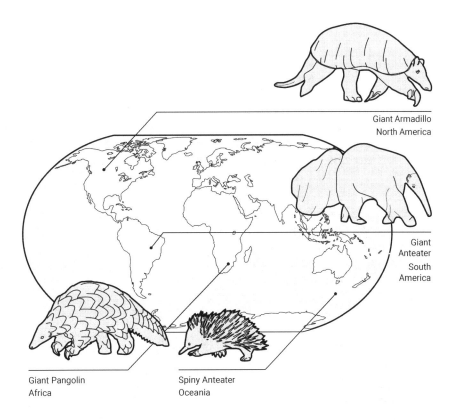

Giant Armadillo
North America

Giant Anteater
South America

Giant Pangolin
Africa

Spiny Anteater
Oceania

DIVERGENT EVOLUTION

Divergent evolution is the evolutionary process in which organisms of one species become increasingly dissimilar in appearance. As several small adaptations occur due to natural selection, the organisms will finally reach a point at which two new species are formed. Then, these two species will further diverge from each other as they continue to evolve. Adaptive radiation is an example of divergent evolution. Another example is the divergent evolution of the wooly mammoth and the modern elephant from a common ancestor.

FOSSIL RECORD

The fossil record provides many types of support for evolution including comparisons from rock layers, transition fossils, and homologies with modern organisms. First, fossils from rock layers from all over the world have been compared, enabling scientists to develop a sequence of life from simple to complex. Based on the fossil record, the geologic timeline chronicles the history of all living things. For example, the fossil record clearly indicates that invertebrates developed before vertebrates and that fish developed before amphibians. Second, numerous transitional fossils have been found. Transitional fossils show an intermediate state between an ancestral form of an organism and the form of its descendants. These fossils show the path of evolutionary change. For example, many transition fossils documenting the evolutionary change from fish to amphibians have been discovered. In 2004, scientists discovered *Tiktaalik roseae*, or the "fishapod," which is a 375-million-year-old fossil that exhibits both fish and amphibian characteristics. For example, scientists have determined that *Pakicetus,* an extinct land mammal, is an early ancestor of modern whales and dolphins based on the specialized structures of the inner ear. Most fossils exhibit homologies with modern organisms. For example, extinct horses are similar to modern horses, indicating a common ancestor.

CEPHALIZATION

Two major evolutionary trends are cephalization and multicellularity. Cephalization is the evolutionary trend that can be summarized as "the evolution of the head." In most animals, nerve tissue has been concentrated into a brain at one end of an organism over many generations. Eventually, a head enclosing a brain and housing sensory organs was produced at one end of the organism. Many invertebrates, such as arthropods and annelids and all vertebrates, have undergone cephalization. However, some invertebrates, such as echinoderms and sponges, have not undergone cephalization, and these organisms literally do not have a head.

MULTICELLULARITY

Another evolutionary trend is multicellularity. Life has evolved from simple, single-celled organisms to complex, multicellular organisms. Over millions of years, single-celled organisms gave rise to biofilms, which gave rise to multicellular organisms, which gave rise to all of the major phyla of multicellular organisms present today..

MODELS OF EVOLUTIONARY RATES

GRADUALISM

Gradualism is a model of evolutionary rates that states that evolutionary changes occurred slowly or gradually by a divergence of lineages due largely to natural selection. These accumulated changes occurred over millions of years. Many transitional forms occurred between ancestors and modern descendants. Although not all of these transitional forms were preserved in the fossil record, the fossil record clearly supports gradualism. Many transition fossils show adaptations as organisms evolve. The geologic time scale describes this gradual change from simple to complex organisms over millions of years.

PUNCTUATED EQUILIBRIUM

Punctuated equilibrium is a model of evolutionary rates that states that in some instances, evolutionary changes occurred in relatively short burst that "punctuate" long periods of equilibrium of little or no change. These "short" periods would still consist of hundreds of thousands of years. Most scientists believe that punctuated equilibrium occurred along with

gradualism. The fossil record supports punctuated equilibrium for many organisms. Punctuated equilibrium provides an explanation for the supposed numerous "missing links" in the fossil record. If punctuated equilibrium is validated, then there actually are no missing links.

EXPLANATIONS FOR THE ORIGIN OF LIFE ON EARTH

PANSPERMIA

The word *panspermia* is a Greek work that means "seeds everywhere." Panspermia is one possible explanation for the origin of life on Earth that states that "seeds" of life exist throughout the universe and can be transferred from one location to another. Three types of panspermia based on the seed-dispersal method have been proposed. Lithopanspermia is described as rocks transferring microorganisms between solar systems. Ballistic panspermia is described as rocks transferring microorganisms within a solar system. Directed panspermia is described as intelligent extraterrestrials spreading the seeds to other planets and solar systems. The panspermia hypothesis only proposes the origin of life on Earth. It does not offer an explanation for the origin of life in the universe or explain the origin of the seeds themselves.

ABIOTIC SYNTHESIS OF ORGANIC COMPOUNDS

Scientists have performed sophisticated experiments to determine how the first organic compounds appeared on Earth. First, scientists performed controlled experiments that closely resembled the conditions similar to an early Earth. In the classic Miller–Urey experiment (1953), the Earth's early atmosphere was simulated with water, methane, ammonia, and hydrogen that were stimulated by an electric discharge. The Miller–Urey experiment produced complex organic compounds including several amino acids, sugars, and hydrocarbons. Later experiments by other scientists produced nucleic acids. Recently, Jeffrey Bada, a former student of Miller, was able to produce amino acids in a simulation using the Earth's current atmospheric conditions with the addition of iron and carbonate to the simulation. This is significant because in previous studies using Earth's current atmosphere, the amino acids were destroyed by the nitrites produced by the nitrogen.

ATMOSPHERIC COMPOSITION

The early atmosphere of Earth had little or possibly no oxygen. Early rocks had high levels of iron at their surfaces. Without oxygen, the iron just entered into the early oceans as ions. In the same time frame, early photosynthetic algae were beginning to grow abundantly in the early ocean. During photosynthesis, the algae would produce oxygen gas, which oxidized the iron at the rocks' surfaces, forming an iron oxide. This process basically kept the algae in an oxygen-free environment. As the algae population grew much larger, it eventually produced such a large amount of oxygen that it could not be removed by the iron in the rocks. Because the algae at this time were intolerant to oxygen, the algae became extinct. Over time, a new iron-rich layer of sediments formed, and algae populations reformed, and the cycle began again. This cycle repeated itself for millions of years. Iron-rich layers of sediment alternated with iron-poor layers. Gradually, algae and other life forms evolved that were tolerant to oxygen, stabilizing the oxygen concentration in the atmosphere at levels similar to those of today.

CAUSES OF EXTINCTION OF SPECIES

LACK OF GENETIC DIVERSITY

Genetic diversity provides a mechanism for populations to adapt to changing environments or even human impacts. With a diverse genome, individuals possessing genes making them better suited for the environment are more likely to exist. Without genetic diversity, populations cannot develop adaptations. Populations cannot resist diseases or adapt to changes in the habitat. As the populations of endangered species decrease, genetic diversity decreases even further. Normally, natural selection selects genes that resist diseases or help the organism to adapt to changes in the habitat, but if those genes have drifted out of the population, the population cannot evolve and may become extinct. A small gene pool does not provide much variety for selection. For example, tigers in India are now in danger of extinction. Studies show that more than 90% of the genome has been lost largely due to a period when tigers were heavily killed by British officials and Indian royalty. With fewer than 2,000 tigers in the world and these in small populations, the genetic diversity can continue to decrease, possibly leading to extinction if much effort is not made to preserve the remaining genetic diversity.

ENVIRONMENTAL PRESSURES

A changing environment may lead to the extinction of a species. If an animal has a small tolerance range to food sources and habitat needs or if a population is small, it is less likely to adapt to changes in the environment. Climate change and global warming can affect an ecosystem. Some species may not be able to adapt even to seemingly minor temperature changes especially if their populations are small. Animals needing cooler climates may need to move to cooler habitats. Melting ice caps and glaciers and rising sea levels can seriously disrupt many ecosystems and affect numerous species. For example, the giant panda feeds almost exclusively on bamboo. Bamboo is being threatened by global warming. Due to the dwindling of their food source, giant pandas are less able to adapt to a changing environment. The polar bear may become extinct due to global warming as the polar bears' habitat is destroyed. Sea turtles may become extinct as the rising sea levels destroy the beaches needed for egg laying. Even if the beaches are not destroyed, increasing temperatures affect the incubation process and the number of offspring being produced.

HUMAN IMPACTS

Humans are responsible for impacting the environment in such a way as to endanger or harm species that may even lead to extinction. Humans destroy habitats directly through deforestation and clearing land for agriculture, logging, mining, and urbanization. Humans also threaten or endanger species through overfishing and overhunting. Pollution can destroy a habitat, and if a species is unable to relocate, this can cause extinction. Introduction of an invasive species that introduces a new predator or competitor to the ecosystem can cause extinction. An example of human impacts leading to the extinction of a species is the case of the passenger pigeon. Millions of passenger pigeons were killed for meat from around 1850 to 1880. Because passenger pigeons only laid one egg at a time, huge flocks were destroyed. The last passenger pigeon died in 1914.

> **Review Video: Genetic vs. Environmental Traits**
> Visit mometrix.com/academy and enter code: 750684

INTERSPECIFIC COMPETITION

Interspecific competition is competition between individuals of different species for the same limited resources such as food, water, sunlight, and living space. This is especially threatening if the two species share a limiting resource and that resource is not in abundant supply. Interspecific competition can limit the population size of a species. With reduced population size, there is less genetic variation. The species may not be able to adapt to environmental changes. For example, firs and spruces compete for resources in coniferous forests. Cheetahs and lions compete for prey in savannas.

ECOLOGY AND BEHAVIOR

POPULATION MODELS

Ecologists use population models to study the populations in an ecosystem and their interactions of populations with the environment. Population models are mathematical models that are designed to study population dynamics. Ecologists can model the growth of a population. For example, models can be designed to describe increases, decreases, or fluctuations in the size of populations due to births, deaths, and migrations. Ecologists can model the interactions of populations with other populations. For example, models of the interactions between predator and prey describe the fluctuating cycles associated with these relationships. Models can also include other factors such as diseases and limiting resources.

ADAPTATION TO ENVIRONMENT

Organisms must be able to adapt to their environment in order to thrive or survive. Individual organisms must be able to recognize stimuli in their surroundings and adapt quickly. For example, an individual euglena can sense light and respond by moving toward the light. Individual organisms must also be able to adapt to changes in the environment on a larger scale. For example, plants must be able to respond to the change in the length of the day to flower at the correct time. Populations must also be able to adapt to a changing environment. Evolution by natural selection is the process by which populations change over many generations. For example, wooly mammoths were unable to adapt to a warming climate and are now extinct, but many species of deer did adapt and are abundant today.

BIOSPHERE
COMPONENTS

The biosphere is the region of the earth inhabited by living things. The components of the biosphere from smallest to largest are organisms, populations, communities, ecosystems, and biomes. Organisms of the same species make up a population. All of the populations in an area make up the community. The community combined with the physical environment for a region forms an ecosystem. Several ecosystems are grouped together to form large geographic regions called biomes.

POPULATION

A population is a group of all the individuals of one species in a specific area or region at a certain time. A species is a group of organisms that can breed and produce fertile offspring. There may be many populations of a specific species in a large geographic region. Ecologists study the size, density, and growth rate of populations to determine their stability. The population density is the number of individuals per unit of area. Growth rates may be exponential or logistic. Population size continuously changes with births, deaths, and migrations. Ecologists also study how the individuals are dispersed within a population. Some species form clusters. Others are evenly or randomly spaced. Every population has limiting factors. Changes in the environment can reduce population size. Geography can limit population size. The individuals of a population react with each other and with other organisms in the community. Competition and predation affect population size.

COMMUNITY INTERACTIONS

A community is all of the populations of different species that live in an area and interact with each other. Community interaction can be intraspecific or interspecific. Intraspecific interactions occur between members of the same species. Interspecific interactions occur between members of different species. Different types of interactions include competition, predation, and symbiosis. Communities with high diversity are more complex and more stable than communities with low diversity. The level of diversity can be seen in a food web of the community, which shows all the feeding relationships within the community.

ECOSYSTEMS

An ecosystem is the basic unit of ecology. An ecosystem is the sum of all the biotic and abiotic factors in an area. Biotic factors are all living things such as plants, animals, fungi, and microorganisms. Abiotic factors include the light, water, air, temperature, and soil in an area. Ecosystems obtain the energy they need from sunlight. Ecosystems contain biogeochemical cycles such as the hydrologic cycle and the nitrogen cycle. Ecosystems are generally classified as either terrestrial or aquatic. All of the living things within an ecosystem are called its community. The number and variety of living things within a community describes the ecosystem's biodiversity. Each ecosystem can only support a limited number of organisms known as the carrying capacity.

BIOTIC AND ABIOTIC FACTORS IN AN ECOSYSTEM

Every ecosystem consists of multiple abiotic and biotic factors. Abiotic factors are the nonbiological physical and chemical factors that affect the ecosystem. Abiotic factors include soil type, atmospheric conditions, sunlight, water, wind, chemical elements, and natural disturbances. In aquatic ecosystems, abiotic factors include salinity, turbidity, water depth, current, temperature, and light. Biotic factors are all of the living organisms in the ecosystem. Biotic factors include plants, algae, fungi, bacteria, archaea, animals, and protozoa.

BIOMES

The biosphere consists of numerous biomes. A biome is a large region that supports a specific community. Each biome has a characteristic climate and geography. Differences in latitude, altitude, and worldwide patterns affect temperature, precipitation, and humidity. Biomes can be classified as terrestrial or aquatic biomes. Terrestrial biomes include ecosystems with land environments, such as tundra, coniferous forest, temperate broadleaf forest, temperate grassland, chaparral, desert, savannas, and tropical forests. Terrestrial biomes tend to grade into each other in regions called ecotones. Aquatic biomes are water-dwelling ecosystems. Aquatic biomes include lakes, coral reefs, rivers, oceanic pelagic zone, estuaries, intertidal zone, and the abyssal zone.

AQUATIC BIOMES

Aquatic biomes are characterized by multiple factors including the temperature of the water, the amount of dissolved solids in the water, the availability of light, the depth of the water, and the material at the bottom of the biome. Aquatic biomes are classified as marine regions or freshwater biomes based on the amount of dissolved salt in the water. Marine biomes include the pelagic zone, the benthic zone, coral reefs, and estuaries. Marine biomes have a salinity of at least 35 parts per thousand. Freshwater biomes include lakes, ponds, rivers, and streams. Freshwater biomes have a salinity that is less than 0.5 parts per thousand. Lakes and ponds, which are relatively stationary, consist of two zones: the littoral zone and the limnetic zone. The littoral zone is closest to the shore and is home to many plants (floating and rooted), invertebrates, crustaceans, amphibians, and fish. The limnetic zone is further from the shore and has no rooted plants. Rivers and streams typically originate in the mountains and make their way to the oceans. Because this water is running and colder, it contains different plants and animals than lakes and ponds. Salmon, trout, crayfish, plants, and algae are found in rivers and streams.

MARINE REGIONS

Marine regions are located in three broad areas: the ocean, estuaries, and coral reefs. The ocean consists of two general regions—the pelagic zone and the benthic zone. The pelagic zone is in the open ocean. Organisms in the pelagic zone include phytoplankton such as algae and bacteria; zooplankton such as protozoa and crustaceans; and larger animals such as squid, sharks, and whales. The benthic zone consists of the floor and the ocean floor. Organisms in the benthic zone can include sponges, clams, oysters, starfish, sea anemones, sea urchins, worms, and fish. The deepest part of the benthic zone is called the abyssal plain. This is the deep ocean floor, which is home to numerous scavengers, many of which have light-generating capability. Estuaries are somewhat-enclosed coastal regions where water from rivers and streams is mixed with seawater. Coral reefs are located in warm, shallow water. Corals are small colonial animals that share a mutualistic relationship with algae.

TERRESTRIAL BIOMES

Terrestrial biomes are classified predominantly by their vegetation, which is primarily determined by precipitation and temperature. Tropical rainforests experience the highest annual precipitation and relatively high temperatures. The dominant vegetation in tropical forests is tall evergreen trees. Temperate deciduous forests experience moderate precipitation and temperatures. The dominant vegetation is deciduous trees. Boreal forests experience moderate precipitation and lower temperatures. The dominant vegetation is coniferous trees. The tundra experiences lower precipitation and cold temperatures. The dominant vegetation is shrubs. The savanna experiences lower precipitation and high temperatures. The dominant vegetation is grasses. Deserts experience the lowest precipitation and the hottest temperatures. The dominant vegetation is scattered thorny plants.

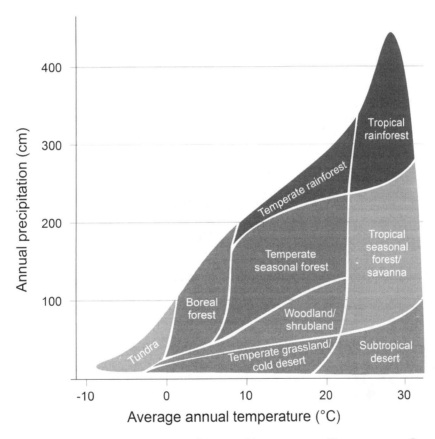

INFLUENCE OF RESOURCE AVAILABILITY AND ABIOTIC FACTORS ON POPULATION SIZE

Population size is affected by resource availability and abiotic factors. As the population density increases, intraspecific competition for available resources intensifies. If the availability of resources decreases, death rates may increase and birth rates may decrease. For example, territoriality for mating or nesting may limit available resources for individuals in a population and limit the population size. Abiotic factors such as temperature, rainfall, wind, and light intensity all influence the population size. For example, temperatures near a species' tolerance limit may

203

decrease the population. Natural disasters such as fire or flood can destroy resources and greatly decrease a population's size. In general, any abiotic factor that reduces or limits resources will also reduce or limit population size.

SIGNIFICANCE OF HABITAT AND NICHE TO POPULATIONS

The habitat of an organism is the type of place where an organism usually lives. A habitat is a piece of an environmental area. A habitat may be a geographic area or even the body of another organism. The habitat describes an organism's natural living environment. A habitat includes biotic and abiotic factors such as temperature, light, food resources, and predators. Whereas a habitat describes an organism's "home," a niche can be thought of as an organism's "occupation." A niche describes an organism's functional role in the community and how the organism uses its habitat. A niche can be quite complex because it should include the impacts that the organism has on the biotic and abiotic surroundings. Niches can be broad or narrow.

INFLUENCE OF COMPETITION AND PREDATION ON POPULATION SIZE

Feeding relationships between organisms can affect population size. Competition and predation both tend to limit population size. Competition occurs when two individuals need the same resource. Predation occurs when one individual is the resource for another individual. Competition occurs when individuals share a resource in the habitat. This competition can be intraspecific, which is between members of the same species, or interspecific, which is between members of different species. Intraspecific competition reduces resources as that species' own population increases. This limits population growth. Interspecific competition reduces resources as a different species uses those same resources. Predation occurs when one species is a food resource for another species. Predator and prey populations can cycle over a range of years. If prey resources increase, predator numbers increase. An example of the predator-prey population cycle is the Canadian lynx and snowshoe hare.

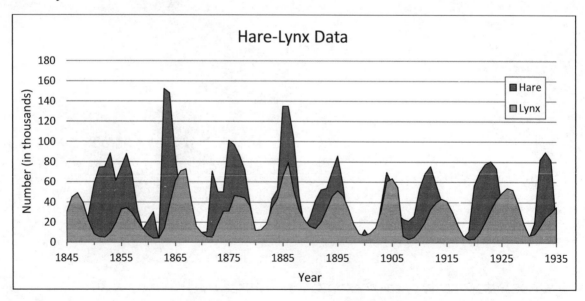

LOGISTIC POPULATION GROWTH MODEL

Populations vary over time due to deaths, births, immigration, and emigration. In most situations, resources such as food, water, and shelter are limited. Each environment or habitat can only support a limited number of individuals. This is known as the carrying capacity. Population growth models that factor in the carrying capacity are called logistic growth models. With logistic population growth models, the rate of population growth decreases as the population size increases. Logistic growth graphs as an S-shaped curve. Comparing logistic growth and exponential growth shows that the graph for exponential growth continues to become steeper, but the graph for logistics growth levels off once the population reaches the carrying capacity. As the population increases, fewer resources are available per individual. This limits the number of individuals that can occupy that environment or habitat.

EXPONENTIAL POPULATION GROWTH MODEL

Populations change over time due to births, deaths, and migrations. Sometimes, conditions are near ideal and populations can increase at their maximum rate exhibiting exponential growth. Exponential growth is growth in which the rate of change is proportional to the increasing size in an exponential progression. Exponential growth graphs as a J-shaped curve. Exponential growth is often observed in single-celled organisms such as bacteria or protozoa in which the population or number of cells increases by a factor of two per unit of time. One cell divides into two cells, which divide into four cells, and so forth. The exponential growth model describes population growth under ideal conditions. It does not take limiting factors or carrying capacity into account. Realistically, exponential growth cannot occur indefinitely, but it may occur for a period of time. It does show a species' capacity for increase and may be helpful when studying a particular species or ecosystem. For example, if a species with no natural predator is introduced into a new habitat, that species may experience exponential growth. If this growth is allowed to go unchecked, the population may overshoot the carrying capacity and then starve. Efforts may need to be taken to reduce the population before this occurs.

ADVANTAGES AND DISADVANTAGES OF ASEXUAL REPRODUCTION IN ANIMALS

Very few species of animals reproduce by asexual reproduction, and nearly all of those species also have the ability to reproduce sexually. While not common, asexual reproduction is useful for animals that tend to stay in one place and may not find mates. Asexual reproduction takes considerably less effort and energy than sexual reproduction. In asexual reproduction, all of the offspring are genetically identical to the parent. This can be a disadvantage because of the lack of genetic variation. Although asexual reproduction is advantageous in a stable environment, if the environment changes, the organisms may lack the genetic variability to survive or selectively adapt.

LIFE HISTORIES

The life history of a species describes the typical organism's life cycle from birth through reproduction to death. Life histories can typically be classified as opportunistic life histories or equilibrial life histories. Species exhibiting opportunistic life histories are typically small, short-lived organisms that have a high reproductive capacity but invest little time and care into their offspring. Their population sizes tend to oscillate significantly over periods of several years. Species exhibiting equilibrial life histories are typically large, long-lived organisms that have a low reproductive capacity but invest much time and care into their offspring. Their populations tend to fluctuate within a smaller range. A general observation is that species that tend to produce numerous offspring typically tend to invest little care into that offspring, resulting in a high mortality rate of that offspring. Organisms of species that tend to produce few offspring typically invest much more care into that offspring, resulting in a lower mortality rate.

SYMBIOSIS

Many species share a special nutritional relationship with another species, called symbiosis. The term symbiosis means "living together." In symbiosis, two organisms share a close physical relationship that can be helpful, harmful, or neutral for each organism. Three forms of symbiosis are parasitism, commensalism, and mutualism. Parasitism is a relationship between two organisms in which one organism is the parasite, and the other organism is the host. The parasite benefits from the relationship because the parasite obtains its nutrition from the host. The host is harmed from the relationship because the parasite is using the host's energy and giving nothing in return. For example, a tick and a dog share a parasitic relationship in which the tick is the parasite, and the dog is the host. Commensalism is a relationship between two organisms in which one benefits, and the other is not affected. For example, a small fish called a remora can attach to the belly of a shark and ride along. The remora is safe under the shark, and the shark is not affected. Mutualism is a relationship between two organisms in which both organisms benefit. For example, a rhinoceros usually can be seen with a few tick birds perched on its back. The tick birds are helped by the easy food source of ticks, and the rhino benefits from the tick removal.

PREDATION

Predation is a special nutritional relationship in which one organism is the predator, and the other organism is the prey. The predator benefits from the relationship, but the prey is harmed. The predator hunts and kills the prey for food. The predator is specially adapted to hunt its prey, and the prey is specially adapted to escape its predator. While predators harm (kill) their individual prey, predation usually helps the prey species. Predation keeps the population of the prey species under control and prevents them from overshooting the carrying capacity, which often leads to starvation. Also, predation usually helps to remove weak or slow members of the prey species leaving the healthier, stronger, and better adapted individuals to reproduce. Examples of predator-prey relationships include lions and zebras, snakes and rats, and hawks and rabbits.

COMPETITION AND TERRITORIALITY

Competition is a relationship between two organisms in which the organisms compete for the same vital resource that is in short supply. Typically, both organisms are harmed, but one is usually harmed more than the other. They could be competing for resources such as food, water, mates, and space. Interspecific competition is between members of different species. Intraspecific competition is between members of the same species. Competition provides an avenue for natural selection. Territoriality can be considered to be a type of interspecific competition for space. Many animals including mammals, birds, reptiles, fish, spiders, and insects have exhibited territorial behavior. Once territories are established, there are fewer conflicts between organisms. For example, a male redwing blackbird can establish a large territory. By singing and flashing his red patches, he is able to warn other males to avoid his territory, and they can avoid fighting.

ALTRUISTIC BEHAVIORS BETWEEN ANIMALS

Altruism is a self-sacrificing behavior in which an individual animal may serve or protect another animal. For example, in a honey bee colony, there is one queen, many workers (females), and drones (males) only during the mating seasons. Adult workers do all the work of the hive and will die defending it. Another example of altruism is seen in a naked mole rat colony. Each colony has one queen that mates with a few males, and the rest of the colony is nonbreeding and lives to service the queen, her mates, and her offspring.

> **Review Video: Mutualism, Commensalism, and Parasitism**
> Visit mometrix.com/academy and enter code: 757249

CHANGES DURING PRIMARY AND SECONDARY SUCCESSION

Ecological succession is the process by which climax communities come into existence or are replaced by new climax communities when they are greatly changed or destroyed. The two types of ecological succession are primary succession and secondary succession. Primary succession occurs in a region where there is no soil and that has never been populated such as a new volcanic island or a region where a glacier has retreated. During the pioneer stage, the progression of species is typically lichen and algae, followed by small annual plants, then perennial herbs and grasses. During the intermediate stage, shrubs, grasses, and shade-intolerant trees are dominant. Finally, after hundreds of years, a climax community is reached with shade-tolerant trees. Secondary succession occurs when a climax community is destroyed or nearly destroyed such as after a forest fire or in an abandoned field. With secondary succession, the area starts with soil and seeds from the original climax community. Typically, in the first two years, weeds and annuals are dominant. This is followed by grasses and biennials. In a few years, shrubs and perennials are dominant followed by pine trees, which are eventually replaced by deciduous trees. Secondary succession takes place in less than 100 years.

ENERGY FLOW IN THE ENVIRONMENT
USING TROPHIC LEVELS WITH AN ENERGY PYRAMID

Energy flow through an ecosystem can be tracked through an energy pyramid. An energy pyramid shows how energy is transferred from one trophic level to another. Producers always form the base of an energy pyramid, and the consumers form successive levels above the producers. Producers only store about 1% of the solar energy they receive. Then, each successive level only uses about 10% of the energy of the previous level. That means that primary consumers use about 10% of the energy used by primary producers, such as grasses and trees. Next, secondary consumers use 10% of primary consumers' 10%, or 1% overall. This continues up for as many trophic levels as exist in a particular ecosystem.

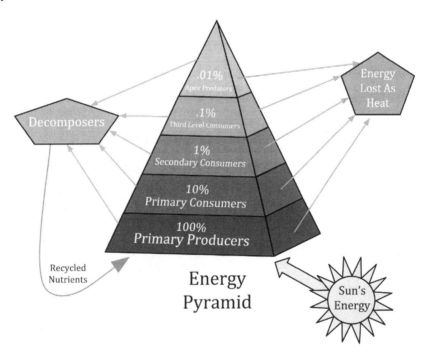

FOOD WEB

Energy flow through an ecosystem can be illustrated by a food web. Energy moves through the food web in the direction of the arrows. In the food web below, producers such as grass, trees, and shrubs use energy from the sun to produce food through photosynthesis. Herbivores or primary consumers such as squirrels, grasshoppers, and rabbits obtain energy by eating the producers. Secondary consumers, which are carnivores such as snakes and shrews, obtain energy by eating the primary consumers. Tertiary consumers, which are carnivores such as hawks and mountain lions, obtain energy by eating the secondary consumers. Note that the hawk and the mountain lion can also be considered quaternary consumers in this food web if a different food chain within the web is followed.

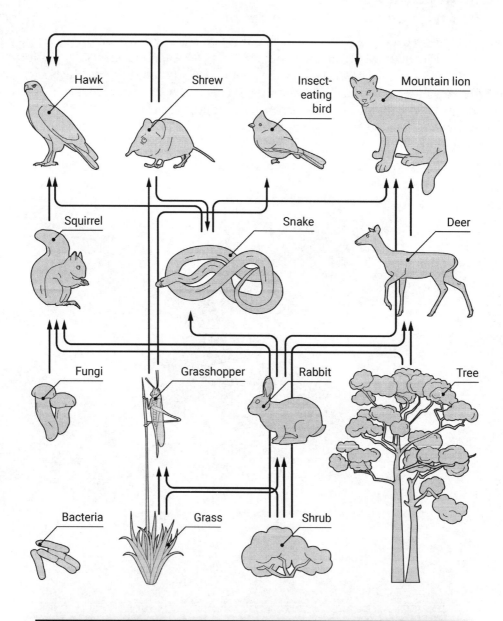

Review Video: <u>Food Webs</u>
Visit mometrix.com/academy and enter code: 853254

WATER CYCLE

The water cycle, also referred to as the hydrologic cycle, is a biogeochemical cycle that describes the continuous movement of the Earth's water. Water in the form of precipitation such as rain or snow moves from the atmosphere to the ground. The water is collected in oceans, lakes, rivers, and other bodies of water. Heat from the sun causes water to evaporate from oceans, lakes, rivers, and other bodies of water. As plants transpire, this water also undergoes evaporation. This water vapor collects in the sky and forms clouds. As the water vapor in the clouds cools, the water vapor condenses or sublimes depending on the conditions. Then, water moves back to the ground in the form of precipitation.

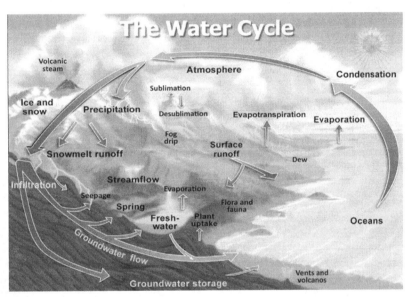

CARBON CYCLE

The carbon cycle is a biogeochemical cycle that describes the continuous movement of the Earth's carbon. Carbon is in the atmosphere, the soil, living organisms, fossil fuels, oceans, and freshwater systems. These areas are referred to as carbon reservoirs. Carbon flows between these reservoirs in an exchange called the carbon cycle. In the atmosphere, carbon is in the form of carbon dioxide. Carbon moves from the atmosphere to plants through the process of photosynthesis. Carbon moves from plants to animals through food chains. Carbon moves from living organisms to the soil when these organisms die. Carbon moves from living organisms to the atmosphere through cellular respiration. Carbon moves from fossil fuels to the atmosphere when fossil fuels are burned. Carbon moves from the atmosphere to the oceans and freshwater systems through absorption.

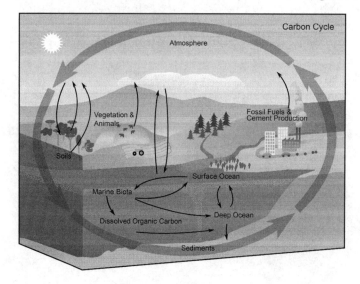

NITROGEN CYCLE

The nitrogen cycle is a biogeochemical cycle that describes the continuous movement of the Earth's nitrogen. Approximately 78% of the Earth's atmosphere consists of nitrogen in its elemental form N_2. Nitrogen is essential to the formation of proteins, but most organisms cannot use nitrogen in this form and require the nitrogen to be converted into some form of nitrates. Lightning can cause nitrates to form in the atmosphere, which can be carried to the soil by rain to be used by plants. Legumes have nitrogen-fixing bacteria in their roots, which can convert the N_2 to ammonia (NH_3). Nitrifying bacteria in the soil can also convert ammonia into nitrates. Plants absorb nitrates from the soil, and animals can consume the plants and other animals for protein. Denitrifying bacteria can convert unused nitrates back to nitrogen to be returned to the atmosphere.

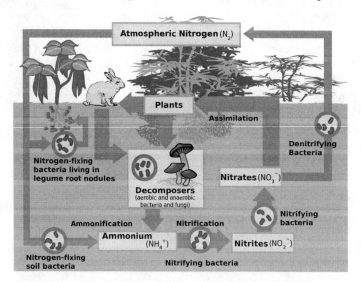

PHOSPHORUS CYCLE

The phosphorus cycle is a biogeochemical cycle that describes the continuous movement of the Earth's phosphorus. Phosphorus is found in rocks. When these rocks weather and erode, the phosphorus moves into the soil. The phosphorus found in the soil and rocks is in the form of phosphates or compounds with the PO_4^{3-} ion. When it rains, phosphates can be dissolved into the water. Plants are able to use phosphates from the soil. Plants need phosphorus for growth and development. Phosphorus is also a component of DNA, RNA, ATP, cell membranes, and bones. Plants and algae can absorb phosphate ions from the water and convert them into many organic compounds. Animals can get phosphorus by eating food or drinking water. When organisms die, the phosphorus is returned to the soil. This is the slowest of all biogeochemical cycles.

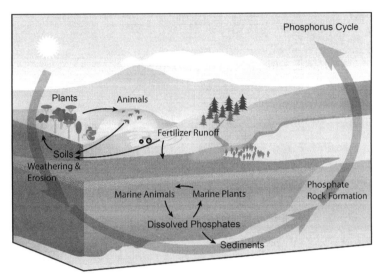

NATURAL DISTURBANCES THAT AFFECT ECOSYSTEMS

A natural disturbance is an event caused by nature, not human activity. Natural disturbances can be brought on by weather such as fires from lightning, droughts, storms, wind, and freezing. Other natural disturbances include earthquakes, volcanic eruptions, and diseases. Natural disturbances can disrupt or disturb the ecosystem in many ways such as altering resources or removing individuals from the community. Natural disturbances can cover small regions, or they can affect an entire ecosystem. The effect may be long lasting and take several years to recover, or the effect may be minor and take only a few months to recover.

EFFECT OF FRAGMENTATION OF ECOSYSTEMS ON BIODIVERSITY

Habitats can become fragmented due to natural disturbances such as fire, volcanic activity, and climate change. Some of the original habitat is destroyed during fragmentation, reducing the total area of the habitat. As a result, there may be insufficient food or other resources to support a species. The resulting habitats may also be reproductively isolated from each other, thus limiting genetic variation and biodiversity. Small fluctuations in resources or climate can be catastrophic in small populations. Larger populations may be able to overcome these fluctuations in variation.

EFFECTS OF HUMAN POPULATION ON ECOLOGICAL SYSTEMS AND BIODIVERSITY

Human population has been increasing at a near-exponential rate for the past 50 years. As the human population increases, the demand for resources such as food, water, land, and energy also increases. As the human population increases, the number of species decreases due to habitat destruction, introduced species, and overhunting. The increased greenhouse gases and resulting climate changes have also significantly affected many ecosystems as temperatures rise and habitats are slowly changed or even destroyed. Increasing human population means increasing pollution, which harms habitats. Many animals have become extinct due to the effects of an exponentially increasing human population. High rates of extinction greatly reduce biodiversity.

EFFECTS OF HABITAT DESTRUCTION BY HUMANS ON ECOLOGICAL SYSTEMS AND BIODIVERSITY

Many habitats have been altered or destroyed by humans. In fact, habitat destruction brought about by human endeavors has been the most significant cause of species extinctions resulting in the decrease in biodiversity throughout the world. As the human population has increased exponentially, the extinction rate has also increased exponentially. This is largely due to habitat destruction by humans. Humans use many resources in their various enterprises including agriculture, industry, mining, logging, and recreation. Humans have cleared much land for agriculture and urban development. As habitats are destroyed, species are either destroyed or displaced. Often, habitats are fragmented into smaller areas, which only allow for small populations that are under threat by predators, diseases, weather, and limited resources. Especially hard hit are areas near the coastline, estuaries, and coral reefs. Nearly half of all mangrove ecosystems have been destroyed by human activity. Coral reefs have nearly been decimated from pollution such as oil spills and exploitation from the aquarium fish market and coral market.

EFFECTS OF INTRODUCED SPECIES ON ECOLOGICAL SYSTEMS AND BIODIVERSITY

Introduced species are species that are moved into new geographic regions by humans. They are also called invasive or nonnative species. Introduction can be intentional, such as the introduction of livestock, or unintentional, such as the introduction of Dutch elm disease. Introduced species can disrupt their new communities by using limited resources and preying on other members of the community. Introduced species are often free from predators and can reproduce exponentially. This typically causes a decrease in biodiversity. Introduced species are contributors or even responsible for numerous extinctions. For example, zebra mussels, which are native to the Black Sea and the Caspian Sea, were accidentally introduced to the Great Lakes. The zebra mussels greatly reduced the amount of plankton available for the native mussel species, many of which are now endangered.

IMPACT OF NONPOINT SOURCES OF POLLUTION ON THE ENVIRONMENT

Nonpoint-source pollution is the leading cause of water pollution in the United States. Nonpoint-source pollution is pollution that does not flow through a pipe, channel, or container. Most nonpoint-source pollution is due to agricultural runoff. Urban runoff from lawns, streets, and parking lots is also treated as nonpoint-source pollution because much of that storm water does not go into a storm drain before entering streams, rivers, lakes, or other bodies of water. Urban runoff contains chemicals such as lawn fertilizers, motor oils, grease, pesticides, soaps, and detergents, each of which is harmful to the environment.

EFFECTS OF REMEDIATION ON ECOLOGICAL SYSTEMS AND BIODIVERSITY

In remediation, or land rehabilitation, environmental damages is reversed or stopped by attempting to restore land to its prior condition. Examples of remediation are reforestation and mine reclamation. Mining reclamation includes the backfilling of open-pit mines and covering ores containing sulfides to prevent rain from mixing with them to produce sulfuric acid. Reforestation is the restocking of forests and wetlands. This can at least partially offset the damaging effects brought about by the deforestation. Reforestation can help reduce global warming due to an increase in the absorption of light by the trees. Restoration can also help to restore the carbon cycle and counter erosion. Reforestation can help maintain or preserve the biodiversity of the region and possibly increase biodiversity if new organisms immigrate into the region.

POLLUTION MITIGATION AND THE CLEAN AIR ACT

Pollution mitigation has greatly reduced pollution and its effects during the past 40 years. The Clean Air Act has reduced pollution by requiring that new industrial sites contain pollution-control technology. These technologies avoid or minimize the negative effects on the environment. For example, new coal-fired power plants are fitted with pollution-control devices that greatly reduce and nearly eliminate sulfur dioxide and nitrogen oxide emissions. This greatly reduces acid rain, improves water quality, and improves the overall health of ecosystems. Reducing acid rain improves soil quality, which in turn improves the health of producers, which consequently improves the health of consumers, essentially strengthening the entire ecosystem. Reduced greenhouse gas emissions have lessened the impact of global warming such as rising sea levels due to melting glaciers and the resulting loss of habitats and biodiversity. Reduced smog and haze improves the intensity of sunlight required for photosynthesis.

RESOURCE MANAGEMENT

Resource management such as waste management and recycling greatly impacts the environment. Waste management is the monitoring, collection, transportation, and recycling of waste products. Well-managed landfills include using clay or another lining material to prevent liquid leachate and layers of soil on top to reduce odors and vermin. Wastes can be incinerated to reduce waste volume. Hazardous biomedical waste can be incinerated. However, incineration does emit pollutants and greenhouse gases. Proper waste management always includes recycling. Recycling is a method to recover resources. Recycled materials can be reprocessed into new products. Metals such as aluminum, copper, and steel are recycled. Plastics, glass, and paper products can be recycled. Organic materials such as plant materials and food scraps can be composted. The current trend is to shift from waste management to resource recovery. Wastes should be minimized and reduced to minimize the need for disposal. Unavoidable nonrecyclable wastes should be converted to energy by combustion if at all possible.

IMPACT OF GLOBAL WARMING, RISING SEA LEVELS, AND FLOODING ON SOCIETY

Global warming caused largely by greenhouse gas emission will greatly affect society in the next several years. The increase in global temperature leads to more extreme weather events such hurricanes, tornadoes, floods, and droughts. Rising temperatures mean warmer summers. Warmer temperatures may shift tourism and improve agriculture, but global mortality rates may rise due to hotter heat waves. Rising temperatures cause weather patterns to shift, leading to more floods and droughts. Rising temperatures mean a decrease in glaciers, sea ice, ice sheets, and snow cover, which all contribute to rising sea levels. Rising sea levels lead to habitat change or loss, which greatly affects numerous species. Some motile species are already moving north to cooler climates. Earlier snowmelt and runoff may overwhelm water management systems. Diseases such as malaria that are spread by mosquitoes could spread further, possibly even to temperate regions. Rising sea levels mean higher storm surges and related issues.

ENDANGERED SPECIES ACT

The Endangered Species Act (ESA) of 1973 has had a positive impact on many species. The law was designed to protect "imperiled species" from extinction due to factors such as loss of habitat, overhunting, and lack of conservation. The ESA also protects the species' ecosystems and removes threats to those ecosystems. If an animal is placed on the endangered or threatened list, it is prohibited to "harass, harm, pursue, hunt, shoot, wound, kill, trap, capture, or collect, or to attempt to engage in any such conduct" with the endangered animal. The populations of many species have increased significantly, including the whooping crane, the gray wolf, the red wolf, and the Hawaiian goose. Some species have even been removed from the endangered species list, including the bald eagle, the peregrine falcon, the gray whale, and the grizzly bear. The ESA has protected numerous species while balancing human economic needs and rights to private property.

NATIONAL PARK SYSTEM

The purpose of the National Park System is to "conserve the scenery and the natural and historic objects and the wildlife therein and to provide for the enjoyment of the same in such manner and by such means as will leave them unimpaired for the enjoyment of future generations." The National Park System protects complete ecosystems and houses great biodiversity. National parks are an integral part of the survival of many species. National parks provide a home to hundreds of endangered or threatened species. Studies show that preserved habitats near national parks helps many species better survive. This will prevent fragmentation and further habitat loss. Nevertheless, National parks may be threatened by invasion species or pressure for use of land along park boundaries. Also, biodiversity is threatened even within national parks. Although many are vast, they still may not be large enough to support a species population.

EFFECTS OF EXTRACTION OF MINERALS AND OIL DRILLING

The extraction of mineral and energy resources by mining and drilling has harmful effects on the environment including pollution and alterations to ecosystems. Mining requires large amounts of land, which harms habitats and affects biodiversity. Mining causes water pollution. Rainwater mixes with the heavy metals in mines and produces an acid runoff that harms aquatic life, birds, and mammals. The pollution is especially bad in countries without proper mining regulations. Open-pit mines and mountaintop removal techniques are especially harsh to the environment, and reclamation is often not regulated in developing countries. Mining often requires large-scale deforestation leading to a loss of habitat for many species. Toxic chemicals such as mercury and sulfuric acid are used in the mining process and are released into bodies of water, harming the aquatic life. If these toxic chemicals are leaked, the ground water is polluted. Oil drilling is controversial due to habitat disruption or loss. Oil spills are toxic to wildlife and difficult to clean up. Offshore drilling uses seismic waves to locate oil, which disturbs whales and dolphins and has been tied to hundreds of beached whales.

SUSTAINABLE AGRICULTURE

The management of natural resources and the renewability or sustainability of those natural resources greatly impact society. Sustainable agriculture involves growing foods in economical ways that do not harm resources. If left unchecked, farming can deplete the soil of valuable nutrients. Crops grown in these depleted soils are less healthy and more susceptible to disease. Sustainable agriculture uses more effective pest control such as insect-resistant corn, which reduces runoff and water pollution in the surrounding area. Sustainable forestry involves replenishing trees as trees are being harvested, which maintains the environment.

RENEWABLE AND NONRENEWABLE ENERGY RESOURCES

Energy sources such as wind, solar power, and biomass energy are all renewable. Wind power is clean with no pollution and no greenhouse gas emissions. Disadvantages of wind power include the use of land for wind farms, threats to birds, and the expense to build. Solar power has no greenhouse gas emissions, but some toxic metal wastes result in the production of photovoltaic cells, and solar power requires large areas of land. Biomass energy is sustainable, but its combustion produces greenhouse emissions. Farming biomass requires large areas of land. Fossil fuels, which are nonrenewable, cause substantially more air pollution and greenhouse gas emissions, contributing to habitat loss and global warming.

General Chemistry

Stoichiometry

MOLECULAR WEIGHT

The molecular weight of a compound, also called molecular mass, is the mass of a single molecule of the compound, generally given in atomic mass units. It can be determined using the periodic table by looking up the atomic weight of each atom in the compound and adding them together. For example, sodium sulfate has the chemical formula Na_2SO_4: it contains two sodium atoms, one sulfur atom, and four oxygen atoms. The atomic weights of sodium, sulfur, and oxygen are 22.990, 32.065, and 15.999, respectively; the molecular weight of sodium sulfate is therefore

$$2(22.990) + 32.065 + 4(15.999) = 142.04$$

EMPIRICAL VERSUS MOLECULAR FORMULA

The molecular formula of a compound consists of the symbols for the elements in the compound, with a subscript indicating the number of atoms of that element if that number is greater than one. Water contains two hydrogen atoms and one oxygen atom, so its molecular formula is H_2O. Hydrogen peroxide contains two hydrogen atoms and two oxygen atoms, so its molecular formula is H_2O_2. Glucose contains six carbon atoms; 12 hydrogen atoms; and six oxygen, so it is $C_6H_{12}O_6$.

The empirical formula, on the other hand, only gives the ratios of elements in the compound. If the numbers of atoms of each element have no common divisor, then the empirical and molecular formula are the same: thus, the empirical formula for water is still H_2O. Otherwise, the subscripts are reduced by their common divisor: the empirical formula for hydrogen peroxide is HO, and for glucose is CH_2O. Two compounds may have the same empirical formula but different molecular formulas: the molecular formula for ethylene is C_2H_4, propylene is C_3H_6, and butylene is C_4H_8, but all would have the same empirical formula of CH_2.

DESCRIPTION OF COMPOSITION BY PERCENT MASS

The percent mass of an element in a compound is the ratio of the mass of the element in question to the total mass of the compound, expressed as a percentage. For example, in water, H_2O, the mass of the hydrogen in each molecule is $2(1.008 \text{ u}) = 2.016$ u; the mass of the oxygen is 15.999 u; the total mass of the molecule is $2.016 \text{ u} + 15.999 \text{ u} = 18.015$ u. The percent mass of hydrogen in the molecule is then $\frac{2.016 \text{ u}}{18.015 \text{ u}} = 0.1112 = 11.12\%$, and the percent mass of the oxygen is $\frac{15.999 \text{ u}}{18.015 \text{ u}} = 0.8881 = 88.81\%$. The chemical composition of water can therefore be said to be 11.12% hydrogen and 88.81% oxygen by mass.

The percent mass of the elements in a compound and the empirical formula are related—if the percent mass of each element is known, the empirical formula can be determined by dividing the percent mass of each element by the atomic mass of that element and finding the ratios of the results. The full molecular formula, however, cannot be found from the percent masses without more information.

AVOGADRO'S NUMBER

Avogadro's Number, abbreviated N_A, is the number of atoms or molecules in one mole of a substance. It is a constant equal to about $6.022 \times 10^{23} \text{ mol}^{-1}$. Avogadro's Number is named after

Italian physicist Lorenzo Romano Amedeo Carlo Avogadro, remembered for his contributions to molecular theory.

Avogadro's Number forms the basis of the definition of the mole, and it was not chosen arbitrarily. The number was originally defined as equal to the number of atoms in 1 gram of hydrogen and was later redefined as the number of atoms in 12 grams of carbon-12. As such, in addition to the number of atoms or molecules in a mole, Avogadro's Number is also the number of atomic mass units in 1 gram. Avogadro's Number is therefore useful in converting between microscopic and macroscopic units, including converting between moles and molecules or grams and atomic mass units.

DEFINITION OF DENSITY

Density is the amount of mass in a substance or object per unit volume. It is usually abbreviated in science by the lowercase Greek letter rho, ρ. It is important to note that although this letter looks somewhat like a lowercase P, it is a different symbol, with a different meaning, and the two should not be confused, especially because there are some significant formulae (such as Bernoulli's equation) in which both symbols appear. The units for density are the units of mass divided by the units of volume, so in SI units they are kg/m^3.

Unlike mass and volume themselves, density is an intrinsic property, independent of the quantity of matter present. If you break a rock in two, the pieces have a smaller mass and volume than the original rock but the same density. Of course, for a gas, the density does depend on other properties, such as temperature and pressure; this is also true for liquids and solids but to a much smaller degree.

OXIDATION NUMBER

The oxidation number of an atom in a compound is a measurement of its effective charge within the molecule. Essentially, the oxidation number is the number of electrons that have been removed from or (for a negative oxidation number) added to the atom in question. The more electronegative atom in a compound generally has a lower oxidation state.

The oxidation state of a monatomic ion is the charge of the ion; the oxidation state of a neutral pure element is zero (even if the element forms polyatomic molecules, such as H_2 or S_8). Some elements have consistent oxidation states: the oxidation state of alkali metals in compounds is always +1 and of alkaline earths always +2. Hydrogen usually has an oxidation state of +1, halogens of −1, and oxygen of -2, although there are exceptions.

The oxidation states of the atoms in a neutral molecule must add to zero and in a polyatomic ion must add to the charge of the ion. This often makes it possible to solve for the oxidation states of elements where the oxidation states are not consistent by plugging in the oxidation states of atoms that are known and solving for the unknowns.

Hydrogen atoms in a compound usually have an oxidation number of −1. However, this is not the case when the hydrogen is bonded to a metal (which has a lower electronegativity), such as in sodium hydride, NaH, or lithium aluminum hydride, $LiAlH_4$.

Oxygen atoms in a compound usually have an oxidation number of −2. However, there are two important exceptions. In the peroxide ion, O_2^{2-}, the ion as a whole has an oxidation number of −2, so each atom in the ion has an oxidation number of −1. This still holds when the ion is part of a compound, as in hydrogen peroxide, H_2O_2. The other exception is when the oxygen is bonded to fluorine. Fluorine is even more electronegative than oxygen, so in this case the fluorine will get a negative oxidation number, and the oxygen's oxidation number will be positive. In a molecule of oxygen difluoride, OF_2, the oxidation number of the oxygen atom is +2.

COMMON OXIDIZING AND REDUCING AGENTS

An oxidizing agent is an element or compound that takes electrons from another substance, causing it to be oxidized. A reducing agent is an element or compound that donates electrons to another compound, causing it to be reduced. Note that in an oxidation-reduction reaction, the oxidizing agent is itself reduced, whereas the reducing agent is oxidized.

Common oxidizing agents include oxygen, chlorine and other halogens, hydrogen peroxide, and sulfuric acid. Common reducing agents include hydrogen gas, sodium and other alkali metals, iron, and carbon monoxide.

REDOX EQUATIONS

Redox equation is short for reduction-oxidation equation, a chemical equation for a reaction involving the reduction of one element or compound and the oxidation of another. When balancing a redox equation, not just the number of atoms of each element on each side must match, but the total oxidation number of all the atoms must match on the left or right as well. Generally, this is done by separating the reaction into half-reactions for oxidation and reduction—adding electrons to the reactions as necessary—and then combining the two reactions such that the electrons cancel.

For instance, take the simple redox reaction $Fe^{3+} + Sn^{2+} \rightarrow Fe^{2+} + Sn^{4+}$. The number of atoms of each element on each side matches, but the oxidation numbers do not: we have a total of +5 on the left and +6 on the right. We first write the separate half-reactions:

$$Fe^{3+} + e^- \rightarrow Fe^{2+}$$
$$Sn^{2+} \rightarrow 2e^- + Sn^{4+}$$

For the electrons to cancel when we combine the half-reactions, the first half-reaction must be multiplied by two. Our final balanced equation is then

$$2Fe^{3+} + Sn^{2+} \rightarrow 2Fe^{2+} + Sn^{4+}$$

Note the matching total oxidation number of +8 on each side.

DISPROPORTIONATION OF REACTION BY CHEMICAL EQUATIONS

A disproportionation reaction is a redox reaction in which the same chemical species is both oxidized and reduced: that is, some of the molecules of the compound are reduced, whereas others are oxidized. One well-known example of a disproportionation reaction is the decomposition of hydrogen peroxide: $2H_2O_2 \rightarrow 2H_2O + O_2$. Note that in the reactant, H_2O_2, the oxygen atoms have an oxidation number of –1. In the product H_2O, the oxygen atoms have an oxidation number of –2— these atoms have been reduced. But in the other product, O_2, the oxygen atoms have an oxidation number of 0—these atoms have been oxidized.

Other examples of disproportionation reactions are the disproportionation of copper(I) ions in solution, $2Cu_{(aq)}^+ \rightarrow Cu_{(s)} + Cu_{(aq)}^{2+}$ (the oxidation number of the copper goes from +1 on the left to 0 and +2 on the right); the disproportionation of carbon monoxide, $2CO \rightarrow C + CO_2$ (the oxidation number of the carbon goes from +2 to 0 and +4); and the disproportionation of mercury chloride, $Hg_2Cl_2 \rightarrow Hg + HgCl_2$ (the oxidation number of the mercury goes from +1 to 0 and +2).

CONVENTIONS FOR WRITING A CHEMICAL EQUATIONS

When writing a chemical equation, the reactants—the elements and compounds initially present before the reaction—go on the left, separated by plus signs, and the products—the elements and compounds produced in the reaction—go on the right, likewise separated. An arrow points from the reactants to the products. The relative number of particles of each reactant and product is shown by a number preceding them, such that the reaction is balanced—each element is represented in equal numbers on the left and right. Optionally, a parenthetical after each species can be written for its state: (s) for solid, (l) for liquid, (g) for gas, and (aq) for aqueous (in solution with water).

For example, take the reaction of sulfuric acid (H_2SO_4) with sodium hydroxide (NaOH) in solution to form water (H_2O) and sodium hydroxide (Na_2SO_4). The first two are the reactants, and the last two the products, so we would write $H_2SO_4 + NaOH \rightarrow H_2O + Na_2SO_4$. This, however, is not balanced; there are, for instance, three hydrogen atoms on the left but only two on the right. The full balanced equation, with states, would be $H_2SO_{4(aq)} + 2NaOH_{(aq)} \rightarrow H_2O_l + 2Na_2SO_{4(aq)}$.

BALANCING EQUATIONS

Balancing a chemical equation means putting the correct coefficient on each species in the reaction so that the total number of atoms of each element is the same on both sides of the equation. For complex equations, this may involve some trial and error, but there are some steps that make it easier. It is generally simplest to balance one element at a time and to start by balancing the elements that appear in the fewest species. One may end up with fractional coefficients; if this is the case, one can simply multiply all the coefficients by the lowest common denominator.

For instance, take the reaction $NH_3 + O_2 = NO + H_2O$. H only appears in one compound on each side, so we can start there: $2NH_3 + O_2 = NO + 3H_2O$. N likewise only appears in one compound on each side and can be balanced by writing 2 in front of NO. That leaves the oxygen. There are now five oxygen atoms on the right, so we need $\frac{5}{2}$ in front of the O_2 on the left. We can multiply all the coefficients by 2 to remove the fraction, giving finally $4NH_3 + 5O_2 = 4NO + 6H_2O$.

LIMITING REACTANTS

The limiting reactant is the reactant that determines how much of the product will be produced—essentially, it is the reactant that runs out first when the reaction takes place. The other reactants that remain after the limiting reactant has been expended are called excess reactants. One way to determine which reactant is the limiting reactant, given the quantities of each reactant, is to calculate how much of one of the products could be formed from each reactant (assuming that sufficient quantities of the other reactants are available). Whichever reactant yields the smallest amount of product is the limiting reactant.

For instance, consider the reaction $Si + 2NaOH + H_2O \rightarrow Na_2SiO_3 + 2H_2$, and suppose we are given that we have 20 grams of Si, 30 grams of NaOH, and 10 grams of H_2O. Dividing by the respective molecular masses, this means that we have 0.712 moles of Si, 0.750 moles of NaOH, and 0.555 moles of water. These would each be sufficient to produce, respectively, 0.712 moles, 0.375 moles, and 0.555 moles of Na_2SiO_3; 0.375 moles, the amount produced by the NaOH, is smallest, so NaOH is the limiting reactant.

THEORETICAL YIELDS

The theoretical yield of a chemical product is the amount that would be produced if the maximum amount of the reactants reacted—that is, if all of the limiting reactant participated. The theoretical yield can be determined by identifying the limiting reactant and determining how much of the product it would produce based on the ratios of the coefficients in the chemical equation. For example, consider the reaction $Fe_2O_3 + 3C \rightarrow CO + 2Fe$, and suppose that we know that the limiting reactant is carbon, of which we have 500 grams; we want to determine the theoretical yield of iron. Five hundred grams of carbon is 41.6 moles; because there are two atoms of elemental iron produced for every three atoms of elemental carbon that reacts, this would produce $\frac{2}{3}(41.6 \text{ mol}) = 27.8$ mol of iron, or 1.55 kg.

The experimental yield is the amount of product that is actually produced in a reaction and empirically measured. It is possible that not all the limiting reactant participates in the reaction—because other reactions occur or because the system reaches an equilibrium state. Therefore, the experimental yield may be (and generally is) less than the theoretical yield but never greater.

States of Matter

The four states of matter are solids, liquids, gases, and plasma. Solids have a definite shape and a definite volume. Because solid particles are held in fairly rigid positions, solids are the least compressible of the four states of matter. Liquids have definite volumes but no definite shapes. Because their particles are free to slip and slide over each other, liquids take the shape of their containers, but they still remain fairly incompressible by natural means. Gases have no definite shape or volume. Because gas particles are free to move, they move away from each other to fill their containers. Gases are compressible. Plasmas are high-temperature, ionized gases that exist only under very high temperatures at which electrons are stripped away from their atoms.

> **Review Video: Properties of Liquids**
> Visit mometrix.com/academy and enter code: 802024
>
> **Review Video: Chemical and Physical Properties of Matter**
> Visit mometrix.com/academy and enter code: 717349

ABSOLUTE TEMPERATURE, (K) KELVIN SCALE

The size of 1 Kelvin is the same as the size of 1° Celsius; the only difference between the two scales is where the zero is: 0°C corresponds to 273.15 K, so to convert from degrees Celsius to Kelvins, it is only necessary to add 273.15. Conversely, Kelvins can be converted to degrees Celsius by subtracting 273.15. For example, the typical room temperature of 25°C corresponds to 298.15 K.

What makes the Kelvin scale particularly useful in science is the fact that 0 K corresponds to the absolute zero of temperature. Multiplying or dividing temperatures is only meaningful in such a scale; it doesn't make sense, for instance, to double a temperature expressed in degrees Celsius because doubling a negative temperature would result in a lower temperature (among other reasons). The Kelvin scale has no negative temperatures, and such an operation is entirely reasonable. In any calculation that involves multiplying or dividing by temperatures (such as some applications of the Ideal Gas Law), the temperature must be expressed in Kelvins, not degrees Celsius. If only differences of temperature are involved, however, then the two scales are interchangeable.

PRESSURE, SIMPLE MERCURY BAROMETER

A mercury barometer in its simplest form consists of a tube closed at one end and filled with mercury inverted in an open container of mercury. The pressure of the surrounding air will press on the mercury in the open container; due to Pascal's Law, this pressure is propagated throughout the mercury. At equilibrium, the hydrostatic pressure due to the mercury column will precisely equal the atmospheric pressure of the surroundings, so the atmospheric pressure can be calculated from the height h of the column of mercury: $P_{atm} = \rho_{Hg} g h$.

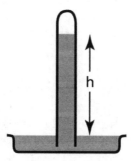

In principle, this would work the same with any incompressible liquid, not just mercury. In practice, mercury is chosen because of its high density. The higher the density of the fluid, the lower the height of the column, so for fluids of low density, the height becomes impractical. At normal atmospheric pressure, the column of mercury in a mercury barometer is about 76 centimeters high. A similar instrument using water instead of mercury would require a column more than 10 meters high!

MOLAR VOLUME

Molar volume is the volume occupied by one mole of a substance: by definition, the number of molecules or atoms in one mole of a substance is Avogadro's number, about 6.022×10^{23}. Although the molar volume cannot be measured directly (you can't count 6.022×10^{23} atoms), it can be calculated from the molar mass and the mass density: $V_m = \frac{M}{\rho}$, where V_m is the molar volume, M is the molar mass, and ρ is the mass density. Because the mass density varies with temperature and pressure, so does the molar volume; it is therefore not correct to say that a particular substance has a specific molar volume but rather that it has a specific molar volume at some particular temperature and pressure.

For instance, nitrogen gas has a molar mass of 28.0135 g/mol and a mass density at 25°C of 1.145 kg/m^3, or 0.001145 g/cm^3. This means that at 25°C, nitrogen gas has a molar volume of $\frac{28.0135 \text{ g/mol}}{0.001145 \text{ g/cm}^3} = 24470$ cm^3/mol, equivalent to 0.02447 m^3/mol or 24.47 L/mol.

At a temperature of 0°C and a pressure of 1 atm, an ideal gas has a molar volume of 0.0224 m^3/mol, or 22.4 liters/mol.

IDEAL GAS

An ideal gas is a gas made up of particles with the following characteristics:

- Their volume is negligible compared to the volume of the container.
- They do not interact except during collisions.
- All collisions are perfectly elastic (no kinetic energy is lost).
- Between collisions, the particles travel at constant speed in straight lines.

Although an ideal gas is an abstract concept, and no real gases have exactly these characteristics, the ideal gas concept is useful because it allows certain calculations and predictions to be made about the gas's properties and behavior—and these predictions turn out to hold to a high level of precision for many real gases, even if they aren't exactly ideal. Essentially, a real gas behaves as an ideal gas to a very good approximation as long as its pressure isn't too high and its temperature isn't too low.

IDEAL GAS LAW

The **ideal gas law** is an equation that relates the pressure, volume, temperature, and number of moles or molecules of an ideal gas. It combines Boyle's law, Charles's law, and Avogadro's law, although each of these laws was originally separately determined on empirical grounds. Like these other laws, and like its name implies, the Ideal Gas Law only holds exactly for a nonexistent ideal gas, but for most real gases it is a very good approximation.

The ideal gas law can be stated as $PV = nRT$, where P is the pressure of the gas, V is the volume, n is the number of moles, T is the temperature (in Kelvin), and R is the ideal gas constant, equal to about 8.314 J/(mol K) or 0.08205 L atm/(mol K).

The ideal gas law can be used to solve for the pressure, volume, temperature, or number of moles of gas if the other quantities are known. For instance, consider a room with a volume of 60.0 m^3 filled with air at 25°C and a pressure of 1.000 atmosphere. We can use the Ideal Gas Law to determine the number of moles of air in the room: $n = \frac{PV}{RT} = \frac{(1.013\times10^5\,\text{Pa})(60.0\ \text{m}^3)}{(8.314\,\text{J/(mol K)})(298\ \text{K})} = 2450$ mol.

By definition, the particles of an ideal gas have negligible volume and do not interact except during collisions. The particles of a real gas, of course, do have some finite volume, and there are long-range forces between them, such as the van der Waals forces arising due to their charge distributions. The difference from ideal behavior is most notable at high pressures and low temperatures. At very high pressures, the effect of the volume of the particles may become important and $PV > nRT$, whereas at very low temperatures the intermolecular forces play a role and $PV < nRT$.

The Dutch physicist Johannes Diderik van der Waals derived a generalization of the Ideal Gas Law that takes these features of a real gas into account: what is now called the van der Waals equation, $\left(P + \frac{an^2}{V^2}\right)(V - nb) = nRT$. Although still not exact, this equation gives closer results for real gases for a broad range of circumstances. Unfortunately, however, it relies on two constants, a and b, that are not universal and must be determined separately for each gas.

> **Review Video: Ideal Gas Law**
> Visit mometrix.com/academy and enter code: 381353

BOYLE'S LAW

Boyle's law states that for a gas at constant temperature, the pressure of the gas is inversely proportional to the volume: all else being equal, $P \propto \frac{1}{V}$, or $P_1V_1 = P_2V_2$. It is named after the Irish chemist and physicist Robert William Boyle, who was among the first to define the modern study of chemistry.

Boyle's law can be used to solve for an unknown pressure or volume, when the other is known and when both quantities are known at a different time. For instance, consider an air bubble deep under the ocean at a pressure of 20 atm. As it rises to the surface, the bubble will expand due to the decreased pressure. If the bubble initially has a volume of 1.0 cm^3, we can find its volume at the surface using Boyle's law: $(20 \text{ atm})(1.0 \text{ cm}^3) = (1.0 \text{ atm})V_2$, so we can solve for V_2 yielding $V_2 = 20 \text{ cm}^3$.

CHARLES'S LAW

Charles's law states that for a gas at constant pressure, the volume of the gas is proportional to the temperature: all else being equal, $V \propto T$, or $\frac{V_1}{T_1} = \frac{V_2}{T_2}$. The law is named after French physicist and inventor Jacques Alexandre César Charles, also known for his development of hydrogen balloons.

Charles's law can be used to solve for an unknown volume or temperature, when the other is known and when both quantities are known at a different time. For instance, consider a balloon that at room temperature (25°C) has a volume of 12.0 m³. If the gas inside the balloon is heated, the balloon will expand. If the gas is heated to a temperature of 300°C, we can find the balloon's new volume using Charles's law, $\frac{12.0 \text{ m}^3}{298 \text{ K}} = \frac{V_2}{573 \text{ K}}$, so $V_2 = 23.1 \text{ m}^3$. Note that we had to convert the temperatures from degrees Celsius into Kelvins—this is necessary whenever we're multiplying or dividing by temperatures.

AVOGADRO'S LAW

Avogadro's law states that at constant temperature and pressure, the volume of gas is proportional to the number of molecules or moles. That is, all else being equal, $V \propto n$, or $\frac{V_1}{n_1} = \frac{V_2}{n_2}$. Alternatively, we can write $V \propto N$, or $\frac{V_1}{N_1} = \frac{V_2}{N_2}$. (In gas equations, it is common to use n for the number of moles and N for the number of molecules.)

Avogadro's law can be used to solve for an unknown volume or number of molecules or moles when the other is known and when both quantities are known at a different time. For instance, consider two chambers filled with gas at equal pressure and temperature. One chamber has a volume of 500 m³, the other 200 m³. If we are given that the larger chamber contains 20,000 moles of gas, we can use Avogadro's law to determine the number of moles of gas in the smaller chamber: $\frac{500 \text{ m}^3}{20000 \text{ mol}} = \frac{200 \text{ m}^3}{n_2}$, so $n_2 = 8,000 \text{ mol}$.

KINETIC MOLECULAR THEORY OF GASES
HEAT CAPACITY

Heat capacity is a measurement of the amount of heat that must be transferred to an object to raise its temperature by a specific amount (or, equivalently, the amount of heat that is released when its temperature lowers). It can be expressed as $C = \frac{Q}{\Delta T}$, where Q is the heat and ΔT the change in temperature. (Technically, the heat capacity itself varies slightly by temperature, so this equation isn't exactly valid, but it holds well for relatively small changes in temperature.) Because heat capacity depends on the amount of material, however, it is also useful to define the specific heat capacity, or specific heat, $c = \frac{C}{m} = \frac{Q}{m\Delta T}$. (Heat capacity is represented by an uppercase C, specific heat by a lower-case c.) The specific heat capacity depends only on the material and not on the quantity present.

Because heat has units of joules and temperature has units of Kelvins or degrees Celsius, the units of heat capacity are J/K or J/°C. For differences in temperature, Kelvins and degrees Celsius are interchangeable, so these two units are equivalent. Because $c = \frac{C}{m}$, the specific heat has units of J/(kg K) or J/(kg °C)

For a gas, the heat capacity is not a constant; it depends on what other quantities are changing. The ideal gas equation, $PV = nRT$, shows that temperature cannot change without affecting other properties of the gas; assuming that the amount of gas (the number of molecules) doesn't change, then either the pressure or the volume must change or both. The heat capacity depends on which of these is changing, and so a gas is said to have a heat capacity at constant pressure, C_P, and a heat capacity at constant volume, C_V.

These two heat capacities are not the same—the heat capacity at constant pressure is always higher than the heat capacity at constant volume because some energy is required to do work on the gas as it expands. However, for an ideal gas there is a simple relationship between the two. The derivation is a bit complicated, but it can be shown that for an ideal gas $C_P - C_V = nR$, where n is the number of moles of gas and R is the ideal gas constant.

BOLTZMANN'S CONSTANT

Boltzmann's constant, abbreviated k or k_B, is a constant that arises in multiple places in thermodynamics. It is named after Austrian physicist Ludwig Eduard Boltzmann, best known for his development of statistical mechanics. Boltzmann's constant is equal to about 1.38×10^{-23} J/K.

One place Boltzmann's constant arises is as the ratio of the ideal gas constant to Avogadro's number: $k_B = \frac{R}{N_A}$. In fact, by using the number of molecules instead of the number of moles, it is possible to rewrite the ideal gas law in terms of Boltzmann's constant instead of the ideal gas constant: $PV = Nk_BT$. This may be useful if you actually know (or want to determine) the number of molecules rather than the number of moles. Boltzmann's constant also turns up in the relationship of kinetic energy to temperature: the average kinetic energy of a molecule in a gas at temperature T turns out to be equal to $\frac{3}{2}k_BT$.

DEVIATION OF REAL GAS BEHAVIOR FROM IDEAL GAS LAW

The main property of an ideal gas that is affected by the number of atoms per molecule is the gas's heat capacity. It can be shown that the heat capacity of a gas at constant pressure is equal to $\frac{1}{2}nR$ for each degree of freedom of the gas particles—roughly, each direction in which the gas particles can meaningfully move or rotate. A single atom is spherically symmetrical, so rotations don't matter, but it can move along any of three axes, so it has three degrees of freedom: its heat capacity at constant pressure is therefore $\frac{3}{2}nR$. A diatomic molecule, on the other hand, has in addition two axes of rotation, so it has five total degrees of freedom and a heat capacity at constant pressure of $\frac{5}{2}nR$. (There's a sixth degree of freedom in the ability of the bond to change its length, but near room temperature it can be ignored due to energy limitations.) Because for an ideal gas $C_P = C_V + nR$, we can also find the heat capacities at constant pressure: $\frac{5}{2}nR$ for a monatomic gas or $\frac{7}{2}nR$ for a diatomic. Once the molecules have more than two atoms, the degrees of freedom become more difficult to determine.

Most instruments that measure the pressure inside a container, including manometers, the gauges used to check tire pressures, and the sphygmomanometers doctors use to measure blood pressure, don't actually measure the total pressure. What they're really measuring is the difference in pressure between the inside of the container and the outside. Because this is the pressure read by gauges, this is called the gauge pressure.

Although the gauge pressure is often useful, at other times it is important to know not just the difference in pressure but the total pressure of the gas inside a container—for example, if one has to use that pressure to calculate some other property using the ideal gas law. This pressure is called the absolute pressure. There is a simple relationship between the two pressures: the absolute pressure is equal to the gauge pressure plus the atmospheric pressure.

For instance, if a gauge used to measure the pressure in a car's tire gives a reading of 32.5 psi, then the gauge pressure is 32.5 psi, but the absolute pressure is:

$$P_{gauge} + P_{atm} = 32.5 \text{ psi} + 14.7 \text{ psi} = 47.2 \text{ psi}$$

PARTIAL PRESSURE AND MOLE FRACTION

The partial pressure of a gas in a container is the pressure that a particular gas within a mixture of gases would have in the absence of the other gases in the mixture. For example, if two ideal gases are mixed together in equal quantities, the partial pressure of each gas is just half the total pressure of the two gases.

The mole fraction of a particular element or compound in a mixture is the ratio of the number of moles of the substance in question to the total number of moles of all the substances in the compound. In a mixture of 10 moles of oxygen and 30 moles of nitrogen, for instance, the mole fraction of oxygen would be $\frac{10}{10+30} = 0.25$, and the mole fraction of nitrogen would be $\frac{30}{10+30} = 0.75$.

For an ideal gas, or rather a mixture of ideal gases, the partial pressure of any constituent is proportional to the mole fraction of that constituent. This follows from the ideal gas law: $PV = nRT$, and the volumes and temperatures of all the constituent gases are the same, so $P_i \propto n_i$.

DALTON'S LAW

Dalton's Law states that the sum of the partial pressures of all the constituents of a particular mixture of (ideal) gases is equal to the total pressure of the gas. It is named after the English chemist and physicist John Dalton, perhaps best known for his seminal role in the development of modern atomic theory.

Dalton's Law has applications to medicine and meteorology, among other fields. In medicine, it is often important to know the partial pressures of individual gases because it is that partial pressure that determines its effect on the body; this also applies, for instance, to scuba divers, who can't let the partial pressure of nitrogen in the mixture they're breathing get too large without risking adverse effects. In meteorology, the partial pressures of different gases in the atmosphere are responsible for many weather phenomena.

Review Video: Dalton's Law of Partial Pressure
Visit mometrix.com/academy and enter code: 355830

UNITS OF PRESSURE

The standard SI unit of pressure is the Pascal, Pa, where $1 \text{ Pa} = 1 \text{ N/m}^2$. However, there are several other units of pressure in common use under certain circumstances. Some other common units of pressure include the following:

- **Atmospheres** (atm): one atmosphere is the (approximate) mean atmospheric pressure at sea level on Earth. It is defined as exactly 101,325 Pa.
- **Pounds per square inch** (psi): this is the standard unit of pressure in traditional avoirdupois (English) units, and although rarely used in science, is still often seen elsewhere: pressure in car tires, for instance, is usually measured in psi. One psi is about 6890 N/m^2; $1 \text{ atm} = 14.70$ psi.
- **Millimeters of mercury** (mmHg): this is a pressure scale based on the height of a column of mercury in a standard mercury barometer. One mmHg is about 133.3 Pa; 1 atm is about 760 mmHg. Historically, the mmHg was also called a torr; now these units have been redefined to be slightly different but still very close to the same: 1 torr is about 0.99999985 mmHg.

INTERMOLECULAR FORCES

HYDROGEN BONDING

Hydrogen bonding refers to an intermolecular force between two polar molecules arising because a hydrogen atom with a partial positive charge in one molecule is attracted to an atom in another molecule with a partial negative charge. Although hydrogen bonds are not as strong as molecular covalent bonds, the fact that they do cause the molecules to "stick together" better is responsible for increasing the boiling points and viscosities of the compounds in which hydrogen bonds occur. For example, water molecules form hydrogen bonds—between a hydrogen atom in one molecule and the oxygen atom in another—and it is this that gives water its relatively high boiling point and viscosity as well as allowing it to form an open lattice in the solid form that gives solid water (ice) its low density.

When two molecules form a hydrogen bond, due to a positively charged hydrogen atom in one molecule being attracted to a negatively charged atom in the other, the negatively charged atom that the hydrogen atom is attracted to is called the hydrogen bond acceptor, whereas the atom bonded to the hydrogen atom in the first molecule (not the hydrogen atom itself) is called the hydrogen bond donor. The hydrogen bond acceptor must have an unbonded electron pair for the hydrogen atom to be attracted to. Both the donor and the acceptor tend to be highly electronegative atoms—the acceptor because it is this electronegativity that results in the atom remaining negatively charged while part of a molecule, the donor because the electronegativity of the atom the hydrogen is bonded to results in the hydrogen atom being positively charged. Oxygen, nitrogen, and fluorine, due to their high electronegativities, are common as both hydrogen bond donors and hydrogen bond acceptors.

DIPOLE INTERACTIONS

A dipole-dipole interaction is an intermolecular force arising because of the attraction between the negative end of one polar molecule and the positive end of another. Generally, the more polar the molecules, the stronger this force, although dipole-dipole interactions are never as strong as covalent or ionic bonds. Hydrogen bonding is one kind of dipole-dipole interaction, but dipole-dipole interactions can occur between any polar compounds—molecules in which one end has a partial positive charge and one end has a slight negative charge. Dipole-dipole interactions play important parts in biological systems; for example, the shape of a protein is largely determined by the dipole-dipole interactions between its parts.

DIPOLE-INDUCED DIPOLE INTERMOLECULAR FORCES

Whereas dipole–dipole intermolecular forces are between two polar molecules, a dipole-induced intermolecular force is between a polar molecule and a nonpolar molecule. Dipole-induced dipole intermolecular forces are forces that occur when a dipole induces a temporary dipole in a molecule that is nonpolar. The electron cloud of the nonpolar molecule is distorted when it comes near the electron cloud of a dipole. This is typically a weak intermolecular force. However, this dipole-induced dipole intermolecular force is responsible for the stability of hydrates formed from hydrocarbons and some of the noble gases.

VAN DER WAALS' FORCES

London dispersion forces are weak forces that arise between molecules because of temporary polarization—even if a molecule is nonpolar, it may have a temporary dipole moment at a given time because the electrons happen to be at that time distributed more toward one side of the nucleus, and two molecules with such temporary dipole moments may be attracted to each other similarly to a dipole-dipole interaction. London dispersion forces and dipole-dipole interactions, the other main kind of intermolecular force, are collectively called Van der Waals forces (although sometimes this term is used to refer only to dispersion forces).

Although London dispersion forces can occur between any molecules, polar or nonpolar, they tend to be stronger between larger molecules and atoms than smaller ones and stronger in long, thin molecules than in more compact ones. That is because the larger the molecule or atom, and the less compact it is, the easier it is for the electrons to become displaced and for the molecule to become temporarily polar—this property is referred to as the molecule's polarizability.

INTERMOLECULAR INTERACTIONS EXAMPLES

NH_3 - The intermolecular forces present in a sample of NH_3 are London forces and hydrogen bonds. London forces are present between all molecules. Hydrogen bonds are present between molecules with hydrogen covalently bonded to nitrogen, fluorine, and oxygen.

CH_4 - The intermolecular forces present in a sample of CH_4 are only London forces. London forces are present between all molecules. Because CH_4 is a nonpolar molecular molecule, no dipole–dipole forces are present.

H_2S - The intermolecular forces present in a sample of H_2S are London forces and dipole–dipole forces. London forces are present between all molecules. Dipole–dipole forces are present between polar molecules, and because H_2S is a polar molecule, dipole–dipole forces are present.

PHASE DIAGRAM

A **phase diagram** is a diagram that shows the phase (solid, liquid, or gas) that a particular compound or element is in at different pressures and temperatures. It is conventionally drawn with pressure on the y axis and temperature on the x-axis; lines on the diagram mark the boundaries of the regions in the diagram where the compound is in each phase. At points on these lines, the two phases are in equilibrium; the points on these lines at particular pressures mark the compound's freezing or boiling points at those pressures. The point where all three phases are in equilibrium is the triple point, the unique pressure and temperature where all three phases of the compound are in equilibrium.

For example, below is a phase diagram of water, with the triple point marked as well as the boiling and freezing points at atmospheric pressure:

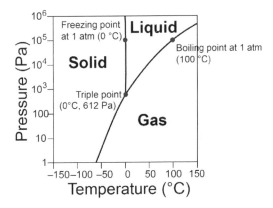

Note that in this diagram the pressure is given a logarithmic scale; this is common in phase diagrams to depict a wide range of pressures, but it is not required; phase diagrams can also be drawn with linear pressure scales.

HEAT OF FUSION AND HEAT OF VAPORIZATION

The **heat of fusion** of a compound, abbreviated L_f, is the amount of heat released when a particular quantity of the compound changes from liquid to solid state—or, equivalently, the amount of heat required to change that quantity of the compound from solid to liquid. The **heat of vaporization**, L_v, is the amount of heat released when a particular quantity of the compound changes from gas to liquid state—or, equivalently, the amount of heat required to change that quantity of the compound from liquid to gas. Typically, in metric units, the quantity is taken to be 1 gram, and L_f and L_v are both measured in Joules per gram (J/g).

For instance, suppose we want to know the amount of heat required to convert 1.0 kilogram of ice into water vapor. This requires first melting the ice into water, then heating the water from 0 °C to 100 °C then vaporizing the water. Water has a heat of fusion of 334 J/g, a heat of vaporization of 2230 J/g, and a specific heat of 4.184 J/g°C; the total heat involved is therefore:

$$mL_f + mC\Delta T + mL_v = (1000 \text{ g})(334 \text{ J/g}) + (1000 \text{ g})(4.184 \text{ J/g°C})(100°C) + (1000 \text{ g})(2230 \text{ J/g})$$
$$= 2.98 \times 10^6 \text{ J or } 2980 \text{ kJ}$$

Enthalpy, abbreviated H, is a measurement of the total energy of a thermodynamic system. Specifically, it is equal to the internal energy of the system plus the product of its pressure and volume: $H = U + PV$. (It should not be confused with entropy, which has a similar name but is an entirely different concept.)

During a process at constant pressure, the change in enthalpy is $\Delta H = \Delta U + P\Delta V = \Delta U - W$, where W is the work on the system (or $\Delta U + W$, where W is the work done by the system). The First Law of Thermodynamics says that $\Delta U = Q + W$; therefore, $\Delta U - W = Q$, and the change in enthalpy is equal to the heat added to the system. Because of this, the heat of reaction of a chemical process is also called its enthalpy of reaction; the two terms are equivalent because the heat added to the system is equal to its change in enthalpy.

POLAR AND NONPOLAR COVALENT BONDS

Polar covalent bonds result when electrons are shared unequally between atoms. **Nonpolar covalent bonds** result when electrons are shared equally between atoms. The unequal sharing of electrons is due to the differences in the electronegativities of the two atoms sharing the electrons. Partial charges develop due to this unequal sharing of electrons. The greater the difference in electronegativities between the two atoms, the stronger the dipole is. For example, the covalent bonds formed between the carbon atom and the two oxygen atoms in carbon dioxide are polar covalent bonds because the electronegativities of carbon and oxygen differ slightly. If the electronegativities are equal, then the covalent bonds are nonpolar. For example, the covalent double bond between two oxygen atoms is nonpolar because the oxygen atoms have the same electronegativities.

> **Review Video: Nonpolar Covalent Bonds**
> Visit mometrix.com/academy and enter code: 986465
>
> **Review Video: What are Covalent Bonds**
> Visit mometrix.com/academy and enter code: 482899

IDENTIFYING POLAR OR NONPOLAR EXAMPLES:

CH_4 - Nonpolar: Methane or CH_4 has a tetrahedral geometry with four hydrogen atoms covalently bonded around the central carbon atom. These four bonds are polar covalent bonds, but because they are arranged symmetrically around the central carbon atom, the molecule is nonpolar.

CO_2 - Nonpolar: Carbon dioxide, or CO_2, is a linear molecule with two oxygen atoms covalently double bonded to a central carbon atom. These two double bonds are polar covalent bonds, but because they are arranged symmetrically around the carbon atom, the molecule is nonpolar.

H_2S - Polar: Dihydrogen sulfide, or H_2S, is an angular molecule with the two hydrogen atoms covalently bonded to a sulfur atom. This molecule has two bonding pairs and one nonbonding pair. Because of the nonbonding pair, the molecule is bent or angular. Because the polar bonds do not cancel each other out in this arrangement, the molecule is polar.

NH_3 - Polar: Ammonia, or NH_3, is a trigonal pyramidal molecule with the three hydrogen atoms bonded asymmetrically around the central nitrogen atom. The molecule has three bonding pairs and one nonbonding pair of electrons. Because the polar covalent bonds are arranged asymmetrically, the molecule is polar.

BF_3 - Nonpolar: Boron trifluoride is a trigonal planar molecule with three fluorine atoms bonded symmetrically around the central boron atom. Because the molecule is an exception to the octet rule and only has three bonding pairs and no nonbonding pairs around the central boron atom, these fluorine atoms are arranged symmetrically around the boron atom canceling out the effect of the polar covalent bonds and resulting in a nonpolar molecule.

INTENSIVE AND EXTENSIVE PROPERTIES

Physical properties are categorized as either intensive or extensive. **Intensive** properties *do not* depend on the amount of matter or quantity of the sample. This means that intensive properties will not change if the sample size is increased or decreased. Intensive properties include color, hardness, melting point, boiling point, density, ductility, malleability, specific heat, temperature, concentration, and magnetization.

Extensive properties *do* depend on the amount of matter or quantity of the sample. Therefore, extensive properties do change if the sample size is increased or decreased. If the sample size is increased, the property increases. If the sample size is decreased, the property decreases. Extensive properties include volume, mass, weight, energy, entropy, number of moles, and electrical charge.

BONDING AND STRUCTURE

PROPERTIES AFFECTED BY BONDING AND STRUCTURE

Bonding and structure determine whether a substance exists naturally as a solid, liquid, or gas. Properties that are affected by bonding and structure include boiling point, freezing point, and vapor pressure. Bonding and structure determine if a substance is soluble in water or in nonpolar solvents. Also affected are the viscosity of liquids and whether a solid material is hard or soft and whether or not a substance forms crystals or is amorphous. Bonding affects the conductivity of heat and electricity and whether a substance is a good insulator or conductor.

EFFECT OF BONDING AND STRUCTURE ON BOILING POINTS AND MELTING POINTS

The types of bonds within molecules affect boiling and melting points. Compounds with ionic bonds typically have high melting and boiling points, whereas compounds with covalent bonds typically have low melting and boiling points. Intermolecular forces also affect these points. Substances with hydrogen bonds typically have high boiling and melting points. For example, hydrogen bonds are responsible for the high boiling and melting points of water.

> **Review Video: <u>Differences in Boiling Points</u>**
> Visit mometrix.com/academy and enter code: 810110

EFFECT OF BONDING AND STRUCTURE ON SOLUBILITY

Bonding and structure affect solubility. The basic idea behind solubility is *like dissolves like*. This means that solutes with polar molecules typically dissolve in solvents with polar molecules. The polarity of the molecules is determined by the type of bonds and the arrangement of those bonds in the molecules. For example, both salt and table sugar (sucrose) dissolve in water because salt, table sugar, and water are polar molecules. Solutes with nonpolar molecules typically dissolve in solvents with nonpolar molecules. For example, a grease stain will not rinse out with water because water consists of polar molecules and grease is a nonpolar lipid.

EFFECT OF BONDING AND STRUCTURE ON EQUILIBRIUM VAPOR PRESSURE

Vapor pressure is related to the boiling point of a substance. The boiling point of a substance is the temperature at which the vapor pressure equals the atmospheric pressure. In general, as the vapor pressure increases, the boiling point decreases. Compounds with ionic bonds typically have high boiling points and low vapor pressures. Compounds with covalent bonds typically have low boiling points and high vapor pressures. Substances with the strongest intermolecular forces, hydrogen bonds, typically have high boiling points and low vapor pressures.

Solutions

MIXTURE, SOLUTION, AND COLLOID

A **mixture** is made of two or more substances that are combined in various proportions. The exact proportion of the constituents is the defining characteristic of any mixture. There are two types of mixtures: homogeneous and heterogeneous. **Homogeneous** means that the mixture's composition and properties are uniform throughout. Conversely, **heterogeneous** means that the mixture's composition and properties are not uniform throughout.

A **solution** is a homogeneous mixture of substances that cannot be separated by filtration or centrifugation. Solutions are made by dissolving one or more solutes into a solvent. For example, in an aqueous glucose solution, glucose is the solute and water is the solvent. If there is more than one liquid present in the solution, then the most prevalent liquid is considered the solvent. The exact mechanism of dissolving varies depending on the mixture, but the result is always individual solute ions or molecules surrounded by solvent molecules. The proportion of solute to solvent for a particular solution is its **concentration**.

A **colloid** is a heterogeneous mixture in which small particles (<1 micrometer) are suspended, but not dissolved, in a liquid. As such, they can be separated by centrifugation. A commonplace example of a colloid is milk.

DILUTE AND CONCENTRATED

The terms **dilute** and **concentrated** have opposite meanings. In a solution, the solute is dissolved in the solvent. The more solute that is dissolved, the more concentrated is the solution. The less solute that is dissolved, the less concentrated and the more dilute is the solution. The terms are often associated with the preparation of a stock solution for a laboratory experiment. Stock solutions are typically ordered in a concentrated solution. To prepare for use in a chemistry lab, the stock solutions are diluted to the appropriate molarity by adding a specific amount of solvent such as water to a specific amount of stock solution.

SATURATED, UNSATURATED, AND SUPERSATURATED

The terms saturated, unsaturated, and supersaturated are associated with solutions. In a solution, a solute is added to a solvent. In a **saturated** solution, the solute is added to the solvent until no more solute is able to dissolve. The undissolved solute will settle down to the bottom of the beaker. A solution is considered **unsaturated** as long as more solute is able to go into solution under ordinary conditions. The solubility of solids in liquids typically increases as temperature increases. If the temperature of a solution is increased as the solute is being added, more solute than is normally possible may go into solution, forming a **supersaturated** solution.

SOLUBILITY OF IONS IN WATER

Some general guidelines regarding solubility include the following:

- All nitrates and acetates are soluble;
- All chlorides, bromides, and iodides are soluble except those of silver, mercury(I), and lead(II);
- All sulfates are soluble except those of strontium, barium, mercury(I), and lead(II);
- All sulfides are insoluble except those of ammonium, the alkali metal cations, calcium, strontium, and barium;
- All carbonates are insoluble except those of ammonium and the alkali metal cations;
- All phosphates are insoluble except those of ammonium and the alkali metal cations; and
- All hydroxides are insoluble except those of the alkali metal cations and calcium, strontium, and barium.

IONS IN SOLUTIONS
ANION, CATION COMMON NAMES

A monatomic anion is named by the element of the atom with the suffix "-ide." For example, a monatomic chlorine ion is called chloride, a monatomic iodine atom iodide, a monatomic sulfur ion sulfide, and so on.

With rare exceptions, the charge of a monatomic anion depends on its group. A halogen (group 17) has a charge of –1, an element in the oxygen group (group 16) has a charge of –2, and an element in group 15 has a charge of –3. Elements of other groups do not generally appear as monatomic anions. So, for instance, because iodine is a halogen, it has a charge of -1 and iodide is I^-; sulfur is in the oxygen group, so a sulfide ion is S^{2-}; because nitrogen is in group 15, a nitride ion is N^{3-}.

The prefixes "hypo-" and "per-" are used for oxyanions, which consist of one or more oxygen atoms and one atom of another element. For a given element, the most common such anion is named with the suffix "-ate" and the anion with one less oxygen atom with the suffix "-ite." For some elements, however, there are more than two such ions, and in these cases the prefixes "hypo-" and "per-" are used for the additional anions. The prefix "per-" always accompanies the suffix "-ate" and identifies the anion with one more oxygen atom than the anion named with -ate. The prefix "hypo-" always accompanies the suffix "-ite" and identifies an anion with one fewer oxygen atom than the anion named with -ite.

The best-known anions using these prefixes are oxyanions of chlorine. Chlorine has four oxyanions: chlorate is ClO_3^-, chlorite is ClO_2^-, perchlorate is ClO_4^-, and hypochlorite is ClO^-. There are likewise four oxyanions of bromine: bromate is BrO_3^-, bromite is BrO_2^-, perbromate is BrO_4^-, and hypobromite is BrO^-. Iodine has the oxyanions iodate, IO_3^-; iodite, IO_2^-; periodate, IO_4^-; and hypoiodite, IO^-.

One of the most common types of anion is the oxyanion, consisting of one or more oxygen atoms and one atom of a different element. There are also some anions that are similar to oxyanions but with the addition of a hydrogen atom (and with one less negative charge). These anions are named by the name of the corresponding oxyanion preceded by hydrogen. For instance, CO_3^{2-} is carbonate, and HCO_3^- is hydrogen carbonate; PO_4^{3-} is phosphate, and HPO_4^{2-} is hydrogen phosphate; SO_4^{2-} is sulfate, and HSO_4^- is hydrogen phosphate. Hydrogen carbonate and hydrogen sulfate are also called bicarbonate and bisulfate, respectively.

The oxyanion may also have two hydrogen atoms added to it; in which case its name is preceded by dihydrogen. The only common example is dihydrogen phosphate, $H_2PO_4^-$.

As the prefix "di-" implies, the dichromate ion includes two chromium atoms. The suffix "-ate" is the same suffix used for oxyanions, and like an oxyanion, dichromate includes a number of oxygen atoms. Unfortunately, there's nothing in the name of the ion to specify exactly how many oxygen atoms it contains, or its charge, so those may have to be memorized. The dichromate ion is $Cr_2O_7^{2-}$.

The prefix "thio-" is applied to anions that are similar to oxyanions but have one of the oxygen atoms replaced by a sulfur ion. Cyanate is OCN^-—the cyanide ion, CN^-, with the addition of an oxygen atom. In thiocyanate, that oxygen atom is replaced by sulfur to make SCN^-. Sulfate is SO_4^{2-}; although it already contains a sulfur atom, in thiosulfate, one of the oxygen atoms is replaced by an additional sulfur atom to make $S_2O_3^{2-}$.

The suffixes "-ate" and "-ite" are used for oxyanions, a common class of polyatomic ions that combine one or more oxygen atoms with one atom of a different element. These ions are generally named after the non-oxygen atom, with the suffix "-ate" or "-ite." Different anions exist with the same element but with different oxidation values and different numbers of oxygen atoms. They are distinguished by the suffixes: the most common such ion, or the one considered in some sense the more fundamental, gets the suffix "-ate," whereas an anion with the same element but one less oxygen atom gets the "-ite" suffix.

Polyatomic cations are in general less common and less numerous than polyatomic anions (at least in terms of relatively simple ions, one can construct arbitrarily many complex examples of both). One important polyatomic cation, however, is ammonium, NH_4^+. Chemicals including ammonium include ammonium chloride, commonly used as in fertilizers; ammonium nitrate, used in fertilizers and explosives; and ammonium carbonate, used as a leavening agent (although today largely replaced by sodium bicarbonate).

Another important polyatomic ion *is hydronium,* H_3O^+, which is notable as one of the products of the dissociation of water: $2H_2O \rightleftharpoons H_3O^+ + OH^-$. Despite its importance in the chemistry of water, hydronium is not a component of any common stable compounds.

One other relatively common polyatomic ion is the mercury (I) ion, Hg_2^{2+}. This ion is found in compounds including mercury (I) chloride, also known as calomel, and is used in electrochemistry, and mercury (I) iodide, formerly used as a medicine despite its (then unrecognized) toxicity.

There are other polyatomic cations, but they are much less common. They include phosphonium (PH_4^+), arsonium (AsH_4^+), methanium (CH_5^+), and tropylium ($C_7H_7^+$).

As monatomic ions, metals are most likely to be cations, whereas nonmetals are most likely to be anions. This is because metals in general have only a few electrons in their outer shells, so they can most easily obtain full valence shells by donating electrons, turning them into positive ions. Nonmetals, on the other hand, have mostly filled valence shells, so they can most easily fill their valence shells by gaining electrons. (Carbon and silicon are exceptions because their valence shells are half full, but these elements do not commonly occur as monatomic ions.)

Hydrogen can be either a cation or an anion because it can fill its valence shell either by gaining one electron or by losing one electron. Most often it is a cation (as in hydrochloric acid, HCl, or hydrofluoric acid, HF), but it can also bond with a metal with a lower electronegativity to become an anion (as in lithium hydride, LiH).

> **Review Video: Anion, Cation, and Octet Rule**
> Visit mometrix.com/academy and enter code: 303525

There is, unfortunately, no easy way to tell from the name how many oxygen atoms a particular ion has, so it is useful to memorize some common ions. Some of the most important such anions include the following:

$$
\begin{array}{rl}
\text{Carbonate:} & CO_3^{2-} \\
\text{Nitrate:} & NO_3^- \\
\text{Nitrite:} & NO_2^- \\
\text{Phosphate:} & PO_4^{3-} \\
\text{Sulfate:} & SO_4^{2-} \\
\text{Sulfite:} & SO_3^{2-}
\end{array}
$$

FORMULAS AND CHARGES FOR FAMILIAR IONS

Hydroxide is OH^-. Hydroxide ions are found in many strong bases including sodium hydroxide and potassium hydroxide as well as in water.

Cyanide is CN^-. Cyanide salts such as sodium cyanide are noted for their high toxicity.

Acetate is $C_2H_3O_2^-$. This organic anion is found in acetic acid, the main component of vinegar as well as in fatty acids and many other organic compounds.

Peroxide is O_2^-. Many peroxide compounds are used as bleaching agents. The simplest common peroxide compound is hydrogen peroxide, H_2O_2, used as a household disinfectant.

HYDRATION

Hydration refers to the addition of water to a chemical species. Although other reactions with water are sometimes called by this name, one common phenomenon referred to as hydration involves water molecules surrounding an ion or a polar molecule to form a hydration shell. The water molecules are attracted to the ion or molecule because the water molecules are themselves slightly polar—the oxygen atom slightly positive and the hydrogen atoms slightly negative—so the oxygen atoms in water are attracted to positive ions or to the positive ends of polar molecules, and the hydrogen atoms are attracted to negative ions or the negative ends of polar molecules.

Hydration helps polar molecules dissolve in water; when sodium chloride dissociates in water, for instance, the water molecules surrounding the ions help disperse them through the solution. Hydration also plays an important role in the functioning of proteins; the water molecules surrounding parts of the proteins affect their shapes.

SOLUBILITY

FREEZING POINT DEPRESSION

Freezing point depression is a colligative property of solutions that depends only on the number of particles in solution, not on the identity of those particles. Adding a nonvolatile solute to a solution will lower the freezing point of that solution. This decrease in temperature is known as **freezing point depression**. Basically, the particles of the nonvolatile solute occupy spaces near the surface and block or inhibit the solvent particles from escaping from the surface of the solution. As fewer particles escape, the vapor pressure lowers. This decrease in vapor pressure causes a decrease in the freezing point known as freezing point depression. The amount of depression can be calculated from the equation $\Delta T_{FP} = mk_f$, where m is the molality of the solution and k_f is the molal freezing point constant for that particular solvent.

> **Review Video: Freezing Point Depression of an Aqueous Solution**
> Visit mometrix.com/academy and enter code: 274630

BOILING POINT ELEVATION

Boiling point elevation is a colligative property of solutions that depends only on the number of particles in solution, not on the identity of those particles. Adding a nonvolatile solute to a solution will raise the boiling point of that solution. This rise in temperature is known as boiling point elevation. Basically, the particles of the nonvolatile solute occupy spaces near the surface and block or inhibit the solvent particles from escaping from the surface of the solution. As fewer particles escape, the vapor pressure lowers. This decrease in vapor pressure causes an increase in the boiling point known as **boiling point elevation**. The amount of elevation can be calculated from the equation $\Delta T_{BP} = mk_b$, where m is the molality of the solution and k_b is the molal boiling point constant for that particular solvent.

SOLUBILITY PRODUCT CONSTANT

The **solubility product constant**, K_{sp}, is a constant that relates to the equilibrium conditions for the concentrations of ions in a slightly soluble ionic compound. It is a special case of the general equilibrium constant K_{eq}. In the case of an arbitrary ionic compound A_mC_n with anion A^{n-} and cation C^{m+}, the equilibrium condition is $K_{sp} = [A^{n+}]^m[C^{m-}]^n$. (The original compound A_mC_n does not contribute to the equilibrium condition because of its solid state; the concentrations of solids and liquids do not change in a reaction, so they do not appear in the equilibrium equation.)

If an ion is present from sources other than the dissolved chemical, the solubility product constant can be used to find out how much of the other ion is present. For example, consider calcium fluoride; CaF_2. K_{sp} for calcium fluoride is 3.45×10^{-11}. If all the calcium and fluoride ions in a solution come from dissolved CaF_2, then there must be twice as many fluoride ions as calcium. Setting the number of fluoride ions to x gives:

$$K_{sp} = (x)(2x)^2 = 4x^3$$

$$[Ca^{2+}] = x = \sqrt[3]{\frac{K_{sp}}{4}} = \sqrt[3]{3.45 \times \frac{10^{-11}}{4}} = 2.05 \times 10^{-4}$$

This must also be the moles per liter of the calcium fluoride that it dissolved; multiplying by the molar mass of CaF_2 gives a solubility of 0.016 g/mol.

The **mass percent** of a solution is a ratio of the mass of the solute in a solution to the total mass of the solution. Molarity is a measurement of the moles of solute to the volume of the solution in moles per liter. You can convert mass percent to molarity by first dividing by the molar mass to convert the mass of solution to moles and then multiplying by the density of the solution to convert the mass of solute to liters. To convert molarity to mass percent, just do the reverse.

For example, suppose you have a 4.00 M solution of NaCl, with a density of 1150 kg/m^3. The molar mass of sodium chloride is 58.443 g/mol, so the mass percent of this solution is:

$$\frac{(4.00 \text{ mol/l})(0.058443 \text{ kg/mol})}{1.15 \text{ kg/l}} = 0.203 \text{ or } 20.3\%$$

Parts per million, sometimes abbreviated ppm, is a unit that is sometimes used for very dilute solutions when the concentration expressed in traditional units like molarity or mass percent would be an inconveniently small number. It literally refers to the number of grams of solute per million grams of solution. One ppm is therefore equal to 0.0001% as a mass percent. For an aqueous solution, which if sufficiently dilute will have essentially the same density as water, 1.00 g/mL; 1 ppm equals 1 mg/L.

For even more dilute solutions, other, similar units are sometimes used such as parts per billion (ppb), parts per trillion (ppt), and so on.

COMMON-ION EFFECT
The common-ion effect refers to the fact that a slightly soluble ionic compound will become less soluble in a solution that contains one of the same ions as the compound. For example, calcium carbonate ($CaCO_3$) already has a low solubility in water, but in a solution of potassium carbonate (K_2CO_3), its solubility is even lower because the calcium carbonate and the potassium carbonate share the carbonate ion in common. The common ion effect follows from the solubility equilibrium condition that the product of the concentrations of the ions is constant. Therefore, an increase in the concentration of one ion must result in a decrease of the other; this is only possible if some ions combine to precipitate the solid compound. The effect can be considered a special case of Le Châtelier's principle.

The common-ion effect is useful in preparing laboratory separations because it can be used to precipitate out a desired compound from a solution by adding another compound that shares an ion with it. For instance, sodium chloride (NaCl) can be precipitated out of saltwater by the addition of hydrochloric acid (HCl).

EFFECTS OF TEMPERATURE, SURFACE AREA, AGITATION, AND PRESSURE ON THE DISSOLUTION RATE

Temperature, pressure, surface area, and agitation affect the dissolution rate. Increasing the temperature increases the kinetic energy of the molecules, which increases the number of collisions with the solute particles. Increasing the surface area of contact by stirring (agitation) or crushing a solid solute also increases the dissolution rate and helps prevent recrystallization. Increasing the pressure will increase the dissolution rate for gas solutes in liquid solvents because the added pressure will make it more difficult for the gas to escape. Increasing the pressure will have virtually no effect on the dissolution rate for solid solutes in liquid solvents under normal conditions.

EFFECT OF TEMPERATURE AND PRESSURE ON SOLUBILITY

Temperature and pressure affect solubility. For gas solutes in liquid solvents, increasing the temperature increases the kinetic energy causing more gas particles to escape the surface of the liquid solvents and therefore decreasing the solubility of the solutes. For most solid solutes in liquid solvents, increasing the temperature increases the solubility, as shown in this solubility curve for selected salts. For gas solutes in liquid solvents, increasing the pressure increases the solubility. Increasing the pressure of liquid or solid solutes in liquid solvents has virtually no effect under normal conditions.

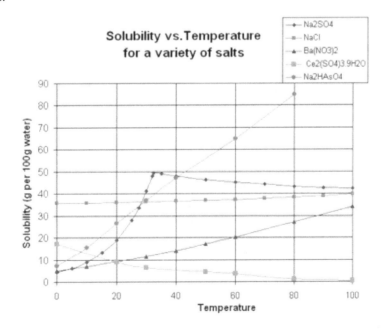

OSMOSIS

Osmosis can be defined as diffusion through a semipermeable membrane. Typically, small solvent particles can pass through, but larger solute particles are too large to pass through. This means that osmosis is the net flow of solvent from a solution with a lower concentration to a solution with a higher concentration until a state of equilibrium is reached. The pressure that must be applied to the semipermeable membrane to stop the flow of solvent to reach this equilibrium state is called *osmotic pressure*. Osmotic pressure is a colligative property that depends on the number of nonvolatile solute particles, not the identity.

UNITS OF CONCENTRATION

Molarity, molality, and normality are all measures of the concentration of a solution, but they are measured in different ways. Molarity (abbreviated M) is a measurement of the number of atoms or molecules of solute by volume of the solution; it has units of moles per liter. Molality (abbreviated m) is a measurement of the number of atoms or molecules of solute by mass of the solution; it has units of moles per kilogram.

Normality (abbreviated N) is a measurement of concentration that is used for acids. It measures the number of H^+ ions—of donatable protons—per liter of solution. For monoprotic acids, which only donate one proton per molecule, the normality is equal to the molarity. For polyprotic atoms, which donate multiple protons per molecule, the normality is equal to the molarity times the number of protons potentially donated by each atom. For example, sulfuric acid, H_2SO_4, is diprotic; it can donate up to two protons per molecule. The normality of a sulfuric acid solution is therefore double its molarity.

CALCULATING THE MOLARITY AND MOLALITY OF A SOLUTION

Molarity and molality are measures of the concentration of a solution. Molarity (M) is the amount of solute in moles per the amount of solution in liters. A 1.0 M solution consists of 1.0 mole of solute for each 1.0 L of solution. Molality (m) is the amount of solute in moles per the amount of solvent in kilograms. A 1.0 m solution consists of 1.0 mole of solute for each 1.0 kg of solvent. Often, when performing these calculations, the amount of solute is given in grams. To convert from grams of solute to moles of solute, multiply the grams of solute by the molar mass of the solute:

$$\text{Molarity (M)} = \frac{\text{moles of solute (mol)}}{\text{liters of solution (L)}}$$

$$\text{Molality (m)} = \frac{\text{moles of solute (mol)}}{\text{kilograms of solvent (kg)}}$$

Review Video: <u>Molarity of a Solution</u>
Visit mometrix.com/academy and enter code: 810121

CALCULATING MOLE FRACTION, PARTS PER MILLION, PARTS PER BILLION, AND PERCENT BY MASS OR VOLUME

Concentrations can be measured in mole fractions, parts per million, parts per billion, and percent by mass or volume. Mole fraction (χ) is calculated by dividing the number of moles of one component by the total number of moles of all of the components of the solution. Parts per million (ppm) is calculated by dividing the mass of the solute in grams by the mass of the solvent and solute in grams and then multiplying the quotient by 1,000,000 ppm. Parts per billion (ppb) is calculated similarly, except the quotient is multiplied by 1,000,000,000 ppb. Percent concentration can be calculated by mass or by volume by dividing the mass or volume of the solute by the mass or volume of the solution. This quotient is a decimal that can be converted to a percent by multiplying by 100.

CALCULATING THE MOLARITY OF 100.0 G OF $CaCl_2$ IN 500.0 ML OF SOLUTION

To calculate molarity, use the formula molarity (M) $= \frac{\text{moles of solute (mol)}}{\text{liters of solution (L)}}$. The necessary conversions from grams $CaCl_2$ to moles $CaCl_2$ and from 500.0 mL to liters may be performed using dimensional analysis. An alternate method of working this problem would be doing the conversions first and then substituting those values directly into the equation. Using the method of dimensional analysis

236

and substituting the given information into the equation yields molarity $= \frac{100.0 \text{ grams CaCl}_2}{500.0 \text{ mL of solution}}$. Adding the necessary conversions using dimensional analysis yields

$$\text{molarity} = \left(\frac{100.0 \text{ g CaCl}_2}{500.0 \text{ mL of solution}}\right)\left(\frac{\text{mol CaCl}_2}{110.98 \text{ g}}\right)\left(\frac{1000 \text{ mL}}{\text{L}}\right) = 1.802 \text{ M}.$$

PREPARING A DILUTE SOLUTION FROM A STOCK SOLUTION

In order to prepare a dilute solution from a stock solution, the molarity and the needed volume of the diluted solution as well as the molarity of the stock solution must be known. The volume of the stock solution to be diluted can be calculated using the formula $V_{stock}M_{stock} = V_{dilute}M_{dilute}$, where V_{stock} is the unknown variable, M_{stock} is the molarity of the stock solution, V_{dilute} is the needed volume of the dilute solution, and M_{dilute} is the needed molarity of the dilute solution. Solving this formula for V_{stock} yields $V_{stock} = \frac{V_{dilute}M_{dilute}}{M_{stock}}$. Then, dilute the calculated amount of stock solution (V_{stock}) to the total volume required of the diluted solution.

SOLUBILITY AND PH

The pH of a solution will not affect the solubility of all chemicals. In particular, the solubility of neutral salts will generally not be affected by the pH of a solution. However, the solubility of acidic or basic salts will be pH dependent.

A basic salt—the salt of a weak acid—will have a greater solubility the lower the pH of the solution. This is because the H_3O^+ ions in the acidic solution will react easily with the relatively strong basic anions of the salt. By Le Châtelier's principle, the removal of these ions from the solution will shift the equilibrium toward the production of more such ions, leading to more of the salt dissolving. For similar reasons, an acidic salt—the salt of a weak base—will have a greater solubility the higher the pH of the solution.

Acids and Bases

BRØNSTED-LOWRY DEFINITION OF ACIDS AND BASES

According to the Brønsted-Lowry definition of acids and bases—named after Danish chemist Johannes Nicolaus Brønsted and English chemist Thomas Martin Lowry—an acid is a substance that donates protons in a chemical reaction, and a base is a substance that accepts protons. This broadened the earlier Arrhenius definition, by which an acid dissociates in water to form H^+ ions, and a base dissociates in water to form OH^- ions. Because an H^+ ion is basically a proton, and because OH^- ions combine with H^+ ions to form water, in general an Arrhenius acid or base is also an acid or base by the Brønsted-Lowry definition. However, the Brønsted-Lowry definition also includes substances that are not acids or bases by the Arrhenius definition. For example, NH_3 in aqueous solution can accept a hydrogen ion from HCl to form NH_4^+ and Cl^-, making NH_3 a Brønsted-Lowry base even though it does not contain an OH^- ion.

Some substances can both donate and accept electrons and can therefore act as both acids and bases by the Brønsted-Lowry definition. Such substances are called amphoteric; the most prominent example is water.

IONIZATION OF WATER

pH is a measurement of the concentration of hydrogen ions in an aqueous solution and therefore of the solution's acidity. More specifically, it is equal to the negative logarithm base 10 of the ion concentration. Technically, free hydrogen ions in an aqueous solution tend to combine with water to form hydronium ions, H_3O^+, so it is really the concentration of hydronium ions, not free H^+ ions, that the pH measures. For example, if the molar concentration of H^+ (or H_3O^+) ions in a solution is 10^{-4}, then the solution's pH is $-\log_{10} 10^{-4} = 4$.

The pH of pure water is 7, which is considered neutral, neither acidic nor basic. Acidic substances have a lower pH; the pH of most orange juice is between 3.5 and 4, and the pH of white vinegar is about 2.4. Basic substances have a higher pH; the pH of baking soda is about 9, and the pH of strong drain cleaners can be about 14.

HYDRONIUM AND HYDROXIDE IONS

The pH is equal to the negative log base 10 of the concentration of hydroxide ions in an aqueous solution: $pH = -\log_{10}[H_3O^+]$. Turning this around to solve for the concentration of hydronium ions, we get $[H_3O^+] = 10^{-pH}$. For example, in a solution with a pH of 10, the molar concentration of hydronium ions is 10^{-10}.

The dissociation reaction of water is $2H_2O \rightarrow H_3O^+ + OH^-$. The equilibrium condition for this reaction is $K_{eq} = \frac{[H_3O^+][OH^-]}{[H_2O]^2}$. Because the number of the ions for typical solutions is very small in comparison to the number of neutral water molecules, we can treat $[H_2O]$ as being essentially constant and write $K_{eq}[H_2O]^2 = [H_3O^+][OH^-]$. The left-hand side of this equation can be written as a single constant K_w; at room temperature $K_w = 1.0 \times 10^{-14}$, so the concentrations of hydronium and hydroxide ions must multiply to $[H_3O^+][OH^-] = 10^{-14}$. Therefore, given either the concentration of hydronium ions or the concentration of hydroxide ions, you can find the other by dividing the known concentration into 10^{-14}. In the example with a concentration of hydronium ions of 10^{-10}, the concentration of hydroxide ions is $\frac{10^{-14}}{10^{-10}} = 10^{-4}$.

CONJUGATE ACIDS AND BASES

In an acid-base reaction, under Brønsted-Lowry definitions, the acid donates a proton to the base, converting both the acid and the base into new compounds. In general, this reaction is reversible, which means that the new compound formed from the base can donate the proton it received, and the new compound formed from the acid can accept a proton. This means the new compound formed from the base is an acid, and the new compound formed from the acid is a base. The base formed from an acid when it donates a proton is called its conjugate base; the acid formed from a base when it accepts a proton is called its conjugate acid. An acid or base together with its conjugate are known as a conjugate base pair. The stronger an acid, the weaker its conjugate base and vice versa.

For instance, hydrochloric acid, HCl, can donate a proton to become Cl^-, its conjugate base, but because HCl is a very strong acid, Cl^- is a very weak base. On the other end of the range, S^{2-} is a strong base by the Brønsted-Lowry definition; it can accept a proton to become HS^-, a very weak acid.

STRONG AND WEAK ACIDS AND BASES

The strength of an acid or base refers to how readily it donates or accepts a proton. A strong acid dissociates completely in water, with practically every molecule losing a proton. A weak acid only partially dissociates; the smaller the proportion of molecules that donate protons, the weaker the acid is said to be. Similarly, in a strong base, practically every molecule will accept a proton—in most cases because the base dissociates into a cation and a proton-accepting hydroxide ion. A weak base can accept a proton but does so less readily.

Common examples of strong acids are nitric acid (HNO_3), sulfuric acid (H_2SO_4), and hydrochloric acid (HCl). Weak acids include acetic acid (CH_3COOH), citric acid ($C_6H_8O_7$), and hydrofluoric acid (HF). Some strong bases include sodium hydroxide (NaOH), lithium hydroxide (LiOH), and potassium hydroxide (KOH). Weak bases include ammonia (NH_3), calcium carbonate ($CaCO_3$), and ammonium hydroxide (NH_4OH).

CALCULATION OF pH OF A SOLUTIONS

A **salt** is a compound (other than water) formed in a neutralization reaction between an acid and a base. When dissolved in water, a salt undergoes hydrolysis, reacting with the water to split into two products. A salt of a weak base and a strong acid is called an acid salt. To find the pH, given the molarity of the salt and the base dissociation constant K_b of the base, you can find K_a for the conjugate acid and use it to solve for the concentration of H_3O^+ ions. For a salt of a strong base and weak acid, the procedure is similar but using K_b for the acid's conjugate base. A salt of a strong acid and a strong base forms a neutral solution.

For example, suppose you have a 2.00 M solution of potassium cyanide, KCN. Because KOH is a strong base and HCN is a weak acid, this is a basic salt. K_a for HCN is 5.8×10^{-10}, so K_b for its conjugate base is $\frac{1.0 \times 10^{-14}}{5.8 \times 10^{-10}} = 1.7 \times 10^{-5}$. The equilibrium equation is $K_b = \frac{[HCN][OH^-]}{[CN^-]}$; we can set [HCN] and [$OH^-$] (which must be equal) to x and solve it to get

$$x = \sqrt{K_b[CN^-]} = \sqrt{(1.7 \times 10^{-5})(2.00)} = 0.0058 \text{ M}$$

Thus the pH is $-\log_{10} \frac{1.0 \times 10^{-14}}{0.006} = 11.8$.

BUFFERS

A **buffer** is a solution that resists changes in pH. A buffer's pH remains almost constant even after the addition of a strong acid or base (in relatively small amounts). Generally, a buffer solution contains either a weak acid and its conjugate base or a weak base and its conjugate acid. When a strong base is added to a solution containing a weak acid, the weak acid will tend to give up a proton to the base, changing it into its conjugate acid. Because there is no significant change in the concentration of hydronium ions in solution, there is little change in pH. Similarly, when a strong acid is added to a solution containing a weak base, the weak base will accept a proton from that acid, again tending to stabilize the concentration of hydronium ions and therefore the pH.

Buffer systems are present in the human body (and other organisms) because many enzymes and other chemicals only work well at certain pH ranges. Blood, for example, is a buffer solution (with carbonic acid, H_2CO_3, and its conjugate base) that remains at a pH of about 7.4. Buffers are also used in shampoos and detergents, in breweries, and in textile dyeing processes. Some examples of weak acids or bases used in buffer systems include acetic acid (CH_3COOH), ammonia (NH_3), citric acid ($C_6H_8O_7$), and monopotassium phosphate (KH_2PO_4).

Review Video: Buffer
Visit mometrix.com/academy and enter code: 389183

UNIQUE PROPERTIES OF WATER

Although water is so much a part of our lives that we may take it for granted, it has some important chemical properties that lend particularly well to supporting life. For one thing, water has a very high specific heat. This means that water tends to resist changes in temperature and moderate climates and helps maintain homeostasis within living systems. Water is also unusual in that it is less dense as a solid than as a liquid. This is why ponds and lakes freeze over but retain liquid water underneath, maintaining a habitat for underwater organisms.

Other properties of water are less unusual but still important. Water is a powerful solvent, which makes it useful as a medium to carry other chemicals through our bodies. Water has both a boiling point and a freezing point close to the average temperature of our surroundings, which means that it is present in all three states of matter and can easily be cycled through the environment. The hydrogen bonds present in water give it a high surface tension and a high cohesion, which among other things allows trees to draw water up their trunks by capillary action.

TITRATION
INDICATORS

An **indicator** is a substance that when added to a solution, changes color (or some other easily observable property) depending on the pH of the solution (or some other property not easily observed directly). One of the best-known indicators is litmus, a mixture of chemicals extracted from lichens that is red in acidic solutions and blue in basic. It is typically sold in the form of litmus paper, strips of paper impregnated with the chemical. Another class of indicators, anthocyanins, are found in red cabbage and certain other plants. Other widely used indicators include phenolphthalein, methyl orange, and bromothymol blue.

Indicators are useful in titration because they help the observer identify the moment at which the pH changes. Because different indicators differ in the range of pH over which they change color, an appropriate indicator will be chosen for a given titration based on the pH of the expected change. Methyl orange, for instance, changes color at a low pH and phenolphthalein at a high pH; litmus and bromothymol blue both change color around neutral pH, although the range of pH for the color change of litmus is wider.

NEUTRALIZATION

Neutralization in chemistry refers to the reaction of an acid and a base to form a salt. In the case of Arrhenius bases—bases that include a hydroxide (OH^-) ion—the reaction also produces water. Despite the name, neutralization does not necessarily result in a neutral solution. The acid and base are said to be neutralized when no excess acid or base remains, but the resulting solution may be acidic, if it results from a strong acid and a weak base, or basic, if it results from a weak acid and a strong base.

For example, the strong acid hydrochloric acid and the strong base sodium hydroxide neutralize each other to form water and sodium chloride: $HCl + NaOH \rightarrow NaCl + H_2O$. (In this case, because HCl is a strong base and NaOH is a strong acid, the resulting solution is neutral.) Other neutralization reactions include $H_2SO_4 + 2KOH \rightarrow K_2SO_4 + 2H_2O$ and, for an example of a neutralization reaction involving Brønsted-Lowry acids and bases, $H^+ + NH_3 \rightarrow NH_4^+$.

INTERPRETATION OF THE TITRATION CURVES

Titration is the process of slowly adding small amounts of a solution of known concentration—the titrant—to a known volume of solution of unknown concentration—the analyte—until some reaction occurs. The volume of titrant added can then be used to find the concentration of the analyte. One common type of titration is acid-base titration, in which the titrant is acidic and the analyte basic, or vice versa, and the looked-for reaction is neutralization.

The titration curve is a curve used in acid-base titration to chart how the pH of the solution changes as more titrant is added. The independent variable is the total volume of titrant added, and the dependent variable is the pH.

The equivalence point of a titration curve is the point of maximum slope. Generally, a titration curve will start out with a relatively shallow slope, then at some point the slope will sharply increase, only to level off again. The equivalence point is where the curve is at its steepest.

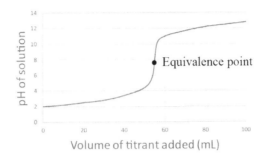

The equivalence point is important because it marks the moment where neutralization occurred. The slope of the titration curve of an acid-base titration indicates the rate of change of the pH of the solution as more titrant is added. It starts out shallow because when the solution is far from neutrality, adding small amounts of acid or base will have little effect. As the concentrations of acid and base become nearly equal, however, a small change in the amount of acid or base can have a large effect on pH, and the slope increases sharply. As the neutralization point is passed, and now the titrant is in excess, again a small increase in the amount of titrant has little effect on the pH, and the slope decreases again.

A monoprotic acid is an acid that can donate only a single proton or that has only a single H^+ ion. Monoprotic acids include hydrochloric acid, HCl; nitric acid, HNO_3; and acetic acid, $HC_2H_3O_2$. (Although acetic acid has four hydrogen atoms, three of them are part of the acetate anion and are not available for donation.) A polyprotic acid is one that has two or more protons or H^+ ions available for donation. Polyprotic acids include sulfuric acid, H_2SO_4; carbonic acid, H_2CO_3; and phosphoric acid, H_2PO_4.

Unlike a monoprotic acid, the titration curve of a polyprotic acid will have more than one equivalence point—the slope of the curve will become steeper and shallower several times. Specifically, it will have one equivalence point for each proton it can donate. This is because a polyprotic acid becomes a different acid when it donates a proton, and that acid has its own inflection point as well. For instance, when H_2SO_4 donates a proton, it becomes HSO_4^-, hydrogen sulfate, which is itself (weakly) acidic. The titration curve for H_2SO_4 shows both an equivalence point at which the H_2SO_4 itself is neutralized and then a second equivalence point where the HSO_4^- is neutralized.

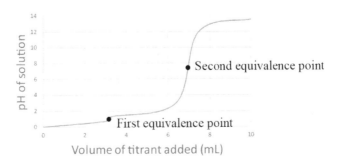

241

A titration curve with a strong acid or base will have a simple, well-defined sigmoid shape; the titration curve will rise or fall relatively slowly at the start, then become much steeper near the inflection point, and then return to a low rate of change. In the case of a weak acid or base, however, including a buffer solution, the shape will be slightly more complex. For a weak acid, at a pH below the equivalence point when the acid is of a higher concentration than the base, the solution will form a buffer, and the slope will become almost flat. Once the concentrations are nearly equalized, the slope will increase again, and the curve will reach an equivalence point as before. At the center of the flat region of the curve is the half-equivalence point, where half the acid has been converted to its conjugate base. At this point, the pH of the solution is equal to the pK_a for the weak acid.

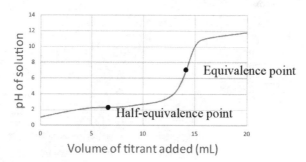

For a weak base, the situation is similar, except that the flat region of the curve and the half-equivalence point will be at a high pH, and at the equivalence point, the pH of the solution is equal to $(14 - pK_b)$.

REDOX TITRATION

A redox titration is a titration based not on a neutralization reaction as with acid-base titration but on a redox reaction. As with other titrations, small amounts of a substance of known concentration (the titrant) are added to a fixed volume of a substance of unknown concentration (the analyte). In a redox titration, the titrant is a reducing agent, and the analyte is an oxidizing agent, or vice versa.

In a redox titration curve, the independent variable is the amount of titrant added, and the dependent variable is the cell potential of the system. A redox titration curve starts out with a shallow slope, as the titrant is almost completely oxidized or reduced by the more abundant analyte, then becomes steeper as the concentrations of titrant and analyte near equality, and then becomes shallower again as the titrant becomes more abundant than the analyte. The point of steepest slope is the equivalence point, where the amount of reducing agent and balancing agent are just enough for each to react completely with the other.

Review Video: <u>Titration</u>
Visit mometrix.com/academy and enter code: 550131

Kinetics and Equilibrium

REACTION RATE

The reaction rate of a chemical reaction is a measurement of what quantity of the reactants reacts per unit time. It is typically measured in units of mol/(L × s) so that a reaction rate r means that in each liter of the substance, r moles of the reactants react each second.

For chemicals to react, their molecules must come into contact. Therefore, increasing the concentration of the reactants will increase the reaction rate—the higher the concentration of the reactants, the more likely it is for molecules of the reactants to meet each other. Temperature affects reaction rate for similar reasons; the higher the temperature, the faster the molecules are moving, and the more frequently molecules of the reactants will collide. For solid reactants, the shape of the solid may also affect things; the larger the surface area, the more molecules of the reactant are exposed and available to contact the other reactants. (This is why finely ground flour is highly flammable, and even aluminum dust may be flammable if the particles are small enough.) In general, however, reactants in the liquid or gas phases have higher reaction rates than solids. Furthermore, the reaction rate of a chemical reaction can be increased by the presence of a catalyst, another compound that facilitates the reaction without itself being consumed.

DEPENDENCE OF REACTION RATE ON CONCENTRATION OF REACTANTS

RATE LAW, RATE CONSTANT

The rate law of a chemical reaction is an equation relating the reaction rate of a chemical reaction to the concentrations of its reactants. It generally (but not always) takes the form of a power law in which the reaction rate is equal to a reaction rate constant k times the product of the concentrations of the reactants, each raised to some exponent. These exponents are called the reaction orders of the associated reactants. That is, if a chemical reaction has reactants $R_1, R_2, R_3, ...,$ then its rate law is $r = k\,[R_1]^{x_1}[R_2]^{x_2}[R_3]^{x_3} ...,$ where x_n is the reaction order of the reactant R_n.

For example, for the reaction $2NO + O_2 \rightarrow 2NO_2$, the rate law is equal to $r = k[NO]^2[O_2]$, where k is about $7100\ L^2/(mol^2 \times s)$. (Note that whereas the reaction orders happen to be the same as the stoichiometric coefficients for this particular equation, this is not necessarily the case in general!) This means that if the concentration of NO is 0.02 mol/L and the concentration of O_2 is 0.1 mol/L, the reaction rate will be $r = \left(7100\ L^2/(mol^2 \times s)\right)(0.02\ mol/L)^2(0.1\ mol/L) = 0.284\ mol/(L \times s)$.

REACTION ORDER

The **reaction order** of a reactant in a chemical reaction is the exponent to which the concentration of that reactant is raised in the rate equation for the chemical reaction. For instance, the reaction $BrO_3^- + 5Br^- + 6H^+ \rightarrow 3Br_2 + 3H_2O$ has the rate law $r = k[BrO_3^-][Br^-][H^+]^2$—the reaction order of BrO_3^- and Br^- is 1, and the reaction order of Br_2 is 2. The overall reaction order of the equation is the sum of the individual reaction orders; for this equation, it would be $1 + 1 + 2 = 4$.

As shown in this example, unlike the exponents in a chemical equilibrium equation, the reaction orders of the reactants are not related to their coefficients in a balanced chemical equation. Rather, the reaction orders of the reactants must be **determined experimentally**. There is no straightforward way to figure out the reaction orders of the reactants just from the chemical equation.

There are some reactions with more complicated reaction laws and in which the reaction orders are not well defined. This may be because the presence of the product slows the reaction; for instance, the reaction $2O_3 \rightarrow 3O_2$ has rate law $r = k\frac{[O_3]^2}{[O_2]^3}$.

RATE CONSTANT

The rate constant of a chemical reaction is the proportionality factor between the reaction rate and the product of the concentrations of the reactants raised to the powers of their reaction orders. That is, it is the constant k in the rate law equation $r = k\,[R_1]^{x_1}[R_2]^{x_2}[R_3]^{x_3}$ .... Like the reaction orders, the rate constant must be determined experimentally. In practice, the rate constant of a reaction is not really a universal constant but depends on the temperature; rate constants are frequently given at a reference temperature of 298 K.

The units of k are chosen so that the reaction rate r has the appropriate units, usually mol/(L × s). This means the units of k are $L^{(\Sigma x-1)}/(mol^{(\Sigma x-1)} \times s)$, where Σx is the reaction order of the reaction, which is equal to the sum of the reaction orders of all the reactants. For instance, the reaction $2ClO_2 + 2OH^- \rightarrow ClO_3^- + ClO_2 + H_2O$ has the rate law $r = k[ClO_2]^2[OH^-]$; the reaction order is $1 + 2 = 3$, and the rate constant must have units of $L^2/(mol^2 \times s)$.

RATE-DETERMINING STEP

When, as is often the case, a chemical reaction actually occurs not all at once but as a series of subsidiary reactions, or steps, the rate-determining step of a reaction is the step that has the slowest reaction rate. The reaction cannot proceed more quickly than its slowest step, so the rate of the overall reaction will be equal to the rate of this step—this slowest step determines the rate of the reaction.

If the steps of the reaction are known, and the reaction order of the equation is known, this is often sufficient to determine the rate-determining step—it is the step at which the total number of molecules of the reactants that have been involved so far is equal to the reaction order. For instance, the reaction $2NO + 2H_2 \rightarrow N_2 + 2H_2O$ proceeds through the following steps:

$$NO + NO \rightarrow N_2O_2$$
$$N_2O_2 + H_2 \rightarrow N_2O + H_2O$$
$$N_2O + H_2 \rightarrow N_2 + 2H_2O$$

The reaction order of this reaction is experimentally determined to be three. After the second step, three molecules are involved (two NO from the first step plus H_2), so the second step must be the rate determining step.

DEPENDENCE OF REACTION RATE UPON TEMPERATURE

ACTIVATION ENERGY

The activation energy of a chemical reaction is the minimum energy required for the reaction to proceed. Even if the total energy of the reactants is less than the total energy of the products, it takes some energy to break bonds in the reactants so that they can form new bonds and make the products; there is some initial energy needed to start, even if the compounds end up getting that energy back when the products are formed. Of course, the higher the temperature of the compound, the more kinetic energy its molecules have that can be used to overcome the activation energy, which is part of the reason that the reaction rate increases with temperature.

The activation energy is usually given not as the energy needed for one molecule of each reactant to react (or a number of molecules each to the stoichiometric coefficient of the compound in the balanced equation), but for a mole of the molecule (or a number of moles equal to the stoichiometric coefficient). The units of the activation energy are therefore equal to joules per mole or, more often, kilojoules per mole.

ACTIVATION ENERGY: ACTIVATED COMPLEX OR TRANSITION STATE

In a chemical reaction, the compounds do not change instantaneously from the reactants to the products but pass through a range of intermediate steps. These intermediate forms may have higher energies than either the initial reactants or the final products, which is why some activation energy is necessary to form them, and they may only exist for very brief periods of time before returning to a lower-energy state, either re-forming the reactants or becoming the products of the chemical reaction. These high-energy intermediate steps are known as activated complexes.

Of all the intermediate forms, there is one that has the highest energy. This form, which the molecules may pass through only briefly as they change from the reactants into the products, is known as the transition state. It is this form that determines the activation energy of the reaction—it is the difference in energy between the transition state and the initial state of the molecules.

ACTIVATION ENERGY: INTERPRETATION OF ENERGY PROFILES

An **energy profile** is a representation of the energy that a chemical system goes through during a chemical reaction. The y axis of the energy profile is the energy of the system (in any appropriate units, but because it is the shape of the energy profile that's important, the units are often omitted); the x-axis is the reaction coordinate, measuring progress of the reaction. (The x-axis is not given in more concrete units such as time or concentration of reactants because the reactants may react at different rates, and the rate depends on concentration and other factors.) Usually an energy profile shows the energy increasing gradually from its initial value to a maximum and then falling back to a lower energy again; multistep reactions may also show some local minima.

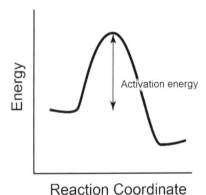

Several useful pieces of data can be drawn from the energy profile. Whether the final energy is higher or lower than the initial shows whether the reaction is endothermic or exothermic. The activation energy can be found as the difference between the maximum energy and the initial energy.

ARRHENIUS EQUATION

The **Arrhenius equation** is an equation showing the relationship between the reaction rate and the temperature. It is named after the Swedish scientist Svante August Arrhenius, who is credited as one of the founders of physical chemistry (and who also formulated the Arrhenius definition of acids and basis). The equation takes the form $k = Ae^{-\frac{E_a}{RT}}$, where A is a constant (which may be different for every reaction), E_a is the activation energy of the reaction, R is the ideal gas constant ($8.314\,J/[mol \times K]$), and T is the temperature in Kelvins.

Although it is not hard to see conceptually why the reaction rate increases with temperature, the Arrhenius equation quantifies the relationship and allows the calculation of the reaction rate at different temperatures as long as the relevant constants are known. The constant A, called the pre-exponential constant, is dependent on the frequency of collisions between molecules as well as their geometry but in practice is determined experimentally.

KINETIC CONTROL VS. THERMODYNAMIC CONTROL OF A REACTION

In many cases, there is more than one set of products that could in principle be formed in a chemical reaction by a given set of reactants. Which products are formed depends on the rates of the related reactions as well as on the products' stability. A product produced by the reaction with the higher reaction rate (and generally the lower activation energy) is called a kinetic product. A product that is more stable (has the lower energy in its final form) is called a thermodynamic product.

Which products actually are formed in a given case, then, depends on which controlling factor becomes more important. At sufficiently low temperatures, there is not enough energy for the reaction forming the kinetic product to reverse despite its relative instability, so as this product has a faster reaction rate, it predominates, and the reaction is said to be under kinetic control. At higher temperatures, when the reaction forming the kinetic product can reverse, this limits the amount of those products that forms, and the thermodynamic product predominates; the reaction is said to be under thermodynamic control.

CATALYSTS

A **catalyst** is a compound that lowers the activation energy of a reaction and thus facilitates that reaction taking place without itself being expended in the reaction—it is said to catalyze the reaction. This may be because the catalyst does react in one step of a multistep reaction, but is then produced in another step, so that the total amount of the catalyst is unchanged. The highest activation energy of any step of the reaction involving the catalyst is smaller than the activation energy of the reaction without the catalyst, so the reaction can proceed at a greater rate.

For example, iron reacts with oxygen to form iron oxide (rust). However, the activation energy is high enough that this does not spontaneously occur at a noticeable rate when iron is exposed to oxygen. It does occur, however, in the presence of water because water acts as a catalyst to this reaction, lowering the activation energy. Important examples of catalysts in biological systems are enzymes, which ensure that metabolic processes occur at a high enough rate to sustain life.

> **Review Video: Catalysts**
> Visit mometrix.com/academy and enter code: 288189

EQUILIBRIUM IN REVERSIBLE CHEMICAL REACTIONS
LAW OF MASS ACTION

The Law of Mass Action states that the rate of a chemical reaction is directly proportional to the product of the concentrations of the reactants. If a reactant or product has a stoichiometric coefficient (a coefficient in the balanced chemical equation) other than 1, then its concentration appears that many times in the product—in other words, its concentration is raised to the power of its stoichiometric coefficient. In other words, the reaction rate is proportional to $[R_1]^{r_1}[R_2]^{r_2}$ ..., where $R_1, R_2, \ldots$ are the reactants and r_n their respective stoichiometric coefficients. This has a number of applications—for instance, it says that we can increase a reaction rate by increasing the concentration of a reactant, although this also follows from Le Châtelier's principle. It is especially useful for systems in equilibrium, in which case it can be used to derive the equilibrium expression $K_{eq} = \frac{[R_1]^{r_1}[R_2]^{r_2}\ldots}{[P_1]^{p_1}[P_2]^{p_2}\ldots}$, where P_1, P_2, ... are the products and p_n their respective stoichiometric coefficients.

EQUILIBRIUM CONSTANT

The equilibrium expression is the constant K_{eq} that appears in the equilibrium expression $K_{eq} = \frac{[R_1]^{r_1}[R_2]^{r_2}\ldots}{[P_1]^{p_1}[P_2]^{p_2}\ldots}$, where R_1, R_2, ... are the reactants, P_1, P_2, ... the products, and r_n and p_n their respective stoichiometric coefficients. (Only gases and chemicals in solution are included in this equation; solid and liquid reactants and products are omitted.) A very large equilibrium constant implies that the products will predominate at equilibrium; a very small constant implies that the reactants will predominate.

The equilibrium constant can be used to determine an unknown concentration of a compound. For example, consider the reversible reaction $3H_2 + N_2 \rightleftharpoons 2NH_3$, which has an equilibrium constant at room temperature of 3.3×10^8, and suppose we know that at equilibrium the concentration of H_2 is 0.0050 M and of N_2 is 0.020 M. The equilibrium expression would be $K_{eq} = \frac{[NH_3]^2}{[H_2]^3[N_2]}$. This means we can find the concentration of NH_3 by solving for it in this equation:

$$[NH_3] = (K_{eq}[H_2]^3[N_2])^{1/2} = ([3.3 \times 10^8][0.0050]^3[0.020])^{1/2} = 2.9 \text{ M}$$

Note that the concentration of the product (NH_3) is much larger than the concentrations of the reactants (H_2 and N_2); this is expected because $K_{eq} \gg 1$.

APPLICATION OF LE CHÂTELIER'S PRINCIPLE

Le Châtelier's principle states that a change in some property of a system in equilibrium will produce a shift in the equilibrium that counteracts the change. For example, if the concentration of one of the reactants is increased, the reaction will tend to proceed toward the right, using up some of the reactants and forming more of the product. A decrease in the concentration of a reactant (or an increase in the concentration of a product) will have the opposite effect. Increasing the pressure on a system of gases in equilibrium will shift the equilibrium toward the side of the reaction with fewer molecules. Increasing the temperature will shift the equilibrium toward the products, if the forward reaction is endothermic, or the reactants, if it is exothermic.

It is possible to take advantage of this principle to move a system's equilibrium in a desired direction. For instance, one step in the production of sulfuric acid involves the reversible reaction $2SO_2 + O_2 \rightleftharpoons 2SO_3$. This reaction can be made to proceed in the forward direction more efficiently by increasing the pressure or by adding oxygen. The reaction is also exothermic in the forward direction, so it works best at lower temperatures.

RELATIONSHIP OF THE EQUILIBRIUM CONSTANT AND ΔG°

The larger the equilibrium constant K_{eq} of a chemical reaction, the more the products will predominate, and the more the reaction will tend to proceed toward the right. The smaller K_{eq}, the more the reactants will predominate, and the more the reaction will tend to proceed toward the left. On the other hand, the reaction will tend to proceed in the direction that decreases the Gibbs free energy, so the larger the change in the free energy, ΔG, the more the equation will proceed toward the left, and the smaller ΔG, the more it will proceed toward the right. This suggests that the change in the Gibbs free energy and the equilibrium constant have an inverse relationship.

It is not, however, a simple matter of the two being inversely proportional (they can't be, because ΔG can be negative, and K_{eq} can't.) Rather, the relationship turns out to be logarithmic. The Gibbs free energy is equal to the negative product of the ideal gas constant $R = 8.314$, the temperature T in Kelvins, and the natural logarithm of the equilibrium constant: $\Delta G = -RT \ln K_{eq}$.

Equilibrium Constants K_a, K_b, pK_a, and pK_b

K_a and K_b are the acid dissociation constant and the base dissociation constant, respectively. They are constants that relate to the equilibrium condition for the dissociation of a particular acid or base. The equilibrium condition for the dissociation of an acid HA with conjugate base A^- is $K_a = \frac{[H^+][A^-]}{[HA]}$; for a base B with conjugate acid HB^+, it is $K_b = \frac{[HB^+][OH^-]}{[B]}$. These constants can be used to determine the concentration of one of the chemical species involved if the concentrations of the others are known—in particular, they can be used to find the concentration of H^+ or OH^- and therefore the pH of the solution.

In practice, these concentrations are typically very small, so it is often more convenient to refer to logarithmic versions of these constants, pK_a and pK_b. These hold the same relation to K_a and K_b as pH does to the concentration of H^+ ions: $pK_a = -\log_{10} K_a$, and $pK_b = -\log_{10} K_b$.

For an acid and its conjugate base, $K_a \times K_b = 10^{-14}$ and $pK_a + pK_b = 14$.

Thermodynamics

State Functions

A state function in thermodynamics is a quantity describing a thermodynamic system that depends only on the current state of the system and not on its history. If a state function changes, the magnitude of that change is entirely determined by the beginning and end states of the system, independent of the path it took between them. Pressure, volume, and temperature are all state functions; the current values of these properties of a system can be measured without requiring any knowledge of a system's past states. Other state functions include internal energy, entropy, enthalpy, and free energy. In contrast, non-state functions include work and heat. The work done by a system as it changes between two states very much depends on the path it takes; it cannot be calculated solely on the basis of the start and end states.

Laws of Thermodynamics
Zeroth Law

The Zeroth Law of Thermodynamics states that two bodies both in thermal equilibrium with a third body are also in thermal equilibrium with each other. Two objects are in thermal equilibrium if they are in contact—or at least they are connected by some method that would allow heat to flow between them—but there is no net heat flow between the objects.

The importance of the Zeroth Law of Thermodynamics is that it establishes that temperature is a meaningful quantity. Two objects in thermal equilibrium can be defined as having the same temperature; two objects in thermal contact but not in thermal equilibrium have different temperatures. The Zeroth Law guarantees that this definition leads to no contradictions. In fact, sometimes the Zeroth Law is written directly in terms of temperature: systems in thermal equilibrium are at the same temperature.

FIRST LAW

The First Law of Thermodynamics states that the total energy of an isolated thermodynamic system is constant. For a non-isolated system, energy may be added or taken away from the system in the form of work or heat, but this means the system's internal energy will change by the same amount. The First Law is also written mathematically as $\Delta U = Q + W$, where ΔU is the change in internal energy of the system, Q is the heat added to the system, and W is the work done on the system. (Sometimes it is instead written in the form $\Delta U = Q - W$, in which case W represents the work done by the system.)

The First Law of Thermodynamics is essentially a restatement of the law of conservation of energy or at least an application of that law to thermodynamics. Among other things, it is the first law that proves the impossibility of perpetual motion machines that provide "free energy." Energy cannot be created arbitrarily; it can only be transferred between systems in the forms of work and heat.

> **Review Video: First Law of Thermodynamics**
> Visit mometrix.com/academy and enter code: 340643

SECOND LAW

The Second Law of Thermodynamics states that the total entropy of an isolated system can never decrease. Over time, the disorder in an isolated system must increase or stay the same. Note that this refers only to isolated systems; the entropy of part of a system can decrease as long as there is an equal or greater increase to make up for it. For instance, the entropy of the water in a pond decreases when it freezes over in winter, but this is countered by an increase in the entropy of the air the water's heat escapes to.

There are several other statements of the law that are (not obviously) equivalent and that do not explicitly refer to entropy. For instance, it is equivalent to the statement that it is not possible for heat to flow from a colder to a warmer body without work being done on the system.

The Second Law of Thermodynamics has many consequences. It determines the maximum efficiency of a heat engine and demonstrates why some chemical reactions and other processes occur preferentially in one direction (because that direction increases entropy).

> **Review Video: Second Law of Thermodynamics**
> Visit mometrix.com/academy and enter code: 251848

ENTROPY AS A MEASURE OF "DISORDER"

Entropy is, roughly speaking, a measurement of the "disorder" in a system. It can be defined more rigorously in terms of the number of possible states that are in a certain sense equivalent. (As a quantitative value, the entropy is conventionally abbreviated S.) As an analogy, if you have a number of coins on the ground, there's only one state in which they are all showing heads, so this is a low-entropy state; there are many states in which roughly equal numbers of coins are heads and tails, so this is a relatively high-entropy state. Entropy tends to increase with temperature, and thanks to the Second Law of Thermodynamics the entropy of a closed system increases (or at best remains constant) over time.

In general, gases have higher entropy than liquids, and liquids have higher entropy than solids. This follows, again roughly speaking, from the fact that as a compound passes from solid to liquid to gas, its molecules or atoms become less constrained, and there are more possible states for them to be in. Crystals have particularly low entropy.

HESS'S LAW

Hess's Law of Heat Summation states that if a chemical reaction can be broken down into smaller steps, then the total heat of the reaction is equal to the sum of the heats of reaction of each step. This can often be used to determine the heat of reaction of a particular chemical reaction if we have no feasible way to measure it directly but can find a way to break it down into sub-reactions with heats of reaction we know or can measure.

For instance, the heat of reaction of $2C + O_2 \rightarrow 2CO$ is not easy to measure directly, but we can measure those of the reactions $C + O_2 \rightarrow CO_2$ and $2CO + O_2 \rightarrow 2CO_2$. Doubling the first reaction and reversing the second, we can combine those into our original reaction:

$$
\begin{array}{rcl}
2C \;+\; 2O_2 &\rightarrow& 2CO_2 \\
2CO_2 &\rightarrow& 2CO \;+\; O_2 \\
\hline
2CO_2 \;+\; 2C \;+\; 2O_2 &\rightarrow& 2CO_2 \;+\; 2CO \;+\; O_2 \\
2C \;+\; O_2 &\rightarrow& 2CO
\end{array}
$$

The heat of reaction of $C + O_2 \rightarrow CO_2$ is –393 kJ/mol and the heat of reaction of $2CO + O_2 \rightarrow 2CO_2$ is –566 kJ/mol; therefore, the heat of reaction of $2C + O_2 \rightarrow 2CO$ is:

$$
2\left(-393\,\frac{kJ}{mol}\right) - \left(-566\,\frac{kJ}{mol}\right) = -220\,\frac{kJ}{mol}
$$

Review Video: Hess's Law
Visit mometrix.com/academy and enter code: 329059

BOND DISSOCIATION ENERGY AS RELATED TO HEATS OF FORMATION

The bond dissociation energy of a compound is the energy required to break a covalent chemical bond in such a way as to leave one of the two shared electrons with each resultant part. (This is called a homolytic cleavage, as contrasted with a heterolytic cleavage, in which both shared electrons go to the same part.) This can be thought of as a measurement of the strength of the bond—the higher the bond dissociation energy, the harder it is to break the bond, and so the stronger the bond.

Knowing the bond dissociation energy of all of the bonds in all the products and reactants of a chemical reaction allows the heat of reaction of any reaction to be determined: it is the sum of the bond dissociation energies of all the bonds in the reactants minus the bond dissociation energies of all the bonds in the products. In particular, the heat of formation of a compound—the heat of reaction of the compound from its elements—is the sum of the bond dissociation energies of all its bonds with the sign changed.

SPONTANEOUS REACTIONS

The Gibbs free energy of a system, abbreviated G, was originally defined by the American chemist and physicist Josiah Willard Gibbs, best known for his work on thermodynamics. Gibbs defined it as the amount of available energy in a chemical system, the energy that could be used to do useful work. Specifically, the Gibbs free energy is equal to the enthalpy of the system minus the product of the temperature and the entropy: $G = H - TS$.

A chemical reaction is said to be spontaneous if it occurs in nature when the reactants are present without any necessary input of energy. A reaction is spontaneous if and only if the total free energy of the reactants is greater than the total free energy of the products—that is, if ΔG of the reactants is negative. This was, in fact, what led Gibbs to formulate this concept in the first place; he was looking for a relatively simple criterion to determine whether or not a reaction would spontaneously occur.

COEFFICIENT OF EXPANSION

The coefficient of (thermal) expansion is a measurement of how much an object or substance expands as heat increases. For a solid, this increase can be measured either linearly or volumetrically. The linear coefficient of expansion, α, is defined as $\alpha = \frac{\Delta L}{L_0 \Delta T}$, where L_0 is the initial length of the object in question, ΔL is the change in length, and ΔT is the change in temperature. (This assumes that the coefficient is independent of temperature, but this is generally a good approximation.) For a liquid, with no fixed shape, only the volume coefficient of expansion is meaningful; this is defined similarly but in terms of volume instead of length as $\beta = \frac{\Delta V}{V_0 \Delta T}$. For a solid, $\beta \approx 3\alpha$.

For example, the linear coefficient of expansion of steel is about $1.3 \times 10^{-5}\ K^{-1}$. This means that if a steel wheel with a diameter of 0.5 meters increases in temperature from 0 °C to 80 °C, its diameter changes by an amount equal to
$\Delta L = \alpha L_0 \Delta T = (1.3 \times 10^{-15} K^{-1})(0.5\ \text{m})(80\ \text{K}) = 0.00052\ \text{m}$, or about half a millimeter. That may not sound like much, but for some high-precision instruments, such a small change may be significant.

MEASUREMENT OF HEAT CHANGES (CALORIMETRY)

Calorimetry is the process of measuring the heat transferred to or from a system. Although the heat cannot be measured directly, it can often be calculated given the change in temperature and the specific heat capacity of the substance. A calorimetry problem is a problem involving heat flow to or from a system or different objects within a system. One common kind of calorimetry problem involves finding the final temperature of two objects in thermal contact. For instance, suppose you drop a 50-gram iron ball with an initial temperature of 500 °C into 100 grams of water with an initial temperature of 25°C in an insulated container. At thermal equilibrium, both will have the same temperature, T_f. Because no net heat is gained or lost by the system as a whole, we can write:

$$0 = Q_{H_2O} + Q_{Fe}$$
$$0 = m_{H_2O} C_{H_2O} \Delta T_{H_2O} + m_{Fe} C_{Fe} \Delta T_{Fe}$$
$$0 = (100\ \text{g})(4.184\ \text{J/g°C})(T_f - 25\ °\text{C}) + (50\ \text{g})(0.450\ \text{J/g°C})(T_f - 500\ °\text{C})$$

Solving for T_f gives $T_f = 49°C$

More complex calorimetry problems may also involve changes of state of matter; this requires the inclusion of terms for the heat gained or lost due to this change of state (in terms of the heat of fusion or heat of vaporization).

PV DIAGRAM

A PV diagram is a diagram of a thermodynamic system in which the pressure is plotted on the y axis and the volume on the x-axis. The thermodynamic state of a system is uniquely determined by these two variables, so any state variable pertaining to the system can be determined from its position on the diagram. Changes in thermodynamic state can be drawn as lines or curves on the PV diagram, representing all the states that the system passes through; changes in non-state functions can be determined from this curve. For instance, the work done by a system as it undergoes a change in state is equal to the area under the curve in a PV diagram.

As an example, the following PV diagram shows a thermodynamic cycle as a system undergoes first an isothermal (constant temperature) expansion, followed by an isobaric (constant pressure) compression, and finally an isochoric (constant volume) increase in pressure:

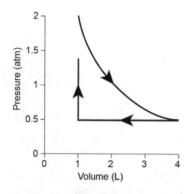

HEAT TRANSFER – CONDUCTION, CONVECTION, RADIATION

Conduction is the transfer of heat between two objects in contact. If you put a pot of water on a hot electric stove, heat is conducted from the stove to the pot and from the pot to the water. Some materials conduct heat better than others; the reason that metal cooking pans often have wood or plastic handles is because these materials conduct heat much more poorly than metals, so you can touch the handle of the hot pan without burning your hand.

Convection is the transfer of heat within a fluid by the movement of the fluid. Warm and cold ocean and air currents are examples of convection. The churning of boiling water in a pan is a consequence of heat convection as the hotter parts of the water rise to the top.

Radiation is the transfer of heat by the emission of electromagnetic radiation. Any object loses heat by such radiation. Compared to conduction and convection, radiation is a very slow method of heat transfer. However, it does not require objects to be in contact and can therefore occur even between objects separated by the vacuum of space—heat from the Sun reaches the Earth through radiation.

Atomic and Molecular Structure

ATOMIC STRUCTURE

The three primary components of an atom are **protons**, **neutrons**, and **electrons**. Protons and neutrons are collectively called nucleons and form the nucleus of the atom; electrons orbit the nucleus at a distance—although they aren't really orbiting in the classical sense, like planets orbit a sun; rather, they are spread out in a probabilistic electron cloud. A neutral atom has the same number of electrons as protons; negative ions have more electrons; positive ions have fewer.

The **atomic number** of an atom is its number of protons. It is this that determines what element it is; carbon has an atomic number of six, so all carbon atoms have six protons. The **mass number** is the number of protons plus the number of neutrons. The number of electrons has no effect on the atomic number or the mass number. (The mass of an electron is only about 1/1800 the mass of a proton or neutron.) The number of electrons does determine the charge of the atom or ion, but an atom can gain or lose electrons and change its charge without altering its atomic number or mass number.

The **atomic weight** of an atom is the mass of the atom in atomic mass units (u), defined as 1/12 the mass of a carbon-12 atom (which contains six protons and six neutrons). Because the proton and the neutron have almost the same mass, the atomic weight is very close to the mass number—but because the protons and neutrons don't have exactly the same mass, and because the electrons also have some mass, they are not precisely equal. (There is also a little mass tied up in the binding energy of the atom.)

For the atomic weights of elements as given on a periodic table, however, there's a further factor to consider. The atomic weight of chlorine, for instance, is given as 35.45—much farther from an integral value than the slight differences in mass between protons and neutrons can account for. This is because the atomic weight given for each element in the periodic table is the average weight of the different isotopes of that element, weighted by their abundance in nature. Most chlorine atoms are chlorine-35, with some chlorine-37 and much smaller amounts of other isotopes; the weighted average of their weights comes out to 35.45.

The **binding energy** of a system in general is the energy required to separate a system into its component parts. In the case of an atom, the atomic binding energy is the energy required to separate the electrons from the atomic nucleus. Because the nth ionization energy of an atom is defined as the energy required to remove one electron after $n-1$ have already been removed, the atomic binding energy can be thought of as the sum of the ionization energies of an atom for all possible values of n (up to the atom's atomic number).

The **nuclear binding energy** is the energy that would be required to completely separate the nucleus of the atom into isolated protons and neutrons. The nuclear binding energies are much larger than the atomic binding energies; the forces holding the atomic nucleus together are very large. For example, the atomic binding energy of a carbon-12 atom is about 7.85×10^{-17} J or (490 eV), whereas its nuclear binding energy is about 1.5×10^{-11} J or (92 MeV)—almost a million times as great. This is why a nuclear fission reaction releases so much energy; a part of the nuclear binding energy is released.

NEUTRONS, PROTONS, ISOTOPES

An **isotope** of an element is an atom of that element with a particular number of neutrons. Two atoms of the same element are said to be different isotopes if their number of neutrons differs. A specific isotope is named in terms of the atomic number and mass number, either by stating the mass number after the element name or writing the atomic number to the lower left and the mass number to the upper right of the chemical symbol. An atom with six protons and eight neutrons, for instance, would be called carbon-14 or $^{14}_{6}$C.

Two isotopes of the same element differ in their mass, of course but often also in their stability. For example, carbon-12 and carbon-13 are stable; carbon-14 is radioactive with a half-life of 5,700 years (making it useful in carbon dating); carbon-15 is extremely radioactive with a half-life of only 2.45 seconds.

RADIOACTIVE DECAY

The three kinds of radioactive decay are alpha, beta, and gamma decay, named after the first three letters of the Greek alphabet. In **alpha decay (α)**, an atomic nucleus emits an alpha particle, consisting of two protons and two neutrons; the atom's atomic number then decreases by two and its mass number by four, altering the atom into a different element. Beta decay actually comes in two varieties: in **beta minus decay (β⁻)**, a neutron turns into a proton, emitting an electron (and a very light particle called an antineutrino), whereas in **beta plus decay (β⁺)** a proton turns into a neutron, emitting a positron, the antimatter version of an electron (along with a neutrino—the very light particle of which the antineutrino is the antimatter version). The atom's atomic number goes up (β⁻) or down (β⁺) by one, whereas its mass number is unchanged. In **gamma decay (γ)**, the atom emits a very high-energy photon; this itself has no effect on the atom's atomic number or mass number, but gamma decay often accompanies one of the other kinds of radioactive decay.

HALF-LIFE

The **half-life** of a radioactive material is the time it takes for half of the atoms in a sample to undergo radioactive decay. This does not mean that after two half-lives there is none of the sample left. Rather, after one half-life half of the original atoms have decayed, and after another half-life, half of the remaining atoms have decayed, which means that one-quarter of the original atoms remain. In general, the amount of a radioactive substance over time decays exponentially. The number of atoms of a radioactive sample remaining after a time t is equal to $N(t) = N_0 \left(\frac{1}{2}\right)^{t/t_{1/2}}$, where N_0 is the number of atoms originally present and $t_{1/2}$ is the half-life. This can be expressed in a base e exponential as:

$$N(t) = N_0 e^{(-\ln 2)\left(\frac{t}{t_{1/2}}\right)}$$

For example, the radioactive isotope nitrogen-13 has a half-life of 9.965 minutes. This means that if you start with 100.0 moles of nitrogen-13, after one hour you would be left with:

$$(100.0 \text{ mol}) \left(\frac{1}{2}\right)^{\frac{60 \text{ min}}{9.965 \text{ min}}} = 1.540 \text{ mol}$$

So, 1.540 moles of the isotope that have not yet decayed.

BOHR ATOM

The Bohr atom was an atomic model developed by and named for Danish physicist Niels Henrik David Bohr. According to the Bohr model of the atom, electrons orbited the nucleus in circular paths, but only in specific, discrete stationary orbits, and were only able to absorb or emit quantities of energy that would transfer them from one stationary orbit to another.

This constraint was intended to explain the observed phenomenon that atoms only emit specific frequencies of light. It improved on the previous atomic model, the Rutherford model of electrons orbiting the nucleus with no constraint on their radii, both by providing this explanation and by avoiding the Rutherford model's problematic prediction that electrons would gradually lose energy and spiral into the nucleus. However, Bohr had no theoretical justification for why the electrons would be constrained to these orbits, and the Bohr model was eventually superseded by the modern Schrödinger model in which the electrons do not occupy specific positions but probabilistic electron clouds, or orbitals. Still, the Bohr model is important in prefiguring the quantization that plays an important part in quantum mechanics.

ELECTRONIC STRUCTURE

The **electron volt**, abbreviated eV, is a unit of energy equal to the change in potential energy of an electron when it moves across a potential difference of one volt. Because this change in potential energy is equal to $U_E = qV$, one electron volt is equal to the magnitude of the charge of an electron multiplied by one volt: $(1.602 \times 10^{-19} \text{ C})(1 \text{ V}) = 1.602 \times 10^{-19} \text{ J}$.

Although it is not an official metric unit, the electron volt is frequently used in atomic and nuclear physics. The energies involved in single atoms are inconveniently small numbers when expressed in Joules but have more manageable values when expressed in electron volts. For instance, the energy of a ground state electron in a hydrogen atom is -2.18×10^{-18} J, which is equal to just -13.6 eV. For energies significantly larger than an electron volt but smaller than a joule, such as nuclear binding energies, units such as megaelectron-volts (MeV) and gigaelectron-volts (GeV) are commonly used.

ORBITAL STRUCTURE OF HYDROGEN ATOM, PRINCIPAL QUANTUM NUMBER N, NUMBER OF ELECTRONS PER ORBITAL

According to quantum mechanics, each electron in an atom can be completely described by four quantum numbers. The values of these quantum numbers are important for the shapes of the electron orbitals, for the electron energies, and for other properties. Each quantum number is constrained to only a discrete set of possible values. The four quantum numbers and their possible values are the following:

- The **principle quantum number, n,** can be any positive integer. This is the only quantum number that can (in principle) have infinitely many possible values, although in practice it will seldom exceed 9 or 10.
- The **angular quantum number, l,** can be any integer between 0 and $n - 1$. Thus, if an electron has a principal quantum number of 1, l must be 0; if $n = 2$, then l may be 0 or 1, and so on.
- The **magnetic quantum number, m,** can be any integer between $-l$ and l. If $l = 0$, then m must be 0; if $l = 1$, then m may be –1, 0, or 1, and so on.
- The **spin quantum number, s,** is always ½ or –½; it does not depend on the other quantum numbers.

The principal quantum number of a hydrogen atom, abbreviated n, is a number characterizing the potential energy of the single electron in the atom. The principal quantum number is always an integer greater than or equal to 1; the higher n, the higher the energy of the hydrogen atom. One of the basic principles of quantum mechanics—in fact, the one that gives the theory its name—is that the energy of atoms, among other quantities, is quantized; rather than being able to take on any value in a continuous range, it is restricted to a discontinuous set of possible values, or quanta. More specifically, if the potential energy of an atom in the lowest state, E_1, is appropriately defined at a certain negative value (-2.18×10^{-18} J for a hydrogen atom, or –13.6 eV), then the potential energy of the state with principal quantum number n is $E_n = \frac{E_1}{n^2}$. As usual with potential energy, it is only the difference in energy between states that really matters, so the assignment of a negative value to the energy is not physically problematic and is done for mathematical convenience.

An **atomic orbital** is a possible state that a pair of electrons can be in in an atom. Therefore, strictly speaking, there are at most only two electrons per orbital. However, the word "orbital" is sometimes used interchangeably with "shell" or "subshell," the former referring to the collection of electrons with the same principal quantum number n, the latter to electrons that also share the angular quantum number l. The subshells are successively symbolized by the letters s, p, d, f, g, and so on; the s subshell contains only one orbital, the p three, the d five, and so on. The first shell contains only an s subshell and so only one orbital. The second contains an s and a p subshell for a total of $1 + 3 = 4$ orbitals. The third contains an s, p, and d, for $1 + 3 + 5 = 9$ orbitals, and so on through 16 and 25, and in general the nth subshell contains n^2 orbitals, and thus $2n^2$ electrons. Because the principal quantum number n corresponds to the energy level of the atom, it would also be correct to say that there are $2n^2$ electrons in each energy level of the hydrogen atom.

CONVENTIONAL NOTATION FOR ELECTRON STRUCTURE

The conventional notation for electron structure of atoms lists the number of electrons in each subshell from lowest to highest energy. To list the electron structure, then, each subshell is listed by a number for n and the appropriate letter for l and then with the number of electrons in that shell as a superscript. For instance, carbon has two electrons in the $n = 1, l = 0$ subshell, and four in the $n = 1, l = 2$; its electron notation is $1s^2 1p^4$.

GROUND STATE AND EXCITED STATES

The **ground state** of an atom is the state with the lowest energy. In a ground-state atom, all the electrons are in the lowest-energy states possible, subject to the Pauli Exclusion Principle and the maximum number of electrons in an orbital. That is, no orbitals in a ground-state atom contain electrons unless all orbitals of lower energy are already full.

An atom that is not in the ground state is said to be in an **excited state**. An atom is in an excited state if there is at least one orbital that is not full despite at least one higher-energy orbital containing electrons.

An atom can change from its ground state to an excited state by one electron moving into an unoccupied, higher-energy state. This can occur if the atom is given energy by, for example, a high-energy photon colliding with it. The excited state is not stable, and an atom in an excited state will after some time spontaneously return to the ground state by the higher-energy electrons dropping back into unoccupied, lower-energy states. This is usually accompanied by emission of a photon.

ABSORPTION AND EMISSION LINE SPECTRA

Emission line spectra are produced by photons emitted as electrons in excited atoms drop back down to lower energy states. The atoms may be put into excited states by high temperatures or electrical currents. Each element or compound has a characteristic emission line spectrum that depends on its possible energy levels. Essentially, there is an emission line corresponding to each possible transition between energy levels—although some transitions are more likely than others, which means the corresponding emission lines will be accordingly more prominent. The frequency of the emission line can be determined by taking the difference in energies between the two energy levels and dividing by Planck's constant, h, 6.626×10^{-34} J/s.

For example, the emission spectrum of mercury vapor has a prominent blue line; this arises from an electron dropping from an excited energy level of 7.70 eV to a still excited but lower energy level of 4.87 eV; then $\Delta E = 7.70$ eV $- 4.87$ eV $= 2.83$ eV $= 4.55 \times 10^{-19}$ J; $f = \frac{\Delta E}{h} = 6.87 \times 10^{14}$ Hz; $\lambda = \frac{c}{f} = 4.36 \times 10^{-7}$ m or 436 nm, in the blue range of visible light.

Absorption line spectra are produced by the absorption by a gas or other transparent medium of photons of particular frequencies from a continuous spectrum. When an atom or molecule absorbs a photon, the absorbed energy puts the particle into an excited state. It is not possible for the atom or molecule to partially absorb the photon; the photon must be absorbed completely or not at all. This places a constraint on the frequencies of photons that can be absorbed: only the photons that have the exact amount of energy to raise the particle to an excited state can be absorbed. Therefore, the energies of photons in the absorption line spectrum correspond to differences in energy between the ground state and the possible excited states; from this energy, the frequency and wavelength of the photons can be determined from the relationships $E = hf$ and $c = \lambda f$.

Unlike the emission line spectrum, the absorption line spectrum does not include lines corresponding to transitions between different excited states. The time that a particle spends in an excited state before returning to its ground state is generally small enough that the chances of its being further excited by another photon while in that state are negligible.

Fluorescence is a phenomenon in which certain materials absorb light at one wavelength and emit light at a wavelength of a lower frequency (and therefore a lower energy). This occurs because each photon of the absorbed light excites an electron in an atom of the material, but rather than fall immediately to the ground state and emit a photon of the same energy as it absorbs, the electron first passes through an intermediate, lower-energy excited state, emitting a photon for each transition and therefore ultimately emitting two or more photons with a total energy equal to the energy of the single-incident photon.

The best-known examples of fluorescence involve materials that absorb ultraviolet light and emit light in the visible range. Because the initial ultraviolet light is not visible to the human eye, the materials when they emit visible light seem to glow. Fluorescent dyes and paints that seem to glow under "black light" (i.e., ultraviolet light) are used for decorative purposes and on amusement park rides as well as in security features on some bills and credit cards. Fluorescence also occurs in nature and even in some living things; many fish and other organisms exhibit biofluorescence.

PAULI EXCLUSION PRINCIPLE

The **Pauli exclusion principle** is a principle in quantum mechanics named after the Austrian theoretical physicist Wolfgang Ernst Pauli, who discovered it. It states that for a certain class of particles called fermions, two such particles in the same system cannot be the same state at the same time. Photons, for example, are not fermions, and the Pauli exclusion principle does not apply to them. Protons, neutrons, and electrons, however, are all fermions, and it is in electrons that the consequences of the principle are most obvious—and in terms of which Pauli first formulated the principle.

It is the Pauli exclusion principle that limits the number of electrons per orbital and the number of orbitals per shell. Specifically, the Pauli exclusion principle states that no two electrons in an atom can have exactly the same quantum numbers. It is this fact that causes shells to be filled by particular numbers of electrons and that ultimately leads to the details of electron structure.

PARAMAGNETISM AND DIAMAGNETISM

Ferromagnetism, paramagnetism, and diamagnetism all refer to a material's ability to be influenced by a magnetic field. **Ferromagnetism** is the type of magnetism present in familiar permanent magnets. Only a few materials are capable of ferromagnetism, including cobalt, nickel, and as the prefix "ferro-" implies, iron. In ferromagnetic materials, adjacent atoms tend to align so that their electrons' spins are in the same direction, causing their individual magnetic moments to build into a significant magnetic field. When the material is not magnetized, the atoms are aligned in parts of the material, called domains, but the magnetic fields of the domains point in different directions and cancel. It is when the domains line up and combine into one large domain that the object as a whole is said to be magnetized.

Paramagnetism and diamagnetism both apply to a broader range of materials but are much weaker effects. In **paramagnetic** materials, unpaired electrons are attracted by a magnetic field, and the rest of the atoms come with them. In **diamagnetic** materials, all electrons are paired, and an induced magnetic field causes the material to be repelled by a magnetic field. Aluminum and myoglobin are examples of paramagnetic materials; carbon and antimony are diamagnetic.

HEISENBERG UNCERTAINTY PRINCIPLE

The **Heisenberg uncertainty principle** states that the position and momentum of an object cannot simultaneously be known with arbitrarily high precision. Quantitatively, it states that $\Delta x \Delta p \geq \frac{h}{4\pi}$, where Δx is the uncertainty in the position, Δp is the uncertainty in the momentum, and h is Planck's constant, 6.626×10^{-34} J/s. This is often written $\Delta x \Delta p \geq \frac{\hbar}{2}$, where $\hbar$, the reduced Planck's constant, is defined as $h/2\pi$. Instead of position and momentum, the uncertainty principle can also be stated in terms of energy and time $\left(\Delta E \Delta t \geq \frac{\hbar}{2} \right)$ or certain other pairs of variables.

Although sometimes it is assumed that the uncertainty principle arises because in observing an object's position, one necessarily must disturb it, it is actually more fundamental than that—it is not just that the object's position and momentum can't be simultaneously measured; it is that—counterintuitively—a particle can't simultaneously have an exact position and momentum. Because Planck's constant is so small, the effects of the principle on macroscopic phenomena are negligible, but for objects on the atomic scale, it is significant. For instance, the Heisenberg uncertainty principle explains quantum tunneling, the ability of a particle to pass through a barrier that classically would be impermeable.

EFFECTIVE NUCLEAR CHARGE

The **effective nuclear charge** on an electron, Z_{eff}, is the effective net nuclear charge experienced by the electrons given the presence of other electrons in the atom. Because each electron is both attracted to the nucleus and repelled by the other electrons present, the electrical force from the other electrons effectively cancels much of the force from a like number of protons. The effective nuclear charge of an atom is therefore always less than the atomic number: $Z_{eff} < Z$ (except in the case of an atom or ion with only one electron). Calculating the exact effective nuclear charge is nontrivial, however, because it depends not only on the number of electrons but also on the shapes of the orbitals.

The effective nuclear charge has a number of ramifications. It affects the atomic binding energy, or ionization energy, as well as the atomic and ionic radius. It is also the reason that in an atom with multiple electrons, different orbitals with the same principal quantum number do not have the exact same energy and that at relatively high n, some of the orbitals fill in a different order than might be expected: for example, the 4s orbital has lower energy than the 3d.

PHOTOELECTRIC EFFECT

The **photoelectric effect** is the phenomenon in which light shined on certain materials causes them to emit electrons. Although this can partly be explained by assuming that the energy of the light knocks electrons from the atom, there are several observed aspects of the phenomenon that this classically failed to explain. The photoelectric effect does not occur when the light's frequency is below a certain threshold, regardless of the intensity of the light. Likewise, the phenomenon can be prevented by applying a stopping voltage, but the necessary voltage depends only on the material and the frequency of the light, not on its intensity.

It was Albert Einstein who recognized that the photoelectric effect could be explained if light came in distinct quanta, now called photons, with an energy dependent on the light's frequency. The number of photons determined the intensity, but only if individual photons had sufficient energy would they be able to remove electrons from atoms. The recognition that light came in discrete quanta helped pave the way for the development of quantum mechanics. Although Einstein is most famous for his theory of relativity, it was for his work on the photoelectric effect that he won his Nobel Prize.

MOLECULAR STRUCTURE
LEWIS ELECTRON DOT FORMULAS
A Lewis Electron Dot formula is a method of visually portraying the bonds between atoms in a molecule or ion and the positions of unbonded electron pairs. In a Lewis formula, each atom is represented by its chemical symbol; a line drawn between atoms represents a bond—with two lines for a double bond and three for a triple—and a dot represents an unbonded electron.

One method to derive Lewis structures starts with totaling the number of valence electrons in all the atoms. Then sum the electrons needed to surround each atom—usually eight for most atoms (the octet rule) and two for hydrogen. Total these electrons, subtract the valence electrons (and the charge, for an ion), and divide by two to find the number of bonds required. Find a way to place this many bonds between the atoms (which may involve some trial and error), and then place the remaining electrons to satisfy the octet rule.

For instance, formic acid is CH_2O_2. There are $4 + 2(1) + 2(6) = 18$ valence electrons; $8 + 2(2) + 2(8) = 28$; $(28 - 18)/2 = 5$. Five bonds are needed, which can be arranged as follows, with the additional electrons:

RESONANCE STRUCTURES
Sometimes when deriving a Lewis dot formula, it turns out that there is more than one possible way to arrange the bonds and electrons so that the necessary conditions are satisfied, without changing the overall structure of the molecule (which atoms are bonded to which other atoms). In this case, the molecule or ion is said to have resonance, and the different possible arrangements are called resonance structures. For example, consider the thiocyanate ion, CNS^-. There are:

$$\overset{C}{(4} + \overset{N}{5} + \overset{S}{6)} + \overset{charge}{1} = 16 \text{ total valence electrons}$$

$3(8) = 24$ are needed, so we need $\frac{24-16}{2} = 4$ bonds. There are three ways to achieve this:

In this case, the third structure is the most accurate; the formal charges are minimized, and the most electronegative atom has the lowest formal charge. But often there is no preferred structure.

For the carbonate ion CO_3^{2-}, we need $[4(8) + 2] - [4 + 3(6)]/2 = 4$ bonds, leading to the following structure:

But there's no reason to choose any particular oxygen atom for the double bond; there are three resonant structures:

In practice, the ion's structure is a hybrid of all of these.

FORMAL CHARGE

To find the formal charge of an atom in a Lewis Electron Dot formula, take the number of valence electrons in a free atom of the element, subtract the number of unbonded electrons, and then subtract half the number of bonded electrons—which is equivalent to subtracting the number of bonds. The total of the formal charges of all the atoms is equal to zero for a neutral molecule or, for an ion, the charge of the ion. If there are multiple possible Lewis structures (resonances), the preferred structure is the one where the atoms have the smallest magnitudes of formal charges, and the most electronegative atom has the most negative formal charge.

For example, consider carbon dioxide, which has three resonances:

In all three, the carbon atom has a formal charge of:

$$\underbrace{\overset{valence}{4} - \overset{bonded}{0}}_{electrons} - \overset{bonds}{4} = 0$$

In the first, the oxygen on the left has a formal charge of $6 - 2 - 3 = +1$ and the oxygen on the right of $6 - 6 - 1 = -1$. In the second, these are reversed. In the third, both oxygen atoms have a formal charge of $6 - 4 - 2 = 0$, so the third is preferred.

LEWIS ACIDS AND BASES

The Lewis theory of acids and basis is named after American physical chemist Gilbert Newton Lewis, noted for his work in thermodynamics and chemical bonding. (This is the same Lewis who developed the Lewis Electron Dot formula.) A Lewis acid is a substance that can accept a pair of electrons. A Lewis base is a substance that can donate a pair of electrons. The Lewis definition of acids and bases further expands the concept beyond the Brønsted-Lowry definition, allowing consideration of chemicals as acids and bases that don't qualify under that theory. Any molecule or ion with an unshared pair of electrons can be a Lewis base, and any with an atom that requires one or more pairs of electrons to fill its valence shell can be a Lewis acid. This means that the H^+ ion

qualifies as a Lewis acid because it needs a pair of electrons to fill its valence shell, but so do other molecules and ions, such as boron trifluoride, BF_3, in which the boron molecule has only six electrons in its valence shell.

FORMATION OF COVALENT BONDS

Unlike an ionic bond, in which one atom "donates" one or more electrons to another and then the two atoms are attracted to each other by their opposite charge, in a covalent bond two atoms share a pair of electrons. Covalent bonds usually occur between nonmetals; the elements in group 14 (carbon, silicon, etc.) are especially prone to form covalent bonds because their valence shells are half full: this makes it impractical to form an ionic bond as they would have to donate or accept four electrons.

It is possible for two atoms to share more than one pair of electrons. If they share two pairs of electrons, then there is said to be a double bond between them. If the atoms share three pairs of electrons, this is said to be a triple bond. Double bonds are shorter than single bonds—that is, the atoms are closer together—as well as stronger—and harder to break. Triple bonds are shorter and stronger still.

LEWIS ELECTRON DOT FORMULA EXCEPTIONS

One of the fundamental rules of creating Lewis electron dot formulas is the octet rule that each atom must be surrounded by eight electrons. Nevertheless, this rule has exceptions. The most common exception is that concerning hydrogen—unlike the heavier elements, hydrogen needs only two electrons to fill its valence shell, not eight. But exceptions sometimes occur, not including hydrogen as well. Most commonly, a compound will have too many electrons to make it possible to satisfy the octet rule, leaving one or more atoms with more than eight electrons surrounding them. Usually these excess electrons will surround the central atom. For instance, in thionyl chloride ($SOCl_2$), the sulfur atom has 10 electrons; in iodine pentafluoride (IF_5) the iodine atom has 12. Other compounds may have too few electrons; this is most common for compounds involving boron and beryllium. (These compounds generally act as Lewis acids.) In boron trichloride (BCl_3), the boron atom has only six electrons; in beryllium iodide (BeI_2) the beryllium has only four. Finally, some molecules contain an odd number of electrons, which makes it impossible to satisfy the octet rule; examples include nitrous oxide (NO) and chlorine dioxide (ClO_2).

PARTIAL IONIC CHARACTER
ROLE OF ELECTRONEGATIVITY IN DETERMINING CHARGE DISTRIBUTION

Although electrons are shared between atoms in a covalent bond, they are not necessarily shared equally. Generally, the electron is more closely associated with the atom with higher electronegativity. If the two atoms have the same electronegativity, then the electron will be shared equally; thus, in a molecule of H_2 or O_2, the electrons in the covalent bonds are shared equally between both atoms. On the other hand, in hydrochloric acid (HCl), the chlorine has a much higher electronegativity than the hydrogen (3.16 vs. 2.20). The electron will thus be more closely associated with the chlorine atom, and although the atom as a whole will be neutrally charged, the chlorine atom will have a slight negative charge, whereas the hydrogen atom is slightly positive. Similarly, because oxygen has a higher electronegativity than hydrogen (3.44 vs. 2.20), the oxygen atom in a molecule of water (H_2O) will have a slight negative charge, and the hydrogen atoms will have a slight positive charge. A covalent bond in which the electrons are shared unequally is called a polar covalent bond.

Review Video: Electronegativity
Visit mometrix.com/academy and enter code: 823348

DIPOLE MOMENT

The **dipole moment** of a molecule is a measurement of the polarity of a molecule—the difference in charge between the ends. More specifically, the magnitude of the dipole moment of an atomic bond in a molecule is equal to the charge difference between the bonded atoms times the length of the bond. It is a vector quantity, pointing from the positive toward the negative charge. For a molecule with more than two atoms, the overall dipole moment can be found by adding together as vectors the dipole moments of each bond.

Polar molecules—molecules with nonzero dipole moments—tend to align themselves to electric fields and to other polar molecules and ions. This makes it possible to determine the dipole moment experimentally by measuring this alignment. For instance, a polar substance placed between the two charged plates of a parallel-plate capacitor will tend to align to the electric field of the capacitor and in doing so will alter the capacitance of the system; by measuring the capacitance, one can in principle derive the dipole moments of the particles.

A polar molecule is a molecule in which two sides of the molecule have opposite charges. A nonpolar molecule is a molecule in which in any orientation of the two sides of the molecule are equally charged. Equivalently, a polar molecule is a molecule with a nonzero dipole moment; a nonpolar molecule has a dipole moment of zero. Thus, for instance, H_2 is a polar molecule; the electrons are shared equally, and the dipole moment is zero. HF is polar; the hydrogen atom has a positive charge, and the fluorine negative.

Note that a molecule can be nonpolar even if the individual bonds are polar. For example, oxygen has a higher electronegativity than carbon, so in a carbon dioxide molecule, the oxygen atoms are slightly negative and the carbon atom positive. However, because the oxygen atoms are positioned symmetrically on either side of the carbon atom, the dipole moments of the bonds cancel, and the carbon dioxide molecule as a whole is nonpolar. The same is true of methane, CH_4, in which each bond is polar but the molecule has tetrahedral symmetry. It is not true, however, of molecules such as water and ammonia, which lack such symmetry and are polar.

SIGMA AND PI BONDS

A **sigma (σ) bond** is a bond formed by two atomic orbitals of similar orientation overlapping end to end. Overlapping s-orbitals always form sigma bonds because they are spherically symmetrical and their orientation is irrelevant, but p-orbitals and higher orbitals can also form sigma bonds if they overlap along their axes of symmetry. A **pi (π) bond** forms when two atomic orbitals overlap along their sides, such as two p-orbitals that are displaced along a line perpendicular to their axes of symmetry.

Single bonds between atoms are almost always sigma bonds (although the bond in B_2 is an exception). Double bonds comprise one sigma bond and one pi bond, whereas triple bonds contain one sigma bond and two pi bonds. Although sigma bonds are stronger than pi bonds, the fact that double bonds consist of a sigma bond and a pi bond make them stronger than single bonds that consist of just a sigma bond, and for the same reason triple bonds are stronger still.

HYBRID ORBITALS SP, SP², AND SP³ AND RESPECTIVE GEOMETRIES

Hybrid orbitals occur when atomic orbitals combine into new configurations to facilitate the pairing of electrons and the formation of bonds by orienting the electrons in such a way as to minimize the repulsive forces between them.

In an **sp hybrid orbital**, one s orbital mixes with one p orbital to form two sp orbitals. This often occurs in molecules that include a triple bond. Ethylene (C_2H_2) is an example of a simple molecule with sp orbitals: the 2s orbital of each carbon atom mixes with one of the 2p orbitals to form two sp orbitals, one of which bonds to the hydrogen atom and the other with the other carbon atom; and the remaining two 2p orbitals bond to the other carbon atom in pi bonds.

In an **sp^2 hybrid orbital**, one s orbital mixes with two p orbitals to form three hybrid orbitals. This often accompanies a double bond and occurs, for example, with the carbon atoms in ethene, C_2H_4. Finally, an **sp^3 hybrid orbital** mixes one s orbital and three p orbitals to form four symmetrically arranged hybrid orbitals; this occurs where bonds have tetrahedral symmetry, such as, for instance, in methane, CH_4.

VALENCE SHELL ELECTRON PAIR REPULSION AND THE PREDICTION OF SHAPES MOLECULES

Valence shell electron pair repulsion, or VSEPR, refers to the tendency of electrons around a given atom to arrange themselves in such a way as to put them maximally distant from each other, including both bonds and unpaired electrons. This can be used to predict the geometry of a molecule. The key to using this technique is to count the number of electron groups around the atom, which is sometimes called the VSEPR number. Any pair of unbonded electrons counts as one electron group; so does an unpaired electron; and so does a bond, regardless of its multiplicity (single, double, or triple). This VSEPR number determines how the electron groups are distributed: linear for 2, in an equilateral triangle for 3, tetrahedrally for 4, and so on. For example, the carbon in CO_2 has two (double) bonds and no unbonded electrons; its VSEPR number is 2. This means carbon dioxide is linear. On the other hand, the oxygen in water has two bonds plus two pairs of unbonded electrons for a VSEPR number of 4. Its electron groups are arranged tetrahedrally, with unbonded electron pairs on two corners of the tetrahedron and the bonded hydrogen atoms on the other two.

MULTIPLE BONDING

The geometries of bonds around atoms in molecules mostly fall into a few classes. A linear geometry describes an atom with another atom bonded on either side, the three forming a straight line. This generally occurs when the atom has two bonds and no unbonded electrons, such as in carbon dioxide (CO_2) or beryllium fluoride (BeF_2). This contrasts with a bent geometry that occurs when there are two bonds but also one or two unbonded electron pairs, as in water (H_2O) or sulfur dioxide (SO_2). A trigonal planar geometry occurs when an atom has three bonds and no unpaired electrons and involves the three bonds all being in a plane and forming (something close to) an equilateral triangle. Examples include the nitrate ion NO_3^- and formaldehyde, CH_2O. In a trigonal pyramidal geometry, the atom's three bonds are all in the same direction, making the central atom the apex of a pyramid; this occurs when the atom has three bonds and one pair of unbonded electrons, as in ammonia (NH_3) and the sulfite ion (SO_3^{2-}). Finally, tetrahedral geometry involves four bonds arranged tetrahedrally, as in methane (CH_4) or the sulfate ion (SO_4^{2-}).

RIGIDITY IN MOLECULAR STRUCTURE

In general, single bonds are able to freely rotate, which may lead to some decrease in molecular rigidity. In some simple molecules, the rotation of a bond may not make a difference; rotating the bonds in a water molecule or a molecule of HF will not change the structure of the molecule at all. On the other hand, rotating the bond between oxygen atoms in a molecule of hydrogen peroxide, H_2O_2, will change the geometry of the molecule significantly. Double and triple bonds do not have this rotational freedom, so a molecule with many double or triple bonds will tend to be more rigid than a molecule of similar size with only single bonds.

NUMBER OF BONDS FOR ATOMS

Hydrogen only has a single electron and needs one more electron to fill its valence shell, so it generally makes only one bond in a molecule.

Oxygen is in group 16 and has six valence electrons. It needs two more to fill its valence shell, so it will typically make two bonds, counting multiplicity—that is, it will make two single bonds or one double bond.

Nitrogen is in group 15 and has five valence electrons. It needs three more to fill its valence shell, so it will typically make three bonds, counting multiplicity—that is, it can make three single bonds, or one single bond and two double bonds, or one triple bond. It can form up to four bonds in some circumstances.

Carbon is in group 14 and has four valence electrons. It needs four more to fill its valence shell, so it will typically make four bonds, counting multiplicity. It is the fact that carbon makes so many bonds, and can bond in so many ways (four single, two double, one single and one triple, etc.) that enables it to form into complex organic molecules and form the foundation of life on Earth.

Fluorine and **chlorine** are both halogens in group 17. They have seven electrons in their valence shells and need one more to fill their shells; they therefore generally form one bond.

Silicon is in group 14, along with carbon; like carbon, it has four valence electrons, and needs four more to fill its valence shell, and so typically makes four bonds, counting multiplicity (i.e., counting a double bond as two bonds and a triple bond as three—although silicon rarely forms double or triple bonds). The bonds formed by silicon are weaker than those formed by carbon, however, and it isn't quite as versatile in the molecules it can make up.

Phosphorus is in group 15; it has five valence electrons and needs another three electrons to fill its valence shell. It often forms three bonds but can form up to five bonds—the reason nitrogen, in the same group, can't form as many bonds is simply because phosphorus is larger and can fit more atoms around it.

Sulfur is in group 16 and needs two electrons to fill its valence shell, but although it often forms two bonds, it can form anywhere from two to six.

DRAWING THE STRUCTURAL FORMULA OF A MOLECULE

The **structural formula** of a molecule is a diagram that shows the atoms of the molecule and the bonds between them. Each atom is represented by its chemical symbol, and a line is drawn between bonded atoms—two lines for a double bond and three lines for a triple bond. Unlike a Lewis Electron Dot formula, the structural formula does not necessarily show unbonded electrons. Common groups of atoms may be depicted as a unit rather than with their bonds; OH and CH_3 may appear in structural formulas in this way.

For complex organic molecules, the structural formula is often simplified by not explicitly representing carbon and hydrogen atoms. The carbon atoms are implied where the lines representing the bonds end and intersect, if no atom is explicitly shown there. Hydrogen atoms bonded to carbon atoms are omitted and can be inferred to exist wherever there are fewer than four bonds shown. This simplified structural formula is also called a skeletal formula.

As examples, shown below are the structural formulas for ammonia, NH_3, and acetaldehyde, C_2H_5O. The latter is shown in three ways: with all bonds shown, with the CH_3 compacted, and as a simplified (skeletal) formula.

DELOCALIZED ELECTRONS

A **delocalized electron** is an electron that may pertain to a particular molecule or ion but is not associated with any one atom or bond. Because of their mobility, the presence of delocalized electrons tends to lead to greater electrical and thermal conductivity. Delocalized electrons are common in metals, which form metallic bonds in which the valence electrons move freely among the atoms in a sort of "electron sea" rather than remaining near one or two atoms. They also can occur under some circumstances, however, in other molecules. When a molecule or ion has two or more resonance structures, no one of which is highly favored over the others, this generally represents one or more electrons being delocalized to combine the resonance structures. One important example of such a structure is the benzene ring, which consists of a ring of six bonded carbon atoms. Although the benzene ring is sometimes depicted with alternating single and double bonds, a more accurate representation involves one electron from each carbon atom becoming delocalized and being free to move around the entire ring; each bond between atoms in the ring is not a "pure" single or double bond but something in between.

> **Review Video: Metallic Bonds**
> Visit mometrix.com/academy and enter code: 230855

ISOMERS

STRUCTURAL ISOMERS

When two molecules have the same elements and the same number of atoms of each element, but have the atoms bonded together in different ways, they are said to be **structural isomers**. Structural isomers have the same molecular formula but different structural formulas. One of the simplest examples is C_2H_2O, which describes three different structural isomers: ethenone, ethynol, and oxirene. The structural formulas for these are depicted below:

More complex organic molecules may have many more structural isomers. The molecular formula $C_6H_{12}O_6$, for instance, describes the sugars glucose and fructose but also hundreds more structural isomers with six carbon, twelve hydrogen, and six oxygen atoms (most of which have no simple names but are given complicated names like alpha-L-altropyranose and (2S,3R,4R,5S)-2,3,4,5,6-pentahydroxyhexanal).

STEREOISOMERS

Two molecules are enantiomers if they are mirror images of each other—but are not identical—so a symmetrical molecule would not be said to be an enantiomer of itself; the term only applies to chiral molecules. For example, the compound chlorofluoroiodomethane, $CHClFI$, exists in two different forms that are enantiomers. Both versions of the molecule are tetrahedral, with the carbon atom in the center and the hydrogen, chlorine, fluorine, and iodine atoms at the points of the tetrahedron. But there are two different ways of choosing the placement of the outer atoms that result in two different mirror-image molecules that cannot be rotated into each other. Despite their structural similarity, enantiomers may be very different in their interactions with biological systems.

There are, of course, much more complicated examples of enantiomers than chlorofluoroiodomethane. Amino acids, for example, are chiral—asymmetrical—and so each amino acid also has a corresponding mirror-image form. However, life on Earth uses almost exclusively only one form of each amino acid; their enantiomers are rarely found in nature.

In general, two molecules are **stereoisomers** if they have the same molecular and structural formulae, but they nevertheless differ in the orientation of the bonds and in their three-dimensional shapes. Enantiomers—different molecules that are mirror images of each other—are one kind of stereoisomer. Two molecules are diastereoisomers (or just diastereomers) if they are stereoisomers but not enantiomers—they differ in their three-dimensional structure but are not just mirror images. Diagrams of diastereomers are sometimes distinguished by drawing them in a sort of quasi-perspective, with black triangles representing bonds coming "out of the page" and dashed triangles representing bonds going "into the page."

For instance, 2,3-butanediol consists of a line of four carbon atoms, with an oxygen atom bonded to each of the middle two atoms, and hydrogen atoms filling all the remaining bonding locations. This chemical has three different stereoisomers, depicted below. (These are skeletal diagrams, so the carbon atoms and the hydrogen atoms bonded to them are implicit.)

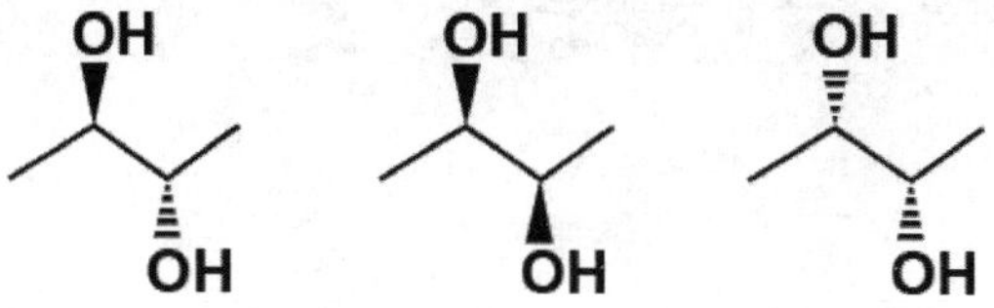

Note that the two molecules on the right are enantiomers of each other, but they are both **diastereoisomers** of the molecule on the left (meso-2, 3-butanediol), which is symmetrical and has no enantiomer.

Two molecules are cis/trans isomers if they are stereoisomers that contain a chain of carbon atoms and that differ as to whether two like atoms or groups of atoms are on the same side (cis) or opposite sides (trans) of the central carbon chain. By definition, all cis/trans isomers are diastereoisomers, but not all diastereoisomers are cis/trans isomers. Note that in all cis/trans isomers, the carbon chain contains at least one double bond or ring structure; this is because parts of molecules can freely rotate around a single bond so that the same molecule can easily change between forms with like parts on the same or opposite side of the central carbon chain if it has only single bonds.

One simple compound that exhibits cis/trans isomerism is 1, 2-dichloroethene, a molecule with two carbon atoms connected by a double bond, and with one chlorine and one hydrogen atom connected to each carbon molecule. The cis and trans forms are shown symbolically below:

A slightly more complicated is 2-butene, a molecule consisting of four carbon atoms with a double bond between the center two and with hydrogen atoms filling the remaining bonding locales:

CONFORMATIONAL ISOMER

Two different molecular structures are **conformational isomers** if they have the same molecules with the same bonds (they are stereoisomers), but they can be converted between each other without breaking any bonds. In other words, the molecules are identical except for rotation around single bonds (double and triple bonds are more rigid and do not allow free rotation). However, this does not necessarily mean that the same molecule can freely change between conformational isomers; it may happen that only certain rotation angles are stable and that an energy barrier inhibits the molecule from readily changing from one stable state to another.

One simple molecule that has different conformational isomers is ethane, C_2H_6. The ends can be rotated about the single bond in the middle to form a so-called eclipsed conformation, in which the hydrogens on each side are directly lined up with each other; a "staggered" conformation, in which the hydrogen atom on one side is in the middle of the gap between hydrogen atoms on the other or anywhere in between.

In practice, the staggered conformation is much more stable than the eclipsed, so ethane molecules will most often be found in or near this conformation.

POLARIZATION OF LIGHT, SPECIFIC ROTATION

A molecule is said to be optically active if the polarization direction of linearly polarized light is rotated when it passes through a substance composed of this molecule. Such molecules can be further classified based on which direction they rotate the light: molecules that rotate light clockwise are said to be dextrorotary; those that rotate light counterclockwise are levorotary.

Molecules are optically active only if they are chiral—that is, they are asymmetrical; they have a mirror image form. If a molecule is levorotary, its enantiomer—the mirror-image version—is

267

dextrorotary and vice versa. An equal mixture of both enantiomers of a compound is said to be racemic and is not optically active because the rotation due to the levorotary and dextrorotary molecules tends to cancel out.

Specific rotation is a measurement of how much an optically active substance rotates linearly polarized light that passes through it. More specifically, it is a measurement of the angle by which the light rotates when it travels 1 decimeter (0.1 m) through a solution of the substance in question with a mass concentration of 1 gram per milliliter. The units of specific rotation are therefore degrees times milliliters (grams times decimeters) but are sometimes given in just degrees, the other units being implied.

The specific rotation of a substance can be measured by a device called a polarimeter, which measures the change in angle of polarization of light after it passes through a solution. Dividing this angle by the light's path length in decimeters and the solution's concentration in grams per milliliter yields the specific rotation.

ABSOLUTE AND RELATIVE CONFIGURATION

Absolute and relative configuration are terms that refer to the arrangement of atoms in chiral molecules—asymmetrical molecules that exist in two mirror-image forms, or enantiomers. The relative configuration of the molecule is its configuration relative to another molecule from which it can be produced. Historically, relative configuration was often stated relative to glyceraldehyde, a particular simple sugar which could be converted into many different compounds (without affecting the configuration of key parts of the molecule). The enantiomers were labeled with the prefix D- if they had the same configuration as the dextrorotary enantiomer of glyceraldehyde (which did not necessarily imply that the molecule in question was itself dextrorotary) and L- if they had the same configuration as levorotary glyceraldehyde. Absolute configuration refers to the precise known geometrical arrangement of the atoms, not relative to any other compounds.

CONVENTIONS FOR WRITING THE R AND S FORMS

The enantiomers of a simple chiral molecule (i.e., the two mirror-image forms of an asymmetrical molecule) can be distinguished by calling one form the R form and one the S form. For a more complex molecule, this terminology can be applied not to a molecule as a whole but to each stereocenter—location in the molecule where there is an atom (usually carbon) with asymmetrical bonds.

To distinguish between the two, determine the "priority" of each constituent bonded to the central atom. The higher the atomic number of the atom bonded directly to the carbon, the higher the priority. If the atom immediately bonded is the same, follow the chain of atoms until you reach a difference. If there's still a tie, double bonds have higher priority than single bonds. Now, picture the lowest-priority constituent pointing away from you, and trace a circle through the others from highest to lowest priority. If this circle runs clockwise, it is an R form; if counterclockwise, it is L.

For instance, consider lactic acid:

Although this has three carbon atoms, only the central one is asymmetrical, so this is our stereocenter. The priority goes H < CH_4 < COOH < OH, so we have:

(R)-lactic acid   (S)-lactic acid

CONVENTIONS FOR WRITING THE E AND Z FORMS

The E and Z terminology is used to distinguish stereoisomers with double bonds, based on the relative positions of the constituents on each side. When there are only two different constituents, they can be distinguished by calling the one with matching constituents on the same side of the central carbon chain cis and the other trans; with more than two constituents, however, these terms are ambiguous, and the E–Z terminology is used.

To distinguish between (E) and (Z) isomers, determine which constituent on each end has a higher "priority." The higher the atomic number of the atom directly connected to the double-bonded atom, the higher the priority; in case of a tie, consider the next atom out, and so on. If the higher priority constituents on each end are on the same side of the double bond, it is a (Z)-isomer; if not, it is an (E)-isomer.

For instance, consider the molecules tiglic acid and angelic acid: two chemicals that are (E) and (Z) isomers:

tiglic acid   angelic acid

CH_3 has a higher priority than H, but COOH has a higher priority than CH_3. So tiglic acid is the (E)-isomer, and angelic acid is the (Z)-isomer.

MASS SPECTROMETER

A mass spectrometer is a device used to separate molecules by mass. Although the spectrometer relies on the particles being charged, uncharged molecules can be separated by a mass spectrometer if they are first ionized. (Technically, the spectrometer separates particles by the mass-to-charge ratio, but it can often be assumed that the charges of most of the particles are the same.)

In a mass spectrometer, charged particles are first accelerated by a voltage that gives all the particles the same kinetic energy. The moving particles are then subjected to a magnetic field. Because the magnetic field deflects some particles more than others, particles of a specific mass (or mass-to-charge ratio) can be selected out. Specifically, the voltage accelerates the particles to an energy of $U = qV$; setting that equal to the kinetic energy gives $qV = \frac{1}{2}mv^2$, and hence $v = \sqrt{\frac{2qV}{m}}$. The magnetic field produces a force of qvB, deflecting the particle in a circular path; setting this equal to the centripetal force yields $qvB = \frac{mv^2}{r}$; putting in our previous formula for v and solving for the radius of the path gives $r = \frac{1}{B}\sqrt{2V\left(\frac{m}{q}\right)}$—the deflection depends on the mass-to-charge ratio.

The Periodic Table

GROUPS

ALKALI METALS

The alkali metals occupy the leftmost column of the periodic table, Group I. They include lithium, sodium, potassium, and so on; hydrogen, however, despite being usually positioned atop the leftmost column, is not conventionally included among the alkali metals.

The alkali metals all have a metallic luster and are soft enough to be easily cut with a knife. One of their most famous properties is their extremely high reactivity. The alkali metals even react with ordinary water, often bursting into flame on contact. Samples of alkali metals must be stored in oil to prevent their oxidation and their reaction with water vapor in the air. All alkali metals have a single valence electron and therefore tend to form singly charged positive ions.

ALKALINE EARTH METALS

The alkaline earth metals occupy the second column from the left on the periodic table. They include barium, magnesium, calcium, and so on.

The alkaline earth metals have a metallic luster and are relatively soft. They tend to react easily, although to a lesser degree than the alkali metals. Still, they are reactive enough that they are never found in nature as pure elements but only in chemical compounds. Their melting points and boiling points are higher than those of the alkali metals but lower than those of most other metals. All the alkaline earth metals have two valence electrons and therefore tend to form doubly charged positive ions.

HALOGENS

The halogens occupy the second column from the right on the periodic table. They include fluorine, chlorine, bromine, and so on. By convention, all the halogens are given names ending in "-ine," and no other elements are, so you can tell from the name whether or not a particular element is a halogen.

The halogens are highly reactive elements, all of which can react with hydrogen to form acids. In their pure elemental state, halogens form diatomic molecules, although because of their reactivity, halogens are never found in their pure elemental state in nature. All of the halogens have seven valence electrons and therefore form singly charged negative ions.

NOBLE GASES

The noble gases occupy the rightmost column in the periodic table. Newly discovered noble gases are given names ending in "-on," but this convention is relatively recent, so there are exceptions among some of the elements discovered earlier: helium is a noble gas but does not have a name ending in "-on," whereas boron, carbon, and silicon have names ending in "-on" but are not noble gases.

The noble gases were formerly also called inert gases; both names come from the nonreactivity of these elements. Although it isn't true that they're completely inert—the noble gases can react with other elements and form compounds—their reactivity is extremely low, and they are almost always found in nature in their pure elemental form. As the name also implies, all known noble gases are in the gaseous state at room temperature, although their melting points increase with their atomic numbers.

TRANSITION METALS

By convention, the transition metals are usually considered to be the elements in groups III through XII of the periodic table, starting with the column topped by scandium (Sc) on the left and usually ending with the column topped by zinc (Zn) on the right. Sometimes the lanthanides and actinides, usually shown in separate rows below the rest of the table, are also included and called inner transition metals. The elements that are not transition metals are called main-group elements or representative elements.

As the name implies, the transition metals are all metals and have the properties shared by most metals: ductility, high electrical and thermal conductivity, and metallic luster. However, they differ from main-group metals in their high electronegativity, which allows them to form covalent compounds and to exist in several different oxidation states. For instance, beryllium, a main-group metal, always forms Be^{2+} ions. On the other hand, iron, a transition metal, can exist in a compound as Fe^{2+} or as Fe^{3+} or, rarely, as Fe^{4-} or in any state from Fe^{2-} to Fe^{7+}.

METALS AND NONMETALS

Most of the elements in the periodic table are considered metals; the nonmetals occupy the upper right corner of the periodic table (plus hydrogen). Metals are characterized in their solid state by malleability and ductility—the former property referring to the fact that they can be reshaped by pressure or hammering, the latter by the fact that they can be stretched into thin wires. Nonmetals, on the other hand, tend to be brittle, cracking under stress or strain rather than reshaping. Metals are also good conductors of both heat and electricity, resulting from the fact that their outer electrons are relatively free to move between atoms. Nonmetals, in general, do not conduct heat or electricity well. Another characteristic of metals is their metallic luster—metals look shiny, whereas nonmetals tend to have a matte and dull appearance. Generally, metals have a higher density and higher melting and boiling points than nonmetals, although this is less reliable; there are metals with relatively low densities (such as lithium) and melting points (such as mercury) and nonmetals with high densities and melting points (such as carbon).

OXYGEN GROUP

The oxygen group is the third column from the right in the periodic table. The elements in the oxygen group are also sometimes called chalcogens. The uppermost element in the group is oxygen, hence the name; the group also includes sulfur, selenium, tellurium, and polonium.

All the elements in the oxygen group have six valence electrons, and the lighter elements in this group usually form doubly negative ions, such as O^{2-} and S^{2-}. Other oxidation states are possible, however, especially for the heavier elements in the group that have smaller electronegativities— polonium more often attains Po^{2+} or Po^{4+} states.

METALLOIDS

The metalloids are elements that lie between the metals and the nonmetals in the periodic table and have properties intermediate between the two. From lowest to highest atomic number, the metalloids include boron (B), silicon (Si), germanium (Ge), arsenic (As), antimony (Sb), tellurium (Te), polonium (Po), and astatine (At), although the last two are not always included. All the elements above and to the right of the metalloids are nonmetals; all the elements below and to the left of the metalloids are metals, with the exception of hydrogen.

Metalloids are solid at room temperature, and have a metallic luster, but are brittle and for the most part behave chemically like nonmetals. Perhaps their most useful property, however, is the ability of some metalloids to act as semiconductors—they can behave either as conductors or as insulators depending on certain conditions. This makes them very useful for various electronic applications and is the reason that computer chips, for example, contain silicon, a semiconductor metalloid.

PERIODIC TRENDS
VALENCE ELECTRONS

Valence electrons are the electrons in the outermost shell of an atom. For a main-group element, it is under normal circumstances solely the valence electrons that are involved in chemical reactions; therefore, it is the number of valence electrons in an atom that primarily determines its chemical properties. This is why elements in the same group have similar chemical properties: elements in the same group have the same number of valence electrons. All the alkali metals have one valence electron, all the halogens have seven, and so on. As a general rule of thumb, atoms will tend to gain or lose electrons in such a way as to be left with a full outer shell of eight valence electrons; this principle is known as the octet rule.

In transition metals, some of the electrons in inner shells can also participate in chemical reactions. The concept of valence electrons is therefore less well defined for transition metals than it is for main-group elements.

FIRST AND SECOND IONIZATION ENERGY

The ionization energy of an element is the amount of energy needed to ionize an atom of that element—that is, to remove an electron from the atom. More specifically, the energy required to remove one electron from a neutral atom is the first ionization energy, the energy required to remove another electron from an atom that has already lost an electron (a singly charged positive ion) is the second ionization energy, and so on; the nth ionization energy is the energy required to remove one electron from an atom that has already lost $n - 1$ electrons.

In general, the closer the outermost electron is to the nucleus, the harder it is to remove, and therefore the greater the ionization energy. This means that the ionization energy increases as the atomic radius decreases. Therefore, the ionization energy within a group tends to decrease as the atomic number increases because the heavier elements in a group have a larger atomic radius. However, across a period the atomic radius decreases from left to right, and therefore the ionization energy increases. So, the atomic energy of elements in the periodic table tends to increase from left to right and from down to up.

ELECTRON AFFINITY

Electron affinity is a measurement of the change in energy when an atom or molecule in the gaseous state gains an electron. Equivalently, the electron affinity can be defined as the amount of energy required to remove an electron from a singly charged negative ion. The larger the electron affinity, the more stable the negative ion.

Electron affinity tends to increase from left to right on the periodic table, although there is no clear trend within groups: electron affinity decreases from top to bottom within the alkali metals, for instance, but mostly increases from top to bottom within the alkaline earths. A few elements do not form negative ions at all or require energy to be added to give them an electron; the electron affinity of these elements is considered to be negative or zero. These elements include the noble gases as well as beryllium, nitrogen, magnesium, manganese, zinc, cadmium, and mercury.

ELECTRONEGATIVITY

Electronegativity is the tendency of an atom to attract electrons. Electronegativity is a unit-less quantity that is only meaningful in terms of the difference in electronegativity between two atoms. It is therefore necessary to decide on a reference point; by convention, the electronegativity of hydrogen is defined as 2.20, and the electronegativities of other atoms are derived based on this. Generally, when two atoms or molecules of different electronegativity interact, the atom that has a smaller electronegativity will tend to "donate" an electron to the atom with a larger electronegativity—or, in the case of a covalent bond, the shared electron will tend to be more closely associated with the latter atom.

Generally, among elements in the periodic table, electronegativity increases from left to right and decreases from top to bottom. (The noble gases are a special case, and because of their nonreactivity are often considered not to have electronegativity.) There are exceptions to these trends among the transition metals and in the boron and carbon groups; lead, for example, has a higher electronegativity than tin despite being positioned below it on the periodic table.

ELECTRON SHELLS AND THE SIZES OF ATOMS

The sizes of atoms of elements in the periodic table tend to increase from top to bottom within a column, and to decrease from left to right within a row. The former trend is easy to understand; as one goes down a row in the periodic table, the atoms have added electron shells that must lie outside the inner shells possessed by the higher atoms and must therefore increase the atomic radius.

The latter trend, however, may be more counterintuitive; as one goes from left to right along a row in the periodic table, the atoms gain more protons and electrons, and one might therefore expect them to become larger, not smaller. The key to understanding the trend is that it is not the size of the nucleus that determines the size of the atom but the size of the electron clouds; as the number of protons increases without adding a new electron shell, the effective nuclear charge on the electrons in the outermost shell increases, pulling these outermost electrons closer to the nucleus.

ELECTRON SHELLS AND THE SIZES OF IONS

In general, negative ions are larger than the neutral atom, whereas positive ions are smaller. Furthermore, the greater the charge of the ion, the greater the difference in size from the neutral atom; for instance, a Ti^{4+} ion is smaller than a Ti^{3+} ion, which is smaller than a Ti^{2+} ion.

The reason for this difference has to do with the effective nuclear charge on the outermost electrons. As an atom gains electrons to become a negative ion, the effective nuclear charge on the outermost electrons decreases because the extra electron partially cancels it; this results in less force holding the electrons to the nucleus, so the electrons' distance from the nucleus is greater. As an atom loses electrons to become a positive ion, the opposite occurs; the effective nuclear charge increases, and the outermost electrons are bound more tightly to the nucleus.

An electron shell is a collection of electrons with the same energy level—the same value of the principal quantum number, n. Very roughly, an electron shell can be thought of as a layer of electrons surrounding an atom. A shell in turn consists of subshells of electrons with the same angular quantum number l. Each shell can hold only a certain maximum number of electrons; the greater the energy of the shell, the more subshells it has, and the more electrons it can hold. The first shell holds up to 2 electrons, the second $2 + 6 = 8$, the third $2 + 6 + 10 = 18$, and so on. It is largely the electron shells that determine the arrangement of the atoms in the periodic table—each row of the periodic table has one more shell than the one above it.

Because each electron shell lies farther from the nucleus than the previous, the more electron shells an atom or ion possesses, the higher its radius. This is the reason that the atomic and ionic radii increase within a group as the atomic number increases.

Nuclear Reactions

RADIOACTIVE DECAY AND HALF-LIFE

Radioactive decay, or radioactivity, is a set of processes that allow unstable atomic nuclei, or nuclides, to emit subatomic particles, or radiation. The decay is a random process and it is not possible to predict an individual atom's decay. Radioactive decay occurs at an exponential rate. This means that the amount of radioactive material, A, present after time t is given by the equation $A = A_0 e^{kt}$, where A_0 is the amount of material present at time $t = 0$, and k is the activity of the material. The activity may be given, but it can also be determined if the amount of material present at two different times is known.

The time required for half the mass of a radioactive material to decay is known as its half-life. Half-life is the most commonly used measure of a material's rate of decay. A half-life can be as short as a fraction of a second or as long as millions of years.

Certain isotopes that are known to be unstable and spontaneously decay are referred to as radioisotopes. One common radioisotope used to determine the age of an object is carbon-14. Over time, this isotope decays to nitrogen-14. The half-life of carbon-14 is about 5,730 years.

An ordinarily stable isotope may be artificially made radioactive by bombarding it with a stream of neutrons. When these neutrons are captured by a previously stable nucleus, it can become unstable and begin to decay.

BETA DECAY

Beta decay is radioactive decay in which there is an emission of a beta particle, a high-energy electron or positron. For an electron emission, it is known as beta minus (β^-) decay. For a positron emission, it is known as beta plus (β^+) decay. In β^- decay, a neutron is converted into a proton, an electron, and an antineutrino, $\bar{v}_e$:

$$n \rightarrow p^+ + e^- + \bar{v}_e$$

This is because a down quark is converted to an up quark, emitting an electron and an antineutrino.

In β^+ decay, a proton is converted into a neutron by means of an up quark becoming a down quark, emitting a positron and a neutrino:

$$energy + p^+ \rightarrow n + e^+ + v_e$$

Unlike β^- decay, β^+ decay cannot occur spontaneously. It requires an input of energy.

In both types of beta decay, the atomic number changes, but the mass number remains constant.

ALPHA DECAY

Alpha decay is a type of radioactive decay in which an alpha particle is ejected from the nucleus. An alpha particle is the nucleus of a helium atom, consisting of 2 protons and 2 neutrons. Ejection of an alpha particle reduces the parent nuclide's atomic number by 2 and its mass number by 4. An example of alpha decay is given by:

$$^{238}U \rightarrow {}^{234}Th + a$$

Alpha decay can be looked at as nuclear fission, in which the parent nucleus splits into a pair of daughter nuclei. Alpha decay is governed by the strong nuclear force, or the force between two or more nucleons. Alpha particles are ejected from the nucleus at speeds around 15,000 km/s with a typical kinetic energy of 5 MeV.

ELEMENTARY PARTICLES

The two basic types of elementary particles are bosons, which have integer spin, and fermions, which have half-integer spin. There are a few different types of bosons, but the type most commonly encountered are photons, which make up the full spectrum of light.

There are only two types of fermions: leptons and quarks. Both leptons and quarks have antiparticles as well, with opposite charge.

Leptons may be one of three different flavors: muon, tauon, or electron. Each of these is accompanied by a small electrically neutral particle called a neutrino, also differentiated by the same three flavors. Each lepton has a charge of -1, while its antiparticle has a charge of +1. The electron's antiparticle is the positron.

Quarks are most commonly encountered as the constituent particles of nucleons. There are six different flavors of quark, of which the two most common are up, having a charge of +2/3, and down, having a charge of -1/3. Neutrons consist of one up quark and two down quarks, while protons have two up quarks and one down quark.

GAMMA RAYS

A gamma ray (γ) is electromagnetic radiation that is produced from radioactive decay or other nuclear processes, such as electron annihilation in which an electron and positron collide. No physical difference exists between X-rays and gamma rays that have the same energy; they are set apart by their origin. Gamma rays are high-energy electromagnetic radiation that result from nuclear transitions, while X-rays are high-energy radiation caused by energy transitions from electrons that are accelerating. Gamma rays penetrate more than either alpha or beta radiation, neither of which is electromagnetic, but they are not as ionizing. Gamma sources have a wide variety of uses ranging from medical to industrial.

NUCLEAR BINDING ENERGY

The nuclear binding energy of an atom is the energy that would be required to disassemble the nucleus into its constituent nucleons. They are held together by a strong nuclear force in the nucleus. Nuclear binding energy may be calculated by determining the difference in mass between the nucleus and the sum of the masses of its constituent particles. This mass, m, is converted to energy by the equation $E = mc^2$, where c is the speed of light in a vacuum.

Nuclei may be transformed by a rearrangement of nucleons. These nuclear transformations may occur by many different means, including radioactive decay, nuclear fusion, and nuclear fission. In nuclear fusion, two light nuclei merge into a single nucleus that is heavier. In nuclear fission, a single large nucleus divides into two or more smaller nuclei. In either case, if the mass of the nuclei before transformation is greater than the mass after transformation, then it is an exothermic process. Conversely, if the mass is greater after transformation, the process is endothermic. Nickel and iron have the most stable nuclei of any elements, having the largest binding energies.

CONSERVATION LAWS THAT APPLY TO NUCLEAR REACTIONS

In nuclear reactions, neither mass nor energy is fully conserved independently. However, the mass-energy relation is conserved. Any mass loss is converted to energy and any energy loss is converted to mass, both by the equation $E = mc^2$, where c is the speed of light in a vacuum. Generally speaking, however, there will not be a significant loss of mass in a reaction and the total number of protons and neutrons will be constant. Additionally, electric charge is conserved in nuclear reactions. For instance, when an alpha particle is ejected, it reduces the charge of the parent nucleus by 2, and itself carries a charge of +2. In beta plus decay, a proton decays to a neutron, reducing the charge of the atom by 1, but a positron with a charge of +1 is also ejected, conserving charge in the reaction. Similarly, in beta minus decay, a neutron is converted to a proton, increasing the atom's charge by 1, but this is accompanied by the ejection of an electron with a charge of -1.

Unknown products in a nuclear reaction can be predicted by balancing those quantities which must be conserved. For instance, if it is known that plutonium-238 decays to cesium-140 upon being impacted by a neutron, ejecting 2 more neutrons in the process, the remaining products may be determined. Since there are no charged particles emitted, the number of protons must remain constant. Of the 94 protons in plutonium, 55 form the cesium atom, leaving 39 protons to form an yttrium atom. Since the number of neutrons must also be constant, this will be an atom of yttrium-97.

FUSION AND FISSION

Fusion generally requires a large input of energy to overcome the repulsive force between nuclei, but after transformation it produces an even greater amount of energy. This makes fusion reactions difficult to control, so fission is generally chosen over fusion for power-generation applications. The energy and radiation given off by stars are the product of countless fusion chain reactions.

Fission is most often initiated by bombarding atoms with a stream of neutrons, destabilizing the atoms and causing a fission into smaller nuclei and emission of numerous radiation particles, including more neutrons, thus perpetuating the reaction. These reactions are easily sustainable and much more easily controlled than fusion, so they are ideal for generating power. However, a fission reaction can be initiated that does not propagate in a controlled manner. This type of reaction is commonly used in nuclear weapons.

Laboratory

SIGNIFICANT FIGURES

Significant figures enable scientists to determine which measurements are very precise and which measurements are not as precise. Every measurement has uncertainty. When recording data, the use of the correct number of significant figures indicates the precision of the equipment being used to measure the data. In general, measurements are recorded only to the first uncertain digit. This means that the final recorded digit is considered to be uncertain. Every calculated value using collected data has uncertainty. Significant figures determine where to round when doing calculations with data. Also, significant figures prevent the answers to calculations from being stated with higher precision than the data used in the calculation would actually support.

When using significant figures in calculations, there are two sets of rules: one for addition and subtraction, and one for multiplication and division. For addition and subtraction calculations, answers should be rounded to the leftmost uncertain digit. For example, when adding measurements of 2.3 g and 10.81 g, the correct answer would be 13.1 g. The first term's uncertain digit is in the tenths place, while the second term's uncertain digit is in the hundredths place. Thus, the answer is rounded to the tenths place. In multiplication and division calculations, answers should be rounded to the exact number of significant figures in the factor that has the smallest number of significant figures. For example, when multiplying 3.2 by 4.001, the correct answer may only have 2 significant figures because 3.2 only has 2 significant figures. Therefore, the correct answer is 13. If the first factor were instead 3.20 or 3.200 (indicating that this value was known with greater precision), the answer would be 12.8 or 12.80, respectively.

PRECISION AND ACCURACY

Most scientific measurements have some uncertainty or error in them, and the precision and accuracy are some ways of describing the extent: The higher the precision or accuracy, the smaller the error or uncertainty. However, precision and accuracy are not the same thing. **Precision** refers to the *consistency* of the measurements: If multiple measurements all yield values that are close to each other, the measurements are *precise*. **Accuracy** refers to how close the measurements are to the real value of the quantity being measured. Significant random error can lead to low precision; *systematic* error leads to low accuracy.

It is possible for measurements to be precise but not accurate or vice versa. Suppose an object has a mass of 50.0 g. One investigator tries to measure its mass and obtains measurements of 39.9, 40.0, 39.8, and 40.1 g. These measurements are precise, but not accurate: They are close to each other, but not to the actual value. Another obtains measurements of 40.5, 46.2, 51.8, and 61.1 g. These measurements are accurate, but not precise: There is a wide spread, but their average is close to the actual value.

DATA ERRORS AND ERROR ANALYSIS

No measurements are ever 100% accurate. There is always some amount of error regardless of how careful the observer or how good his equipment. The important thing for the scientist to know is how much error is present in a given measurement. Two commonly misunderstood terms regarding error are accuracy and precision. Accuracy is a measure of how close a measurement is to the true value. Precision is a measure of how close repeated measurements are to one another. Error is usually quantified using a confidence interval and an uncertainty value. For instance, if the quantity is measured as 100 ± 2 on a 95% confidence interval, this means that there is a 95% chance that the actual value falls between 98 and 102.

When looking for the uncertainty in a derived quantity such as density, the errors in the constituent quantities, mass and volume in this case, are propagated to the derived quantity. The percent uncertainty in the density, U_ρ/ρ, can be found by the equation:

$$U_\rho/\rho = \sqrt{\left(\frac{U_m}{m}\right)^2 + \left(\frac{U_V}{V}\right)^2}$$

MINIMIZING ERROR AND BIAS

Random error, also called statistical error, is one of the two main types of error that arise in a scientific investigation. It gets its name from the fact that it is not consistent but may randomly cause the measured value to be either higher or lower than the actual value.

Random error comes about due to unavoidable variability in measurements. For instance, if you're measuring the diameter of a wire with a micrometer (an instrument for measuring very small distances), you may not get exactly the same measurement each time—perhaps because it's hard to tell when the micrometer is firmly in contact with the wire but not so firmly that you're compressing it, or because the wire isn't perfectly round. If your measurements vary from 0.12 mm to 0.14 mm, we may write that as 0.13 mm $\pm$ 0.01 mm.

Random error can be minimized by taking many measurements and using the average value. Because random error can make the measurement either larger or smaller than the actual value, on average, for many measurements, it tends to cancel out. Although the random error can't be completely eliminated, the more measurements you take, the smaller it tends to become.

Systematic error is one of the two main types of error that arise in a scientific investigation. Unlike the other main type of error, random error, systematic error has a consistent effect on all measurements, making all the measurements off in the same direction and by about the same amount.

Systematic error comes about due to often-subtle defects in the measuring instrument or measurement process. For example, suppose you want to measure the amount of liquid in a cup, and you do so by pouring the liquid into a graduated cylinder. It may be, however, that each time you pour the liquid into the cylinder, a few drops are left behind in the cup. All your measurements are then lower than they should be by the volume of those drops.

There is no universal way to avoid systematic error, but it can often be accounted for by careful consideration of the experimental procedure and calibration of measuring instruments. It may also help to try to measure quantities by two or more different methods; if different methods of measuring the same quantity give consistently different results, then at least one of those methods probably has some systematic error.

A scientific investigation is said to have **experimental bias**—or simply to be **biased**—if researchers or experimental subjects influence the recorded observations toward the results they want or expect. This doesn't necessarily mean that they are deliberately and dishonestly fudging the values. Bias is frequently unconscious; the investigators may not be aware that they are letting their preconceptions influence their observations.

Experimental bias is especially likely in investigations with subjective observations. In a medical trial to test whether a drug can alleviate some symptoms, experimental subjects who expect the drug to help them might convince themselves they're feeling better even if the drug actually has no effect. However, even in studies with more objective measurements, investigators have been known to record wrong values due to unconscious bias.

One way to eliminate bias is to make sure if possible that the experiment is **blinded**—the investigator doesn't know which of the subjects have been treated and which are untreated controls, so the investigator *can't* change the observations in favor of a particular result. An investigation involving human subjects can be **double-blinded**, so that neither the investigator nor the subjects know which subjects are receiving treatment and which are controls.

CONTROLS

A valid experiment must be carefully controlled. All variables except the one being testing must be carefully maintained. This means that all conditions must be kept exactly the same except for the independent variable. Additionally, a set of data is usually needed for a control group. The control group represents the "normal" state or condition of the variable being manipulated. Controls can be negative or positive. Positive controls are the variables that the researcher expects to have an effect on the outcome of the experiment. A positive control group can be used to verify that an experiment is set up properly. Negative control groups are typically thought of as placebos. A negative control group should verify that a variable has no effect on the outcome of the experiment. The better an experiment is controlled, the more valid the conclusions from that experiment will be. A researcher is more likely to draw a valid conclusion if all variables other than the one being manipulated are being controlled.

DATA COLLECTION

A valid experiment must be measurable. Data tables should be formed, and meticulous, detailed data should be collected for every trial. First, the researcher must determine exactly what data are needed and why those data are needed. The researcher should know in advance what will be done with those data at the end of the experimental research. The data should be repeatable, reproducible, and accurate. The researcher should be sure that the procedure for data collection will be reliable and consistent. The researcher should validate the measurement system by performing practice tests and making sure that all of the equipment is correctly calibrated and periodically retesting the procedure and equipment to ensure that all data being collected are still valid.

DESCRIPTIVE STATISTICS

When there are large numbers of data points, it's useful to present them in a summarized way that takes all the data into account but is easier to use and understand than just the raw data points themselves. **Statistics** is a method for doing this: The point of statistics is to take many data points and find trends and properties that describe the data set as a whole, or patterns within it. Common statistical properties of a data set include the **mean**, or average, and the **standard deviation**, a measure of the variability of the data set—how much the data points tend to differ. In addition to describing single data sets, statistics can also be used to characterize the relationships between two or more variables. One statistical property that serves this purpose is **correlation**, which describes to what extent the changes in one variable tend to be mirrored by the other.

Conclusions drawn from statistics are generally not absolute, but they are probabilistic: A statistical analysis can only establish that it is *probable* that a particular relationship holds. However, for very large data sets and repeated trials, this probability can be very high.

EXTENDING RESULTS

In the context of a scientific investigation, a **prediction** is an expression of what you would expect to happen if certain conditions are met. It is not a blanket statement of the future; when you make a scientific prediction, you are not necessarily stating what *will* happen, only what would happen *if* certain conditions hold. For example, we can predict based on what we know about its chemical properties that *if* we place an apple in a solution of concentrated sulfuric acid, it will dissolve.

Predictions are important in science for two reasons: (1) because they permit application of scientific theories—if a theory predicts what will happen under certain circumstances, then we may be able to use that to our benefit—and (2) because they allow hypotheses and theories to be tested—if a theory predicts that something should happen under particular circumstances, and we put that to the test and the event does occur as predicted, that provides further evidence of the validity of the theory. If, on the other hand, the event does *not* match the prediction, the theory may be falsified. A theory that has been validated by numerous successful predictions may come to be widely accepted as valid.

Interpolation is the estimation of the expected value of a dependent variable for a particular value of an independent variable, based on the measured value of the dependent variable at values of the independent variable both smaller and larger than the value in question. For example, suppose we know that the height of a tree was 10 meters in 1960 and 20 meters in 1980; by interpolation, we can guess that it may have been 15 meters tall in 1970.

The preceding example assumes a linear relationship and is therefore a case of **linear interpolation**. However, of course not all relationships are linear, and interpolation can take that into account. Interpolation may be done graphically: We can draw a curve through the known data points and use that curve to estimate the value of the dependent variable (*y*) at some other value of the independent variable (*x*). If we have many data points, interpolation tends to be fairly reliable, though not completely; it could still be the case that there is some large spike or other change that we don't know about between the measured data points.

Extrapolation is the estimation of the expected value of a dependent variable for a particular value of an independent variable, based on the measured value of the dependent variable at values of the independent variable either smaller or larger than the value in question, but not both. For example, suppose we know that the population of a town was 5,000 in the year 1990, 6,000 in the year 2000, and 7,000 in the year 2010; by extrapolation we can guess that its population may be 8,000 in the year 2020.

Like interpolation, extrapolation does not necessarily assume a linear relationship, and it may be done graphically. However, extrapolation may be less reliable than interpolation. Frequently, a relationship that holds for some range of variables breaks down at higher and lower values. For instance, suppose we note that hanging a 1 kg mass on a spring stretches it by 1 cm, a 2 kg mass by 2 cm, and a 3 kg mass by 3 cm. We extrapolate that a 10 kg mass would stretch the spring by 10 cm. But that isn't necessarily true: There's a limit to the weight a spring can hold before it breaks or is damaged, and 10 kg may exceed that limit.

PROCESS OF INFERENCE

Inference is the process of drawing conclusions based on observations. This is an important part of the process of science as well as social studies. It could even be said that the goal of most scientific investigations is to infer an answer to the experimental question.

Often, drawing an inference involves noticing a trend in the data and assuming that the trend continues. For example, if every time an investigator puts a particular chemical in a bacterial culture the bacteria die, it is a reasonable inference that that chemical is deadly to the bacteria. The trend may be more subtle, involving, for example, a relationship between two quantities. An investigator may observe that a certain type of tree tends to be taller at lower altitudes and infer that there is something about higher altitudes that inhibits the trees' growth.

An inference is not necessarily a sure thing; especially if only a few observations have been made, it could be that the relationship on which the inference is based is coincidental, and the inference is not valid. The inference may be used to create a hypothesis that can be tested in further investigations.

TABLES, GRAPHS, AND CHARTS

When reading tables, graphs, and charts, determine if there is a correlation between the data for the independent variable and the data for the dependent variable. The correlation is positive if both data sets increase together. The correlation is negative if one set of data increases while the other set of data decreases. If a scatterplot is drawn, determine if there is a positive correlation, a negative correlation, or no correlation between the variables. If a correlation is found, determine if the correlation is linear or curvilinear. If there is a linear correlation, a line of best fit can be drawn to make predictions. Graphing calculators can be used to perform linear regression of the data and determine the equation for the line of best fit. Use of linear regression will increase the accuracy of predictions.

APPROPRIATE APPAREL AND CONDUCT

General guidelines for appropriate apparel in the chemistry laboratory are as follows. Safety goggles must be worn at all times while in the laboratory. Wear a chemical-resistant laboratory apron. Roll long sleeves up above the elbow. Closed-toe shoes and long pants must be worn in the lab. Contact lenses are not allowed. Long, loose hair should be tied back. Wear disposable gloves when handling hazardous materials. General guidelines for conduct in the chemistry laboratory are as follows. No practical jokes or boisterous conduct in the laboratory. No horseplay. No eating, drinking, or chewing gum. No unauthorized experiments are to be performed. Never taste anything. Never directly smell the source of any vapor or gas; instead, waft a small sample to your nose. Always wash your hands before leaving the lab.

STANDARD SAFETY EQUIPMENT

Eyewash stations and safety showers should be located less than 10 seconds from the laboratory area, according to Occupational Safety and Health Administration (OSHA) standards. Bottles of eyewash solution should be readily available. If chemicals come into contact with your skin or eyes, flush immediately with large amounts of water. Fire extinguishers should be located according to the building code. Fire blankets should be readily available. Fire blankets may be used to smother small fires. Never use a carbon dioxide extinguisher on a person.

SAFE DISPOSAL OF MATERIALS

The safe disposal of materials in the laboratory should include a minimum of the following. Check the Safety Data Sheet (SDS) for the correct disposal procedure for each chemical. Check with local authorities concerning possible restrictions before disposing of materials. Do not pour chemicals down the drain unless approved by local authorities. Usually, dilute solutions of inorganic salts, in which neither ion is highly acidic or basic, are approved for drainage disposal. Some organics may be flushed down the drain with large amounts of water. Use professional waste haulers for all hazardous waste. Provide appropriate waste containers. Properly dispose of unwanted chemicals. Treat spills properly.

Organic Chemistry

Mechanisms

ENERGETICS AND STRUCTURE
EXOTHERMIC AND ENDOTHERMIC REACTIONS

The current convention in defining whether a reaction is exothermic or endothermic lies in the **system perspective** and is manifested in the surroundings. An **exothermic reaction** is any process that gives off heat and transfers that heat energy from the system to its surroundings. Therefore, the temperature (measure of thermal energy) of the surroundings will be warmer. A vivid example is the combustion reaction of alkanes (burning of gasoline). In contrast, an **endothermic reaction** requires heat to be supplied to the system from the surroundings. An example is the hydrolysis of amide bonds (constituent of proteins). That is the reason why we need to heat meat in order to cook it.

BOND DISSOCIATION ENERGY

To illustrate bond dissociation energy (BDE), consider the free radical chlorination of methane to form methyl chloride. **BDE** is the amount of heat required to cause homolytic cleavage (a radical-based process) of a given bond. For example, the BDE of the following bonds (in kJ/mol) are: C–H 410; Cl–Cl 240; C–Cl 330; and H–Cl 430.

Now, consider the free radical monochlorination of methane.

$$CH_4 + Cl_2 \rightarrow CH_3Cl + HCl$$

Homolysis of the CH of methane and Cl_2 bonds requires $(410 + 240)$ kJ/mol . In order to initiate the reaction, 650 kJ/mol must be supplied to the reaction.

CATALYSIS

Every chemical reaction requires an energy of activation (E_{act}). E_{act} can be supplied as heat or light energy. A **catalyst** lowers that E_{act}. Therefore, with a catalyst, a reaction can proceed without harsh conditions. For example, S_N2 reactions can be catalyzed by addition of iodide ions and hydrogenation reactions in the presence of Pt or Pd. Another nice example of catalysts is enzymes (in biochemical reactions). Without enzymes, these biological transformations will require tremendous amounts of heat that an organism may not survive.

TRANSITION STATE AND REACTION INTERMEDIATE

A **transition state (TS)** occurs at the energy maximum, at the top of an energy hill in a reaction coordinate diagram. For a one-step reaction, its energy is the difference between the E_{act} and the energy of the reactants. The TS is highly unstable and short-lived, hence the TS can never be isolated. An example of a transition state is "pentavalent" carbon in an S_N2 reaction.

In contrast, a **reaction intermediate** is found at the energy minimum of two successive energy hills and is more stable than the TS. Relative to the TS, an intermediate has a longer lifetime and may be isolated. However, a reaction intermediate is a transient species and is immediately consumed to generate the product. An example of an intermediate is the carbocation in an S_N1 reaction. The carbocation is subsequently quenched by a nucleophile to give the final reaction product.

HEAT OF HYDROGENATION

Hydrogenation of double bonds, such as alkenes, is an exothermic reaction, i.e. heat is released, which is called $\Delta H°$. $\Delta H°$ is an indicator of the stability of an alkene; lower $\Delta H°$ corresponds to higher stability. The relative stability of alkenes is correlated to their degree of substitution (number of alkyl groups attached to C=C). Hence, tetrasubstituted alkenes are the most stable (and ethene is the least because there are no alkyl groups at all) and has the lowest $\Delta H°$.

FREE RADICAL

A carbon radical (see below) does not satisfy the octet rule, hence is regarded as an electrophile. It attacks electron-rich systems such as the π bonds of unsaturated hydrocarbons. Unlike carbocations, radicals are neutral species.

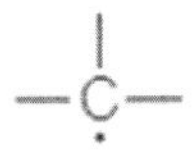

Other examples of radicals are RO· (from the decomposition of organic peroxides) and Br· (from RO· treated with HBr). The stability of carbon radicals is similar to that of carbocations (benzylic, allylic > 3° > 2° > 1°). Notice that the radical is more stable when there are electron-donating groups around the radical.

ELIMINATION

Alcohols do not undergo elimination reactions spontaneously because the –OH group attached to the Csp^3 is a poor leaving group due to the basicity of the hydroxide (OH^-).

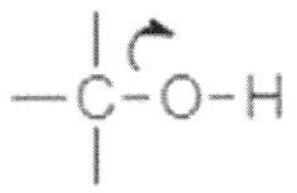

To circumvent this problem, **addition of an acid** (such as H_3PO_4 and H_2SO_4) will do the trick. One of the lone pairs of oxygen will form a coordinate covalent bond to the proton, leaving a positively charged oxygen. Now the leaving group is H_2O, which is less basic than OH^-.

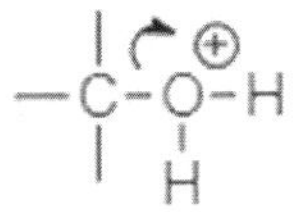

For elimination to occur, there must be a β–hydrogen to be abstracted (X = H_2O in the figure below).

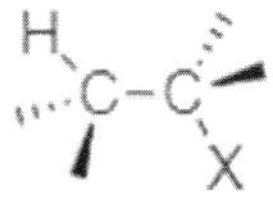

ADDITION

An addition reaction changes the hybridization of the alkenic (olefinic) carbons from Csp^2 to Csp^3. The electrophile (electron sink; Lewis acid) is usually the **proton** (H^+; electrophiles are usually positively charged) from the dissociation of a strong acid such as hydrobromic acid.

$$HBr \rightarrow H^+ + Br^-$$

The nucleophile (electron source; Lewis base) is the π electrons in the double bond, C=C. These π electrons will form a *coordinate covalent bond* to the H^+, leading to the generation of a carbocation. Take note that when the neutral alkene adds to the positively-charged H^+ then the resulting species is positively charged. The order of carbocation stability is benzylic, allylic > 3° > 2° > 1°, where the most stable carbocation is preferentially formed. Finally, the conjugate base from the dissociation of the strong acid (Br^-) attacks the carbocation to form a neutral compound, which is an alkyl bromide in this case. Remember that the bromine atom attaches to the more substituted carbon in the original alkene (Markovnikov rule).

EFFECT OF ORGANIC PEROXIDES

The addition of organic peroxides (ROOR) **reverses** the regioselectivity of electrophilic addition of HBr to alkenes. The presence of peroxides will generate a bromine radical (Br ✕). The radical (the electrophile) adds across the double bond. Again, either site is plausible. However, Br preferentially attaches to the less substituted carbon in order to have a more stable **free radical** (secondary instead of primary). This pattern is known as the reverse (or anti-) Markovnikov orientation.

DIENES: 1,2 COMPARED WITH 1,4 ADDITION

These reactions can be exemplified by the addition of HBr to a conjugated diene (a continuous chain of 4 Csp^2 hybridized carbons). A 1,2–addition can be treated as if the alkene unit is "isolated" from the other alkene group in the diene. An allylic carbocation is formed followed by a nucleophilic attack by Br^-. There is no rearrangement of the other π bonds; that is why the reaction is fast and described as kinetic and favored at lower temperatures. (Note: the figures below omit the hydrogens in the original molecule to highlight the addition of HBr).

In contrast, 1,4–addition involves **rearrangement** of the other π bond. As a result, the HBr is added in the 1st and 4th carbons of the conjugated diene (instead of the 1st and 2nd carbons as in the preceding case).

SUBSTITUTION MECHANISMS

The acronym S_N2 means substitution nucleophilic second-order. Recall that a substitution reaction retains the hybridization of the C involved. This reaction is a **bimolecular reaction**, i.e. the rate is dependent on the concentrations of both the alkyl halide (RX) and the incoming nucleophile (Nu). Cleavage of the C–X bond occurs *simultaneously* with the formation of the C–Nu bond. This backside attack **inverts the configuration** at the chiral carbon atom. A good analogy is a strong wind inverting your umbrella on a windy day. S_N2 reactions are favored using a **polar aprotic solvent** such as DMSO (dimethyl sulfoxide).

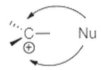

In contrast, an S_N1 reaction is **unimolecular**, i.e. the rate is dependent on the concentration of the alkyl halide (RX) alone. A carbocation is formed as an intermediate and the products are **racemic** (50:50 for both enantiomers). The carbocation is planar, hence the nucleophile can attack on either the top face or the bottom face. **Polar protic solvents** such as alcohols favor S_N1 reactions.

Chemical and Physical Properties of Molecules

SPECTROSCOPY

^1H NMR SPECTROSCOPY

There are four features of a ^1H NMR spectrum. First, the **chemical shift** that is correlated to the surrounding chemical environment (such as the functional group). As a general rule, a proton near an electron-withdrawing group (such as the carbonyl C=O group) is more deshielded (greater ppm value) compared to a proton near an electron-donating group (such as N–containing groups).

Next is the **number of signals** and **integration**. Each type of ^1H nucleus (non-equivalent, i.e. different chemical environment) in a molecule gives rise to a signal, i.e. different peak. Integration indicates the relative number of distinct ^1H nuclei.

Finally is the **multiplicity**. The peaks in the ^1H spectrum may appear as multiple lines (multiplets). The number of lines (*multiplicity* or *splitting pattern*) for a ^1H signal mirrors the number of its neighboring protons, **n**. A signal is split into **$n + 1$** lines. For example, CH_3CH_2-Br: The methyl signal will appear as a triplet $(2 + 1)$ while the methylene signal appears as a quartet $(3 + 1)$.

^1H CHEMICAL SHIFTS

The following is a table of ^1H chemical shifts by type:

^1H Type	Name	Formula	Chemical Shift (ppm)
Carbon Bonded	Alkane	$H–C$	1–1.5
	Carbonyl	$H–C–C=O$	2
	Alkyne	$H–C≡C$	2–3
	Nitrile	$H–C≡N$	2–4
	Heteroatom	$H–C–X$	3–5

^{1}H Type	Name	Formula	Chemical Shift (ppm)
	Alkene	$H-C=C$	5–6
	Aromatic	$H-Ar$	7–8
	Aldehyde	$H-C=O$	9–10
Non-Carbon Bonded	Alcohol	$H-O$	0.5–5
	Amine	$H-N-C$	0.5–5
	Aniline	$H-N-Ar$	3–5
	Phenol	$H-O-Ar$	4–7
	Amide	$H-N-C=O$	5–9
	Imine	$H-N=C$	7–10
	Carboxylic Acid	$H-O-C=O$	10–13

Notice that polar substituents near the ^{1}H nucleus cause deshielding (chemical shifts have higher ppm values).

^{13}C NMR SPECTROSCOPY

The number of distinct ^{13}C NMR signals depends on whether a ^{13}C nucleus is in a non–equivalent chemical environment; an equivalent environment will reduce the number of ^{13}C signals relative to the number of carbon atoms in the molecule. Typically, the number of signals is the same as the number of C atoms. However, this number is reduced if the following are present.

First, a **plane of symmetry.** For example, the compound below has a vertical plane of symmetry. The upper methines (CHs) are equivalent (hence, only one ^{13}C signal for these two C atoms) and so are the two lower methines.

Second, an **unrestricted rotation** around a single bond makes C atoms equivalent. An example of this case is a tert–butyl group, where the three methyls are all equivalent; the three methyls will give a single ^{13}C signal.

In contrast, restricted rotation around double bonds renders the carbons non-equivalent. For example, the two methyl carbons are non-equivalent for the alkene below, giving distinct ^{13}C NMR signals.

^{13}C CHEMICAL SHIFTS

^{13}C chemical shifts are roughly 20 times as large as ^{1}H shifts, as the ^{13}C spectrum (0–220 ppm) is broader than the ^{1}H spectrum (0–12 ppm) for the common functional groups.

^{13}C Type	Formula	Chemical Shift (ppm)
Alkane	Csp^3	0–70
Phenol	HO–Ar	25–65
Amine	R–C–N	30–60
Alcohol	R–C–OH	50–75
Alkyne	Csp	65–90
Aniline	N–Ar	110–130
Alkene	Csp^3	110–150
Nitrile	R–$C\equiv$N	120–130
Aromatic	Ar	120–160
Amide	N–C=O	150–180
Carboxylic Acid	HO–C=O	150–185
Imine	R–C=N	160–170
Aldehyde	R–C=O	190–205
Ketone	R_2–C=O	200–215

INFRARED SPECTROSCOPY

The IR Spectrum has the following ranges for functional group analysis:

Type	Functional Group	Formula	Range (cm^{-1})
Single Bond	Alcohols, Phenols, and Amines	O–H, N–H	3200–3500
	Alkyne	Csp–H	3200–3300
	Alkene	Csp^2–H	3000–3100
	Alkane	Csp^3–H	2800–3000
	Aromatic	Ar–H	1650–2000
Double Bond	Alkene	C=C	1620–1680
	Carbonyl	C=O	1630–1800
Triple Bond	Alkyne	C≡C	2100–2140
	Nitrile	C≡N	2220–2260

The region below 1300 cm^{-1} is the fingerprint region, which is typically cumbersome for functional group analysis. If two compounds are identical, then the fingerprint region will be exactly the same.

MASS–SPECTROSCOPY

In order for a molecule to be observed using mass spectroscopy, the molecule is made to undergo a high energy collision to produce a **molecular ion peak**, either positive $[M + H]^+$ or negative $[M - H]^-$. A signal appears in an m/z scale (where m = molecular mass and z = charge). **Isotope peaks** are also observed, usually 1 and 2 m/z units higher than the molecular ion peak. The isotope peak is useful in identifying heteroatoms such as Br, Cl, and S. Fragmentation may also occur of the molecular ion peak. For example, elimination of a neutral molecule such as water (from alcohols) or carbon dioxide (from carboxylic acids) will result in a signal that is 18 and 44 m/z units lower than the molecular ion peak.

ISOTOPE PEAKS IN A MASS SPECTRUM

Isotope peaks (M + 1, M + 2, etc.) are due to the heavier isotopes. The more abundant lighter isotopes will give rise to the molecular ion peak, M, which is generally more intense than the isotope peaks. For example, ^{12}C is more abundant than ^{13}C. Organic compounds will give an M + 1 signal (with M calculated using the mass of ^{13}C: 13 u), in addition to the M signal (using the mass of ^{12}C: 12 u). The % intensity of M + 1 usually reflects the number of C atoms in the molecule.

The M + 2 peak can be used to determine the presence of some heteroatoms. If the percent intensity of M + 2 is 98% then it is diagnostic for the presence of Br (the abundance of ^{79}Br is roughly equal to that of ^{81}Br). Other useful indicators from the M + 2 isotope peak are 33% (for Cl) and 4% (for S).

STRUCTURE
POLARITY

Bond polarity (i.e. a dipole moment) arises when the participating atoms that form a bond have a substantial difference in electronegativity. (Both atoms in a polar bond are non-metals.) A **polar bond** is a truly covalent bond, hence it excludes ionic bonds (formed between a metal and a non–metal). Examples of polar bonds (and their occurrence in certain functional groups) are the following: O–H (alcohols and phenols), N–H (amines), C–O (ketones, aldehydes, esters, etc.), C–N (amines and nitriles), and C–X (alkyl halides).

INTERMOLECULAR FORCES
SOLUBILITY

Solubilization requires the breakage of intermolecular forces of attraction (IMFA) between solute particles before solute–solvent interactions are formed. The types of IMFAs are (1) **ionic interactions** (2) **hydrogen bonding** (3) **dipole–dipole forces** and (4) **van der Waals/hydrophobic interactions**. Compounds with ionic interactions, such as quaternary ammonium salts, are readily soluble in water because water is highly polar. Compounds that exhibit hydrogen bonding, such as alcohols, have a borderline solubility with water (alcohol must have 4 carbon atoms or fewer in each molecule in order to be water soluble). If the predominant IMFA is a dipole–dipole or van der Waals interaction then expect that such a compound will be immiscible with water.

BOILING POINT

The boiling point marks the transition of the liquid phase to the gas phase. In order for vaporization to occur, intermolecular forces of attraction have to be overcome. Among compounds with comparable molecular weights, the relative boiling point depends on the intermolecular forces. Compounds that exhibit hydrogen bonding, such as carboxylic acids, amines (1° and 2°), amides (1°), and alcohols, have relatively high boiling points. Compounds that have dipole moments, such as aldehydes, ketones, and esters, have moderate boiling points. Lastly, the most volatile (low boiling point) are the compounds that are predominantly hydrophobic in nature, such as the hydrocarbons. Ethers and alkyl halides have boiling points that are not significantly different from their hydrocarbon counterparts.

MELTING POINT

The melting point is dependent on the strength of the intermolecular forces of attraction. For example, organic salts such as amine hydrochlorides and amino acids have high melting points (both are ionic compounds), followed by carboxylic acids (hydrogen bonding). In addition to the type of IMFA, **symmetry** is also an important factor due to crystal packing; a more symmetric

molecule is more efficiently packed in a crystal lattice. For example, the *trans* isomer (higher degree of symmetry) has a higher melting point than its *cis* counterpart. That is the reason why vegetable oil (*cis* double bonds) has a lower melting point compared to margarine (*trans*).

LABORATORY THEORY AND TECHNIQUES
THIN LAYER CHROMATOGRAPHY (TLC)

Rf is a measure of how far a solute travels in a stationary phase (in this case, silica, which is composed of Si–O bonds). Mathematically, Rf = distance travelled by compound / distance traveled by the solvent front. Any strong interaction between the compound and the Si–O of silica will potentially slow the rate of migration (less distance travelled). Ionic bonding is the strongest possible interaction in TLC. Hence, organic salts will have the lowest Rf. Next, compounds with the –OH group, such as alcohols and carboxylic acids, will also be retained in the silica phase strongly because of the H–bond (hence low Rf's). Carboxylic acids have two O atoms (in contrast to alcohol, which has only one O). The aldehyde will have a dipole–dipole interaction (δ+ C=O δ–) with silica, but this interaction is weaker than a hydrogen bond. Finally, there are no polar groups in alkanes, hence there is minimal interaction with the silica (highest Rf value).

ELECTROPHORESIS

Electrophoresis is technique that separates molecules (such as proteins) according to their size or charge. A protein sample is added to a solvent, usually a gel, which behaves like a molecular sieve. The gel is placed in an electrophoresis chamber, which is then connected to a power source. As an electric field is applied, the proteins begin to migrate and separate. The smaller the molecule, the farther it will travel. Because most proteins are charged at any pH, with the exception of their isoelectric point, they will migrate toward the electrode with the opposite charge. The original sample will separate into distinct bands of isolated proteins. The rate at which a protein migrates is dependent on the size of the protein, the net charge, the strength of the electric field, and the viscosity and pore size of the solvent. Two common media used in electrophoresis are agar and polyacrylamide. Polyacrylamide is typically used for proteins because it has the appropriate pore size. SDS-PAGE is a type of electrophoresis that uses polyacrylamide along with a denaturing agent called sodium dodecyl sulfate. Proteins are then separated according to molecular weight.

ISOELECTRIC POINT

Proteins have the ability to be separated according to their properties (such as electrical charge, size, and solubility). One such technique is called isoelectric focusing (IEF). IEF separates molecules by isoelectric point (pI), which is the pH at which the protein is either neutral, or at its lowest ionization. In general, the isoelectric point decreases as the proportion of acidic amino acids increases and vice versa.

The IEF technique spreads the proteins of interest over a medium (usually a gel) with a pH gradient ranging from low to high. A current is passed through the gel, and proteins that carry a positive charge will begin to migrate toward the negative pole (anode), whereas proteins with a negative charge will migrate toward the positive pole (cathode). At some point along the pH gradient, the protein will reach its pI and lose its electric charge to become a zwitterion. Because the protein is now neutral, the electrode will not be able to pull it any further. The result is a banding pattern on the gel, with each band consisting of a species of protein with its unique isoelectric point.

LIQUID–LIQUID EXTRACTION

These types of compounds may be separated easily by adjusting the pH and recovering the compound of interest in the aqueous phase. First, addition of dilute acid (such as 5% HCl) will protonate the amine only and will make it water soluble (as an amine hydrochloride salt). Second, addition of dilute $NaHCO_3$ will deprotonate the carboxylic acid only and will render it water soluble (as carboxylate). Third, addition of dilute NaOH will deprotonate the phenol, which will be transferred to the aqueous phase (as phenolate). Take note that the weaker base ($NaHCO_3$) should be used first when separating carboxylic acid and phenol. Finally, the hydrocarbon will be left in the organic phase.

Stereochemistry

CHIRALITY

A chiral compound will rotate a plane of polarized light. To be able to exhibit this phenomenon, the molecule must have a **stereogenic center,** i.e. there must be a C atom that is bonded to 4 different atoms or groups of atoms (substituents). A chiral molecule is not identical to its corresponding mirror image (non-superimposable). Your left and right hands are perfect examples; in fact, chirality comes from the Greek word for hand. Additionally, a chiral molecule does not have a plane of symmetry.

R/S NOTATION

The designation of R or S is based from the Cahn–Ingold–Prelog (CIP) sequence rules. Do not confuse this with the (+ or −) and (*d* or *l*) notations, as these are determined experimentally: dextrorotatory or levorotatory when the compound rotates the plane of polarized light to the right or left, respectively. The CIP rule requires the substituents to be ranked based on their atomic masses where 1 has the highest u and 4 has the lowest. The example below uses I (127 u) > Br (80 u) > Cl (35.5 u) > H (1 u). The 4th substituent is placed at the back of the plane. Next, determine if the arrangement of the 1st, 2nd and 3rd substituents follows a clockwise pattern (**R**ectus, to the right)

or counterclockwise pattern (**S**inistrus, to the left).

ISOMER RELATIONSHIPS

Enantiomers and diastereomers are configurational isomers; unlike conformational isomers, they are not convertible by bond rotation. These terms are applicable only for chiral compounds (compounds containing a stereogenic center). Enantiomers are non-superimposable mirror images; one will rotate a plane of polarized light to the left and the other one to the right. Enantiomers are difficult to separate by physical means such as fractional distillation. A mixture of 50:50 for both enantiomers is called a *racemic mixture* and will not rotate a plane of polarized light (each enantiomer will cancel the effect of the other). In contrast, diastereomers are not related by mirror image reflection. At least two chiral centers are needed to obtain a diastereomeric relationship. Diastereomers are much easier to separate than enantiomers.

MESO COMPOUND

For a molecule to be classified as a *meso* compound, at least two stereogenic centers must be present, so 4 different groups are attached to the C atom. The peculiar thing about a meso compound is that there is an internal plane symmetry located in the middle of the molecule as exemplified by the compound below.

Etymologically, *meso* means "middle" in Greek. This type of compound is not optically active. Essentially, its property is similar to that of a racemic mixture, albeit rolled into one compound!

CONFORMATIONS

OPEN CHAINS

Conformers are geometrical isomers that arise due to the rotation of a C–C single bond. As a result of free bond rotation, conformers are interconvertible. Do not confuse this with the *cis–trans* isomers arising from a C=C double bond, which is not free to rotate. To illustrate conformers, let us consider 1,2–dibromoethane and use the relative positions of the two bromine atoms as reference. There are three possible orientations for the Br atoms (hydrogens deleted for clarity; the carbon in the front is held fixed).

Conformer	Angle	Example	Stability
anti	180°		Most stable
gauche	60°		
syn	0°		Least stable

CYCLIC SYSTEMS

The chair conformation is a stable arrangement because there is no eclipsing interaction (all *anti*). This is the preferred conformation of hexoses (C6 aldoses/carbohydrates).

In contrast, the boat conformation is relatively unstable due to eclipsing interactions (*syn*).

SUBSTITUTED CYCLIC SYSTEMS

For illustration, isopropylcyclohexane is used. Considering the chair conformation only, there are two possible ways to position the isopropyl group, by placing the bulky substituent in either the axial or the equatorial direction. The interconversion is achievable by a "ring flip" which is feasible due to the free rotation of the C–C single bonds. When the bulky group is in the axial direction, there are 1,3–diaxial interactions (as designated by the double headed arrows) which result in destabilization due to sterics. When the cyclohexane ring is flipped, the substituent is placed in the equatorial position. The **absence of 1,3–diaxial interactions** makes the second conformation more energetically favored. If two substituents are present, priority is given to the bulkier group to be placed in the equatorial position.

CIS–TRANS (DISUBSTITUTED ALKENES)

Cis–trans isomers are examples of geometric isomers. This classification is used to designate the common names of disubstituted alkenes (the substituents must be located at the two carbons). Note that this system of nomenclature is not at all related to E–Z designation.

If the substituents (usually alkyl groups) occur at the same side of the π bond then it is *cis*:

$$\underset{R}{\overset{H}{}}C=C\underset{R}{\overset{H}{}}$$

Otherwise, it is *trans*:

$$\underset{R}{\overset{H}{}}C=C\underset{H}{\overset{R}{}}$$

Cyclic alkenes such as cyclopentene and cyclohexene must be *cis* due to geometrical constraints. The *trans* isomer can only occur in larger ring systems such as cyclooctene.

E/Z NOTATION (TRI/TETRA SUBSTITUTED ALKENES)

The E or Z notation is based from the Cahn–Ingold–Prelog (CIP) rules. These rules depend on the atomic mass of the substituents. The CIP rule requires the substituents of the Csp^2 carbon to be ranked in order of their atomic masses. The example below uses I (127 u) > Br (80 u) > Cl (35.5 u) > F (19 u).

If both the higher–ranked substituents occur at the same side of the π bond then it is a *Z* isomer (from the German *zussamen* which means "together"):

$$\underset{I}{\overset{F}{}}C=C\underset{Br}{\overset{Cl}{}}$$

Otherwise, it is an *E* isomer (from the German *entgegen* which means "opposite"):

CONSTITUTIONAL ISOMERISM

Isomers have the same chemical formulas (Greek *iso* "same" and *meros* "part"). Constitutional isomerism includes skeletal, functional, and positional. Skeletal isomers differ in the relative arrangement of the carbon framework. For example, n–butane and 2–methylpropane, i.e. linear and branched alkane, respectively:

Functional isomers differ in the functional groups present. For example, butanone and tetrahydrofuran, i.e. ketone and cyclic ether, respectively:

Positional isomers differ in the position of the functional group present. For example, 1–butene and 2–butene:

Nomenclature

GENERAL FORMAT OF AN IUPAC NAME

The general format in systematically naming an organic compound is **"prefix + stem + suffix"**.

The **"prefix"** specifies the position (# in the carbon chain or, if not a carbon atom, the heteroatom), number (how many times a substituent appears), and type of substituent (usually an atom or an alkyl group).

The **"stem"** is the number of C atoms in the parent chain, which is determined by finding the longest *continuous* carbon network.

# of C atoms	Stem	# of C atoms	Stem
1	meth–	7	hep–
2	eth–	8	oct–
3	prop–	9	non–
4	but–	10	dec–
5	pent–	11	undec–
6	hex–	12	dodec–

Finally, the **"suffix"** indicates the class or functional group of the compound.

SPECIAL NAMES TO ALKYL SUBSTITUENTS

Consider the butyl group. Drawn below are the butyl isomers (same chemical formula but differ in the skeletal framework), starting from the least branched to the most branched. The leftmost is named **"n–butyl"** or simply **butyl**. n stands for normal, which indicates a straight chain. Next is **"sec–butyl"**. Sec means secondary because the C to which it is attached is secondary i.e., two flanking C atoms. Then, **"isobutyl"**. The prefix "iso" is used for all compounds where there are two methyl groups at the rear end. And finally, **"tert–butyl"** where the C to which it is attached is tertiary.

$$CH_3CH_2CH_2CH_2 \qquad CH_3CHCH_2CH_3 \qquad CH_3CHCH_2 \qquad CH_3CCH_3$$
$$\qquad\qquad\qquad\qquad\qquad\qquad\qquad\qquad\qquad CH_3 \qquad\qquad CH_3$$

The isomers for the pentyl group are: **n–pentyl** (or simply **pentyl**), **isopentyl**, and **neopentyl**. The first two are similar to the corresponding butyl isomers. The salient feature of neopentyl is its quaternary C in the center.

$$CH_3CH_2CH_2CH_2CH_2 \qquad CH_3CHCH_2CH_2 \qquad \begin{array}{c}H_2C\\CH_3CCH_3\\CH_3\end{array}$$
$$\qquad\qquad\qquad\qquad\qquad\qquad\qquad CH_3$$

ALKANES/CYCLOALKANES

For alkanes: First, locate the longest carbon chain. If there are two different chains of equal length then choose the one with more substituents. In the example below, the longest chain is a C9. There are two ways of obtaining the C9: either having an isopropyl substituent or an ethyl and a methyl. The latter, with two substituents, should be chosen. Second, number the chain so that substituents are given the lowest position numbers. In this case, we have to number from left to right (instead of right to left). Therefore, the name is 3–ethyl–2–methylnonane. Notice that the alkyl groups are listed in alphabetical order. Hyphenated prefixes in the names of alkyl groups (*sec–* and *tert–*) are not considered for alphabetization.

For cycloalkanes: Generally, the rules are the same as for alkanes except for the addition of "cyclo" before the alkane. For the compound below, the name is 1–ethyl–2–methylcyclononane.

ALKYL HALIDES

The general rule is to specify the alkyl substituents present and affix the name of the functional group halide (Cl = chloride, Br = bromide, I = iodide). An alternative way of naming is to designate the halide as a substituent. For example, the compound below is named either isopentyl bromide or 3–methyl–1–bromobutane. Note that the lower position number is assigned to the functional group rather than the alkyl substituent.

ALKENES/DIENES

The longest continuous chain (with the C=C) is considered the parent chain and named with the suffix "ene". If the alkene is cyclic, the lowest possible numbering is given to the C=C, i.e. positions 1 and 2. For example, the compound below is named 4–cyclopropyl–1–methyl cyclohexene (non-hyphenated prefixes, such as cyclo, are considered for alphabetization).

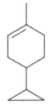

If more than one C=C is present, indicate the position of the C=C and use the suffixes diene, triene, or so on. Hence, the compound below will be named 4–cyclopropyl–1–methyl–1,4–cyclohexadiene.

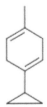

ALKYNES

The longest continuous chain (with the C≡C) is considered the parent chain and named with the suffix "yne". The numbering should give the lower possible position number for the C≡C. For the compound below, the numbering is from left to right (rather than right to left) to give priority to the functional group. The name of the compound below is 6,6–dimethyl–2–heptyne (not 2,2–dimethyl–5–heptyne).

AROMATICS

A monosubstituted benzene ring is represented below. There are various identities for Y (substituents), and their common names are enumerated in the table below.

Substituent (Y)	Name
–OH	Phenol
–OCH₃	Anisole
–NH₂	Aniline
–NH–COCH₃	Acetanilide
–CH₃	Toluene
–CH=CH₂ (vinyl)	Styrene

Substituent (Y)	Name
isopropyl	cumene
–CH₂OH	benzyl alcohol
–CHO	benzaldehyde
–COOH	benzoic acid
–CONH₂	benzamide
–C≡N	benzonitrile

A tip in studying: Memorize the substituents by groups. For example, remember phenol and anisole together, as anisole differs from phenol in that the H (of –OH) is changed to CH_3. Acetanilide is "acetylated" (–$COCH_3$) aniline.

DISUBSTITUTED

Ortho, *meta*, and *para* can be abbreviated by *o*, *m*, and *p*, respectively:

- **Ortho:** The substituents are in 1,2 positions relative to the ring. For example, *ortho*–dimethylbenzene or 1,2–dimethylbenzene. The common name for dimethylbenzene is xylene. Hence, the compound below may be named *ortho*-xylene.

Another example is *ortho*-methylphenol. Methylphenol is commonly referred to as cresol. Hence, the compound below may be named *ortho*–cresol (or alternatively, 2–methylphenol). Do not confuse cresol with anisole (where the methyl is attached to O).

- **Meta**: The substituents are in 1,3 positions relative to the ring. For example, *meta*–methylaniline. Methyl aniline is referred to as toluidine. Hence, the compound below may be named *meta*– toluidine (or, alternatively, 3–methylaniline).

- **Para**: The substituents are in 1,4 positions relative to the ring. For example, *para*–methylbenzoic acid. Methyl benzoic acid is referred to as toluic acid. Hence, the compound below may be named *para*–toluic acid (or, alternatively, 4–methylbenzoic acid).

3 OR MORE SUBSTITUENTS

The numbering is made so that the positions of the substituents receive the lowest possible numbers. In the compound below, the numbering is done counterclockwise, starting from COOH (as a rule of thumb, priority is given to the substituent with the highest degree of oxidation). Therefore, the name for the compound below is 2–isobutyl–4–chlorobenzoic acid.

HETEROATOMS AND FUSED AROMATICS

First, let us consider the N–containing aromatics: pyridine and pyrrole. Pyridine is six-membered while pyrrole is five-membered.

Second, the five-membered heterocycles containing the chalcogens O and S: furan (O) and thiophene (S).

Finally, the fused aromatic rings: naphthalene (two rings) and anthracene (three rings).

ALCOHOLS/THIOLS

For alcohols the longest chain bearing the hydroxyl group is considered the parent chain and the name is derived by replacing the final "e" of the alkane name with "ol". The lowest position number is assigned to the C atom bearing the OH. The compound below is named 4–octanol (not 5–octanol).

For thiols the longest chain containing the –SH group is considered the parent chain and the name is derived by replacing the final "e" of the alkane name with "thiol". The lowest position number is assigned to the C atom containing the SH. The compound below is named 3–octanthiol (not 6–octanthiol).

Alternatively, the –OH and –SH groups are referred to as hydroxy and mercapto when named as substituents.

ETHERS/THIOETHERS

Ethers are named by identifying the alkyl groups and affixing "ether". For example, the compound below is named *sec*–butyl methyl ether. Alternatively, an ether group may be named as a substituent (alkoxy). Another acceptable name of the compound below is 2–methoxybutane.

If the ether is symmetric (both alkyl groups are the same) then it is named as "dialkyl ether". For example, the compound below is named di*tert*–butyl ether.

Thioethers are named by identifying the alkyl groups and affixing "thioether". For example, the compound below is named benzyl phenyl thioether.

KETONES/ALDEHYDES

For ketones the longest chain bearing the hydroxyl group is considered the parent chain and the name is derived by replacing the final "e" of the alkane name with "one". Numbering prioritizes the C=O moiety (which always takes position 1 for cyclic ketones). Hence, the compound below is 2–neopentylcycloheptanone (not 7–neopentylcycloheptanone). Another acceptable system is to use

Greek letters (α for the C position next to C=O, β after α, etc.). An alternative name for the compound below is α–neopentylcycloheptanone.

There are some special names for aromatic ketones: acetophenone (left) and propiophenone (right).

For aldehydes the longest chain bearing the hydroxyl group is considered the parent chain and the name is derived by replacing the final "e" of the alkane name with "al". The aldehyde C is always in position 1. The compound below is named 3–methyl–octanal or β–methyl–octanal.

CARBOXYLIC ACIDS

Below is a list of the linear carboxylic acids, indicating the common names and systematic names. The common names are derived from the Latin names of their sources (like "formicus" from ants: an ant's sting contains formic acid). The longer chains (C12 and beyond) are derived from fats and oils (for example, C12 from coconut oil and C18 from beef tallow).

# C atoms	IUPAC	Common
1	methanoic acid	formic acid
2	ethanoic acid	acetic acid
3	propanoic acid	propionic acid
4	butanoic acid	butyric acid
5	pentanoic acid	valeric acid
6	hexanoic acid	caproic acid
7	heptanoic acid	enanthic acid

# C atoms	IUPAC	common
8	octanoic acid	caprylic acid
9	nonanoic acid	pelargonic acid
10	decanoic acid	capric acid
12	dodecanoic acid	lauric acid
14	tetradecanoic acid	myristic acid
16	hexadecanoic acid	palmitic acid
18	octadecanoic acid	stearic acid

Also important are the diacids series $HOOC-(CH_2)_n-COOH$

N	common name
0	oxalic acid
1	malonic acid
2	succinic acid

n	common name
3	glutaric acid
4	adipic acid
5	pimelic acid

An easy mnemonic is: **O**h **M**y **S**uch **G**ood **A**pple **P**ie!

DERIVATIVES

For acid halides, change the ending "oic acid" from the parent carboxylic acid to "oyl halide." For example:

butanoic acid → butanoyl chloride

For esters: The names for esters are derived from the name of the carboxylate (conjugate base of carboxylic acid), affixing the group attached to the oxygen. For example:

sodium butanoate → phenyl butanoate

For amides: Change the ending "oic acid" from the parent carboxylic acid to "amide." For example:

butanoic acid → butanamide

If a hydrogen on the nitrogen is replaced by an alkyl group then the name of the alkyl group is added and its point of attachment (N heteroatom). Hence, the leftmost amide below is butanamide, and the substituted amides to its right are named N–ethylbutanamide and N–ethyl–N–methylbutanamide, respectively. Do not forget to add "N," otherwise it would mean that the alkyl group is attached to one of the carbons in the parent carboxylic acid.

AMINES

The general rule is to specify the alkyl substituents present and affix the name of the functional group "amine".

Primary: The name of the alkyl group is *sec*–butyl hence the name of the compound below is *sec*–butyl amine. An alternative way of naming is to designate –NH_2 (the amino group) as a substituent. Hence, 2–aminobutane can be an alternative name for this compound.

Secondary: Treating cyclopentyl as a substituent, the compound below is named N–cyclopentyl aniline. Remember to indicate "N," otherwise it would mean that cyclopentyl is attached to the carbons of the parent aromatic compound (aniline).

Tertiary: The compound below is named ethyl diisopropyl amine.

Functional Group Chemistry

ALKENE (PREPARATION)

The difference between the outcomes of these reactions is best illustrated by an internal alkyne. Both reactions involve hydrogenation of alkyne with 1 mole of H_2, hence an alkene is the product (using Pt as catalyst will deliver 2 moles of H_2, yielding an alkane). **Lindlar's catalyst** facilitates a *syn* **addition** of H_2 across the π bond, giving rise to a *cis*–**alkene**.

In contrast, **Na/NH₃**, causes *anti* **addition** of H_2 (across the π bond), resulting to a *trans*–**alkene**. This is sometimes known as dissolving-metal reduction.

ALKENE (POLYMERIZATION)

There are three steps in synthesizing a polymer from an alkene: initiation, propagation, and termination. First, the **initiation step** involves the generation of the radical (homolysis) with either light or heat. Second, the generated radical attacks an alkene molecule, producing a new radical species. This newly formed radical attacks another alkene and so forth and so on (**propagation**). The propagation step makes the actual polymer. Finally, if two radicals react with each other then a stable species is formed, which no longer reacts (**termination**). This process is used to create polymers and plastics such as styrofoam for thermal insulators (from styrene) and polyethylene for bottles (from ethene).

ALKYNE (REACTION)

A terminal alkyne will yield either an aldehyde or a methyl ketone, depending to the method used for the hydration. If a borane-based reagent reacts with an alkyne (see below, top scheme), then the OH is delivered to the less-hindered C, resulting in an enol that tautomerizes to the aldehyde.

On the other hand, if a mercury-based reagent is used (bottom scheme) then the OH is delivered to the more-hindered C, resulting in an enol that tautomerizes to a methyl ketone. In contrast, internal alkynes ($R-C\equiv C-R$) will always produce ketones.

AROMATIC

Electrophilic aromatic substitution (EAS) involves the replacement of one of the aromatic protons of a benzene ring with an electrophile. The regioselective outcome of an EAS reaction is determined by the type of substituents initially attached to the aromatic ring. Electron-donating groups, such as $-OCH_3$ and the halogens, are *ortho/para* directors, while electron-withdrawing groups, such as $-NO_2$ and carbonyl groups, are *meta* directors. Sometimes the substituents reinforce each other for the position of the incoming electrophile (hence there should be no problem). In the event that the substituents oppose each other, the position dictated by the stronger electron-donating group determines the outcome. Rarely (almost never) will the electrophile occupy a position between two groups *meta* to each other due to steric reasons.

DIELS–ALDER

A Diels–Alder reaction is an example of a concerted reaction (bond formation takes place simultaneously with bond breakage). It involves a diene (4 π electrons) and a dienophile (2 π electrons). Sometimes, this process is described as 4 + 2 cycloaddition. The diene must be in the *cisoid* conformation to react. This reaction is used to synthesize cyclohexene and its derivatives.

The reactivity of the diene is enhanced by attaching an electron-releasing group, such as an alkyl group (see below) or alkoxy group (−OR).

302

The dienophile ("diene loving") is usually an alkene or alkyne. Electron-withdrawing groups such as aldehydes (see below), ketones, esters, or nitriles increase the reactivity of dienophiles.

SUBSTITUTION/ELIMINATION

There is always a competition between an elimination reaction and a substitution reaction. An elimination reaction will occur only if β hydrogens are present (for reference, the C attached to the halide is the Cα). Take note that for an elimination reaction, the hybridization of the C involved changes from Csp^3 to Csp^2. The more substituted alkene is the major product for an elimination reaction.

If there are no β hydrogens, then substitution will occur exclusively. Elimination requires strong bases, particularly hindered and bulky bases such as *tert*–butoxide; steric hindrance prevents tert–butoxide from acting as a nucleophile for a substitution reaction. There is a higher tendency to undergo elimination for tertiary alkyl halides over primary alkyl halides. Finally, higher temperatures favor elimination over substitution.

ALDEHYDE/KETONE (REACTIONS)

Direct addition involves the use of hydride reagents (such as $LiAlH_4$) and Grignard reagents (RMgX). The product is an alcohol, after workup with acid.

Addition followed by substitution involves the use of an alcohol, catalyzed with trace acid. The product is an acetal.

Addition followed by elimination involves the use of a primary amine. The product is a Schiff base. If a secondary amine (R_2NH) is used, then the product is an enamine. Tertiary amines (R_3N) don't react.

ALDEHYDE/KETONE (A–ACIDITY)

A carbanion is formed when a sufficiently strong base, such as NaOH or alkoxide, abstracts an α proton of a carbonitrile, carbonyl, or nitro group. The carbanion has a resonance structure that is called enolate. The negatively charged state is stabilized by resonance to the π bond of the carbonitrile, carbonyl, or nitro group. The order of stability is:

$$\text{nitro (pKa} \approx 10) > \text{keto (pKa} \approx 20) > \text{nitrile (pKa} \approx 25)$$

As a trend, better electron-withdrawing groups provide higher degrees of stabilization. Two keto groups can reinforce each other and the stability will be comparable to a nitro group. Electron-releasing groups, such as alkyl groups, attached to the carbanion will result in destabilization.

ALDEHYDE/KETONE (ALDOL CONDENSATION)

First, a carbanion must be formed and act as a nucleophile to a C=O (such as another ketone or aldehyde, but aldehyde is more reactive because of steric reasons), generating a hydroxy compound. Then, dehydration (C=C formation) must take place; it is termed condensation because water is one of the products of the reaction. Dehydration is favored due to the conjugation to C=O (resonance stabilized).

A,B–UNSATURATED ALDEHYDES AND KETONES (CONJUGATE ADDITION)

Conjugate addition, or Michael addition, is the reaction of "soft" nucleophiles to α,β–unsaturated carbonyl compounds. Examples of "soft" nucleophiles are the carbanions and cyanide. The nucleophile adds to the β carbon. Double bond migration takes place and finally, tautomerization to regenerate the C=O (C=O is stronger than C=C hence it is favored by enthalpy).

In contrast, "hard" nucleophiles are the organometallic reagents such as RMgX and RLi. They add directly to the C=O.

CARBOXYLIC ACIDS AND DERIVATIVES (REACTIVITY)

The trend for reactivity is dependent on the nature of Z, the leaving group.

Take note that the C=O is attached to a heteroatom for carboxylic acid derivatives (R or H for ketones and aldehydes, respectively). Z= halide, OCOR, OR, and NR$_2$ for acyl halides, anhydrides, esters, and amides, respectively. The nature of the heteroatom determines the leaving group ability. The less basic the leaving group is, the better is its ability to leave. The least basic are the halides (conjugate bases of strong acids) followed by carboxylate (conjugate base of carboxylic acids) then alkoxide. N has the least propensity to leave. For a note in your memory, nylon is made of amide bonds (resistant to degradation).

CARBOXYLIC ACIDS AND DERIVATIVES (REACTION WITH HYDRIDE REAGENTS)

Due to its small size, $LiAlH_4$ will add twice to an acyl halide, yielding a primary alcohol upon acid workup as the final product.

In contrast, bulky hydride sources, such as DIBAL–H (**di**isobutyl **al**uminum **h**ydride), will only add a hydride once, stopping at the aldehyde stage. The sterically hindered reagent can no longer access the carbonyl of the aldehyde.

CARBOXYLIC ACIDS AND DERIVATIVES (SAPONIFICATION)

Soap is manufactured from fats and oils, which are triacyl glycerides (esters), where R is a hydrocarbon tail such as C12 and its longer analogues.

The fat or oil is heated with an aqueous solution of NaOH or KOH, causing hydrolysis of the ester bond. Saponification is a general term often used to describe alkali-induced hydrolysis of esters. The products are glycerol and a Na^+ or K^+ carboxylate salt (soap).

ALCOHOLS (OXIDATION)

In order for an alcohol (Csp^3 attached to OH) to be oxidizable, there must be a proton attached to the carbon bearing the hydroxy group (H–C–OH). A typical oxidant used is $K_2Cr_2O_7$ in acid. Hence, tertiary alcohols are not oxidizable.

Secondary alcohols will yield ketones.

Primary alcohols will generate aldehydes first, but the aldehyde is also prone to oxidation, resulting in carboxylic acids. An interesting application is a breath analyzer to detect whether a driver is intoxicated with alcohol (ethanol) using $K_2Cr_2O_7$ (orange-colored). The formation of green Cr^{3+} indicates the oxidation of ethanol.

To stop the oxidation at the aldehyde stage, a milder oxidant (such as PCC, pyridinium chlorochromate) is typically used.

ETHERS (HYDROLYSIS)

Ethers are organic derivatives of water, where the two H's are replaced by either alkyl or aryl groups. Ethers are generally resistant to reactions except to acid (HI) hydrolysis. Hydrolysis of a symmetrical dialkyl ether yields 2 moles of alkyl iodide. Initially, an alcohol and an alkyl iodide are produced, but the alcohol reacts again to form another alkyl iodide. In case of an alkyl aryl ether, the hydrolyzed products are phenol and an alkyl iodide (see below).

Unlike alcohol, phenol is resistant to substitution reactions. Phenol has a stronger Csp^2–OH bond compared to alcohol's Csp^3–OH.

AMINES (PREPARATION)

Primary amines are generally prepared from the hydrogenation of the parent nitrile using H_2 and metal catalysts, such as Pt.

Secondary amines are readily available from the reaction of a Schiff base with a mild reducing agent such as $NaBH_3CN$.

Acid–Base Chemistry

RANKING ACIDITY (STRUCTURE ANALYSIS AND PH/PKA DATA ANALYSIS)

Acidity is enhanced when the conjugate base is stabilized either by inductive effects or by resonance effects. All organic acids are subject to **inductive effects**. The **resonance effect** is an extra factor for aromatic carboxylic acids and phenols. Electron-withdrawing groups, such as oxygen, halogens, and nitro groups, stabilize the conjugate base (hence increasing acidity). In contrast, electron-donating groups, such as an alkoxy or alkyl group, destabilize the base (hence reducing acidity). In order for the resonance effect to contribute to the acidity, the substituent should either be *ortho* or *para* relative to the COOH or OH group in the aromatic ring. However, the *para* isomer is usually more acidic than the *ortho* isomer (due to intramolecular hydrogen bonding for the *ortho*).

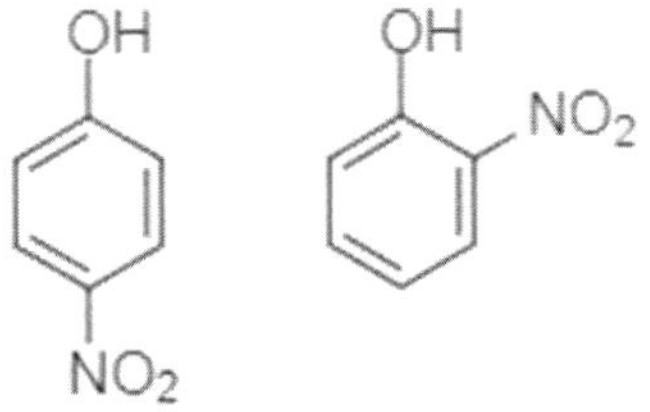

BASICITY (STRUCTURE ANALYSIS AND PH/PKA DATA ANALYSIS)

The basicity of an amine is increased when electron-donating groups are attached to N. Hence, tertiary (R_3N) is the most basic because of the combined inductive effects of three alkyl groups. Then secondary (R_2NH), then finally primary (RNH_2). In contrast, electron-withdrawing groups decrease the basicity of amines. Consider an aromatic amine, aniline (below). The lone pairs are effectively pulled by the benzene ring through resonance. Therefore, the lone pairs are no longer available (less basic) to form a coordinate covalent bond to a proton.

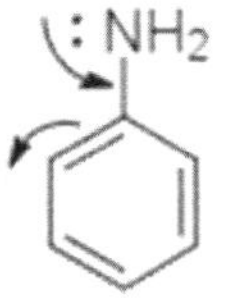

PREDICTION OF PRODUCTS AND EQUILIBRIA

The Gibbs equation ($\Delta G = \Delta H - T\Delta S$) determines the spontaneity of a given reaction; if $\Delta G < 0$, then the forward reaction is favored. Two factors determine the value of ΔG: First, ΔH (enthalpy), which is dependent on the bond strength of the products. Reactions occur when stronger bonds are formed at the expense of weak bonds. For example, dehydration is favored because a double bond (stronger than a single bond) is formed. Second, ΔS (entropy) is favored by an increase of disorder in the system. Reactions that generate more products, especially when these products are gases, are favored in terms of entropy. The entropy factor is more significant at higher temperatures.

Aromatics and Bonding

CONCEPT OF AROMATICITY

To be an aromatic compound, there are three criteria that must be met. First, the number of π electrons must be equal to **4n + 2**, where n is a positive integer, including zero. Sometimes, the π electrons can be substituted with lone pairs from heteroatoms, such as pyrrole.

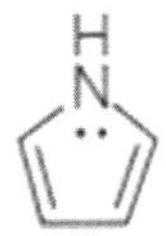

Second, the electrons must lie on a **single plane**. Third, the electrons must be **conjugated** (continuous Csp^2 atoms, or with a lone-pair-bearing atom). The last two conditions ensure that resonance structures can be formed, as aromatic compounds achieve extra stabilization by resonance.

ATOMIC/MOLECULAR ORBITALS

Molecular orbitals (MO) are formed from atomic orbitals (AO). Bonding MOs have lower energy and greater stability compared to the AOs from which they are formed. In contrast, antibonding MOs have higher energy and lower stability compared to their corresponding AOs. The number of electrons from an AO is equal to the number of electrons in the resulting MO. The bond order (BO) is given by the equation:

$$BO = \frac{(\#bonding\ electrons) - (\#\ antibonding\ electrons)}{2}$$

In order for a bond to exist, the BO must be ½ or greater.

RESONANCE STRUCTURES

Resonance structures show the delocalization of the electrons around the molecule. As a rule of thumb, more resonance structures indicate higher stability for a molecule. The "true" representation of the molecule is a hybrid of all resonance structures. However, the greatest contribution will come from the most plausible formation, which can be determined by the following rules. First, absence of formal charge is preferred to the structures with formal charges. If charges are unavoidable, then large formal charges (±2, ±3 and so on) are less likely than small formal charges (±1). Finally, among resonance structures with small charges, the most plausible resonance form is the one in which the negative formal charges are placed on the more electronegative atom. For illustration, see the resonance structures below. The second one is favored because the negative charge is on the O (more electronegative) rather than C.

HYBRIDIZATION

The hybridization of a carbon atom can be quickly determined by counting the number of stereoactive groups. Stereoactive groups can be a bond (double or triple bonds are counted as one group) or a lone pair. An unpaired electron (in free radicals) is not considered a stereoactive group.

Four groups will have sp^3 hybridization (add the superscripts, e.g. s^1p^3).

Three stereoactive groups will have sp^2 hybridization.

Two stereoactive groups will have sp hybridization.

BOND ANGLES/LENGTHS

First, sp^3 hybridized carbons have **tetrahedral** shape, hence the bond angle is approximately 109.5°. This carbon type occurs in alkanes, alkyl halides, alcohols, and amines.

Second, sp^2 hybridized carbons are **trigonal planar**, hence the bond angle is approximately 120°. This carbon hybridization occurs in alkenes, aldehydes, ketones, carboxylic acids, and derivatives.

Finally, sp hybridized carbons are **linear**, hence the bond angle is approximately 180°, characteristic of alkynes and nitriles.

The trend for bond length is as follows: sp^3 > sp^2 > sp, as single bonds are longer than double bonds and double bonds are longer than triple bonds.

BOND STRENGTHS

There are three factors that determine bond strength, as reflected in the **bond dissociation energy** or BDE (energy that must be supplied to break the bond).

First is **bond order**. The higher the bond order, the stronger the bond. Double bonds are stronger than single bonds. For example, BDE for C–C is 350 kJ/mol compared with 610 kJ/mol for C=C.

If the bond order is the same, then evaluate **bond polarity**. Generally, polar bonds are stronger. For example, BDE for C=C is 610 kJ/mol compared with 730 kJ/mol for C=O.

Finally, if bond order and bond polarity are identical then consider **hybridization**. The strongest C–H bond will come from the terminal alkyne, i.e. sp hybridized; the higher the s–character, the stronger it is. Then comes the vinylic C–H, i.e. sp^2. The sp^3-hybridized C–H is the weakest.

Reading Comprehension

Comprehension Skills

One of the most important skills in reading comprehension is the identification of **topics** and **main ideas.** There is a subtle difference between these two features. The topic is the subject of a text, or what the text is about. The main idea, on the other hand, is the most important point being made by the author. The topic is usually expressed in a few words at the most, while the main idea often needs a full sentence to be completely defined. As an example, a short passage might have the topic of penguins and the main idea *Penguins are different from other birds in many ways.* In most nonfiction writing, the topic and the main idea will be stated directly, often in a sentence at the very beginning or end of the text. When being tested on an understanding of the author's topic, the reader can quickly *skim* the passage for the general idea, stopping to read only the first sentence of each paragraph. A paragraph's first sentence is often (but not always) the main topic sentence, and it gives you a summary of the content of the paragraph. However, there are cases in which the reader must figure out an unstated topic or main idea. In these instances, the student must read every sentence of the text, and try to come up with an overarching idea that is supported by each of those sentences.

> ### Review Video: <u>Topics and Main Ideas</u>
> Visit mometrix.com/academy and enter Code: 407801

While the main idea is the overall premise of a story, **supporting details** provide evidence and backing for the main point. In order to show that a main idea is correct, or valid, the author needs to add details that prove their point. All texts contain details, but they are only classified as supporting details when they serve to reinforce some larger point. Supporting details are most commonly found in informative and persuasive texts. In some cases, they will be clearly indicated with words like *for example* or *for instance*, or they will be enumerated with words like *first*, *second*, and *last*. However, they may not be indicated with special words. As a reader, it is important to consider whether the author's supporting details really back up his or her main point. Supporting details can be factual and correct but still not relevant to the author's point. Conversely, supporting details can seem pertinent but be ineffective because they are based on opinion or assertions that cannot be proven.

> ### Review Video: <u>Supporting Details</u>
> Visit mometrix.com/academy and enter Code: 396297

An example of a main idea is: "Giraffes live in the Serengeti of Africa." A supporting detail about giraffes could be: "A giraffe uses its long neck to reach twigs and leaves on trees." The main idea gives the general idea that the text is about giraffes. The supporting detail gives a specific fact about how the giraffes eat.

As opposed to a main idea, themes are seldom expressed directly in a text, so they can be difficult to identify. A **theme** is an issue, an idea, or a question raised by the text. For instance, a theme of William Shakespeare's *Hamlet* is indecision, as the title character explores his own psyche and the results of his failure to make bold choices. A great work of literature may have many themes, and the reader is justified in identifying any for which he or she can find support. One common characteristic of themes is that they raise more questions than they answer. In a good piece of fiction, the author is not always trying to convince the reader, but is instead trying to elevate the

310

reader's perspective and encourage him to consider the themes more deeply. When reading, one can identify themes by constantly asking what general issues the text is addressing. A good way to evaluate an author's approach to a theme is to begin reading with a question in mind (for example, how does this text approach the theme of love?) and then look for evidence in the text that addresses that question.

> **Review Video: Theme**
> Visit mometrix.com/academy and enter Code: 732074

PURPOSES FOR WRITING

In order to be an effective reader, one must pay attention to the author's **position** and purpose. Even those texts that seem objective and impartial, like textbooks, have some sort of position and bias. Readers need to take these positions into account when considering the author's message. When an author uses emotional language or clearly favors one side of an argument, his position is clear. However, the author's position may be evident not only in what he writes, but in what he doesn't write. For this reason, it is sometimes necessary to review some other texts on the same topic in order to develop a view of the author's position. If this is not possible, then it may be useful to acquire a little background personal information about the author. When the only source of information is the text, however, the reader should look for language and argumentation that seems to indicate a particular stance on the subject.

> **Review Video: Author's Position**
> Visit mometrix.com/academy and enter code: 827954

Identifying the **purpose** of an author is usually easier than identifying her position. In most cases, the author has no interest in hiding his or her purpose. A text that is meant to entertain, for instance, should be obviously written to please the reader. Most narratives, or stories, are written to entertain, though they may also inform or persuade. Informative texts are easy to identify as well. The most difficult purpose of a text to identify is persuasion, because the author has an interest in making this purpose hard to detect. When a person knows that the author is trying to convince him, he is automatically more wary and skeptical of the argument. For this reason persuasive texts often try to establish an entertaining tone, hoping to amuse the reader into agreement, or an informative tone, hoping to create an appearance of authority and objectivity.

An author's purpose is often evident in the organization of the text. For instance, if the text has headings and subheadings, if key terms are in bold, and if the author makes his main idea clear from the beginning, then the likely purpose of the text is to inform. If the author begins by making a claim and then makes various arguments to support that claim, the purpose is probably to persuade. If the author is telling a story, or is more interested in holding the attention of the reader than in making a particular point or delivering information, then his purpose is most likely to entertain. As a reader, it is best to judge an author on how well he accomplishes his purpose. In other words, it is not entirely fair to complain that a textbook is boring: if the text is clear and easy to understand, then the author has done his job. Similarly, a storyteller should not be judged too harshly for getting some facts wrong, so long as he is able to give pleasure to the reader.

> **Review Video: Purpose**
> Visit mometrix.com/academy and enter Code: 511819

The author's purpose for writing will affect his writing style and the response of the reader. In a **persuasive essay**, the author is attempting to change the reader's mind or convince him of something he did not believe previously. There are several identifying characteristics of persuasive writing. One is opinion presented as fact. When an author attempts to persuade the reader, he often presents his or her opinions as if they were fact. A reader must be on guard for statements that sound factual but which cannot be subjected to research, observation, or experiment. Another characteristic of persuasive writing is emotional language. An author will often try to play on the reader's emotion by appealing to his sympathy or sense of morality. When an author uses colorful or evocative language with the intent of arousing the reader's passions, it is likely that he is attempting to persuade. Finally, in many cases a persuasive text will give an unfair explanation of opposing positions, if these positions are mentioned at all.

An **informative text** is written to educate and enlighten the reader. Informative texts are almost always nonfiction, and are rarely structured as a story. The intention of an informative text is to deliver information in the most comprehensible way possible, so the structure of the text is likely to be very clear. In an informative text, the thesis statement is often in the first sentence. The author may use some colorful language, but is likely to put more emphasis on clarity and precision. Informative essays do not typically appeal to the emotions. They often contain facts and figures, and rarely include the opinion of the author. Sometimes a persuasive essay can resemble an informative essay, especially if the author maintains an even tone and presents his or her views as if they were established fact.

> **Review Video: Informative Text**
> Visit mometrix.com/academy and enter code: 924964

The success or failure of an author's intent to **entertain** is determined by those who read the author's work. Entertaining texts may be either fiction or nonfiction, and they may describe real or imagined people, places, and events. Entertaining texts are often narratives, or stories. A text that is written to entertain is likely to contain colorful language that engages the imagination and the emotions. Such writing often features a great deal of figurative language, which typically enlivens its subject matter with images and analogies. Though an entertaining text is not usually written to persuade or inform, it may accomplish both of these tasks. An entertaining text may appeal to the reader's emotions and cause him or her to think differently about a particular subject. In any case, entertaining texts tend to showcase the personality of the author more so than do other types of writing.

When an author intends to **express feelings,** she may use colorful and evocative language. An author may write emotionally for any number of reasons. Sometimes, the author will do so because she is describing a personal situation of great pain or happiness. Sometimes an author is attempting to persuade the reader, and so will use emotion to stir up the passions. It can be easy to identify this kind of expression when the writer uses phrases like *I felt* and *I sense*. However, sometimes the author will simply describe feelings without introducing them. As a reader, it is important to recognize when an author is expressing emotion, and not to become overwhelmed by sympathy or passion. A reader should maintain some detachment so that he or she can still evaluate the strength of the author's argument or the quality of the writing.

In a sense, almost all writing is descriptive, insofar as it seeks to describe events, ideas, or people to the reader. Some texts, however, are primarily concerned with **description**. A descriptive text focuses on a particular subject, and attempts to depict it in a way that will be clear to the reader. Descriptive texts contain many adjectives and adverbs, words that give shades of meaning and create a more detailed mental picture for the reader. A descriptive text fails when it is unclear or vague to the reader. On the other hand, however, a descriptive text that compiles too much detail can be boring and overwhelming to the reader. A descriptive text will certainly be informative, and it may be persuasive and entertaining as well. Descriptive writing is a challenge for the author, but when it is done well, it can be fun to read.

WRITING DEVICES

Authors will use different stylistic and writing devices to make their meaning more clearly understood. One of those devices is comparison and contrast. When an author describes the ways in which two things are alike, he or she is **comparing** them. When the author describes the ways in which two things are different, he or she is **contrasting** them. The "compare and contrast" essay is one of the most common forms in nonfiction. It is often signaled with certain words: a comparison may be indicated with such words as *both, same, like, too,* and *as well*; while a contrast may be indicated by words like *but, however, on the other hand, instead,* and *yet*. Of course, comparisons and contrasts may be implicit without using any such signaling language. A single sentence may both compare and contrast. Consider the sentence *Brian and Sheila love ice cream, but Brian prefers vanilla and Sheila prefers strawberry*. In one sentence, the author has described both a similarity (love of ice cream) and a difference (favorite flavor).

> **Review Video: Compare and Contrast**
> Visit mometrix.com/academy and enter code: 171799

One of the most common text structures is **cause and effect**. A cause is an act or event that makes something happen, and an effect is the thing that happens as a result of that cause. A cause-and-effect relationship is not always explicit, but there are some words in English that signal causality, such as *since, because,* and *as a result*. As an example, consider the sentence *Because the sky was clear, Ron did not bring an umbrella*. The cause is the clear sky, and the effect is that Ron did not bring an umbrella. However, sometimes the cause-and-effect relationship will not be clearly noted. For instance, the sentence *He was late and missed the meeting* does not contain any signaling words, but it still contains a cause (he was late) and an effect (he missed the meeting). It is possible for a single cause to have multiple effects, or for a single effect to have multiple causes. Also, an effect can in turn be the cause of another effect, in what is known as a cause-and-effect chain.

Authors often use analogies to add meaning to the text. An **analogy** is a comparison of two things. The words in the analogy are connected by a certain, often undetermined relationship. Look at this analogy: moo is to cow as quack is to duck. This analogy compares the sound that a cow makes with the sound that a duck makes. Even if the word 'quack' was not given, one could figure out it is the correct word to complete the analogy based on the relationship between the words 'moo' and 'cow'. Some common relationships for analogies include synonyms, antonyms, part to whole, definition, and actor to action.

Another element that impacts a text is the author's point of view. The **point of view** of a text is the perspective from which it is told. The author will always have a point of view about a story before he draws up a plot line. The author will know what events they want to take place, how they want the characters to interact, and how the story will resolve. An author will also have an opinion on the topic, or series of events, which is presented in the story, based on their own prior experience and beliefs.

The two main points of view that authors use are first person and third person. If the narrator of the story is also the main character, or *protagonist*, the text is written in first-person point of view. In first person, the author writes with the word *I*. Third-person point of view is probably the most common point of view that authors use. Using third person, authors refer to each character using

313

the words *he* or *she.* In third-person omniscient, the narrator is not a character in the story and tells the story of all of the characters at the same time.

A good writer will use **transitional words** and phrases to guide the reader through the text. You are no doubt familiar with the common transitions, though you may never have considered how they operate. Some transitional phrases (*after, before, during, in the middle of*) give information about time. Some indicate that an example is about to be given (*for example, in fact, for instance*). Writers use them to compare (*also, likewise*) and contrast (*however, but, yet*). Transitional words and phrases can suggest addition (*and, also, furthermore, moreover*) and logical relationships (*if, then, therefore, as a result, since*). Finally, transitional words and phrases can demarcate the steps in a process (*first, second, last*). You should incorporate transitional words and phrases where they will orient your reader and illuminate the structure of your composition.

TYPES OF PASSAGES

A **narrative** passage is a story. Narratives can be fiction or nonfiction. However, there are a few elements that a text must have in order to be classified as a narrative. To begin with, the text must have a plot. That is, it must describe a series of events. If it is a good narrative, these events will be interesting and emotionally engaging to the reader. A narrative also has characters. These could be people, animals, or even inanimate objects, so long as they participate in the plot. A narrative passage often contains figurative language, which is meant to stimulate the imagination of the reader by making comparisons and observations. A metaphor, which is a description of one thing in terms of another, is a common piece of figurative language. *The moon was a frosty snowball* is an example of a metaphor: it is obviously untrue in the literal sense, but it suggests a certain mood for the reader. Narratives often proceed in a clear sequence, but they do not need to do so.

An **expository** passage aims to inform and enlighten the reader. It is nonfiction and usually centers around a simple, easily defined topic. Since the goal of exposition is to teach, such a passage should be as clear as possible. It is common for an expository passage to contain helpful organizing words, like *first, next, for example*, and *therefore*. These words keep the reader oriented in the text. Although expository passages do not need to feature colorful language and artful writing, they are often more effective when they do. For a reader, the challenge of expository passages is to maintain steady attention. Expository passages are not always about subjects in which a reader will naturally be interested, and the writer is often more concerned with clarity and comprehensibility than with engaging the reader. For this reason, many expository passages are dull. Making notes is a good way to maintain focus when reading an expository passage.

A **technical** passage is written to describe a complex object or process. Technical writing is common in medical and technological fields, in which complicated mathematical, scientific, and engineering ideas need to be explained simply and clearly. To ease comprehension, a technical passage usually proceeds in a very logical order. Technical passages often have clear headings and subheadings, which are used to keep the reader oriented in the text. It is also common for these passages to break sections up with numbers or letters. Many technical passages look more like an outline than a piece of prose. The amount of jargon or difficult vocabulary will vary in a technical passage depending on the intended audience. As much as possible, technical passages try to avoid language that the reader will have to research in order to understand the message. Of course, it is not always possible to avoid jargon.

> **Review Video: A Technical Passage**
> Visit mometrix.com/academy and enter code: 478923

A **persuasive** passage is meant to change the reader's mind or lead her into agreement with the author. The persuasive intent may be obvious, or it may be quite difficult to discern. In some cases, a persuasive passage will be indistinguishable from an informative passage: it will make an assertion and offer supporting details. However, a persuasive passage is more likely to make claims based on opinion and to appeal to the reader's emotions. Persuasive passages may not describe alternate positions and, when they do, they often display significant bias. It may be clear that a persuasive passage is giving the author's viewpoint, or the passage may adopt a seemingly objective tone. A persuasive passage is successful if it can make a convincing argument and win the trust of the reader.

A persuasive essay will likely focus on one central argument, but it may make many smaller claims along the way. These are subordinate arguments with which the reader must agree if he or she is going to agree with the central argument. The central argument will only be as strong as the subordinate claims. These claims should be rooted in fact and observation, rather than subjective judgment. The best persuasive essays provide enough supporting detail to justify claims without overwhelming the reader. Remember that a fact must be susceptible to independent verification: that is, it must be something the reader could confirm. Also, statistics are only effective when they take into account possible objections. For instance, a statistic on the number of foreclosed houses would only be useful if it was taken over a defined interval and in a defined area. Most readers are wary of statistics, because they are so often misleading. If possible, a persuasive essay should always include references so that the reader can obtain more information. Of course, this means that the writer's accuracy and fairness may be judged by the inquiring reader.

Opinions are formed by emotion as well as reason, and persuasive writers often appeal to the feelings of the reader. Although readers should always be skeptical of this technique, it is often used in a proper and ethical manner. For instance, there are many subjects that have an obvious emotional component, and therefore cannot be completely treated without an appeal to the emotions. Consider an article on drunk driving: it makes sense to include some specific examples that will alarm or sadden the reader. After all, drunk driving often has serious and tragic consequences. Emotional appeals are not appropriate, however, when they attempt to mislead the reader. For instance, in political advertisements it is common to emphasize the patriotism of the preferred candidate, because this will encourage the audience to link their own positive feelings about the country with their opinion of the candidate. However, these ads often imply that the other candidate is unpatriotic, which in most cases is far from the truth. Another common and improper emotional appeal is the use of loaded language, as for instance referring to an avidly religious person as a "fanatic" or a passionate environmentalist as a "tree hugger." These terms introduce an emotional component that detracts from the argument.

Critical Thinking Skills

OPINIONS, FACTS, & FALLACIES

Critical thinking skills are mastered through understanding various types of writing and the different purposes that authors have for writing the way they do. Every author writes for a purpose. Understanding that purpose, and how they accomplish their goal, will allow you to critique the writing and determine whether or not you agree with their conclusions.

Readers must always be conscious of the distinction between fact and opinion. A **fact** can be subjected to analysis and can be either proved or disproved. An **opinion**, on the other hand, is the author's personal feeling, which may not be alterable by research, evidence, or argument. If the author writes that the distance from New York to Boston is about two hundred miles, he is stating a fact. But if he writes that New York is too crowded, then he is giving an opinion, because there is no objective standard for overpopulation. An opinion may be indicated by words like *believe*, *think*, or *feel*. Also, an opinion may be supported by facts: for instance, the author might give the population density of New York as a reason for why it is overcrowded. An opinion supported by fact tends to be more convincing. When authors support their opinions with other opinions, the reader is unlikely to be moved.

Facts should be presented to the reader from reliable sources. An opinion is what the author thinks about a given topic. An opinion is not common knowledge or proven by expert sources, but it is information that the author believes and wants the reader to consider. To distinguish between fact and opinion, a reader needs to look at the type of source that is presenting information, what information backs-up a claim, and whether or not the author may be motivated to have a certain point of view on a given topic. For example, if a panel of scientists has conducted multiple studies on the effectiveness of taking a certain vitamin, the results are more likely to be factual than if a company selling a vitamin claims that taking the vitamin can produce positive effects. The company is motivated to sell its product, while the scientists are using the scientific method to prove a theory. If the author uses words such as "I think…", the statement is an opinion.

> **Review Video:** Fact or Opinion
> Visit mometrix.com/academy and enter Code: 870899

In their attempt to persuade, writers often make mistakes in their thinking patterns and writing choices. It's important to understand these so you can make an informed decision. Every author has a point of view, but when an author ignores reasonable counterarguments or distorts opposing viewpoints, she is demonstrating a **bias**. A bias is evident whenever the author is unfair or inaccurate in his or her presentation. Bias may be intentional or unintentional, but it should always alert the reader to be skeptical of the argument being made. It should be noted that a biased author may still be correct. However, the author will be correct in spite of her bias, not because of it. A **stereotype** is like a bias, except that it is specifically applied to a group or place. Stereotyping is considered to be particularly abhorrent because it promotes negative generalizations about people. Many people are familiar with some of the hateful stereotypes of certain ethnic, religious, and cultural groups. Readers should be very wary of authors who stereotype. These faulty assumptions typically reveal the author's ignorance and lack of curiosity.

> **Review Video:** Bias and Stereotype
> Visit mometrix.com/academy and enter Code: 644829

Sometimes, authors will **appeal to the reader's emotion** in an attempt to persuade or to distract the reader from the weakness of the argument. For instance, the author may try to inspire the pity of the reader by delivering a heart-rending story. An author also might use the bandwagon approach, in which he suggests that his opinion is correct because it is held by the majority. Some authors resort to name-calling, in which insults and harsh words are delivered to the opponent in an attempt to distract. In advertising, a common appeal is the testimonial, in which a famous person endorses a product. Of course, the fact that a celebrity likes something should not really mean anything to the reader. These and other emotional appeals are usually evidence of poor reasoning and a weak argument.

Certain *logical fallacies* are frequent in writing. A logical fallacy is a failure of reasoning. As a reader, it is important to recognize logical fallacies, because they diminish the value of the author's message. The four most common logical fallacies in writing are the false analogy, circular reasoning, false dichotomy, and overgeneralization. In a **false analogy**, the author suggests that two things are similar, when in fact they are different. This fallacy is often committed when the author is attempting to convince the reader that something unknown is like something relatively familiar. The author takes advantage of the reader's ignorance to make this false comparison. One example might be the following statement: *Failing to tip a waitress is like stealing money out of somebody's wallet.* Of course, failing to tip is very rude, especially when the service has been good, but people are not arrested for failing to tip as they would for stealing money from a wallet. To compare stingy diners with thieves is a false analogy.

Circular reasoning is one of the more difficult logical fallacies to identify, because it is typically hidden behind dense language and complicated sentences. Reasoning is described as circular when it offers no support for assertions other than restating them in different words. Put another way, a circular argument refers to itself as evidence of truth. A simple example of circular argument is when a person uses a word to define itself, such as saying *Niceness is the state of being nice.* If the reader does not know what *nice* means, then this definition will not be very useful. In a text, circular reasoning is usually more complex. For instance, an author might say *Poverty is a problem for society because it creates trouble for people throughout the community.* It is redundant to say that poverty is a problem because it creates trouble. When an author engages in circular reasoning, it is often because he or she has not fully thought out the argument, or cannot come up with any legitimate justifications.

One of the most common logical fallacies is the **false dichotomy**, in which the author creates an artificial sense that there are only two possible alternatives in a situation. This fallacy is common when the author has an agenda and wants to give the impression that his view is the only sensible one. A false dichotomy has the effect of limiting the reader's options and imagination. An example of a false dichotomy is the statement *You need to go to the party with me, otherwise you'll just be bored at home.* The speaker suggests that the only other possibility besides being at the party is being bored at home. But this is not true, as it is perfectly possible to be entertained at home, or even to go somewhere other than the party. Readers should always be wary of the false dichotomy: when an author limits alternatives, it is always wise to ask whether he is being valid.

Overgeneralization is a logical fallacy in which the author makes a claim that is so broad it cannot be proved or disproved. In most cases, overgeneralization occurs when the author wants to create an illusion of authority, or when he is using sensational language to sway the opinion of the reader. For instance, in the sentence *Everybody knows that she is a terrible teacher*, the author makes an assumption that cannot really be believed. This kind of statement is made when the author wants to create the illusion of consensus when none actually exists: it may be that most people have a negative view of the teacher, but to say that *everybody* feels that way is an exaggeration. When a reader spots overgeneralization, she should become skeptical about the argument that is being made, because an author will often try to hide a weak or unsupported assertion behind authoritative language.

Two other types of logical fallacies are **slippery slope** arguments and **hasty generalizations**. In a slippery slope argument, the author says that if something happens, it automatically means that something else will happen as a result, even though this may not be true. (i.e., just because you study hard does not mean you are going to ace the test). "Hasty generalization" is drawing a conclusion too early, without finishing analyzing the details of the argument. Writers of persuasive texts often use these techniques because they are very effective. In order to **identify logical fallacies**, readers need to read carefully and ask questions as they read. Thinking critically means not taking everything at face value. Readers need to critically evaluate an author's argument to make sure that the logic used is sound.

ORGANIZATION OF THE TEXT

The way a text is organized can help the reader to understand more clearly the author's intent and his conclusions. There are various ways to organize a text, and each one has its own purposes and uses.

Some nonfiction texts are organized to **present a problem** followed by a solution. In this type of text, it is common for the problem to be explained before the solution is offered. In some cases, as when the problem is well known, the solution may be briefly introduced at the beginning. The entire passage may focus on the solution, and the problem will be referenced only occasionally. Some texts will outline multiple solutions to a problem, leaving the reader to choose among them. If the author has an interest or an allegiance to one solution, he may fail to mention or may describe inaccurately some of the other solutions. Readers should be careful of the author's agenda when reading a problem-solution text. Only by understanding the author's point of view and interests can one develop a proper judgment of the proposed solution.

Authors need to organize information logically so the reader can follow it and locate information within the text. Two common organizational structures are cause and effect and chronological order. When using **chronological order**, the author presents information in the order that it happened. For example, biographies are written in chronological order; the subject's birth and childhood are presented first, followed by their adult life, and lastly by the events leading up to the person's death.

In **cause and effect**, an author presents one thing that makes something else happen. For example, if one were to go to bed very late, they would be tired. The cause is going to bed late, with the effect of being tired the next day.

It can be tricky to identify the cause-and-effect relationships in a text, but there are a few ways to approach this task. To begin with, these relationships are often signaled with certain terms. When an author uses words like *because*, *since*, *in order*, and *so*, she is likely describing a cause-and-effect relationship. Consider the sentence, "He called her because he needed the homework." This is a simple causal relationship, in which the cause was his need for the homework and the effect was his phone call. Not all cause-and-effect relationships are marked in this way, however. Consider the sentences, "He called her. He needed the homework." When the cause-and-effect relationship is not indicated with a keyword, it can be discovered by asking why something happened. He called her: why? The answer is in the next sentence: He needed the homework.

Persuasive essays, in which an author tries to make a convincing argument and change the reader's mind, usually include cause-and-effect relationships. However, these relationships should not always be taken at face value. An author frequently will assume a cause or take an effect for granted. To read a persuasive essay effectively, one needs to judge the cause-and-effect relationships the author is presenting. For instance, imagine an author wrote the following: "The parking deck has been unprofitable because people would prefer to ride their bikes." The relationship is clear: the cause is that people prefer to ride their bikes, and the effect is that the parking deck has been unprofitable. However, a reader should consider whether this argument is conclusive. Perhaps there are other reasons for the failure of the parking deck: a down economy, excessive fees, etc. Too often, authors present causal relationships as if they are fact rather than opinion. Readers should be on the alert for these dubious claims.

Thinking critically about ideas and conclusions can seem like a daunting task. One way to make it easier is to understand the basic elements of ideas and writing techniques. Looking at the way different ideas relate to each other can be a good way for the reader to begin his analysis. For instance, sometimes writers will write about two different ideas that are in opposition to each other. The analysis of these opposing ideas is known as **contrast**. Contrast is often marred by the author's obvious partiality to one of the ideas. A discerning reader will be put off by an author who does not engage in a fair fight. In an analysis of opposing ideas, both ideas should be presented in their clearest and most reasonable terms. If the author does prefer a side, he should avoid indicating this preference with pejorative language. An analysis of opposing ideas should proceed through the major differences point by point, with a full explanation of each side's view. For instance, in an analysis of capitalism and communism, it would be important to outline each side's view on labor, markets, prices, personal responsibility, etc. It would be less effective to describe the theory of communism and then explain how capitalism has thrived in the West. An analysis of opposing views should present each side in the same manner.

Many texts follow the **compare-and-contrast** model, in which the similarities and differences between two ideas or things are explored. Analysis of the similarities between ideas is called comparison. In order for a comparison to work, the author must place the ideas or things in an equivalent structure. That is, the author must present the ideas in the same way. Imagine an author wanted to show the similarities between cricket and baseball. The correct way to do so would be to summarize the equipment and rules for each game. It would be incorrect to summarize the equipment of cricket and then lay out the history of baseball, since this would make it impossible for the reader to see the similarities. It is perhaps too obvious to say that an analysis of similar ideas should emphasize the similarities. Of course, the author should take care to include any differences that must be mentioned. Often, these small differences will only reinforce the more general similarity.

DRAWING CONCLUSIONS

Authors should have a clear purpose in mind while writing. Especially when reading informational texts, it is important to understand the logical conclusion of the author's ideas. **Identifying this logical conclusion** can help the reader understand whether he agrees with the writer or not. Identifying a logical conclusion is much like making an inference: it requires the reader to combine the information given by the text with what he already knows to make a supportable assertion. If a passage is written well, then the conclusion should be obvious even when it is unstated. If the author intends the reader to draw a certain conclusion, then all of his argumentation and detail should be leading toward it. One way to approach the task of drawing conclusions is to make brief notes of all the points made by the author. When these are arranged on paper, they may clarify the logical conclusion. Another way to approach conclusions is to consider whether the reasoning of the author raises any pertinent questions. Sometimes it will be possible to draw several conclusions from a passage, and on occasion these will be conclusions that were never imagined by the author. It is essential, however, that these conclusions be supported directly by the text.

> **Review Video: Identifying Logical Conclusions**
> Visit mometrix.com/academy and enter code: 281653

The term **text evidence** refers to information that supports a main point or points in a story, and can help lead the reader to a conclusion. Information used as *text evidence* is precise, descriptive, and factual. A main point is often followed by supporting details that provide evidence to back-up a claim. For example, a story may include the claim that winter occurs during opposite months in the Northern and Southern hemispheres. *Text evidence* based on this claim may include countries where winter occurs in opposite months, along with reasons that winter occurs at different times of the year in separate hemispheres (due to the tilt of the Earth as it rotates around the sun).

> **Review Video: Text Evidence**
> Visit mometrix.com/academy and enter code: 486236

Readers interpret text and respond to it in a number of ways. Using textual support helps defend your response or interpretation because it roots your thinking in the text. You are interpreting based on information in the text and not simply your own ideas. When crafting a response, look for important quotes and details from the text to help bolster your argument. If you are writing about a character's personality trait, for example, use details from the text to show that the character acted in such a way. You can also include statistics and facts from a nonfiction text to strengthen your response. For example, instead of writing, "A lot of people use cell phones," use statistics to provide the exact number. This strengthens your argument because it is more precise.

The text used to support an argument can be the argument's downfall if it is not credible. A text is **credible**, or believable, when the author is knowledgeable and objective, or unbiased. The author's motivations for writing the text play a critical role in determining the credibility of the text and must be evaluated when assessing that credibility. The author's motives should be for the dissemination of information. The purpose of the text should be to inform or describe, not to persuade. When an author writes a persuasive text, he has the motivation that the reader will do what they want. The extent of the author's knowledge of the topic and their motivation must be evaluated when assessing the credibility of a text. Reports written about the Ozone layer by an environmental scientist and a hairdresser will have a different level of credibility.

Review Video: Credible
Visit mometrix.com/academy and enter code: 827257

After determining your own opinion and evaluating the credibility of your supporting text, it is sometimes necessary to communicate your ideas and findings to others. When **writing a response to a text**, it is important to use elements of the text to support your assertion or defend your position. Using supporting evidence from the text strengthens the argument because the reader can see how in depth the writer read the original piece and based their response on the details and facts within that text. Elements of text that can be used in a response include: facts, details, statistics, and direct quotations from the text. When writing a response, one must make sure they indicate which information comes from the original text and then base their discussion, argument, or defense around this information.

A reader should always be drawing conclusions from the text. Sometimes conclusions are implied from written information, and other times the information is **stated directly** within the passage. It is always more comfortable to draw conclusions from information stated within a passage, rather than to draw them from mere implications. At times an author may provide some information and then describe a counterargument. The reader should be alert for direct statements that are subsequently rejected or weakened by the author. The reader should always read the entire passage before drawing conclusions. Many readers are trained to expect the author's conclusions at either the beginning or the end of the passage, but many texts do not adhere to this format.

Drawing conclusions from information implied within a passage requires confidence on the part of the reader. **Implications** are things the author does not state directly, but which can be assumed based on what the author does say. For instance, consider the following simple passage: "I stepped outside and opened my umbrella. By the time I got to work, the cuffs of my pants were soaked." The author never states that it is raining, but this fact is clearly implied. Conclusions based on implication must be well supported by the text. In order to draw a solid conclusion, a reader should have multiple pieces of evidence, or, if he only has one, must be assured that there is no other possible explanation than his conclusion. A good reader will be able to draw many conclusions from information implied by the text, which enriches the reading experience considerably.

As an aid to drawing conclusions, the reader should be adept at **outlining** the information contained in the passage; an effective outline will reveal the structure of the passage, and will lead to solid conclusions. An effective outline will have a title that refers to the basic subject of the text, though it need not recapitulate the main idea. In most outlines, the main idea will be the first major section. It will have each major idea of the passage established as the head of a category. For instance, the most common outline format calls for the main ideas of the passage to be indicated with Roman numerals. In an effective outline of this kind, each of the main ideas will be represented by a Roman numeral and none of the Roman numerals will designate minor details or secondary ideas. Moreover, all supporting ideas and details should be placed in the appropriate place on the outline. An outline does not need to include every detail listed in the text, but it should feature all of those that are central to the argument or message. Each of these details should be listed under the appropriate main idea.

Review Video: Outlining
Visit mometrix.com/academy and enter code: 584445

It is also helpful to **summarize** the information you have read in a paragraph or passage format. This process is similar to creating an effective outline. To begin with, a summary should accurately define the main idea of the passage, though it does not need to explain this main idea in exhaustive detail. It should continue by laying out the most important supporting details or arguments from the passage. All of the significant supporting details should be included, and none of the details included should be irrelevant or insignificant. Also, the summary should accurately report all of these details. Too often, the desire for brevity in a summary leads to the sacrifice of clarity or veracity. Summaries are often difficult to read, because they omit all of graceful language, digressions, and asides that distinguish great writing. However, if the summary is effective, it should contain much the same message as the original text.

> **Review Video: Summarizing Text**
> Visit mometrix.com/academy and enter code: 172903

Paraphrasing is another method the reader can use to aid in comprehension. When paraphrasing, one puts what they have read into their own words, rephrasing what the author has written to make it their own, to "translate" all of what the author says to their own words, including as many details as they can.

Testing Tips

SKIMMING

Your first task when you begin reading is to answer the question "What is the topic of the selection?" This can best be answered by quickly skimming the passage for the general idea, stopping to read only the first sentence of each paragraph. A paragraph's first sentence is usually the main topic sentence, and it gives you a summary of the content of the paragraph.

Once you've skimmed the passage, stopping to read only the first sentences, you will have a general idea about what it is about, as well as what is the expected topic in each paragraph.

Each question will contain clues as to where to find the answer in the passage. Do not just randomly search through the passage for the correct answer to each question. Search scientifically. Find key word(s) or ideas in the question that are going to either contain or be near the correct answer. These are typically nouns, verbs, numbers, or phrases in the question that will probably be duplicated in the passage. Once you have identified those key word(s) or idea, skim the passage quickly to find where those key word(s) or idea appears. The correct answer choice will be nearby.

Example: What caused Martin to suddenly return to Paris?

The key word is Paris. Skim the passage quickly to find where this word appears. The answer will be close by that word.

However, sometimes key words in the question are not repeated in the passage. In those cases, search for the general idea of the question.

Example: Which of the following was the psychological impact of the author's childhood upon the remainder of his life?

Key words are "childhood" or "psychology". While searching for those words, be alert for other words or phrases that have similar meaning, such as "emotional effect" or "mentally" which could be used in the passage, rather than the exact word "psychology".

Numbers or years can be particularly good key words to skim for, as they stand out from the rest of the text.

Example: Which of the following best describes the influence of Monet's work in the 20th century?

20th contains numbers and will easily stand out from the rest of the text. Use 20th as the key word to skim for in the passage.

Other good key word(s) may be in quotation marks. These identify a word or phrase that is copied directly from the passage. In those cases, the word(s) in quotation marks are exactly duplicated in the passage.

Example: In her college years, what was meant by Margaret's "drive for excellence"?

"Drive for excellence" is a direct quote from the passage and should be easy to find.

Once you've quickly found the correct section of the passage to find the answer, focus upon the answer choices. Sometimes a choice will repeat word for word a portion of the passage near the answer. However, beware of such duplication – it may be a trap! More than likely, the correct choice will paraphrase or summarize the related portion of the passage, rather than being exactly the same wording.

For the answers that you think are correct, read them carefully and make sure that they answer the question. An answer can be factually correct, but it MUST answer the question asked. Additionally, two answers can both be seemingly correct, so be sure to read all of the answer choices, and make sure that you get the one that BEST answers the question.

Some questions will not have a key word.

Example: Which of the following would the author of this passage likely agree with?

In these cases, look for key words in the answer choices. Then skim the passage to find where the answer choice occurs. By skimming to find where to look, you can minimize the time required.

Sometimes it may be difficult to identify a good key word in the question to skim for in the passage. In those cases, look for a key word in one of the answer choices to skim for. Often the answer choices can all be found in the same paragraph, which can quickly narrow your search.

PARAGRAPH FOCUS

Focus upon the first sentence of each paragraph, which is the most important. The main topic of the paragraph is usually there.

Once you've read the first sentence in the paragraph, you have a general idea about what each paragraph will be about. As you read the questions, try to determine which paragraph will have the answer. Paragraphs have a concise topic. The answer should either obviously be there or obviously not. It will save time if you can jump straight to the paragraph, so try to remember what you learned from the first sentences.

Example: The first paragraph is about poets; the second is about poetry. If a question asks about poetry, where will the answer be? *The second paragraph.*

The main idea of a passage is typically spread across all or most of its paragraphs. Whereas the main idea of a paragraph may be completely different than the main idea of the very next paragraph, a main idea for a passage affects all of the paragraphs in one form or another.

Example: What is the main idea of the passage?

For each answer choice, try to see how many paragraphs are related. It can help to count how many sentences are affected by each choice, but it is best to see how many paragraphs are affected by the choice. Typically the answer choices will include incorrect choices that are main ideas of individual paragraphs, but not the entire passage. That is why it is crucial to choose ideas that are supported by the most paragraphs possible.

ELIMINATE CHOICES

Some choices can quickly be eliminated. "Andy Warhol lived there." Is Andy Warhol even mentioned in the article? If not, quickly eliminate it.

When trying to answer a question such as "the passage indicates all of the following EXCEPT" quickly skim the paragraph searching for references to each choice. If the reference exists, scratch it off as a choice. Similar choices may be crossed off simultaneously if they are close enough.

In choices that ask you to choose "which answer choice does NOT describe?" or "all of the following answer choices are identifiable characteristics, EXCEPT which?" look for answers that are similarly worded. Since only one answer can be correct, if there are two answers that appear to mean the same thing, they must BOTH be incorrect, and can be eliminated.

Example:

1. changing values and attitudes
2. a large population of mobile or uprooted people

These answer choices are similar; they both describe a fluid culture. Because of their similarity, they can be linked together. Since the answer can have only one choice, they can also be eliminated together.

CONTEXTUAL CLUES

Look for contextual clues. An answer can be right but not correct. The contextual clues will help you find the answer that is most right and is correct. Understand the context in which a phrase is stated.

When asked for the implied meaning of a statement made in the passage, immediately go find the statement and read the context it was made in. Also, look for an answer choice that has a similar phrase to the statement in question.

Example: In the passage, what is implied by the phrase "Churches have become more or less part of the furniture"?

Find an answer choice that is similar or describes the phrase "part of the furniture" as that is the key phrase in the question. "Part of the furniture" is a saying that means something is fixed, immovable, or set in their ways. Those are all similar ways of saying "part of the furniture." As such, the correct answer choice will probably include a similar rewording of the expression.

Example: Why was John described as "morally desperate"?

The answer will probably have some sort of definition of morals in it. "Morals" refers to a code of right and wrong behavior, so the correct answer choice will likely have words that mean something like that.

FACT/OPINION

When asked about which statement is a fact or opinion, remember that answer choices that are facts will typically have no ambiguous words. For example, how long is a long time? What defines an ordinary person? These ambiguous words of "long" and "ordinary" should not be in a factual statement. However, if all of the choices have ambiguous words, go to the context of the passage. Often a factual statement may be set out as a research finding.

Example: "The scientist found that the eye reacts quickly to change in light."

Opinions may be set out in the context of words like thought, believed, understood, or wished.

Example: "He thought the Yankees should win the World Series."

OPPOSITES

Answer choices that are direct opposites are usually correct. The paragraph will often contain established relationships (when this goes up, that goes down). The question may ask you to draw conclusions for this and will give two similar answer choices that are opposites.

Example:

1. a decrease in housing starts
2. an increase in housing starts

MAKE PREDICTIONS

As you read and understand the passage and then the question, try to guess what the answer will be. Remember that three of the four answer choices are wrong, and once you being reading them, your mind will immediately become cluttered with answer choices designed to throw you off. Your mind is typically the most focused immediately after you have read the passage and question and digested its contents. If you can, try to predict what the correct answer will be. You may be surprised at what you can predict.

Quickly scan the choices and see if your prediction is in the listed answer choices. If it is, then you can be quite confident that you have the right answer. It still won't hurt to check the other answer choices, but most of the time, you've got it!

ANSWER THE QUESTION

It may seem obvious to only pick answer choices that answer the question, but the test can contain some excellent answer choices that are wrong. Don't pick an answer just because it sounds right, or you believe it to be true. It MUST answer the question. Once you've made your selection, always go back and check it against the question and make sure that you didn't misread the question, and the answer choice does answer the question posed.

BENCHMARK

After you read the first answer choice, decide if you think it sounds correct or not. If it doesn't, move on to the next answer choice. If it does, make a mental note about that choice. This doesn't mean that you've definitely selected it as your answer choice, it just means that it's the best you've seen thus far. Go ahead and read the next choice. If the next choice is worse than the one you've already selected, keep going to the next answer choice. If the next choice is better than the choice you've already selected, then make a mental note about that answer choice.

As you read through the list, you are mentally noting the choice you think is right. That is your new standard. Every other answer choice must be benchmarked against that standard. That choice is correct until proven otherwise by another answer choice beating it out. Once you've decided that no other answer choice seems as good, do one final check to ensure that it answers the question posed.

NEW INFORMATION

Correct answers will usually contain the information listed in the paragraph and question. Rarely will completely new information be inserted into a correct answer choice. Occasionally the new information may be related in a manner that the test is asking for you to interpret, but seldom.

Example:

The argument above is dependent upon which of the following assumptions?

1. Charles's Law was used

If Charles's Law is not mentioned at all in the referenced paragraph and argument, then it is unlikely that this choice is correct. All of the information needed to answer the question is provided for you, and so you should not have to make guesses that are unsupported or choose answer choices that have unknown information that cannot be reasoned.

VALID INFORMATION

Don't discount any of the information provided in the passage, particularly shorter ones. Every piece of information may be necessary to determine the correct answer. None of the information in the paragraph is there to throw you off (while the answer choices will certainly have information to throw you off). If two seemingly unrelated topics are discussed, don't ignore either. You can be confident there is a relationship, or it wouldn't be included in the paragraph, and you are probably going to have to determine what that relationship is for the answer.

TIME MANAGEMENT

In technical passages, do not get lost on the technical terms. Skip them and move on. You want a general understanding of what is going on, not a mastery of the passage.

When you encounter material in the selection that seems difficult to understand, it often may not be necessary and can be skipped. Only spend time trying to understand it if it is going to be relevant for a question. Understand difficult phrases only as a last resort.

Answer general questions before detail questions. A reader with a good understanding of the whole passage can often answer general questions without rereading a word. Get the easier questions out of the way before tackling the more time consuming ones.

Identify each question by type. Usually the wording of a question will tell you whether you can find the answer by referring directly to the passage or by using your reasoning powers. You alone know which question types you customarily handle with ease and which give you trouble and will require more time. Save the difficult questions for last.

Final Warnings

WORD USAGE QUESTIONS

When asked how a word is used in the passage, don't use your existing knowledge of the word. The question is being asked precisely because there is some strange or unusual usage of the word in the passage. Go to the passage and use contextual clues to determine the answer. Don't simply use the popular definition you already know.

SWITCHBACK WORDS

Stay alert for "switchbacks". These are the words and phrases frequently used to alert you to shifts in thought. The most common switchback word is "but". Others include although, however, nevertheless, on the other hand, even though, while, in spite of, despite, regardless of.

AVOID "FACT TRAPS"

Once you know which paragraph the answer will be in, focus on that paragraph. However, don't get distracted by a choice that is factually true about the paragraph. Your search is for the answer that answers the question, which may be about a tiny aspect in the paragraph. Stay focused and don't fall for an answer that describes the larger picture of the paragraph. Always go back to the question and make sure you're choosing an answer that actually answers the question and is not just a true statement.

Physics

Mechanical Motion

UNITS AND DIMENSIONS

The standard unit of length is the meter, abbreviated m. The meter is currently defined as the distance that light travels in a vacuum in $\frac{1}{299,792,458}$ seconds.

The standard unit of mass is the kilogram, abbreviated kg. The kilogram is currently defined as being equal to the mass of a particular reference weight kept in the International Bureau of Weights and Measures in Sèvres, France. (It is the only standard metric unit defined in terms of a specific object rather than fundamental physical constants.)

The standard unit of time is the second, abbreviated s. The second is currently defined as being equal to 9,192,631,770 times the time associated with the transition between two specific states of the cesium 133 atom.

Derived units based on these units include the units of velocity, m/s; the units of acceleration, m/s^2; the units of force, N or $(kg\ m)/s^2$; the units of energy, J or $(kg\ m^2)/s^2$; the units of pressure, Pa or kg/m^2, and the units of frequency, Hz or s^{-1}.

VECTORS, COMPONENTS

If a vector has a magnitude of v and its angle from the x-axis is θ, then the x component of the vector is $v\cos\theta$, and the y component of the vector is $v\sin\theta$.

These aren't formulas that need to be memorized—although it doesn't hurt to memorize them to speed up your work. They can be derived straightforwardly through trigonometry. The vector v, its x component v_x, and its y component v_y can be arranged to form a right triangle, with θ as one of its angles:

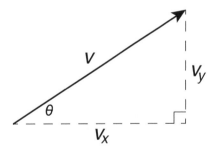

Because the cosine of an angle in a right triangle is equal to the length of the adjacent side over the length of the hypotenuse, that means $\cos\theta = \frac{v_x}{v}$; solving for v_x gives $v_x = v\cos\theta$. A similar argument for the sine yields $v_y = v\sin\theta$.

If a vector has an x component of v_x and a y component of v_y, then the magnitude of the vector is $\sqrt{v_x^2 + v_y^2}$, and the angle from the x axis satisfies the formula $\tan\theta = \frac{v_y}{v_x}$.

Note that it is not necessarily the case that $\theta = \tan^{-1}\frac{v_y}{v_x}$: the arctangent is always by definition in the first or fourth quadrant, so this equation holds if the angle is in one of those quadrants, but if the angle is in the second or third quadrant, then it is 180° off. This can be accounted for by considering the sign of the x component: if $v_x > 0$ then $\theta = \tan^{-1}\frac{v_y}{v_x}$, whereas if $v_x < 0$, then $\theta = \tan^{-1}\frac{v_y}{v_x} + 180°$. And if $v_x = 0$, then $\theta = 90°$ if $v_y > 0$ or 270° if $v_y < 0$.

VECTOR ADDITION

It is possible to add two vectors graphically by drawing them to scale and joining them from head to tail. A vector drawn from the tail of the first vector to the head of the second vector will then represent the sum of the two vectors.

However, adding two vectors graphically can lead to considerable imprecision. A more precise way of adding vectors is to add the components. Suppose the first vector has a magnitude of v_1 and an angle from the x-axis of θ_1, and the second vector has a magnitude of v_2 and an angle from the x-axis of θ_2. The x and y components of the first vector are $v_1\cos\theta_1$ and $v_1\sin\theta_1$, respectively, and the components of the second vector are $v_2\cos\theta_2$ and $v_2\sin\theta_2$. To find the components of the sum, just add together the individual components: $v_x = v_{1x} + v_{2x} = v_1\cos\theta_1 + v_2\cos\theta_2$ and $v_y = v_{1y} + v_{2y} = v_1\sin\theta_1 + v_2\sin\theta_2$. Finally, if you need the magnitude and angle of the total angle, you can find those from the components: $\sqrt{v_x^2 + v_y^2}$ and $\tan\theta = \frac{v_y}{v_x}$.

SPEED, VELOCITY (AVERAGE AND INSTANTANEOUS)

Velocity is the rate of change of position over time. The average velocity is, as the name implies, the average velocity over an interval of time; it can be found by finding the change in position over that interval and dividing by the change in time. In other words, if the position at time t_1 is x_1 and the position at time t_2 is x_2, then the average velocity over the interval (t_1, t_2) is equal to $\frac{x_2 - x_1}{t_2 - t_1}$.

The instantaneous velocity is equal to the rate of change of the position at a particular point in time. It can be found from the slope of a graph of position versus time. This follows from the definition of velocity: the slope of a graph is the rate of change of the dependent variable relative to the independent variable, and velocity is the rate of change of position over time. If the portion of the graph at that time is linear, then the instantaneous velocity is simply the slope of that linear segment of the graph. If the graph is not linear, then the instantaneous velocity is equal to the slope of the tangent line at that point.

Acceleration is the rate of change of velocity over time. The average acceleration is, as the name implies, the average acceleration over an interval of time; it can be found by finding the change in velocity over that interval and dividing by the change in time. In other words, if the velocity at time t_1 is v_1 and the velocity at time t_2 is v_2, then the average acceleration in the interval (t_1, t_2) is equal to $\frac{v_2 - v_1}{t_2 - t_1}$.

The instantaneous acceleration is equal to the rate of change of the velocity at a particular point in time. It can be found from the slope of a graph of velocity versus time. This follows from the definition of acceleration: the slope of a graph is the rate of change of the dependent variable relative to the independent variable, and acceleration is the rate of change of velocity over time. If the portion of the graph at that time is linear, then the instantaneous acceleration is simply the slope of that linear segment of the graph. If the graph is not linear, then the instantaneous acceleration is equal to the slope of the tangent line at that point.

The change in velocity is the area under the graph of acceleration versus time. More specifically, it is the area between the graph and the x-axis, where areas under the x-axis are counted as negative. The following diagram shows an example:

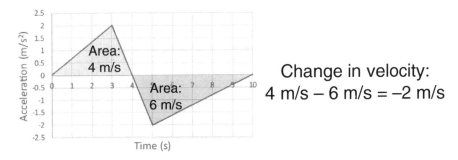

Change in velocity:
4 m/s – 6 m/s = –2 m/s

It is important to note that this area gives the change in velocity over a particular interval, which is not the same thing as the absolute velocity. To find the velocity at the end of this interval, you would have to add this change in velocity to the initial velocity at the beginning of the interval.

The change in position is the area under the graph of velocity versus time. More specifically, it is the area between the graph and the x-axis, where areas under the x-axis are counted as negative. The following diagram shows an example:

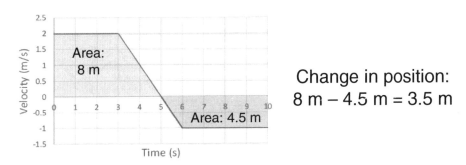

Change in position:
8 m – 4.5 m = 3.5 m

It is important to note that this area gives the change in position over a particular interval, which is not the same thing as the absolute position. To find the position at the end of this interval, you would have to add this change in position to the initial position at the beginning of the interval.

FORCE
NEWTON'S FIRST LAW

Newton's First Law, also called the Law of Inertia, is often stated as follows: An object at rest tends to remain at rest, and an object in motion tends to remain in motion, unless acted on by an outside force. Although Newton's First Law is purely qualitative, it has important consequences; the idea that only external forces can change the motion of an object contradicts previous ideas such as Aristotle's theory that a force was necessary to keep an object in motion and that objects without force acting on them would gradually slow and stop.

Technically, Newton's First Law (like Newton's other laws) only applies in an inertial reference frame—a reference frame that is itself either stationary or moving at a constant velocity (relative to other inertial reference frames). For example, a ball on the floor of a car may seem to move on its own when the car turns, but that's because while it is turning, the car is not an inertial reference frame—relative to the street below the car, the ball is still moving at constant speed (ignoring friction and until the ball hits the side of the car).

NEWTON'S SECOND LAW

Newton's Second Law states that the net force on an object is equal to the product of the object's mass and its acceleration. It is often written in the simple equation form $\vec{F} = m\vec{a}$. Newton's First Law follows directly from Newton's Second Law; in fact, Newton's Second Law can be thought of as a quantification of the first.

Newton's Second Law is very useful in physics because it can be used to predict the acceleration of an object if the net force on the object is known or vice versa. If the force and acceleration are known, it can be used to predict the mass—this is, in fact, how a typical spring scale works; what it is actually measuring is the gravitational force on an object, and the mass it displays is this force divided by the known acceleration of gravity. A special case that frequently occurs is when the object is not moving or when the object is moving at a constant velocity. In this case, the acceleration of the object is zero, so Newton's Second Law shows that the net force on the object must also be zero.

NEWTON'S THIRD LAW

Newton's Third Law is often stated as follows: For every action, there is an equal and opposite reaction. This wording, however, is somewhat misleading because it implies that one force applies first and the other is a later reaction in response to it. In fact, the two forces apply simultaneously, and which one is the "action" and which is the "reaction" is entirely semantic. A more accurate phrasing of the law, then, is that forces always occur in equal and opposite action/reaction pairs. Action/reaction pairs of forces reverse the object acting and the object being acted on: If object A exerts a force on object B, then the reaction force is exerted by object B on object A.

For example, the gravitational force the Earth exerts on you is paired with the gravitational force you exert on the Earth. When a man pushes a car, the car pushes back on the man with an equal force. When a block slides along a table, the block and the table exert equal frictional forces on each other but in opposite directions.

FRICTION, STATIC AND KINETIC

Whenever two objects are in contact and there exists a normal force between them, then there is a frictional force between those objects. If the two objects are in motion relative to each other—such as a block sliding across a table or a child going down a slide—then this is *kinetic* friction. If the two objects are *not* in relative motion—such as a book resting on a shelf, or a car parked on a slope—then it is *static* friction.

One significant difference between static and kinetic friction is that the coefficient of static friction between two objects is always greater than the coefficient of kinetic friction. It takes more force to overcome friction and start moving an object than it does to keep it moving despite friction once it is already in motion.

The coefficient of friction is a value that characterizes the frictional force between two objects depending on their materials and textures. It is not equal to the force of friction between the objects because the force of friction depends not only on the materials of the objects but also on the normal force between them. However, there is a simple relationship between the coefficient of friction μ and the force of friction f: $f = \mu n$, where n is the normal force. More specifically, this relationship always holds for kinetic friction, $f_k = \mu_k n$; for *static* friction this formula gives the maximum force before friction is overcome and the objects start moving: $f_s \leq \mu_s n$. As long as the net force excluding friction is less than this threshold, the static friction is just enough to balance this force and make the total net force equal to zero. However, as soon as the net force excluding friction on an object exceeds $\mu_s n$, friction is no longer sufficient to prevent it from moving.

Review Video: Friction
Visit mometrix.com/academy and enter code: 716782

CENTER OF MASS

One way to find the object's center of mass experimentally is to suspend it from a point (e.g., by tying a string to the object at that point). The center of mass will always be directly below the point from which it is suspended. This locates a line along which the center of mass lies; to find the exact location of the center, repeat the process by suspending the object from a different point, determining another such line. The center of mass is located at the intersection of these two lines.

Finding the center of mass mathematically involves dividing the object into pieces that are considered separately. Define a system of axes, multiply the mass of each part by its position along the x-axis, add those products together, and divide by the total mass. Formulaically, $x_{CM} = \frac{\sum m_i x_i}{\sum m_i}$. Repeat for the other axes. If the object consists of a collection of point masses, this formula is exact; otherwise, finding the center of mass exactly requires calculus.

UNITS OF FORCE

The units of force are newtons, abbreviated N. The unit takes its name after the English mathematician and physicist Sir Isaac Newton, who is credited with discovering the laws of motion that relate force to mass and acceleration.

One newton is equal to 1 kilogram times meter per second squared ([kg m]/s^2). This relationship can be derived by considering Newton's second law: because force equals mass times acceleration, the units of force must be equal to the units of mass (kg) times the units of acceleration (m/s^2).

EQUILIBRIUM

FREE BODY

A free body diagram is a diagram showing all the forces acting on an object with their magnitudes and directions. The forces are drawn as arrows radiating from a point that represents the object. The lengths of the arrows are in proportion to the magnitudes of the forces they represent, and their directions match the directions of these forces. The following is an example representing perhaps the forces on an object being pulled by a rope up an incline, and therefore subject to the force of gravity, the normal force from the incline, the tension in the rope, and kinetic friction:

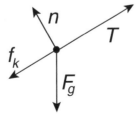

Free body diagrams are useful because they make it easy to visualize the forces acting on the object and to write a formula for the net force based on the individual components. For instance, for the free body diagram drawn here, the net force parallel to the incline would be equal to:

$$T - f_k - F_g \sin \theta$$

Where θ is the angle of the incline. Additionally, the net force perpendicular to the incline would be $n - F_g \cos\theta$—which, because the object is not accelerating along this direction, should be equal to zero.

STATIC EQUILIBRIUM VS. DYNAMIC EQUILIBRIUM

An object is in equilibrium if the net force (or torque) on the object is zero. This means that the acceleration (or angular acceleration) of the object must also be zero, and therefore the object is not moving (or rotating). This is certainly true if the object is stationary, but it is also true if the object is moving at constant velocity (or angular velocity). In the former case—if the object is not moving (or rotating) and if its velocity (or angular velocity) is zero—the object is said to be in *static equilibrium*. If the object is moving (or rotating), but its velocity (or angular velocity) is constant, then the object is said to be in *dynamic equilibrium*.

TRANSLATIONAL EQUILIBRIUM VS. ROTATIONAL EQUILIBRIUM

Equilibrium refers to the balance of opposing influences. In physics, these influences can be forces or torques.

If the forces on an object are balanced—that is, the net force on the object is zero—then the object is said to be in translational equilibrium. An object in translational equilibrium is either not moving or moving at constant velocity.

If the torques on an object are balanced—that is, the net torque on the object is zero—then the object is said to be in rotational equilibrium. An object in rotational equilibrium is either not rotating, or rotating at constant angular velocity.

It is possible—and indeed quite common—for an object to be in both translational and rotational equilibrium. In fact, when an object is said to be in equilibrium, this is often assumed to be the case.

VECTOR ANALYSIS OF FORCES ACTING ON A POINT OBJECT

The net force on an object is simply the total force on the object, that is, the sum of all the individual forces. However, because force is a vector, the forces on the object must be added as vectors; it is not sufficient to simply add their magnitudes. For example, if there are two forces acting on an object, one of 3 N and one of 4 N, then the net force on the object may be anywhere from 1 N to 7 N, depending on the directions. If the two forces are acting in the same direction, then the net force is 7 N; if they're acting in opposite directions, the net force is 1 N in the direction of the larger force; if they're acting at right angles to each other, the net force is 5 N at an angle of about 37° from the larger force.

If the net force on an object is zero, it does not necessarily follow that the object is motionless. According to Newton's Second Law, $\vec{F} = m\vec{a}$, which means if the net force on an object is zero, then the acceleration of the object is zero. However, acceleration is equal to change in velocity over time, so all this means is that the velocity is not changing. If the net force on the object is zero, its velocity must be constant, but not necessarily zero, which means the object may still be moving—it just can't be accelerating.

TORQUES, LEVER ARMS

Torque is something of a rotational analogue of force. Just as a greater force will, all else being equal, produce a greater acceleration, a greater torque will, all else being equal, produce a greater angular acceleration. However, torque is not simply equal to force; there are other factors affecting it. For instance, if you try pushing on a door's outer edge, you will close the door faster than if you exert the same force near the hinges. So, the distance between the axis of rotation and the point at which the force is exerted also matters. A vector pointing from the axis to where the force is exerted is called the lever arm, and the length of the lever arm is the distance in question. There's one more factor that also matters: the angle at which the force is exerted. You'll get the most angular acceleration by exerting a force perpendicular to the lever arm, whereas a force parallel to the lever arm will produce no angular acceleration. The full formula is $\tau = r\,F \sin \phi$, where τ is the torque, r is the lever arm, F is the force, and ϕ is the angle between the force and the lever arm.

Qualitatively, the greater the torque, the greater the angular acceleration—just as for linear motion, the greater the force, the greater the acceleration. In fact, the quantitative formula is similar as well: just like for linear motion we have Newton's Second Law, $\vec{F} = m\vec{a}$, for rotational motion, we have the analogous relationship $\tau = I\alpha$, where τ is the torque and α is the angular acceleration. The remaining factor is not the mass, however, because the torque required for a given angular acceleration depends not just on the mass of an object but on the mass distribution as well and also on the axis of rotation: it is much easier, for instance, to rotate a sledgehammer about a lengthwise axis than it is to rotate it about a crosswise axis through the end of the handle. Therefore, the mass is replaced in this equation by another value, the moment of inertia, abbreviated I, that takes these other factors into account. The units of the moment of inertia are kg m^2.

The units of torque are N × m, newtons times meters. Because a newton is equal to a $(\text{kg m})/\text{s}^2$, an N × m is equal to $(\text{kg m})/\text{s}^2$ × m, which comes out to $(\text{kg m}^2)/\text{s}^2$. This is the same combination of units as the unit of energy, joules, but joules are never used as units of torque. Even though they have the same units, in terms of their relationship to fundamental units, torque and energy are two very different things, and the joule is reserved for energy. The units of torque are simply written N × m, and unlike many other derived units (including joules and newtons themselves), they are not given a shorthand name.

ENERGY
UNITS OF ENERGY

The units of energy are joules, abbreviated J. They are named after the English physicist James Prescott Joule, best known for his discovery of the equivalence between heat and mechanical work.

One joule is equal to 1 kilogram times meter squared per second squared: $(\text{kg m}^2)/\text{s}^2$. This can be derived by considering any of the various equations for work or energy. For example, the work done by a constant force is $W = F\,d \cos \theta$, so the units of work must be equal to the units of force times the units of distance. (The cosine is unit-less.) That means the units of force are newtons times meters, or $(\text{kg m})/\text{s}^2$ × m, which comes out to $(\text{kg m}^2)/\text{s}^2$.

KINETIC ENERGY

The kinetic energy of an object depends on its mass and its velocity. Specifically, the equation for the kinetic energy is $K = \frac{1}{2}mv^2$: the kinetic energy is equal to half the mass of the object times the square of its velocity. Although velocity is a vector, its square is a scalar, so the kinetic energy is a scalar quantity.

One way to derive this formula is by starting with the formula for the gravitational potential energy and considering an object that falls through a distance y. The potential energy lost is mgy because gravity is a conservative force that must be equal to the kinetic energy gained. Because the gravitational acceleration is a constant g (as long as the distances are sufficiently small), we can calculate the final velocity of the object:

$$v_f^2 = v_0^2 + 2ay$$
$$v_f^2 = 0 + 2gy$$
$$\frac{1}{2}v_f^2 = gy$$
$$\frac{1}{2}mv_f^2 = mgy$$

For example, a 2000-kg car moving at 30 m/s has a kinetic energy of:

$$K = \frac{1}{2}mv^2 = \frac{1}{2}(2000 \text{ kg})(30 \text{ m/s})^2 = 900{,}000 \text{ J}$$

POTENTIAL ENERGY
GRAVITATIONAL, LOCAL

The gravitational potential energy of an object can be calculated as $U = mgy$, where m is the mass of the object, g is the acceleration of gravity (which is equal to about 9.8 m/s^2 on Earth), and y is the altitude of the object. Where the altitude is calculated from (the ground, the surface of the table, etc.) is not important as long as you're consistent within a given problem; it is really the change in potential energy that's important.

This formula can be derived simply from the equation for work due to a constant force. Because the force of gravity on an object is mg, when an object falls a distance Δy, then the work gravity does on it is equal to $Fd = mg\Delta y$. Because gravity is a conservative force, this must be equal to the change in potential energy.

For example, a 10-kg weight at the top of a 2.0-m ladder has a potential energy of:

$$mgh = (10 \text{ kg})(9.8 \text{ m/s}^2)(2.0 \text{ m}) = 196 \text{ J}$$

(This is assuming that you consider the height to be zero at the bottom of the ladder.)

SPRING

The spring constant is a value related to the elasticity of a spring: the harder it is to stretch the spring, the higher the spring constant. As such, despite the name, it is not a universal constant; it is only constant for a given spring.

An equation defining the spring constant is Hooke's law: $F = -k\Delta x$: the greater the force applied, the greater the displacement of the end of the spring from the equilibrium position (where it would be with no force applied), with the spring constant as the constant of proportionality. The negative sign in this equation arises because F and Δx are in opposite directions; the spring constant itself is always positive. (Hooke's law only holds as long as the spring is not stretched too far; there is a threshold called the elastic limit beyond which Hooke's law breaks down, and the spring may become permanently deformed.)

Solving for k in Hooke's law gives $k = -\frac{F}{\Delta x}$. From this we can determine the units of the spring constant: it must have units of force (newtons) over units of displacement (meters), so its units are N/m, or kg/s^2.

The potential energy of a spring is equal to $\frac{1}{2}k(\Delta x)^2$, where Δx is the displacement of the end of the spring from its equilibrium position (where it would be with no force applied), and k is the spring constant. As one would expect, a spring in its equilibrium state has no potential energy, whereas the more the spring is stretched or compressed, the higher its potential energy.

For example, consider a spring with a spring constant of 10.0 N/m. If this spring is stretched by 5.0 centimeters, its potential energy is $\frac{1}{2}(10.0 \text{ N/m})(0.050 \text{ m})^2 = 0.013$ J. If it is compressed by 20.0 centimeters, its potential energy is $\frac{1}{2}(10.0 \text{ N/m})(0.200 \text{ m})^2 = 0.200$ J.

CONSERVATION OF ENERGY

Saying that energy is conserved means that whereas energy may be changed from one form to another (such as kinetic energy to potential energy), the total amount of energy in a system does not change. For a closed system, energy is always conserved, if you include thermal energy and other dissipative forms of energy (at least, on the macroscopic scale—technically in certain reactions involving subatomic particles it is possible for energy to be converted to mass, or vice versa, but that's beyond the scope of what's covered here.)

However, thermal energy is not generally easy to convert to another form, or easy to measure, and often it is more useful to exclude it and refer only to the conservation of mechanical energy—where mechanical energy refers only to kinetic and potential energy. Mechanical energy is conserved only when the only forces acting on the system are conservative forces—that is, in the absence of friction and air resistance and other dissipative forces.

Generally, conservation of energy can be used to solve for physical quantities by writing expressions for the total energy of a system at two different times, setting these two expressions equal to each other (because the total energy isn't changing), and then solving for unknown quantities. For example, consider a block starting from rest and sliding down a frictionless ramp 2.0 meters tall. At the top of the ramp, the block has a kinetic energy of zero and a potential energy of:

$$mgh = m(9.8 \text{ m/s}^2)(2.0 \text{ m}) = m(19.6 \text{ m}^2/\text{s}^2)$$

So, its total energy is $m(19.6 \text{ m}^2/\text{s}^2)$, where m is the (unknown) mass of the block. At the bottom of the ramp, the block has a potential energy of zero and a kinetic energy of $\frac{1}{2}mv^2$, so its total energy is $\frac{1}{2}mv^2$. Because mechanical energy is conserved in this situation, we can set these total energies equal: $m(19.6 \text{ m}^2/\text{s}^2) = \frac{1}{2}mv^2$; the mass cancels, and we can solve for the velocity to get $v = \sqrt{2(19.6 \text{ m}^2/\text{s}^2)} = 6.3$ m/s. Note that this result is independent of the mass of the block or the angle of the ramp.

UNITS OF POWER

The units of power are **watts**, named after the Scottish engineer James Watt, best known for his popularization of the steam engine. Although Watt did not invent the steam engine, it was his refinements to its design that allowed its use to become widespread.

In terms of the fundamental metric units, 1 watt is equal to 1 kilogram times meter squared per second cubed: $1 \text{ W} = 1 \text{ (kg m}^2)/\text{s}^3$. This can be derived from the definition of power: power is change in energy over time, so the units of power must be the units of energy divided by the units of time: joules divided by seconds, or $[(\text{kg m}^2)/\text{s}^2]/\text{s} = (\text{kg m}^2)/\text{s}^3$.

One simple equation to calculate power derives from the definition of power: power is change in energy over time, so $P = \frac{\Delta E}{\Delta t}$ or $P = \frac{W}{\Delta t}$ (where W is work). For instance, a machine that uses 30 kJ of energy per hour is using a power of $\frac{30,000\,\text{J}}{3600\,\text{s}} = 830$ W.

Another equation can be used to determine the power exerted by a constant force: $P = F\,v$. This can be derived from the previous equation: because $W = F \times d = F \times \Delta x$, that means:

$$P = \frac{W}{\Delta t} = \frac{F\,\Delta x}{\Delta t} = F\frac{\Delta x}{\Delta t} = F\,v$$

For instance, if a man pushes an appliance across the floor, exerting a force of 150 N to keep it moving at 0.2 m/s, then the power he exerts is $(150\,\text{N})(0.2\,\text{m/s}) = 30$ W.

WORK
WORK DONE BY A CONSTANT FORCE

The work done by a constant force depends on the magnitude of the force and on the distance over which the object that the force is acting on moves. Specifically, if the object is moving in the same direction as the force, the work done by the force is just $W = F \times d$. If the motion is not in the same direction as the force, then the angle between the force and the distance also becomes a factor: then the work done by the force is $W = F \times d\cos\theta$. For example, suppose a boy exerts a 50-N force to pull a wagon 3 meters along the ground by a rope that makes an angle of 30° with the horizontal. The total work the boy does pulling the wagon is then $F\,d\cos\theta = (50\,\text{N})(3\,\text{m})(\cos 30°) = 75$ J.

MECHANICAL ADVANTAGE

Mechanical advantage is the factor by which a machine decreases the necessary force to perform a task; it is the ratio of the force produced to the force applied. Pulleys, inclined planes, and other simple machines are useful because they grant a mechanical advantage; they allow a task to be done with a smaller force than would be necessary without the machine. The smaller force must be exerted over a larger distance, however, so the total work done remains the same.

For a **lever**, the mechanical advantage is simply the ratio of the distance from the fulcrum to the point where the force is applied to the distance from the fulcrum to the point where the force is exerted. For example, if an object is placed 10 cm from the fulcrum of a lever, and a force is exerted 30 cm from the fulcrum, the mechanical advantage is 3; the object can be lifted with a force one-third the object's weight.

For a **pulley system**, the mechanical advantage is equal to the number of rope systems that hold up the object being lifted. (The rope that the force is being applied to doesn't count.)

WORK KINETIC ENERGY THEOREM

The **work kinetic energy theorem** states that the work done on an object by the net force on that object is equal to the change in the object's kinetic energy. This can be used either to find the work given the change in kinetic energy, or to find the kinetic energy given the work, and then possibly to use these results to find other unknown values. For example, suppose a 2.0 N constant horizontal force pushes a 5-kg object 8 meters across a table against friction, accelerating it from rest to a final speed of 2 m/s. This means the object's change in kinetic energy is $\frac{1}{2}(5\,\text{kg})(2\,\text{m})^2 = 10$ J. The work kinetic energy theorem tells us that this is also equal to the work done by the net force. For a

338

constant force in the direction of motion $W = F \times d$, we can derive that $F_{net} = \frac{10\,J}{8\,m} = 1.25$ N. Because this net force must be the applied force minus the force of friction, we can conclude that the force of friction on the object must be 2.0 N − 1.25 N = 0.75 N.

CONSERVATIVE FORCES

The work done on an object by some forces depends on the path it takes, whereas for other forces the work only depends on the start and end points. A force of the latter type is called a **conservative force**. For example, gravity is a conservative force; gravity does the same amount of work on an object that falls directly as it does on an object that slides down a ramp of the same height. Friction, on the other hand, is not a conservative force; friction does much less work on an object sliding straight across a table than it does on one that reaches the same point along a longer, zigzag path.

Aside from gravity, other conservative forces include electric force and the elastic force of a spring.

Aside from friction, other non-conservative forces include tension and air drag.

MOMENTUM

LINEAR MOMENTUM AND IMPULSE

In physics, **linear momentum** can be found by multiplying the mass and velocity of a particle: $P = mv$. Momentum has units of [kg m]/s. Like velocity, momentum is a vector quantity and will always have the same direction as the velocity. Newton's second law describes momentum, stating that the rate of change of momentum is proportional to the force exerted, and is in the direction of the force. **Impulse** is the application of force over a period of time. If a constant net force of 10 N is exerted on an object for 5 seconds, it gives the object an impulse of 50 N s. An impulse of 50 N s corresponds to a change in momentum of 50 [kg m]/s in the direction of the force. In equation form, $Ft = \Delta mv$, where F is a constant net force. If the force is varying, it will be necessary to integrate the force over time.

For example, suppose a 2 kg block is initially at rest on a frictionless surface and a constant net force of 8 N is exerted on the block for 5 seconds. In order to determine how fast the block is moving, we need to calculate the impulse that was given to it, $Ft = 40$ N s. This means that the change in momentum of the block was 40 [kg m]/s. Since the block has a mass of 2 kg, this translates to an increase in velocity of 20 m/s. Thus, the block will be traveling at 20 m/s after 5 seconds.

LINEAR MOMENTUM AND COLLISIONS

If we assume a closed and isolated system (that is, one in which no particles leave or enter, and on which the sum of external forces is zero), then we can assume that the momentum of the system will neither increase nor decrease. That is, if we write the equation for the linear momentum of the system such that the net external force $F_{ext} = 0$, then we will find that linear momentum, P, is a constant. The equation for linear momentum is a vector equation, and as such it can be divided into component equations for each dimension.

Some of the most popular examples to demonstrate conservation of linear momentum involve two objects colliding on a frictionless surface. A perfectly elastic collision is one in which both total momentum and kinetic energy are conserved. A perfectly inelastic collision is one in which only momentum is conserved, as the two bodies combine to form a single body. Most actual collisions fall somewhere between these two extremes. Unless a collision is specified as being elastic, it should be assumed that only momentum is conserved.

Mometrix

EXAMPLES OF ONE-DIMENSIONAL COLLISIONS

All examples assume a frictionless surface.

If a 0.01 kg bullet traveling at 400 m/s strikes a stationary 10 kg block of wood, and buries itself in the wood, find the final velocity of the block and the bullet.

The bullet initially has 4 [kg m]/s of momentum. The block of wood, beginning at rest, has no momentum. Thus, the final momentum is 4 [kg m]/s. Given the new combined mass of 10.01 kg, the final velocity is approximately 0.4 m/s.

Two blocks, having masses of 10 kg and 40 kg, are traveling toward one another with velocities of -20 m/s and 10 m/s, respectively. If the collision was perfectly elastic, find the final velocities of each body. If it was perfectly inelastic, find the final velocity of the resulting single body.

For elastic collisions, two conditions hold: $KE_i = KE_f$ and $P_i = P_f$. Calculating initial conditions yields $KE_i = 4000$ J and $P_i = 200$ [kg m]/s total for both blocks. Equating these to the final values of each yields $5(v_{1f})^2 + 20(v_{2f})^2 = 4000$ J and $10v_{1f} + 40v_{2f} = 200$ [kg m]/s. Solving both equations simultaneously gives $v_{1f} = 28$ m/s and $v_{2f} = -2$ m/s.

The inelastic case is much simpler. Since the two blocks merge to form one, the final momentum, 200 [kg m]/s, is divided by the combined mass to give the final velocity of 4 m/s.

TWO-DIMENSIONAL COLLISIONS

All examples assume a frictionless surface.

Two blocks of mass, 5 kg and 10 kg, having velocities $v_1 = 9\mathbf{i}$ m/s and $v_2 = 3\mathbf{j}$ m/s, respectively, are on a collision course. If the collision is perfectly inelastic, find the velocity of the combined block after collision.

Since each block initially has velocity in only one dimension, it is a simple calculation to find intial momentum values: $P_x = 45$ [kg m]/s and $P_y = 30$ [kg m]/s. With the new combined mass of 15 kg, the final velocity vector will be $v_f = 3\mathbf{i} + 2\mathbf{j}\frac{m}{s}$.

Two hockey pucks, each with a mass of 0.15 kg, having velocity vectors $v_{1i} = 20\mathbf{i} + 30\mathbf{j}$ m/s and $v_{2i} = -50\mathbf{i} - 10\mathbf{j}$ m/s, are headed toward a collision. If the final velocity of one puck is $v_{2f} = -10\mathbf{i} + 15\mathbf{j}$ m/s, find the final velocity vector of the other puck.

We must ensure that momentum is conserved in both dimensions. The initial momentum in the x- and y-directions is calculated to be $P_{xi} = -4.5$ [kg m]/s and $P_{yi} = 3$ [kg m]/s. Since we know the final velocity of one of the pucks, we can find the other's final velocity to be $v_{1f} = -20\mathbf{i} + 5\mathbf{j}$ m/s.

POLAR COORDINATE SYSTEM

Polar coordinates were designed to be useful in situations in which circular arcs are more common than straight lines and right angles. Instead of having x- and y-coordinates, an object's location is described by its distance from the origin, r, and the angle between its position vector and the positive x-axis, commonly denoted as θ.

The two coordinate systems are related by the following equations:

$$x = r\,\cos(\theta), \qquad y = r\,\sin(\theta)$$

$$r = sqrt(x^2 + y^2), \qquad \theta = \tan^{-1}(y/x)$$

The direction and nature of the conversion will dictate which set of equations to use.

The polar coordinate system simplifies many calculations of circular motion. Instead of a velocity in the x- or y-direction, velocity may be described by velocity toward or away from the origin and an increase or decrease in the angle θ. For uniform circular motion, the change in r is zero, and the rate of change of angle θ is constant. The only acceleration on the body is the centripetal acceleration, given by $a_c = |v|^2/r = r\omega^2$, where ω is the rate of change in angle θ, known as the rotational velocity, keeping the body in its circular arc. This acceleration is caused by a centripetal force that pulls the object toward the center of the circle. By Newton's second law, this force has a magnitude given by $F = ma_c = m|v|^2/r = mr\omega^2$.

ANGULAR MOTION AND THE AXIS OF ROTATION

When a body is moving in a straight line, it is said to be moving in **translation**. When, on the other hand, it is moving around some fixed axis, it is said to be in **rotation**. For a rotating object, the fixed axis is called the axis of rotation. Every point on the body will move in a circle that has this axis as its center, and every point will move through the same angle over the same interval of time. Angles may be measured in one of three units: degrees, radians, or revolutions. A full rotation is equal to 360 degrees, 2π radians, or 1 revolution. On a circle, one radian is the angle that measures an arc length equal to the radius of the circle. Since a circle's circumference is 2π times the radius, one full rotation is equal to 2π radians.

Angular motion has many correlations to linear motion. For an angle of rotation, θ, the linear distance traveled is $x = r\theta$. For angular velocity, ω, the linear velocity is $v = r\omega$. For angular acceleration, α, the linear acceleration is $a = r\alpha$. When discussing angular motion in this way, the angular unit is always radians.

ROTATIONAL MOTION

Newton's second law, commonly stated as $F = ma$, is applied to rotational motion by the equation $\tau = I\alpha$. That is, the **torque** is equal to the moment of inertia times the angular acceleration. Torque is calculated as the magnitude of an applied force times its perpendicular distance from the body's center of mass. A body's **moment of inertia** depends on both its mass and its configuration. Each particle in a body contributes a moment of $I = mr^2$, where m is the particle's mass and r is its distance from the center of mass. Thus, for a thin ring or a thin hollow sphere, the moment for the body is $I = mr^2$. Some other commonly encountered shapes are spheres ($I = (2/5)mr^2$) and disks ($I = (1/2)mr^2$). A closely related property of these shapes is the **radius of gyration**, k. This quantity is the average distance of mass from the center. It can be found by the equation $k = \sqrt{I/m}$. Similarly, the moment of inertia may be found as $I = mk^2$.

Another important corollary with linear motion is momentum. An object's angular momentum may be calculated as $L = I\omega$. All the same conservation rules for linear momentum apply to angular momentum as well. Additionally, there is a kinetic energy associated with rotational motion. It is calculated as $KE_r = I\omega^2/2$. When calculating kinetic energy for an object that is in both linear and angular motion, the total kinetic energy is the sum of the translational and rotational kinetic energy, $KE = mv^2/2 + I\omega^2/2$.

APPLYING CONSERVATION OF ENERGY AND MOMENTUM

A metal hoop of mass m and radius r is released from rest at the top of a hill of height h. Assuming that it rolls without sliding and does not lose energy to friction or drag, what will be the hoop's angular and linear velocities upon reaching the bottom of the hill?

The hoop's initial energy is all potential energy, $PE = mgh$. As the hoop rolls down, all of its energy is converted to translational and rotational kinetic energy. Thus, $mgh = \frac{mv^2}{2} + \frac{I\omega^2}{2}$. Since the moment for a hoop is $I = mr^2$, and $\omega = \frac{v}{r}$, the equation may be rewritten as $mgh = \frac{mv_2}{2} + \frac{mr^2}{2}\left(\frac{v^2}{r^2}\right)$, which further simplifies to $mgh = mv^2$. Thus, the resulting velocity of the hoop is $v_f = \sqrt{gh}$, with an angular velocity of $\omega_f = \frac{v_f}{r}$. Note that if you were to forget about the energy converted to rotational motion, you would calculate a final velocity of $v_f = \sqrt{2gh}$, which is the impact velocity of an object dropped from height h.

Consider a planet orbiting the sun through an elliptical orbit with small radius r_S and large radius r_L. Find the angular velocity of the planet when it is at distance r_S from the sun if its velocity at r_L is ω_L.

Since the size of a planet is almost insignificant compared to the interplanetary distances, the planet may be treated as a single particle of mass m, giving it a moment about the sun of $I = mr^2$. Since the gravitational force is incapable of exerting a net torque on an object, we can assume that the planet's angular momentum about the sun is a constant. Thus, $m(r_L)^2\,\omega_L = m(r_S)^2\omega_S$. Solving this equation for ω_S yields $\omega_S = \omega_L\left(\frac{r_L}{r_S}\right)^2$.

PERIODIC MOTION

AMPLITUDE, FREQUENCY, PHASE

The frequency, f, is the number of waves that pass a point per unit of time. The wavelength, λ, is the length of one wave. The speed, v, is, of course, how fast the wave is moving. (This does not refer to how fast the particles of the medium are moving, which may be very different; v is the speed of the wave itself.) To see how these quantities are related, consider this: the reciprocal of the frequency is the period, T, the amount of time it takes one wave to pass a given point. By definition, then, because exactly one wave passes in one period, the distance that the wave travels in one period is its wavelength. Because speed is distance over time, the speed of the wave must therefore be equal to $v = \frac{\lambda}{T}$. And because $T = 1/f$, this reduces to $v = \frac{\lambda}{1/f} = f\lambda$: the speed of the wave is equal to its frequency times its wavelength.

The phase of a wave is its shift along its own direction of propagation, or where in the cycle the wave starts. Two waves with the same frequency and wavelength have different phases if they start at different parts of the wave's cycle, as in these examples:

The phase is usually given as an angle, where one full wave corresponds to an angle of 360° or 2π radians. The difference in phase between two waves is called the phase shift. Two waves with a phase shift of zero are said to be in phase. Two waves with a phase shift of 180° or π radians are maximally out of phase. In the previous diagram, the lower wave is shifted left by about a quarter cycle relative to the upper wave, so it has a phase shift of $-\frac{360°}{4} = -90°$ or $-\frac{\pi}{2}$ radians.

Roughly speaking, the amplitude of a wave is a measurement of how "big" the wave is—not in the sense of the wavelength but in the sense of how much the medium moves to create the wave. More specifically, for a transverse wave, the amplitude is the difference between the maximum displacement and the equilibrium position—between the crest of a wave and its center line. The amplitude in this case is measured in units of distance. For a longitudinal wave, the amplitude is often measured not in units of distance but in units of pressure and represents the difference in pressure between the regions of maximum compression or rarefaction and the equilibrium pressure.

The amplitude of a wave can be easily determined from a graph of displacement versus time (or pressure vs. time, in the case of a longitudinal wave): it is the vertical distance between the crest of the wave and its center, or half the distance between the crest and the trough. For example, the wave graphed here would have an amplitude of 10 centimeters:

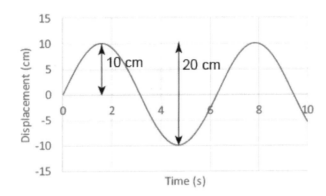

The frequency of a wave, abbreviated f, is the number of waves that pass a point per unit time. The standard metric unit of frequency is the Hertz, abbreviated Hz, named after the nineteenth-century German physicist Heinrich Rudolph Hertz, best known for proving the existence of electromagnetic waves. One Hertz is simply equal to one inverse second: that is, $1 \text{ Hz} = 1 \text{ s}^{-1}$.

The period of a wave, abbreviated T, is the time it takes for a wave to pass a particular point, or equivalently, the time for a wave to complete one full cycle. Because the period is just a time, it is measured in seconds. There is a simple reciprocal relationship between the period and the frequency: $T = \frac{1}{f}$.

TRANSVERSE AND LONGITUDINAL WAVES

A transverse wave is a wave in which the displacement of the medium (the object or substance the wave is traveling through) is perpendicular to the velocity of the wave itself. For example, if the wave is traveling left to right, the displacement of the medium occurs either up and down or forward and backward (or at some angle between the two). A wave on a string is a transverse wave; the wave travels along the string, but the points on the string itself oscillate perpendicular to the string. Electromagnetic waves are also transverse waves, though the vibration is of the intangible electric and magnetic fields and can't be perceived directly.

A longitudinal wave is a wave in which the displacement of the medium is along the same axis as the wave itself. They are also called compression waves because they involve an alternating compression and rarefaction of the medium. Sound waves are perhaps the most common example of compression waves.

It is not hard to produce both kinds of wave in a slinky: transverse waves by moving an end of the slinky side to side, longitudinal by moving it forward and backward. Earthquakes also combine transverse and longitudinal waves.

Electricity and Circuits

ELECTROSTATICS
CHARGE, CONDUCTORS, CHARGE CONSERVATION, INSULATORS

To say that charge is conserved means that the total charge in a closed system does not change. Charge may be transferred from one object to another, but the total must remain the same. If a system is initially electrically neutral, for instance, one part of the system cannot become positively charged without another part becoming negatively charged.

Charge conservation is important because it allows prediction of unknown charges. If an object initially has a charge of 2 C, and after touching another (initially neutral) object it has a charge of 3 C, the other object must have acquired a charge of –1 C for the total charge to remain the same. Charge conservation also places restrictions on possible events; it is because of charge conservation, for instance, that we know that the total current flowing into a point in a circuit must be equal to the total current out because otherwise a charge would be building up at that point.

An electrical conductor is a substance that conducts electricity—that is, a substance through which electrical charge is able to freely flow. Electrical conductors tend to have loosely bound electrons, or free ions. For instance, metals are good conductors because they share their electrons in such a way that it is easy for electrons to move between atoms; solutions of ionic compounds such as saltwater are also good conductors because the positive and negative dissolved ions are themselves free to move through the solution.

An electrical insulator is a substance that does not conduct electricity; an electrical charge does not easily flow through it. Rubber is known as a good insulator; other insulating materials include glass, asbestos, and PVC.

Whether a material is a conductor or an insulator is not an all-or-nothing affair; there are no perfect insulators, and the only perfect conductors are special superconductor materials that only hold that property under certain circumstances (most notably, all known superconductors require very low temperatures). Therefore, when we call a material a conductor or an insulator, these are relative terms, and there are some materials—semiconductors—that lie right in between and can't easily be classified as one or the other.

COULOMB'S LAW

Coulomb's Law is an equation giving the electric force between two charged particles: $F = \frac{kq_1q_2}{r^2}$, where q_1 and q_2 are the magnitudes of the charges, r is the distance between them, and k is Coulomb's constant, equal to about 8.99×10^9 (N m^2)/C^2. The direction of the force on either particle is directly toward the other particle if their charges have opposite signs or directly away from the other particle if the charges have the same sign. Like the coulomb, the SI unit of charge, Coulomb's Law is named after the French physicist Charles-Augustin de Coulomb.

For example, the charge on an electron is about -1.602×10^{-19} C. Suppose we have two electrons separated by the diameter of a hydrogen atom, about 5×10^{-11} m. The electric force these atoms exert on each other would then be $\frac{(8.99\times10^9 \text{ N m}^2/\text{C}^2)(1.602\times10^{-19}\text{C})^2}{(5\times10^{-11}\text{m})^2}$ = about 9×10^{-8} N. Because the electrons are both negatively charged, the force on each electron would be directed away from the other.

ELECTRIC FIELD
FIELD LINES

The electric field lines are lines that trace the direction of the electric field in space. Although the exact places the lines are drawn are arbitrary, the direction of the electric field lines represents the direction of the electric field, and the density of the electric field lines represents its magnitude.

The equipotential lines are lines that connect points in space with the same electrical potential in much the same way that the lines in a topological map connect points of equal altitude.

The most salient relationship between the electric field lines and the equipotential lines are that they are always perpendicular. This stands to reason from the definition of electrical potential: the electrical potential is the amount of work done in moving a unit charge from one point to another. The electrical force is in the same direction as the electric field and does work on the charge in that direction. Therefore, if there were any component of the electric field parallel to the equipotential line, there would be work done on the charge in that direction, which means there would be a difference in potential, which contradicts the definition of the equipotential line.

The electric field at a given point in space is defined as the force that would be exerted on a positive unit charge at that point. Turning that around and solving for the force, the force on a unit charge at a particular point is equal to the field at that point times 1 C. Because the electric force is proportional to the charge, for a charge of a different magnitude we have to multiply by that charge instead of by 1 C, so in general the force on an arbitrary charged particle at a given point is equal to the field times that charge: $\vec{F} = q\vec{E}$. For instance, a 3.0 C charge in an electric field with a magnitude of 0.4 N/C would experience a force of $(3.0 \text{ C})(0.4 \text{ N/C}) = 1.2$ N. (Note that the force and the field are both vectors, whereas the charge is a scalar, so the force will simply be in the same direction as the field.)

FIELD DUE TO CHARGE DISTRIBUTION

The electric field lines point in the same direction as the electric force on a positive particle. Positively charged particles repel each other, so the electric force—and therefore the electric field—points directly away from a positively charged particle. A negatively charged particle attracts a positively charged particle, so the electric field points toward a negatively charged particle. So, the electric field lies near a positively charged particle point radially away from the particle, whereas the electric field lines near a negatively charged particle point radially toward the particle.

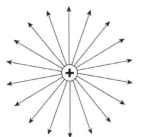 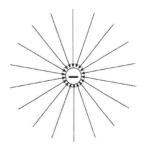

ELECTROSTATIC ENERGY, ELECTRIC POTENTIAL AT A POINT IN SPACE

To find the electric field near a point charge Q, we can consider a hypothetical charge q at that point and use Coulomb's Law to determine the force on that charge: $F = \frac{kQq}{r^2}$. Because the field at a point is equal to the force on a charge at that point divided by the magnitude of the charge, we can find the field by dividing the force by q, giving $E = \frac{kQ}{r^2}$. This field points directly away from the point charge if it is positive or toward the point charge if it is negative.

In the case of a distribution of multiple point charges, we have to find the contribution to the electric field of each charge and then add those fields together. Because the electric field is a vector, we have to add the component fields as vectors, not just add their magnitudes. For example, the net electric field at a point directly between two equal charges is zero because the contributions from each charge are equal in magnitude but opposite in direction, so they cancel each other out.

UNITS OF ELECTRIC POTENTIAL AND ELECTRIC FIELD

We can determine the units of the electric potential by considering the relationship between electric potential and electric potential energy: $U_E = qV$, so $V = \frac{U_E}{q}$. Because the electric potential energy has units of joules and the charge has units of coulombs, the electric potential must have units of J/C. This unit—joules per coulomb—is also known as a volt, abbreviated V and named after the Italian physicist and chemist Alessandro Giuseppe Antonio Anastasio Volta.

As for the electric field, we can determine its units from the equation relating electric field to electric force: $\vec{F} = q\vec{E}$, so $\vec{E} = \frac{\vec{F}}{q}$. Because the force has units of newtons and the charge has units of coulombs, the units of electric field must therefore be N/C, or equivalently, V/m. (That these are equivalent is not immediately obvious but can be shown by expressing both in terms of the fundamental metric units.)

CIRCUIT ELEMENTS

CURRENT

Current is the rate of flow of charge past a given point. In other words, it is equal to the amount of charge that passes through a given point per unit of time.

The unit of current is the ampere, abbreviated A. The ampere is named after the French mathematician and physicist André-Marie Ampère, considered one of the pioneers of the study of electromagnetism. We can see what the ampere must be in terms of the fundamental units by considering its definition. Because current is the rate of flow of charge, the units of current must be units of charge divided by the units of time: coulombs per second. So, 1 A = 1 C/s. (The coulomb is itself a fundamental unit and cannot be broken down further.)

SIGN CONVENTIONS

The current is defined to be positive in the direction that positive charge is flowing. This may seem a little backward because in solid conductors what's actually moving is the electrons, which are negatively charged—so the direction of the current is in the opposite direction that the electrons are moving! However, the sign convention for the current was defined before it was understood exactly what particles were moving to cause the current.

The voltage is defined to have the same sign as the potential energy that a positively charged particle would have at that point. As with gravitational potential energy, however, it is really the difference in potential energies that matters, and where to set the zero is arbitrary; by convention, the potential energy of a particle is usually defined to be zero when it is infinitely far away from other charged particles.

ELECTROMOTIVE FORCE, VOLTAGE

Electromotive force is a bit of a misleading term because what it describes is not a force in the usual sense and not measured in newtons. Rather, it is a measurement of voltage but specifically the voltage produced by a source of electrical energy in a circuit. Electromotive force is often abbreviated to EMF, or simply to $\mathcal{E}$. (Note that this is always a script $\mathcal{E}$, not a block E; in electromagnetism, the symbol E conventionally refers to electric field.)

One common source of electromotive force is a battery, which uses its stored chemical energy to produce a potential difference across its terminals. Other possible sources of electromotive force include solar cells and electric generators.

The voltage, also known as electrical potential, is defined as the potential energy difference that a unit charge would experience between two points. Its units are equal to the units of energy divided by the units of charge, joules per coulomb, which—unsurprisingly—is equivalent to volts.

For example, if a 2 C charge had a potential energy of 30 J at one point and a potential energy of 20 J at another point, then the voltage between the two points is $\frac{30\,J-20\,J}{2\,C} = 5$ J/C, or 5 V.

Note that formally voltage is defined only in terms of the voltage difference between two points. In practice, however, it is common to designate one particular point as having a voltage of zero (e.g., the ground of a circuit) and to state the voltage difference between another point and this point as the voltage at the other point.

The voltage difference is defined as the difference in potential energy experienced by a unit charge as it travels between two points. A uniform electric field exerts a force on the charge of $F = qE$. From the equation for work done by a constant force, the work done by this force is equal to $F\,d\cos\theta = q\,E\,d\cos\theta$. The electrical force is a conservative force, so this work must be equal to the change in potential energy. The voltage difference is therefore equal to the potential energy divided by the charge, or $\Delta V = E\,d\cos\theta$, where d is the distance between the two points and θ is the angle between the electric field and a line drawn between the two points.

For example, consider two points 5.0 cm apart in an electric field with a magnitude of 0.20 N/C. If a line drawn between the points is parallel to the electric field, then the voltage difference between the points is $\Delta V = (0.20 \text{ N/C})(0.05 \text{ m})(\cos 0) = 0.01$ V. If, on the other hand, a line drawn between the points is perpendicular to the electric field, then the voltage difference is $\Delta V = (0.20 \text{ N/C})(0.05 \text{ m})(\cos 90°) = 0$—the two points are at the same voltage.

ELECTRICAL CIRCUIT GROUND

The ground in an electrical circuit is a part of the circuit that is connected to a large electrically neutral reservoir that can absorb or provide charge as needed without its own charge changing appreciably. This prevents the circuit from building up too much charge itself. If an excess negative charge builds up in the circuit, electrons flow to the ground; if an excess positive charge builds up, electrons flow from the ground into the circuit. In either case, the circuit itself remains neutral. A circuit or object connected to the ground is said to be grounded. Many electrical appliances are grounded when in use; in a standard three-prong plug, the third plug connects to the ground.

The ground gets its name from the fact that generally it is literally the ground; the ground wire connects ultimately to the Earth itself, which is certainly a very large neutral reservoir. Likewise, a person working on a sensitive electrical project who doesn't want to risk any buildup of static electricity can ground himself or herself by touching some conductive object that is in contact with the Earth, such as a metal faucet.

RESISTANCE

OHM'S LAW

Ohm's Law is an equation relating some of the most important properties of an electrical circuit. It is usually written in the form $V = IR$ or sometimes $\mathcal{E} = IR$ if the voltage is provided by a battery or other source of electromotive force. V (or $\mathcal{E}$) is the voltage, I is the current, and R is the resistance.

Ohm's Law can therefore be used to solve for any of these three quantities if given the other two. For instance, if 45 mA of current flow through a lightbulb attached to a 9 V battery, then the resistance of the lightbulb must be $R = \frac{V}{I} = \frac{9\,V}{0.045\,A} = 200\ \Omega$.

RESISTANCE

Electrical resistance is the tendency of a material to oppose the passage of current. The higher the resistance, the less current will be produced by application of a given voltage. Conductors have a low resistance; insulators have a high resistance.

The units of resistance are ohms, abbreviated by the upper-case Greek letter omega, Ω. The ohm is named after Georg Simon Ohm, the German mathematician and physicist credited with discovering the relationship between the voltage and current in a circuit. It is this relationship that shows how the ohm is related to other units: because $V = IR$, the units of resistance must be units of voltage over units of current, that is, volts over amperes. So $1\ \Omega = 1$ V/A or, put in terms of the fundamental metric units, $1\ (\mathrm{kg\ m^2})/(C^2 s)$.

RESISTORS IN SERIES AND PARALLEL

series   parallel

For resistors in series (joined linearly end to end so current must pass sequentially through each of them), the resistances simply add together: $R_{net} = R_1 + R_2 + \cdots$. For example, if you connect a 200 Ω and a 300 Ω resistor in series, their net resistance is 200 Ω + 300 Ω = 500 Ω.

For resistors in parallel (with each end of each resistor connected to the corresponding end of the others so that current may pass through any of the resistors), the reciprocals of the resistances add together: $R_{net} = \frac{1}{\frac{1}{R_1}+\frac{1}{R_2}+\cdots}$. For example, if you connect a 200 Ω and a 300 Ω resistor in parallel, the net resistance is $\frac{1}{\frac{1}{200\,\Omega}+\frac{1}{300\,\Omega}} = 120\ \Omega$.

Note that when the resistors are joined in series, the net resistance is greater than any of the individual resistances, whereas when they're connected in parallel, the net resistance is smaller than any of the individual resistances. This makes sense because for resistors in series, the current must flow through all of the resistors, meaning it is affected by each one, whereas for resistors in parallel, the current has more paths it can take and isn't wholly affected by any one resistor.

RESISTIVITY

Resistivity is the tendency of a particular material to prevent the flow of current through it. The higher the resistivity of a material, the more voltage it takes to produce a given current, all else being equal. The difference between resistivity and resistance is that the resistivity depends only on the material; an object's resistance also depends on its shape and dimensions. (Technically, resistivity may also be affected by temperature, but it is independent of the material's shape and size.) Specifically, for a wire or other cylindrical (or prism-shaped) object, $R = \frac{\rho L}{A}$, where R is the object's resistance, ρ is its resistivity, L is its length, and A its cross-sectional area. We can also use this equation to figure out the units of resistivity: for the units on both sides of this equation to match, resistivity must have units of $\Omega \times$ m, or ohms times meters.

CAPACITANCE

Capacitance is the ability of an object to store electrical charge. Although almost any object can store some charge and technically has a nonzero capacitance, the term is typically used mostly in relation to circuit elements called capacitors, which are specially designed for this purpose. In the case of parallel-plate capacitors, it is used not for the total charge of both plates (which remains zero) but for the charge stored by each plate of a capacitor, in which case it is technically called mutual capacitance. The units of capacitance are farads, abbreviated F, and named after Michael Faraday, an English physicist and chemist who was responsible for many fundamental discoveries regarding electromagnetism.

As capacitance can be thought of as the ratio of the charge of an object to the voltage across it, the units of capacitance are equal to the units of charge over the units of voltage: 1 F = 1 C/V. In terms of the fundamental metric units, $1 \text{ F} = 1 \ (s^2 C^2)/m^2 kg$. Compared to the capacitances of the capacitors traditionally used in circuits, the farad is a very large unit, and in practice capacitances have been usually stated in millifarads, microfarads, nanofarads, or even picofarads.

PARALLEL PLATE CAPACITOR

One way to conceive of capacitance is as the amount of charge that can be induced in an object by a unit voltage. This definition leads directly to the equation relating charge to voltage in a capacitor: $Q = CV$, where Q is the charge, C is the capacitance (the ability of the particular capacitor or object to store charge), and V is the voltage. This means that for a given capacitor, the charge is directly proportional to the voltage across the capacitor. Of course, this only holds as long as the voltage is not too large; if the voltage exceeds a quantity known as the breakdown voltage of the material, the proportional relationship no longer applies.

For instance, if a 2.0 µF parallel-plate capacitor has a charge of 5 mC on each plate, then the voltage across the capacitor is $V = \frac{Q}{C} = \frac{5 \times 10^{-3} \text{C}}{2.0 \times 10^{-6} \text{ µF}} = 2{,}500$ V.

ENERGY OF CHARGED CAPACITOR

The energy stored in a charged capacitor is equal to $U = \frac{1}{2}\frac{Q^2}{C}$, where Q is the charge of the capacitor and C is the capacitance. The most straightforward way to derive this formula is through calculus, but it is possible to justify it without use of calculus, using the equation for the work done in moving a charge across a potential difference: $W = qV$. Because the voltage changes as the charge accumulates, we can't simply assume that the work is equal to the total charge Q times the voltage, but as the voltage changes linearly with the charge, we can use the average voltage. The initial voltage is zero, and the final voltage is $V = \frac{Q}{C}$, so the average voltage is $\frac{1}{2}\frac{Q}{C}$. The potential difference is then $Q\left(\frac{1}{2}\frac{Q}{C}\right) = \frac{1}{2}\frac{Q^2}{C}$.

The relationship among charge, voltage, and capacitance, $Q = CV$, can be used to rewrite the equation for the energy in several different ways: $U = \frac{1}{2}\frac{Q^2}{C} = \frac{1}{2}CV^2 = \frac{1}{2}QV$.

PARALLEL-PLATE CAPACITORS

In a parallel-plate capacitor, two conductive plates are separated by a thin layer of vacuum or polarizable insulating material (dielectric). The electric field within the capacitor depends on the charge on each capacitor and the area of the plates: for a capacitor where the plates are separated by a vacuum, it is equal to $E = \frac{Q}{\varepsilon_0 A}$, where Q is the charge on each plate, A is the area of the plates, and ε_0 is a constant called the permittivity of free space, equal to 8.854×10^{-12} F/m.

Knowing the electric field within the capacitor, we can use this to determine the capacitance. We know from the relationship between voltage and electric field that the voltage across the capacitor must be $V = Ed$, where d is the distance between the plates, and we know that for a capacitor $Q = CV$. So $C = \frac{Q}{V} = \frac{Q}{Ed} = \frac{Q}{\left(\frac{Q}{\varepsilon_0 A}\right)d} = \frac{\varepsilon_0 A}{d}$.

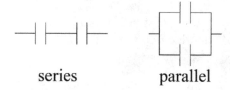

series   parallel

For capacitors in series (joined linearly end to end), the reciprocals of the capacitances add together: $C_{net} = \frac{1}{\frac{1}{C_1} + \frac{1}{C_2} + \cdots}$. For example, if you connect a 200 μF and a 300 μF capacitor in series, the net capacitance is $\frac{1}{\frac{1}{200 \text{ μF}} + \frac{1}{300 \text{ μF}}} = 120$ μF.

For capacitors in parallel (with each end of each the capacitor connected to the corresponding end of the others), capacitances simply add together: $C_{net} = C_1 + C_2 + \cdots$. For example, if you connect a 200 μF and a 300 μF capacitor in series, their net capacitance is 200 μF + 300 μF = 500 μF.

Note that this is reversed from how resistors join together: mathematically, capacitors in series work like resistors in parallel, and capacitors in parallel work like resistors in series.

DIELECTRICS

A dielectric is a polarizable insulating material that can be placed between the plates of a capacitor to increase its capacitance. In fact, although capacitors are often introduced by first discussing those with vacuums between the plates, in practice most real-world capacitors do include a dielectric, largely because keeping the plates of a capacitor separated with nothing between them but a vacuum is impractical.

Dielectrics are characterized by a quantity called the dielectric constant—sometimes also called the relative permittivity—that measures the strength of the dielectric: how much it affects the properties of the capacitor. The dielectric constant, commonly abbreviated k, is a unit-less value. The dielectric constant of vacuum is 1, that of air is very close to 1 (about 1.00059 at room temperature), but other materials may have dielectric constants in the thousands.

Because of the polarization of the dielectric, the effective electric field inside a capacitor with a dielectric is divided by the dielectric constant. It follows that the dielectric also affects the capacitance: $C = kC_0$, where C_0 would be the capacitance without the dielectric. For a parallel plate capacitor, $C = \frac{k\varepsilon_0 A}{d}$. The energy stored in the capacitor is likewise multiplied by the dielectric constant.

CONDUCTIVITY

METALLIC VS. ELECTROLYTIC CONDUCTIVITY

Metallic conductivity is conductivity due to the flow of electrons. It is so called because it is this process that leads to the conductivity of solid metals; the nuclei of the metal atoms stay in place, while electrons flow between them.

Electrolytic conductivity is conductivity due to the flow of ions. It is this that leads to the conductivity, for example, of saltwater; not just electrons but entire Na^+ and Cl^- ions (and H^+ and OH^- ions) flow through the solution.

Among the differences in the effects of these two kinds of conductivity, electrolytic conductivity leads to chemical change as different ions accumulate at the positive and negative terminals; there is no chemical change involved in metallic conductivity as the nuclei of the atoms remain in place. Furthermore, the conductivity of a metallic conductor tends to decrease with temperature, whereas the conductivity of an electrolytic conductor tends to increase with temperature.

METERS

There are a number of kinds of meters that can measure properties of electric circuits, but perhaps the most common are these:

- Voltmeters are used to measure the voltage across a circuit element or a part of the circuit. Voltmeters are always connected in parallel to the circuit element(s), the voltage of which they are measuring.
- Ammeters are used to measure the current through a particular part of the circuit. The ammeter must be connected in series; the circuit is broken and the ammeter inserted. An ammeter that works by generating a magnetic field in a coil is called a galvanometer.
- Ohmmeters measure the resistance of a circuit element; they are connected across individual elements or collections of elements when the circuit is disconnected and no current is flowing.

Now, instruments are common that depending on their settings, can work as voltmeters, ammeters, or ohmmeters; these versatile instruments are called multimeters.

Other less common types of meters include capacitance meters, which as their name implies measure the capacitance of a circuit element, and wattmeters, which measure electric power.

Waves: Sound and Light

SOUND

PRODUCTION OF SOUND

Sound is, in essence, a vibration in a medium that propagates through the medium as a compression wave. All that is necessary to produce a sound, therefore, is to produce a vibration in some medium. Sound can pass from one medium to another; so, for example, a sound wave in air could have originated from the vibration of a metal plate in contact with the air. In fact, often when we produce a sound, it isn't by generating a vibration in the air directly but by producing a vibration in some solid object, which vibration is then transmitted to the air.

For example, when the skin of a drum is hit, it vibrates, producing a characteristic sound. Plucking a string, or drawing a bow across it, causes the string to vibrate, which is the basis of the working of pianos and string instruments. We produce sound with our voices by blowing air across taut mucous membranes in our larynges called vocal cords. In a wind or brass instrument such as a flute or trumpet, the air is more or less set in motion directly, but the shape of the instrument affects how the waves interfere and build up.

RELATIVE SPEED OF SOUND IN SOLIDS, LIQUIDS, AND GASES

Sound is a compression wave that travels through a medium. It is transmitted through the medium as particles collide and interact. Therefore, the greater the forces between the particles, the more readily the disturbance will propagate through the medium, and the faster the wave will travel. In a solid, the atoms or molecules are subject to significant intermolecular forces, which is why a solid tends to hold its shape. In a liquid, the intermolecular forces are smaller than those in a solid, but they are still sufficient to cause the liquid to maintain its volume. In a gas, the intermolecular forces are very small, and the particles may be very far apart. Therefore, sound will tend to travel faster through solids than through liquids and faster through liquids than gases.

The speed of sound also depends on the density—all else being equal, the denser the material, the slower sound travels through it because it takes more energy to set the material in motion. In practice, however, this effect tends to be less significant than the effect of the intermolecular forces.

INTENSITY OF SOUND

The absolute intensity of a sound, abbreviated I, is the amount of power contained in the sound per unit area: $I = \frac{P}{A}$. This intensity is measured in watts per square meter. However, we don't really hear a sound with twice the intensity as twice as loud; the apparent volume of a sound, or intensity level, has a logarithmic relationship to the intensity. This intensity level is measured in a unit called decibels. The decibel, abbreviated dB, originated as one-tenth of a now rarely used unit called the bel, named after Scottish-American engineer and inventor Alexander Graham Bell, most famous for inventing, or at least being first to patent, the telephone.

The relationship between the intensity I and the intensity level L_I is $L_I = 10 \text{ dB} \log_{10} \frac{I}{I_0}$, where I is a reference intensity, conventionally 10^{-12} W/m^2 (approximately the lowest intensity of sound that the average human can hear). For instance, a sound with an absolute intensity of 0.5 W/m^2 would have an intensity level of $10 \text{ dB} \log \frac{0.5 \text{ W/m}^2}{10^{-12} \text{W/m}^2} = 10 \text{dB} \log(5 \times 10^{11} \text{W/m}^2) = 117 \text{ dB}$.

ATTENUATION (DAMPING)

A sound is attenuated, or damped, when there are dissipative forces that turn some of the energy of the wave into thermal energy. In a substance such as an ideal gas with no intermolecular forces, or with perfectly elastic intermolecular forces, no attenuation will occur, and the sound will propagate indefinitely at the same intensity. In reality, of course, no such perfect substances exist, and the internal forces between molecules will tend to dissipate some of the energy and cause the sound to be attenuated over time. (Even in a superfluid, an exotic liquid with zero viscosity, sound attenuation occurs due to interactions between pairs of particles.) Of course, it is possible to intentionally damp a sound by applying an external force—such as pressing down on a vibrating guitar string with a finger to stop its vibration.

The effect of attenuation is to decrease the sound's amplitude. Due to attenuation, a damped sound will gradually "die out" over time, its amplitude decreasing until it can no longer be detected. In most cases, the amplitude of the sound follows an exponential decay model.

DOPPLER EFFECT
MOVING SOUND SOURCE OR OBSERVER

If a source is emitting a sound as it moves toward an observer, the successive crests of the sound wave will reach the observer at a higher frequency than if the source were stationary because when the source emits each wave, it is slightly closer to the observer than it was when it emitted the last one, so each new wave has a shorter distance to travel. A careful consideration of the quantities involved shows that the apparent frequency of the sound to the observer is $f = \left(\frac{v}{v - v_s}\right) f_0$, where v is the velocity of sound in the medium, v_s the velocity of the source, and f_0 the frequency of the sound as it is emitted. By similar arguments if the source is moving away from the observer or the observer is moving toward or away from the source, ultimately, we get the general equation $f = \left(\frac{v + v_o}{v - v_s}\right) f_0$, where v_o is the velocity of the observer, and v_o and v_s are each considered positive if the source or observer is moving toward the other and negative if it is moving away.

In general, then, a sound seems higher pitched if the source is moving toward the observer, or vice versa, and lower-pitched if it is moving away.

REFLECTION OF SOUND FROM A MOVING OBJECT

If a sound is reflected off a moving object, its frequency appears to change—the frequency seems higher if the object is moving toward the source and lower if it is moving away. To see why this is the case, and to quantify it, we can consider two adjacent crests hitting a moving object. We'll call the speed of the object v_s and the speed of sound in the medium v. Suppose a crest of the sound wave emitted at time $t = 0$ hits the object when it is at a distance D_1 from the observer; this will occur at time $t_1 = \frac{D_1}{v}$. A second crest is emitted at time T_0, where T_0 is the period of the wave, and will hit the object at a distance D_2 from the observer at time $t_1 + \Delta t = T_0 + \frac{D_2}{v}$. Using the fact that $D_2 - D_1 = v_s \Delta t$, some algebraic manipulation yields $\Delta t = \frac{T_0}{1 - \frac{v_s}{v}}$. But the time for each reflected crest to return to the source is twice the time it takes to reach the object, so the apparent period $T = 2\Delta t = \frac{2T_0}{1 - \frac{v_s}{v}}$. The apparent frequency is then $f = \frac{1}{T} = \frac{1}{T_0}\left(1 - \frac{v_s}{v}\right) = f_0\left(1 - \frac{v_s}{v}\right)$, where v_s is positive if the source is moving away from the object and negative if it is moving toward it.

PITCH

The pitch of a sound is how high or low it seems to the ear. A siren has a very high pitch and a foghorn a very low pitch. The keys to the right on a piano produce higher-pitched sounds than the keys to the left.

The pitch of a sound depends on the frequency of the sound wave—the number of vibrations per second. The higher the frequency, the higher the pitch. The frequency of a wave can in turn be affected by other factors. For a wave in a string, for instance, all else being equal, the higher the tension in the string, the higher the frequency, and the heavier the string, the lower the frequency. (Technically, these factors directly affect the velocity of the wave in the string, but this has an indirect effect on the frequency.) This is why the lower-pitched strings of a string instrument are thicker than the higher-pitched strings and why the instrument can be tuned by altering the strings' tensions.

RESONANT FREQUENCY

The resonant frequencies on a string are frequencies at which the waves will constructively interfere and reinforce each other, leading to "standing waves" that have fixed positions of zero amplitude (nodes) and of maximum amplitude (antinodes). An important constraint on the resonant frequencies is that the ends of the string must be nodes because they are stationary. Because each full wave contains one node at each end and one in the middle, the only way for standing waves in the string to be possible is if the string contains an integral or half-integral number of wavelengths: $L = \frac{n\lambda}{2}$, where L is the length of the string, λ the wavelength of the waves, and n an arbitrary positive integer.

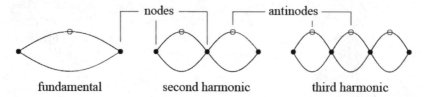

| | | |
| fundamental | second harmonic | third harmonic |

The frequency is related to the wavelength by the equation $v = f\lambda$. So $f = \frac{v}{\lambda} = \frac{v}{\frac{2L}{n}} = \frac{nv}{2L}$. This can be rewritten as $f = nf_0$, where f_0 is the lowest possible frequency, $f_0 = \frac{v}{2L}$. This lowest frequency is called the fundamental frequency, whereas higher resonant frequencies are called the harmonics.

We can even go a little further: the velocity of a wave in a string is $v = \sqrt{\frac{T}{\mu}}$, where T is the tension in the string and μ its mass per unit length, so $f_0 = \frac{1}{2L}\sqrt{\frac{T}{\mu}}$.

A standing wave in a pipe must have a node where the pipe's end is closed and an antinode where it is open. Therefore, a pipe with open ends must have an antinode on each end; a pipe with closed ends must have a node on each end; and a pipe with one open and one closed end must have a node on one end and an antinode on the other.

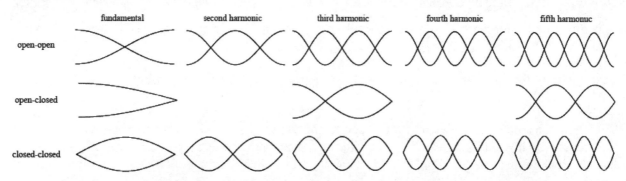

A pipe with open ends and a pipe with closed ends both must have a length that is an integral number of half-wavelengths: $L = \frac{n\lambda}{2}$, so $\lambda = \frac{2L}{n}$. For an open/closed pipe, there's a quarter wavelength between a node and an antinode, but because antinodes and nodes alternate, we have to have an odd number of quarter wavelengths. Thus, for this case $L = \frac{n\lambda}{4}$, or $\lambda = \frac{4L}{n}$, with the additional constraint that n must be odd.

Now, using $v = f\lambda$, we can find the frequency: $f = \frac{nv}{2L}$ for an open-open or open-closed pipe and for an open-closed pipe $f = \frac{nv}{4L}$, where n must be odd.

ULTRASOUND

Ultrasound is sound with a frequency too high for humans to hear. The typical range of human hearing is from about 20 Hz to 20,000 Hz, although the upper end of this range tends to decline with age. Ultrasound includes frequencies above 20,000 Hz.

Although it is inaudible, ultrasound has many applications. High-frequency sound waves can travel efficiently through solid and liquid matter, so ultrasound can be used to generate an image of the interior of an object—most famously, ultrasonic imagery can be used to "look at" fetuses still in the womb. Ultrasound is also useful for range finding; sonar works by sending out ultrasonic pulses, detecting their return, and using the time elapsed to determine how far they had traveled before encountering and reflecting off an object.

SHOCK WAVES

A shock wave is an abrupt pressure difference that propagates through a medium; it is similar to a single, very intense sound wave, although the sharp, almost discontinuous nature of the pressure change makes it qualitatively different from ordinary sound waves. A shock wave in air is heard as a loud cracking or booming sound.

A shock wave occurs whenever a disturbance in a fluid travels faster than the speed of sound in that fluid. Essentially, the particles of the medium can't "keep up" with the change, so instead of the gradual, continuous change in pressure that would normally occur, the pressure and other properties change nearly instantaneously. An object moving through the fluid faster than the speed of sound will disturb the fluid enough to produce a shock wave. This is why supersonic air craft produce "sonic booms"—the "boom" is the effect of a shock wave produced by the plane's supersonic disturbance of the medium. On a smaller scale, the crack of a whip is produced by the tip of the whip traveling at supersonic speeds and producing a similar sudden disturbance in the air.

LIGHT, ELECTROMAGNETIC RADIATION

ELECTROMAGNETIC RADIATION

The speed of propagation of electromagnetic radiation, otherwise known as the speed of light, abbreviated c, is about 3.00×10^8 m/s. More specifically, it is 299,792,458 m/s; this value is exact because the meter is currently defined as the distance traveled by light in 1/299,729,458 seconds.

Technically, this value is the speed of light in a vacuum. Under these circumstances, it is invariant; perhaps counterintuitively, the speed of light in a vacuum is always the same regardless of the relative motion of the source and observer. However, when passing through a medium, the speed of light is slower due to interaction between the light and the medium. The ratio of the speed of light in a vacuum to the speed of light in a transparent material is called that material's index of refraction, n. The index of refraction of air is very close to one; light travels at almost the same speed in air as in a vacuum. The index of refraction of water is about 1.33; light travels about three-quarters as fast in water as it does in a vacuum.

In electromagnetic radiation, the electric and magnetic fields and the direction of propagation are all mutually perpendicular. As the light wave moves, the electric and magnetic fields both oscillate perpendicular to the direction of propagation (as is usual for a transverse wave) as well as perpendicular to each other. This is true even for circularly polarized waves in which the field direction rotates; the electric and magnetic fields both rotate in the same direction at the same speed and maintain their perpendicularity.

We can be more specific about the relationship between these quantities. The magnitudes of the electric and magnetic fields in electromagnetic radiation are related by the equation $E = cB$, where c is the speed of light in a vacuum. The direction of propagation is the same direction as the vector $\vec{E} \times \vec{B}$, where "×" represents the vector cross product.

CLASSIFICATION OF ELECTROMAGNETIC SPECTRUM

Electromagnetic radiation comes in a broad range of wavelengths. Although the spectrum is continuous, different ranges have different effects on living things and the environment, so certain ranges of wavelengths and frequencies are given names. From longest to shortest wavelength (smallest to highest frequency), the conventional divisions include the following:

- Radio (roughly 100 cm to 100 km)—these waves can travel large distances and are useful for communication
- Microwave (10 mm to 100 cm)—aside from their use in microwave ovens, these can also be used for communication
- Infrared (700 nm to 1 mm)—objects at human body temperature radiate infrared light, which is why night vision goggles work
- Visible (400 to 700 nm)—this very small range of wavelengths comprises what we see as visible light; not coincidentally, the radiation from the sun peaks in this range
- Ultraviolet (10 nm to 400 nm)—ultraviolet light plays a part in the phenomenon of fluorescence as well as causing sunburn
- X-ray (10 pm to 10 nm)—these rays can penetrate many solid objects, which is why they are used in X-ray machines
- Gamma ray (less than 10 pm)—often produced in nuclear reactions, gamma rays can be very hazardous to living tissue

PHOTON ENERGY

The energy of a photon depends on its frequency. The exact equation that can be used to calculate the energy of a photon is $E = hf$, where h is a constant called Planck's constant, equal to 6.626×10^{-34} J × s. (Planck's constant, which also plays a large part in quantum mechanics, is named after the German physicist Max Karl Ernst Ludwig Planck, best known for the pioneering role he played in the development of quantum theory.) Sometimes the symbol v, the lowercase Greek letter nu, is used instead of f to stand for the frequency of light, and this equation is written $E = hv$.

Note that this equation implies that the higher the frequency of light, the greater the energy of the photons. This relationship is responsible for many of the different effects of different frequency ranges of light. X-rays can penetrate animal tissue because they have a very short wavelength and therefore a high frequency and consequently a high energy. Gamma rays have an even shorter wavelength and an even higher energy, which is what makes them dangerous; their energy is high enough to damage important molecules within cells, including DNA.

VISUAL SPECTRUM

The color of light depends on the wavelength of the electromagnetic radiation. Equivalently, it could be said to depend on the frequency because the two are related: in a vacuum, $f = c/\lambda$. (This follows from the general wave equation $v = f\lambda$, putting c in for v and solving for f.) Light near the low-wavelength end of the visible spectrum, 400 nm, appears violet. The colors then progress through blue, green, yellow, and orange, till reaching the high-wavelength end of the visible spectrum, about 700 nm, which appears red. Other colors not in this progression (such as reddish-purple, brown, or gray) do not correspond to individual wavelengths but to mixtures of colors.

Ultraviolet, the range of electromagnetic radiation with a wavelength slightly shorter than the visible range, gets its name from the fact that it has a frequency above ("ultra-") violet. Similarly, infrared, the range of electromagnetic radiation with a wavelength slightly longer than visible, has a frequency slightly below ("infra-") red.

WAVE INTERFERENCE

Wave interference occurs when two waves overlap and combine. Essentially, the displacements of two overlapping waves add together at each point. It can be classified into constructive interference, in which the combined wave is larger than either individual wave, and destructive interference, in which it is smaller. If two identical waves are perfectly in phase, they will constructively interfere into a wave twice as large; if they are perfectly out of phase, they will destructively interfere and completely cancel.

Wave interference is fundamental to the understanding of resonance and standing waves. The interference of light waves is responsible for the colors of bubbles and thin films of oil. Interference also has applications such as noise-cancelling headphones and interferometry, the use of interference between two beams of light following different paths to measure very small distances.

YOUNG DOUBLE-SLIT EXPERIMENT

Named after English physicist and physiologist Thomas Young (although others had done versions of the experiment earlier), the Young Double-Slit Experiment is an experiment in which, in its usual modern form, a coherent light source such as a laser beam is shined through two thin slits onto a screen some distance behind them. Rather than an image of the slits, what is produced on the screen is an interference pattern of dark and light bands, their spacing dependent on the wavelength of the light and on the distance between the slits. Specifically, for a distant screen, the bright bands appear at the positions $y_m = \frac{m\lambda L}{d}$, where λ is the wavelength, L the distance to the screen, d the distance between the slits, and m an arbitrary integer.

Young's purpose in performing a version of this experiment was to demonstrate the wave nature of light. Although the experiment is still considered a classic demonstration of this principle, later variations involving particles instead of waves suggested wave-particle duality and laid some of the foundation for the theory of quantum mechanics.

THIN FILMS, DIFFRACTION GRATING, SINGLE-SLIT DIFFRACTION

Light shined through a thin single slit onto a screen some distance behind it will form an interference pattern of bright and dark lines. The positions of the dark lines are given by the equation $y_m = \frac{m\lambda L}{a}$, where λ is the wavelength, L the distance to the screen, d the distance between the slits, and m a nonzero integer. This occurs because the slit, although thin, still has a finite width, and the light passing through some positions in the slit interferes with the light passing through others.

The single-slit diffraction equation is very similar to the equation for double-slit diffraction but differs in that whereas the single-slit equation shows the position of the dark lines, the double-slit diffraction equation gives the positions of the bright lines—as well as, of course, the constraint in the single-slit case that m cannot be zero. In practice, light shined through a double slit shows not a perfect single-slit pattern but the superimposed patterns from the single- and double-slit interference because single-slit interference occurs at each slit.

Ideal double-slit pattern:

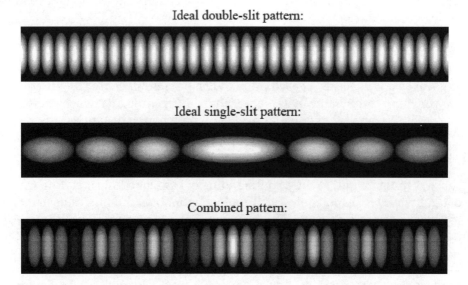

Ideal single-slit pattern:

Combined pattern:

Thin-film interference refers to the interference between light that reflects off the surface of a thin film of a transparent material and light that passes through the film and reflects off a surface behind it. Because the light that passed through the film has traveled a slightly larger distance, it will be slightly out of phase with the light that reflected from the surface of the film, which is what causes the interference. In terms of the thickness of the film t, the film's index of refraction n, the angle of incidence θ, and the wavelength of the light λ, the condition for constructive interference is either $2nt \cos \theta = m\lambda$ if the index of refraction of the film is greater than the index of refraction behind it (like an anti-reflective coating or a soap film on water) or $2nt \cos \theta = \left(m - \frac{1}{2}\right)\lambda$ if the index of refraction of the film is less than the index of refraction behind it (like a soap bubble in air or an oil film on water). In these equations, m is an arbitrary positive integer. The difference in the equations arises because the light reflecting off a material with a greater index of refraction undergoes a 180° phase change.

OTHER DIFFRACTION PHENOMENA

A diffraction grating is an instrument consisting of an opaque plate with a number of very thin open or transparent slits or grooves, evenly and closely spaced. Typical diffraction gratings used in labs may have hundreds or thousands of slits per millimeter.

Diffraction gratings produce diffraction patterns like double slits, but the large number of slits allows the patterns to be brighter and more easily measurable. The spacing of the bright lines on the diffraction pattern follows the same relationship as for the double slit: $m\lambda = d \sin \theta$, where d is the spacing of the grating, λ is the wavelength of the light, θ is the angle at which the light is deflected from the slit to the position on the screen, and m is an arbitrary integer. When the distance L of the grating to the screen or detector is very large compared to d, this can be rewritten as $y_m = \frac{m\lambda L}{d}$, where y_m is the distance from the center of the diffraction pattern to the mth bright line on that side.

Because diffraction gratings diffract different wavelengths to different positions, they are useful for separating wavelengths of light and for finding what wavelengths of light are present in a source.

POLARIZATION OF LIGHT

Light waves are transverse waves, and as such the oscillation of the electromagnetic fields in a light wave occurs in some particular direction perpendicular to the direction of propagation. In an ordinary beam of light, the directions of oscillation of different waves that make up the beam are randomly distributed; there are likely to be just as many waves oscillating in one direction as another. Light is said to be polarized if the directions of oscillation of the waves match up with each other if all the waves are oscillating in the same direction.

Although our eyes can't easily detect a difference between polarized and non-polarized light (although this isn't true of the eyes of bees and some other animals), it is possible to make filters that only let through light oscillating in a particular direction. Light reflecting in certain ways off flat surfaces is naturally polarized, such as the glare off of water or concrete. Polarized sunglasses eliminate the glare by filtering out the light polarized parallel to the ground. Polarization also is commonly used in 3-D movies; the light intended for the left and right eye is polarized in perpendicular directions and filtered accordingly by the 3-D glasses.

LINEAR VS. CIRCULAR POLARIZATION

Most of the time, when one speaks of polarization of light, it refers to linear polarization. Light, as a transverse wave, oscillates in a direction perpendicular to the direction of propagation; if all the light waves from a source oscillate in the same direction, the light is linearly polarized.

However, what is oscillating in light is the electromagnetic fields, and waves in these behave a little differently than, say, waves in a string. Instead of just oscillating in a constant direction, it is possible for the oscillations in a light wave to rotate over time. (This can be conceived of as two superimposed linear oscillations equal in magnitude but in perpendicular directions and 90° out of phase.) If all the light waves from a particular source are rotating in the same direction, then the light is said to be circularly polarized. There is also an intermediate case (similarly corresponding to two superimposed linear oscillations but with a phase shift less than 90°) called elliptical polarization.

GEOMETRICAL OPTICS

REFLECTION FROM PLANE SURFACE

Total internal reflection occurs when light hitting a boundary between transparent materials at a sufficiently large angle of incidence completely reflects off the boundary rather than being partially reflected and partially transmitted. Total internal reflection is the principle behind fiberoptics; the light hits the side of the optical fiber at a large enough angle to be reflected down the fiber rather than leaking out of the fiber and being lost. Some reflectors in streets also work by this principle.

Total internal reflection occurs when Snell's Law cannot otherwise be satisfied. By Snell's Law, $\sin \theta_r = \frac{n_i \sin \theta_i}{n_r}$. Because the sine of an angle cannot be greater than one, this suggests that refraction cannot occur when $\frac{n_i \sin \theta_i}{n_r} > 1$, that is, when $\sin \theta_i > \frac{n_r}{n_i}$. It is worth noting that this shows that total internal reflection can occur only when passing from a material of higher index of refraction into lower, never the reverse.

ANGLE OF INCIDENCE AND ANGLE OF REFLECTION

The relationship between the angle of incidence and the angle of reflection from a smooth surface is very simple: the angle of incidence equals the angle of refraction. Although this relationship may seem trivial, it can be useful; knowing that the angle of reflection equals the angle of refraction allows the use of ray tracing to locate the images formed by a mirror and even allows the treatment of more complicated scenarios such as reflections in curved mirrors, concave or convex.

For example, one can apply this principle to show that a mirror must be at least half a person's height for the person to see his or her whole body in it. Light rays from the top of the person's head reflect off the mirror to enter the person's eye, and because of the equal angles, the vertical distances from the top of the head to the point the light hits the mirror and from that point to eye level must be equal, and the top of the mirror must be halfway between the person's eye level and the top of the person's head. The same argument applies to the light from the bottom of the person's feet.

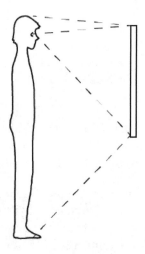

REFRACTION

REFRACTIVE INDEX

Although the index of refraction of a material is often given as a single number, it actually has some dependence on wavelength as well. For example, the index of refraction of pure water at room temperature is generally given as 1.33, but it actually varies from about 1.342 for 400 nm to 1.330 at 700 nm.

As this example shows, the dependence of index of refraction on wavelength is not necessarily large, but it still can have notable effects. It is because of this, for instance, that a prism splits white light into a spectrum because each wavelength is refracted a slightly different amount. The same phenomenon leads to rainbows, with tiny drops of water each acting like miniature prisms.

SNELL'S LAW

Snell's Law relates the amount that light is refracted (bent) on passing through the interface between two different materials to the respective indices of refraction of the materials. If the index of refraction of the material in which the light begins is n_i, that of the material in which the light ends up is n_r, and the angles of incidence and refraction are θ_i and θ_r respectively, then Snell's Law states that $n_i \sin \theta_i = n_r \sin \theta_r$.

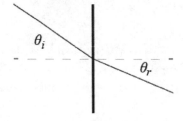

Snell's Law follows from the definition of the index of refraction as the ratio of the speed of light in a vacuum to its speed in the material. Because the frequency of the light does not change as it passes into a different material, $v = f\lambda$ implies that the wavelength must change proportionately to the speed, and it is possible (although nontrivial) to show geometrically that for the wavefronts to be continuous at the boundary, Snell's Law must hold.

Snell's Law can be used to determine an unknown index of refraction; by measuring the angles of incidence and refraction when light passes between two materials, one of which has a known index of refraction, the unknown n of the other material can be calculated.

REAL AND VIRTUAL IMAGES

Real and virtual describe two kinds of images that can be formed by lenses or curved mirrors. A real image is an image that is formed where the reflected or refracted light rays actually converge. A virtual image is formed when the reflected or refracted rays diverge, but tracing their paths back reaches a point on the other side of the lens or mirror that they seem to be diverging from; this point is the location of the virtual image.

For an image formed by a single lens, a real image is always inverted (upside-down) and on the opposite side of the lens from the object, whereas a virtual image is always upright and on the same side of the lens as the object. For an image formed by a curved mirror, a real image is always inverted and on the same side of the mirror as the object, whereas a virtual image is upright and on the opposite side of the mirror (seeming to be behind the mirror).

SPHERICAL MIRRORS

The focal length of a spherical mirror is approximately half the radius of the mirror (i.e., the radius of the spherical surface of which the mirror is a section). This is true for both convex and concave mirrors, but the focal point will be in a different place. For a convex mirror, the focal point will be one focal length in front of the mirror (and for the purposes of the thin lens equation, the focal length can be regarded as positive). For a concave mirror, the focal point will be one focal length behind the mirror (and for the purposes of the thin lens equation, the focal length can be regarded as negative).

LENSES

CONVERGING AND DIVERGING LENSES

Applied to a lens, the words "converging" and "diverging" refer to the effect of the lens on parallel, incident light rays. In the case of a **converging lens**, these rays will converge on the opposite side of the lens. In the case of a **diverging lens**, the rays will diverge. Generally, converging lenses are thicker in the middle than they are at the edges, whereas diverging lenses are thicker at the edges and thinner in the middle.

Converging and diverging lenses differ in the way they form images. A diverging lens always forms a virtual image, regardless of the location of the object. A converging lens, however, can form either a real or a virtual image, depending on whether the object is closer or farther away from the lens than one focal length.

When an optical system includes more than one lens, the effective focal length and magnification of the system can be determined by considering the lenses in the order that the light passes through them and taking the image from each lens as the object of the next.

For instance, suppose you have a converging lens with a focal length of 25 cm and a diverging lens of 40 cm. The lenses are 50 cm apart, and the object is 30 cm in front of the converging lens. We first apply the thin lens equation for the converging lens: $\frac{1}{30 \text{ cm}} = \frac{1}{25 \text{ cm}} + \frac{1}{d_i}$; solving for d_i yields an image position of 150 cm. Because the two lenses are 50 cm apart, an image 150 cm behind the converging lens is 100 cm behind the diverging lens, so now we apply the thin lens equation again for the second lens, with an object position of –100 cm. (A multiple-lens problem like this is the only time the object distance can be negative.) So $\frac{1}{-40 \text{ cm}} = \frac{1}{-100 \text{ cm}} + \frac{1}{d_i}$; $d_i = -31.0$ cm. The image is 31.0 cm behind the diverging lens.

For thin lenses in contact, the effective combined focal length satisfies the equation $\frac{1}{f_{eq}} = \frac{1}{f_1} + \frac{1}{f_2}$.

THIN LENS EQUATION

The **thin lens equation** relates the focal length f of a lens to the position of an object d_o and the position of the image of the object formed by the lens, d_i, where both d_o and d_i are measured from the center of the lens: $\frac{1}{f} = \frac{1}{d_o} + \frac{1}{d_i}$. (Other choices of symbol are common; instead of d_o and d_i, one often sees s_o and s_i or p and q.) Despite the name of this equation, it also works for curved, spherical mirrors.

By convention, f is positive for a converging lens (or mirror) and negative for a diverging lens (or mirror); d_i is positive for a real image (one formed where the light rays actually converge), and negative for a virtual image (one formed where the light rays only seem to converge as traced back through the lens or mirror). Note that for a lens, a real image is on the opposite side from the image, and a virtual image is on the same side. For a mirror these are reversed; d_o is always positive except in the special case of a "virtual object" that is the image from a previous lens in a multiple-lens system and that is on the far side of the lens in question.

LENS STRENGTH, DIOPTERS

A **diopter**, abbreviated D, is a unit used to measure the optical power of a lens (or a curved mirror)—a measurement of how much it bends the light passing through it and how markedly it causes the light to converge or diverge. As such, the optical power has an inverse relationship to the focal length: the longer the focal length, the lower the optical power, and the shorter the focal length, the higher the optical length. As a matter of fact, the optical power is just the reciprocal of the focal length, and one diopter is simply equal to one inverse meter: $1 \text{ D} = 1 \text{ m}^{-1}$. For example, a lens with a focal length of 20 cm has an optical power of $\frac{1}{0.20 \text{ m}} = 5.0 \text{ m}^{-1} = 5.0 \text{ D}$.

The diopter is not an official metric unit and is not commonly used by scientists but remains in use by optometrists and photographers.

LENS ABERRATION

Lens aberration is the tendency of lenses to not form perfect images. Although mathematically lenses are often treated as if they cause parallel rays to all converge to or diverge from a single point, in reality not all the parallel rays will meet at the same point. For the same reason, an image of an object in a single lens will not necessarily be perfectly clear and focused.

There are two main causes of lens aberration: spherical aberration and chromatic aberration. Spherical aberration occurs simply because a spherical lens does not form a perfect focus. It can be avoided by using lenses of other shapes; a parabolic lens, for instance, actually will focus parallel rays at a single point. Chromatic aberration occurs because the index of refraction is different for different wavelengths, so if the lens is perfectly focused for one wavelength, it can't be perfectly focused for others. Chromatic aberration can't be eliminated by using a lens of a different shape, but it is possible to arrange a system of a converging and diverging lenses so that their chromatic aberrations more or less cancel out.

<u>FINDING AN IMAGE OF AN OBJECT BY RAY TRACING</u>

The image of an object can be found by choosing a point on the object and tracing three principle rays from it. Where these rays intersect—or, in the case of a virtual image, where the rays would intersect if traced back—is the location of the image. Technically, only two of the rays are sufficient to locate the object, but the third acts as a useful check.

The general principles of ray tracing work the same for any lens or mirror, but there are slight differences depending on whether it is a lens or mirror and whether it is converging or diverging. For a **convex lens**, these rays are the following:

- One ray that passes through the center of the lens and continues straight
- One ray that begins parallel to the optical axis (the line perpendicular through the center of the lens) and then refracts directly toward the focus on the other side
- One ray that begins by passing through the focus on the near side and then reflects or refracts parallel to the optical axis.

Depending on the position of the object, this can result in either a real or a virtual image:

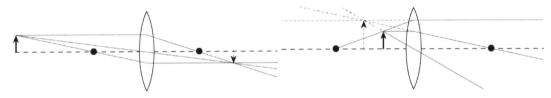

For a **concave lens**, these rays are:

- One ray that passes through the center of the lens and continues straight
- One ray that begins parallel to the optical axis (the line perpendicular through the center of the lens) and then refracts directly away from the focus on the near side
- One ray that begins by going toward the focus on the far side and then refracts parallel to the optical axis.

For a concave lens, this always results in a virtual image.

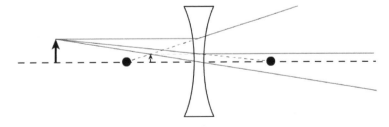

For a **spherical mirror**, these rays include the following:

- One ray that passes through the center of the mirror and reflects at the same angle
- One ray that begins parallel to the optical axis (the line perpendicular through the center of the mirror) and then reflects directly toward (convex) or away from (concave) the focus
- One ray that begins by going toward (convex) or through (concave) the focus and then reflects parallel to the optical axis.

For a **convex mirror**, this always results in a virtual image.

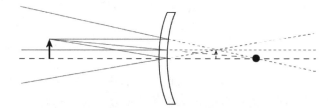

For a **concave mirror**, it can result in either a real or a virtual image.

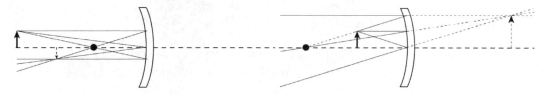

MAGNIFICATION

The magnification of an image is the ratio of the size of the image to the size of the object. The sign of the magnification is positive for an upright image and negative for an inverted image.

The magnification can be found by the same ray tracing techniques that are used to find the image position; the sizes of the object and the ray-traced image can be measured and their ratio calculated. The magnification can also be found more accurately from the equation $\frac{s_i}{s_o} = -\frac{d_i}{d_o}$, where s_i and s_o are the sizes of the image and object, respectively, and d_i and d_o their distance from the lens or mirror. The ratio on the left, $\frac{s_i}{s_o}$, is equal to the magnification. This means that the magnification is the same as the ratio of the image distance to the object distance but with the sign flipped. For example, if when an object is placed 20 cm in front of a given lens a real image is produced 50 cm behind it, then $\frac{s_i}{s_o} = -\frac{50 \text{ cm}}{20 \text{ cm}} = -2.5$: the image will be inverted and 2.5 times the size of the object. If the object is 4.0 cm tall, the image height will be $(-2.5)(4.0 \text{ cm}) = 10.0 \text{ cm}$.

OPTICAL INSTRUMENTS

As an optical instrument, the human eye focuses images on the retina, where they can be sensed by the rods and cones and the information transmitted to the brain. The specific part primarily responsible for the focusing is the lens, which sits in the front of the eye and acts as exactly that. Because the distance of the lens to the object depends on the distance of the lens to the image, the lens must adjust its focal length to the distance of the object; this is why your eye refocuses depending on the distance of the object you're looking at and why you won't see a distant object and a close-up object in focus at the same time. (The cornea in front of the lens also helps focus light on the retina, but unlike the lens its focal length is not adjustable.)

Some eyes are incapable of focusing the full necessary range, which leads to certain optical disorders. If the eye cannot focus properly on distant objects, then the eye is said to be nearsighted; if the eye cannot focus properly on close-up objects, the eye is said to be farsighted. Both conditions are treatable with corrective lenses.

A compound microscope, which includes most of the optical microscopes used in labs and classrooms, contains two convex lenses, an eyepiece and an objective lens. (This is something of a simplification because the eyepiece and the objective lens each often consist of multiple lenses, and there may be additional components such as mirrors to direct the light, but the basic working of the microscope can be explained in terms of these two lenses.) The object to be viewed is placed very close to the focal point of the objective lens, which then produces a virtual image at the focal point of the eyepiece; this virtual image then acts as the object of the eyepiece, which forms an image that the eye sees as infinitely far away.

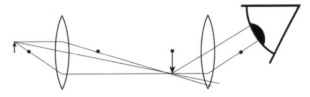

A microscope with an eyepiece of focal length f_e, an objective lens of focal length f_o, and a distance L between the two lenses is capable of magnifying an image by a factor of $M = -\frac{(25 \text{ cm})L}{f_o f_e}$. (The 25 cm comes about from the near point of the average human eye.)

A telescope is used to increase the apparent size of very distant objects. Simple refracting telescopes do this with a pair of convex lenses, an eyepiece and an objective lens. The two lenses are placed a distance apart equal to the sum of their focal lengths. The light rays from the distant object are nearly parallel, which means that as they pass through the objective lens, they are focused at its focal point. The eyepiece, which has a shorter focal length, then forms a magnified image at infinity. If the telescope's objective lens has a focal length of f_o and the eyepiece of f_e, then the magnification of the telescope as a whole is just $M = -\frac{f_o}{f_e}$.

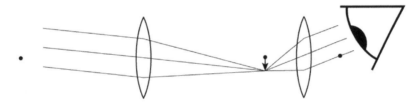

In practice, the largest telescopes in use today are not refracting telescopes but reflecting telescopes, which rely not just on lenses but on converging mirrors. The primary reason for this is because larger objective lenses are better for gathering light, but there is a limit on how large a high-quality lens can be made; large mirrors are much more practical.

Static Fluids

FLUIDS

It sounds obvious, perhaps, but fluids can best be defined as substances that flow. A fluid will conform, slowly or quickly, to any container in which it is placed. This is because a fluid is unable to maintain a force tangential to its surface. In other words, fluids cannot withstand shearing stress. They can, on the other hand, exert a force perpendicular to their surface. Both liquids and gases are considered to be fluids. Fluids, essentially, are those substances in which the atoms are not arranged in any permanent, rigid way. In ice, for instance, molecules are all lined up in a crystalline lattice, while in water and steam the only intermolecular arrangements are haphazard connections between neighboring molecules.

DENSITY, SPECIFIC GRAVITY

The specific gravity of a fluid is the ratio of its density to the density of some reference substance—most commonly water for liquids or air for gases. (More specifically, it is water at the temperature at which it is densest (about 4°C) or air at room temperature (25°C).) Because specific gravity is a ratio between two quantities with the same units, the specific gravity itself is unit-less.

For instance, the density of mercury is about 13,500 kg/m³, whereas the density of water is 1,000 kg/m³. This means mercury is 13.5 times as dense as water, so the specific gravity of mercury is 13.5.

BUOYANCY

Any time that an object is immersed in a fluid, there is a buoyant force exerted on it that acts upward, against gravity. If the buoyant force is greater than the object's weight, the object floats; if less, the object sinks. If the buoyant force is equal to the object's weight, the object will neither float nor sink but remain at the same height within the fluid; in this case, the object is said to have neutral buoyancy.

The buoyant force results from the difference in pressure on the top and bottom of the object. Because the hydrostatic pressure increases with depth, the pressure on the bottom of the object is slightly more than the pressure on the top of the object. This in turn means that the force on the bottom of the object will be slightly greater than the force on the top of the object, which results in an upward net force.

An object can float in a less dense liquid provided that the object displaces a weight of water greater than its own weight—which requires it to displace a greater volume of water than its own volume. This is possible if the object has a cavity or depression in it that increases its fluid displacement; metal boats can float because they are hollow, whereas a solid block of metal would sink.

For instance, consider a hemispherical shell of lead, 1.000 meter in diameter and 1 millimeter thick. Lead is much denser than water: 22,600 kg/m³ as opposed to 1,000 kg/m³ for water. The volume of the lead shell would be $\frac{1}{2}4\pi[(0.500 \text{ m})^3 - (0.499 \text{ m})^3)] = 0.0047 \text{ m}^3$; its weight would be $(0.0047 \text{ m}^3)(22,600 \text{ kg/m}^3)(9.80 \text{ m/s}^2) = 1,040$ N. However, if it is placed in the water up to its rim, open side up, the volume of water it displaces is $\frac{1}{2}(4\pi(0.500 \text{ m})^3) = 0.196 \text{ m}^3$; the weight of water (and thus the buoyant force) is $(0.0196 \text{ m}^3)(1,000 \text{ kg/m}^3)(9.80 \text{ m/s}^2) = 1,920$ N. The buoyant force is greater than the weight of the lead shell, so the shell would float!

(Be careful not to confuse P and ρ—the symbols look similar but have very different meanings!)

HYDROSTATIC PRESSURE

The hydrostatic pressure within a fluid is the pressure exerted by a fluid at equilibrium. The hydrostatic pressure arises because of gravity; as gravity exerts a downward force on each part of the fluid, the fluid will therefore also exert a downward force on the fluid below it. This implies that the hydrostatic pressure increases with the depth in the fluid as there's more fluid above to press down.

To derive a formula for the hydrostatic pressure, consider a small cube of fluid a distance h below the surface, with an area of A on each face. Directly above the cube is a column of fluid with a height h and an area A, which means its volume is Ah. The mass of the column of fluid pressing down on the cube is the density times the volume, ρAh, and its weight—the force of gravity acting on the column—is its mass times gravity, ρAhg. The pressure on the small cube of fluid is the force exerted on its top surface divided by the area of that surface, $\frac{\rho Ahg}{A} = \rho gh$. So, the hydrostatic pressure at a depth h within a fluid is equal to ρgh.

UNITS OF PRESSURE

The units of pressure are pascals, abbreviated Pa, named after Blaise Pascal, a French mathematician and physicist also known for his contributions to the fields of probability theory and fluid flow. Because pressure is defined as force over area, the units of pressure must be equal to the units of force divided by the units of area: newtons divided by meters squared. So, $1 \text{ Pa} = 1 \text{ N/m}^2$. Because a newton is equal to a $(\text{kg m})/\text{s}^2$, this can be expressed in terms of fundamental units as $1 \text{ Pa} = 1 \text{ kg}/(\text{m} \times \text{s}^2)$, although it is rarely written this way.

ARCHIMEDES' PRINCIPLE

Archimedes' Principle states that the buoyant force on a body immersed in a fluid is equal to the weight of the fluid the body displaces. Equivalently, $B = \rho V g$, where B is the buoyant force, ρ is the density of the fluid, V is the volume of fluid displaced, and g is the acceleration of gravity.

This principle can be derived by considering a cube of side length s immersed at a depth h under the fluid. The hydrostatic pressure on the top of the cube is $\rho g h$, so the downward force is the pressure times area, $\rho g h s^2$. On the bottom of the cube, the pressure is $\rho g(h + s)$, and the upward force is $\rho g(h + s)s^2$. The net force is the difference between the two, which is $\rho g s^3 = \rho g V$. Although this was derived for the special case of a cube, it holds for objects of any shape.

For example, consider a sphere with a radius of 1.00 meter submerged in water. Its volume is $4\pi r^3 = 12.6 \text{ m}^3$, so the buoyant force on it is $\rho V g = \left(9.81 \frac{\text{m}}{\text{s}^2}\right)\left(1,000 \frac{\text{kg}}{\text{m}^3}\right)(12.6 \text{ m}^3) = 123 \text{ N}$. Note that the mass of the sphere is irrelevant—that affects the weight of the sphere but not the buoyant force on it.

SURFACE TENSION

Surface tension is the tendency of the surface of a liquid to "stick together," as if the liquid were enclosed in a thin film or membrane. It is a consequence of the attractive forces between molecules of the liquid: because the molecules of the liquid are more strongly attracted to each other than they are to the molecules of the air or other surrounding gas, the molecules at the surface of the liquid are subject to a net inward force. Because of the relatively strong hydrogen bonds between water molecules, water has a higher surface tension than most liquids.

It is because of surface tension that small quantities of water and other liquids tend to form into rounded droplets rather than spreading evenly over a surface. Surface tension also can be sufficient to support small objects that are too dense to float because of the buoyant force—it is possible, with care, to place a paper clip such that it floats on a glass of water. Some small animals, such as water striders, are able to walk on the surface of water due to surface tension.

PASCAL'S LAW

Pascal's Law states that a change in pressure exerted anywhere in an incompressible fluid in a closed container is propagated throughout the fluid. In other words, if the pressure of a fluid is increased at one point in the fluid, it increases everywhere in the fluid.

One of the best-known applications of Pascal's Law is hydraulics. Hydraulic brakes in a car, for instance, work because pushing down on the brake pedal exerts a pressure on the brake fluid below, and then that pressure is transmitted through the fluid to the brakes themselves, causing the brake pads to press against the rotor. A hydraulic lift works by a piston exerting a downward pressure on a fluid, and the pressure is then transmitted through the fluid to exert upward pressure elsewhere.

Thermodynamics

TEMPERATURE SCALES

Each of the temperature scales, Celsius and Fahrenheit, has a corresponding absolute temperature scale, Kelvin and Rankine, respectively. A temperature of zero Kelvin or zero Rankine is known as absolute zero, at which point there is theoretically no atomic motion or thermal energy. Kelvins and degrees Celsius are related by the equation, $T_{°C} = T_K - 273.15$. Similarly, Rankines and degrees Fahrenheit are related as $T_{°F} = T_R - 459.67$. From these relations, we can see that within both individual pairs of temperature scales, the magnitude of the unit is the same; that is, an increase of 1 °C is the same an increase of 1 K, while an increase of 1 °F equals an increase of 1 R. Converting from Fahrenheit to Celsius is slightly more complicated: $T_{°C} = \left(\frac{5}{9}\right)(T_{°F} - 32)$, or in reverse, $T_{°F} = \left(\frac{9}{5}\right)T_{°C} + 32$. From these equations, we can see that a degree Celsius is greater than a degree Fahrenheit.

HEAT AND TEMPERATURE

Heat, or thermal energy, is a measure of the kinetic energy of the atoms within a substance. Heat, being a form of energy, has SI units of joules, but is also commonly measured in calories. The amount of heat a substance contains is generally quantified as a **temperature**. Temperature has SI units of degrees Celsius, though degrees Fahrenheit are also widely used.

It is often useful to know how much heat is required to cause a certain amount of material to reach a desired temperature. Each material has a property called **specific heat**, which allows this calculation. To bring about a temperature increase ΔT to a mass m made of a material with specific heat C, the required heat input is found by the equation $Q = mC\Delta T$. This equation can also be used to calculate the amount of heat absorbed during a given temperature increase. The amount of heat required to raise the temperature of a gram of water by one degree Celsius, or one Kelvin, is one calorie, or 4.184 J. Thus, the specific heat of water is 1 cal/(g K).

LATENT HEAT AND SPECIFIC HEAT

Suppose we wish to convert ice initially at -5 °C to water at 5 °C. We must provide heat to accomplish this. The amount of heat required to raise the temperature of a given quantity of a material is a property known as specific heat. This is most often given on a mass basis, with units of J/(g K), but may also be given as a molar property as J/(mol K). If the given quantity of material and the given specific heat are not unit compatible, it will be necessary to multiply or divide by the molar weight of the material to achieve compatibility. Returning to the problem at hand, in order for ice initially at -5 °C to reach 5 °C, it must undergo a phase change, from a solid to a liquid. When the ice is heated, it does not simply become water when it reaches 0 °C. In order for the ice to become water, additional heat must be added to break the bonds of the solid. This heat is called the **latent heat of fusion** and, like the specific heat, may be given on a mass or a molar basis, with common units of kJ/g or kJ/mol, respectively. This heat input for the phase change occurs while the material remains at a constant temperature. Once the phase change has been completed, the water temperature will begin to rise again with heat input, though the specific heat of liquid water will be different from that of ice. If the water need be heated above 100 °C, it will have to undergo a second phase change, overcoming the **latent heat of vaporization**, and its temperature will subsequently be governed by a third specific heat, that of the gas phase.

THERMAL EXPANSION

When heated, most materials will undergo some amount of expansion. Though this is generally quite small, it is important to know how much of an impact this thermal expansion might have on the size of the object in question. Each material has a **linear coefficient of thermal expansion, α,** generally having units of 1/°C or 1/°F, that relates the additional length to the original length. The percentage change in length is found by the equation $\Delta L/L_0 = \alpha\Delta T$, or to find the absolute change, $\Delta L = L_0\alpha\Delta T$. Just as heating the material causes it to expand, cooling it will cause it to contract.

Assuming that the material is able to expand in all directions, there will similarly be a change in areas and volumes. The change in an area A_0 will be $\Delta A = 2\alpha A_0\Delta T + \alpha^2\Delta T^2$. Because α is generally much less than 1, $\alpha^2\Delta T^2$ will most often be negligible. Thus, the change in area becomes $\Delta A = 2\alpha A_0\Delta T$. From this we can see that the **area coefficient of thermal expansion** is $\gamma = 2\alpha$, and $\Delta A = \gamma A_0\Delta T$. By making similar assumptions with the equation for change in volume, we find that the **volume coefficient of thermal expansion** is $\beta = 3\alpha$ and that $\Delta V = \beta V_0\Delta T$.

CONVECTION

Heat always flows from a region of higher temperature to a region of lower temperature. If two regions are at the same temperature, there is a thermal equilibrium between them and there will be no net heat transfer between them. **Convection** is a mode of heat transfer in which a surface in contact with a fluid experiences a heat flow. The **heat rate for convection** is given as $q = hA\Delta T$, where h is the convection coefficient. The convection coefficient is dependent on a number of factors, including the configuration of the surface and the nature and velocity of the fluid. For complicated configurations, it often has to be determined experimentally.

Convection may be classified as either free or forced. In free convection, when a surface transfers heat to the surrounding air, the heated air becomes less dense and rises, allowing cooler air to descend and come into contact with the surface. Free convection may also be called natural convection. Forced convection in this example would involve forcibly cycling the air: for instance, with a fan. While this does generally require an additional input of work, the convection coefficient is always greater for forced convection.

CONDUCTION

Heat always flows from a region of higher temperature to a region of lower temperature. If two regions are at the same temperature, there is a thermal equilibrium between them and there will be no net heat transfer between them. **Conduction** is a form of heat transfer that requires contact. Since heat is a measure of kinetic energy, most commonly vibration, at the atomic level, it may be transferred from one location to another or one object to another by contact. The rate at which heat is transferred is proportional to the material's **thermal conductivity** k, cross-sectional area A, and temperature gradient $\frac{dT}{dx}$, $q = kA\left(\frac{dT}{dx}\right)$. If two ends of a rod are each held at a constant temperature, the heat transfer through the rod will be given as $q = kA(T_H - T_L)/d$, where d is the length of the rod. The heat will flow from the hot end to the cold end. The thermal conductivity is generally given in units of W/(m K). Metals are some of the best conductors, many having a thermal conductivity around 400 W/(m K). The thermal conductivity of wood is very small, generally less than 0.5 W/(m K). Diamond is extremely thermally conductive and may have a conductivity of over 2,000 W/(m K). Although fluids also have thermal conductivity, they will tend to transfer heat primarily through convection.

KINETIC MOLECULAR THEORY

The **kinetic molecular theory of gases** states that the pressure exerted by a gas is due to numerous collisions of molecules with one another and with container walls. This assertion led to the development of what is now known as the **ideal gas law**: $PV = nRT$, where P is pressure, V is volume, T is temperature, n is the number of moles of gas present, and R is the universal gas constant. Different aspects of this law have different names, but there are many simple relations that may be derived from it. For instance, if an ideal gas is contained such that no molecules can escape, then it may be said that $(P_1V_1)/T_1 = (P_2V_2)/T_2$, where the subscripts indicate distinct sets of conditions. Generally, one of the three variables will be held constant while the other two change. If an ideal gas in a container with a constant volume is heated, the effect this has on the pressure can be determined both analytically and numerically. Additional energy imparted to the gas particles will cause them to move faster and, by the kinetic molecular theory, faster particles mean more collisions and a higher resulting pressure. Numerically, $P_1/T_1 = P_2/T_2$. This means that if T_2 is higher than T_1, then P_2 must be equivalently higher than P_1 to maintain the same ratio.

Other derivations from the ideal gas law include calculating molarity or moles per unit volume $\left(\frac{n}{V} = \frac{P}{RT}\right)$, gas density if the molecular weight M is known $\left(\rho = \frac{PM}{RT}\right)$, or conversely, molecular weight if the density is known $\left(M = \frac{\rho RT}{P}\right)$.

RADIATION

Heat always flows from a region of higher temperature to a region of lower temperature. If two regions are at the same temperature, there is a thermal equilibrium between them and there will be no net heat transfer between them. **Radiation heat transfer** occurs via electromagnetic radiation between two bodies. Unlike conduction and convection, radiation requires no medium in which to take place. Indeed, the heat we receive from the sun is entirely radiation since it must pass through a vacuum to reach us. Everything at a temperature above absolute zero emits heat radiation at a rate given by the equation $q = e\sigma A T^4$, where e is the **surface emissivity** and σ is the **Stefan-Boltzmann constant**. The net radiation heat-transfer rate for a body is given by $q = e\sigma A(T^4 - (T_0)^4)$, where T_0 is the temperature of the surroundings. Emissivity, which has a value between 0 and 1, is a measure of how well a surface absorbs and emits radiation. Dark-colored surfaces tend to have high emissivity, while shiny or reflective surfaces have low emissivity. In the radiation heat-rate equation, it is important to remember to use absolute temperature units, since the temperature value is being raised to a power.

LAWS OF THERMODYNAMICS
FIRST LAW

The **first law of thermodynamics** states that energy cannot be created or destroyed, but only converted from one form to another. It is generally applied as $Q = \Delta U + W$, where Q is the net heat energy added to a system, ΔU is the change in internal energy of the system, and W is the work done by the system. For any input of heat energy to a system, that energy must be either converted to internal energy through a temperature increase or expended in doing work. For a system that gives off heat, either the temperature of the system must decrease or work must be done on the system by its surroundings. By convention, work done by the system is positive while work done on the system is negative.

For instance, suppose a gas is compressed by a piston while the gas temperature remains constant. If we consider the gas to be the system, the work is negative, since the work is being performed on the gas. Since the temperature remains constant, $\Delta U = 0$. Thus, Q must be a negative quantity, indicating that heat is lost by the gas. Conversely, if the gas does positive work on the piston while remaining at a constant temperature, the gas must be receiving heat input from the surroundings.

SECOND LAW

The **second law of thermodynamics** is primarily a statement of the natural tendency of all things toward disorder rather than order. It deals with a quantity called **entropy**, which is an inverse measure of the remaining useful energy in a system. If we take a system of a pot of hot water and an ice cube, the system entropy initially has a value of S_1. After the ice cube melts in the water and the system reaches an equilibrium temperature, the system has larger entropy value S_2, which is the maximum entropy for the system. The system cannot return to its initial state without work input to refreeze the ice cube and reheat the water. If this is done and the system returns to a state with entropy S_1, then the entropy of the surroundings must at the same time increase by more than $S_2 - S_1$, since the net entropy from any process is always greater than zero. Reversible processes are those that may be accomplished in reverse without requiring additional work input. These processes do not exist in the real world, but can be useful for approximating some situations. All real processes are irreversible, meaning they require additional work input to accomplish in reverse. Another important concept is that of spontaneity, the ability of a process to occur without instigation. An ice cube located in an environment at a temperature above the freezing point will spontaneously melt. Although some processes can decrease system entropy at a cost to the entropy of the surroundings, all spontaneous processes involve an increase in system entropy.

THIRD AND ZEROTH LAWS

The **third law of thermodynamics** regards the behavior of systems as they approach absolute zero temperature. Actually, reaching a state of absolute zero is impossible. According to this law, all activity disappears as molecules slow to a standstill near absolute zero, and the system achieves a perfect crystal structure while the system entropy approaches its minimum value. For most systems, this would in fact be a value of zero entropy. Note that this does not violate the second law since causing a system to approach absolute zero would require an immense increase in the entropy of the surroundings, resulting in a positive net entropy. This law is used to determine the value of a material's standard entropy, which is its entropy value at the standard temperature of 25 °C.

The **zeroth law of thermodynamics** deals with thermal equilibrium between two systems. It states that if two systems are both in thermal equilibrium with a third system, then they are in thermal equilibrium with each other. This may seem intuitive, but it is an important basis for the other thermodynamic laws.

THERMODYNAMIC PROCESSES OF GASES

In discussing thermodynamic processes applied to gases, it is important to understand what is meant by some of the different types of processes that can take place. Most real processes do not strictly hold to one of these types, but most can be reasonably approximated by one of them. A process in which the pressure remains constant is known as an **isobaric process**. In this type of process, the volume-to-absolute-temperature ratio remains constant. In an **isothermal process**, the temperature remains constant, as does the product of the pressure and volume. For isothermal processes, the internal energy of the gas is constant and, by the first law of thermodynamics, the heat added is equal to the work done by the gas. An **adiabatic process** is one in which no heat is transferred between the gas or its surroundings. This does not mean that the temperature of the gas remains the same, but only that any temperature changes are due to changes in pressure or volume or, by the first law, the change in internal energy of the gas is equal to the amount of work done on the gas by its surroundings.

HEAT ENGINES AND THE CARNOT CYCLE

A **heat engine** is a mechanical device that takes in heat energy Q_H from a high-temperature region, uses that energy to produce work W, and then expels heat Q_C to a lower-temperature region. When the machine is operating at steady state, such that it does not change temperature, the first law of thermodynamics tells us that the net heat input is equal to the work achieved, $Q_H - Q_C = W$. We can define the **efficiency of a heat engine**, η, as the work received divided by the work put in, or

$\eta = W/Q_H$. The rejected heat Q_C is not considered work received because it is not usable for work. The efficiency may also be calculated as $\eta = 1 - Q_C/Q_H$. From this, we can see that 100% efficiency can only be achieved if $Q_C = 0$. However, constructing a heat engine that expels no heat is impossible.

A **Carnot engine** is a heat engine that operates on the **Carnot cycle**, an ideal reversible gas cycle that consists of the following processes: high-temperature isothermal expansion, adiabatic expansion, low-temperature isothermal compression, and adiabatic compression. The efficiency of this ideal engine is given as $\eta = 1 - T_C/T_H$, where T_C and T_H are the low and high temperatures of the gas during the cycle. Carnot's theorem states that no heat engine operating between T_C and T_H can have a higher efficiency than that of the Carnot engine.

CONVERSION OF ENERGY

There are many different types of energy that exist. These include mechanical, sound, magnetic, electrical, light, heat, and chemical. From the first law of thermodynamics, we know that no energy can be created or destroyed, but it may be converted from one form to another. This does not mean that all forms of energy are useful. Indeed, the second law states that net useful energy decreases in every process that takes place. Most often this occurs when other forms of energy are converted to heat through means such as friction. In these cases, the heat is quickly absorbed into the surroundings and becomes unusable. There are many examples of energy conversion, such as in an automobile. The chemical energy in the gasoline is converted to mechanical energy in the engine. Subsequently, this mechanical energy is converted to kinetic energy as the car moves. Additionally, the mechanical energy is converted to electrical energy to power the radio, headlights, air conditioner, and other devices. In the radio, electrical energy is converted to sound energy. In the headlights, it is converted to heat and light energy. In the air conditioner, it does work to remove heat energy from the car's interior. It is important to remember that, in all of these processes, a portion of the energy is lost from its intended purpose.

Quantitative Reasoning

Numerical Calculations

NUMBERS AND THEIR CLASSIFICATIONS

Numbers are the basic building blocks of mathematics. Specific features of numbers are identified by the following terms:

Integers – The set of whole positive and negative numbers, including zero. Integers do not include fractions $\left(\frac{1}{3}\right)$, decimals (0.56), or mixed numbers $\left(7\frac{3}{4}\right)$.

Prime number – A whole number greater than 1 that has only two factors, itself and 1; that is, a number that can be divided evenly only by 1 and itself.

Composite number – A whole number greater than 1 that has more than two different factors; in other words, any whole number that is not a prime number. For example: The composite number 8 has the factors of 1, 2, 4, and 8.

Even number – Any integer that can be divided by 2 without leaving a remainder. For example: 2, 4, 6, 8, and so on.

Odd number – Any integer that cannot be divided evenly by 2. For example: 3, 5, 7, 9, and so on.

Decimal number – a number that uses a decimal point to show the part of the number that is less than one. Example: 1.234.

Decimal point – a symbol used to separate the ones place from the tenths place in decimals or dollars from cents in currency.

Decimal place – the position of a number to the right of the decimal point. In the decimal 0.123, the 1 is in the first place to the right of the decimal point, indicating tenths; the 2 is in the second place, indicating hundredths; and the 3 is in the third place, indicating thousandths.

The decimal, or base 10, system is a number system that uses ten different digits (0, 1, 2, 3, 4, 5, 6, 7, 8, 9). An example of a number system that uses something other than ten digits is the binary, or base 2, number system, used by computers, which uses only the numbers 0 and 1. It is thought that the decimal system originated because people had only their 10 fingers for counting.

Rational numbers include all integers, decimals, and fractions. Any terminating or repeating decimal number is a rational number.

Irrational numbers cannot be written as fractions or decimals because the number of decimal places is infinite and there is no recurring pattern of digits within the number. For example, pi (π) begins with 3.141592 and continues without terminating or repeating, so pi is an irrational number.

Real numbers are the set of all rational and irrational numbers.

> **Review Video: Numbers and their Classifications**
> Visit mometrix.com/academy and enter Code: 461071

373

OPERATIONS

There are four basic mathematical operations:

Addition increases the value of one quantity by the value of another quantity. Example: $2 + 4 = 6$; $8 + 9 = 17$. The result is called the sum. With addition, the order does not matter. $4 + 2 = 2 + 4$.

Subtraction is the opposite operation to addition; it decreases the value of one quantity by the value of another quantity. Example: $6 - 4 = 2$; $17 - 8 = 9$. The result is called the difference. Note that with subtraction, the order does matter. $6 - 4 \neq 4 - 6$.

Multiplication can be thought of as repeated addition. One number tells how many times to add the other number to itself. Example: 3×2 (three times two) $= 2 + 2 + 2 = 6$. With multiplication, the order does not matter. $2 \times 3 = 3 \times 2$ or $3 + 3 = 2 + 2 + 2$.

Division is the opposite operation to multiplication; one number tells us how many parts to divide the other number into. Example: $20 \div 4 = 5$; if 20 is split into 4 equal parts, each part is 5. With division, the order of the numbers does matter. $20 \div 4 \neq 4 \div 20$.

An **exponent** is a superscript number placed next to another number at the top right. It indicates how many times the base number is to be multiplied by itself. Exponents provide a shorthand way to write what would be a longer mathematical expression. Example: $a^2 = a \times a$; $2^4 = 2 \times 2 \times 2 \times 2$. A number with an exponent of 2 is said to be "squared," while a number with an exponent of 3 is said to be "cubed." The value of a number raised to an exponent is called its power. So, 8^4 is read as "8 to the 4th power," or "8 raised to the power of 4." A negative exponent is the same as the reciprocal of a positive exponent. Example: $a^{-2} = \frac{1}{a^2}$.

Parentheses are used to designate which operations should be done first when there are multiple operations. Example: $4 - (2 + 1) = 1$; the parentheses tell us that we must add 2 and 1, and then subtract the sum from 4, rather than subtracting 2 from 4 and then adding 1 (this would give us an answer of 3).

Order of Operations is a set of rules that dictates the order in which we must perform each operation in an expression so that we will evaluate it accurately. If we have an expression that includes multiple different operations, Order of Operations tells us which operations to do first. The most common mnemonic for Order of Operations is PEMDAS, or "Please Excuse My Dear Aunt Sally." PEMDAS stands for Parentheses, Exponents, Multiplication, Division, Addition, Subtraction. It is important to understand that multiplication and division have equal precedence, as do addition and subtraction, so those pairs of operations are simply worked from left to right in order.

Example: Evaluate the expression $5 + 20 \div 4 \times (2 + 3)^2 - 6$ using the correct order of operations.

P: Perform the operations inside the parentheses, $(2 + 3) = 5$.

E: Simplify the exponents, $(5)^2 = 25$. The equation now looks like this: $5 + 20 \div 4 \times 25 - 6$.

MD: Perform multiplication and division from left to right, $20 \div 4 = 5$; then $5 \times 25 = 125$. The equation now looks like this: $5 + 125 - 6$.

AS: Perform addition and subtraction from left to right, $5 + 125 = 130$; then $130 - 6 = 124$.

> **Review Video: <u>Order of Operations</u>**
> Visit mometrix.com/academy and enter Code: 259675

The laws of exponents are as follows:

- Any number to the power of 1 is equal to itself: $a^1 = a$.
- The number 1 raised to any power is equal to 1: $1^n = 1$.
- Any number raised to the power of 0 is equal to 1: $a^0 = 1$.
- Add exponents to multiply powers of the same base number: $a^n \times a^m = a^{n+m}$.
- Subtract exponents to divide powers of the same number; that is $a^n \div a^m = a^{n-m}$.
- Multiply exponents to raise a power to a power: $(a^n)^m = a^{n \times m}$.
- If multiplied or divided numbers inside parentheses are collectively raised to a power, this is the same as each individual term being raised to that power: $(a \times b)^n = a^n \times b^n$; $(a \div b)^n = a^n \div b^n$.

Note: Exponents do not have to be integers. Fractional or decimal exponents follow all the rules above as well. Example: $5^{\frac{1}{4}} \times 5^{\frac{3}{4}} = 5^{\frac{1}{4} + \frac{3}{4}} = 5^1 = 5$.

> **Review Video: Laws of Exponents**
> Visit mometrix.com/academy and enter Code: 532558

A **root**, such as a square root, is another way of writing a fractional exponent. Instead of using a superscript, roots use the radical symbol ($\sqrt{}$) to indicate the operation. A radical will have a number underneath the bar, and may sometimes have a number in the upper left: $\sqrt[n]{a}$, read as "the nth root of a." The relationship between radical notation and exponent notation can be described by this equation: $\sqrt[n]{a} = a^{\frac{1}{n}}$. The two special cases of $n = 2$ and $n = 3$ are called square roots and cube roots. If there is no number to the upper left, it is understood to be a square root ($n = 2$). Nearly all of the roots you encounter will be square roots. A square root is the same as a number raised to the one-half power. When we say that a is the square root of b ($a = \sqrt{b}$), we mean that a multiplied by itself equals b: ($a \times a = b$).

A **perfect square** is a number that has an integer for its square root. There are 10 perfect squares from 1 to 100: 1, 4, 9, 16, 25, 36, 49, 64, 81, 100 (the squares of integers 1 through 10).

Scientific notation is a way of writing large numbers in a shorter form. The form $a \times 10^n$ is used in scientific notation, where a is greater than or equal to 1, but less than 10, and n is the number of places the decimal must move to get from the original number to a. Example: The number 230,400,000 is cumbersome to write. To write the value in scientific notation, place a decimal point between the first and second numbers, and include all digits through the last non-zero digit ($a = 2.304$). To find the appropriate power of 10, count the number of places the decimal point had to move ($n = 8$). The number is positive if the decimal moved to the left, and negative if it moved to the right. We can then write 230,400,000 as 2.304×10^8. If we look instead at the number 0.00002304, we have the same value for a, but this time the decimal moved 5 places to the right ($n = -5$). Thus, 0.00002304 can be written as 2.304×10^{-5}. Using this notation makes it simple to compare very large or very small numbers. By comparing exponents, it is easy to see that 3.28×10^4 is smaller than 1.51×10^5, because 4 is less than 5.

POSITIVE AND NEGATIVE NUMBERS

A precursor to working with negative numbers is understanding what absolute values are. A number's **absolute value** is simply the distance away from zero a number is on the number line. The absolute value of a number is always positive and is written $|x|$.

When adding signed numbers, if the signs are the same simply add the absolute values of the addends and apply the original sign to the sum. For example, $(+4) + (+8) = +12$ and $(-4) + (-8) = -12$. When the original signs are different, take the absolute values of the addends and subtract the smaller value from the larger value, then apply the original sign of the larger value to the difference. For instance, $(+4) + (-8) = -4$ and $(-4) + (+8) = +4$.

For subtracting signed numbers, change the sign of the number after the minus symbol and then follow the same rules used for addition. For example, $(+4) - (+8) = (+4) + (-8) = -4$.

If the signs are the same the product is positive when multiplying signed numbers. For example, $(+4) \times (+8) = +32$ and $(-4) \times (-8) = +32$. If the signs are opposite, the product is negative. For example, $(+4) \times (-8) = -32$ and $(-4) \times (+8) = -32$. When more than two factors are multiplied together, the sign of the product is determined by how many negative factors are present. If there are an odd number of negative factors then the product is negative, whereas an even number of negative factors indicates a positive product. For instance, $(+4) \times (-8) \times (-2) = +64$ and $(-4) \times (-8) \times (-2) = -64$.

The rules for dividing signed numbers are similar to multiplying signed numbers. If the dividend and divisor have the same sign, the quotient is positive. If the dividend and divisor have opposite signs, the quotient is negative. For example, $(-4) \div (+8) = -0.5$.

FACTORS AND MULTIPLES

Factors are numbers that are multiplied together to obtain a product. For example, in the equation $2 \times 3 = 6$, the numbers 2 and 3 are factors. A prime number has only two factors (1 and itself), but other numbers can have many factors.

A **common factor** is a number that divides exactly into two or more other numbers. For example, the factors of 12 are 1, 2, 3, 4, 6, and 12, while the factors of 15 are 1, 3, 5, and 15. The common factors of 12 and 15 are 1 and 3.

A **prime factor** is also a prime number. Therefore, the prime factors of 12 are 1, 2, and 3. For 15, the prime factors are 1, 3, and 5.

The **greatest common factor (GCF)** is the largest number that is a factor of two or more numbers. For example, the factors of 15 are 1, 3, 5, and 15; the factors of 35 are 1, 5, 7, and 35. Therefore, the greatest common factor of 15 and 35 is 5.

> **Review Video: Factors**
> Visit mometrix.com/academy and enter Code: 920086

The **least common multiple (LCM)** is the smallest number that is a multiple of two or more numbers. For example, the multiples of 3 include 3, 6, 9, 12, 15, etc.; the multiples of 5 include 5, 10, 15, 20, etc. Therefore, the least common multiple of 3 and 5 is 15.

> **Review Video: Multiples**
> Visit mometrix.com/academy and enter Code: 626738

FRACTIONS, PERCENTAGES, AND RELATED CONCEPTS

A **fraction** is a number that is expressed as one integer written above another integer, with a dividing line between them $\left(\frac{x}{y}\right)$. It represents the quotient of the two numbers "x divided by y." It can also be thought of as x out of y equal parts.

The top number of a fraction is called the **numerator**, and it represents the number of parts under consideration. The 1 in $\frac{1}{4}$ means that 1 part out of the whole is being considered in the calculation. The bottom number of a fraction is called the **denominator**, and it represents the total number of equal parts. The 4 in $\frac{1}{4}$ means that the whole consists of 4 equal parts. A fraction cannot have a denominator of zero; this is referred to as "undefined."

Fractions can be manipulated, without changing the value of the fraction, by multiplying or dividing (but not adding or subtracting) both the numerator and denominator by the same number. If you divide both numbers by a common factor, you are reducing or simplifying the fraction. Two fractions that have the same value, but are expressed differently are known as equivalent fractions. For example, $\frac{2}{10}, \frac{3}{15}, \frac{4}{20}$, and $\frac{5}{25}$ are all equivalent fractions. They can also all be reduced or simplified to $\frac{1}{5}$.

When two fractions are manipulated so that they have the same denominator, this is known as finding a **common denominator**. The number chosen to be that common denominator should be the least common multiple of the two original denominators. Example: $\frac{3}{4}$ and $\frac{5}{6}$; the least common multiple of 4 and 6 is 12. Manipulating to achieve the common denominator: $\frac{3}{4} = \frac{9}{12}; \frac{5}{6} = \frac{10}{12}$.

If two fractions have a common denominator, they can be added or subtracted simply by adding or subtracting the two numerators and retaining the same denominator. Example: $\frac{1}{2} + \frac{1}{4} = \frac{2}{4} + \frac{1}{4} = \frac{3}{4}$. If the two fractions do not already have the same denominator, one or both of them must be manipulated to achieve a common denominator before they can be added or subtracted.

Two fractions can be multiplied by multiplying the two numerators to find the new numerator and the two denominators to find the new denominator. Example: $\frac{1}{3} \times \frac{2}{3} = \frac{1 \times 2}{3 \times 3} = \frac{2}{9}$.

Two fractions can be divided flipping the numerator and denominator of the second fraction and then proceeding as though it were a multiplication. Example: $\frac{2}{3} \div \frac{3}{4} = \frac{2}{3} \times \frac{4}{3} = \frac{8}{9}$.

A fraction whose denominator is greater than its numerator is known as a **proper fraction**, while a fraction whose numerator is greater than its denominator is known as an **improper fraction**. Proper fractions have values less than one and improper fractions have values greater than one.

A **mixed number** is a number that contains both an integer and a fraction. Any improper fraction can be rewritten as a mixed number. Example: $\frac{8}{3} = \frac{6}{3} + \frac{2}{3} = 2 + \frac{2}{3} = 2\frac{2}{3}$. Similarly, any mixed number can be rewritten as an improper fraction. Example: $1\frac{3}{5} = 1 + \frac{3}{5} = \frac{5}{5} + \frac{3}{5} = \frac{8}{5}$.

Percentages can be thought of as fractions that are based on a whole of 100; that is, one whole is equal to 100%. The word percent means "per hundred." Fractions can be expressed as percentages by finding equivalent fractions with a denomination of 100. Example: $7/10 = 70/100 = 70\%$; $1/4 = 25/100 = 25\%$.

To express a percentage as a fraction, divide the percentage number by 100 and reduce the fraction to its simplest possible terms. Example: $60\% = \frac{60}{100} = \frac{3}{5}$; $96\% = \frac{96}{100} = \frac{24}{25}$.

Converting decimals to percentages and percentages to decimals is as simple as moving the decimal point. To convert from a decimal to a percent, move the decimal point two places to the right. To convert from a percent to a decimal, move it two places to the left. Example: $0.23 = 23\%$; $5.34 = 534\%$; $0.007 = 0.7\%$; $700\% = 7.00$; $86\% = 0.86$; $0.15\% = 0.0015$. It may be helpful to remember that the percentage number will always be larger than the equivalent decimal number.

A percentage problem can be presented three main ways: (1) Find what percentage of some number another number is. Example: What percentage of 40 is 8? (2) Find what number is some percentage of a given number. Example: What number is 20% of 40? (3) Find what number another number is a given percentage of. Example: What number is 8 20% of? The three components in all of these cases are the same: a whole (W), a part (P), and a percentage (%). These are related by the equation: $P = W \times \%$. This is the form of the equation you would use to solve problems of type (2). To solve types (1) and (3), you would use these two forms: $\% = \dfrac{P}{W}$ and $W = \dfrac{P}{\%}$.

The thing that frequently makes percentage problems difficult is that they are most often also word problems, so a large part of solving them is figuring out which quantities are what. Example: In a school cafeteria, 7 students choose pizza, 9 choose hamburgers, and 4 choose tacos. Find the percentage that chooses tacos. To find the whole, you must first add all of the parts: $7 + 9 + 4 = 20$. The percentage can then be found by dividing the part by the whole ($\% = \dfrac{P}{W}$): $\dfrac{4}{20} = \dfrac{20}{100} = 20\%$.

> **Review Video: Fractions, Decimals, and Percentages**
> Visit mometrix.com/academy and enter Code: 350606

A **ratio** is a comparison of two quantities in a particular order. Example: If there are 14 computers in a lab, and the class has 20 students, there is a student to computer ratio of 20 to 14, commonly written as 20:14. Ratios are normally reduced to their smallest whole number representation, so 20:14 would be reduced to 10:7 by dividing both sides by 2.

A **proportion** is a relationship between two quantities that dictates how one changes when the other changes. A direct proportion describes a relationship in which a quantity increases by a set amount for every increase in the other quantity, or decreases by that same amount for every decrease in the other quantity. Example: Assuming a constant driving speed, the time required for a car trip increases as the distance of the trip increases. The distance to be traveled and the time required to travel are directly proportional.

Inverse proportion is a relationship in which an increase in one quantity is accompanied by a decrease in the other, or vice versa. Example: the time required for a car trip decreases as the speed increases, and increases as the speed decreases, so the time required is inversely proportional to the speed of the car.

Algebra

EQUATIONS AND GRAPHING

When algebraic functions and equations are shown graphically, they are usually shown on a **Cartesian coordinate plane**. The Cartesian coordinate plane consists of two number lines placed perpendicular to each other, and intersecting at the zero point, also known as the origin. The horizontal number line is known as the x-axis, with positive values to the right of the origin, and negative values to the left of the origin. The vertical number line is known as the y-axis, with positive values above the origin, and negative values below the origin. Any point on the plane can be identified by an ordered pair in the form (x, y), called coordinates. The x-value of the coordinate is called the abscissa, and the y-value of the coordinate is called the ordinate. The two number lines divide the plane into four quadrants: I, II, III, and IV.

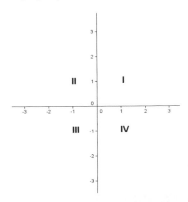

Review Video: <u>Cartesian Coordinate Plane and Graphing</u>
Visit mometrix.com/academy and enter code: 115173

Before learning the different forms equations can be written in, it is important to understand some terminology. A ratio of the change in the vertical distance to the change in horizontal distance is called the **slope**. On a graph with two points, (x_1, y_1) and (x_2, y_2), the slope is represented by the formula $= \frac{y_2 - y_1}{x_2 - x_1}$; $x_1 \neq x_2$. If the value of the slope is positive, the line slopes upward from left to right. If the value of the slope is negative, the line slopes downward from left to right. If the y-coordinates are the same for both points, the slope is 0 and the line is a **horizontal line**. If the x-coordinates are the same for both points, there is no slope and the line is a *Vertical Line*. Two or more lines that have equal slopes are **parallel lines**. **perpendicular lines** have slopes that are negative reciprocals of each other, such as $\frac{a}{b}$ and $\frac{-b}{a}$.

Equations are made up of monomials and polynomials. A **monomial** is a single variable or product of constants and variables, such as x, $2x$, or $\frac{2}{x}$. There will never be addition or subtraction symbols in a monomial. Like monomials have like variables, but they may have different coefficients. **polynomials** are algebraic expressions which use addition and subtraction to combine two or more monomials. Two terms make a binomial; three terms make a trinomial; etc. The **degree of a monomial** is the sum of the exponents of the variables. The **degree of a polynomial** is the highest degree of any individual term.

As mentioned previously, equations can be written many ways. Below is a list of the many forms equations can take.

- **Standard form**: $Ax + By = C$; the slope is $\frac{-A}{B}$ and the y-intercept is $\frac{C}{B}$
- **Slope intercept form**: $y = mx + b$, where m is the slope and b is the y-intercept
- **Point-slope form**: $y - y_1 = m(x - x_1)$, where m is the slope and (x_1, y_1) is a point on the line
- **Two-point form**: $\frac{y-y_1}{x-x_1} = \frac{y_2-y_1}{x_2-x_1}$, where (x_1, y_1) and (x_2, y_2) are two points on the given line
- **Intercept form**: $\frac{x}{x_1} + \frac{y}{y_1} = 1$, where $(x_1, 0)$ is the point at which a line intersects the x-axis, and $(0, y_1)$ is the point at which the same line intersects the y-axis

Equations can also be written as $ax + b = 0$, where $a \neq 0$. These are referred to as **one variable linear equations**. A solution to such an equation is called a **root**. In the case where we have the equation $5x + 10 = 0$, if we solve for x we get a solution of $x = -2$. In other words, the root of the equation is -2. This is found by first subtracting 10 from both sides, which gives $5x = -10$. Next, simply divide both sides by the coefficient of the variable, in this case 5, to get $x = -2$. This can be checked by plugging -2 back into the original equation $(5)(-2) + 10 = -10 + 10 = 0$.

The **solution set** is the set of all solutions of an equation. In our example, the solution set would simply be -2. If there were more solutions (there usually are in multivariable equations) then they would also be included in the solution set. When an equation has no true solutions, this is referred to as an **empty set**. Equations with identical solution sets are **equivalent equations**. An **identity** is a term whose value or determinant is equal to 1.

OTHER IMPORTANT CONCEPTS

Commonly in algebra and other upper-level fields of math you find yourself working with mathematical expressions that do not equal each other. The statement comparing such expressions with symbols such as < (less than) or > (greater than) is called an **inequality**. An example of an inequality is $7x > 5$. To solve for x, simply divide both sides by 7 and the solution is shown to be $x > \frac{5}{7}$. Graphs of the solution set of inequalities are represented on a number line. Open circles are used to show that an expression approaches a number but is never quite equal to that number.

conditional inequalities are those with certain values for the variable that will make the condition true and other values for the variable where the condition will be false. **absolute inequalities** can have any real number as the value for the variable to make the condition true, while there is no real number value for the variable that will make the condition false. Solving inequalities is done by following the same rules as for solving equations with the exception that when multiplying or dividing by a negative number the direction of the inequality sign must be flipped or reversed. **double inequalities** are situations where two inequality statements apply to the same variable expression. An example of this is $-c < ax + b < c$.

A **weighted mean**, or weighted average, is a mean that uses "weighted" values. The formula is weighted mean $= \frac{w_1 x_1 + w_2 x_2 + w_3 x_3 ... + w_n x_n}{w_1 + w_2 + w_3 + \cdots + w_n}$. Weighted values, such as $w_1, w_2, w_3, ... w_n$ are assigned to each member of the set $x_1, x_2, x_3, ... x_n$. If calculating weighted mean, make sure a weight value for each member of the set is used.

CALCULATIONS USING POINTS

Sometimes you need to perform calculations using only points on a graph as input data. Using points, you can determine what the midpoint and distance are. If you know the equation for a line you can calculate the distance between the line and the point.

To find the **midpoint** of two points (x_1, y_1) and (x_2, y_2), average the x- coordinates to get the x-coordinate of the midpoint, and average the y-coordinates to get the y-coordinate of the midpoint. The formula is midpoint $= \left(\frac{x_1+x_2}{2}, \frac{y_1+y_2}{2}\right)$.

The **distance** between two points is the same as the length of the hypotenuse of a right triangle with the two given points as endpoints, and the two sides of the right triangle parallel to the x-axis and y-axis, respectively. The length of the segment parallel to the x-axis is the difference between the x-coordinates of the two points. The length of the segment parallel to the y-axis is the difference between the y-coordinates of the two points. Use the Pythagorean Theorem $a^2 + b^2 = c^2$ or $c = \sqrt{a^2 + b^2}$ to find the distance. The formula is: distance $= \sqrt{(x_2 - x_1)^2 + (y_2 - y_1)^2}$.

When a line is in the format $Ax + By + C = 0$, where A, B, and C are coefficients, you can use a point (x_1, y_1) not on the line and apply the formula $d = \frac{|Ax_1 + By_1 + C|}{\sqrt{A^2 + B^2}}$ to find the distance between the line and the point (x_1, y_1).

SYSTEMS OF EQUATIONS

Systems of equations are a set of simultaneous equations that all use the same variables. A solution to a system of equations must be true for each equation in the system. **Consistent systems** are those with at least one solution. **Inconsistent systems** are systems of equations that have no solution.

To solve a system of linear equations by **substitution**, start with the easier equation and solve for one of the variables. Express this variable in terms of the other variable. Substitute this expression in the other equation, and solve for the other variable. The solution should be expressed in the form (x, y). Substitute the values into both of the original equations to check your answer. Consider the following problem.

Solve the system using substitution:

$$x + 6y = 15$$
$$3x - 12y = 18$$

Solve the first equation for x:

$$x = 15 - 6y$$

Substitute this value in place of x in the second equation, and solve for y:

$$3(15 - 6y) - 12y = 18$$
$$45 - 18y - 12y = 18$$
$$30y = 27$$
$$y = \frac{27}{30} = \frac{9}{10} = 0.9$$

381

Plug this value for y back into the first equation to solve for x:

$$x = 15 - 6(0.9) = 15 - 5.4 = 9.6$$

Check both equations if you have time:

$$9.6 + 6(0.9) = 9.6 + 5.4 = 15$$
$$3(9.6) - 12(0.9) = 28.8 - 10.8 = 18$$

Therefore, the solution is (9.6, 0.9).

To solve a system of equations using **elimination**, begin by rewriting both equations in standard form $Ax + By = C$. Check to see if the coefficients of one pair of like variables add to zero. If not, multiply one or both of the equations by a non-zero number to make one set of like variables add to zero. Add the two equations to solve for one of the variables. Substitute this value into one of the original equations to solve for the other variable. Check your work by substituting into the other equation. Next we will solve the same problem as above, but using the addition method.

Solve the system using elimination:

$$x + 6y = 15$$
$$3x - 12y = 18$$

If we multiply the first equation by 2, we can eliminate the y terms:

$$2x + 12y = 30$$
$$3x - 12y = 18$$

Add the equations together and solve for x:

$5x = 48$

$$x = \frac{48}{5} = 9.6$$

Plug the value for x back into either of the original equations and solve for y:

$9.6 + 6y = 15$

$$y = \frac{15 - 9.6}{6} = 0.9$$

Check both equations if you have time:

$$9.6 + 6(0.9) = 9.6 + 5.4 = 15$$
$$3(9.6) - 12(0.9) = 28.8 - 10.8 = 18$$

Therefore, the solution is (9.6, 0.9).

POLYNOMIAL ALGEBRA

To multiply two binomials, follow the *FOIL* method. FOIL stands for:

- First: Multiply the first term of each binomial
- Outer: Multiply the outer terms of each binomial

- Inner: Multiply the inner terms of each binomial
- Last: Multiply the last term of each binomial

Using FOIL, $(Ax + By)(Cx + Dy) = ACx^2 + ADxy + BCxy + BDy^2$.

To divide polynomials, begin by arranging the terms of each polynomial in order of one variable. You may arrange in ascending or descending order, but be consistent with both polynomials. To get the first term of the quotient, divide the first term of the dividend by the first term of the divisor. Multiply the first term of the quotient by the entire divisor and subtract that product from the dividend. Repeat for the second and successive terms until you either get a remainder of zero or a remainder whose degree is less than the degree of the divisor. If the quotient has a remainder, write the answer as a mixed expression in the form: $\text{quotient} + \frac{\text{remainder}}{\text{divisor}}$.

Rational Expressions are fractions with polynomials in both the numerator and the denominator; the value of the polynomial in the denominator cannot be equal to zero. To add or subtract rational expressions, first find the common denominator, then rewrite each fraction as an equivalent fraction with the common denominator. Finally, add or subtract the numerators to get the numerator of the answer, and keep the common denominator as the denominator of the answer. When multiplying rational expressions factor each polynomial and cancel like factors (a factor which appears in both the numerator and the denominator). Then, multiply all remaining factors in the numerator to get the numerator of the product, and multiply the remaining factors in the denominator to get the denominator of the product. Remember – cancel entire factors, not individual terms. To divide rational expressions, take the reciprocal of the divisor (the rational expression you are dividing by) and multiply by the dividend.

> **Review Video: Rational Expressions**
> Visit mometrix.com/academy and enter code: 415183

Below are patterns of some special products to remember: perfect trinomial squares, the difference between two squares, the sum and difference of two cubes, and perfect cubes.

- **Perfect trinomial squares**: $x^2 + 2xy + y^2 = (x + y)^2$ or $x^2 - 2xy + y^2 = (x - y)^2$
- **Difference between two squares**: $x^2 - y^2 = (x + y)(x - y)$
- **Sum of two cubes**: $x^3 + y^3 = (x + y)(x^2 - xy + y^2)$
  Note: the second factor is NOT the same as a perfect trinomial square, so do not try to factor it further.
- **Difference between two cubes**: $x^3 - y^3 = (x - y)(x^2 + xy + y^2)$
  Again, the second factor is NOT the same as a perfect trinomial square.
- **Perfect cubes**: $x^3 + 3x^2y + 3xy^2 + y^3 = (x + y)^3$ and $x^3 - 3x^2y + 3xy^2 - y^3 = (x - y)^3$

In order to **factor** a polynomial, first check for a common monomial factor. When the greatest common monomial factor has been factored out, look for patterns of special products: differences of two squares, the sum or difference of two cubes for binomial factors, or perfect trinomial squares for trinomial factors. If the factor is a trinomial but not a perfect trinomial square, look for a factorable form, such as:

$$x^2 + (a + b)x + ab = (x + a)(x + b)$$
$$\text{or}$$
$$(ac)x^2 + (ad + bc)x + bd = (ax + b)(cx + d)$$

383

For factors with four terms, look for groups to factor. Once you have found the factors, write the original polynomial as the product of all the factors. Make sure all of the polynomial factors are prime. Monomial factors may be prime or composite. Check your work by multiplying the factors to make sure you get the original polynomial.

SOLVING QUADRATIC EQUATIONS

The **quadratic formula** is used to solve quadratic equations when other methods are more difficult. To use the quadratic formula to solve a quadratic equation, begin by rewriting the equation in standard form $ax^2 + bx + c = 0$, where a, b, and c are coefficients. Once you have identified the values of the coefficients, substitute those values into the quadratic formula $x = \frac{-b \pm \sqrt{b^2 - 4ac}}{2a}$. Evaluate the equation and simplify the expression. Again, check each root by substituting into the original equation. In the quadratic formula, the portion of the formula under the radical ($b^2 - 4ac$) is called the **discriminant**. If the discriminant is zero, there is only one root: zero. If the discriminant is positive, there are two different real roots. If the discriminant is negative, there are no real roots.

To solve a quadratic equation by **factoring**, begin by rewriting the equation in standard form, if necessary. Factor the side with the variable then set each of the factors equal to zero and solve the resulting linear equations. Check your answers by substituting the roots you found into the original equation. If, when writing the equation in standard form, you have an equation in the form $x^2 + c = 0$ or $x^2 - c = 0$, set $x^2 = -c$ or $x^2 = c$ and take the square root of c. If $c = 0$, the only real root is zero. If c is positive, there are two real roots—the positive and negative square root values. If c is negative, there are no real roots because you cannot take the square root of a negative number.

To solve a quadratic equation by **completing the square**, rewrite the equation so that all terms containing the variable are on the left side of the equal sign, and all the constants are on the right side of the equal sign. Make sure the coefficient of the squared term is 1. If there is a coefficient with the squared term, divide each term on both sides of the equal side by that number. Next, work with the coefficient of the single-variable term. Square half of this coefficient, and add that value to both sides. Now you can factor the left side (the side containing the variable) as the square of a binomial. $x^2 + 2ax + a^2 = C \Rightarrow (x + a)^2 = C$, where x is the variable, and a and C are constants. Take the square root of both sides and solve for the variable. Substitute the value of the variable in the original problem to check your work.

> **Review Video: <u>Factoring Quadratic Equations</u>**
> Visit mometrix.com/academy and enter Code: 336566

Probability and Statistics

Probability is a branch of statistics that deals with the likelihood of something taking place. One classic example is a coin toss. There are only two possible results: heads or tails. The likelihood, or probability, that the coin will land as heads is 1 out of 2 (1/2, 0.5, 50%). Tails has the same probability. Another common example is a 6-sided die roll. There are six possible results from rolling a single die, each with an equal chance of happening, so the probability of any given number coming up is 1 out of 6.

Terms frequently used in probability:

- **Event** – a situation that produces results of some sort (a coin toss)
- **Compound event** – event that involves two or more independent events (rolling a pair of dice; taking the sum)
- **Outcome** – a possible result in an experiment or event (heads, tails)
- **Desired outcome (or success)** – an outcome that meets a particular set of criteria (a roll of 1 or 2 if we are looking for numbers less than 3)
- **Independent events** – two or more events whose outcomes do not affect one another (two coins tossed at the same time)
- **Dependent events** – two or more events whose outcomes affect one another (two cards drawn consecutively from the same deck)
- **Certain outcome** – probability of outcome is 100% or 1
- **Impossible outcome** – probability of outcome is 0% or 0
- **Mutually exclusive outcomes** – two or more outcomes whose criteria cannot all be satisfied in a single event (a coin coming up heads and tails on the same toss)

> **Review Video: Intro to Probability**
> Visit mometrix.com/academy and enter Code: 212374

Probability is the likelihood of a certain outcome occurring for a given event. The **theoretical probability** can usually be determined without actually performing the event. The likelihood of a outcome occurring, or the probability of an outcome occurring, is given by the formula:

$$P(A) = \frac{\text{Number of acceptable outcomes}}{\text{Number of possible outcomes}}$$

Where $P(A)$ is the probability of an outcome A occurring, and each outcome is just as likely to occur as any other outcome. If each outcome has the same probability of occurring as every other possible outcome, the outcomes are said to be equally likely to occur. The total number of acceptable outcomes must be less than or equal to the total number of possible outcomes. If the two are equal, then the outcome is certain to occur and the probability is 1. If the number of acceptable outcomes is zero, then the outcome is impossible and the probability is 0.

Example: There are 20 marbles in a bag and 5 are red. The theoretical probability of randomly selecting a red marble is 5 out of 20, (5/20 = 1/4, 0.25, or 25%).

When trying to calculate the probability of an event using the $\frac{desired\ outcomes}{total\ outcomes}$ formula, you may frequently find that there are too many outcomes to individually count them. Permutation and combination formulas offer a shortcut to counting outcomes. A permutation is an arrangement of a specific number of a set of objects in a specific order. The number of **permutations** of r items given a set of n items can be calculated as $_nP_r = \frac{n!}{(n-r)!}$. Combinations are similar to permutations, except there are no restrictions regarding the order of the elements. While ABC is considered a different permutation than BCA, ABC and BCA are considered the same combination. The number of **combinations** of r items given a set of n items can be calculated as $_nC_r = \frac{n!}{r!(n-r)!}$ or $_nC_r = \frac{_nP_r}{r!}$.

Example: Suppose you want to calculate how many different 5-card hands can be drawn from a deck of 52 cards. This is a combination since the order of the cards in a hand does not matter. There are 52 cards available, and 5 to be selected. Thus, the number of different hands is $_{52}C_5 = \frac{52!}{5! \times 47!} = 2,598,960$.

Sometimes it may be easier to calculate the possibility of something not happening, or the **complement of an event**. Represented by the symbol $\bar{A}$, the complement of A is the probability that event A does not happen. When you know the probability of event A occurring, you can use the formula $P(\bar{A}) = 1 - P(A)$, where $P(\bar{A})$ is the probability of event A not occurring, and $P(A)$ is the probability of event A occurring.

The **addition rule** for probability is used for finding the probability of a compound event. Use the formula $P(A \text{ or } B) = P(A) + P(B) - P(A \text{ and } B)$, where $P(A \text{ and } B)$ is the probability of both events occurring to find the probability of a compound event. The probability of both events occurring at the same time must be subtracted to eliminate any overlap in the first two probabilities.

Conditional probability is the probability of an event occurring once another event has already occurred. Given event A and dependent event B, the probability of event B occurring when event A has already occurred is represented by the notation $P(A|B)$. To find the probability of event B occurring, take into account the fact that event A has already occurred and adjust the total number of possible outcomes. For example, suppose you have ten balls numbered 1–10 and you want ball number 7 to be pulled in two pulls. On the first pull, the probability of getting the 7 is $\frac{1}{10}$ because there is one ball with a 7 on it and 10 balls to choose from. Assuming the first pull did not yield a 7, the probability of pulling a 7 on the second pull is now $\frac{1}{9}$ because there are only 9 balls remaining for the second pull.

The **multiplication rule** can be used to find the probability of two independent events occurring using the formula $P(A \text{ and } B) = P(A) \times P(B)$, where $P(A \text{ and } B)$ is the probability of two independent events occurring, $P(A)$ is the probability of the first event occurring, and $P(B)$ is the probability of the second event occurring.

The multiplication rule can also be used to find the probability of two dependent events occurring using the formula $P(A \text{ and } B) = P(A) \times P(B|A)$, where $P(A \text{ and } B)$ is the probability of two dependent events occurring and $P(B|A)$ is the probability of the second event occurring after the first event has already occurred.

Before using the multiplication rule, you MUST first determine whether the two events are dependent or independent.

Use a combination of the multiplication rule and the rule of complements to find the probability that at least one outcome of the element will occur. This given by the general formula $P(\text{at least one event occurring}) = 1 - P(\text{no outcomes occurring})$. For example, to find the probability that at least one even number will show when a pair of dice is rolled, find the probability that two odd numbers will be rolled (no even numbers) and subtract from one. You can always use a tree diagram or make a chart to list the possible outcomes when the sample space is small, such as in the dice-rolling example, but in most cases it will be much faster to use the multiplication and complement formulas.

Expected value is a method of determining expected outcome in a random situation. It is really a sum of the weighted probabilities of the possible outcomes. Multiply the probability of an event occurring by the weight assigned to that probability (such as the amount of money won or lost). A practical application of the expected value is to determine whether a game of chance is really fair. If the sum of the weighted probabilities is equal to zero, the game is generally considered fair because the player has a fair chance to at least to break even. If the expected value is less than zero, then players lose more than they win. For example, a lottery drawing might allow the player to choose any three-digit number, 000–999. The probability of choosing the winning number is 1:1000. If it costs $1 to play, and a winning number receives $500, the expected value is:

$$\left(-\$1 \times \frac{999}{1,000}\right) + \left(\$500 \times \frac{1}{1,000}\right) = -0.499 \text{ or } -\$0.50$$

On average, you can expect to lose 50 cents for every dollar you spend.

Most of the time, when we talk about probability, we mean theoretical probability. **Empirical probability**, or experimental probability or relative frequency, is the number of times an outcome occurs in a particular experiment or a certain number of observed events. While theoretical probability is based on what *should* happen, experimental probability is based on what *has* happened. Experimental probability is calculated in the same way as theoretical, except that actual outcomes are used instead of possible outcomes.

Theoretical and experimental probability do not always line up with one another. Theoretical probability says that out of 20 coin tosses, 10 should be heads. However, if we were actually to toss 20 coins, we might record just 5 heads. This doesn't mean that our theoretical probability is incorrect; it just means that this particular experiment had results that were different from what was predicted. A practical application of empirical probability is the insurance industry. There are no set functions that define life span, health, or safety. Insurance companies look at factors from hundreds of thousands of individuals to find patterns that they then use to set the formulas for insurance premiums.

Objective probability is based on mathematical formulas and documented evidence. Examples of objective probability include raffles or lottery drawings where there is a pre-determined number of possible outcomes and a predetermined number of outcomes that correspond to an event. Other cases of objective probability include probabilities of rolling dice, flipping coins, or drawing cards. Most gambling games are based on objective probability.

Subjective probability is based on personal or professional feelings and judgments. Often, there is a lot of guesswork following extensive research. Areas where subjective probability is applicable include sales trends and business expenses. Attractions set admission prices based on subjective probabilities of attendance based on varying admission rates in an effort to maximize their profit.

The total set of all possible results of a test or experiment is called a **sample space**, or sometimes a universal sample space. The sample space, represented by one of the variables S, Ω, or U (for universal sample space) has individual elements called outcomes. Other terms for outcome that may be used interchangeably include elementary outcome, simple event, or sample point. The number of outcomes in a given sample space could be infinite or finite, and some tests may yield multiple unique sample sets. For example, tests conducted by drawing playing cards from a standard deck would have one sample space of the card values, another sample space of the card suits, and a third sample space of suit-denomination combinations. For most tests, the sample spaces considered will be finite.

An event, represented by the variable E, is a portion of a sample space. It may be one outcome or a group of outcomes from the same sample space. If an event occurs, then the test or experiment will generate an outcome that satisfies the requirement of that event. For example, given a standard deck of 52 playing cards as the sample space, and defining the event as the collection of face cards, then the event will occur if the card drawn is a J, Q, or K. If any other card is drawn, the event is said to have not occurred.

For every sample space, each possible outcome has a specific likelihood, or probability, that it will occur. The probability measure, also called the **distribution**, is a function that assigns a real number probability, from zero to one, to each outcome. For a probability measure to be accurate, every outcome must have a real number probability measure that is greater than or equal to zero and less than or equal to one. Also, the probability measure of the sample space must equal one, and the probability measure of the union of multiple outcomes must equal the sum of the individual probability measures.

Probabilities of events are expressed as real numbers from zero to one. They give a numerical value to the chance that a particular event will occur. The probability of an event occurring is the sum of the probabilities of the individual elements of that event. For example, in a standard deck of 52 playing cards as the sample space and the collection of face cards as the event, the probability of drawing a specific face card is $\frac{1}{52} = 0.019$, but the probability of drawing any one of the twelve face cards is $12(0.019) = 0.228$. Note that rounding of numbers can generate different results. If you multiplied 12 by the fraction $\frac{1}{52}$ before converting to a decimal, you would get the answer $\frac{12}{52} = 0.231$.

For a simple sample space, possible outcomes may be determined by using a **tree diagram** or an organized chart. In either case, you can easily draw or list out the possible outcomes. For example, to determine all the possible ways three objects can be ordered, you can draw a tree diagram:

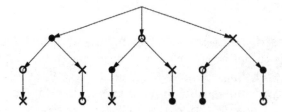

You can also make a chart to list all the possibilities:

First object	Second object	Third object
●	×	0
●	0	×
0	●	×
0	×	●
×	●	0
×	0	●

Either way, you can easily see there are six possible ways the three objects can be ordered.

If two events have no outcomes in common, they are said to be **mutually exclusive**. For example, in a standard deck of 52 playing cards, the event of all card suits is mutually exclusive to the event of all card values. If two events have no bearing on each other so that one event occurring has no influence on the probability of another event occurring, the two events are said to be independent. For example, rolling a standard six-sided die multiple times does not change that probability that a particular number will be rolled from one roll to the next. If the outcome of one event does affect the probability of the second event, the two events are said to be dependent. For example, if cards are drawn from a deck, the probability of drawing an ace after an ace has been drawn is different than the probability of drawing an ace if no ace (or no other card, for that matter) has been drawn.

In probability, the odds in favor of an event are the number of times the event will occur compared to the number of times the event will not occur. To calculate the odds in favor of an event, use the formula $\frac{P(A)}{1-P(A)}$, where $P(A)$ is the probability that the event will occur. Many times, odds in favor is given as a ratio in the form $\frac{a}{b}$ or $a:b$, where a is the probability of the event occurring and b is the complement of the event, the probability of the event not occurring. If the odds in favor are given as 2:5, that means that you can expect the event to occur two times for every 5 times that it does not occur. In other words, the probability that the event will occur is $\frac{2}{2+5} = \frac{2}{7}$.

In probability, the odds against an event are the number of times the event will not occur compared to the number of times the event will occur. To calculate the odds against an event, use the formula $\frac{1-P(A)}{P(A)}$, where $P(A)$ is the probability that the event will occur. Many times, odds against is given as a ratio in the form $\frac{b}{a}$ or $b:a$, where b is the probability the event will not occur (the complement of the event) and a is the probability the event will occur. If the odds against an event are given as 3:1, that means that you can expect the event to not occur 3 times for every one time it does occur. In other words, 3 out of every 4 trials will fail.

STATISTICS

In statistics, the **population** is the entire collection of people, plants, etc., that data can be collected from. For example, a study to determine how well students in the area schools perform on a standardized test would have a population of all the students enrolled in those schools, although a study may include just a small sample of students from each school. A **parameter** is a numerical value that gives information about the population, such as the mean, median, mode, or standard deviation. Remember that the symbol for the mean of a population is μ and the symbol for the standard deviation of a population is σ.

A **sample** is a portion of the entire population. Where as a parameter helped describe the population, a **statistic** is a numerical value that gives information about the sample, such as mean, median, mode, or standard deviation. Keep in mind that the symbols for mean and standard deviation are different when they are referring to a sample rather than the entire population. For a sample, the symbol for mean is $\bar{x}$ and the symbol for standard deviation is s. The mean and standard deviation of a sample may or may not be identical to that of the entire population due to a sample only being a subset of the population. However, if the sample is random and large enough, statistically significant values can be attained. Samples are generally used when the population is too large to justify including every element or when acquiring data for the entire population is impossible.

Inferential statistics is the branch of statistics that uses samples to make predictions about an entire population. This type of statistics is often seen in political polls, where a sample of the population is questioned about a particular topic or politician to gain an understanding about the attitudes of the entire population of the country. Often, exit polls are conducted on election days using this method. Inferential statistics can have a large margin of error if you do not have a valid sample.

Statistical values calculated from various samples of the same size make up the sampling distribution. For example, if several samples of identical size are randomly selected from a large population and then the mean of each sample is calculated, the distribution of values of the means would be a **sampling distribution**.

The **sampling distribution of the mean** is the distribution of the sample mean, $\bar{x}$, derived from random samples of a given size. It has three important characteristics. First, the mean of the sampling distribution of the mean is equal to the mean of the population that was sampled. Second, assuming the standard deviation is non-zero, the standard deviation of the sampling distribution of the mean equals the standard deviation of the sampled population divided by the square root of the sample size. This is sometimes called the standard error. Finally, as the sample size gets larger, the sampling distribution of the mean gets closer to a normal distribution via the **Central Limit Theorem**.

A **survey study** is a method of gathering information from a small group in an attempt to gain enough information to make accurate general assumptions about the population. Once a survey study is completed, the results are then put into a summary report. Survey studies are generally in the format of surveys, interviews, or questionnaires as part of an effort to find opinions of a particular group or to find facts about a group. It is important to note that the findings from a survey study are only as accurate as the sample chosen from the population.

Correlational studies seek to determine how much one variable is affected by changes in a second variable. For example, correlational studies may look for a relationship between the amount of time a student spends studying for a test and the grade that student earned on the test or between student scores on college admissions tests and student grades in college. It is important to note that correlational studies cannot show a cause and effect, but rather can show only that two variables are or are not potentially correlated.

Experimental studies take correlational studies one step farther, in that they attempt to prove or disprove a cause-and-effect relationship. These studies are performed by conducting a series of experiments to test the hypothesis. For a study to be scientifically accurate, it must have both an experimental group that receives the specified treatment and a control group that does not get the treatment. This is the type of study pharmaceutical companies do as part of drug trials for new medications. Experimental studies are only valid when proper scientific method has been followed. In other words, the experiment must be well-planned and executed without bias in the testing process, all subjects must be selected at random, and the process of determining which subject is in which of the two groups must also be completely random.

Observational studies are the opposite of experimental studies. In observational studies, the tester cannot change or in any way control all of the variables in the test. For example, a study to determine which gender does better in math classes in school is strictly observational. You cannot change a person's gender, and you cannot change the subject being studied. The big downfall of observational studies is that you have no way of proving a cause-and-effect relationship because you cannot control outside influences. Events outside of school can influence a student's performance in school, and observational studies cannot take that into consideration.

For most studies, a **random sample** is necessary to produce valid results. Random samples should not have any particular influence to cause sampled subjects to behave one way or another. The goal is for the random sample to be a **representative sample**, or a sample whose characteristics give an accurate picture of the characteristics of the entire population. To accomplish this, you must make sure you have a proper **sample size**, or an appropriate number of elements in the sample.

In statistical studies, biases must be avoided. **Bias** is an error that causes the study to favor one set of results over another. For example, if a survey to determine how the country views the president's job performance only speaks to registered voters in the president's party, the results will be skewed because a disproportionately large number of responders would tend to show approval, while a disproportionately large number of people in the opposite party would tend to express disapproval.

Extraneous variables are, as the name implies, outside influences that can affect the outcome of a study. They are not always avoidable, but could trigger bias in the result.

DATA ANALYSIS

The **measure of central tendency** is a statistical value that gives a general tendency for the center of a group of data. There are several different ways of describing the measure of central tendency. Each one has a unique way it is calculated, and each one gives a slightly different perspective on the data set. Whenever you give a measure of central tendency, always make sure the units are the same. If the data has different units, such as hours, minutes, and seconds, convert all the data to the same unit, and use the same unit in the measure of central tendency. If no units are given in the data, do not give units for the measure of central tendency.

The statistical **mean** of a group of data is the same as the arithmetic average of that group. To find the mean of a set of data, first convert each value to the same units, if necessary. Then find the sum of all the values, and count the total number of data values, making sure you take into consideration each individual value. If a value appears more than once, count it more than once. Divide the sum of the values by the total number of values and apply the units, if any. Note that the mean does not have to be one of the data values in the set, and may not divide evenly.

$$\text{mean} = \frac{\text{sum of the data values}}{\text{quantity of data values}}$$

While the mean is relatively easy to calculate and averages are understood by most people, the mean can be very misleading if used as the sole measure of central tendency. If the data set has outliers (data values that are unusually high or unusually low compared to the rest of the data values), the mean can be very distorted, especially if the data set has a small number of values. If unusually high values are countered with unusually low values, the mean is not affected as much. For example, if five of twenty students in a class get a 100 on a test, but the other 15 students have an average of 60 on the same test, the class average would appear as 70. Whenever the mean is skewed by outliers, it is always a good idea to include the median as an alternate measure of central tendency.

The statistical **median** is the value in the middle of the set of data. To find the median, list all data values in order from smallest to largest or from largest to smallest. Any value that is repeated in the set must be listed the number of times it appears. If there are an odd number of data values, the median is the value in the middle of the list. If there is an even number of data values, the median is the arithmetic mean of the two middle values.

The statistical **mode** is the data value that occurs the most number of times in the data set. It is possible to have exactly one mode, more than one mode, or no mode. To find the mode of a set of data, arrange the data like you do to find the median (all values in order, listing all multiples of data values). Count the number of times each value appears in the data set. If all values appear an equal number of times, there is no mode. If one value appears more than any other value, that value is the mode. If two or more values appear the same number of times, but there are other values that appear fewer times and no values that appear more times, all of those values are the modes.

The big disadvantage of using the median as a measure of central tendency is that is relies solely on a value's relative size as compared to the other values in the set. When the individual values in a set of data are evenly dispersed, the median can be an accurate tool. However, if there is a group of rather large values or a group of rather small values that are not offset by a different group of values, the information that can be inferred from the median may not be accurate because the distribution of values is skewed.

The main disadvantage of the mode is that the values of the other data in the set have no bearing on the mode. The mode may be the largest value, the smallest value, or a value anywhere in between in the set. The mode only tells which value or values, if any, occurred the most number of times. It does not give any suggestions about the remaining values in the set.

The **measure of dispersion** is a single value that helps to "interpret" the measure of central tendency by providing more information about how the data values in the set are distributed about the measure of central tendency. The measure of dispersion helps to eliminate or reduce the disadvantages of using the mean, median, or mode as a single measure of central tendency, and give a more accurate picture of the data set as a whole. To have a measure of dispersion, you must know or calculate the range, standard deviation, or variance of the data set.

The **range** of a set of data is the difference between the greatest and lowest values of the data in the set. To calculate the range, you must first make sure the units for all data values are the same, and then identify the greatest and lowest values. Use the formula range = highest value – lowest value. If there are multiple data values that are equal for the highest or lowest, just use one of the values in the formula. Write the answer with the same units as the data values you used to do the calculations.

Standard deviation is a measure of dispersion that compares all the data values in the set to the mean of the set to give a more accurate picture. To find the standard deviation of a population, use the formula

$$\sigma = \sqrt{\frac{\sum_{i=1}^{n}(x_i - \bar{x})^2}{n}}$$

Where σ is the standard deviation of a population, x represents the individual values in the data set, $\bar{x}$ is the mean of the data values in the set, and n is the number of data values in the set. The higher the value of the standard deviation is, the greater the variance of the data values from the mean. If a constant is added to every value in the population, the mean will increase by that constant, but the standard deviation will remain the same. If every value in the population is multiplied by a constant factor, both the mean and standard deviation will increase by that factor.

The **variance** of a population, or just variance, is the square of the standard deviation of that population. While the mean of a set of data gives the average of the set and gives information about where a specific data value lies in relation to the average, the variance of the population gives information about the degree to which the data values are spread out and tell you how close an individual value is to the average compared to the other values. The units associated with variance are the same as the units of the data values.

Percentiles and Quartiles are other methods of describing data within a set. **Percentiles** tell what percentage of the data in the set fall below a specific point. For example, achievement test scores are often given in percentiles. A score at the 80th percentile is one which is equal to or higher than 80 percent of the scores in the set. In other words, 80 percent of the scores were lower than that score.

Quartiles are percentile groups that make up quarter sections of the data set. The first quartile is the 25th percentile. The second quartile is the 50th percentile; this is also the median of the data set. The third quartile is the 75th percentile.

Skewness is a way to describe the symmetry or asymmetry of the distribution of values in a data set. If the distribution of values is symmetrical, there is no skew. In general the closer the mean of a data set is to the median of the data set, the less skew there is. Generally, if the mean is to the right of the median, the data set is **positively skewed**, or right-skewed, and if the mean is to the left of the median, the data set is **negatively skewed**, or left-skewed. However, this rule of thumb is not infallible. When the data values are graphed on a curve, a set with no skew will be a perfect bell curve. To estimate skew, use the formula

$$\text{skew} = \frac{\sqrt{n(n-1)}}{n-2}\left(\frac{\frac{1}{n}\sum_{i=1}^{n}(x_i - \bar{x})^3}{\left(\frac{1}{n}\sum_{i=1}^{n}(x_i - \bar{x})^2\right)^{\frac{3}{2}}}\right)$$

Where n is the number of values is the set, x_i is the ith value in the set, and $\bar{x}$ is the mean of the set.

In statistics, **simple regression** is using an equation to represent a relation between an independent and dependent variables. The independent variable is also referred to as the explanatory variable or the predictor, and is generally represented by the variable x in the equation. The dependent variable, usually represented by the variable y, is also referred to as the response variable. The equation may be any type of function – linear, quadratic, exponential, etc. The best way to handle this task is to use the regression feature of your graphing calculator. This will easily give you the curve of best fit and provide you with the coefficients and other information you need to derive an equation.

In a scatter plot, the **line of best fit** is the line that best shows the trends of the data. The line of best fit is given by the equation $\hat{y} = ax + b$, where a and b are the regression coefficients. The regression coefficient a is also the slope of the line of best fit, and b is also the y-coordinate of the point at which the line of best fit crosses the x-axis. Not every point on the scatter plot will be on the line of best fit. The differences between the y-values of the points in the scatter plot and the corresponding y-values according to the equation of the line of best fit are the residuals. The line of best fit is also called the least-squares regression line because it is also the line that has the lowest sum of the squares of the residuals.

The **correlation coefficient** is the numerical value that indicates how strong the relationship is between the two variables of a linear regression equation. A correlation coefficient of –1 is a perfect negative correlation. A correlation coefficient of +1 is a perfect positive correlation. Correlation coefficients close to –1 or +1 are very strong correlations. A correlation coefficient equal to zero indicates there is no correlation between the two variables. This test is a good indicator of whether or not the equation for the line of best fit is accurate. The formula for the correlation coefficient is

$$r = \frac{\sum_{i=1}^{n}(x_i - \bar{x})(y_i - \bar{y})}{\sqrt{\sum_{i=1}^{n}(x_i - \bar{x})^2}\sqrt{\sum_{i=1}^{n}(y_i - \bar{y})^2}}$$

where r is the correlation coefficient, n is the number of data values in the set, (x_i, y_i) is a point in the set, and $\bar{x}$ and $\bar{y}$ are the means.

A **z-score** is an indication of how many standard deviations a given value falls from the mean. To calculate a z-score, use the formula $= \frac{x-\mu}{\sigma}$, where x is the data value, μ is the mean of the data set, and σ is the standard deviation of the population. If the z-score is positive, the data value lies above the mean. If the z-score is negative, the data value falls below the mean. These scores are useful in interpreting data such as standardized test scores, where every piece of data in the set has been counted, rather than just a small random sample. In cases where standard deviations are calculated from a random sample of the set, the z-scores will not be as accurate.

According to the **central limit theorem**, regardless of what the original distribution of a sample is, the distribution of the means tends to get closer and closer to a normal distribution as the sample size gets larger and larger (this is necessary because the sample is becoming more all-encompassing of the elements of the population). As the sample size gets larger, the distribution of the sample mean will approach a normal distribution with a mean of the population mean and a variance of the population variance divided by the sample size.

DISPLAYING INFORMATION

Charts and **tables** are ways of organizing information into separate rows and columns that are labeled to identify and explain the data contained in them. Some charts and tables are organized horizontally, with row lengths giving the details about the labeled information. Other charts and tables are organized vertically, with column heights giving the details about the labeled information.

Frequency tables show how frequently each unique value appears in the set. A **relative frequency table** is one that shows the proportions of each unique value compared to the entire set. Relative frequencies are given as percentages; however, the total percent for a relative frequency table will not necessarily equal 100 percent due to rounding. An example of a frequency table with relative frequencies is below.

Favorite Color	Frequency	Relative Frequency
Blue	4	13%
Red	7	22%
Purple	3	9%
Green	6	19%
Cyan	12	38%

Circle graphs, also known as **pie charts**, provide a visual depiction of the relationship of each type of data compared to the whole set of data. The circle graph is divided into sections by drawing radii to create central angles whose percentage of the circle is equal to the individual data's percentage of the whole set. Each 1% of data is equal to 3.6° in the circle graph. Therefore, data represented by a 90° section of the circle graph makes up 25% of the whole. When complete, a circle graph often looks like a pie cut into uneven wedges. The pie chart below shows the data from the frequency table referenced earlier where people were asked their favorite color.

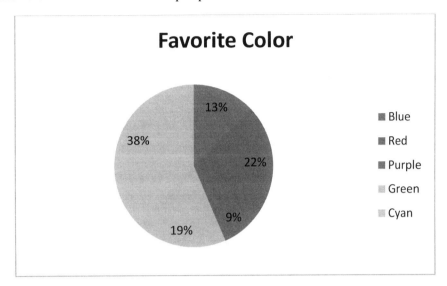

A **bar graph** is one of the few graphs that can be drawn correctly in two different configurations – both horizontally and vertically. A bar graph is similar to a line plot in the way the data is organized on the graph. Both axes must have their categories defined for the graph to be useful. Rather than placing a single dot to mark the point of the data's value, a bar, or thick line, is drawn from zero to the exact value of the data, whether it is a number, percentage, or other numerical value. Longer bar lengths correspond to greater data values. To read a bar graph, read the labels for the axes to find the units being reported. Then look where the bars end in relation to the scale given on the corresponding axis and determine the associated value. The bar chart below represents the responses from our favorite color survey.

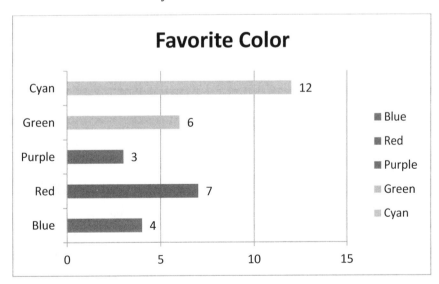

Line graphs have one or more lines of varying styles (solid or broken) to show the different values for a set of data. The individual data are represented as ordered pairs, much like on a Cartesian plane. In this case, the *x*- and *y*- axes are defined in terms of their units, such as dollars or time. The individual plotted points are joined by line segments to show whether the value of the data is increasing (line sloping upward), decreasing (line sloping downward) or staying the same (horizontal line). Multiple sets of data can be graphed on the same line graph to give an easy visual comparison. An example of this would be graphing achievement test scores for different groups of students over the same time period to see which group had the greatest increase or decrease in performance from year-to-year (as shown below).

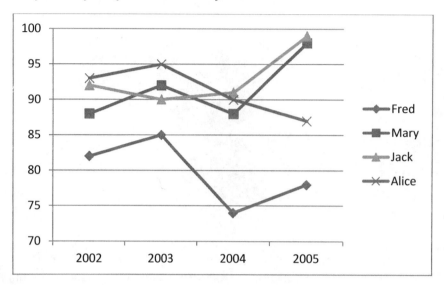

A **line plot**, also known as a **dot plot**, has plotted points that are NOT connected by line segments. In this graph, the horizontal axis lists the different possible values for the data, and the vertical axis lists the number of times the individual value occurs. A single dot is graphed for each value to show the number of times it occurs. This graph is more closely related to a bar graph than a line graph. Do not connect the dots in a line plot or it will misrepresent the data.

A **pictograph** is a graph, generally in the horizontal orientation, that uses pictures or symbols to represent the data. Each pictograph must have a key that defines the picture or symbol and gives the quantity each picture or symbol represents. Pictures or symbols on a pictograph are not always shown as whole elements. In this case, the fraction of the picture or symbol shown represents the same fraction of the quantity a whole picture or symbol stands for. For example, a row with $3\frac{1}{2}$ ears of corn, where each ear of corn represents 100 stalks of corn in a field, would equal $3\frac{1}{2} \times 100 = 350$ stalks of corn in the field.

A **stem and leaf plot** is useful for depicting groups of data that fall into a range of values. Each piece of data is separated into two parts: the first, or left, part is called the stem; the second, or right, part is called the leaf. Each stem is listed in a column from smallest to largest. Each leaf that has the common stem is listed in that stem's row from smallest to largest. For example, in a set of two-digit numbers, the digit in the tens place is the stem, and the digit in the ones place is the leaf. With a stem and leaf plot, you can easily see which subset of numbers (10s, 20s, 30s, etc.) is the largest. This information is also readily available by looking at a histogram, but a stem and leaf plot also allows you to look closer and see exactly which values fall in that range. Using all of the test scores from above, we can assemble a stem and leaf plot like the one below.

Test Scores

7	4	8						
8	2	5	7	8	8			
9	0	0	1	2	2	3	5	8	9

At first glance, a **histogram** looks like a vertical bar graph. The difference is that a bar graph has a separate bar for each piece of data and a histogram has one continuous bar for each **range** of data. For example, a histogram may have one bar for the range 0–9, one bar for 10–19, etc. While a bar graph has numerical values on one axis, a histogram has numerical values on both axes. Each range is of equal size, and they are ordered left to right from lowest to highest. The height of each column on a histogram represents the number of data values within that range. Like a stem and leaf plot, a histogram makes it easy to glance at the graph and quickly determine which range has the greatest quantity of values. A simple example of a histogram is below.

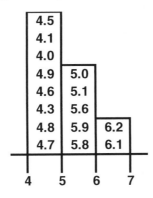

Bivariate data is simply data from two different variables. (The prefix *bi-* means *two*.) In a **scatter plot**, each value in the set of data is plotted on a grid similar to a Cartesian plane, where each axis represents one of the two variables. By looking at the pattern formed by the points on the grid, you can often determine whether or not there is a relationship between the two variables, and what that relationship is, if it exists. The variables may be directly proportionate, inversely proportionate, or show no proportion at all. It may also be possible to determine if the data is linear, and if so, to find an equation to relate the two variables. The following scatter plot shows the relationship between preference for brand "A" and the age of the consumers surveyed.

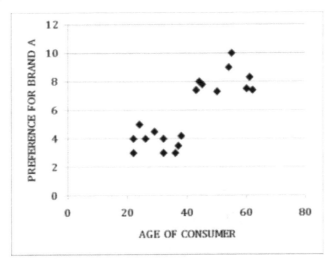

Scatter Plots are also useful in determining the type of function represented by the data and finding the simple regression. Linear scatter plots may be positive or negative. Nonlinear scatter plots are generally exponential or quadratic. Below are some common types of scatter plots:

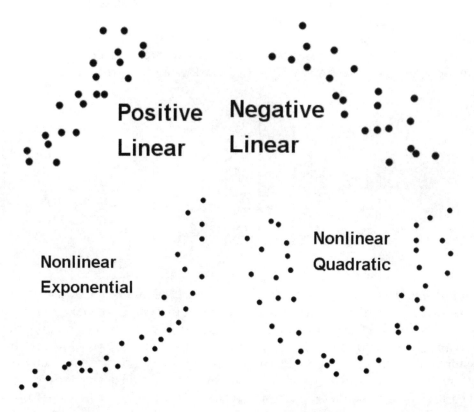

The **5-number summary** of a set of data gives a very informative picture of the set. The five numbers in the summary include the minimum value, maximum value, and the three quartiles. This information gives the reader the range and median of the set, as well as an indication of how the data is spread about the median.

A **box-and-whiskers plot** is a graphical representation of the 5-number summary. To draw a box-and-whiskers plot, plot the points of the 5-number summary on a number line. Draw a box whose ends are through the points for the first and third quartiles. Draw a vertical line in the box through the median to divide the box in half. Draw a line segment from the first quartile point to the minimum value, and from the third quartile point to the maximum value.

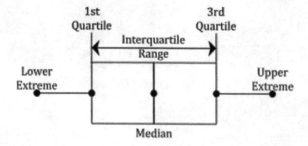

The **68–95–99.7 rule** describes how a normal distribution of data should appear when compared to the mean. This is also a description of a normal bell curve. According to this rule, 68 percent of the data values in a normally distributed set should fall within one standard deviation of the mean

(34 percent above and 34 percent below the mean), 95 percent of the data values should fall within two standard deviations of the mean (47.5 percent above and 47.5 percent below the mean), and 99.7 percent of the data values should fall within three standard deviations of the mean, again, equally distributed on either side of the mean. This means that only 0.3 percent of all data values should fall more than three standard deviations from the mean. On the graph below, the normal curve is centered on the y-axis. The x-axis labels are how many standard deviations away from the center you are. Therefore, it is easy to see how the 68-95-99.7 rule can apply.

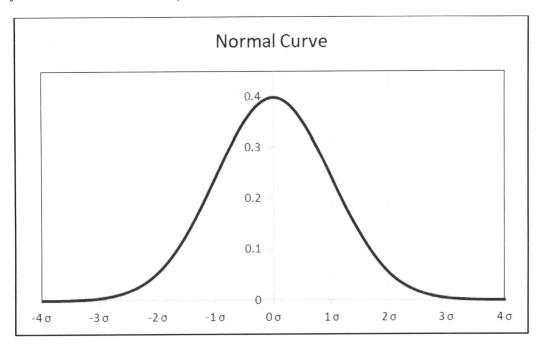

The five general shapes of frequency curves are **symmetrical**, **U-shaped**, **skewed**, **J-shaped**, and **multimodal**. Symmetrical curves are also known as bell curves or normal curves. Values equidistant from the median have equal frequencies. U-shaped curves have two maxima – one at each end. Skewed curves have the maximum point off-center. Curves that are negative skewed, or left skewed, have the maximum on the right side of the graph so there is longer tail and lower slope on the left side. The opposite is true for curves that are positive skewed, or right skewed. J-shaped curves have a maximum at one end and a minimum at the other end. Multimodal curves have multiple maxima. For example, if the curve has exactly two maxima, it is called a bimodal curve.

Geometry

LINES AND PLANES

A **point** is a fixed location in space; has no size or dimensions; commonly represented by a dot.

A **line** is a set of points that extends infinitely in two opposite directions. It has length, but no width or depth. A line can be defined by any two distinct points that it contains. A line segment is a portion of a line that has definite endpoints. A ray is a portion of a line that extends from a single point on that line in one direction along the line. It has a definite beginning, but no ending.

> **Review Video: Geometric Symbols: Segments, Lines, Rays, and Vectors**
> Visit mometrix.com/academy and enter Code: 122404

A **plane** is a two-dimensional flat surface defined by three non-collinear points. A plane extends an infinite distance in all directions in those two dimensions. It contains an infinite number of points, parallel lines and segments, intersecting lines and segments, as well as parallel or intersecting rays. A plane will never contain a three-dimensional figure or skew lines. Two given planes will either be parallel or they will intersect to form a line. A plane may intersect a circular conic surface, such as a cone, to form conic sections, such as the parabola, hyperbola, circle or ellipse.

Perpendicular lines are lines that intersect at right angles. They are represented by the symbol ⊥. The shortest distance from a line to a point not on the line is a perpendicular segment from the point to the line.

Parallel lines are lines in the same plane that have no points in common and never meet. It is possible for lines to be in different planes, have no points in common, and never meet, but they are not parallel because they are in different planes.

> **Review Video: Parallel and Perpendicular Lines**
> Visit mometrix.com/academy and enter Code: 815923

A **bisector** is a line or line segment that divides another line segment into two equal lengths. A perpendicular bisector of a line segment is composed of points that are equidistant from the endpoints of the segment it is dividing.

Intersecting lines are lines that have exactly one point in common. Concurrent lines are multiple lines that intersect at a single point.

A **transversal** is a line that intersects at least two other lines, which may or may not be parallel to one another. A transversal that intersects parallel lines is a common occurrence in geometry.

ANGLES

An **angle** is made when two lines or line segments meet at a point. The angle may be a starting point for a pair of segments or rays. Also, angles come from the intersection of lines. The symbol ∠ stands for angles.

Angles that are opposite to one another are called vertical angles, and their measures are equal. The vertex is the point where two segments or rays meet to make an angle. Angles that are made from intersecting rays, lines, and/or line segments have four angles at the vertex.

An **acute angle** is an angle with a degree measure less than 90°. A **right angle** is an angle with a degree measure of exactly 90°. An **obtuse angle** is an angle with a degree measure greater than 90° but less than 180°. A **straight angle** is an angle with a degree measure of exactly 180°. A **reflex angle** is an angle with a degree measure greater than 180° but less than 360°. A **full angle** is an angle with a degree measure of exactly 360°.

Two angles with a sum of exactly 90° are known as **complementary**. The two angles may or may not be adjacent (i.e., *next to* or *beside*). In a right triangle, the two acute angles are complementary.

Two angles with a sum that is exactly 180° are known as **supplementary**. The two angles may or may not be adjacent. Two intersecting lines always make two pairs of supplementary angles. Adjacent supplementary angles will always make a straight line.

Two angles that have the same vertex and share a side are known as **adjacent**. **Vertical angles** are not adjacent because they share a vertex, but they have no common side.

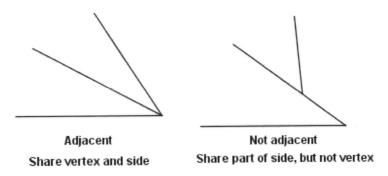

Adjacent
Share vertex and side

Not adjacent
Share part of side, but not vertex

When two parallel lines are cut by a transversal, the angles that are between the two parallel lines are interior angles. In the diagram below, angles 3, 4, 5, and 6 are **interior angles**.

When two parallel lines are cut by a transversal, the angles that are outside the parallel lines are exterior angles. In the diagram below, angles 1, 2, 7, and 8 are **exterior angles**.

When two parallel lines are cut by a transversal, the angles that match the position of other angles are corresponding angles. The diagram below has four pairs of corresponding angles: angles 1 and 5; angles 2 and 6; angles 3 and 7; and angles 4 and 8. Corresponding angles made by parallel lines are congruent. For congruent angles, we mean that they have the same angle measures.

When two parallel lines are cut by a transversal, the two interior angles that are on opposite sides of the transversal are alternate interior angles. In the diagram below, there are two pairs of alternate interior angles: angles 3 and 6 and angles 4 and 5. Alternate interior angles made by parallel lines are congruent.

When two parallel lines are cut by a transversal, the two exterior angles that are on opposite sides of the transversal are alternate exterior angles. In the diagram below, there are two pairs of alternate exterior angles: angles 1 and 8 and angles 2 and 7. Alternate exterior angles made by parallel lines are congruent.

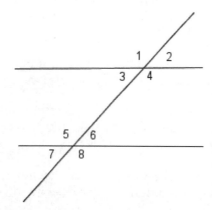

When two lines intersect, four angles are formed. The non-adjacent angles at this vertex are called vertical angles. Vertical angles are congruent. In the diagram, $\angle ABD \cong \angle CBE$ and $\angle ABC \cong \angle DBE$.

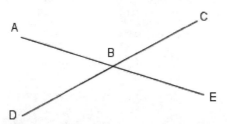

Review Video: Angles
Visit mometrix.com/academy and enter Code: 264624

TRIANGLES

An **equilateral triangle** is a triangle with three congruent sides. Also, an equilateral triangle will have three congruent angles and each angle will be 60°. All equilateral triangles are acute triangles.

An **isosceles triangle** is a triangle with two congruent sides. An isosceles triangle will have two congruent angles as well.

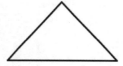

A **scalene triangle** is a triangle with no congruent sides. Also, a scalene triangle will have three angles of different measures. The angle with the largest measure is opposite from the longest side. The angle with the smallest measure is opposite from the shortest side.

An **acute triangle** is a triangle whose three angles are all less than 90°. If two of the angles are equal, the acute triangle is also an isosceles triangle. If the three angles are all equal, the acute triangle is also an equilateral triangle.

A **right triangle** is a triangle with exactly one angle equal to 90°. All right triangles follow the Pythagorean Theorem. A right triangle can never be acute or obtuse.

An **obtuse triangle** is a triangle with one angle greater than 90°. The other two angles may or may not be equal. If the two remaining angles are equal, the obtuse triangle is also an isosceles triangle.

TERMINOLOGY

Altitude of a triangle: A line segment drawn from one vertex perpendicular to the opposite side. In the diagram below, $\overline{BE}$, $\overline{AD}$, and $\overline{CF}$ are altitudes. The three altitudes in a triangle are always concurrent.

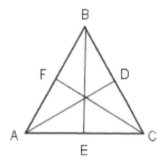

Height of a triangle: The length of the altitude, although the two terms are often used interchangeably.

Orthocenter of a triangle: The point of concurrency of the altitudes of a triangle. Note that in an obtuse triangle, the orthocenter will be outside the triangle, and in a right triangle, the orthocenter is the vertex of the right angle.

Median of a triangle: A line segment drawn from one vertex to the midpoint of the opposite side. This is not the same as the altitude, except the altitude to the base of an isosceles triangle and all three altitudes of an equilateral triangle.

Centroid of a triangle: The point of concurrency of the medians of a triangle. This is the same point as the orthocenter only in an equilateral triangle. Unlike the orthocenter, the centroid is always inside the triangle. The centroid can also be considered the exact center of the triangle. Any shape triangle can be perfectly balanced on a tip placed at the centroid. The centroid is also the point that is two-thirds the distance from the vertex to the opposite side.

PYTHAGOREAN THEOREM

The side of a triangle opposite the right angle is called the hypotenuse. The other two sides are called the legs. The **Pythagorean theorem** states a relationship among the legs and hypotenuse of a right triangle: $a^2 + b^2 = c^2$, where a and b are the lengths of the legs of a right triangle, and c is the length of the hypotenuse. Note that this formula will only work with right triangles.

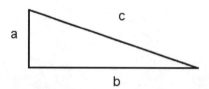

Review Video: Pythagorean Theorem
Visit mometrix.com/academy and enter Code: 906576

GENERAL RULES

The **triangle inequality theorem** says that the sum of the measures of any two sides of a triangle is always greater than the measure of the third side. For example, one side of a triangle is 5, and the other side is 10. So, the third side must be less than 15. The third side cannot be 15.

If the sum of the measures of two sides were equal to the third side, a triangle would be impossible. The reason is that the two sides would lie flat across the third side, and there would be no vertex. If the sum of the measures of two of the sides was less than the third side, a closed shape would be impossible. The reason is that the two shortest sides would never meet.

The **triangle sum theorem** says that the sum of the measures of the interior angles of a triangle is always 180°. So, a triangle can never have more than one angle that is greater than or equal to 90°.

In any triangle, the angles that are opposite to congruent sides are congruent. The sides that are opposite to congruent angles are congruent. The largest angle is always opposite the longest side. The smallest angle is always opposite to the shortest side.

The line segment that joins the midpoints of any two sides of a triangle is always parallel to the third side. Also, this line segment is exactly half the length of the third side.

SIMILARITY AND CONGRUENCE RULES

Similar triangles are triangles whose corresponding angles are equal and whose corresponding sides are proportional. Represented by **AA**. Similar triangles whose corresponding sides are congruent are also congruent triangles.

Three sides of one triangle are congruent to the three corresponding sides of the second triangle. Represented as **SSS**.

Two sides and the included angle (the angle formed by those two sides) of one triangle are congruent to the corresponding two sides and included angle of the second triangle. Represented by **SAS**.

Two angles and the included side (the side that joins the two angles) of one triangle are congruent to the corresponding two angles and included side of the second triangle. Represented by **ASA**.

Two angles and a non-included side of one triangle are congruent to the corresponding two angles and non-included side of the second triangle. Represented by **AAS**.

Note that AAA is not a form for congruent triangles. This would say that the three angles are congruent, but says nothing about the sides. This meets the requirements for similar triangles, but not congruent triangles.

AREA AND PERIMETER FORMULAS

The **perimeter of any triangle** is found by summing the three side lengths; $P = a + b + c$. For an equilateral triangle, this is the same as $P = 3s$, where s is any side length, since all three sides are the same length.

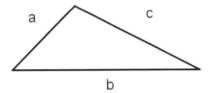

The **area of any triangle** can be found by taking half the product of one side length (base or b) and the perpendicular distance from that side to the opposite vertex (height or h). In equation form, $A = \frac{1}{2}bh$. For many triangles, it may be difficult to calculate h, so using one of the other formulas given here may be easier.

Another formula that works for any triangle is $A = \sqrt{s(s - a)(s - b)(s - c)}$, where A is the area, s is the semiperimeter $s = \frac{a+b+c}{2}$, and a, b, and c are the lengths of the three sides.

The **area of an equilateral triangle** can be found by the formula $A = \frac{\sqrt{3}}{4}s^2$, where A is the area and s is the length of a side. You could use the $30° - 60° - 90°$ ratios to find the height of the triangle and then use the standard triangle area formula, but this is faster.

The **area of an isosceles triangle** can be found by the formula, $A = \frac{1}{2}b\sqrt{a^2 - \frac{b^2}{4}}$, where A is the area, b is the base (the unique side), and a is the length of one of the two congruent sides. If you do not remember this formula, you can use the Pythagorean Theorem to find the height so you can use the standard formula for the area of a triangle.

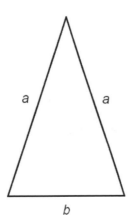

TRIGONOMETRIC FORMULAS

In the diagram below, angle C is the right angle, and side c is the hypotenuse. Side a is the side adjacent to angle B and side b is the side adjacent to angle A. These formulas will work for any acute angle in a right triangle. They will NOT work for any triangle that is not a right triangle. Also, they will not work for the right angle in a right triangle, since there are not distinct adjacent and opposite sides to differentiate from the hypotenuse.

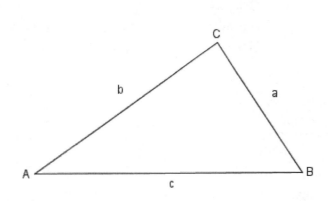

$$\sin A = \frac{\text{opposite side}}{\text{hypotenuse}} = \frac{a}{c}$$

$$\cos A = \frac{\text{adjacent side}}{\text{hypotenuse}} = \frac{b}{c}$$

$$\tan A = \frac{\text{opposite side}}{\text{adjacent side}} = \frac{a}{b}$$

$$\csc A = \frac{1}{\sin A} = \frac{\text{hypotenuse}}{\text{opposite side}} = \frac{c}{a}$$

$$\sec A = \frac{1}{\cos A} = \frac{\text{hypotenuse}}{\text{adjacent side}} = \frac{c}{b}$$

$$\cot A = \frac{1}{\tan A} = \frac{\text{adjacent side}}{\text{opposite side}} = \frac{b}{a}$$

LAWS OF SINES AND COSINES

The **law of sines** states that $\frac{\sin A}{a} = \frac{\sin B}{b} = \frac{\sin C}{c}$, where A, B, and C are the angles of a triangle, and a, b, and c are the sides opposite their respective angles. This formula will work with all triangles, not just right triangles.

> **Review Video: (Upper Level Trig) Law of Sines**
> Visit mometrix.com/academy and enter code: 206844

The **law of cosines** is given by the formula $c^2 = a^2 + b^2 - 2ab(\cos C)$, where a, b, and c are the sides of a triangle, and C is the angle opposite side c. This formula is similar to the Pythagorean theorem, but unlike the Pythagorean theorem, it can be used on any triangle.

POLYGONS

Each straight line segment of a polygon is called a **side**. The point at which two sides of a polygon intersect is called the **vertex**. In a polygon, the number of sides is always equal to the number of vertices. A polygon with all sides congruent and all angles equal is called a **regular polygon**. A line segment from the center of a polygon that is perpendicular to a side of the polygon is called the **apothem**. A line segment from the center of a polygon to a vertex of the polygon is called a **radius**.

> **Review Video: Polygons**
> Visit mometrix.com/academy and enter code: 271869

In a regular polygon, the apothem can be used to find the area of the polygon using the formula $A = \frac{1}{2}ap$, where a is the apothem, and p is the perimeter.

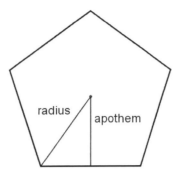

Naming polygons:

Triangle = 3 sides
Quadrilateral = 4 sides
Pentagon = 5 sides
Hexagon = 6 sides
Heptagon = 7 sides
Octagon = 8 sides
Nonagon = 9 sides
Decagon = 10 sides
Dodecagon = 12 sides

Generally, an n-gon is a polygon that has more than 12 angles and sides. The space of n is for the number of sides. Also, an 11-sided polygon is known as an 11-gon.

The sum of the interior angles of an n-sided polygon is $(n - 2) \times 180°$. For example, in a triangle $n = 3$. So, the sum of the interior angles is $(3 - 2) \times 180° = 180°$. In a quadrilateral, $n = 4$, and the sum of the angles is $(4 - 2) \times 180° = 360°$.

A **diagonal** is a line segment that joins two non-adjacent vertices of a polygon. The number of diagonals that a polygon has can be found by using the formula: $\frac{n(n-3)}{2}$; where n is the number of sides in the polygon. This formula works for all polygons.

A **convex polygon** is a polygon whose diagonals all lie within the interior of the polygon. A **concave polygon** is a polygon with a least one diagonal that is outside the polygon. In the diagram below, quadrilateral $ABCD$ is concave because diagonal $\overline{AC}$ lies outside the polygon.

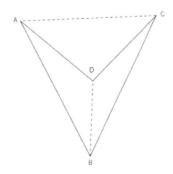

Congruent figures are geometric figures that have the same size and shape. All corresponding angles are equal, and all corresponding sides are equal. Congruence is shown by the symbol ≅.

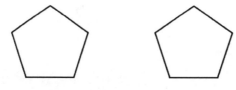

Congruent polygons

Similar figures are geometric figures that have the same shape, but may not have the same size. All corresponding angles are equal, and all corresponding sides are proportional. However, they do not have to be equal. Similarity is shown by the symbol ~.

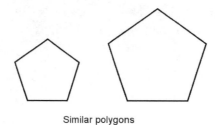

Similar polygons

Note that all congruent figures are also similar. However, not all similar figures are congruent.

Line of Symmetry: The line that divides a figure or object into equal parts. Each part is congruent to the other. An object may have no lines of symmetry, one line of symmetry, or multiple (i.e., more than one) lines of symmetry.

Lines of symmetry:

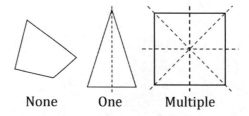

None   One   Multiple

Quadrilateral: A closed two-dimensional geometric figure that has four straight sides. The sum of the interior angles of any quadrilateral is 360°.

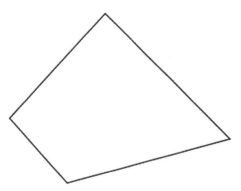

Kite: A quadrilateral with two pairs of adjacent sides that are congruent. A result of this is perpendicular diagonals. A kite can be concave or convex and has one line of symmetry.

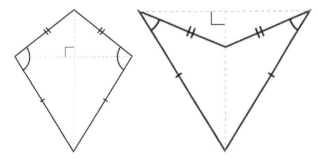

Trapezoid: Normally, a quadrilateral has one pair of parallel sides. Some define a trapezoid as a quadrilateral that has at least one pair of parallel sides. There are no rules for the second pair of sides. So, there are no rules for the diagonals and no lines of symmetry for a trapezoid.

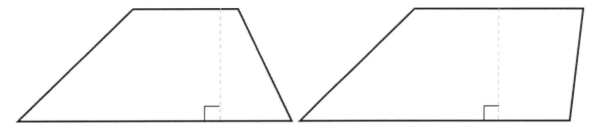

Parallelogram: A quadrilateral that has two pairs of opposite parallel sides. As such it is a special type of trapezoid. The sides that are parallel are also congruent. The opposite interior angles are always congruent, and the consecutive interior angles are supplementary. The diagonals of a parallelogram divide each other. Each diagonal divides the parallelogram into two congruent triangles. A parallelogram has no line of symmetry, but does have 180-degree rotational symmetry about the midpoint.

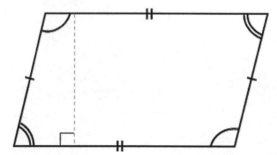

Isosceles Trapezoid: A trapezoid with equal base angles. This gives rise to other properties including: the two nonparallel sides have the same length, the two non-base angles are also equal, and there is one line of symmetry through the midpoints of the parallel sides.

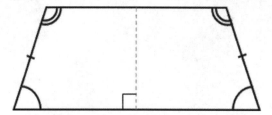

Rectangle: A quadrilateral with four right angles. All rectangles are parallelograms and trapezoids, but not all parallelograms or trapezoids are rectangles. The diagonals of a rectangle are congruent. Rectangles have 2 lines of symmetry (through each pair of opposing midpoints) and 180-degree rotational symmetry about the midpoint.

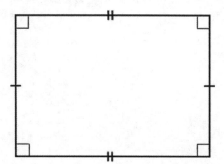

Rhombus: A quadrilateral with four congruent sides. All rhombuses are parallelograms and kites; thus, they inherit all the properties of both types of quadrilaterals. The diagonals of a rhombus are perpendicular to each other. Rhombi have 2 lines of symmetry (along each of the diagonals) and 180-degree rotational symmetry.

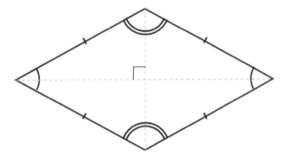

Square: A quadrilateral with four right angles and four congruent sides. Squares satisfy the criteria of all other types of quadrilaterals. The diagonals of a square are congruent and perpendicular to each other. Squares have 4 lines of symmetry (through each pair of opposing midpoints and along each of the diagonals) as well as 90-degree rotational symmetry about the midpoint.

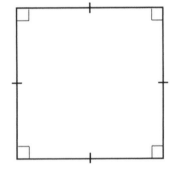

The hierarchy of quadrilaterals can be shown as follows:

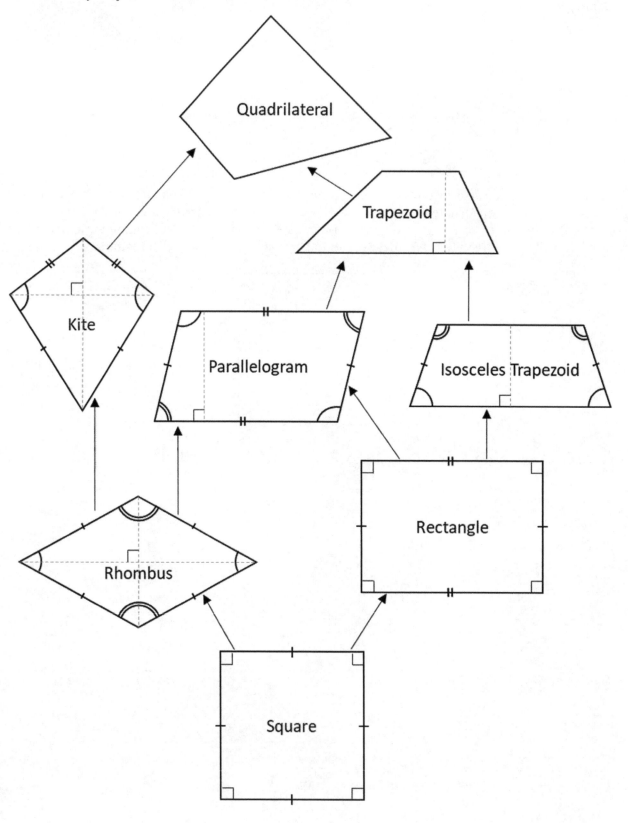

AREA AND PERIMETER FORMULAS

The **area of a square** is found by using the formula $A = s^2$, where and s is the length of one side.

The perimeter of a square is found by using the formula $P = 4s$, where s is the length of one side. Because all four sides are equal in a square, it is faster to multiply the length of one side by 4 than to add the same number four times. You could use the formulas for rectangles and get the same answer.

The **area of a rectangle** is found by the formula $A = lw$, where A is the area of the rectangle, l is the length (usually considered to be the longer side) and w is the width (usually considered to be the shorter side). The numbers for l and w are interchangeable.

The **perimeter of a rectangle** is found by the formula $P = 2l + 2w$ or $P = 2(l + w)$, where l is the length, and w is the width. It may be easier to add the length and width first and then double the result, as in the second formula.

The **area of a parallelogram** is found by the formula $A = bh$, where b is the length of the base, and h is the height. Note that the base and height correspond to the length and width in a rectangle, so this formula would apply to rectangles as well. Do not confuse the height of a parallelogram with the length of the second side. The two are only the same measure in the case of a rectangle.

The **perimeter of a parallelogram** is found by the formula $P = 2a + 2b$ or $P = 2(a + b)$, where a and b are the lengths of the two sides.

The **area of a trapezoid** is found by the formula $A = \frac{1}{2}h(b_1 + b_2)$, where h is the height (segment joining and perpendicular to the parallel bases), and b_1 and b_2 are the two parallel sides (bases). Do not use one of the other two sides as the height unless that side is also perpendicular to the parallel bases.

The **perimeter of a trapezoid** is found by the formula $P = a + b_1 + c + b_2$, where a, b_1, c, and b_2 are the four sides of the trapezoid.

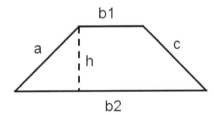

CIRCLES

The **center** is the single point inside the circle that is equidistant from every point on the circle. (Point O in the diagram below.)

The **radius** is a line segment that joins the center of the circle and any one point on the circle. All radii of a circle are equal. (Segments OX, OY, and OZ in the diagram below.)

The **diameter** is a line segment that passes through the center of the circle and has both endpoints on the circle. The length of the diameter is exactly twice the length of the radius. (Segment XZ in the diagram below.)

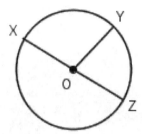

The **area of a circle** is found by the formula $A = \pi r^2$, where r is the length of the radius. If the diameter of the circle is given, remember to divide it in half to get the length of the radius before proceeding.

The **circumference** of a circle is found by the formula $C = 2\pi r$, where r is the radius. Again, remember to convert the diameter if you are given that measure rather than the radius.

Concentric circles are circles that have the same center, but not the same length of radii. A bulls-eye target is an example of concentric circles.

An **arc** is a portion of a circle. Specifically, an arc is the set of points between and including two points on a circle. An arc does not contain any points inside the circle. When a segment is drawn from the endpoints of an arc to the center of the circle, a sector is formed.

A **central angle** is an angle whose vertex is the center of a circle and whose legs intercept an arc of the circle. Angle XOY in the diagram above is a central angle. A minor arc is an arc that has a measure less than $180°$. The measure of a central angle is equal to the measure of the minor arc it intercepts. A major arc is an arc having a measure of at least $180°$. The measure of the major arc can be found by subtracting the measure of the central angle from $360°$.

A **semicircle** is an arc whose endpoints are the endpoints of the diameter of a circle. A semicircle is exactly half of a circle.

An **inscribed angle** is an angle whose vertex lies on a circle and whose legs contain chords of that circle. The portion of the circle intercepted by the legs of the angle is called the intercepted arc. The measure of the intercepted arc is exactly twice the measure of the inscribed angle. In the diagram below, angle ABC is an inscribed angle. $\overset{\frown}{AC} = 2(m\angle ABC)$

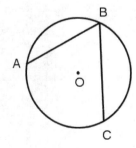

Any angle inscribed in a semicircle is a right angle. The intercepted arc is 180°, making the inscribed angle half that, or 90°. In the diagram below, angle *ABC* is inscribed in semicircle *ABC*, making angle *ABC* equal to 90°.

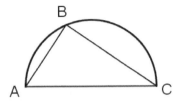

A **chord** is a line segment that has both endpoints on a circle. In the diagram below, $\overline{EB}$ is a chord.

Secant: A line that passes through a circle and contains a chord of that circle. In the diagram below, $\overleftrightarrow{EB}$ is a secant and contains chord $\overline{EB}$.

A **tangent** is a line in the same plane as a circle that touches the circle in exactly one point. While a line segment can be tangent to a circle as part of a line that is tangent, it is improper to say a tangent can be simply a line segment that touches the circle in exactly one point. In the diagram below, $\overleftrightarrow{CD}$ is tangent to circle *A*. Notice that $\overline{FB}$ is not tangent to the circle. $\overline{FB}$ is a line segment that touches the circle in exactly one point, but if the segment were extended, it would touch the circle in a second point. The point at which a tangent touches a circle is called the point of tangency. In the diagram below, point *B* is the point of tangency.

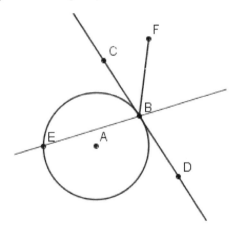

When two secants intersect inside a circle, the measure of each of two vertical angles is equal to half the sum of the two intercepted arcs. In the diagram below, $m\angle AEB = \frac{1}{2}(\widehat{AB} + \widehat{CD})$ and $m\angle BEC = \frac{1}{2}(\widehat{BC} + \widehat{AD})$.

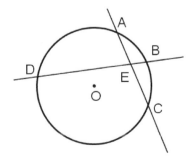

When two secants intersect outside a circle, the measure of the angle formed is equal to half the difference of the two arcs that lie between the two secants. In the diagram below, $m\angle AEB = \frac{1}{2}(\widehat{AB} - \widehat{CD})$.

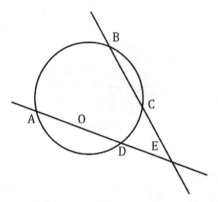

The **arc length** is the length of that portion of the circumference between two points on the circle. The formula for arc length is $s = \frac{\pi r \theta}{180°}$ where s is the arc length, r is the length of the radius, and θ is the angular measure of the arc in degrees, or $s = r\theta$, where θ is the angular measure of the arc in radians (2π radians = 360 degrees).

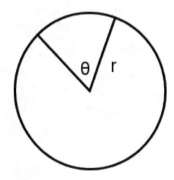

A **sector** is the portion of a circle formed by two radii and their intercepted arc. While the arc length is exclusively the points that are also on the circumference of the circle, the sector is the entire area bounded by the arc and the two radii.

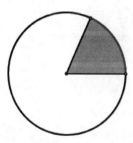

The **area of a sector** of a circle is found by the formula, $A = \frac{\theta r^2}{2}$, where A is the area, θ is the measure of the central angle in radians, and r is the radius. To find the area when the central angle is in degrees, use the formula, $A = \frac{\theta \pi r^2}{360}$, where θ is the measure of the central angle in degrees and r is the radius.

A circle is inscribed in a polygon if each of the sides of the polygon is tangent to the circle. A polygon is inscribed in a circle if each of the vertices of the polygon lies on the circle.

A circle is circumscribed about a polygon if each of the vertices of the polygon lies on the circle. A polygon is circumscribed about the circle if each of the sides of the polygon is tangent to the circle.

If one figure is inscribed in another, then the other figure is circumscribed about the first figure.

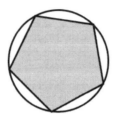

Circle circumscribed about a pentagon
Pentagon inscribed in a circle

OTHER CONIC SECTIONS

An **ellipse** is the set of all points in a plane, whose total distance from two fixed points called the **foci** (singular: focus) is constant, and whose center is the midpoint between the foci.

The standard equation of an ellipse that is taller than it is wide is $\frac{(y-k)^2}{a^2} + \frac{(x-h)^2}{b^2} = 1$, where a and b are coefficients. The center is the point (h, k) and the foci are the points $(h, k + c)$ and $(h, k - c)$, where $c^2 = a^2 - b^2$ and $a^2 > b^2$.

The major axis has length $2a$, and the minor axis has length $2b$.

Eccentricity (e) is a measure of how elongated an ellipse is, and is the ratio of the distance between the foci to the length of the major axis. Eccentricity will have a value between 0 and 1. The closer to 1 the eccentricity is, the closer the ellipse is to being a circle. The formula for eccentricity is $= \frac{c}{a}$.

Parabola: The set of all points in a plane that are equidistant from a fixed line, called the **directrix**, and a fixed point not on the line, called the focus.

Axis: The line perpendicular to the directrix that passes through the focus.

For parabolas that open up or down, the standard equation is $(x - h)^2 = 4c(y - k)$, where $h, c,$ and k are coefficients. If c is positive, the parabola opens up. If c is negative, the parabola opens down. The vertex is the point (h, k). The directrix is the line having the equation $y = -c + k$, and the focus is the point $(h, c + k)$.

For parabolas that open left or right, the standard equation is $(y - k)^2 = 4c(x - h)$, where $k, c,$ and h are coefficients. If c is positive, the parabola opens to the right. If c is negative, the parabola opens to the left. The vertex is the point (h, k). The directrix is the line having the equation $x = -c + h$, and the focus is the point $(c + h, k)$.

A **hyperbola** is the set of all points in a plane, whose distance from two fixed points, called foci, has a constant difference.

The standard equation of a horizontal hyperbola is $\frac{(x-h)^2}{a^2} - \frac{(y-k)^2}{b^2} = 1$, where a, b, h, and k are real numbers. The center is the point (h, k), the vertices are the points $(h + a, k)$ and $(h - a, k)$, and the foci are the points that every point on one of the parabolic curves is equidistant from and are found using the formulas $(h + c, k)$ and $(h - c, k)$, where $c^2 = a^2 + b^2$. The asymptotes are two lines the graph of the hyperbola approaches but never reaches, and are given by the equations $y = \left(\frac{b}{a}\right)(x - h) + k$ and $y = -\left(\frac{b}{a}\right)(x - h) + k$.

A vertical hyperbola is formed when a plane makes a vertical cut through two cones that are stacked vertex-to-vertex.

The standard equation of a vertical hyperbola is $\frac{(y-k)^2}{a^2} - \frac{(x-h)^2}{b^2} = 1$, where a, b, k, and h are real numbers. The center is the point (h, k), the vertices are the points $(h, k + a)$ and $(h, k - a)$, and the foci are the points that every point on one of the parabolic curves is equidistant from and are found using the formulas $(h, k + c)$ and $(h, k - c)$, where $c^2 = a^2 + b^2$. The asymptotes are two lines the graph of the hyperbola approaches but never reach, and are given by the equations $y = \left(\frac{a}{b}\right)(x - h) + k$ and $y = -\left(\frac{a}{b}\right)(x - h) + k$.

SOLIDS

The surface area of a solid object is the area of all sides or exterior surfaces. For objects such as prisms and pyramids, a further distinction is made between base surface area (B) and lateral surface area (LA). For a prism, the total surface area (SA) is $SA = LA + 2B$. For a pyramid or cone, the total surface area is $SA = LA + B$.

The **surface area of a sphere** can be found by the formula $A = 4\pi r^2$, where r is the radius. The volume is given by the formula $V = \frac{4}{3}\pi r^3$, where r is the radius. Both quantities are generally given in terms of π.

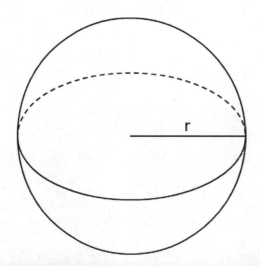

Review Video: <u>Volume and Surface Area of a Sphere</u>
Visit mometrix.com/academy and enter Code: 786928

The **volume of any prism** is found by the formula $V = Bh$, where B is the area of the base, and h is the height (perpendicular distance between the bases). The **surface area of any prism** is the sum of the areas of both bases and all sides. It can be calculated as $SA = 2B + Ph$, where P is the perimeter of the base.

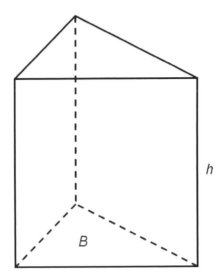

The **volume of a rectangular prism** can be found with the formula $V = lwh$, where V is the volume, l is the length, w is the width, and h is the height. The **surface area of a rectangular prism** can be calculated as $SA = 2lw + 2hl + 2wh$ or $SA = 2(lw + hl + wh)$.

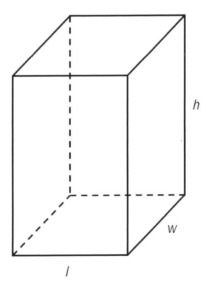

The **volume of a cube** can be found by the formula $V = s^3$, where s is the length of a side. The **surface area of a cube** is calculated as $SA = 6s^2$, where SA is the total surface area and s is the length of a side. These formulas are the same as the ones used for the volume and surface area of a rectangular prism, but simplified since all three quantities (length, width, and height) are the same.

Review Video: <u>Volume and Surface Area of a Cube</u>
Visit mometrix.com/academy and enter Code: 664455

The **volume of a cylinder** can be calculated by the formula $V = \pi r^2 h$, where r is the radius, and h is the height. The **surface area of a cylinder** can be found by the formula $SA = 2\pi r^2 + 2\pi rh$. The first term is the base area multiplied by two, and the second term is the perimeter of the base multiplied by the height.

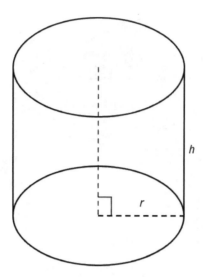

The **volume of a pyramid** is found by the formula $V = \frac{1}{3}Bh$, where B is the area of the base, and h is the height (perpendicular distance from the vertex to the base). Notice this formula is the same as $\frac{1}{3}$ times the volume of a prism. Like a prism, the base of a pyramid can be any shape. Finding the surface area of a pyramid is not as simple as the other shapes we've looked at thus far. If the pyramid is a right pyramid, meaning the base is a regular polygon and the vertex is directly over the center of that polygon, the **surface area** can be calculated as $SA = B + \frac{1}{2}Ph_s$, where P is the perimeter of the base, and h_s is the slant height (distance from the vertex to the midpoint of one side of the base). If the pyramid is irregular, the area of each triangle side must be calculated individually and then summed, along with the base.

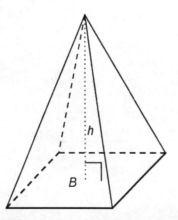

Review Video: <u>Volume and Surface Area of a Pyramid</u>
Visit mometrix.com/academy and enter Code: 621932

The **volume of a cone** is found by the formula $V = \frac{1}{3}\pi r^2 h$, where r is the radius, and h is the height. Notice this is the same as $\frac{1}{3}$ times the volume of a cylinder. The **surface area** can be calculated as $SA = \pi r^2 + \pi rs$, where s is the slant height. The slant height can be calculated using the Pythagorean Thereom to be $\sqrt{r^2 + h^2}$, so the surface area formula can also be written as $SA = \pi r^2 + \pi r\sqrt{r^2 + h^2}$.

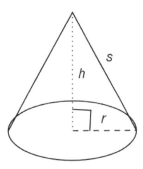

Trigonometry

BASIC TRIGONOMETRIC FUNCTIONS

The three basic trigonometric functions are sine, cosine, and tangent.

SINE

The **sine (sin) function** has a period of 360° or 2π radians. This means that its graph makes one complete cycle every 360° or 2π. Because $\sin 0 = 0$, the graph of $y = \sin x$ begins at the origin, with the x-axis representing the angle measure, and the y-axis representing the sine of the angle. The graph of the sine function is a smooth curve that begins at the origin, peaks at the point $\left(\frac{\pi}{2}, 1\right)$, crosses the x-axis at $(\pi, 0)$, has its lowest point at $\left(\frac{3\pi}{2}, -1\right)$, and returns to the x-axis to complete one cycle at $(2\pi, 0)$.

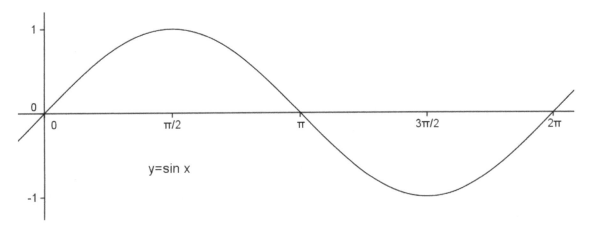

y=sin x

COSINE

The **cosine (cos) function** also has a period of 360° or 2π radians, which means that its graph also makes one complete cycle every 360° or 2π. Because $\cos 0° = 1$, the graph of $y = \cos x$ begins at the point $(0, 1)$, with the x-axis representing the angle measure, and the y-axis representing the cosine of the angle. The graph of the cosine function is a smooth curve that begins at the point $(0, 1)$, crosses the x-axis at the point $\left(\frac{\pi}{2}, 0\right)$, has its lowest point at $(\pi, -1)$, crosses the x-axis again at the point $\left(\frac{3\pi}{2}, 0\right)$, and returns to a peak at the point $(2\pi, 1)$ to complete one cycle.

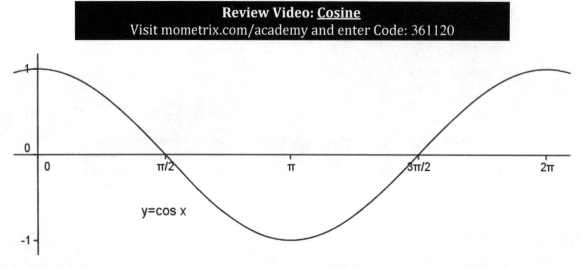

TANGENT

The **tangent (tan) function** has a period of 180° or π radians, which means that its graph makes one complete cycle every 180° or π radians. The x-axis represents the angle measure, and the y-axis represents the tangent of the angle. The graph of the tangent function is a series of smooth curves that cross the x-axis at every 180° or π radians and have an asymptote every $k \times 90°$ or $\frac{k\pi}{2}$ radians, where k is an odd integer. This can be explained by the fact that the tangent is calculated by dividing the sine by the cosine, since the cosine equals zero at those asymptote points.

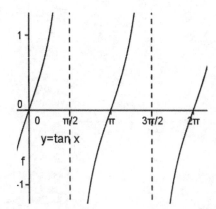

The tangent function is defined as the ratio of the sine to the cosine:

$$\tan x = \frac{\sin x}{\cos x}$$

Mometrix

DEFINED AND RECIPROCAL FUNCTIONS

To take the **reciprocal** of a number means to place that number as the denominator of a fraction with a numerator of 1. The reciprocal functions are thus defined quite simply.

$$\text{Cosecant:} \quad \csc x = \frac{1}{\sin x}$$

$$\text{Secant:} \quad \sec x = \frac{1}{\cos x}$$

$$\text{Cotangent:} \quad \cot x = \frac{1}{\tan x}$$

It is important to know these reciprocal functions, but they are not as commonly used as the three basic functions.

INVERSE FUNCTIONS

Each of the trigonometric functions accepts an angular measure, either degrees or radians, and gives a numerical value as the output. The **inverse functions** do the opposite; they accept a numerical value and give an angular measure as the output. The inverse sine, or arcsine, commonly written as either $\sin^{-1} x$ or $\arcsin x$, gives the angle whose sine is x. Similarly:

- The inverse of $\cos x$ is written $\cos^{-1} x$ or $\arccos x$ and means the angle whose cosine is x.
- The inverse of $\tan x$ is written $\tan^{-1} x$ or $\arctan x$ and means the angle whose tangent is x.
- The inverse of $\csc x$ is written $\csc^{-1} x$ or $\text{arccsc } x$ and means the angle whose cosecant is x.
- The inverse of $\sec x$ is written $\sec^{-1} x$ or $\text{arcsec } x$ and means the angle whose secant is x.
- The inverse of $\cot x$ is written $\cot^{-1} x$ or $\text{arccot } x$ and means the angle whose cotangent is x.

IMPORTANT NOTE ABOUT SOLVING TRIGONOMETRIC EQUATIONS

Trigonometric and algebraic equations are solved following the same rules, but while algebraic expressions have one unique solution, trigonometric equations could have multiple solutions, and you must find them all. When solving for an angle with a known trigonometric value, you must consider the sign and include all angles with that value. Your calculator will probably only give one value as an answer, typically in the following ranges:

- For the inverse sine function, $\left[-\frac{\pi}{2}, \frac{\pi}{2}\right]$ or $[-90°, 90°]$
- For the inverse cosine function, $[0, \pi]$ or $[0°, 180°]$
- For the inverse tangent function, $\left[-\frac{\pi}{2}, \frac{\pi}{2}\right]$ or $[-90°, 90°]$

It is important to determine if there is another angle in a different quadrant that also satisfies the problem. To do this, find the other quadrant(s) with the same sign for that trigonometric function and find the angle that has the same reference angle. Then check whether this angle is also a solution.

- In the first quadrant, all six trigonometric functions are positive (sin, cos, tan, csc, sec, cot).
- In the second quadrant, sin and csc are positive.
- In the third quadrant, tan and cot are positive.
- In the fourth quadrant, cos and sec are positive.

423

TRIGONOMETRIC IDENTITIES
SUM AND DIFFERENCE

To find the sine, cosine, or tangent of the **sum or difference of two angles**, use one of the following formulas:

$$\sin(\alpha \pm \beta) = \sin \alpha \cos \beta \pm \cos \alpha \sin \beta$$
$$\cos(\alpha \pm \beta) = \cos \alpha \cos \beta \mp \sin \alpha \sin \beta$$
$$\tan(\alpha \pm \beta) = \frac{\tan \alpha \pm \tan \beta}{1 \mp \tan \alpha \tan \beta}$$

Where α and β are two angles with known sine, cosine, or tangent values as needed.

HALF ANGLE

To find the **sine or cosine of half of a known angle**, use the following formulas:

$$\sin \frac{\theta}{2} = \pm \sqrt{\frac{1 - \cos\theta}{2}}$$

$$\cos \frac{\theta}{2} = \pm \sqrt{\frac{1 + \cos\theta}{2}}$$

Where θ is an angle with a known exact cosine value.

To determine the sine of the answer, you must notice the quadrant the given angle is in and apply the correct sign for the trigonometric function you are using. If you need to find the exact sine or cosine of an angle that you do not know, such as sine 22.5°, you can rewrite the given angle as a half angle, such as sine $\frac{45°}{2}$, and use the formula above.

To find the **tangent or cotangent of half of a known angle**, use the following formulas:

$$\tan \frac{\theta}{2} = \frac{\sin\theta}{1 + \cos \theta}$$
$$\cot \frac{\theta}{2} = \frac{\sin \theta}{1 - \cos \theta}$$

Where θ is an angle with known exact sine and cosine values. These formulas will work for finding the tangent or cotangent of half of any angle unless the cosine of θ happens to make the denominator of the identity equal to 0.

DOUBLE ANGLES

To find the **sine or cosine of twice a known angle**, use one of the following formulas:

$$\sin(2\theta) = 2 \sin \theta \cos \theta$$
$$\cos(2\theta) = \cos^2 \theta - \sin^2 \theta \ \text{ or}$$
$$\cos(2\theta) = 2 \cos^2 \theta - 1 \ \text{ or}$$
$$\cos(2\theta) = 1 - 2 \sin^2 \theta$$

To find the **tangent or cotangent of twice a known angle**, use the formulas:

$$\tan(2\theta) = \frac{2\tan\theta}{1 - \tan^2\theta}$$
$$\cot(2\theta) = \frac{\cot\theta - \tan\theta}{2}$$

In each case, θ is an angle with known exact sine, cosine, tangent, and cotangent values.

PRODUCTS

To find the product of the sines and cosines of two different angles, use one of the following formulas:

$$\sin\alpha\sin\beta = \frac{1}{2}[\cos(\alpha - \beta) - \cos(\alpha + \beta)]$$
$$\cos\alpha\cos\beta = \frac{1}{2}[\cos(\alpha + \beta) + \cos(\alpha - \beta)]$$
$$\sin\alpha\cos\beta = \frac{1}{2}[\sin(\alpha + \beta) + \sin(\alpha - \beta)]$$
$$\cos\alpha\sin\beta = \frac{1}{2}[\sin(\alpha + \beta) - \sin(\alpha - \beta)]$$

Where α and β are two unique angles.

COMPLEMENTARY

The trigonometric cofunction identities use the trigonometric relationships of complementary angles (angles whose sum is 90°). These are:

$$\cos x = \sin(90° - x)$$
$$\csc x = \sec(90° - x)$$
$$\cot x = \tan(90° - x)$$

PYTHAGOREAN THEOREM AND TRIGONOMETRIC IDENTITIES

The Pythagorean theorem states that $a^2 + b^2 = c^2$ for all right triangles. The trigonometric identity that derives from this principle is stated in this way:

$$\sin^2\theta + \cos^2\theta = 1$$

Dividing each term by either $\sin^2\theta$ or $\cos^2\theta$ yields two other identities, respectively:

$$1 + \cot^2\theta = \csc^2\theta$$
$$\tan^2\theta + 1 = \sec^2\theta$$

UNIT CIRCLE

A **unit circle** is a circle with a radius of 1 that has its center at the origin. The equation of the unit circle is $x^2 + y^2 = 1$. Notice that this is an abbreviated version of the standard equation of a circle. Because the center is the point $(0, 0)$, the values of h and k in the general equation are equal to zero and the equation simplifies to this form.

Standard position is the position of an angle of measure θ whose vertex is at the origin, the initial side crosses the unit circle at the point $(1, 0)$, and the terminal side crosses the unit circle at some other point (a, b). In the standard position, $\sin \theta = b$, $\cos \theta = a$, and $\tan \theta = \frac{b}{a}$.

> **Review Video: Unit Circles and Standard Position**
> Visit mometrix.com/academy and enter Code: 333922

TABLE OF COMMONLY ENCOUNTERED ANGLES

$0° = 0$ radians, $30° = \frac{\pi}{6}$ radians, $45° = \frac{\pi}{4}$ radians, $60° = \frac{\pi}{3}$ radians, and $90° = \frac{\pi}{2}$ radians

$\sin 0° = 0$	$\cos 0° = 1$	$\tan 0° = 0$
$\sin 30° = \frac{1}{2}$	$\cos 30° = \frac{\sqrt{3}}{2}$	$\tan 30° = \frac{\sqrt{3}}{3}$
$\sin 45° = \frac{\sqrt{2}}{2}$	$\cos 45° = \frac{\sqrt{2}}{2}$	$\tan 45° = 1$
$\sin 60° = \frac{\sqrt{3}}{2}$	$\cos 60° = \frac{1}{2}$	$\tan 60° = \sqrt{3}$
$\sin 90° = 1$	$\cos 90° = 0$	$\tan 90° = undefined$
$\csc 0° = undefined$	$\sec 0° = 1$	$\cot 0° = undefined$
$\csc 30° = 2$	$\sec 30° = \frac{2\sqrt{3}}{3}$	$\cot 30° = \sqrt{3}$
$\csc 45° = \sqrt{2}$	$\sec 45° = \sqrt{2}$	$\cot 45° = 1$
$\csc 60° = \frac{2\sqrt{3}}{3}$	$\sec 60° = 2$	$\cot 60° = \frac{\sqrt{3}}{3}$
$\csc 90° = 1$	$\sec 90° = undefined$	$\cot 90° = 0$

The values in the upper half of this table are values you should have memorized or be able to find quickly.

RECTANGULAR AND POLAR COORDINATE SYSTEMS

Rectangular coordinates are those that lie on the square grids of the Cartesian plane. They should be quite familiar to you. The **polar coordinate system** is based on a circular graph, rather than the square grid of the Cartesian system. Points in the polar coordinate system are in the format (r, θ), where r is the distance from the origin (think radius of the circle) and θ is the smallest positive angle (moving counterclockwise around the circle) made with the positive horizontal axis.

To convert a point from rectangular (x, y) format to polar (r, θ) format, use the formula:

$$(x, y) \text{ to } (r, \theta) \Rightarrow \begin{matrix} r = \sqrt{x^2 + y^2} \\ \theta = \arctan\frac{y}{x} \end{matrix}, \quad \text{when } x \neq 0$$

If x is positive, use the positive square root value for r. If x is negative, use the negative square root value for r.

If $x = 0$, use the following rules:

- If $x = 0$ and $y = 0$, then $\theta = 0$
- If $x = 0$ and $y > 0$, then $\theta = \frac{\pi}{2}$
- If $x = 0$ and $y < 0$, then $\theta = \frac{3\pi}{2}$

To convert a point from polar (r, θ) format to rectangular (x, y) format, use the formula:

$$(r, \theta) \text{ to } (x, y) \Rightarrow \begin{matrix} x = r\cos\theta \\ y = r\sin\theta \end{matrix}$$

Practice Test

Natural Science

BIOLOGY

1. The hydrogen bonds in a water molecule make water a good

    A. Solvent for lipids
    B. Participant in replacement reactions
    C. Surface for small particles and living organisms to move across
    D. Solvent for polysaccharides such as cellulose
    E. Example of an acid

2. When an animal takes in more energy that it uses over an extended time, the extra chemical energy is stored as:

    A. Fat
    B. Starch
    C. Protein
    D. Enzymes
    E. Cholesterol

3. Which of the following is an example of a cofactor?

    A. Zinc
    B. Actin
    C. Cholesterol
    D. GTP
    E. Chlorophyll

4. Which of the following statements regarding chemiosmosis in mitochondria is not correct?

    A. ATP synthase is powered by protons flowing through membrane channels
    B. Energy from ATP is used to transport protons to the intermembrane space
    C. Energy from the electron transport chain is used to transport protons to the intermembrane space
    D. An electrical gradient and a pH gradient both exist across the inner membrane
    E. The waste product of chemiosmosis is water

5. DNA replication occurs during which of the following phases?

    A. Prophase I
    B. Prophase II
    C. Interphase I
    D. Interphase II
    E. Telophase I

6. Which of the following parts of an angiosperm give rise to the fruit?

   A. Pedicel
   B. Filament
   C. Sepal
   D. Ovary
   E. Meristem

Questions 7 and 8 pertain to the following diagram representing a cross section of a tree trunk

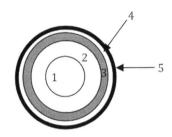

7. Which structure contains tissue that is dead at maturity?

   A. 1
   B. 2
   C. 3
   D. 4
   E. 5

8. Which structure transports carbohydrates to the roots?

   A. 1
   B. 2
   C. 3
   D. 4
   E. 5

9. When Ca^{2+} channels open in a presynaptic cell (doesn't the cell also depolarize?)

   A. The cell depolarizes
   B. The cell hyperpolarizes
   C. An action potential is propagated
   D. Synaptic vesicles release neurotransmitter
   E. The nerve signal is propagated by salutatory conduction

10. Which hormone is secreted by the placenta throughout pregnancy?

   A. Human chorionic gonadotropin (HCG)
   B. Gonadotropin releasing hormone (GnRH)
   C. Luteinizing hormone (LH)
   D. Follicle stimulating hormone (FSH)
   E. None of these

11. On a standard biomass pyramid, level 3 corresponds to which trophic level?

   A. Producers
   B. Decomposers
   C. Primary consumers
   D. Primary carnivores
   E. Secondary carnivores

12. The diagram below represents the three types of survivorship curves, describing how mortality varies as species age. Which of the following species is most likely to exhibit Type I survivorship?

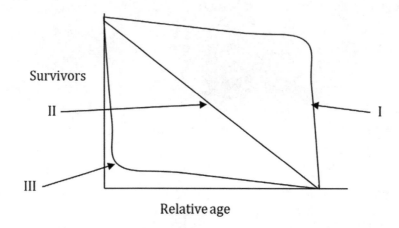

   A. Frogs
   B. Oysters
   C. Salmon
   D. Dolphins
   E. Shrimp

13. Which of the following is NOT a natural dispersal process that would lead to species colonization on an island?

   A. Mussels carried into a lake on the hull of a ship
   B. Drought connecting an island to other land
   C. Floating seeds
   D. Animals swimming long distances
   E. Birds adapted to flying long distances

14. A population of pea plants has 25% dwarf plants and 75% tall plants. The tall allele, T is dominant to the dwarf allele, t. What is the frequency of the T allele?

   A. 0.75
   B. 0.67
   C. 0.5
   D. 0.25
   E. 0.16

15. All of the following are homologous structures EXCEPT

A. Bird feathers
B. Elephant eyelashes
C. Human fingernails
D. Dog fur
E. Insect exoskeleton

16. The chemical bonds between hydrogen and oxygen in an H_2O molecule are an example of?

A. Nonpolar covalent bonds
B. Polar covalent bonds
C. Ionic bonds
D. Hydrogen bonds
E. Van der Waals bonds

17. Phosphate is a chemical moiety found in all but which of the following metabolic compounds?

A. Amino acids
B. DNA
C. RNA
D. Phospholipids
E. Nucleotides

18. An example of a coenzyme is:

A. Iron
B. Catalase
C. Vitamin B1
D. Glucose
E. ATP

19. The graph below shows the potential energy of molecules during a chemical reaction. Which of the following statements about the reaction is true?

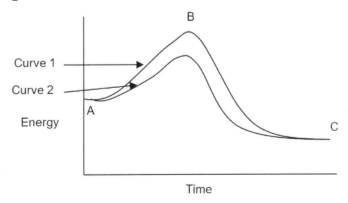

A. An enzyme could have increased the potential energy at point C
B. An enzyme was probably present in curve 2
C. This is an exergonic reaction
D. The curves show the potential energy of the enzyme
E. The energy of the substrate is less than the energy of the products

20. In oxidative phosphorylation, high-energy electrons are passed from NAD and $FADH_2$ down the electron transport chain to a final electron acceptor. Which of the following is that electron acceptor?

A. CO_2
B. NAD^+
C. Pyruvate
D. O_2
E. ATP

21. Plant shoots demonstrate negative gravitropism, whereas roots demonstrate positive gravitropism. Which of the following plant hormones mediates this response?

A. Ethylene
B. Abscisic acid
C. Jasmonic acid
D. Gibberellins
E. Auxin

22. Most of the CO_2 in blood is converted to carbonic acid in red blood cells. When a body is active, CO_2 production increases. Which of the following changes in pH would stimulate increased respiratory rate?

A. A drop in pH
B. A return to normal pH after a drop in pH
C. A rise in pH
D. A return to normal pH after a rise in pH
E. No change in pH is needed to stimulate increased respiratory rate

23. The major inhibitory neurotransmitter in the central nervous system is:

A. Acetylcholine
B. Epinephrine
C. GABA
D. Dopamine
E. Serotonin

24. A pea plant with purple flowers is crossed with a pea plant with white flowers. Half the progeny have purple flowers and half have white flowers. The allele for purple flowers is _____ to the allele for white flowers.

A. Dominant
B. Co-dominant
C. Recessive
D. Incompletely dominant
E. Impossible to determine from the information provided

25. In a dihybrid cross between bean plants with red (R) wrinkled (w) seeds and white (r) smooth (W) seeds, the F$_1$ progeny is all red and smooth. F$_1$ plants are selfed, and the progeny are 1/2 red and smooth, 1/4 red and wrinkled, and 1/4 white and smooth. Red is dominant to white and smooth is dominant to wrinkled. Which is true of the R and W genes?

    A. They are linked
    B. They are unlinked
    C. They are sex-linked
    D. They are on different chromosomes
    E. They cause abnormal chromosome segregation

26. What is the largest reservoir of phosphorous on the planet?

    A. The ocean
    B. Plants
    C. Soil
    D. The atmosphere
    E. Rocks and ocean sediments

27. Species that inhabit an island because they were transported there by humans are called

    A. Invasive species
    B. Introduced species
    C. Dispersed species
    D. Native species
    E. Mutualistic species

28. The combination of natural selection and Mendelian genetics is known as:

    A. Inheritance of acquired characters
    B. Microevolution
    C. Macroevolution
    D. The modern synthesis
    E. Natural transformation of species

29. New mutations

    A. Are rare
    B. Are usually beneficial
    C. Result from sexual reproduction
    D. Result from reproductive isolation
    E. Are the raw material for natural selection

30. In the absence of selective pressure, but in a small population, allele frequencies will likely change because of:

    A. Genetic drift
    B. Gene flow
    C. The founder effect
    D. Nonrandom mating

31. All but which of the following processes are ways of moving solutes across a plasma membrane?

    A. Osmosis
    B. Passive transport
    C. Active transport
    D. Facilitated diffusion
    E. Endocytosis

32. Prokaryotic and eukaryotic cells are similar in having which of the following?

    A. Membrane-bound organelles
    B. Protein-studded DNA
    C. Presence of a nucleus
    D. Integral membrane proteins in the plasma membrane
    E. Flagella composed of microtubules

33. Enzymes catalyze biochemical reactions by

    A. Lowering the potential energy of the products
    B. Separating inhibitors from products
    C. Forming a complex with the products
    D. Lowering the activation energy of the reaction
    E. Providing energy to the reaction

34. In a strenuously exercising muscle, NADH begins to accumulate in high concentration. Which of the following metabolic process will be activated to reduce the concentration of NADH?

    A. Glycolysis
    B. The Krebs cycle
    C. Lactic acid fermentation
    D. Oxidative phosphorylation
    E. Acetyl CoA synthesis

35. The combination of DNA with histones is called

    A. A centromere
    B. Chromatin
    C. A chromatid
    D. Nucleoli
    E. A plasmid

36. Which of the following is true of the enzyme telomerase?

    A. It is active on the leading strand during DNA synthesis
    B. It requires a chromosomal DNA template
    C. It acts in the $3' \rightarrow 5'$ direction
    D. It adds a repetitive DNA sequence to the end of chromosomes
    E. It takes the place of primase at the ends of chromosomes

37. Which section of the digestive system is responsible for water reabsorption?

   A. The large intestine
   B. The duodenum
   C. The small intestine
   D. The gallbladder
   E. The stomach

38. Which of the following hormones triggers ovulation in females?

   A. Estrogen
   B. Progesterone
   C. Serotonin
   D. Luteinizing hormone
   E. Testosterone

39. Which of the following is not a mechanism that contributes to cell differentiation and development in embryos?

   A. Asymmetrical cell division
   B. Asymmetrical cytoplasm distribution
   C. Organizer cells
   D. Location of cells on the lineage map
   E. Homeotic genes

40. An individual with an AB blood type needs a blood transfusion. Which of the following types could NOT be a donor?

   A. O
   B. AB
   C. A
   D. B
   E. All can be donors.

GENERAL CHEMISTRY

1. Which substance is most likely to be a solid at STP?

 A. Kr
 B. Na
 C. NH_3
 D. Xe

2. A weather balloon is filled with 1000 mol of He gas at 25 °C and 101 kPa of pressure. What is the volume of the weather balloon?

 A. 24518 m^3
 B. 24.5 m^3
 C. 2 m^3
 D. 245 m^3

3. Which is the correct order of increasing intermolecular attractive forces?

 A. Dipole-dipole < ionic < hydrogen bonding < London dispersion
 B. Ionic < dipole-dipole < London dispersion < hydrogen bonding
 C. Hydrogen bonding < London dispersion < ionic < dipole-dipole
 D. London dispersion < dipole-dipole < hydrogen bonding < ionic

4. Three liquids, X, Y and Z are placed in separate flasks, each of which is suspended in a water bath at 75 °C. The boiling points of each liquid are

 X, 273 K
 Y, 340 K
 Z, 360 K

Which of the three liquids will begin to boil after warming to 75 °C?

 A. X, Y, and Z
 B. X and Z
 C. X and Y
 D. Y and Z

5. Gas X is in a cylinder at 1 atm of pressure and has a volume of 10 L at 0° C. Gas X spontaneously decomposes to gas Y, according to the equation:

$$X \rightarrow 3Y$$

The temperature in the cylinder remains the same during the reaction. What is the pressure in the cylinder now?

 A. 1 atm
 B. 3 atm
 C. 4 atm
 D. Cannot be determined

6. 100 g of H_3PO_4 is dissolved in water, producing 400 mL of solution. What is the normality of the solution?

 A. 2.55 N
 B. 1.02 N
 C. 7.65 N
 D. 0.25 N

7. 100 mL of a 0.1 M solution of NaOH is neutralized to pH 7 with H_2SO_4. How many grams of H_2SO_4 are required to achieve this neutralization?

   A. 4.9 g
   B. 0.98 g
   C. 9.8 g
   D. 0.49 g

8. Place the following in the correct order of increasing solubility in water.

   A. butanol < ethanol < octane < NaCl
   B. ethanol < NaCl < octane < butanol
   C. NaCl < octane < butanol < ethanol
   D. octane < butanol < ethanol < NaCl

9. Which of the following represents the correct increasing order of acidity?

   A. $CH_3COOH < CH_3OH < CH_3CH_3 < HCl$
   B. $CH_3CH_3 < CH_3OH < CH_3COOH < HCl$
   C. $CH_3CH_3 < CH_3COOH < CH_3OH < HCl$
   D. $CH_3OH < CH_3CH_3 < HCl < CH_3COOH$

10. Which of the following radioactive emissions results in an increase in atomic number?

   A. Alpha
   B. Negative Beta
   C. Positive Beta
   D. Gamma

11. The best way to separate isotopes of the same element is to exploit:

   A. Differences in chemical reactivity
   B. Differences in reduction potential
   C. Differences in toxicity
   D. Differences in mass

12. Describe the correct outer shell electronic arrangement of phosphorus.

   A. $4s^2 4p^3$
   B. $3s^2 3p^3$
   C. $2s^2 3p^3$
   D. $2s^2 2p^3$

13. Place the following elements in order of decreasing electronegativity: N, As, Bi, P, Sb

   A. As > Bi > N > P > Sb
   B. N > P > As > Sb > Bi
   C. Bi > Sb > As > P > N
   D. P > N > As > Sb > Bi

14. Atoms that are sp^2 hybridized will have what sort of hybrid orbital geometry around them?

   A. Tetrahedral
   B. Trigonal planar
   C. Linear
   D. Angled

15. Balance the following reaction between sulfuric acid and aluminum hydroxide by filling in the correct stoichiometric values for each chemical.

$$\_\_H_2SO_4 + \_\_Al(OH)_3 \rightarrow \_\_Al_2(SO_4)_3 + \_\_H_2O$$

- A. 3, 2, 1, 6
- B. 2, 3, 1, 3
- C. 3, 3, 2, 6
- D. 1, 2, 1, 4

16. Methane gas is burned in pure oxygen at 200 °C and 1 atm of pressure to produce CO_2 and H_2O according to the equation

$$CH_4 + 2O_2 \rightarrow CO_2 + 2H_2O$$

If 10 L of methane gas were burned, and the final temperature and pressure remained the same, how many liters of gaseous products are produced by the reaction?

- A. 10 L
- B. 20 L
- C. 30 L
- D. 40 L

17. 10 g of salt XY (MW = 100 g/mol) is added to 1 liter of water with stirring. The salt dissociates into ions X^+ and Y^-. After equilibrium is established, the undissolved portion of the salt was removed by filtration, weighed, and found to be 9.5 g. What is the K_{sp} for this salt?

- A. 5×10^{-2}
- B. 5×10^{-3}
- C. 1×10^{-2}
- D. 2.5×10^{-5}

18. What will be the pH of 2 L of a 0.1 M aqueous solution of HCl?

- A. 2
- B. -1
- C. 1
- D. 0.05

19. For the conversion of water into steam, which of the following is true?

- A. $\Delta T = 0, \Delta S > 0$
- B. $\Delta T > 0, \Delta S = 0$
- C. $\Delta T = 0, \Delta S < 0$
- D. $\Delta T > 0, \Delta S > 0$

20. What would be the correct IUPAC name for the following compound?

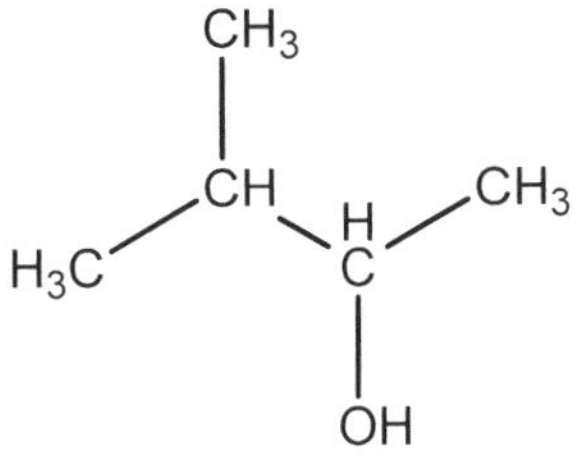

    A. 3-methyl-2-butanol
    B. 2-methyl-3-butanol
    C. 3,3-dimethyl-2-propanol
    D. 2-Hydroxy-3-methyl butane

21. Which of the following molecules are cis alkenes?

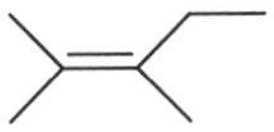

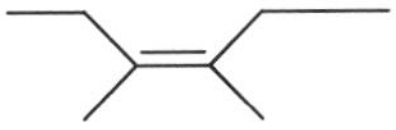

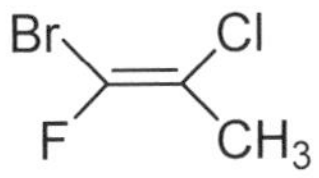

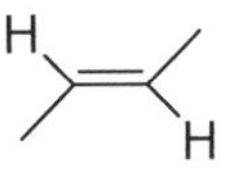

    A. I, II
    B. II, III
    C. III, IV
    D. I, IV

22. A liquid is held at its freezing point and slowly allowed to solidify. Which of the following statements about this event are true?

    A. During freezing, the temperature of the material decreases
    B. While freezing, heat is given off by the material
    C. During freezing, heat is absorbed by the material
    D. During freezing, the temperature of the material increases

23. Nuclear chain reactions, such as the one that is exploited in nuclear power plants, are propagated by what subatomic particle(s)?

    A. Protons
    B. Neutrons
    C. Electrons
    D. Neutrons and protons

24. An alpha particle consists of

    A. Two electrons and two protons
    B. Two electrons and two neutrons
    C. Four neutrons
    D. Two protons and two neutrons

25. Arrange the following elements in order of increasing atomic radius:

   A. K < Zn < Fe < As < Kr

   B. K < Fe < Zn < Kr < As

   C. Kr < As < Fe < K < Zn

   D. Kr < As < Zn < Fe < K

26. When a solid is heated and transforms directly to the gaseous phases, this process is called:

   A. sublimation

   B. fusion

   C. diffusion

   D. condensation

27. Which bond has the shortest length?

   A. sp^2

   B. sp^3

   C. sp

   D. pi

28. Resonance structures can be defined as:

   A. Two or more structures that have different atoms bound to different atoms

   B. Two structures that have a similar structure but different formula

   C. Two or more structures that have the same formula, but are different in shape

   D. Two or more structures that differ only in the arrangement of electrons in the structures

29. How many electrons are in the atom $^{45}_{20}Ca$?

   A. 20

   B. 45

   C. 65

   D. 25

30. For the reaction $CO_2(g) + H_2(g) \rightarrow CO(g) + H_2O(l)$, which of the following will occur if the pressure of the reaction is increased?

   A. The reaction rate will increase

   B. The reaction rate will decrease

   C. The reaction equilibrium will shift to the right

   D. The reaction equilibrium will shift to the left

ORGANIC CHEMISTRY

1. Alkanes increase in molecular weight

    A. by 14 units per mole per carbon atom
    B. by 15 units per mole per carbon atom
    C. by 14 grams per mole per carbon atom
    D. by 12 grams per mole per carbon atom

2. A specific combination of atoms that imparts common properties to a series of compounds is

    A. a functional group
    B. a substituent
    C. a diluent
    D. an eluent

3. Benzene, C_6H_6,

    A. has three sites of unsaturation
    B. is aromatic
    C. is non-flammable
    D. is a waxy solid at room temperature

4. Ethanol, C_2H_5OH, and propanol, C_3H_7OH, are

    A. homologous alcohols
    B. isomers
    C. not water soluble
    D. gases at room temperature

5. The structural formulas CH_3CH_2OH and CH_3OCH_3 are

    A. the same
    B. non-isomeric
    C. ethanol and methanol
    D. ethanol and dimethyl ether

6. Water adds to the carbonyl group to form

    A. acetals and ketals
    B. hydroxy ketones
    C. saccharides
    D. esters

7. An sp^3 carbon atom that has a completely asymmetric arrangement of four substituent groups is called

    A. a conformer
    B. a chiral center
    C. a reactive center
    D. a stereoisomer

8. Enantiomers

    A. have identical physical properties
    B. rotate plane polarized light in equal but opposite directions
    C. can be separated from each other by various methods
    D. all of the above

9. Triple bonds to carbon atoms are found in

    A. alkynes and cycloalkenes
    B. alkynes and alkenones
    C. nitriles and alkynes
    D. aromatic compounds

10. Aldehydes react with Tollens' reagent to produce

    A. ketones and silver ions
    B. carboxylic acids and silver atoms
    C. carboxylic acids and silver ions
    D. no reaction

11. Jones oxidation of alcohols and aldehydes is used to produce carboxylic acids by reaction with

    A. $K_2Cr_2O_7$ in concentrated H_2SO_4
    B. CrO_3 in sulfuric acid
    C. $KMnO_4$ in sulfuric acid
    D. MnO_2 in hydrochloric acid

12. High-boiling liquids should be distilled under reduced pressure because

    A. they have high vapor pressures
    B. they have low melting points
    C. they can decompose at temperatures below their boiling points
    D. they do not boil at normal pressure

13. A monosaccharide is

    A. a cyclic ketone
    B. a branched chain aldehyde
    C. a simple sugar
    D. an α-hydroxycarboxylic acid

14. Removal of an α hydrogen atom from a carbonyl compound is favored by

    A. delocalization of the remaining negative charge
    B. enolate formation
    C. 3° amines
    D. none of the above

15. Substituent groups can be added to benzene rings by a

    A. Claisen condensation reaction
    B. Wittig reaction
    C. Friedel-Crafts reaction
    D. bicycloannulation reaction

16. **Reaction of benzaldehyde with diborane and mild acid produces**

    A. benzoic acid
    B. benzyl alcohol
    C. 9-borabicyclononane (9-BBN)
    D. dibenzoyl

17. **Reaction between alkyl halides and primary amines**

    A. produce 2o amines
    B. produce 2o and 3o amines
    C. produce 2o and 3o amines and quaternary ammonium salts
    D. do not occur

18. **The reaction of P_2O_5 with water to produce phosphoric acid is**

    A. $P_2O_5 + 2H_2O \rightarrow 2H_2PO_3$
    B. $P_2O_5 + 3H_2O \rightarrow 2H_3PO_4$
    C. $2P_2O_5 + 5H_2O \rightarrow 4H_3PO_5$
    D. $2P_2O_5 + 6H_2O \rightarrow 4H_3PO_4$

19. **In a redox reaction**

    A. the reducing agent gains electrons
    B. the oxidizing agent loses electrons
    C. the oxidizing agent is reduced as the reducing agent is oxidized
    D. oxidation occurs first followed by reduction

20. **The following molecule is**

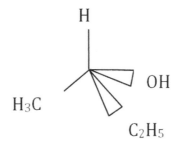

    A. S-2-butanol
    B. R-2-butanol
    C. d-butyl alcohol
    D. l-butyl alcohol

21. **The addition of an anionic species to the β position of an α, β-unsaturated ketone is called a**

    A. Michaelson-Morley experiment
    B. Michaelson reaction
    C. Michael addition
    D. Mitchell addition

22. Anthracene, phenanthrene and other similar compounds are known as

    A. simple hydrocarbons

    B. diketo carbonyl compounds

    C. polycyclic aromatic hydrocarbons

    D. dioxins

23. Carbon and nitrogen

    A. only bond to each other in primary amines

    B. form a double bond to each other in imines

    C. cannot bond to each other

    D. cannot form a triple bond to each other

24. Lactones and lactams are

    A. cyclic esters and amides

    B. cyclic ketones and amines

    C. hydroxy ketones and hydroxy aldehydes

    D. cyclic ketones and ethers

25. Molecules of compounds such as β-carotene have alternating C=C and C-C bonds. Such double bonds are known as

    A. repeating

    B. segregated

    C. conjugated

    D. non-alternant

26. Side-by-side overlap of p orbitals in a molecular structure results in

    A. π bonding and delocalization of the p orbital electrons

    B. resonance destabilization

    C. non-aromaticity

    D. steric strain

27. A mixture of equal quantities of enantiomers is called

    A. a diastereomeric mixture

    B. a meso- structure

    C. a racemic mixture

    D. a eutectic mixture

28. When drops of a solution of Br_2 in CCl_4 are added to a similar solution of an unknown compound, the color due to Br_2 disappears. This indicates that

    A. a carbonyl group is present in the unknown molecule

    B. the unknown compound is a carboxylic acid

    C. the unknown compound has C=C or C≡C bonds

    D. an amide has been formed

29. Ketones and aldehydes

    A. form a colorless adduct with 2,4-DNP

    B. form a colored iminium salt with 2,4-DNP

    C. form a highly colored solid adduct with 2,4-DNP

    D. do not react with 2,4-DNP

30. In a haloform test, a positive result indicates

    A. a methyl group adjacent to a carbonyl group

    B. a cyclic ketone

    C. a cyclic aldehyde

    D. an α-methylene ester

Reading Comprehension

Questions 1 – 10 are based on the following passage:

Cilia and flagella are tubular structures found on the surfaces of many animal cells. They are examples of organelles, sub-cellular structures that perform a particular function. By beating against the surrounding medium in a swimming motion, they may endow cells with motility or induce the medium to circulate, as in the case of gills. Ciliated cells typically each contain large numbers of cilia 2 -10 μm (micrometer) long. In contrast, flagellated cells usually have one or two flagella, and the structures can be as long as 200 μm. For both types of structure, the diameters are less than 0.5 μm.

Although they share similar structures, the motion of the two organelles is somewhat different. Flagella beat in a circular, undulating motion that is continuous. The effective stroke of a cilium's beat, which generates the power, is followed by a more languid recovery to the original position. During the recovery stroke, they are brought in close to the membrane of the cell. Cilia usually beat in coordinated waves, so that at any given moment some are in the midst of their power stroke while others are recovering. This provides for a steady flow of fluid past gill surfaces or the epithelia lining the lungs or digestive tract.

The construction of both organelles is very similar. A portion of the cell membrane appears to be stretched over a framework made of tubulin polymers. A polymer is a long, chain-like molecule made of smaller units that are strung together. In this case, the subunits are molecules of the protein tubulin. The framework, or skeleton, of a cilium or flagellum consists of 9 pairs of tubulin polymers spaced around the periphery, and two more single polymers of tubulin that run along the center of the shaft. This is called a 9+2 pattern.

The motion of the organelles results from chemical reactions that cause the outer polymers to slide past one another. By doing so, they force the overall structure to bend. This is similar to the mechanism of contraction of skeletal muscle. In cilia and flagella, the nine outer polymer pairs of the skeleton have along their lengths molecules of a rod-shaped protein called dynein. The dynein rods can grasp, or bind to, the neighboring tubulin polymer. Energy is then used to drive a chemical reaction that causes the dynein arms to bend, causing one tubulin polymer to move along the length of the other. Through a coordinated series of thousands of such reactions, the cilium or flagellum will beat.

Cilia have also provided some of the best evidence for the inheritance of traits by a mechanism that does not involve DNA. Paramecium is a single-celled ciliated protist that lives in ponds. In one variety, the stroke cycle of the cilia is clockwise (right-handed). In another variety, it is counter-clockwise (left-handed). When the cells divide, left-handed cells give rise to more left-handed cells, and vice versa. T.M. Sonneborn of Indiana University managed to cut tiny pieces of cell membrane from a left-handed Paramecium and graft them onto a right-handed one. The cell survived, and the direction of the stroke did not change, despite the fact that cilia were now in a cell with a right-handed nucleus and surrounded by right-handed cilia, they continued to rotate to the left. A paramecium reproduces by dividing, and Sonneborn followed the transplanted patch for several generations, but it did not change direction. This suggested that the direction of rotation is a property of the cilium itself, and is not influenced by the DNA in the nucleus. In another experiment, Sonneborn transplanted the nucleus of a right-handed cell into a left-handed cell from which the original nucleus had been removed. The cell's cilia kept their counter-clockwise direction of rotation. Further, when this cell divided, all subsequent generations maintained it as well. This proved that the direction of rotation could be inherited in a manner completely independent of the chromosomal DNA.

One theory to explain this is the concept of nucleation. According to this idea, the tubulin proteins in left- and right-handed Paramecia are the same, so that the genes that give rise to them are also identical. However, once they begin to chain together in a left- or right-handed manner, they continue to do so. Therefore the direction of rotation does not depend upon the genes, but rather on some basal structure that is passed on to the cell's offspring when it divides.

1. Cilia and flagella are both

    A. Proteins.
    B. Sub-cellular structures that perform a particular function.
    C. Organelles that beat in a continuous undulating motion.
    D. Single-celled protists

2. According to the passage, where would you expect to find cilia?

    A. Stomach lining
    B. Back of the hand
    C. Lining of the heart
    D. Circulatory system

3. According to the passage, how many tubulin polymers make up the entire 9 + 2 pattern seen in cilia and flagella?

    A. 11
    B. 9
    C. 20
    D. Passage doesn't say

4. Two proteins mentioned in this passage are

    A. Tubulin and Paramecium.
    B. Tubulin and dynein.
    C. Tubulin and flagellin.
    D. Tubulin and Sonneborn.

5. Which of the following describes how the beating motion of flagella is caused?

    A. The two central polymers slide past one another.
    B. Dynein causes the outer polymer pairs to slide past one another.
    C. Dynein causes each of the outer polymers to bend.
    D. The organelle increases in diameter.

6. Polymers are always

    A. Made of protein.
    B. Made of tubulin.
    C. Made of subunits.
    D. Arranged in a 9 + 2 array.

7. The passage implies that T.M. Sonneborn was

    A. A zookeeper.
    B. A scientist at Indiana University.
    C. A chemist.
    D. A medical practitioner.

8. It was shown that, if cilia with a counterclockwise rotation are grafted onto a cell whose native cilia beat clockwise, the transplants will

    A. Beat clockwise.
    B. Stop beating.
    C. Beat randomly.
    D. Beat counterclockwise.

9. The passage describes cilia and flagella and tells us that

    A. Cilia may be 200 μm long.
    B. Flagella are less than 0.5 μm long.
    C. Cells can have more than two flagella.
    D. Flagella are less than 0.5 μm in diameter.

10. Sonneborn's experiments showed that

    A. Chromosomes influence the inheritance of rotational direction in cilia.
    B. Rotational direction in cilia is inherited by a mechanism that does not involve DNA.
    C. Chromosomes do not influence the inheritance of rotational direction in flagella.
    D. Rotational direction in cilia is random.

Questions 11 – 22 are based on the following passage:

Annelids

The phylum Annelida, named for the Latin word anellus, meaning "ring", includes earthworms, leeches, and other similar organisms. In their typical form, these animals exhibit bilateral symmetry, a cylindrical cross section, and an elongate body divided externally into segments (metameres) by a series of rings (annuli). They are segmented internally as well, with most of the internal organs repeated in series in each segment. This organization is termed metamerism. Metameric segmentation is the distinguishing feature of this phylum, and provides it with a degree of evolutionary plasticity in that certain segments can be modified and specialized to perform specific functions. For example, in some species certain of the locomotor parapodia, or feet, may be modified for grasping, and some portions of the gut may evolve digestive specializations.

The gut is a straight, muscular tube that functions independently of the muscular activity in the body wall. The Annelida resemble the nematodes, another worm phylum, in possessing a fluid-filled internal cavity separating the gut from the body wall. In both phyla, this cavity is involved in locomotion. However, in the annelids this space is formed at a much later time during the development of the embryo, and presumably evolved much later as well. This fluid-filled internal space is called a true coelum.

The annelid excretory and circulatory systems are well developed, and some members of the phylum have evolved respiratory organs. The nervous system offers a particular example of metameric specialization. It is concentrated anteriorly into enlarged cerebral ganglia connected to a ventral nerve cord that extends posteriorly and is organized into repeating segmental ganglia.

This phylum includes members bearing adaptations required for aquatic (marine or freshwater) or terrestrial habitats. They may be free-living entities or exist as parasites. Among the best known are the earthworm Lumbricus, the water leech Hirudo, and the marine worm Nereis.

11. What is the purpose of this passage?
  A. To describe the annelid nervous system.
  B. To describe the annelid digestive system.
  C. To introduce distinctive features of annelid anatomy.
  D. To define metamerism.
  E. To tell readers about earthworms.

12. What is meant by the term metamerism?
  A. Segmentation of the anatomy
  B. A series of rings
  C. Bilateral symmetry
  D. Evolutionary plasticity
  E. Specialization

13. What is meant by the term parapodia?
  A. Specialization
  B. Grasping appendages
  C. Locomotion
  D. Metameres
  E. Feet

14. One evolutionary advantage of segmentation is that
  A. Segmented animals have many feet.
  B. Segmented animals have a fluid-filled coelum.
  C. Parts of some segments can become specialized to perform certain functions.
  D. Segments can evolve.
  E. Segments are separated by rings.

15. A group of worms other than the Annelida are called
  A. Lumbricus
  B. Nematodes
  C. Leeches
  D. Parapodia
  E. Metameres

16. Some annelid feet may be specialized in order to

    A. be used for locomotion.
    B. be segmented.
    C. be fluid-filled.
    D. evolve.
    E. grasp things.

17. A difference between the annelid coelum and the fluid-filled cavity of other worms is that

    A. the annelid coelum is involved in locomotion.
    B. the annelid coelum is formed later.
    C. the annelid coelum is formed before the embryonic stage.
    D. the annelid coelum is cylindrical in cross section.
    E. the annelid coelum separates the gut from the body wall.

18. An example of metameric specialization in the nervous system is

    A. segmental ganglia.
    B. the ventral nerve cord.
    C. respiratory organs.
    D. parpapodia
    E. cerebral ganglia

19. The main difference between the Annelida and all other animal phyla is that

    A. the Annelida are worms.
    B. the Annelida include the leeches.
    C. the Annelida are metameric.
    D. the Annelida are aquatic.
    E. the Annelida are specialized.

20. The purpose of the last paragraph in the passage is to

    A. give familiar examples of members of the annelid phylum.
    B. show that annelids may be parasites.
    C. tell the reader that annelids may be adapted to aquatic environments.
    D. show that there are many annelids in nature and that they are adapted to a wide variety of habitats.
    E. tell the reader that earthworms are annelids.

21. The fluid-filled cavity in the nematodes is used for

    A. defense.
    B. reproduction.
    C. feeding.
    D. the gut.
    E. movement.

22. Members of the Annelida are

    A. free-living animals.
    B. parasites.
    C. aquatic.
    D. terrestrial.
    E. all the above

Questions 23 – 30 are based on the following passage:

VISUAL PERCEPTION

It is tempting to think that your eyes are simply mirrors that reflect whatever is in front of them. Researchers, however, have shown that your brain is constantly working to create the impression of a continuous, uninterrupted world.

For instance, in the last ten minutes, you have blinked your eyes around 200 times. You have probably not been aware of any of these interruptions in your visual world. Something you probably have not seen in a long time without the aid of a mirror is your nose. It is always right there, down in the bottom corner of your vision, but your brain filters it out so that you are not aware of your nose unless you purposefully look at it.

Nor are you aware of the artery that runs right down the middle of your retina. It creates a large blind spot in your visual field, but you never notice the hole it leaves. To see this blind spot, try the following: Cover your left eye with your hand. With your right eye, look at the O on the left. As you move your head closer to the O, the X will disappear as it enters the blind spot caused by your optical nerve.

O   X

Your brain works hard to make the world look continuous!

23. The word filters, as used in this passage, most nearly means:
A. Alternates
B. Reverses
C. Ignores
D. Depends

24. The word retina, as used in this passage, most nearly means:
A. Optical illusion
B. Part of the eye
C. Pattern
D. Blindness

25. Which of the following statements can be inferred from this passage?
A. Not all animals' brains filter out information.
B. Visual perception is not a passive process.
C. Blind spots cause accidents.
D. The eyes never reflect reality.

26. What is the author's purpose for including the two letters in the middle of the passage?
A. To demonstrate the blind spot in the visual field.
B. To organize the passage.
C. To transition between the last two paragraphs of the passage.
D. To prove that the blind spot is not real.

27. What is the main purpose of this passage?

    A. To persuade the reader to pay close attention to blind spots.

    B. To explain the way visual perception works.

    C. To persuade the reader to consult an optometrist if the O and X disappear.

    D. To prove that vision is a passive process.

28. Based on the passage, which of the following statements is true?

    A. The brain cannot accurately reflect reality.

    B. Glasses correct the blind spot caused by the optical nerve.

    C. Vision is the least important sense.

    D. The brain fills in gaps in the visual field.

29. The author mentions the nose to illustrate what point?

    A. The brain filters out some visual information.

    B. Not all senses work the same way.

    C. Perception is a passive process.

    D. The sense of smell filters out information.

30. Which of the following statements can be inferred from the second paragraph?

    A. The brain filters out the sound created by the shape of the ears.

    B. The brain does not perceive all activity in the visual field.

    C. Closing one eye affects depth perception.

    D. The brain evolved as a result of environmental factors.

Questions 31 – 36 are based on the following passage:

The immune system is a network of cells, tissues, and organs that defends the body against attacks by foreign invaders. These invaders are primarily microbes—tiny organisms such as bacteria, parasites, and fungi—that can cause infections. Viruses also cause infections, but are too primitive to be classified as living organisms. The human body provides an ideal environment for many microbes. It is the immune system's job to keep the microbes out or destroy them.

The immune system is amazingly complex. It can recognize and remember millions of different enemies, and it can secrete fluids and cells to wipe out nearly all of them. The secret to its success is an elaborate and dynamic communications network. Millions of cells, organized into sets and subsets, gather and transfer information in response to an infection. Once immune cells receive the alarm, they produce powerful chemicals that help to regulate their own growth and behavior, enlist other immune cells, and direct the new recruits to trouble spots.

Although scientists have learned much about the immune system, they continue to puzzle over how the body destroys invading microbes, infected cells, and tumors without harming healthy tissues. New technologies for identifying individual immune cells are now allowing scientists to determine quickly which targets are triggering an immune response. Improvements in microscopy are permitting the first-ever observations of living B cells, T cells, and other cells as they interact within lymph nodes and other body tissues.

In addition, scientists are rapidly unraveling the genetic blueprints that direct the human immune response, as well as those that dictate the biology of bacteria, viruses, and parasites. The combination of new technology with expanded genetic information will no doubt reveal even more about how the body protects itself from disease.

31. What is the main idea of the passage?
A. Scientists fully understand the immune system.
B. The immune system triggers the production of fluids.
C. The body is under constant invasion by malicious microbes.
D. The immune system protects the body from infection.

32. Which statement is not a detail from the passage?
A. Most invaders of the body are microbes.
B. The immune system relies on excellent communication.
C. Viruses are extremely sophisticated.
D. The cells of the immune system are organized.

33 What is the meaning of the word ideal as it is used in the first paragraph?
A. thoughtful
B. confined
C. hostile
D. perfect

34. Which statement is not a detail from the passage?
A. Scientists can now see T cells.
B. The immune system ignores tumors.
C. The ability of the immune system to fight disease without harming the body remains mysterious.
D. The immune system remembers millions of different invaders.

35. What is the meaning of the word enlist as it is used in the second paragraph?
A. call into service
B. write down
C. send away
D. put across

36. What is the author's primary purpose in writing the essay?
A. to persuade
B. to analyze
C. to inform
D. to entertain

Questions 37 – 40 are based on the following passage:

It is most likely that you have never had diphtheria. You probably don't even know anyone who has suffered from this disease. In fact, you may not even know what diphtheria is. Similarly, diseases like whooping cough, measles, mumps, and rubella may all be unfamiliar to you. In the nineteenth and early twentieth centuries, these illnesses struck hundreds of thousands of people in the United States each year, mostly children, and tens of thousands of people died. The names of these diseases were frightening household words. Today, they are all but forgotten. That change happened largely because of vaccines.

You probably have been vaccinated against diphtheria. You may even have been exposed to the bacterium that causes it, but the vaccine prepared your body to fight off the disease so quickly that you were unaware of the infection. Vaccines take advantage of your body's natural ability to learn how to combat many disease-causing germs, or microbes. What's more, your body remembers how to protect itself from the microbes it has encountered before. Collectively, the parts of your body that remember and repel microbes are called the immune system. Without the proper functioning of the immune system, the simplest illness—even the common cold—could quickly turn deadly.

On average, your immune system needs more than a week to learn how to fight off an unfamiliar microbe. Sometimes, that isn't enough time. Strong microbes can spread through your body faster than the immune system can fend them off. Your body often gains the upper hand after a few weeks, but in the meantime you are sick. Certain microbes are so virulent that they can overwhelm or escape your natural defenses. In those situations, vaccines can make all the difference.

Traditional vaccines contain either parts of microbes or whole microbes that have been altered so that they don't cause disease. When your immune system confronts these harmless versions of the germs, it quickly clears them from your body. In other words, vaccines trick your immune system in order to teach your body important lessons about how to defeat its opponents.

37. What is the main idea of the passage?
A. The nineteenth and early twentieth centuries were a dark period for medicine.
B. You have probably never had diphtheria.
C. Traditional vaccines contain altered microbes.
D. Vaccines help the immune system function properly.

38. Which statement is not a detail from the passage?
A. Vaccines contain microbe parts or altered microbes.
B. The immune system typically needs a week to learn how to fight a new disease.
C. The symptoms of disease do not emerge until the body has learned how to fight the microbe.
D. A hundred years ago, children were at the greatest risk of dying from now-treatable diseases.

39. What is the meaning of the word virulent as it is used in the third paragraph?

    A. tiny
    B. malicious
    C. contagious
    D. annoying

40. What is the author's primary purpose in writing the essay?

    A. to entertain
    B. to persuade
    C. to inform
    D. to analyze

Physics

1. Which of the following measurements has the most significant digits?

    A. 0.2990
    B. 2.9900
    C. 2.997
    D. 0.00209

2. A person walks 4 meters in a single direction. He or she then changes directions and walks an additional 9 meters. What is the total magnitude of the displacement of the person?

    A. It is 13 meters.
    B. It is always larger than 9 meters but less than 13 meters.
    C. It is less than 13 meters and as small as 5 meters.
    D. It is less than 5 meters.

3. An automobile increased its speed uniformly from 20 m/s to 30 m/s at rate 5 m/s^2. During this time, it traveled 50 meters. How long did it take the automobile to make this change?

    A. 5 seconds
    B. 2 seconds
    C. 10 seconds
    D. Can't be determined.

4. Which of the following demonstrations best illustrates Newton's first law?

    A. Giving a billiard ball at rest on a smooth level table a small push and letting it roll on the table.
    B. Dragging a box on a table at a constant speed by exerting a force just enough to overcome the force of friction.
    C. Trying without success to move a heavy bureau or filing cabinet on the floor.
    D. Running a current through two parallel wires.

5. A lead sphere 10 centimeters in diameter is attached to a 10-meter wire and suspended from a beam in a large warehouse. A lead sphere 1 meter in diameter is hung next to the smaller sphere, almost touching. Ignoring friction, which statement is true?

    A. The small sphere will move slightly towards the big sphere, but the big sphere will not move.
    B. The big sphere will move slightly toward the small sphere, but the small sphere will not move.
    C. Neither sphere will move.
    D. Both spheres will move slightly towards each other.

6. Two spring scales having negligible mass are connected together and used to weigh a 10 kg object, as shown below.

What will be the reading on the scales?

    A. Both scales will read 10 pounds.
    B. Each scale will read 49 newtons.
    C. The sum of the two readings will be 196 newtons.
    D. The bottom scale will read 98 newtons and the top scale will read 0 newtons.

7. The ideal mechanical advantage (IMA) of a pulley system indicates how much force is required to lift a mass. A fixed pulley has an IMA of 1 because all it only changes the direction of the force. A floating pulley has an IMA of 2. The total IMA is the product of the individual pulleys' IMAs. What is the ideal mechanical advantage of the pulley system below?

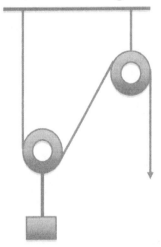

    A. 1
    B. 2
    C. 3
    D. 4

8. A piece of art of mass 200 kg is suspended from two nails so that the angle the hanging wires make is 40° with the horizontal. What is the tension in the hanging wires? (Note: $\sin(40°) = 0.64$ and $\cos(40°) = 0.77$).

    A. 1279 N
    B. 1524 N
    C. 1960 N
    D. 3048 N

9. Two cars driving in opposite directions collide. If you ignore friction and any other outside interactions, which of the following statements is always true?

    A. The total momentum is conserved.
    B. The sum of the potential and kinetic energy are conserved.
    C. The total velocity of the cars is conserved.
    D. The total impulse is conserved.

10. A bowling ball with a mass of 4 kilograms moving at a speed of 10 meters per second hits a stationary 1 kg bowling ball in a head-on elastic collision. What is the speed of the stationary ball after the collision?

    A. 0 m/s
    B. 10 m/s.
    C. Less than 10 m/s, but not 0 m/s.
    D. More than 10 m/s

11. Which statement best explains why the work done by a gravitational force on an object does not depend on the path the object takes?

    A. Work depends on the path when there is friction. The longer the path the more energy is required to overcome friction.
    B. Gravitational fields that arise from the interaction between point masses always produce elliptical paths of motion.
    C. A falling object experiences a change in potential energy.
    D. When an object falls down the work done by gravity is positive and when an object is thrown up the work done by gravity is negative.

12. A motorcycle weighs twice as much as a bicycle and is moving twice as fast. Which of the following statements is true?

    A. The motorcycle has four times as much kinetic energy as the bicycle.
    B. The motorcycle has eight times as much kinetic energy as the bicycle.
    C. The bicycle and the motorcycle have the same kinetic energy.
    D. The bicycle has four times as much kinetic energy as the motorcycle.

13. Two objects of masses m and M are a distance R apart. The force of their gravitational attraction is given by GmM/R^2. Their gravitational potential energy is given by $-GmM/R$. If the distance between these two objects doubles from 100 km to 200 km, what happens to the ratio of the gravitational force to the gravitational potential energy?

    A. Doubled
    B. Quadrupled
    C. Halved
    D. Quartered

14. How much does it cost to operate a 5 kilowatt electric motor for 12 hours if electricity is 6 cents per kilowatt-hour?

  A. $0.025
  B. $3.60
  C. $14.40
  D. $360

15. The equation for the amplitude of the motion of an object undergoing simple harmonic motion is $A\sin(5t)$. Assuming the wave's phase is measured in radians, what is the period of the motion?

  A. $\sin(5t)$
  B. 0.2 seconds
  C. 1.26 seconds
  D. A

16. What is the speed of a wave with a frequency of 12 Hz and a wavelength of 3 meters?

  A. 12 meters per second
  B. 36 meters per second
  C. 4 meters per second
  D. 0.25 meters per second

17. Transverse travelling waves propagate through a taut string of length 20 meters at a speed of 4 m/s. Standing waves are set up in this string which is fixed at both ends. What is the smallest frequency possible for the standing waves?

  A. 0.1 Hz
  B. 0.05 Hz
  C. 0.2 Hz
  D. 0.4 Hz

18. The speed of a travelling wave in a stretched string is given by $\sqrt{T/\mu}$, where T is the tension in the string and μ is the mass per unit length. A 2 meter long stretched string with a mass of 0.010 kilograms is made to resonate with standing waves at 50 Hz. What tension in the string is needed to produce the fourth harmonic? (Note: the fourth harmonic fits 2 full waves into the length of the string).

  A. 12.5 newtons
  B. 25 newtons
  C. 50 newtons
  D. 10,000 newtons

19. A hydraulic lift needs to raise a 3.5×10^3 newton truck. The input piston has a diameter of 2.0 cm and the output piston has a diameter of 24 cm. What minimum force must be applied to the input piston?

  A. 24 N
  B. 292 N
  C. 42,000 N
  D. 504,000 N

20. An incompressible ideal fluid is flowing through a pipe 5.0 cm in radius at a speed of 6.0 m/s. The pipe narrows to 3.0 cm. What is the speed of flow in the narrower section?

    A. 10 m/s
    B. 3.6 m/s
    C. 16.7 m/s
    D. Can't be determined from the given information.

21. Which statement correctly describes the elastic limit of a metal rod?

    A. The elastic limit occurs when a deformed object will no longer return to its original shape.
    B. The elastic limit occurs when the rod breaks.
    C. The elastic limit occurs when the stress stops producing a strain.
    D. The elastic limit assumes that the forces between molecules in a metal act like springs.

22. A charge $+2q$ is placed at the origin of a coordinate system and a charge of $-q$ is placed at a distance d from the origin. How far from the origin must a third charge $+q$ be placed so that the net force on it is 0 newtons?

    A. Less than $d/2$
    B. Between $d/2$ and d
    C. Between d and $2d$
    D. Greater than $2d$

23. An electron moves in a uniform electric field in the same direction as the electric field from point A to point B. Which of the following statements is true?

    A. The potential energy of the electron decreased
    B. The potential energy of the electron increased
    C. The potential energy of the electron remained constant
    D. The potential energy of the electron was converted into kinetic energy

24. The charged particle moving through a magnetic field will be subject to a force of $F = qvB\sin\theta$, where q is the charge, v is the particle's velocity, B is the magnetic field strength, and θ is the particle's angle between the magnetic field vector and the velocity vector. Charged particles from space enter the earth's atmosphere all the time. For example, the Aurora Borealis or Northern Lights are created by positive and negative charges passing through the Earth's magnetic field. Assume a proton with a speed of 8.0×10^6 meters per second enters the Earth's magnetic field at an angle of 45°, at a point where the magnetic field is 0.5 Teslas. What is the magnetic force acting on the proton? (Note: the proton has a charge of 1.6×10^{-19} coulombs.)

    A. 6.4×10^{-17} newtons
    B. 4.5×10^{-17} newtons
    C. 4.5×10^{-13} newtons
    D. 5.5×10^{-17} tesla

25. A solenoid is made of loops of wire, through which a current is run. What is the purpose of putting a lot of loops into a solenoid?

    A. To increase the magnetic field inside the solenoid.
    B. To increate the magnetic field outside the solenoid.
    C. To decrease the magnetic field inside the solenoid.
    D. To decrease the magnetic field outside the solenoid.

26. Which of the following gives the correct order of electromagnetic radiation from the lowest frequency to the highest frequency?

    A. microwaves, UHF radio waves, x-rays, visible light
    B. UHF radio waves, microwaves, visible light, x-rays
    C. UHF radio waves, microwaves, visible light, x-rays
    D. microwaves, x-rays, visible light, UHF radio waves

27. Which of the following statements about electricity flowing through a circuit can be correctly derived from Ohm's law?

    A. Increasing the voltage decreases the current if the resistance remains unchanged.
    B. Increasing the current and the resistance decreases the voltage.
    C. Increasing the current increases the voltage if the resistance is unchanged.
    D. Decreasing the resistance increases the current if the voltage remains unchanged.

28. Consider one tungsten wire of length L and cross-sectional area A and another tungsten wire of length 2L and area 2A. Assuming both wires are the same temperature, which of the following statements is true?

    A. The resistance of the two wires is the same.
    B. The resistance of the longer wire is twice the resistance of the shorter wire.
    C. The resistance of the longer wire is half the resistance of the shorter wire.
    D. The resistance of the longer wire is four times the resistance of the shorter wire.

29. Adding multiple capacitors to a circuit is much the opposite as adding multiple resistors. Adding resistors in series, for example, creates an effective resistance equal to their sum. To add resistors in parallel, you must add the reciprocals of their resistance. With capacitors, however, you use reciprocals when adding them in series and you sum the capacitance when adding in parallel. Given the following diagram, what is the total capacitance of the circuit?

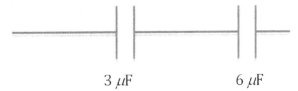

$$3 \; \mu F \qquad\qquad 6 \; \mu F$$

    A. 2-microfarads
    B. 9-microfarads
    C. 0.5-microfarads
    D. 4.5 microfarads

30. A miniature heater has a power rating of 50 watts and is connected to a battery with an electromotive force of 10 volts. What current flows through the heater?

    A. 500 amperes
    B. 5 amperes
    C. 200 milliamperes
    D. 3.1×10^{19} electrons per second

31. A lens forms an upright image 19 cm from a lens of an object 49 cm from the lens. The object and image are on the same side of the lens. What is the magnification of the image?

   A. 0.39
   B. 2.6
   C. 13.7
   D. 31.2

32. Which of the forces depicted below produces a counter-clockwise torque around the pivot point?

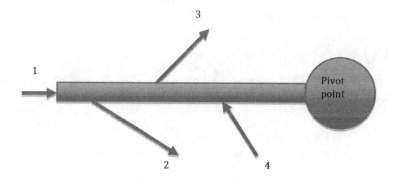

   A. 1
   B. 2
   C. 3
   D. 4

33. You blow up a rubber balloon and hold the opening tight with your fingers. You then release your fingers, causing air to blow out of the balloon. This pushes the balloon forward, causing the balloon shoots across the room. Which of Newton's laws best explains the cause of this motion?

   A. First law
   B. Second law
   C. Third law
   D. Law of gravity

34. Which has a greater moment of inertia about an axis through its center: a solid cylinder or a hollow cylinder? Both cylinders have the same mass and radius.

   A. Solid cylinder
   B. Hollow cylinder
   C. Both have same moment of inertia.
   D. It depends on how quickly the cylinders are rolling.

35. Astronauts in orbit are sometimes considered to be "weightless." Consider the four propositions about weightlessness and determine which ones are true.

> I. Weightlessness occurs in outer space because the force of gravity becomes negligible.
> II. Weightlessness occurs when a ski jumper makes a jump.
> III. Weightlessness occurs when you roll a baseball on the ground.

A. I only.
B. II only.
C. I and II.
D. I, II and III.

36. The potential energy of a spring is represented as $\frac{1}{2}kx^2$, where k represents the spring constant and x is the displacement of the spring from its position when it is not stretched. A massless spring is suspended from a support and a 100 g mass is attached, stretching it 2 cm. If another 100 g mass is attached, what is the new potential energy of the spring?

A. Half as much as with one 100 g mass attached.
B. One-fourth as much as with one 100 g mass attached.
C. Twice as much as with one 100 g mass attached.
D. Four times as much as with one 100 g mass attached.

37. Which of the following statements about refraction is true?

A. Refraction means a change in direction of the wave.
B. The angle of reflection equals the angle of refraction.
C. The frequency in a refracted wave changes.
D. The phase of a refracted wave changes.

38. What corresponds to the amplitude of a sound wave?

A. loudness
B. pressure differential of fluctuations
C. magnitude of motion of air molecules
D. power

39. The density of helium is much lower than that of air. How does the speed of sound traveling through helium gas compare to the speed of sound in air?

A. It is faster
B. It is slower
C. It is the same speed
D. It cannot be determined without knowing their atomic masses

40. What property of a sound wave in air corresponds to the frequency of the sound?

A. pitch
B. high and low
C. timbre
D. overtones

Quantitative Reasoning

1. A man decided to buy new furniture from Futuristic Furniture for $2600. Futuristic Furniture gave the man two choices: pay the entire amount in one payment with cash, or pay $1000 as a down payment and $120 per month for two full years in the financial plan. If the man chooses the financial plan, how much more would he pay?

    A. $1480 more
    B. $1280 more
    C. $1600 more
    D. $2480 more

2. What is the value of *r* in the following equation?

$$29 + r = 420$$

    A. $r = 29/420$
    B. $r = 420/29$
    C. $r = 391$
    D. $r = 449$

3. If 35% of a paycheck was deducted for taxes and 4% for insurance, what is the total percentage taken out of the paycheck?

    A. 20%
    B. 31%
    C. 39%
    D. 42%

4. In the year 2000, 35% of the company sales were in electronics. The table below shows how electronic sales have changed for the company over the years. Find the percentage of electronics sold in 2005.

Years	Change
2000 − 2001	−2%
2001 − 2002	−1%
2002 − 2003	+6%
2003 − 2004	−1%
2004 − 2005	+2%

    A. 2%
    B. 11%
    C. 39%
    D. 42%

5. A woman wants to stack two small bookcases beneath a window that is $26\frac{1}{2}$ inches from the floor. The larger bookcase is $14\frac{1}{2}$ inches tall. The other bookcase is $8\frac{3}{4}$ inches tall. How tall will the two bookcases be when they are stacked together?

    A. 12 inches tall
    B. $23\frac{1}{4}$ inches tall
    C. $35\frac{1}{4}$ inches tall
    D. 41 inches tall

464

6. Solve for y in the following equation if $x = -3$

$$y = x + 5$$

A. $y = -2$
B. $y = 2$
C. $y = 3$
D. $y = 8$

7. Put the following integers in order from greatest to least:

-52, 16, -12, 14, 8, -5, 0

A. -52, 16, -12, 14, 8, -5, 0
B. 0, -5, 8, -12, 14, 16, -52
C. -5, -12, -52, 0, 8, 14, 16
D. 16, 14, 8, 0, -5, -12, -52

8. If number x is subtracted from 27, the result is -5. What is number x?

A. 22
B. 25
C. 32
D. 35

9. What is the simplest way to write the following expression?

$$5x - 2y + 4x + y$$

A. $9x - y$
B. $9x - 3y$
C. $9x + 3y$
D. $x - y$

10. Find the sum.

$$\left(3x^2 + x + 3\right) + 8x^2 + 5x + 16$$

A. $7x^2 + 29x^2$
B. $11x^2 + 6x + 19$
C. $30x + 19$
D. $(3x^2 + 3x) + 13x^2 + 16$

11. What is the perimeter of the following figure?

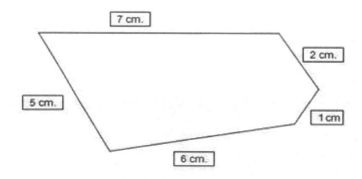

A. 15 cm
B. 18 cm
C. 21 cm
D. 36 cm

12. To begin making her soup, Jennifer added four containers of chicken broth with 1 liter of water into the pot. Each container of chicken broth contains 410 milliliters. How much liquid is in the pot?

A. 1.64 liters
B. 2.64 liters
C. 5.44 liters
D. 6.12 liters

13. According to the table below, which snack is made with no more than 4 grams of sugar and between 4-6 grams of carbohydrates?

Snack (amount per serving)	Grams of Sugar per Serving	Grams of Carbohydrates per Serving
Snappy Cookies (3)	6	8
Snappy Crackers (8)	6	4
Snappy Cheese (2)	0	0
Snappy Twisters (4)	4	5
Snappy Chews (20)	0	8

A. Snappy Cookies
B. Snappy Crackers
C. Snappy Cheese
D. Snappy Twisters

14. Which of the following fractions is halfway between $\frac{2}{5}$ and $\frac{4}{9}$?

A. $\frac{2}{3}$
B. $\frac{2}{20}$
C. $\frac{17}{40}$
D. $\frac{19}{45}$

15. Which of the following is the largest number?

    A. $1/2$

    B. $3/8$

    C. $7/16$

    D. $13/54$

16. Of the following expressions, which is equal to $6\sqrt{10}$?

    A. 36

    B. $\sqrt{600}$

    C. $\sqrt{360}$

    D. $\sqrt{6}$

17. Which number equals 2^{-3}?

    A. $1/2$

    B. $1/4$

    C. $1/8$

    D. $1/16$

18. What is the average of $7/5$ and 1.4?

    A. 5.4

    B. 1.4

    C. 2.4

    D. 7.4

19. Two numbers are said to be reciprocal if their product equals 1. Which of the following represents the reciprocal of the variable x?

    A. $x - 1$

    B. $\dfrac{1}{-x}$

    C. x^{-1}

    D. $-x^1$

20. A taxi service charges \$5.50 for the first 1/5 of a mile, \$1.50 for each additional 1/5 of a mile, and 20¢ per minute of waiting time. Joan took a cab from her place to a flower shop 8 miles away, where she bought a bouquet, then another 3.6 miles to her mother's place. The driver had to wait 9 minutes while she bought the bouquet. What was the fare?

    A. \$20

    B. \$120.20

    C. \$92.80

    D. \$91

21. Which of the following expressions is equivalent to the equation $3x^2 + 4x - 15$?

    A. $(x - 3)(x + 5)$

    B. $(x + 5)(3 + x^2)$

    C. $x(3x + 4 - 15)$

    D. $(x + 3)(3x - 5)$

22. Prizes are to be awarded to the best pupils in each class of an elementary school. The number of students in each grade is shown in the table, and the school principal wants the number of prizes awarded in each grade to be proportional to the number of students. If there are twenty prizes, how many should go to fifth grade students?

Grade	1	2	3	4	5
Students	35	38	38	33	36

    A. 5
    B. 4
    C. 7
    D. 3

23. Which of the following numbers is a prime number?

    A. 15
    B. 11
    C. 33
    D. 4

24. Which of the following expressions is equivalent to $3\left(\frac{6x-3}{3}\right) - 3(9x - 9)$?

    A. $-3(7x + 10)$
    B. $-3x + 6$
    C. $(x + 3)(x - 3)$
    D. $3x^2 - 9$

25. Evaluate the expression $(x - 2y)^2$ where $x = 3$ and $y = 2$.

    A. -1
    B. +1
    C. +4
    D. -2

26. Bob decides to go into business selling lemonade. He buys a wooden stand for $45 and sets it up outside his house. He figures that the cost of lemons, sugar, and paper cups for each glass of lemonade sold will be 10¢. Which of these expressions describes his cost for making g glasses of lemonade?

    A. $\$45 + \$0.1 \times g$
    B. $\$44.90 \times g$
    C. $\$44.90 \times g + 10¢$
    D. $\$90$

27. Which of the following expressions is equivalent to $(3x^{-2})^3$?

    A. $9x^{-6}$
    B. $9x^{-8}$
    C. $27x^{-6}$
    D. $27x^{-8}$

28. **Sally wants to buy a used truck for her delivery business. Truck A is priced at $450 and gets 25 miles per gallon. Truck B costs $650 and gets 35 miles per gallon. If gasoline costs $4 per gallon, how many miles must Sally drive to make truck B the better buy?**

    A. 600
    B. 7500
    C. 340
    D. 740

29. **Given the equation $\frac{3}{y-5} = \frac{15}{y+4}$, what is the value of y?**

    A. 45
    B. 54
    C. $\frac{29}{4}$
    D. $\frac{4}{29}$

30. **Which of the following expressions is equivalent to $(a)(a)(a)(a)(a)$ for all values of a, positive or negative?**

    A. $5a$
    B. a^{-5}
    C. $a^{-\frac{1}{5}}$
    D. a^{5}

31.

English-Metric Equivalents	
1 meter	1.094 yard
2.54 centimeter	1 inch
1 kilogram	2.205 pound
1 liter	1.06 quart

A sailboat is 19 meters long. What is its length in inches?

    A. 254
    B. 1094
    C. 4826
    D. 748

Questions 32 and 33 are based upon the following table:

Kyle bats third in the batting order for the Badgers baseball team. The table shows the number of hits that Kyle had in each of 7 consecutive games played during one week in July.

Day of Week	Number of Hits
Monday	1
Tuesday	2
Wednesday	3
Thursday	1
Friday	1
Saturday	4
Sunday	2

32. What is the mode of the numbers in the distribution shown in the table?
- A. 1
- B. 2
- C. 3
- D. 4

33. What is the mean of the numbers in the distribution shown in the table?
- A. 1
- B. 2
- C. 3
- D. 4

34. $\left(2a^2 b - 3c^3\right)\left(3a^3 b + 4c\right) =$
- A. $5a^6 b^2 + 12c^4 - 9a^3 bc^3 - 12c^4$
- B. $5a^5 b^2 + 8a^2 bc - 9a^3 bc^3 + 12c^4$
- C. $6a^5 b^2 + 8a^2 bc - 9a^3 bc^3 + 12c^4$
- D. $6a^5 b^2 + 8a^2 bc - 9a^3 bc^3 - 12c^4$

35. In the following inequality, solve for x.

$-4x + 8 \geq 48$
- A. $x \geq 10$
- B. $x \geq -10$
- C. $x \leq 10$
- D. $x \leq -10$

36. Two even integers and one odd integer are multiplied together. Which of the following could be their product?
- A. 3.75
- B. 9
- C. 16.2
- D. 24

37. There are 80 mg / 0.8 ml in concentrated acetaminophen drops for children. If the proper dosage for a four year old child is 240 mg, how many milliliters should the child receive?

    A. 0.8 ml
    B. 1.6 ml
    C. 2.4 ml
    D. 3.2 ml

38. Using the chart below, which equation describes the relationship between x and y?

x	y
2	6
3	9
4	12
5	15

    A. $x = 3y$
    B. $y = 3x$
    C. $y = 1/3x$
    D. $x/y = 3$

39. On a highway map, the scale indicates that 1 inch represents 45 miles. If the distance on the map is 3.2 inches, how far is the actual distance?

    A. 45 miles
    B. 54 miles
    C. 112 miles
    D. 144 miles

40. What fractional part of an hour is 400 seconds?

    A. 1/5
    B. 1/6
    C. 1/7
    D. 1/9

Answers and Explanations

Natural Science

BIOLOGY

1. C: The hydrogen bonds between water molecules cause water molecules to attract each other (negative pole to positive pole. and "stick" together. This gives water a high surface tension, which allows small living organisms, such as water striders, to move across its surface. Since water is a polar molecule, it readily dissolves other polar and ionic molecules such as carbohydrates and amino acids. Polarity alone is not sufficient to make something soluble in water, however; for example, cellulose is polar but its molecular weight is so large that it is not soluble in water.

2. A: Long term energy storage in animals takes the form of fat. Animals also store energy as glycogen, and plants store energy as starch, but these substances are for shorter-term use. Fats are a good storage form for chemical energy because fatty acids bond to glycerol in a condensation reaction to form fats (triglycerides). This reaction, which releases water, allows for the compacting of high-energy fatty acids in a concentrated form.

3. A: A cofactor is an inorganic substance that is required for an enzymatic reaction to occur. Cofactors bind to the active site of the enzyme and enable the substrate to fit properly. Many cofactors are metal ions, such as zinc, iron, and copper.

4. B: Proteins in the inner membrane of the mitochondrion accept high-energy electrons from NAD and $FADH_2$, and in turn transport protons from the matrix to the intermembrane space. The high proton concentration in the intermembrane space creates a gradient which is harnessed by ATP synthase to produce ATP.

5. C: Although there are two cell divisions in meiosis, DNA replication occurs only once. It occurs in interphase I, before M phase begins.

6. D: The ovary houses the ovules in a flower. Pollen grains fertilize ovules to create seeds, and the ovary matures into a fruit.

7. A: The central, supporting pillar of the tree is known as heartwood. Heartwood does not function in the transport of water, and even though it is dead it will not decay or lose strength as long as the outer layers remain intact.

8. D: The phloem is the pipeline through which carbohydrates are transported to the roots. It is located outside of the xylem and lives for only a short time before becoming part of the outer bark.

9. D: When Ca^{2+} channels open, calcium enters the axon terminal and causes synaptic vesicles to release neurotransmitter into the synaptic cleft.

10. E: The placenta secretes progesterone and estrogen once a pregnancy is established. Early in pregnancy, the placenta secretes hCG.

11. D: At the lowest trophic level are the producers, followed by primary consumers. Primary carnivores follow consumers, followed by secondary carnivores.

12. D: Type I curves describe species in which most individuals survive to middle age, after which deaths increase. Dolphins have few offspring, provide extended care to the young, and live a long time.

13. A: Transportation by humans or human-associated means is not considered a natural dispersal process.

14. C: According to Hardy-Weinberg equilibrium, $p + q = 1$ and $p^2 + 2pq + q^2 = 1$. In this scenario, $q^2 = 0.25$, so $q = 0.5$. p must also be 0.5.

15. E: Structures are homologous because they derive from a common ancestor. Insects do not share a common ancestor with birds and mammals. Birds and mammals share a reptile ancestor.

16. B: The bonds between hydrogen and oxygen in water involve shared electrons and are therefore covalent. But the electrons are shared unequally because oxygen is more electronegative than hydrogen, so the shared electrons are more attracted to oxygen. Hydrogen – oxygen bonding between water molecules is an example of hydrogen bonding.

17. A: Amino acids contain carbon, oxygen, nitrogen, hydrogen, and sometimes sulfur. Polypeptides do not contain phosphate as an integral component. However, they may be phosphorylated by an enzyme following translation.

18. C: Coenzymes are organic cofactors that are necessary for certain enzymatic reactions. Cofactors bind to the active site and allow the substrate to fit properly. Many coenzymes are vitamins, some of which are not made by cells but must be obtained through the diet.

19. B: The activation energy, or peak, is lower in curve 2, which means that a catalyst was present. Enzymes work by lowering the activation energy of reactions.

20. D: Oxygen is the final electron acceptor, which is why oxygen is required for cellular respiration. Oxygen combines with two electrons and two protons to form water, one of the waste products of cellular respiration. The other waste product is carbon dioxide.

21. E: Auxin controls cell wall plasticity and is produced at root and shoot tips. It controls the responses of these structures to light and gravity.

22. A: When the CO_2 concentration is high, more carbonic acid is formed, and the body needs to increase respiration to remove it from the blood. Thus, a drop in pH causes an increase in the respiratory rate.

23. C: GABA is an inhibitory neurotransmitter in the brain, although it may occasionally function as an excitatory neurotransmitter.

24. E: Because we are not told whether the parent plants are homozygous or heterozygous, it is not possible to determine the dominance of one allele over another.

25. A: If the genes were unlinked, a 9:3:3:1 distribution of phenotypes would appear in the F_2 generation because of independent segregation of the traits.

26. E: Phosphorus, like other minerals such as calcium and magnesium, is found in its largest quantities in rocks and other sediments. It is released into the environment through erosion. Synthetic fertilizer is the main source of phosphorous for crop plants.

27. B: Species that inhabit a particular ecosystem that were transported by humans to that location are called introduced species. They may or may not be invasive, depending on whether or not they displace native species.

28. D: Darwin and Mendel were contemporaries but were apparently not aware of each other's work. Around the beginning of the 20th century, Mendel's discoveries about genetics were incorporated into Darwinism, resulting in what is called the modern synthesis.

29. E: The variation caused by mutation is the raw material for natural selection.

30. A: Genetic drift is the random change in allele frequencies. In a small population, some alleles may increase or decrease for no other reason than by chance.

31. A: Osmosis is the movement of water molecules (not solutes) across a semi-permeable membrane. Water moves from a region of higher concentration to a region of lower concentration. Osmosis occurs when the concentrations of a solute differ on either side of a semi-permeable membrane. For example, a cell (containing a higher concentration of water) in a salty solution (containing a lower concentration of water) will lose water as water leaves the cell. This continues until the solution outside the cell has the same salt concentration as the cytoplasm.

32. D: Both prokaryotes and eukaryotes interact with the extracellular environment and use membrane-bound or membrane-associated proteins to achieve this. They both use diffusion and active transport to move materials in and out of their cells. Prokaryotes have very few proteins associated with their DNA, whereas eukaryotes' DNA is richly studded with proteins. Both types of living things can have flagella, although with different structural characteristics in the two groups. The most important differences between prokaryotes and eukaryotes are the lack of a nucleus and membrane-bound organelles in prokaryotes.

33. D: Enzymes act as catalysts for biochemical reactions. A catalyst is not consumed in a reaction, but, rather, lowers the activation energy for that reaction. The potential energy of the substrate and the product remain the same, but the activation energy—the energy needed to make the reaction progress—can be lowered with the help of an enzyme.

34. C: Lactic acid fermentation converts pyruvate into lactate using high-energy electrons from NADH. This process allows ATP production to continue in anaerobic conditions by providing NAD^+ so that ATP can be made in glycolysis.

35. B: DNA wrapped around histone proteins is called chromatin. In a eukaryotic cell, DNA is always associated with protein; it is not "naked" as with prokaryotic cells.

36. D: Each time a cell divides; a few base pairs of DNA at the end of each chromosome are lost. Telomerase is an enzyme that uses a built-in template to add a short sequence of DNA over and over at the end of chromosomes—a sort of protective "cap". This prevents the loss of genetic material with each round of DNA replication.

37. A: The large intestine's main function is the reabsorption of water into the body to form solid waste. It also allows for the absorption of vitamin K produced by microbes living inside the large intestine.

38. D: Positive feedback from rising levels of estrogen in the menstrual cycle produces a sudden surge of luteinizing hormone (LH). This high level triggers ovulation.

39. D: A lineage map describes the fates of cells in the early embryo: in other words, it tells which germ layer different cells will occupy. In some small organisms such as the nematode Caenorhabditis elegans, all of the adult cells can be traced back to the egg. A lineage map is not a mechanism of embryo development, but rather a tool for describing it.

40. E: An individual with AB blood is tolerant to both the A carbohydrate on red blood cells and the B carbohydrate as "self" and can therefore accept any of the 4 different blood types.

GENERAL CHEMISTRY

1. B: Na (sodium) is a solid at standard temperature and pressure, which is 0°C (273 K) and 100 kPa (0.986 atm), according to IUPAC. The stronger the intermolecular forces, the greater the likelihood of the material being a solid. Kr and Xe are noble gases and have negligible intermolecular attraction. NH_3 has some hydrogen bonding but is still a gas at STP. Sodium is an alkali metal whose atoms are bonded by metallic bonding and is therefore a solid at STP.

2. B: The ideal gas law $PV = nRT$ is rearranged to solve for V, and we get $V = nRT/P$. R is the gas constant, 0.08206 (L atm)/(mol K), and the Celsius temperature must be converted to Kelvin, by adding 273 to 25°C to obtain 298 K. The pressure must be converted to atmospheres, which 101 kPa is essentially 1 atm (0.9967 atm). Plugging the numbers into the equation we get:

$$V = \frac{1000 \text{ mol} \left(0.08206 \frac{\text{L atm}}{\text{mol K}}\right)(298 \text{ K})}{1 \text{ atm}}$$

which gives $V = 24,453$ L. A liter is a cubic decimeter (dm^3) and when converted gives $V = 24.5 \text{ m}^3$.

3. D: London dispersion forces are the weakest intermolecular forces. These interactions occur in all molecules due to unequal electron density around the nucleus, which results in a momentary dipole. Dipole-dipole interactions are those between two polar molecules. The more positive portion of one molecule is attracted to the negative portion of a different molecule. Hydrogen bonding is a stronger type of dipole-dipole interaction which occurs between a hydrogen in one molecule and a nitrogen, oxygen or fluorine atom in another molecule. Hydrogen bonding only occurs between molecules containing H-F, H-O or H-N bonds. Ionic bonds are the strongest intermolecular forces. In ionic molecules, a positive ion is attracted to a negative ion. NaCl is entirely ionic with full charge separation, and the ions are tightly bound to each other in an organized crystalline network.

4. C: To convert from degrees Celsius to Kelvin, add 273. 75° C is equivalent to 348 K. Both X and Y have lower boiling points, which means that they will each boil in the water bath. Z will never become warm enough to boil.

5. B: Since both the volume and the temperature remain fixed, the only variable that changes is the number of moles of particles. Because there are now 3 times the number of particles as there were originally, the pressure must increase proportionately and so the pressure must be 3 atm.

6. C: Normality refers to the concentration of acid equivalents (H^+ ions), not the concentration of the solute. 100 g of phosphoric acid has a MW of 98 g/mol. So, (100 g)/(98 g/mol) = 1.02 moles of phosphoric acid are in solution. The total volume of the solution is 0.4 L, so the molarity of the solution is 1.02 mol/0.4 L = 2.55 M. Since there are three acid equivalents for every mole of phosphoric acid, the normality is $3 \times 2.55 = 7.65$ N.

7. D: 100 mL of a 0.1 M solution of NaOH contains 0.01 moles of NaOH. That means 0.01 moles of acid are required to completely neutralize the solution. The MW of sulfuric acid is 98, so 0.98 g of sulfuric acid is 0.01 mole. But since sulfuric acid has two equivalents of acid per mole, only 0.005 mole of the acid is required or 0.49 g.

8. D: Octane is a nonpolar hydrocarbon with little or no water solubility. Butanol is an alcohol with a small amount of solubility due to its polar –OH group. Ethanol is a smaller, more polar alcohol that is very soluble in water. NaCl is an ionic salt that is highly soluble in water.

9. B: Ethane is an alkane and only very weakly acidic. Methanol, an alcohol, has a slightly acidic proton attached to the oxygen. Acetic acid is much more acidic than methanol with the acidic proton attached to the carboxyl group. Hydrochloric acid is highly acidic and completely dissociates in water.

10. B: Negative beta emission represents the spontaneous decay of a neutron into a proton with the release of an electron. Therefore, the resulting nucleus will have one more proton than it did before the reaction, and protons represent the atomic number of an atom. Alpha decay results in the emission of a helium nucleus. The resulting nucleus of an alpha decay would lose two protons and two neutrons, causing a decrease in both the atomic number and the mass number. Gamma decay does not affect the numbers of protons or neutrons in the nucleus. It is an emission of a photon, or packet of energy.

11. D: Isotopes of the same element must have the same chemical behavior, so A, B, and C all represent, in one form or another, chemical behavior. Isotopes differ in mass, and this can be used to separate them by some appropriate physical property.

12. B: Phosphorus is in the third period, so the outermost levels must be 3s, 3p. Phosphorus is in Group 5A, which indicates that it has 5 valence electrons. To fill the 3s and 3p, 2 electrons first fill the s orbital, and then the remaining 3 electrons enter the p orbitals. So, $3s^2 3p^3$.

13. B: The trend within any column of the periodic table is that electronegativity decreases going down the column.

14. B: Hybrid orbitals arrange themselves to be as far from each other as possible. An sp^2 atom has three hybrid orbitals, so they arrange themselves to be trigonal planar, with 120° between the bonds.

15. A: By comparing the products to the reactants, there must be at least two Al atoms in the starting material, and at least three sulfate groups. Therefore, a coefficient of 2 must be placed in front of $Al(OH)_3$ and a coefficient of 3 must be placed in front of H_2SO_4. To make the number of hydrogen and oxygen atoms equal on both sides of the equation, a coefficient of 6 must be placed in front of H_2O.

16. C: The equation shows that for every liter of methane reacted, one liter of CO_2 and 2 liters of water vapor will be produced. So a total of three liters of gaseous products will be formed for every liter of methane burned. Because the temperature of the reaction products is 200 °C, the water produced will be in vapor (gas) form and not in liquid form. Since 10L of methane were burned, 30 L of gaseous products were formed.

17. D: 0.5 g of the salt dissolved, which is 0.005 mol of the salt. Since the volume is 1 L, the molarity of the salt is 0.005 M. This means that both species X and Y are present at 0.005 M concentration. The $K_{sp} = [X][Y]$, or $[0.005][0.005]$ which equals 2.5×10^{-5}.

18. C: HCl is a strong acid that will completely dissociate. $pH = -\log_{10}[H^+]$, which for this problem is $pH = -\log_{10}(0.1) = 1$. The volume of the solution has no bearing on the pH since we know the concentration.

19. A: When liquid water changes to steam, the temperature is constant, as in all phase changes. The entropy increases due to the increase in disorder from a liquid to a gas.

20. A: The longest straight chain of carbons is four, so the parent name is butane. The alcohol takes number precedence, so it is in the -2- position, placing the methyl in the -3- position. The suffix becomes –ol since it is an alcohol, so the name is 3-methyl-2-butanol.

21. B: Cis isomers have substituent groups that are on the same side of the molecule across the double bond. Trans isomers are those with substituent groups that are on opposite sides of the molecule across the double bond. I is neither cis nor trans, since both substituents on the same carbon are identical. IV is trans because the two methyl groups are on opposite sides of the molecule. II is cis due to both ethyl groups being on the same side of the molecule. III is also considered cis, although each substituent is different. The heaviest groups on each end of the double bond must be on the same side of the double bond to be cis.

22. B: Freezing is an exothermic event; therefore, heat must be given off. The temperature of the material remains unchanged at the freezing point during the process.

23. B: Neutrons are neutral in charge, and can impact a nucleus in order to break it.

24. D: An alpha particle is a helium nucleus, which contains two protons and two neutrons.

25. D: All of the elements belong to the same row in the periodic table. Atomic radii increase going from right to left in any row of the periodic table. Although these elements belonged to the same row, it is important to also know that atomic radii increase from top to bottom in the groups of the periodic table.

26. A: Sublimation is the process of a solid changing directly into a gas without entering the liquid phase. Fusion refers to a liquid turning into a solid. Diffusion is the process of a material dispersing throughout another. Condensation is generally a gas turning into a liquid.

27. C: The more s character the bond has, the shorter it will be. A triple bond is stronger and shorter than a double bond, which is stronger and shorter than a single bond. An sp orbital is found in a triple bond. An sp^2 orbital is found in a double bond and sp^3 orbitals are found in single bonds.

28. D: Resonance structures have the same atoms connected to the same atoms, but differ only in electronic structure amongst the atoms. Isomers are molecules that have the same formula but differ in structure. Structural isomers differ in how the atoms are bonded to each other. Stereoisomers are isomers that have the same bonding structure but different arrangements, for example, cis- and trans- isomers.

29. A: Since the atomic number is 20, which represents the number of protons in the atom, there must be an equal number of electrons in a neutral atom. Protons have a positive charge and electrons are negative. Equal numbers of protons and electrons will result in a neutral atom, or zero charge.

30. C: A pressure increase will force the reaction to go further to the right, which lowers gas pressure to restore equilibrium. Since the water formed is in the liquid phase, it does not appear in the equilibrium equation, so only 1 mole of gas is produced and is part of the equation.

ORGANIC CHEMISTRY

1. C: Molecular weights are expressed as grams per mole. Each additional carbon atom to the alkane requires two additional hydrogen atoms. The molecular formula of the alkane will therefore increase by $-CH_2-$, which incrementally increases the molecular weight by 14 g per mole.

2. A: This is the definition of a functional group. "Substituent" refers to an atom or group of atoms attached to a specific carbon atom within a molecule and describes the structure of the molecule rather than its chemical behavior. A "diluent" is a solvent used to dilute the concentration of a solution. An "eluent" is a solvent used to elute materials in a chromatographic separation process.

3. B: The saturated hydrocarbon formula for a six-carbon molecule is C_6H_{14}. Two H atoms are lost for each site of unsaturation (a ring or a double bond to C). The difference of 8 H atoms in the two formulas means there are four sites of unsaturation, not three. Benzene is a highly flammable, sweet-smelling, oily liquid at room temperature. "Aromatic" refers to the electronic structure of the molecule, not to its odor.

4. A: Isomers must have the same molecular formula. Ethanol and propanol are both very soluble in water, and both are clear, colorless liquids at room temperature. The two formulas differ by one $-CH_2-$ unit, and are therefore two members of the homologous series of alcohols.

5. D: The two standard formulas, as written, portray different molecular structures and are therefore not the same. They do represent the same molecular formula, C_2H_6O, though not the same molecular structure, and therefore are isomeric. The molecular formula of methanol is CH_3OH, or CH_4O.

6. A: The carbonyl group is somewhat polarized by the electronegativity of the O atom relative to that of the C atom. With a mild acid catalyst, the carbonyl O atom can be protonated to form a carbonium ion stabilized by two –OH groups. Addition of a molecule of H_2O to the C atom, followed by the loss of H^+ produces an acetal from an aldehyde or a ketal from a ketone. With a mild base catalyst, an OH^- first adds to the carbonyl C atom and the resulting alkoxy anion extracts a proton from a water molecule to form the acetal or ketal and regenerate the OH^- ion.

7. B: An asymmetrically substituted sp^3 carbon atom is optically active and rotates the plane of plane-polarized light either clockwise or counter-clockwise. The order of priority of substituents about the axis of one of the bonds is either clockwise or counter-clockwise. The atom is thus described as having "handedness" or "chirality", as in left-handed or right-handed. It is a chiral center.

A conformer is a conformational isomer, such as the chair and boat conformations of the cyclohexane ring. It is a reactive center only if it is the location in the molecule at which a particular reaction occurs, which is not always the case. Stereoisomer describes the relative configurations of two or more chiral centers in a molecule.

8. D: Enantiomers are left-handed and right-handed versions of the same chemical compound. They therefore have identical physical properties. As enantiomers, their only difference is that they rotate the plane of plane-polarized light in opposite direction by an equal amount. Numerous methods have been developed by which enantiomers in a mixture can be separated from each other. When reacted with a compound having a single chiral center of known configuration, two new compounds are formed that have different molecular structures. These new compounds have different chemical and physical properties that permit their separation by normal methods. After being separated in this way, reversing or undoing the addition reaction releases the original enantiomers as a single pure isomer. Chromatographic methods that employ a chiral adsorbent also have the ability to separate enantiomers in a mixture.

9. C: Nitriles are characterized by the –CN functional group, in which the carbon atom is triply bonded to the nitrogen atom. Alkynes are characterized by a triple bond between two carbon atoms. Cycloalkenes are ringed structures which have a double bond between two carbon atoms. Alkenones contain both carbon-carbon double bonds and ketone carbonyl groups. "Aromatic" refers to the electronic structure of certain molecules, such as benzene, and describes the greater stability of the molecule due to the delocalization of electrons between adjacent and overlapping p-orbitals.

10. B: The oxidizing agent in Tollens' reagent is silver ion from silver oxide, Ag_2O. It will oxidize an aldehyde to a carboxylic acid. In this redox reaction, the silver ion is reduced from Ag^+ to AgO, or neutral silver atoms. This is a classic characterization test in which a positive result is indicated by the formation of a silver 'mirror' coating in the test tube.

11. B: Jones oxidations are carried out by the treatment of an alcohol or an aldehyde with a solution of CrO_3 in mild sulfuric acid solution. A solution of $K_2Cr_2O_7$ in concentrated sulfuric acid produces "chromic acid", a very strongly oxidizing solution sometimes used as a 'last resort' to clean chemical residues from laboratory glassware. Chromic acid oxidizes organic compounds completely to CO_2 and H_2O, and does not stop at the carboxylic acid stage of the process. Potassium permanganate, $KMnO_4$, and manganese dioxide, MnO_2, are also used as oxidizing agents, but neither of these is the Jones' reagent.

12. C: It is entirely possible that the molecules of the compound can decompose at the elevated temperatures before the boiling point of the material is attained. Reducing the pressure lowers the temperature at which materials boil, so distillation can occur before the material ever becomes hot enough to decompose. High-boiling materials do boil at normal pressure, but at temperatures that are high enough to be a concern in regard to safety, energy use, etc. Boiling point and vapor pressure are inversely related; higher vapor pressure means lower boiling point. The melting point of a compound is not related to its boiling point.

13. C: Monosaccharides are simple sugar molecules, or single carbohydrate molecules, such as glucose and fructose. They are cyclic compounds but do not have a carbonyl group when they are in that form, so they cannot be classified as either ketones or aldehydes. They have several –OH groups, as carbohydrates do, but they are not carboxylic acids.

14. A: The electron-withdrawing power of the carbonyl O atom draws electron density through the C=O π bond away from the α C-H bonds. This makes it easier for the sp^3 α carbon atom to hybridize to sp^2 + p and form an extended π system. This renders the α position sufficiently acidic that a proton can be extracted by a strong base. The extra electron of the negative charge in the free p orbital is stabilized by delocalization into the carbonyl π orbital system. The negatively-charged ion formed by the extraction of an α proton is called an enolate ion because its structure is similar to the enol form of a carbonyl compound. Tertiary amines are generally not sufficiently strong bases to extract an α proton.

15. C: Friedel-Crafts reactions use strong Lewis acids to activate the benzene ring to the replacement of H atoms by alkyl or aryl substituent groups. The Lewis acid catalyst coordinates the π system of the benzene ring and the halide of the alkyl or aryl halide. This produces a good electrophile that can add to the benzene ring and displace a proton. The reaction can also be used for halogenation and acylation of benzene ring structures. Claisen condensation involves the addition of an enolate ion to an ester with loss of H_2O from the initial product to form an enone structure. Wittig reactions add a phosphine to a carbonyl group. Bicycloannulation reactions add two new ring structures to a substrate molecule in one step.

16. B: Diborane (B_2H_6) is a reducing agent used to convert aldehydes and ketones to alcohols. Therefore, the reaction of benzaldehyde with diborane produces benzyl alcohol. Benzoic acid is produced by oxidation of benzaldehyde. 9-BBN is a bulky, sterically hindered borane compound used to reduce aldehydes, ketones and other compounds in specific ways. Dibenzoyl has the structure indicated as C_6H_5-(C=O)-(C=O)-C_6H_5 and is not formed in the reaction.

17. C: The amine N atom coordinates one alkyl halide molecule to form a dialkylammonium halide species, which then loses HX to form a secondary amine. The secondary amine undergoes the same coordination–elimination sequence to form a tertiary amine from the intermediate trialkylammonium halide species. The tertiary amine coordinates the alkyl halide to form a tetraalkylammonium halide, but cannot eliminate HX. All three secondary and tertiary amines and quaternary ammonium salts are produced in the reaction.

18. B: This is the balanced equation. The other three are not balanced.

19. C: In simple terms, the loss of electrons is oxidation, and the gain of electrons is reduction. In a redox reaction, one species is reduced and another is oxidized. There must always be one of each for a redox reaction to occur. One species will be the reducing agent and the other will be the oxidizing agent. They have an equal but opposite effect on each other in that the reducing agent gives up the same number of electrons as the oxidizing agent accepts. Since the reducing agent gives up electrons, it is oxidized, and similarly since the oxidizing agent accepts electrons, it is reduced.

20. A: The R- and S- designations of stereochemistry refer to the absolute order of substituents about an asymmetric center. To determine the order, one visualizes the molecule as seen in the direction of the bond to the lowest priority substituent, which in this case was the C-H bond. The priorities of the remaining three substituents are assigned from highest to lowest using the same rules as for E- and Z- designations. Their order then determines the designation as R- for clockwise order and S- for counterclockwise order. The D- and L- designations refer to the direction in which the compound rotates the plane of plane-polarized light passing through the molecules, D- for dextrorotatory, or to the right, and L- for levorotatory, or to the left.

21. C: The α,β-unsaturated ketone system is polarized by the carbonyl group through its extended π bond system. The carbonyl C atom and the β C atom are both subject to attack by a nucleophile. The Michael addition takes advantage of this to add a carbon nucleophile at the β position. This forms a new C-C bond and is irreversible because of that. The actual product of the reaction upon completion is an enol, but this immediately rearranges to the ketone form. The "Michelson-Morley experiment" was an exercise to measure the speed of light. "Michaelson reaction" and "Mitchell addition" are made-up terms and have no meaning.

22. C: The benzene ring is described as "aromatic" because of the extra stability imparted by the geometry of the molecule, the continuous overlap of the p orbitals in its π bond system, and the number of π electrons. The naphthalene molecule has the structure of two benzene rings fused together. That is, one of the C-C bonds is common to both rings. A vast array of molecules up to and including graphene can be constructed from fused benzene rings. This includes the compounds anthracene and phenanthrene. Compounds of three or more fused benzene rings are referred to as polyaromatic hydrocarbons, or PAHs. Simple hydrocarbons are the alkanes and other such compounds. PAHs do not contain carbonyl groups at all and therefore are not "diketo carbonyl compounds". Nor do they contain O atoms in a heterocyclic structure and so are not dioxins. PAHs are known to produce dioxins through incomplete combustion and reactions with molecular oxygen.

23. B: Carbon and nitrogen atoms are found bonded to each other in many types of compounds, not just in 1o amines. Thus they obviously do bond to each other, and the nitrile group, -CN, is characterized by the triple bond between the C and N atoms. An imine is characterized by the double bond between the C and N atoms, analogous to the double bond between C and O in the carbonyl group.

24. A: Lactones are formed by molecules that have both an –OH group and a –COOH group in their molecular structures. Lactams are formed by molecules that have both an –NH$_2$ or –NHR group and a –COOH group in their molecular structures. Intramolecular condensation reactions form a cyclic structure through formation of an ester or amide linkage.

25. C: The correct term is "conjugated", which refers to an alternating arrangement of single bonds and multiple bonds. Their relationship is alternant in some conjugated systems and non-alternant in other conjugated systems, such as in an amide. Conjugated bonds are not segregated, or isolated from each other, within the molecule.

26. A: The main bond between two sp or sp^2 hybridized atoms is the σ (sigma) bond directly between them. A second bond is formed between the two atoms by the sideways overlap of the adjacent p orbitals. This is called a π (pi) bond. Electrons in the adjacent p orbitals are able to move freely, or delocalize, through the π bond system.

27. C: A racemic mixture contains exactly equal quantities of the two enantiomers of a chiral compound, and is therefore not optically active itself. A eutectic mixture consists of two or more different compounds in which the mixture has a lower melting point than the individual compounds. A diastereomeric mixture is a mixture of diastereomeric compounds, each having two or more chiral centers. A meso- structure is a molecule that contains two chiral centers in which the orientation of substituents about one of the centers is the mirror image of the orientation of substituents about the other center.

28. C: The Br$_2$/CCl$_4$ test is the characteristic test for the presence of C=C and C≡C bonds in an organic compound. The color due to Br$_2$ disappears as the Br$_2$ adds across the double or triple bond to form the corresponding dibromo compound. For example, cyclohexene would react with Br$_2$/CCl$_4$ to produce colorless 1,2-dibromocyclohexane.

29. C: 2,4-Dinitrophenylhydrazine adds as a nucleophile to the carbonyl carbon atom of aldehydes and ketones. Rearrangement and elimination of H$_2$O results in the formation of a 2,4-dintrophenylhydrazone, which is usually a highly-colored crystalline solid. This is a classic derivatization test used to identify and characterize aldehydes and ketones.

30. D: Proton signals in NMR exhibit "spin splitting" according to the number of different protons on adjacent carbon atoms. Protons experiencing identical magnetic environments produce identical signals, so the three protons of a single methyl group produce just one peak at about 1.0. In an ethyl group, -CH$_2$CH$_3$, the three methyl protons are affected by the two -CH$_2$- protons and their signal is split into three slightly different peaks called a "triplet". The -CH$_2$- proton signal is split by the three

–CH3 protons into four slightly different peaks called a quartet. Integration of the quartet and the triplet sets of peaks is in the ratio of 2:3 respectively, according to the number of each different type of proton. There is certainly one ethyl group present indicated by this pattern, but it does not preclude the possibility that there may be two or more identical ethyl groups in the molecule. They would still have a 2:3 integration ratio, so in this case the correct answer is (D).

Reading Comprehension

1. B: Cilia and flagella are both organelles, which are defined in the first paragraph as sub-cellular structures that perform a particular function.

2. A: The second paragraph describes the function of cilia as providing fluid flow across the gills or the epithelia lining the digestive tract. The stomach is part of the digestive tract.

3. C: The third paragraph of the text describes 9 peripheral pairs of polymers, and 2 central ones, or 20 in all.

4. B: Tubulin and dynein are both defined as proteins in the text. Flagellin is a protein, but it is not mentioned in the text. Sonneborn is not a protein; he was a scientist.

5. B: The mechanism is described in detail in the fourth paragraph. Dynein causes the outer polymer pairs to slide past each other, not to bend. The inner polymers do not have dynein associated with them, so they are not involved in the bending. And the passage cites no evidence to suggest that the organelles contract.

6. C: Although the polymers in this passage are made of protein subunits, the definition is more general. The third paragraph tells us that in this case the subunits are tubulin proteins.

7. B: The fifth paragraph describes Sonneborn as "of Indiana University" and doing scientific research.

8. D: The experiment described in the fifth paragraph showed that the cilia always retained their original direction of rotation.

9. D: This is mentioned in the first paragraph.

10. B: The experiment demonstrated that the cilia's rotational direction was not dependent upon the DNA in their nuclei. Sonneborn performed his experiment with cilia, not with flagella.

11. C: The passage describes several distinctive features of annelid anatomy and tells how some of them differ from other worms.

12. A: The term is defined in the text as an organization of the anatomy into segments.

13. E: The term is defined in the text between commas.

14. C: The text gives the example of feet specializing into grasping organs to illustrate this evolutionary advantage of segmental plasticity.

15. B: Nematodes differ from the annelids in the structure of the coelum. Lumbricus and leeches are both members of the Annelida.

16. E: The text gives the example of parapodia modified for grasping to illustrate evolutionary plasticity among metameres.

17. B: The text states that the annelid coelum is formed later in the embryonic stage and probably evolved at a later time, as well.

18. E: The text indicates that the cerebral ganglia are enlarged, whereas the remaining ganglia in the nerve cord are merely repeating (unspecialized) units.

19. C: The text defines metemeres as segments, and discusses segmentation as the distinguishing feature of the phylum.

20. D: The paragraph tells us that annelids can live in salt or fresh water and on land, and then gives examples.

21. E: The text indicates that both nematodes and annelids possess a fluid-filled cavity which is involved in locomotion, or movement.

22. E: The last paragraph indicates that annelids occupy all the habitats listed and gives examples.

23. C: Sentence reads, "Your brain filters [your nose] out," which means your brain ignores it.

24. B: Only choice B reflects the meaning of the term "retina," which is a part of the eye's anatomy.

25. B: The final sentence reads, "Your brain works hard to make the world look continuous." It follows that visual perception is an active process, not a passive one, making choice B the best answer.

26. A: If the reader follows the instructions given in the paragraph, the O and X in the middle of the passage can be used to demonstrate the blind spot in the visual field. Choice A is the best answer.

27. B: The passage explains the way that visual perception works. Choice B is the best answer.

28. D: Much of the information in the passage is provided to show examples of how the brain fills in gaps in the visual field. Choice D is the best answer.

29. A: The author of the passage mentions the nose to demonstrate how the brain filters information out of the visual field. Choice A is the best answer.

30. B: Choice B can be inferred from the second paragraph. The paragraph states that the brain filters out information, which means that the brain does not perceive all activity in the visual field.

31. D: The main idea of the passage is that the immune system protects the body from infection. The author repeatedly alludes to the complexity and mystery of the immune system, so it cannot be true that scientists fully understand this part of the body. It is true that the immune system triggers the production of fluids, but this description misses the point. Similarly, it is true that the body is under constant invasion by malicious microbes; however, the author is much more interested in the body's response to these microbes. For this reason, the best answer choice is D.

32. C: The passage never states that viruses are extremely sophisticated. In fact, the passage explicitly states the opposite. The passage says that viruses are too primitive, or early in their development, to be classified as living organisms.

33. D: In the first paragraph, the word ideal means "perfect." Take a look at the context in which the word is used. The author is describing how many millions of microbes can live inside the human body. It would not make sense, then, for the author to be describing the body as a hostile environment for microbes. Moreover, whether or not the body is a confined environment would not seem to have much bearing on whether it is good for microbes. Rather, the paragraph suggests that the human body is a perfect environment for microbes.

34. B: The passage never states that the immune system ignores tumors. Indeed, at the beginning of the third paragraph, the author states that scientists remain puzzled by the body's ability to fight

484

tumors. This question is a little tricky, because it is common knowledge that many tumors prove fatal to the human body. However, you should not take this to mean that the body does not at least try to fight tumors.

35. A: In the second paragraph, the word enlist means "call into service." The use of this word is an example of figurative language. In this case, the author is describing the efforts of the immune system as if they were a military campaign. The immune system enlists other cells, and then directs these recruits to areas where they are needed.

36. C: The author's primary purpose in writing this essay is to inform. The passage is written in a clear, declarative style with no obvious prejudice on the part of the author. The primary intention of the passage seems to be providing information about the immune system to a general audience.

37. D: The main idea of this passage is that vaccines help the immune system function properly. Answer choices A, B, and C express details from the passage, but only answer choice D is a comprehensive summary of the author's message.

38. C: This passage does not state that the symptoms of disease will not emerge until the body has learned to fight the disease. On the contrary, the passage implies that a person may become quite sick and even die before the body learns to effectively fight the disease.

39. B: In the third paragraph, the word virulent means "malicious." The word virulent could in some circumstances mean contagious or annoying. However, since the passage is not talking about transfer of the disease and is referring to a serious illness, malicious is the more appropriate answer.

40. C: The author's primary purpose in writing this essay is to inform. If the above passage took an objective look at the pros and cons of various approaches to fighting disease, we would say that the passage was a piece of analysis. Because the purpose of this passage is to present new information to the reader in an objective manner, however, it is clear that the author's intention is to inform.

Physics

1. B: Significant digits indicate the precision of the measurement. Answer B has 5 significant figures. A and C each have 4. D has 3. The leading zeros in Answers A and D and are not counted as significant digits, but zeros at the end of the number (as in Answers A and B) do count. In answer D, the zero in between 2 and 9 is significant.

2. C: Displacement is a vector that indicates the change in the location of an object. Answer A would be correct if the question asked for the total distance the person walked or if the person didn't change direction. If the person turned around 180°, the displacement could be as small as 5 meters. If the person changed directions only a fraction of a degree, its magnitude would be less than 13 meters, not as large as 13 meters.

3. B: The answer can be determined because the rate of acceleration is uniform. Since the acceleration is 5 m/s^2, the velocity increases by 5 m/s every second. If it starts at 20 m/s, after 1 second it will be going 25 m/s. After another second it will be going 30 m/s, so the total time is 2 seconds. You can also calculate this time by using the average speed. Since the object undergoes uniform acceleration, the average speed is 25 m/s. Using the distance traveled, the same result is obtained. $t = d/v = (50 \text{ m})/(25 \text{ m/s}) = 2$ seconds.

4. A: Newton's first law (inertia) says an object in motion stays in motion, and an object at rest stays at rest, unless external forces act on them. *I* is an excellent demonstration because it shows the ball at rest and in motion. At rest, the ball stays at rest until a force acts on it. When the ball is moving, there is no force acting on the ball in the direction of motion. Thus, the natural state of the ball is to be at rest or moving with a constant speed. Answer C is not a good demonstration because the force of friction is what makes it hard to move the heavy object. Answer B is a good demonstration of equilibrium and friction. Answer D, running a current through wires, has nothing to do with Newton's first law.

5. D: There will be a gravitational force of attraction between the two spheres determined by the universal constant of gravity, the distance between the spheres, and the mass of the spheres. Since both objects are affected by this force (remember, Newton's 3rd law says the force needs to be equal and opposite), both objects will experience a slight acceleration and start moving towards each other a tiny amount (when we ignore friction). Using $F = ma$, you know that the less massive sphere will experience a larger acceleration than the more massive one.

6. C: The weight of an object near Earth's surface is given by $w = mg$, where $g = 9.8$ m/s^2. The Earth exerts a force on the 10 kg object equal 10 kg $\times$ 9.8 m/s^2 = 98 N. This weight pulls on the lower spring, stretching it until it reads 98 N. The lower spring then exerts a force of 98 N on the upper spring, causing it to read 98 N.

7. B: The ideal mechanical advantage (IMA) of a simple machine ignores friction. It is the effort force divided into the resultant force. It is also the distance the effort force moves divided by the distance the resultant force moves. The IMA of a fixed pulley is 1 because all a fixed pulley does is change the direction of the effort force. A moveable pulley, however, doubles the force by increasing the distance by two. In this case, there is one fixed pulley and one floating pulley. Since the IMA of the fixed pulley is 1, and the floating pulley doubles this, the total IMA is 2.

8. D: The weight of the art is 200 kg $\times$ 9.8 m/s^2 = 1960 N. This is the total force pulling DOWN on the wires. However, the tension acts along a 40° angle, and the vertical force is $T \sin \theta$. However, there are two ends to the wire, which splits the tension, meaning the weight is spread across $2T \sin \theta$. So $2T \sin \theta = w$. Therefore, $T = 1/2 \times (1960 \text{ N})/\sin(40°) = 1524$ N. Note: There's also a horizontal component to the tension forces, each expressed as $T \cos \theta$. The net force of the left and right tensions is zero. Answer A is calculated using the $\cos(40°)$ instead of $\sin(40°)$.

9. A: In a closed system (when you ignore outside interactions), the total momentum is constant and conserved. The total energy would also be conserved, although not the sum of the potential and kinetic energy. Some of the energy from the collision would be turned into thermal energy (heat) for example. Nor is the total velocity conserved, even though the velocity is a component of the momentum, since the momentum also depends on the mass of the cars. The impulse is a force over time that causes the momentum of a body to change. It doesn't make sense to think of impulse as conserved, since it's not necessarily constant throughout a collision.

10. D: Since this is a head-on elastic collision, you could use conservation of kinetic energy and momentum to actually solve this problem. However, in this case, you only need to think through the answers to arrive at a correct conclusion. Clearly the ball after it's struck won't be going 0 m/s. And since this is an elastic collision, and it is hit by a much larger ball, it must be going faster than the larger ball was originally moving. Therefore, the ball will be moving at more than 10 m/s. If this were an inelastic collision where the balls stuck together, the ball would final velocity would be less than 10 m/s.

11. C: To determine how much work is done by a gravitational force, you should calculate the change in that object's potential energy $= mgh$, where $m =$ mass, $g =$ gravitational acceleration (9.8 m/s^2), and $h =$ height. Therefore, the work done only depends on the change in height and not on the path taken. In Answer A, the work done by gravity doesn't have anything to do with friction, so this is not a good explanation. Friction is a separate force. Answer D, although true, doesn't explain why the work doesn't depend on the path.

12. B: Kinetic energy is the energy of motion and is defined as $\frac{1}{2}mv^2$. Using this equation, if you double the mass and the velocity of an object, you find $KE = \frac{1}{2}(2m')(2v')^2$ or 8 times the original KE. Therefore, the motorcycle has 8 times as much kinetic energy as the bicycle.

13. C: From the question, doubling distance would lower the gravitational force by a factor of 1/4, since the force is proportional to 1/R2. The gravitational potential would be 1/2 of the original because it is proportional to 1/R. Therefore, the ratio of the new force to the new potential would be $1/4 \div 1/2$, or 1/2 of the original ratio.

14. B: Power is the amount of work done divided by the time it took to do the work. A kilowatt-hour is a unit of work. A 5 KW engine running for 12 hours produces $5 \times 12 = 60$ kilowatt-hours of work. At $0.06 per Kw-h, this is $60 \times 0.06 = \$3.60$. The other answers all occur from simple math mistakes.

15. C: The phase will cycle through 2π radians. Therefore, $5t = 2\pi$ and $t = \frac{2\pi}{5} = 1.26$ seconds.

16. B: The speed of a wave is the product of its wavelength and frequency. $v = \lambda f$. Here, $v = 12 \times 3 = 36$ m/s.

17. A: A standing wave remains stationary, and the fixed points at both ends are the wave's nodes. Nevertheless, a standing waves with nodes at both ends of the string can have several forms. It may have one anti-node (i.e., it will arc across), two anti-nodes (this looks like a sine wave), three anti-nodes (with 1.5 sine waves), etc. However, waves with just one anti-node will the longest wavelength and thus the smallest frequency. For a wave with one anti-node, the string will have only 1/2 of a wave, so 20 m represents a half-wavelength and the full wavelength is 40 m. Using the wave equation ($v = \lambda f$) gives the correct answer. $f = v/\lambda = (4 \text{ m/s})/(40 \text{ m}) = 0.1$ Hz.

18. A: For standing waves, the string must be fixed at both ends. The wavelength at the fundamental frequency is 4 meters and the wavelength when the string resonates at the fourth harmonic is 1 meter. Using the wave equation $v = \lambda f$, the frequency at the fourth harmonic is $v/(1 \text{ m}) = 50$ Hz. Hence the necessary speed is 50 m/s. Furthermore, the mass per unit length is $(0.01 \text{ kg})/(2 \text{ m}) = 0.005$ kg/m. Thus, the tension is the string is $v^2 \times \mu = 50^2 \times 0.005 = 12.5$ N.

19. A: Pascal's law is that the pressure on the input piston is equal to the pressure on the output piston. (To move the truck, of course, the input piston moves a much greater distance than the output piston.) Since the pressure depends on the area of the pistons, and the area $= \pi r^2$, you need only find the ratio of the two areas to find the necessary force. Since the diameter is twice the radius, you can simplify this step by taking the ratio of the square of the diameters. $2^2/24^2 = 0.007$. Multiplying this by the weight of the car gets $0.007 \times 3500 \text{ N} = 24$ N. Remember also that the point of a hydraulic lift is to reduce the force, not increase it.

20. C: In an ideal fluid, from the conservation of mass, $\rho v A$ is constant. Since the area (A) decreases by a factor $3^2/5^2 = 0.36$, the speed increases by $5^2/3^2$. So $(6 \text{ m/s}) \times 5^2/3^2 = 16.7$ m/s. Incompressible means the density (ρ) is a constant. An ideal fluid has no viscosity, there is no rotational flow, and the flow is the same throughout the liquid, so answer D is not correct.

21. A: When an external force deforms a solid material, it will return to its initial position when the force is removed. This is called elasticity and is exhibited by springs. If too much force is applied and the elastic limit is exceeded, the rod won't return to its original shape any longer. As with springs, the deformation is directly proportional to the stress. The elastic limit occurs in rods subjected to a tensile force when the strain stops being directly proportional to the stress. The typical pattern when the force increases is that the strain increases linearly, then it doesn't increase as much, and then it breaks.

22. D: The third charge, which is positive, will be repelled by the charge of $+2q$ and attracted to the charge of $-q$. For this reason, the third charge can't be between the two other charges and have a net force of 0, since it would always jointly be pushed and pulled towards the negative charge. It must be past the more distant negative charge. If the charge were situated at a distance of $2d$ from the origin, which is distance d from the negative charge, it would have a repulsive force of $F = [k(q)(2q)]/(2d)^2$ and an attractive force of $F = [k(q)(q)]/(d)^2$, meaning the attractive force is still too small by 1/2 the repulsive force. Thus, the particle must be past the distance of $2d$, or Answer D. If you solve this distance quadratically, the particle is at $3.41d$.

23. B: The direction of the electric field is the same as the direction of the force on a positive test charge. Moving a negative charge in the direction of the electric field requires an external force to oppose the electric field. This would increase the electron's potential energy.

24. C: The force $F = qvB \sin \theta = (1.6 \times 10^{-19} \text{C}) \left(8.0 \times 10^6 \frac{\text{m}}{\text{s}}\right) (0.5 \text{ T}) \sin(45) = 4.5 \times 10^{-13}$ N.

25. A: Solenoids create a magnetic field inside the coils. Outside the solenoid, the magnetic field is practically zero, so increasing the number of coils won't have much effect on the exterior field strength. Inside the coils, increasing the number and density of coils increases the field strength.

26. C: Radio waves have the lowest frequency and the longest wavelength. Microwaves also have low frequencies and long wavelengths compared to visible light. X-rays are highly energetic and have higher frequencies and smaller wavelengths than visible light.

27. C: Ohm's law is that $V = IR$. Answer C is the only relation that holds true using this equation. If the resistance doesn't change, increasing the current on the right side must cause the voltage to also increase on the left side.

28. A: Answer A would be correct if the temperature of the two wires was the same. Wires have the least resistance when they are short and fat. This is expressed as $R = \rho L/A$, where ρ is the resistivity of the substance, L is the length and A is the area. Since both wires are tungsten, they must have the same resistivity. So, doubling the length and area adds a factor of 2 to both the top and bottom of the equation, giving no change in overall resistance.

29. A: Since these capacitors are connected in series you must add the reciprocals of their capacitance. $\frac{1}{C_{total}} = \frac{1}{C_1} + \frac{1}{C_2}$. So, $\frac{1}{C_{total}} = \frac{1}{3} + \frac{1}{6} = \frac{1}{2}$. Thus, $C_{total} = 2$ microfarads.

30. B: Power is the rate at which work is done. It can be expressed as $P = VI$ or $P = IR^2$. With 10 volts and 50 watts, the current is $I = \frac{P}{V} = \frac{50\text{ W}}{10\text{ V}} = 5$ A. Current is measured in coulombs/second, watts in joules/second, and volts in joules/coulomb. Answer D is equivalent to 5 amps since the charge on an electron is 1.6×10^{-19} coulombs.

31. A: The magnification of a lens can be calculated from its image distance, i, and its object distance, o. $M = i/o$. Here $M = 19/49 = 0.39$.

32. B: Clockwise is the direction the hands of a clock rotate when looking at the clock, so a counterclockwise torque would require a force that pushes or pulls down on the lever. The pivot point is the axis of rotation. We don't care about the components of these forces that push either to the left or right, since these components do not produce any torque. Force 1 is directed into the axis, so it produces no torque. Forces 3 and 4 both push up on the lever. The only force producing a counter-clockwise rotation is Force 2.

33. C: All three laws are operating, but the third law (forces come in equal and opposite pairs) best explains the motion. The first law (inertia) is shown from the fact that the balloon doesn't move until a force acts upon it. The second law ($F = ma$) is shown because you can see the force and the acceleration. The force comes from the contraction of the rubber balloon. The stretched rubber exerts a force on the air inside the balloon. This causes the air to accelerate in accordance with the second law. You can't see this acceleration because the air is invisible and because it is all the air in the room that the balloon is exerting a force on. However, the air in the room exerts and equal and opposite force on the balloon (this is Newton's third law), which causes the balloon to accelerate in the direction it did.

34. B: The moment of inertia of a point mass about any axis is given by mR^2, where R is the distance from the axis. The moment of inertia of a solid object is calculated by imagining that the object is made up of point masses and adding the moments of inertia of the point masses. The average radius of the particles in a hollow cylinder will be R (all the mass is at radius R). For a solid cylinder, however, the average radius is less than R, meaning the overall moment of inertia will be smaller, which means Answer B is correct. To actually calculate the moment of inertia of a cylinder of thickness $R_2 - R_1$ is $\frac{1}{2}m(R_1^2 + R_2^2)$. For a solid cylinder, $R_1 = 0$ meters. For a hollow cylinder, $R_1 = R_2$.

35. B: The phenomenon known as weightlessness is caused by an object being in free fall. An object in space still experiences a gravitational force due to the earth, but if that object is in orbit, it's effectively free falling around the earth, which causes it to experience weightlessness. Here, proposition I is wrong because you have to be pretty far away from a star for gravity to become negligible. In fact, objects only stay in orbit because the earth's gravity pulls on them and causes them to change direction. This means the usual experience of weight is lost, as you can see by the floating objects and people inside an orbiting spaceship. The same thing happens to a ski jumper, who is in free fall after he or she jumps. If the jumper is carrying a rock, for example, that rock will feel weightless while the jumper is in the air. A rolled baseball is not in freefall and does not experience weightlessness.

36. D: The formula for the potential energy of a spring comes from calculating how much work is required to stretch a spring an amount x. Hooke's law applies so the force increases uniformly from 0 N to kx, where k is the spring constant. Hence, $PE = \frac{1}{2}kx^2$. There are two ways to solve this problem. If you recognize that doubling the mass will double how much the spring is stretched, you can easily see that $(2x)^2$ shows the potential energy of the spring quadruples. If you don't realize that the displacement doubles, you can easily prove it, since $F = ma = -kx$ for a spring. Doubling the mass would double the force, and thereby double the displacement x. The spring constant is just that, a constant, and will not change unless you use a different type of spring.

37. A: Refraction occurs when a wave enters a new medium. The boundary between the old medium and the new medium produces a reflected wave and a refracted wave. Since the medium is different, the speed and direction of the refracted wave changes. This changes the wavelength, but the frequency remains the same. The angle of reflection depends on the angle of incidence of the wave that strikes the boundary. The angle of refraction depends partly on this angle of incidence, but also on the indices of refraction of the two substances. Although refraction is defined as a wave changing direction when it enters a new substance, a wave will not change direction if it enters this new medium exactly perpendicular to the surface.

38. B: When a tuning fork vibrates it creates areas of condensation (higher pressure) and rarefactions (lower pressure) that propagate through the air because of the air's elasticity. The distance between the condensations or rarefactions is the wavelength of the sound. The amplitude of the sound is half the difference between the pressure of the condensation and the pressure of the rarefaction. Loudness and power are both logarithmic measures that depend on the amplitude, but are not directly proportional to it. For example, doubling the amplitude will not double the loudness or power; those quantities will increase just slightly.

39. A: Sound travels much faster through helium than through air. Generally, the speed of sound can be calculated by speed $= \sqrt{k \times P / \rho}$, where k is the index of specific heats, P is pressure and ρ is density. Since helium has a much lower density, it would have a higher speed.

40. A: The frequency of a sound wave directly determines its pitch. We say the pitch of 480 Hz is higher than the pitch of 440 Hz. High and low are the words we use to describe pitch. Overtones refer to the frequencies above the fundamental frequency in a musical instrument. Two singers singing the same note at the same loudness will sound differently because their voices have different timbres.

Quantitative Reasoning

1. B: Multiply $120 by 24 months (a full two years) to get $2880. Add the thousand dollars for the down payment to get $3880. Find the difference between the entire amount all at once ($2600) and the amount paid in the plan ($3880). To find the difference, you subtract. The difference shows that $1280 more is paid with the installment plan.

2. C: Solve the equation as follows:

$$29 + r = 420$$
$$29 + r - 29 = 420 - 29$$
$$r = 391$$

3. C: To solve, find the sum. $35\% + 4\% = 39\%$

4. C: Let the percentage of sales in electronics be $x\%$, then add each change to the original 35%

$$x = 35 + (-2) + (-1) + (+6) + (-1) + (+2)$$
$$x = (35 + 6 + 2) + (-2 + (-1) + (-1))$$
$$x = (43) + (-4)$$
$$x = 39$$

5. B: Add to solve. The height of the window from the floor is not needed in this equation. It is extra information. You only need to add the heights of the two bookcases. Change the fractions so that they have a common denominator. After you add, simplify the fraction.

$$14\frac{1}{2} + 8\frac{3}{4} = 14\frac{2}{4} + 8\frac{3}{4}$$
$$= 22\frac{5}{4}$$
$$= 23\frac{1}{4}$$

6. B: Given $y = x + 5$ and $x = -3$. Substitute the value of x, then solve.

$$y = (-3) + 5$$
$$y = 2$$

7. D: Think of the numbers as they would be on a number line to place them in the correct order.

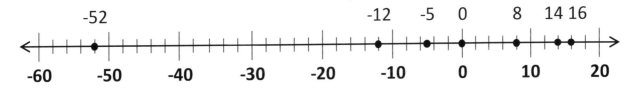

8. C: In this problem, if you do not know how to solve, try filling in the answer choices to see which one checks out. Many math problems may be solved by a guess and check method when you have a selection of answer choices.

$$27 - x = -5$$
$$x = 32$$

9. A: Add the coefficients of the 'x-terms' together as follows: $5x + 4x = 9x$

Add the coefficients of the 'y-terms' as follows: $-2y + y = -y$

Put the x- and y-terms back into the same equation: $9x - y$.

10. B: To solve, line up the like terms, as follows:

$$
\begin{array}{rrrr}
 & 3x^2 & +x & +3 \\
+ & 8x^2 & +5x & +16 \\
\hline
 & 11x^2 & +6x & +19
\end{array}
$$

11. C: To find perimeter, add the sides. $7\text{ cm} + 2\text{ cm} + 1\text{ cm} + 6\text{ cm} + 5\text{ cm} = 21\text{ cm}$

12. B: Since there are 4 containers of broth: $410\text{ ml} \times 4 = 1640\text{ ml}$

Change to liters: $1640\text{ mL} \times \frac{1\text{ L}}{1000\text{ mL}} = 1.64\text{ L}$

Add the liter of water that was already in the pot: $1.64\text{ L} + 1\text{ L} = 2.64\text{ L}$

13. D: Snappy Twisters are the only ones that fall into the criteria listed in the question. The use of the words "no more than" is important to notice.

14. D: Find the common denominator for the two fractions so that you can compare them. You can use the common denominator of 45, as follows:

$$
\frac{2}{5} = \frac{18}{45}, \qquad \frac{4}{9} = \frac{20}{45}
$$

Look at the numerators: 18 and 20. The number halfway between them is 19, so the answer is $\frac{19}{45}$

15. A: Convert each to the lowest common denominator and then compare the numerators. Since 2 and 8 are factors of 16, we only need to use 16 and 54 to find the common denominator.

$$
\begin{aligned}
16 &= 2 \times 2 \times 2 \times 2 \\
54 &= 2 \times 3 \times 3 \times 3 \\
LCD &= 2 \times 2 \times 2 \times 2 \times 3 \times 3 \times 3 = 432
\end{aligned}
$$

$$
\begin{aligned}
A &\rightarrow \frac{1}{2} = \frac{216}{432} \\
B &\rightarrow \frac{3}{8} = \frac{162}{432} \\
C &\rightarrow \frac{7}{16} = \frac{189}{432} \\
D &\rightarrow \frac{13}{54} = \frac{104}{432}
\end{aligned}
$$

1/2 is clearly the largest.

16. C: Check each of the answer choices:

$$A \to 36 = 6^2 \neq 6\sqrt{10}$$
$$B \to \sqrt{600} = \sqrt{6 \times 100} = 10\sqrt{6} \neq 6\sqrt{10}$$
$$C \to \sqrt{360} = \sqrt{36 \times 10} = \sqrt{6^2 \times 10} = 6\sqrt{10}$$
$$D \to \sqrt{6} \neq 6\sqrt{10}$$

17. C: Check each of the answer choices:

$$A \to \frac{1}{2} = 2^{-1}$$
$$B \to \frac{1}{4} = \frac{1}{2^2} = 2^{-2}$$
$$C \to \frac{1}{8} = \frac{1}{2^3} = 2^{-3}$$
$$D \to \frac{1}{16} = \frac{1}{2^4} = 2^{-4}$$

18. B: The value of the fraction $\frac{7}{5}$ can be evaluated by dividing 7 by 5, which yields 1.4. The average of 1.4 and 1.4 is $\frac{1.4+1.4}{2} = 1.4$.

19. C: The expression x^{-1} is equivalent to $\frac{1}{x}$. The product of x and $\frac{1}{x}$ is $\frac{1}{x} \times x = \frac{x}{x} = 1$.

$$A \to (x-1) \times x = x^2 - x \neq 1$$
$$B \to \frac{1}{(-x)} \times x = -1 \neq 1$$
$$D \to -x^1 \times x = -x^2 \neq 1$$

20. C: The total distance traveled was $8 + 3.6 = 11.6$ miles. The first 1/5 of a mile is charged at the higher rate. Since $1/5 = 0.2$, the remainder of the trip is 11.4 miles. Thus, the fare for the distance traveled is computed as $\$5.50 + 5 \times 11.4 \times \$1.50 = \$91$. To this the charge for waiting time must be added, which is $9 \times 20¢ = 180¢ = \$1.80$. Finally, add the two charges, $\$91 + \$1.80 = \$92.80$.

21. D: Each term of each expression in parentheses must be multiplied by each term in the other:

$$A \to (x-3)(x+5) = x^2 - 3x + 5x - 15 = x^2 + 2x - 15 \neq 3x^2 + 4x - 15$$
$$B \to (x+5)(3+x^2) = 3x + 15 + x^3 + 5x^2 \neq 3x^2 + 4x - 15$$
$$C \to x(3x + 4 - 15) = 3x^2 + 4x - 15x = 3x^2 - 11x \neq 3x^2 + 4x - 15$$
$$D \to (x+3)(3x-5) = 3x^2 + 9x - 5x - 15 = 3x^2 + 4x - 15$$

22. B: First determine the proportion of students in Grade 5. Since the total number of students is 180, this proportion is $\frac{36}{180} = 0.2$, or 20%. Then determine the same proportion of the total prizes, which is 20% of twenty, or $0.2 \times 20 = 4$.

$$A \to 5 \neq 0.2 \times 20$$
$$C \to 7 \neq 0.2 \times 20$$
$$D \to 3 \neq 0.2 \times 20$$

23. B: A prime number is a natural, positive, non-zero number which can be factored only by itself and by 1. $15 = 5 \times 3, 33 = 11 \times 3, 4 = 2 \times 2$.

24. A: Simplify the starting expression:

$$3\left(\frac{6x-3}{3}\right) - 3(9x+9) = 3(2x-1) - 27x - 27$$
$$= 6x - 3 - 27x - 27$$
$$= -21x - 30$$

A $\to -3(7x+10) = -21x - 30$
B $\to -3x + 6 \neq -21x - 30$
C $\to (x+3)(x-3) = x^2 + 3x - 3x - 9 = x^2 - 9 \neq -21x - 30$
D $\to 3x^2 - 9 \neq -21x - 30$

25. B: Substitute the given values and compute as follows: $(3 - 2 \times 2)^2 = (3-4)^2 = (-1)^2 = +1$.

26. A: Each glass of lemonade costs 10¢, or $0.10, so that g glasses will cost $g = \$0.10$. To this, add Bob's fixed cost of $45, giving the expression in A.

27. C: Evaluate as follows:

$$(3x^{-2})^3 = 3^3 \times (x^{-2})^3 = 27x^{(-2\times 3)} = 27x^{-6}$$

28. D: Let P_A = the price of truck A and P_B that of truck B. Similarly let M_A and M_B represent the gas mileage obtained by each truck. The total cost of driving a truck n miles is

$$C = P + n \times \frac{\$4}{M}$$

To determine the break-even mileage, set the two cost equations equal and solve for n:

$$P_A + n \times \frac{\$4}{M_A} = P_B + n \times \frac{4}{M_B}$$
$$n \times \left(\frac{\$4}{M_A} - \frac{\$4}{M_B}\right) = P_B - P_A$$
$$n = \frac{P_B - P_A}{\frac{\$4}{M_A} - \frac{\$4}{M_B}}$$

Plugging in the given values:

$$n = \frac{650 - 450}{\frac{4}{25} - \frac{4}{35}} = \frac{200}{0.16 - 0.11} = 740 \text{ miles}$$

29. C: Cross multiply and solve for y:

$$3(y+4) = 15(y-5)$$
$$15y - 3y = 12 + 75$$
$$12y = 87$$
$$y = \frac{87}{12} = \frac{29}{4}$$

30. D: The product $(a)(a)(a)(a)(a)$ is defined as a to the fifth power, a^5.

31. D: Convert meters to centimeters and then use the conversion factor in the table to convert centimeters to inches. Recall that there are 100 centimeters in a meter (centi means "hundredth"). Therefore, 19 m = 1900 cm = $\frac{1900}{2.54}$ = 748 inches.

32. A: The mode is the number that appears most often in a set of data. If no item appears most often, then the data set has no mode. In this case, Kyle achieved one hit a total of three times, two hits twice, three hits once, and four hits once. One hit occurred the most times, therefore the mode of the data set is 1.

33. B: The mean, or average, is the sum of the numbers in a data set divided by the total number of items. This data set contains seven items, one for each day of the week. The total number of hits that Kyle had during the week is the sum of the numbers in the right-hand column, or 14. This gives: Mean = $\frac{14}{7}$ = 2.

34. D: To multiply two binomials, use the FOIL method. FOIL stands for first, outside, inside, last. When multiplying each pair of terms, remember to multiply the coefficients, then add the exponents of each separate variable. So the product of the first terms is $2a^2b \times 3a^3b = 6a^5b^2$. The product of the outside terms is $2a^2b \times 4c = 8a^2bc$. The product of the inside terms is $-3c^3 \times 3a^3b = -9a^3bc^3$. The product of the last terms is $-3c^3 \times 4c = -12c^4$. The final answer is simply the sum of these four products: $6a^5b^2 + 8a^2bc - 9a^3bc^3 - 12c^4$

35. D: To solve for x, first isolate the variable. Remember: when an inequality is divided by a negative number, the sign must change directions.

$$-4x + 8 \geq 48$$
$$-4x \geq 48 - 8$$
$$-4x \geq 40$$
$$-\frac{4x}{-4} \geq \frac{40}{-4}$$
$$x \leq -10$$

36. D: Integers include all positive and negative whole numbers and the number zero. The product of three integers must be an integer, so you can eliminate any answer choice that is not a whole number: choices (A) and (C). The product of two even integers is even. The product of even and odd integers is even. The only even choice is 24.

37. C: Divide the mg the child should receive by the number of mg in 0.8 ml to determine how many 0.8 ml doses the child should receive: $240 \div 80 = 3$. Multiply the number of doses by 0.8 to determine how many ml the child should receive: $3 \times 0.8 = 2.4$ ml

38. B: The chart indicates that each x value must be tripled to equal the corresponding y value, so $y = 3x$. One way you can determine this is by plugging corresponding pairs of x and y into the answer choices.

39. D: Using the proportion, $\frac{1 \text{ in.}}{45 \text{ miles}} = \frac{3.2 \text{ inches}}{x \text{ miles}}$, cross multiply to solve: $x = (45)(3.2) = 144$ miles

40. D: Each hour has 60 minutes, and each of those minutes has 60 seconds. Expressed in seconds, then, an hour is $60 \times 60 = 3600$ seconds. Thus, we can find that $400/3600 = 1/9$.

How to Overcome Test Anxiety

Just the thought of taking a test is enough to make most people a little nervous. A test is an important event that can have a long-term impact on your future, so it's important to take it seriously and it's natural to feel anxious about performing well. But just because anxiety is normal, that doesn't mean that it's helpful in test taking, or that you should simply accept it as part of your life. Anxiety can have a variety of effects. These effects can be mild, like making you feel slightly nervous, or severe, like blocking your ability to focus or remember even a simple detail.

If you experience test anxiety—whether severe or mild—it's important to know how to beat it. To discover this, first you need to understand what causes test anxiety.

Causes of Test Anxiety

While we often think of anxiety as an uncontrollable emotional state, it can actually be caused by simple, practical things. One of the most common causes of test anxiety is that a person does not feel adequately prepared for their test. This feeling can be the result of many different issues such as poor study habits or lack of organization, but the most common culprit is time management. Starting to study too late, failing to organize your study time to cover all of the material, or being distracted while you study will mean that you're not well prepared for the test. This may lead to cramming the night before, which will cause you to be physically and mentally exhausted for the test. Poor time management also contributes to feelings of stress, fear, and hopelessness as you realize you are not well prepared but don't know what to do about it.

Other times, test anxiety is not related to your preparation for the test but comes from unresolved fear. This may be a past failure on a test, or poor performance on tests in general. It may come from comparing yourself to others who seem to be performing better or from the stress of living up to expectations. Anxiety may be driven by fears of the future—how failure on this test would affect your educational and career goals. These fears are often completely irrational, but they can still negatively impact your test performance.

Review Video: 3 Reasons You Have Test Anxiety
Visit mometrix.com/academy and enter code: 428468

Elements of Test Anxiety

As mentioned earlier, test anxiety is considered to be an emotional state, but it has physical and mental components as well. Sometimes you may not even realize that you are suffering from test anxiety until you notice the physical symptoms. These can include trembling hands, rapid heartbeat, sweating, nausea, and tense muscles. Extreme anxiety may lead to fainting or vomiting. Obviously, any of these symptoms can have a negative impact on testing. It is important to recognize them as soon as they begin to occur so that you can address the problem before it damages your performance.

Review Video: 3 Ways to Tell You Have Test Anxiety
Visit mometrix.com/academy and enter code: 927847

The mental components of test anxiety include trouble focusing and inability to remember learned information. During a test, your mind is on high alert, which can help you recall information and stay focused for an extended period of time. However, anxiety interferes with your mind's natural processes, causing you to blank out, even on the questions you know well. The strain of testing during anxiety makes it difficult to stay focused, especially on a test that may take several hours. Extreme anxiety can take a huge mental toll, making it difficult not only to recall test information but even to understand the test questions or pull your thoughts together.

Review Video: How Test Anxiety Affects Memory
Visit mometrix.com/academy and enter code: 609003

Effects of Test Anxiety

Test anxiety is like a disease—if left untreated, it will get progressively worse. Anxiety leads to poor performance, and this reinforces the feelings of fear and failure, which in turn lead to poor performances on subsequent tests. It can grow from a mild nervousness to a crippling condition. If allowed to progress, test anxiety can have a big impact on your schooling, and consequently on your future.

Test anxiety can spread to other parts of your life. Anxiety on tests can become anxiety in any stressful situation, and blanking on a test can turn into panicking in a job situation. But fortunately, you don't have to let anxiety rule your testing and determine your grades. There are a number of relatively simple steps you can take to move past anxiety and function normally on a test and in the rest of life.

Review Video: How Test Anxiety Impacts Your Grades
Visit mometrix.com/academy and enter code: 939819

Physical Steps for Beating Test Anxiety

While test anxiety is a serious problem, the good news is that it can be overcome. It doesn't have to control your ability to think and remember information. While it may take time, you can begin taking steps today to beat anxiety.

Just as your first hint that you may be struggling with anxiety comes from the physical symptoms, the first step to treating it is also physical. Rest is crucial for having a clear, strong mind. If you are tired, it is much easier to give in to anxiety. But if you establish good sleep habits, your body and mind will be ready to perform optimally, without the strain of exhaustion. Additionally, sleeping well helps you to retain information better, so you're more likely to recall the answers when you see the test questions.

Getting good sleep means more than going to bed on time. It's important to allow your brain time to relax. Take study breaks from time to time so it doesn't get overworked, and don't study right before bed. Take time to rest your mind before trying to rest your body, or you may find it difficult to fall asleep.

Review Video: <u>The Importance of Sleep for Your Brain</u>
Visit mometrix.com/academy and enter code: 319338

Along with sleep, other aspects of physical health are important in preparing for a test. Good nutrition is vital for good brain function. Sugary foods and drinks may give a burst of energy but this burst is followed by a crash, both physically and emotionally. Instead, fuel your body with protein and vitamin-rich foods.

Also, drink plenty of water. Dehydration can lead to headaches and exhaustion, especially if your brain is already under stress from the rigors of the test. Particularly if your test is a long one, drink water during the breaks. And if possible, take an energy-boosting snack to eat between sections.

Review Video: <u>How Diet Can Affect your Mood</u>
Visit mometrix.com/academy and enter code: 624317

Along with sleep and diet, a third important part of physical health is exercise. Maintaining a steady workout schedule is helpful, but even taking 5-minute study breaks to walk can help get your blood pumping faster and clear your head. Exercise also releases endorphins, which contribute to a positive feeling and can help combat test anxiety.

When you nurture your physical health, you are also contributing to your mental health. If your body is healthy, your mind is much more likely to be healthy as well. So take time to rest, nourish your body with healthy food and water, and get moving as much as possible. Taking these physical steps will make you stronger and more able to take the mental steps necessary to overcome test anxiety.

Review Video: <u>How to Stay Healthy and Prevent Test Anxiety</u>
Visit mometrix.com/academy and enter code: 877894

Mental Steps for Beating Test Anxiety

Working on the mental side of test anxiety can be more challenging, but as with the physical side, there are clear steps you can take to overcome it. As mentioned earlier, test anxiety often stems from lack of preparation, so the obvious solution is to prepare for the test. Effective studying may be the most important weapon you have for beating test anxiety, but you can and should employ several other mental tools to combat fear.

First, boost your confidence by reminding yourself of past success—tests or projects that you aced. If you're putting as much effort into preparing for this test as you did for those, there's no reason you should expect to fail here. Work hard to prepare; then trust your preparation.

Second, surround yourself with encouraging people. It can be helpful to find a study group, but be sure that the people you're around will encourage a positive attitude. If you spend time with others who are anxious or cynical, this will only contribute to your own anxiety. Look for others who are motivated to study hard from a desire to succeed, not from a fear of failure.

Third, reward yourself. A test is physically and mentally tiring, even without anxiety, and it can be helpful to have something to look forward to. Plan an activity following the test, regardless of the outcome, such as going to a movie or getting ice cream.

When you are taking the test, if you find yourself beginning to feel anxious, remind yourself that you know the material. Visualize successfully completing the test. Then take a few deep, relaxing breaths and return to it. Work through the questions carefully but with confidence, knowing that you are capable of succeeding.

Developing a healthy mental approach to test taking will also aid in other areas of life. Test anxiety affects more than just the actual test—it can be damaging to your mental health and even contribute to depression. It's important to beat test anxiety before it becomes a problem for more than testing.

Review Video: <u>Test Anxiety and Depression</u>
Visit mometrix.com/academy and enter code: 904704

Study Strategy

Being prepared for the test is necessary to combat anxiety, but what does being prepared look like? You may study for hours on end and still not feel prepared. What you need is a strategy for test prep. The next few pages outline our recommended steps to help you plan out and conquer the challenge of preparation.

STEP 1: SCOPE OUT THE TEST

Learn everything you can about the format (multiple choice, essay, etc.) and what will be on the test. Gather any study materials, course outlines, or sample exams that may be available. Not only will this help you to prepare, but knowing what to expect can help to alleviate test anxiety.

STEP 2: MAP OUT THE MATERIAL

Look through the textbook or study guide and make note of how many chapters or sections it has. Then divide these over the time you have. For example, if a book has 15 chapters and you have five days to study, you need to cover three chapters each day. Even better, if you have the time, leave an extra day at the end for overall review after you have gone through the material in depth.

If time is limited, you may need to prioritize the material. Look through it and make note of which sections you think you already have a good grasp on, and which need review. While you are studying, skim quickly through the familiar sections and take more time on the challenging parts. Write out your plan so you don't get lost as you go. Having a written plan also helps you feel more in control of the study, so anxiety is less likely to arise from feeling overwhelmed at the amount to cover.

STEP 3: GATHER YOUR TOOLS

Decide what study method works best for you. Do you prefer to highlight in the book as you study and then go back over the highlighted portions? Or do you type out notes of the important information? Or is it helpful to make flashcards that you can carry with you? Assemble the pens, index cards, highlighters, post-it notes, and any other materials you may need so you won't be distracted by getting up to find things while you study.

If you're having a hard time retaining the information or organizing your notes, experiment with different methods. For example, try color-coding by subject with colored pens, highlighters, or post-it notes. If you learn better by hearing, try recording yourself reading your notes so you can listen while in the car, working out, or simply sitting at your desk. Ask a friend to quiz you from your flashcards, or try teaching someone the material to solidify it in your mind.

STEP 4: CREATE YOUR ENVIRONMENT

It's important to avoid distractions while you study. This includes both the obvious distractions like visitors and the subtle distractions like an uncomfortable chair (or a too-comfortable couch that makes you want to fall asleep). Set up the best study environment possible: good lighting and a comfortable work area. If background music helps you focus, you may want to turn it on, but otherwise keep the room quiet. If you are using a computer to take notes, be sure you don't have any other windows open, especially applications like social media, games, or anything else that could distract you. Silence your phone and turn off notifications. Be sure to keep water close by so you stay hydrated while you study (but avoid unhealthy drinks and snacks).

Also, take into account the best time of day to study. Are you freshest first thing in the morning? Try to set aside some time then to work through the material. Is your mind clearer in the afternoon or evening? Schedule your study session then. Another method is to study at the same time of day that you will take the test, so that your brain gets used to working on the material at that time and will be ready to focus at test time.

STEP 5: STUDY!

Once you have done all the study preparation, it's time to settle into the actual studying. Sit down, take a few moments to settle your mind so you can focus, and begin to follow your study plan. Don't give in to distractions or let yourself procrastinate. This is your time to prepare so you'll be ready to fearlessly approach the test. Make the most of the time and stay focused.

Of course, you don't want to burn out. If you study too long you may find that you're not retaining the information very well. Take regular study breaks. For example, taking five minutes out of every hour to walk briskly, breathing deeply and swinging your arms, can help your mind stay fresh.

As you get to the end of each chapter or section, it's a good idea to do a quick review. Remind yourself of what you learned and work on any difficult parts. When you feel that you've mastered the material, move on to the next part. At the end of your study session, briefly skim through your notes again.

But while review is helpful, cramming last minute is NOT. If at all possible, work ahead so that you won't need to fit all your study into the last day. Cramming overloads your brain with more information than it can process and retain, and your tired mind may struggle to recall even previously learned information when it is overwhelmed with last-minute study. Also, the urgent nature of cramming and the stress placed on your brain contribute to anxiety. You'll be more likely to go to the test feeling unprepared and having trouble thinking clearly.

So don't cram, and don't stay up late before the test, even just to review your notes at a leisurely pace. Your brain needs rest more than it needs to go over the information again. In fact, plan to finish your studies by noon or early afternoon the day before the test. Give your brain the rest of the day to relax or focus on other things, and get a good night's sleep. Then you will be fresh for the test and better able to recall what you've studied.

STEP 6: TAKE A PRACTICE TEST

Many courses offer sample tests, either online or in the study materials. This is an excellent resource to check whether you have mastered the material, as well as to prepare for the test format and environment.

Check the test format ahead of time: the number of questions, the type (multiple choice, free response, etc.), and the time limit. Then create a plan for working through them. For example, if you have 30 minutes to take a 60-question test, your limit is 30 seconds per question. Spend less time on the questions you know well so that you can take more time on the difficult ones.

If you have time to take several practice tests, take the first one open book, with no time limit. Work through the questions at your own pace and make sure you fully understand them. Gradually work up to taking a test under test conditions: sit at a desk with all study materials put away and set a timer. Pace yourself to make sure you finish the test with time to spare and go back to check your answers if you have time.

After each test, check your answers. On the questions you missed, be sure you understand why you missed them. Did you misread the question (tests can use tricky wording)? Did you forget the information? Or was it something you hadn't learned? Go back and study any shaky areas that the practice tests reveal.

Taking these tests not only helps with your grade, but also aids in combating test anxiety. If you're already used to the test conditions, you're less likely to worry about it, and working through tests until you're scoring well gives you a confidence boost. Go through the practice tests until you feel comfortable, and then you can go into the test knowing that you're ready for it.

Test Tips

On test day, you should be confident, knowing that you've prepared well and are ready to answer the questions. But aside from preparation, there are several test day strategies you can employ to maximize your performance.

First, as stated before, get a good night's sleep the night before the test (and for several nights before that, if possible). Go into the test with a fresh, alert mind rather than staying up late to study.

Try not to change too much about your normal routine on the day of the test. It's important to eat a nutritious breakfast, but if you normally don't eat breakfast at all, consider eating just a protein bar. If you're a coffee drinker, go ahead and have your normal coffee. Just make sure you time it so that the caffeine doesn't wear off right in the middle of your test. Avoid sugary beverages, and drink enough water to stay hydrated but not so much that you need a restroom break 10 minutes into the test. If your test isn't first thing in the morning, consider going for a walk or doing a light workout before the test to get your blood flowing.

Allow yourself enough time to get ready, and leave for the test with plenty of time to spare so you won't have the anxiety of scrambling to arrive in time. Another reason to be early is to select a good seat. It's helpful to sit away from doors and windows, which can be distracting. Find a good seat, get out your supplies, and settle your mind before the test begins.

When the test begins, start by going over the instructions carefully, even if you already know what to expect. Make sure you avoid any careless mistakes by following the directions.

Then begin working through the questions, pacing yourself as you've practiced. If you're not sure on an answer, don't spend too much time on it, and don't let it shake your confidence. Either skip it and come back later, or eliminate as many wrong answers as possible and guess among the remaining ones. Don't dwell on these questions as you continue—put them out of your mind and focus on what lies ahead.

Be sure to read all of the answer choices, even if you're sure the first one is the right answer. Sometimes you'll find a better one if you keep reading. But don't second-guess yourself if you do immediately know the answer. Your gut instinct is usually right. Don't let test anxiety rob you of the information you know.

If you have time at the end of the test (and if the test format allows), go back and review your answers. Be cautious about changing any, since your first instinct tends to be correct, but make sure you didn't misread any of the questions or accidentally mark the wrong answer choice. Look over any you skipped and make an educated guess.

At the end, leave the test feeling confident. You've done your best, so don't waste time worrying about your performance or wishing you could change anything. Instead, celebrate the successful

completion of this test. And finally, use this test to learn how to deal with anxiety even better next time.

Important Qualification

Not all anxiety is created equal. If your test anxiety is causing major issues in your life beyond the classroom or testing center, or if you are experiencing troubling physical symptoms related to your anxiety, it may be a sign of a serious physiological or psychological condition. If this sounds like your situation, we strongly encourage you to seek professional help.

Thank You

We at Mometrix would like to extend our heartfelt thanks to you, our friend and patron, for allowing us to play a part in your journey. It is a privilege to serve people from all walks of life who are unified in their commitment to building the best future they can for themselves.

The preparation you devote to these important testing milestones may be the most valuable educational opportunity you have for making a real difference in your life. We encourage you to put your heart into it—that feeling of succeeding, overcoming, and yes, conquering will be well worth the hours you've invested.

We want to hear your story, your struggles and your successes, and if you see any opportunities for us to improve our materials so we can help others even more effectively in the future, please share that with us as well. **The team at Mometrix would be absolutely thrilled to hear from you!** So please, send us an email (support@mometrix.com) and let's stay in touch.

> **If you'd like some additional help, check out these other resources we offer for your exam:**
> **http://mometrixflashcards.com/OAT**

Additional Bonus Material

Due to our efforts to try to keep this book to a manageable length, we've created a link that will give you access to all of your additional bonus material.

Please visit https://www.mometrix.com/bonus948/oat to access the information.